For Clint —

This book was a
favorite of my dad's —
and full of well-written and
thought-provoking stuff. I hope you
enjoy it!

Lindy

Willmoore Kendall Contra Mundum

WILLMOORE KENDALL

CONTRA MUNDUM

Willmoore Kendall

<small>Edited by Nellie D. Kendall</small>

ARLINGTON HOUSE   *New Rochelle, N.Y.*

Library of Congress Catalog Card Number 71-115353

ISBN 0-87000-101-9

MANUFACTURED IN THE UNITED STATES OF AMERICA BY HADDON CRAFTSMEN, INC., SCRANTON, PA.

Acknowledgements

I wish to express my gratitude for moral support and actual help to George Anastaplo, George W. Carey, Donald A. Cowan, Louise S. Cowan, Leo Paul de Alvarez, Jeffrey Hart, Yvona K. Mason and Garry Wills.

—MRS. NELLIE D. KENDALL

Permission to publish material from the following sources is hereby gratefully acknowledged:

"The Majority Principle and the Scientific Elite," *The Southern Review,* Winter, 1939.

"On the Preservation of Democracy for America," *The Southern Review,* Summer, 1939.

"Bipartisanship and Majority-Rule Democracy," in a symposium "Is the Bipartisan Policy Democratic?," *American Perspective,* Vol. IV, No. 2, Spring, 1950.

"Prolegomena to any Future Work on Majority Rule," *Journal of Politics,* Vol. 12, 1950.

"The People Versus Socrates Revisited," *Modern Age,* Vol. III, No. 1, Winter, 1958-59.

"How to Read Milton's Areopagitica," *Journal of Politics,* Vol. 22, 1960.

"The Two Majorities," reprinted from *Midwest Journal of Political Science,* Vol. IV, No. 4, November, 1960, by permission of the Wayne State University Press.

"Subversion in the Twentieth Century," in *The Committee and Its Critics,* by the Staff of *National Review,* Putnam, 1962.

"Toward a Definition of 'Conservatism,' " with George W. Carey, *Journal of Politics,* Vol. 26, 1964.

"The Congress," debate with James McGregor Burns, in *Dialogues in Americanism,* Henry Regnery Co., 1964.

"Deadlock" (a review), *Claremont Quarterly,* Spring, 1964. Used by permission of *Claremont Quarterly.*

"Jefferson and Civil Liberties: The Darker Side" (a review), *Stanford Law*

Review, Vol. 16, No. 3, May, 1964. Copyright © 1964 by the Board of Trustees of the Leland Stanford Junior University.

"The Bill of Rights & American Freedom," in *What is Conservatism?,* edited by Frank S. Meyer. Copyright © 1964 by Intercollegiate Society of Individualists, Inc. Reprinted by permission of Holt, Rinehart and Winston, Inc.

"American Conservatism and the 'Prayer' Decisions," *Modern Age,* Vol. VIII, No. 3, Summer, 1964.

"Equality and the American Political Tradition," *Politeia,* Vol. 2, No. 1, Winter, 1964-65. Copyright © by Alexander R. Landi.

"The Civil Rights Movement and the Coming Constitutional Crisis," *The Intercollegiate Review,* Vol. I, No. 2, Feb.-March, 1965.

"How to Read Richard Weaver: Philosopher of 'We the (Virtuous) People,'" *The Intercollegiate Review,* Vol. 2, No. 1, September, 1965.

"How to Read *The Federalist,*" from "Introduction" to *The Federalist Papers,* with George W. Carey, Arlington House, 1965.

"John Locke Revisited," *The Intercollegiate Review,* Vol. 2, No. 4, Jan.-Feb., 1966.

"Thoughts on Machiavelli" (a review), *The Philosophical Review,* Vol. LXXV, No. 2, April, 1966.

"What Killed the Civil Rights Movement?," *Phalanx,* Vol. I, No. 2, Summer, 1967.

"The 'Intensity' Problem and Democratic Theory," with George W. Carey, *The American Political Science Review,* Vol. LXII, No. 1, March, 1968.

"The 'Roster Device': J.S. Mill and Contemporary Elitism," with George W. Carey, *The Western Political Quarterly,* Vol. XXI, No. 1, March, 1968.

Table of Contents

Willmoore Kendall: American

By Jeffrey Hart

Willmoore Kendall remains, beyond any possibility of challenge, the most important political theorist to have emerged in the twenty-odd years since the end of World War II. Nevertheless, he was, for all the immense sanity of his genius, a strange and solitary figure, isolated not only from the academic establishment—though he was a great teacher, and profoundly changed the lives of some of his students—but from any establishment whatsoever. It is only the first of the terrible polarities with which he grappled that he was, personally and intellectually, so solitary, and yet—it was the other truth—also the rediscoverer of the historic American political orthodoxy.

There are many ways in which Kendall was deeply, indeed almost terrifyingly American, but surely his isolation was one of them. It was undoubtedly an isolation inextricable from his genius itself—his capacity to think his way through convention and assumption finally to arrive at the irreducible and crystalline truth. Talking with him, reading his essays, one saw that his was, so to speak, a "typical strangeness"—analogous to that of the pioneer pushing West alone, developing idiosyncrasies, yet never doubting his own American "orthodoxy," or of the captain of a whaler, Ahab, say, moving through strange and lonely seas. One side of the American character is its optimism, its capability, its health and gregariousness. But how often it is that the American genius is isolated and driven by obscure furies —Melville, Hawthorne, Hemingway. Kendall was in this vein—and in this rank. Yet even Thorstein Veblen, to compare the two, seems almost a genial conformist.

I first met Willmoore Kendall in Paris in the fall of 1965 when I was driving up from Catalonia on the way to an academic winter at Oxford. He was living in a rather grim Paris suburb, Meudon-Bellvue, and working on Rousseau. I had admired his essays and we had corresponded; I looked him up. I also knew his legend. And so was entirely unprepared for the considerate and civilized individual, elegant, to the point of self-consciousness, whom I met. A black turtleneck shirt and splendid checked sport coat; tall, handsome, almost courtly, though also worn and deeply lined. We had drinks in a left-bank cafe and went on to dinner in a Greek restaurant where the food was superb.

For this initial impression I was, as I say, totally unprepared, for I was aware of the legend. It was said at *National Review* that Kendall was never on speaking terms with more than one member of the group there at a time, though the identity of that one favored individual changed from month to month, Kendall disengaging from one communicant and, simultaneously, sending out feelers to the next one. His drinking feats were referred to with awe. He had been replaced as book editor of the magazine, it seemed, because he had been obliged to defend his conduct of the section *after* lunch. And embedded in the major mythology of the U.S. Congress is the time he passed out noisily in the House dining room. Once, it is also said, he was arrested for speeding on the Jersey turnpike, only to inform an incredulous judge that, no, your honor, he had no driver's license, never, in fact had had one, and, no, now did not feel the need of one. The judge, in despair, in touch with the incommensurate, let him go.

At Yale Kendall has also passed into the realm of legend, for as a member of the faculty he was absolutely unique. From his first appointment in 1947 he had been embroiled in controversy, and, though tenured, he was never given a promotion or a salary raise. His personal impact upon his colleagues was so shattering that he was encouraged to take frequent leaves of absence, and never in fact remained at Yale for more than two consecutive years at a time. Nevertheless he was one of the most popular teachers on the scene, and had a decisive effect upon the lives of many students. Everywhere he appeared he was a felt force. One well-known but uncomprehending journalist described him as a wild Yale don, of extreme and highly abstract views who could get a conversation into the shouting stage faster than anyone within memory. This description does suggest something of Kendall's violence of personality, but is misleading as to the character of his "views." They were civilized, central, and startlingly gentle.

In 1961, Yale said goodbye. The episode was bizarre, and so far as I know unique in academic history. Kendall, on one of his frequent leaves, had settled in Spain, and, as the humor struck him, had phoned the administration and said, well, you don't seem to be able to take me, how about paying me off and calling it quits? The check was instantly on the way. Yale bought back his tenure for twenty-five thousand dollars and gratefully bade farewell.

Of all this bizarre history there was not so much as a hint in the scholarly and urbane gentleman with whom I sipped cool drinks in the Paris dusk that fall. The waiters bustled about. Over *there* was the site of Cluny, whence pilgrims had journeyed south to Santiago da Compastella in the northeast corner of Spain, one of the great, and *civilizing*, pilgrimages of the European middle-ages. What would Europe have been without Cluny, without Santiago? Did I realize that Camus' *Plague* was a parable of the Social Contract? We must all go to the San Fermin next spring in Pamplona. He might visit us in Oxford. It would be good to see Pembroke College again. But then, almost in passing, came the touch consonant with his legend: he was, it seemed—and he was impatient with the delay—processing his first two marriages simultaneously through the annulment proceedings before the Vatican Rota. Ah, his Roman lawyer was a pedant. And to be sure, though others—one man, perhaps two—had had *two* marriages annuled, his was the *first* time, in the two-thousand-year history of the Church, that anyone had tried to annul two *simultaneously.* He thought he would succeed. We speculated about the astonishment of Paul VI.

Later that year he visited me and my family at Oxford. While he was there it became apparent that he was suffering from a dangerous heart condition, and could sustain himself only through sudden recourse to nitro pills. He loved Oxford. He had been an incredibly precocious student, and his Rhodes Scholarship in 1932 had brought him here to Pembroke, introduced him to political philosophy, and changed his life. Nevertheless, he was a terribly sick man; I remember once, walking along High Street with him, he suddenly stopped and said go on; he leaned against the New College wall and took a nitro pill, which revived him temporarily. Still, it was a marvellous week or so. He had brought his evening clothes and he went back to some ceremonial event at his old college; he found to his immense delight that his peers there knew his work, and knew his stature. The dons, he thought, were much less ideological than American academics.

Meanwhile, his marvellous talk went on. "What *was* the relationship between the Philadelphia Constitution—the Preamble especially—and the Bill of Rights, which seems to embody an entirely different theory of government? Not the whole Bill—really only the First Amendment. The rest are common-law specificities. And *what* do *you* think is the relationship between these two documents and the Declaration's abstractions? What *individual* rights do *you* have under the Constitution? And how would you sustain them against legislation by the *Congress?*" The great deep questions opened up; he seemed to roll the matter back to the terms in which it must have been considered by the founders. "What do you make of the fact that the Preamble *deliberately* puts 'justice' and the 'domestic tranquility' in rhetorical balance—neither having primacy? How does that fit in with the *theory* of the Constitution?"

Thinking back to these conversations now, in 1970, as American perplexities in Indochina deepen, I remember one startling thing he said. At the time I thought it part of the violence of emotion that lurked in some corner of his being. I was full of Strausz-Hupé and protracted conflict, of Maxwell Taylor and graduate response, of both Kissinger and Kahn and the impulse to analyze international conflict in terms of game theory. Kendall brushed this aside. No, neither the American character nor the American *system,* he said, could wage protracted conflict. Not the year after year grinding, boring conflict. This would be bound to fragment the consensus upon which American institutional authority rests. He then terrified the workmen around us in the English pub. "Only two countries today," he said, "can plausibly contemplate atomic war. And only one can seriously contemplate it." Said leeringly.

II

Another time we sat in an inn called the Rose about ten miles from Oxford, where the Thames is a fresh and tiny river, actually patrolled by swans. Matthew Arnold country. I learned that he had been born in a small town in Oklahoma, his family having come westward from Kentucky. We have lately been hearing a great deal about Middle America, but for Kendall it was a felt fact, part of his mind and his identity. He liked to call himself an "Appalachians-to-the-Rockies patriot." The overwhelming emotional fact of his life was his father, a blind Methodist minister, clearly a formidable mind, whose ministry took him from one small Oklahoma town to another as he attended to the needs of their independent citizenry. His father's blindness and consequent need for someone to read to him accelerated what would in any event have been a precocious development. The boy taught himself to read by the time he was two by picking out words and then sentences on a typewriter he had been given as a toy. By the time he was four he was able to read aloud to his father from adult texts, and to this early habit of oral reading may be traced the spoken quality of his own later prose, a prose which represents one of the distinctive stylistic achievements in twentieth-century writing. In other ways, too, the blind minister had a lasting effect upon his son. As a mature man Kendall retained undiminished the awe a child is likely to feel for his father, and so exacting was the standard he felt his father to have set that until the last years of his teaching career he did not presume to lecture extemporaneously; everything had to be organized, in correct proportion, everything had to be *there* on the page.

Kendall graduated from high-school at the age of thirteen, a year earlier than most students enter it, and became the youngest freshman ever, until then, to enter Northwestern University. Simultaneously, he became the youngest full-time reporter on the Chicago *Herald & Examiner.* When he completed his B.A. he toyed with the idea of many careers—he would teach, he would go to Europe, he would enter the foreign service or become a drama critic. At length he decided to do graduate work in Romance Languages, first at Northwestern, later at Illinois, where he completed the course work for a doctorate. At this point a Rhodes Scholarship, taking him to Oxford where he read Politics and Economics, turned him in a new direction. Henceforth his language skills—he spoke Spanish and French, and read Russian, German, and Italian—would be ancillary to his work as a political theorist. In 1938 he returned to Illinois with his Oxford B.A. and M.A. and finished a Ph.D. in Political Science. His dissertation, *John Locke and Majority Rule* (1941) has become a classic in the field of political theory, and points to what would be the dominant theme of his political thought: the conditions under which majority rule could produce good government.

This question was deeply rooted in his background and experience. The middle-America in which he had grown up had as part of its identity its historical experience as a free—that is, a self-governing—people. It had shown the world that majority rule could work. But how, and under what theoretical conditions?

Earlier than most American intellectuals, Kendall became aware of the threat posed to the people's liberties by alien ideologies, for his academic career was punctuated by jobs which took him to South America and to Spain as a journalist. Initially in Spain he supported the Republic, but he quickly became aware of the extent of Communist influence on the government side and thereafter favored the Nationalists. Subsequently, when the hard choice was between Communism and some right-wing authoritarian regime, he chose the latter as by far the lesser evil. Despite the fury shown toward them by the American press, the right-wing regimes were generally much less oppressive than the Communist alternative, and, above all, they posed no threat to the United States, whereas the expansion of Communist power most certainly did. Kendall's support for such foreign authoritarian regimes, however, did not mean for a moment any abatement in his allegiance to the unique system of government established by his beloved Constitution; it was, rather, perfectly consistent with that allegiance—and indeed probably intensified it. The American system *must* be made to work, all of his writings say in effect, and to be sure that it does work we *must* understand its principles. For if it does fail, the alternatives are only too clear—the abandonment of self-government for an authoritarian government of the left or the right. "What I do take sides on," he concludes in the last paragraph of the last essay he ever wrote, "is the thesis of the *Federalist Papers,* namely: That America's mission in the world is to prove to the world that self-government—that is, government by the people through a representative assembly which, by definition, calls the plays—is possible. What I do take sides on is our solemn obligation, as Americans, to value the good health of the American political system—the system we have devised in order to prove to the world that self-government is possible—above the immediate demands, however just and right, of any minority. What I do take sides on is government by consensus, which, I repeat, requires of minorities demanding drastic change that they bide their time until they have pleaded their case successfully before the bar of public—not merely majority—opinion. What I do take sides on is the Preamble of the Constitution which gives equal status to justice and domestic tranquility, and so pledges us to pursue them simultaneously and not even in the 'case' that seems 'dearest' to a protesting minority, subordinate domestic tranquility to justice."

III

For all his urbanity and cosmopolitanism, Willmoore Kendall cherished the vernacular, and especially the regional habits of speech. They preserved, in their own way, the particular and the concrete and could strike through the more polished, the more conventional, and the more academic words to convey the feeling of recognition. His own prose style is characterized by a sort of dialogue between the vernacular and the polite, the long sentences with their oral rhythms winding and unwinding between the two modes. It is much to the point here that his first publication was a book called *Baseball: How to play it and how to watch it.* He liked to use, as I recall, a striking and oddly disturbing phrase which I had never heard before and have never heard since, but which probably he recalled from his Oklahoma childhood. The American people, he would remark, continued to live their political tradition "in their hips." He meant that while they continued to live according to their traditional modes and orders, they had forgotten in their articulate life what those modes and orders were. In the life of the nation there had opened up a gap between doxa and episteme, between, on the one hand, unconscious assumption and practice, and, on the other, conscious idea. The division was reflected, Kendall saw, in the "two majorities," presidential and congressional. Typically, the president appealed to the regnant abstractions, he adumbrated vast new "frontiers" and "great societies"; he spoke of the unfinished agenda of democracy, of things like "equality of opportunity," and of idealistic goals abroad. Moreover *both* presidential candidates, competing for "swing" constituencies in the large states, were likely to employ this mode. Presidential rhetoric was much more in tune with the language of the academy and the media, and the thrust of presidential action was likely, though not always, to be in the direction this rhetoric adumbrated. Congress, on the other hand, represented a different constituency. The Congressman was closer to local feeling and interest. His concerns were less sweeping and ideal, and did not go so easily with the customary rhetoric of idealism. Congress, he saw, was much less articulate, but also much more successful. It usually prevailed, to the endless frustration of ideologues desiring to actualize the abstractions.

Kendall's brilliant discussion of "equality of opportunity" in his late essay on "Basic Issues Between Conservatives and Liberals," provides a concrete instance of the way this works. On the one hand, in the public forum, no articulate resistance exists to the idea that "equality of opportunity" is at the very top of our political agenda. The man who challenged it openly would soon find himself publicly discredited. But on the other hand, writes Kendall, "Any way you look at it, progress on the equalization of opportunity front, if there be progress at all (which I doubt), is glacially slow. New born babies in the United States are *not* born to the equality of opportunity that liberals claim for them as, literally, their birthright, but what is more, nobody thinks they are. More important still: even measures that might move things just a little towards making good the supposed right to equal opportunity are stoutly—and on the whole successfully —resisted all along the front. Most important of all: really drastic measures on behalf of equality of opportunity are not even proposed —not, I imagine, because liberals cannot think up such meaures, and not, I imagine, because they wouldn't be in favor of such measures, but because sound strategic instinct tells them that such measures are not politically possible." The paradox thus is surfaced: equality of opportunity is the only morally respectable case in the public forum; but it is politically impossible. It is not that another case does not exist, a counter-argument, but that it is "silent"—both known and not known—and never articulated. The "congressional majority" defeats or tables or ignores the liberal measures when they do come before it; but it does so without articulating a "position." An important aspect of Kendall's political writing is his effort to give voice to that silent case—to the majority position. Edmund Burke once compared the English people to oxen, grazing in a meadow. Large and silent, they fill the meadow with their bulk and their numbers. But it is the swarm of tiny crickets that fills the air with its chirping. Kendall's view of the American people was similar, and he tried—with brilliant success—to make the argument in opposition to the crickets.

For example, here is the known but unarticulated case against equality of opportunity. "The equality of opportunity goal, they [the majority] would say, is unrealistic, impossible to achieve, *utopian*— and because utopian, *dangerous.* In order to equalize opportunity in any meaningful way you would have, first of all—as clear-headed political philosophers have always seen—to neutralize that great carrier and perpetrator of unequal opportunity, the *family,* and you can do that, really do it, only by abolishing the family, which we will not let you do because that would be wrong. You would have, in the second place, to abolish poverty, and we do not believe anybody knows how to do that ... and the schemes one hears of now and then for making [the pie] big enough to go around do not commend themselves to us, either intellectually or morally; usually they involve one kind or another of *socialism,* about which we believe *both* that it is morally wrong and that it won't work—that it will in fact impoverish people rather than improve their lot. In a word, you can't equalize opportunity, and it is wrong to talk as if you could—wrong, to go no further, because you encourage many people to think themselves entitled to things they cannot have, to think they are being treated unjustly when in fact all is being done for them that can be done— more, indeed, in many cases, than ought to be done because more than is good for them. All that creates unnecessary and unwarranted resentment, and causes dissension among us, kicks up trouble. Finally, we repudiate your equality of opportunity goal because it rests on a false reading of the all-men-are-created-equal clause, and makes us forget, keeps us from acting on, the true meaning of those words ..."

To perceive the split between doxa and episteme, Kendall saw, led logically to an investigation of its sources. Where and when did it occur? Was it always part of our political history, or did it appear at some point or other? What *was* our political tradition? What really was—in the above passage—"the true meaning of those words," the all-men-are-created-equal clause?

IV

The "ordinary" books—as Kendall liked to call them—on American political history, books like those of Farrand, Curti, Hartz, or Rossiter, assume as a matter of course that we have a single political tradition enshrined in the Declaration of Independence, the Constitution, and the Bill of Rights. At the center of Kendall's work is the recognition that profound problems exist as regards this received assumption, that in these "founding documents"—*at least as conventionally interpreted*—there exists a contradiction in political theory, and further, that this contradiction, if fully explicated, defines the political issues that now divide us. Kendall concludes that contemporary students of American politics must take the analysis of this apparent contradiction as their starting point, and in this I think there can be little doubt that he is correct.

Though the bulk of Kendall's writing consists of a complex meditation upon the issues to be raised here, his most extended treatment of the matter occurs in a series of lectures he delivered several years ago at Vanderbilt University, now published by the Louisiana State University Press under the title *The Basic Symbols of the American Political Tradition* (co-authored with George W. Carey).

He observes, to begin with, that the Philadelphia Convention in 1787 almost unanimously opposed the adoption of a Bill of Rights, and he raises the question of whether a Bill of Rights—or, more precisely, the theory of inalienable individual rights—is compatible with the government established by the Philadelphia Constitution, or with the political theory of the Preamble. He notices that while the Declaration does talk about inalienable rights and about equality, the Preamble, which sets forth the purposes for which the new government is being established, says nothing at all about rights or about equality—though surely this was the place to talk about them if it were thought proper to do so. Is the American tradition, then, one of individual rights and their protection and of equality, or is it that of the Preamble? The question presses itself upon us, for it is obvious enough that in a given situation the goals of the Preamble might come into conflict with a "right." Which takes precedence, the goal of "domestic tranquility" or the supposed "right" of free speech? Suppose the goal of equality, allegedly implicit in the Declaration, comes into conflict with the obligation to provide for the common defense? or the maintenance of a more perfect union? The goals set forth in the Preamble might come into conflict at any number of points with the rights said to be enumerated or implied in the Declaration or in the Bill of Rights, especially the First Amendment. Kendall also reminds us that the men who were prominent at the outbreak of the War of Independence and who might be called the "rights" men—

Sam Adams, Tom Paine, Patrick Henry, etc.—tended to recede from view as the war went on and to give way to another breed altogether. Patrick Henry refused to attend the Philadelphia Convention, other "rights" men walked out and refused to sign—George Mason is a prominent example—and the Constitution itself was widely accused of betraying the "spirit" of the Declaration.

I would like to set aside for just one moment the question of whether the contradiction adduced here is real or only apparent; Kendall at length concluded that it was apparent, and that it has its source in a later misinterpretation of the key documents. But even that misinterpretation, it is clear, derives from something profoundly true about American culture. No misinterpretation, which becomes not only widespread but pervasive, could come from nowhere—its roots must be deep in the national identity. And the sense of contradiction—apparent or real—that Kendall defines in these documents has a familiar ring to the student of American literature, for that literature tells us that the very form of American experience is one of contradiction and polarity, that it exhibits, as Henry James remarked, a "rich passion for extremes." In his well-known book on the American novel, Richard Chase observes—indeed, it is the thesis of his book—that "the best and most characteristic American fiction has been shaped by the contradictions and not by the unities and harmonies of our culture"; and he adduces a number of such polarities, beginning with those of New England Calvinism with its opposition of the kingdom of light and the kingdom of darkness, of election and damnation. Elsewhere Chase, sharpening a formulation of Lionel Trilling's, describes American culture as divided between conservative feeling and radical idea, a contrast which might well seem to be adumbrated in the contrast between the government established by the Constitution, designed to reflect the deliberate sense of the community, and the universals and absolutes allegedly to be found in the Declaration and in the First Amendment.

Kendall has a number of profound things to say about this contradiction, but in his Vanderbilt lectures and in his later writings he reaches the following conclusion: Yes, there are at the *present* time alternative political traditions virtually at war in America—but no, when read carefully and in the context of their own time, the founding documents do not in fact reveal the contradiction and thus do not themselves provide the basis for our current ideological war. It is true,

he says, that the language of the Declaration has been read as asserting a "right" of "equality"—but it was Abraham Lincoln who in fact
first articulated such a reading and *made it* part of the political
tradition, or rather, part of one of the two political traditions. In its
own time, the language did not carry this meaning and need not
necessarily be so read today. The Declaration means to say only that
men are created equal in their right to set up a system of government,
by which they then shall be governed by majority consent—not that
the task of that government shall be thenceforth to render them
equal. One of the paradoxes of the American system, in fact, is that
though men are "equal" in the sense that they equally grant or withhold consent, they are part of a social system that has always been
hierarchical. Kendall traces this paradox back to the beginnings, to
the Mayflower Compact: all the free men aboard the ship gave their
consent to the Compact, but only eleven out of forty-one were called
"Mister." Read as stipulating a right of equality, the Declaration
would contradict the theory of the Preamble; read, correctly, as
affirming men's equality in having their consent solicited, the clause
is logically ancillary to the Constitution and not at all in conflict with
it. Men are equal in their right to govern themselves through a representative assembly and to enjoy, as individuals, those (but only those)
rights which the assembly confers in its pursuit of the general good.

When the clause is read as implying a mission to establish an overall
equality of condition, Kendall argues, this is clearly something quite
different from the intent of both Declaration and Preamble, and in
fact is one of our leading heresies. It expresses itself not by appeal
to the meaning of the founding documents, but to a series of quasi-
messianic Leaders—Washington, Jefferson, Lincoln, Roosevelt,
Kennedy—"each of whom sees more deeply into the specifically
American problem, which is posed by the all-men-are-created-equal
clause of the Declaration of Independence. America will build a New
Jerusalem which will be a commonwealth of free and equal men, free
men yes, but especially equal men, and will cause it to spread over
the face of the entire earth." If that requires the remaking of human
nature, making the unequal equal, well, no task is too great for the
genius of the messianic and—significantly—*suffering* Leader.
Through Him we shall be reborn.

But what of the other famous right, the right of free speech? One
reading of the First Amendment, Kendall points out, would mean,

definitively, that the United States is an "open society," that no questions are in fact closed, and that sanctions of any sort against the right of free speech are illegitimate and unconstitutional. This might be called the Hugo Black reading of the Amendment. And yet the language of the Amendment, Kendall points out, mentions no such right, is careful *not* to, and cannot legitimately be construed as sustaining one. "Congress," indeed, "shall make no law ... abridging the freedom of speech"—but the Tenth Amendment makes it clear that this applies specifically to *Congress* and not to the state governments, and that the thrust of the Amendment as it stands is to strengthen the authority of the state governments as against the central one, and *not* the individual against all government. The First Amendment, says Kendall, gives the states a legislative monopoly in the area of speech. Thus James Madison, the author of the Bill of Rights, could validly claim in answer to its opponents that the amendments would not "endanger the beauty of the government" established by the Philadelphia Constitution, and would not "weaken its frame or abridge its usefulness"—would not, that is, introduce a theoretical contradiction. The contradiction comes to the fore only when the later idea of the "open society" is read back into the original language.

To bring these issues to the fore in just this way illuminates the grounds of the argument which is at the center of our political conflict at the present time. Is the American government or is it not committed to the establishment of equality amongst its citizens? Does the First Amendment or does it not mean that America is an "open" society, has no "orthodoxy"?

Related to this argument are contrasting conceptions of the role of the different branches of the government. What is the form of the American government which, according to Kendall, emerged from the founding documents? His answer is complex, original and convincing. The Philadelphia Convention (as indeed the *Federalist* explains) established a government not, as we are now generally told, of three independent and equal or "balanced" branches, but a government of legislative supremacy—a supremacy nowhere inhibited by individual rights. In the last resort, Congress has final weapons which it may use against the other two branches, but which they lack against it. Does the Supreme Court have the last word on a given issue? Most certainly not. Congress can remove an act from the jurisdiction of the Court, can "pack" the Court, can initiate the amendment process, can impeach justices and refuse to pay them.

Why then, does the Court so often have its way; why does Congress so seldom employ a weapon of the last resort, as it did when the Court declared the income tax unconstitutional? Kendall proposes a variety of explanations: such as that the issues generally are not of sufficient urgency, or that the Court, aware of the power of Congress, tailors its decisions so as not to force a showdown. More important, he concludes, we have in historical fact been governed by an "understanding" of the Constitution which enjoins "restraint" upon the three branches. Congress does not forget that it possesses ultimate weapons, but it believes that it should not throw its weight around, and the condition of such restraint is a similar restraint on the part of the others. In Kendall's view, this morality of restraint is articulated in the *Federalist,* and has become the political ethos according to which the branches have historically functioned. The Constitution will work to permit the emergence of the deliberate sense of the nation only if the three branches move together on the great issues.

But there exists an alternative to this historic working of the Constitution, an alternative rooted in the theory of absolute and inalienable individual rights. The Court might assert such a right independently of the deliberate sense of the nation. If the Court deems the "right" to exist and to be inalienable, it need not wait upon the deliberate sense. The Court might thus force a showdown, which it could not win, but which would fracture the ethos of restraint upon which we historically have been governed. Such a danger is implicit in the entire "rights" theory of government, and in the aggrandizement of the Court and its mystique. Kendall considers the Court now to be embarked upon a course that will lead to such a confrontation; he prays that it will forbear.

But, it might now be asked: What prevents Congress—if under the central or orthodox American tradition Congress is really supreme—what prevents *Congress* from violating the deliberate sense of the community? Kendall gives his answer in several places—in the just-published Vanderbilt lectures, in his famous essay on "The Two Majorities in American Politics," and in various other essays. The founders deliberately designed Congress, and Congress has so evolved, that it would resist the transmission to its floors of "waves of popular enthusiasm." Congress is bicameral; its upper chamber is not apportioned according to population; its elections are staggered;

and it has developed procedures, such as the committee system, the filibuster, and the seniority system, which function to frustrate action by a temporary majority. The Congressional process thus slows down the decision of important matters until the deliberate sense of the community may be discerned. On important matters—so the founders clearly thought—a majority position must remain in being over a considerable length of time before being embodied in legislation. On important matters, the system really provides for government by consensus, and not by slender majorities. Finally, because Congress by its nature is so deeply involved with particular and local interests in its constituencies it functions to de-ideologize and de-fanaticize the issues before it. The orthodox American political tradition, wrote Kendall in his last essay,

> says to the movement seeking drastic change through the rewriting of the nation's laws: you must cool your heels in, so to speak, the legislative antechamber until a) the legislation you demand can pass Congress, with overwhelming majorities, and until b) the legislation can go into effect with the acquiescence not merely of Congress but of the President and the Supreme Court. Put the other way 'round, the system says to the movement seeking drastic change through governmental action, you must settle, from moment to moment, year to year, decade to decade, for whatever the three branches of our government (one of them, I repeat, acting by overwhelming majorities) are willing to give you; for whatever, in the first instance, the generality of our Congressmen and Senators can get together on. And that means, in practice: you must settle, from year to year and decade to decade for just as much, just as much and no more of your "objectives," as you can "sell" to the generality of politically active men and women out in American society.

It is on this line that Kendall takes his stand against modern liberalism as he understands it. Acting through their representatives, the American people have resisted, on the whole quite successfully, the set of policies which constitute the liberal program. The greatest breaches in the defenses of the "deliberate sense" conception of governing America have in fact most recently been made by the Supreme Court. The advocates of the liberal policies recognize the foot-dragging character of the "deliberate sense" mechanisms set up

by the Constitution and embodied in the Congress: like James Mac-
Gregor Burns in his *Deadlock of Democracy,* they are committed to
a set of policies, and are determined that those policies will be effectuated; the question then arises of what must be done *to* our political
institutions and habits in order to break the "deadlock" that keeps
them from being effectuated. "What is *really* new in Burns," as Kendall writes, "is on the one hand the problem to which he reduces
American political theory, and on the other hand his repudiation, no
less flat and un-ambiguous than that of Machiavelli himself, of the
whole range of concerns, principles . . . and above all inhibitions
handed down to him from the past. The nation's political regime is,
for Burns, the *ancilla* of a set of policies that he and his friends have
declared good. Let the liberal program prevail, and *ruat coelum!*"
The substance of justice and common good is preserved, in the orthodox American political tradition, through loyalty to a process—a process the delicate design of which reflects the founders' perceptions
regarding human nature and the nature of the body politic, perceptions continuous with the traditional wisdom of the West. The political heretic desires to short-circuit the process in the interest of a set
of prescribed absolutes, which reflect a different and opposite conception of human nature and politics. The confrontation is inherently
revolutionary.

V

But in the last resort the representative assembly, Congress, no
matter how carefully buffered against waves of popular enthusiasm,
no matter how systematically designed to ensure consensus government, does respond to the will of the people. The system presupposes
what Kendall, consciously employing the categories of our first
"founding" document, the Mayflower Compact, calls the "virtue" of
the people—that combination of civility, Christian conscience, and
recognition of a higher moral law which was a principal presumption
of the founding documents. Suppose the presupposed "virtue" is lost,
suppose the people becomes "corrupt"? In a sense, Kendall says in
his essay on Richard Weaver, there is a missing *Federalist* paper, for
Publius never answered the question, how are the people to be kept
virtuous? The people are to be kept virtuous, Kendall answers, by
teachers who keep alive—or, if necessary, recover—the nation's "his-

torical memory": the nation's knowledge of its own traditions, "lest, in ignorance of them, they forget, like madmen, what and who they are." The teachers then, who care enough for the past, not just because it *is* past, but for what it knows—those teachers can keep the people "virtuous": and it is good to have that word, with its ancient roots, cleaned off, purified of all priggishness. The Latin *virtu:* strength, ability, knowledge, courage—it is one of those deep and complex words.

Willmoore Kendall was such a teacher. He knew instinctively, and he succeeded in resurfacing historically, the American political tradition. In his last years his academic wandering ceased; he was, in fact, ready to admit that his difficulties had been in part those of a difficult personality, but only in part. He knew too how intense the ideological animus had been. The University of Dallas, however, proved hospitable, and he founded there a graduate program which is reminiscent in modern terms of the curriculum of the Renaissance humanists, a Ph.D. program in Politics and Literature. The students would go back to fundamentals in political theory, and they would also partake of the moral insights of the poets and novelists. In modern terms, it is the equivalent of the program advocated by Erasmus, St. Thomas More, or Sir Thomas Elyot, and taught at Milton's St. Paul's. It would be "rhetoric" and "logic" plus the historical consciousness. At Dallas both professionally and personally everything seemed to come together for him: he said that his days of wandering were at an end. He was surrounded by promising students and a first-rate staff; he at last was happily married. One senses here a liberation. He had begun to lecture extemporaneously, not laboriously writing everything out. The small child's awe of the blind but powerful father no longer operated to overpower. He knew, and he knew that he knew.

One almost parenthetical note is necessary here. Kendall was, for excellent reasons, almost defiantly American. He talked of being an Appalachians-to-the-Rockies patriot; he liked Dallas for itself and because it was only a few hours drive from his Oklahoma birthplace. But though this middle-America was part of his identity, and part of his historical sense—he knew how America is hated, even by some Americans—he knew that the American crisis was part of a broader Western crisis. He did not want *Americans* to be *Burkeans,* but he knew Burke's power as a diagnostician of the disease. Nowhere is it more clear that Kendall, precisely as an American, saw himself as part

of the West, than in the concluding paragraph of his review of Leo
Strauss' book on Machiavelli. Again the role of the "teacher" is central. Machiavelli, Strauss had shown, was a very great teacher, a very
successful teacher, but also a great negator. How is he now to be
counteracted? "Strauss's silence on this point is perhaps as explicit
a statement as the 'situation' and the 'quality of the times' call for, and
what it says is: the mischief can be undone only by a great teacher
who feels within himself a strength and a vocation not less than
Machiavelli's own, who possesses a store of learning not inferior to
Machiavelli's own, who will take the best of the young, of this generation and future generations, and, leading them by the hand without
arguing with them, habituate them to the denial of Machiavelli's
denials."

Kendall's was a great and a generous ambition, an ambition conceived in national and even world-historic terms. In his students, and
in his writings, he would negate the negation. I do not know, of
course, but I think he will win.

On June 30, 1967, at the age of 58, he decided to take an afternoon
nap and died in his sleep. For some months he had been functioning
at full capacity, and he had recently felt a special vitality and confidence in the importance of what he was doing. He died after a most
ordinary academic day—he had gone down to get his mail, read,
talked with one of his students about a term paper, and laid himself
down to rest.*

*The foregoing account of the final phase of Willmoore Kendall's life is indebted to
an unpublished memorial sketch by Prof. Leo Paul de Alvarez of the University of
Dallas.

Part I

THREE CHAPTERS
FROM THE NEVER-PUBLISHED
Sages of Conservatism

The Benevolent Sage of Mecosta*

Let us listen first to Mr. Russell Kirk, in his now-famous opening pages of *The Conservative Mind:*[1]

There is, we learn first-off, a "conservative principle" (it has been defended, during the past 150 years, by "men of genius," both in Britain and in America [p. 3])—or, what appears to be the same thing, an "essence" of conservatism, a "system of ideas" that has "sustained men of conservative *instincts* in their *resistance* against *radical* theories and social transformation ever since the beginning of the French Revolution [italics added, *ibid.*]. The resistance has, however, fared poorly: the "radical thinkers" have, by and large, "won the day"; put otherwise, the world has "clutched at Rousseau, swallowed him whole," as the conservatives have "yielded ground in a manner which . . . must be described as a rout" (p. 4); through the period in question, "things" have been in the saddle (as, apparently, Rousseau had wished them to be!); "unreasoning forces" have prevailed, which is to say: "industrialism, centralization, secularism, and the *levelling impulse*" [italics added] have prevailed, presumably over the impotent protest of the "conservatives." (Let us note, in passing, the tacit premise: *had* the conservatives prevailed, industrialism, centralization, secularism, and the levelling impulse, all four on the same footing it would seem, would *not* have triumphed, as triumphed they have.) Nor, in this context, is there any difficulty about placing the American Revolution: it was "substantially" a "conservative reaction, in the English political tradition, against royal innovation (p. 6).

What *is* the conservative principle—or rather *the* conservative principle? Well, Conservatism is *not*, we must understand, a "fixed and immutable body of ideas"; conservatives "re-express" their "convictions" to "fit" the times; at most we can hazard, on the main point, a "working premise," which we may state variously as "preservation of the ancient moral traditions of humanity" (presumably Kirk's own preferred way of putting it), or, with Lincoln, as "adher-

---

*Work notes found in Willmoore Kendall's files indicate that the three chapters in this section were to be re-worked and enlarged. They are not finished material.—Ed.

ence to the old and tried, against the new and untried." Or, if we wish to be more specific, we can identify certain "canons" of "conservative thought," as follows:

The conservative believes (I do not follow Kirk's numbering, and to some extent I paraphrase):

1. Society is ruled by, on the one hand, divine intent, and by, on the other hand, conscience.

2. There is an "eternal chain of right and duty."

3. One of the characteristics of the "eternal chain" is: it "links" the "great and obscure", the "living and dead."

4. Political problems are, "at bottom . . . religious and moral problems."

5. "Narrow rationality" cannot "of itself satisfy human needs."

6. Satisfying human needs is at least one standard by which we should judge principles.

7. There are "great forces in heaven and earth that man's philosophy cannot plumb or fathom."

8. Human reason is not to be trusted.

9. "Traditional life" was characterized by "proliferating variety and mystery," as over against the "narrowing uniformity and equalitarianism and utilitarian aims of most radical systems"; of these it is the former that merits "affection."

10. "Civilized society requires orders and classes."

11. Society longs for leadership.

12. There are natural distinctions among men.

13. Society should respect, not try to set aside, give free rein to, the natural distinctions among men.[2]

14. The natural distinctions among men are compatible with "equality," if by equality we understand "moral equality"; society should strive to bring about moral equality among its members.

15. Attempts at levelling, if *"enforced by positive legislation,"* lead to despair; society should (for that reason? for, among other reasons, that reason?) not make such attempts.

16. Attempts at levelling which are *not* enforced by positive legislation do not lead to despair, and are not to be quarreled with (because they do not lead to despair).

17. Despair is a bad thing.

18. If society destroys natural distinctions among men, dictatorship will ensue.

19. Freedom is inseparably connected with property; property is inseparable from "private possession"; if property *is* separated from private possession liberty disappears.

20. Economic levelling is not economic progress (and is *therefore* a bad thing, economic progress being a good thing).

21. Prescriptive rights should be respected.

22. Man is governed more by emotion than by reason; he has an "anarchic impulse."

23. Man must put a control upon his will and appetite, *because* he is governed more by emotion than reason.

24. Tradition and sound prejudice are good things, at least insofar as they put checks on man's anarchic impulse.

25. Change and reform are not identical.

26. Innovation is more often a "devouring conflagration" than a "torch of progress."

27. Slow change, however, is the means of society's conservation, wherefore "society must alter."

28. The proper instrument for change in a society is Providence.

29. Real statesmen are statesmen who have cognized the real tendency of Providential social forces.

There the creed is, then. "Deviations," says Kirk, have indeed occurred, but

> "in general conservatives have adhered to these articles of belief with a consistency rare in political history."

Their opponents, by contrast, he deems more difficult to pin down (there are five major schools: the rationalism of the *philosopher;* the "romantic emancipation" of Rousseau and his "allies"; the utilitarianism of the Benthamites; the positivism of the Comtists; collective materialism, that is, Marx and other socialists). Nevertheless, Kirk sees a "common denominator," and here again we can discern a creed. The radical believes that:

1. Humanity does *not* have a proclivity toward "violence and sin."

2. Education, positive legislation, alterations in the environment can (variously) produce "men like gods," or (not quite the same thing, surely) improve men.

3. Unlimited social progress is possible.

4. Where social welfare is concerned, the wisdom of "our ances-

tors" is a poorer guide than "reason, impulse, and materialistic determinism."

5. "Formal religion" should be rejected in favor of "anti-Christian
systems."

6. The ideal form of government is "total democracy, as direct as
practicable."

7. "Old parliamentary arrangements" should go by the board, in
favor of centralization and consolidation.

8. "Order and privilege" are bad things.

9. Private property, especially in land, is at best suspect, and short
of best ought to be abolished.

10. The state is not a "divinely ordained moral essence, a spiritual
union of the dead, the living, and those yet unborn."

Or, to summarize *both* creeds, the conservative believes "Conserve that which was seen by the eyes of your fathers." The radical
is "in love with change."

One shudders at this point as one thinks—well, of several people:
the student, assigned to write a term-paper on "modern conservatism," whose instructor has steered him (as there are many good
reasons for his instructor's doing) to Kirk's *Conservative Mind;* the
undergraduate who, in the context of all the current talk about "conservatism" and "liberalism," would like to know whose "side" he is
on; the conscious "young conservative," who begins to deem himself
part of a "conservative movement," and wishes to clear up for himself
the question, What do "we" stand for; the university teacher who
wishes to include in his course on contemporary politics a spate of
lectures on contemporary American conservatism, and turns (as,
given Kirk's reputation, he *must*) to the Sage of Mecosta for help.
One shudders because it is clear, once you lay Kirk's analysis out in
front of you in black and white, and subject it to even the most casual
textual winnowing, that Kirk can only confuse them; and one asks
oneself, here at the beginning of a series of lectures on contemporary
American conservatism, how many of the difficulties one should
pounce upon at once, how many of them postpone, push forward to
some later moment. But at least the following cry up at one in such
fashion that postponing them seems dishonest:

a) Mr. Kirk, *in this statement,* seems something less than clear on
where his conservatives stand with regard to *reason.* They are, we
readily see, opposed to letting "narrow rationality" (no. 5) call the

turns in human affairs (partly because it "of itself" cannot "satisfy human needs," but it would be gratuitous to suppose that that is Mr. Kirk's only objection to it). If, on the other hand, we pass along to no. 8, attention has shifted from "narrow rationality" to reason itself, and we are being told that conservatives "distrust" it. Yet in no. 23, where we learn of man's "anarchic impulse," the latter seems to be a matter of man's being governed more often by "emotion" than by "reason," and we get the impression that, the "anarchic impulse" being a bad thing, being governed by "emotion" is also a bad thing—and being governed by reason a *good* thing, presumably because reason *is* to be trusted. (I do not suggest that a satisfactory position on these questions cannot be extracted from Mr. Kirk's *opera* in general, but I am concerned here only with his widely-quoted statement in *The Conservative Mind.*)

　　b) Several of the propositions are clearly as can be (I put it that way because some of them, *e.g.,* no. 1, no. 4, appear to be but are not) "empirical" propositions, that is, statements about reality, about how things work. This is certainly true of no. 11, "Society longs for leadership," possibly of no. 15, *in re* the "despair" to which "attempts at levelling... enforced by positive legislation" lead, possibly (assuming we all know what we mean by "natural distinctions") of no. 18, *in re* levelling and dictatorship, possibly again (assuming we can agree what "liberty" is), of no. 19, in the destruction of private property and liberty. Now: this raises the question, Do such propositions conceivably have any proper place in such a "Creed" as Mr. Kirk is trying to construct?—where the off-hand answer would appear to be, Probably not. What Conservatives and Radicals disagree about are (as they are fashionably called) "values" or ends, or goals, or goods, which cannot be expressed in "empirically" "verifiable" propositions —not, of course, that men do not often differ about empirical propositions, propositions about how things work, what reality is like, and sometimes so deeply that they seem actually to be talking about different worlds. But the matter is not quite so simple as that. There are, in the first place (as the point is anticipated in two parenthetical remarks just above), some propositions that, though ultimately empirical, cannot be stated without employing *words* that involve, or may involve, difference in value. Take, for example, the proposition, "Good men make more money than bad men." It is, once we have agreed as to which men are good and which bad, empirically verifiable, and once "we" had looked up the relevant income-tax returns "we" should be able, quite without regard to our differing "value judgments," to agree as to whether or not the proposition is valid. Kirk's no. 15, about "levelling" and "despair," his no. 18, about levelling and dictatorship, and his no. 19, about the destruction of private property and dictatorship, are all propositions of this kind, and differences about them might well arise between conservatives and liberals because of differing views as to what despair is, or what liberty is, or what "natural distinctions" are. Insofar as this is true, we should perhaps not, *a priori*, exclude such propositions from such a creed. (Put otherwise, some apparently empirical propositions contain concealed value judgments, and so easily become fighting matters between persons of differing political philosophies.) Secondly, almost but not quite the same point, there are indeed competing "worldviews," views of reality, which is half the point, and possessors of differing views often do observe different things when they look out upon the world, which is the other half, and it is conceivable that there is a "conservative" view of reality and a "radical" view of reality, in which case empirical propositions describing the behavior of that reality might very *well* find a place in our creeds. Third, there are propositions that, even after the component terms are agreed upon, are so difficult of proof, that they easily become matters of dispute even though they are inherently proveable or disproveable "empirically." Mr. Kirk's writings are full, for example, of statements about the unavoidable effects, in any society, of the pursuance of "materialistic" ends, and these are good illustrations of the kind of thing I have in mind. Here again, a close student of the clash between conservatives and radicals might possibly conclude that a given proposition of that kind belongs in the creed. Fourth, we may anticipate a little by saying that the strongest claimants in this area, that is the "empirical" propositions about which the strongest claim can be made that they belong in a conservative creed, are propositions about the nature of man, about which, in my view, conservatives do not so much agree among themselves, but are united, or uniteable, against the Liberal view of the nature of man. (But of that more later.) We might conclude, of a much later moment, that one of the weaknesses of Kirk's creed is that it does not focus attention, at least not directly, upon the "nature-of-man" issue. (Due to the asymmetry between his two creeds, the second is the less open to this objection.)

a) The creed does *not* seem to bear out Mr. Kirk's initial reference to "the" conservative principle. Even in the statement *preceding* the creed, Kirk appears to have two candidates: preservation of the ancient moral traditions of mankind *and,* since the two things are, clearly, not one and the same thing, adherence to the old and tried (many things that confront us as very old, very tried, clearly fly in the face of *anybody's* statement of the ancient moral traditions of mankind) or, to put that differently, the first of the two *mots d'ordre* bids us cling to the tried in one "area," that or morals, while the second appears to embody the general animus against "change" that is often attributed to conservatives. In any case, the creed as it stands cannot possibly be regarded as a specification or "reading out" of either of the two; rather it seems to add *further* principles that would appear to be projected *on the same level* with the two, especially those relating to "divine intent" and "Providence." (One of the theses of this book will be that there *is* a conservative principle, that is, *a* principle that ultimately underlies the positions adopted by contemporary American conservatism, but that it cannot be either of the two Mr. Kirk puts forward.)

In any case, b) and even on the loosest reading of the creed, the latter would seem to make *non*-conservatives out of all non-theists. The conservative, we are assured, believes that society is ruled by *divine* intent and that *Providence* is the "proper instrument for change," both of which are propositions of which we can say that they are clearly unacceptable to persons who do not, so to speak, believe in God to begin with, and worse still that they are unacceptable to many theists, including this theist. This—the equating of conservatism with Christian or even "Judaeo-Christian" belief, or *qui est pire* with some particular aspect of such belief—poses very great problems, to which we must recur often in these pages. Here we merely note that Mr. Kirk is one of the contemporary analysts of conservatism who poses the problem.

c) The *most* obvious of the difficulties that cry up at you out of the creed we may point up with the question, Where, when Mr. Kirk has done, where do we end up about conservatism and "change"? *If* conservatism is adherence to the old and tried, then presumably it opposes "change," as, again, *if* conservatives believe that "innovation" (= change) is most often a "devouring conflagration," then presumably we would expect conservatives, unless they are arsonists, to oppose it. But No, *one* kind of change, "slow" change, is the "means of society's preservation" (= "society must alter"), and conservatives are not only no longer opposed to change, but in *favor* of it, or at least in favor of it provided it proceed *slowly*—which seems an astonishing criterion to try to saddle off on the conservative movement, if only because we have no standards by which, in this connection, to say what change *is* slow. Or, as no. 23 would seem to suggest, conservatives favor "reform" (= slow change) over against change (= rapid change). Evidently Kirk, at least as we see him here, needs to go off in the corner and make up his mind about this: as it stands, the creed here is hopelessly confusing. And, anticipating once again, let me say that, on this point unlike some others, we cannot clarify matters much by fanning out into Kirk's other writings: he is himself mixed up about conservatism and change, as, whether in large part thanks to him (and Rossiter) we need not say, contemporary American conservatives in general are mixed up about it—understandably, perhaps, since on the showing of this book the problem involved is *not* an easy one to square off to, but all mixed up all the same. (I shall "move in" on the matter in the chapter on the Pseudo-Sage of Ithaca.)[3] Suffice it to say here that *any* attempt to define conservatism as adherence to the old and tried must trip up over some difficulties that should be obvious to a high school boy.

d) A further difficulty, once we have grasped the foregoing, leaps to the eye, which we may put tentatively as follows (this time in the hope of Yes, getting some mileage): 'If we were to assume, *arguendo,* that conservatism = adherence to the old and tried = opposition to change, which is indeed always one possibility, then we must look askance at the contention that *both* Burke and the Founders of the American Republic were conservatives. For, even if we grant (as if we are in a mood for the somewhat far-fetched we might conceivably do) that the American Revolution was *on one side* (yes, the qualification *is* necessary) a "conservative reaction" against innovation by that wicked fellow George III, even I say if we grant that, the feat of fitting the Founding Fathers into the category "opponents of change" or "adherents to the old and tried" is one that, quite simply, no one, not even someone with Russell Kirk's gifted pen, is going to bring off, because it cannot be done. "Change," and not "slow" change either by a long sight, was the watchword on these shores from the moment of the Mayflower Compact, which in and of itself was a breathtaking political innovation—as, in due course, the Declaration of Independence and the Constitution of the United States were also to be innovations. Yes, yes, I know that all that was done in accordance with the traditional rights of Englishmen, and anyway under intolerable pressures that made it impossible to perpetuate the "old and tried" political *status quo* of 1775, but after you have milked all that dry you are still up against the fact that principled, general opposition to change (political, social, economic, what have you) was *not* characteristic of our Founding Fathers, was never in American conditions, and is not today, a possible political posture, save perhaps as we confine our purview to the ancient moral traditions of mankind, and then only if you can work "all men are created equal" into your picture of those ancient moral traditions. Put otherwise; take Burke as your Bible for this purpose, take as your premise that what Burke taught is conservatism, and you will indeed find yourself with passages on your hands that point you to adherence to the old and tried as the essence of conservatism. But take the *Federalist* as your Bible, and you will find few such passages, and very guarded ones when you do find them.

e) Let us note, for what it is worth, that there is nothing in the creed we have before us—nothing unless, just possibly, the reference to "natural distinctions" among men, and the references to "levelling"—that would suggest any connection between conservatism and capitalism, or conservatism and the "defense of the free market." Some readers, especially those familiar with the what-conservatism-is pronouncements of some of Mr. Kirk's putative political allies, may well find this a little confusing; as we shall have much to say, in what follows, about the kind of problem this kind of thing poses for the emergent conservative movement.

f) Let us note, again for what it may be worth at a later point, the —well, defeatism of the statement with which Mr. Kirk introduces the creed: he thinks of the conservative force as, quite simply, having been "routed," and, as many a passage in his subsequent works show even more clearly, of himself and his contemporary allies as fighting a rear-guard or delaying action. Nor, as we shall see in subsequent chapters, is he alone in this—indeed the battle-cry of contemporary American conservatives often seems to be: "We are losing! We are losing! But in how beautiful, how fine, how *noble* a cause!"

g) *Some* at least of the apparently empirical propositions in the

creed would appear to be open to attack on the grounds not so much
that they are empirical and thus seem a little out of place, as that it
is difficult to believe, in the absence of convincing proof to the contrary, that they could possibly be "issues" between conservatives and
their opponents. Is Russell Kirk, conservative, really more deeply
persuaded than John F. Kennedy, radical, that "society longs for
leadership"? Can we imagine a falling out between Russell Kirk,
conservative, and the editors of *America,* liberals surely, over
whether there is "an eternal chain of right and duty"—or over
whether political problems are "at bottom . . . religious and moral
problems"? Is Russell Kirk, conservative, likely to hold out more
stubbornly than, say, Dr. Albert Schweitzer, pacifist, for the truth that
there are "great forces in heaven and earth that man's philosophy
cannot plumb or fathom"? Is Russell Kirk, conservative, more persuaded that "despair is a bad thing" in society than, say, the editors
of *The New Republic?* So, too, with at least one item that is clearly
a "straight" moral precept. Does Russell Kirk, conservative, really
think there is something peculiarly conservative about the belief that
"man must put a control on his will and appetites"? Obviously not;
and this comment, which I believe to be of the first importance for
the emergent conservative movement in the United States, seems to
me in order. One understands, upon a moment's reflection, how all
these copybook maxims got into Mr. Kirk's creed, namely as follows:
Many "radicals," that is, liberals, either openly deny the maxims in
question, or hold beliefs that can be shown to involve their denial;
conservatives regard such denial, whether explicit or implicit, as
wrong, pernicious even; and the temptation arises to include the
assertion of the maxims in the conservative creed, where what *should*
appear in the creed is, at most, repudiation of the denial of the
maxims (which if echoed from some liberal quarters merely strength-
ens the conservatives' hands). But we must not, on pain of sounding
trivial, yield to the temptation. Put otherwise: a conservative creed
should include only items demonstrably *central* to the conservatives'
position over against their opponents. Put otherwise again: one clear
objection to Mr. Kirk's creed, distributed as it is on a very high level of generality, is that there is too much of it. Put otherwise again:
any item of belief that conservatives share with large numbers
of their political opponents is suspect as an item for inclusion in a
conservative creed, and should be offered up to Occam's razor

however ardently conservatives may believe it.

h) If we assume, as it seems natural to do and as the very remarks with which Kirk introduces the creed would dispose us to do, that the issues that have divided conservatives and radicals over the decades since Burke are the selfsame issues that divide conservatives and liberals in contemporary America, many of us will find the creed hard to square with what we know about the contemporary discussion process. That omnipresent phenomenon of the contemporary American discussion process, the debate between Mr. William F. Buckley, Jr. and whatever unfortunate Liberal the program committee has served up for Mr. Buckley's kind and capable ministrations, simply is *not* a debate about the kind of thing with which, for the most part, the creed deals—either directly, or, another possibility of course, indirectly (in the sense that Mr. Kirk's issues are those on which the debaters, had they time and leisure, would ultimately be forced back). That, as I have intimated, is partly a matter of Kirk's writing and thinking with an eye too much to Burke and not enough to the Framers, so that he addresses himself to, for Americans, the wrong topics in an inappropriate vocabulary. Partly, however, and more importantly on the showing of this book, it is a matter of Mr. Kirk's actually being, except where education is concerned, too far above the fray, that is, above the kind of thing over which, in for example the Congress of the United States, conservatives and liberals actually divide; he is, therefore, on the showing of this book, an improbable spokesman for the emergent conservative movement, because he simply does not "identify" with those who are fighting the battles on which the outcome of the war must ultimately turn. The free market is, as we shall see, only one of the central issues between conservatives and liberals that the creed not only does not touch upon, but does not, so to speak, even prepare us for. The appropriate creed, if and when we are able to formulate it, is likely to be set down by someone with, if I may put it so, a little more blood showing on his hands and a little more smell of sweat emanating from his armpits. We shall see why, or rather why in greater detail, in what follows.

i) It remains, in all fairness, to indicate those points on which, on the ultimate showing of this book, the Kirk creed is *not* open to the kind of criticism I have been urging—that is, to say what ones, out of all the concepts and ideas we now have before us, I would advise the reader to seize upon and cherish. They are, briefly, these: The

idea that conservatism, as or especially as it presents itself in the
arena of political conflict and conflict over social and economic
policy, is a *resistance,* and a resistance to proposals put forward by
those whom Kirk, for his purposes, calls radicals, and whom in contemporary America, we call liberals. The idea that the clash between
conservatives and liberals is somehow reducible, on one side at least,
to a disagreement about the rôle of "reason" in human affairs. The
idea, in our view quite insufficiently stressed in Kirk's creed but
certainly present, that the conservatives find themselves forever resisting the radicals (*i.e.* liberals) because the liberals are "levellers,"
and, finally, the idea that there are, on the one hand, "conservatives
by instinct," and, on the other, conservative intellectuals, whose
function it is to *articulate* the principles and premises that demonstrably underlie the political and social action of the "instinctives"—
or, as I would prefer to add, fail to articulate them. As regards all these
points, Mr. Kirk seems to me to be on solid ground.

If Kirk's creed is open to all that many objections, why have I
tarried thus long over it? Well, for a number of reasons: First, as I have
already intimated, because of the place it occupies in the literature
of our topic. It was, in point of time, the first recent attempt, by an
American, to offer a succinct answer to the question to which this
book is addressed; and, because of the fame and prestige that have
been justly accorded to the book in which it appears, *The Conservative Mind;* because, if you like, so many other writers and speakers
have used it as a point of departure for a discussion of contemporary
American conservatism, so that it has itself entered into and become
part of our problem, acquiring something approaching semi-official
status and authority. Second, because whatever its shortcomings for
the purpose for which it was intended, in part *because* of its shortcomings, it provides, when subjected to the kind of criticism I have
just attempted, an excellent means of opening up some of the problems and pitfalls with which our topic abounds, so that, as I hope, we
shall the more easily come to grips with the Pseudo-Sage of Ithaca,
and the Muscleminded Sage of Kent,[4] as a result of having dwelt
upon it so long.

The temptation to pass along at once to the Pseudo-Sage of Ithaca
is, let me confess it, considerable, but I propose, before doing that,
to raise and try to answer, and at some little length, two questions
about Russell Kirk over and above the question (What, according to

him, *do* conservatives believe?) with which I have just dealt. Mr. Kirk regards himself, and is regarded by others, as a conservative in his own right. Put otherwise, he is not merely a would-be definer and historian of modern British and American conservatism, but also a political thinker, observer, commentator, with ideas of his own that might or might not be subsumable under his own definition of conservatism and, what is more important, might or might not be subsumable under a more accurate and realistic definition of conservatism. Put otherwise: he is himself a conspicuous and honored figure in the emergent conservative movement in America, and in the two-fold capacity of *evangelist,* selflessly devoted to the task of bringing converts into the fold, and *theorist,* with notions of his own as to the *doctrines* the movement should adopt and, that being by no means necessarily the same thing, the *program* it should espouse. Put still otherwise: he has himself entered into and become part of our problem, so that it would be unjust, alike to him and to my readers, not to take cognizance here of his characteristic doctrines and proposals and, however briefly, square off to them from the point of view defended in these pages.

Three remarks, by way of propaedeutic, before entering on this phase of our inquiry:

We now distinguish, I say, between Russell Kirk, the author of a celebrated definition of conservatism, and Russell Kirk, the teacher, especially (as we shall see) the *moral* teacher, of his contemporaries, and propose to fix attention upon his *teachings.* In order to do this, however, we must adopt a rather arbitrary procedure the necessity for which we may put as follows: Kirk's characteristic manner of putting a teaching forward is not the "verily, verily, I, Russell Kirk, say unto you" of the New Testament, but rather the sentence or paragraph or statement that begins "The intelligent conservative feels" or "The reasoning conservative will support" or "The true conservative believes, etc," which is to say that if we read him "literally" we shall find him forever at the stage of defining conservatism. There may (I do not exclude the possibility) be some cases where such sentences or statements are really intended as parts of a "compleat" definition of conservatism, that is, where the phrase "the reasoning conservative will, etc." is intended *sensu stricto.* I give it as my opinion, however, that these cases are rare, and that "the reasoning conservative" is merely Kirkian shorthand for saying what a less (or is it more?) modest man would express with a simple "I," and I shall, in what follows, so read it. (Put otherwise: Mr. Kirk does *not* distinguish between the two questions, "What is conservatism?" and "What are my teachings?") We, if only because we cannot accept the tacit premise involved (the archetype of the reasoning conservative is Russell Kirk), must and will distinguish between the two questions.

Second, I happen, for the most part, to agree with the moral teachings of Russell Kirk, and would like nothing better than to see them taken to heart, and lived by, not only in the emergent conservative movement but in the American Republic as a whole; put otherwise, I wish Russell Kirk the moral teacher well, and in my own part-time activities as a moral teacher propose, in future as in the past, to echo and second and underline the main body of his teachings. But it seems to me, as apparently it does not to Kirk, that it is one thing to say, "I deem this moral teaching sound," another thing to say, "Because and in virtue of being sound, this moral teaching has a place in the doctrine of the emergent conservative movement," and still another thing to say, "This moral teaching, because sound, has a place in the doctrine of the emergent conservative movement, and furthermore I think there *is* anyhow a prayer of the movement's adopting it in the foreseeable future." Quixotism is always admirable —the place of honor in the living room of the Old Sage of Northford is occupied by two beautiful editions of *Don Quixote*—but somewhere, in the course of building a political movement, we must draw the line between teachings whose reception could come, at the earliest, only at the end of sustained educational effort, by Church and Academy, over many decades or even many generations, and those for which we might, in the foreseeable future, win enough adherents to actually affect the course of events.

Thirdly, no treatment of the doctrines and program of a man who is, on the face of it, one of the contenders for intellectual leadership of the emergent conservative movement, could (what with the movement burgeoning all about us) be complete without a certain amount of attention to what let us call, borrowing the phrase from Leo Strauss, his "silences"—the points he might fairly be expected to make but never gets around to, the further thing that, in this context or that, he might say but doesn't. In Kirk's case, on the showing of this book, the silences are perhaps equally important with the characteristic doctrines and the program.

The Characteristic Teachings of Russell Kirk.

The teaching concerning tradition.

Let us examine the teaching first in its programmatic aspect. Mr. Kirk would, first, like to see the conservative movement adopt as part of its program measures calculated to decentralize industry, deconcentrate population, and to "prevent further diminution of our rural population"—measures, in a word, calculated to keep as many as possible of our people close to the world of nature and of custom. He would like, second, for the movement to work for the "humanization" of urban life, that is, the revival, in our cities, of the "old ways and old things," and of concern for the preservation of, for example, "old houses and neighborhoods." And he would like, third, for the movement to throw the weight of its influence against the claim, on the part of public educators, to a "right" to "train the whole child," while, at the same time, "encouraging" parents to resume responsibility for instructing the young in morality and in "the ways of the world," and supporting the churches in their "endeavors to make religious knowledge the most important part" of education. (Mr. Kirk does not go into the question of how a conservative movement might go about achieving these, for me at least, worthy objectives or how the second and the third, as opposed to the first—decentralization and deconcentration could, presumably, be accomplished by legislation, though probably not without granting to "the state" powers that some conservatives would wish to think twice about—could conceivably become the business of a political movement. We have, clearly, come almost at once upon one of those teachings that, however sound their moral basis, must be left to grow by a slow process of persuasion and that, even if finally accepted by, say, a majority of Americans, could for the most part be translated into reality only in the personal lives of the persuaded. There seems nothing to be gained, except confusing matters, by labelling it conservative, though one *might* give a different answer here if the proposals were, so to speak, turned 'round, and the conservative movement called upon to resist any and all state action calculated to produce further centralization and concentration, further undermining of the rural community, further transfers to public agencies, from the family and the churches, of responsibility for education.)

The doctrinal theme common to the three foregoing proposals is, as my heading indicates, a teaching concerning tradition, which we may summarize briefly but I think not unfairly as follows: We should feel a deep sense of gratitude to the "generations that have preceded us in this life" (and, beyond or above them, to the "eternal order" and, finally, to the source of that order, that is, God). If we are to maintain a just civilization, we must keep ourselves, and others, reminded of the value of *continuity*—continuity in "religious and ethical conviction," in "literature and schooling," in (if I interpret Kirk correctly) our political institutions and economic policy, and, finally, in the "physical fabric of life" (down, one supposes, to the town and city planners). Men who have interrupted such continuity, men that is who break with tradition, in due course lose all sense of community with their fellows, become impatient of any restraints upon appetite, and give themselves up to, on the one hand, a "levelling envy" that undermines the achievements of mind and spirit, and, on the other hand, the "violence" that is congenital in "fallen human nature." Put otherwise: to interrupt the continuity is to break an "eternal contract" that imposes upon the living sacred obligations toward the dead—the forefathers that is, and the unborn—future generations that is. What obligations? An obligation, *inter alia* it seems, to live in accordance with the "wisdom" of the ancestors (p. 298); to keep alive recognition of the "divine element in social institutions" (p. 299), to —well, not so much to keep things as they are, since society must be continuously "renewed" and "change" is the instrument by which its renewal is accomplished (p. 301), but to see to it (Kirk is not easy to follow here) that such changes as are made shall be "beneficent," and in "continuous train" with the past (p. 301); finally, to "look forward with solicitude to the interests of posterity" (p. 298). Why does the obligation obligate, why should the living observe the contract? Not, it appears, because they are bidden to by Reason, which Kirk seems, in this connection, to equate with "abstract rationality," or "simple rationality," which, in turn, he seems to equate with being guided by "self-interest" (p. 298)—as, so far as I can see, he seems to equate the two questions, "Why should the living obey the contract?" and "Why do the living obey the contract?", letting his answer to the second of the two stand as his answer to both: the living obey the contract because of their "beliefs": "The eternal contact . . . has been made known to succeeding generations, from the dawn of civilization, by

. . . tradition. Tradition is the process of handing on beliefs, . . . [especially] through the life of the family and the observance of the church" (pp. 301-302). "Tradition [is] . . . the principal source of our moral beliefs and our worldly wisdom . . . [It is] that body of knowledge that is bound up with prescription and prejudice and authority, the accepted beliefs of a people . . ." Just any old beliefs the people may happen to have "accepted"? Apparently so.

Let us observe at once: if the teaching is sound, the programmatic proposals are unexceptionable. Let us observe, too: the teaching is a teaching about *the* important problems of politics. Let us observe, finally, that no attempt is made to conceal the extent of the author's indebtedness to Burke: it would be easy, as I am sure Mr. Kirk would agree, to send the reader, point by point, to the parallel passages in Burke's writings; much even of the vocabulary is Burke's. The question might well arise, therefore, whether the teaching is a faithful rendition of Burke's teaching, though we must be careful, because it would take us too far afield, *not* to let it arise. Let us ask, rather, Is the teaching *sound,* that is, a teaching that contemporary American conservatism would be well-advised to let the Benevolent Sage of Mecosta talk it into accepting? And let us give at once the only possible answer, which is No, and for, to go no further, the following reasons:

a) Mr. Kirk's teaching on tradition is, on the face of it, an assertion of the very relativism and positivism that, in other contexts, he abhors. For it is, on the face of it, a teaching about the role and binding force of tradition in societies-in-general, and what it says about societies-in-general is that they are all somehow based on an "eternal contract," which enjoins a moral and religious tradition which is and, one gathers, ought to be transmitted from generation to generation by the family and, one gathers again, the local equivalent of "churches" (presumably shrines in Japan, mosques in Turkey, and temples in ancient Greece). Having, as I do, no objection to certain "circular" arguments, I shall not dwell on the patent circularity of the teaching (the contract is the source of the morality, the morality the source of the obligation to obey the contract), that is, the weakness of its weak side, but rather shall insist merely upon the dangerousness of its dangerous side: Because it declares all traditions equal, it reduces the American tradition to the level of, say, the tradition that will obtain in the Soviet Union once the latter has succeeded in

getting the Russian family and the Russian churches into the business
of transmitting Communist doctrine. Contemporary American conservatism, one of whose basic quarrels *must* be the quarrel with
relativism and positivism *in all their forms,* must give the teaching
a wide berth.

b) Even if we shook the teaching loose from its relativist emphases,
which we could do by abstracting from societies-in-general and tra-
ditions-in-general and restating it as a teaching about *American* society and the *American* tradition, matters would not be greatly
improved. For the teaching then becomes: We Americans are parties
to an "eternal contract" which imposes upon us certain obligations
to our forefathers and to our descendants, and which we ought to
obey because we are taught to obey it by our families and by our
churches—one, moreover, which we would *not* be led to obey
through reliance on Reason, which merely points us in the direction
of "self-interest" (and, Mr. Kirk assures us, cannot teach us the "real
veneration" we owe to the "wisdom of our ancestors"). Such a teaching—let me lay it on the line—would be an insult to the American
tradition that contemporary American conservatism must conserve,
and the latter must, in this area anyhow, find itself a teacher who can
teach it *why* it is an insult. For one thing, American traditionalists do
not have to speak vaguely of an "eternal contract," like that which
Burke pulls out of thin air in his famous metaphor (which he surely
never intended as anything *but* a metaphor), which we ought to
observe merely or even primarily because our families and churches
taught us to; when, in connection with the American tradition, we
speak of a contract (which I, for one, have no objection to our doing)
we know perfectly well what contract we are referring to, namely
that of the Declaration of Independence as renewed and specified
in the Constitution of the United States and as explicated in a book
entitled *The Federalist,* and have no reason, when we speak of it, not
to put a name to it. And we ought to obey that contract not because
our families and churches taught us to (which, as we saw Mr. Kirk
recognize a moment ago, they may very well not have got around to
doing), but for one thing because contracts, which are *promises,*
ought to be kept (=we ought to obey the contract, and live up to and
perpetuate the morality it enjoins, because to begin with we have
promised to), and for another because the contract is *reasonable* (=
we ought to obey because that which it specifies was worked out by

reasonable men locked in discourse, and the *law of reason* accordingly bids us to obey it). *Our* contract, moreover, is *not* understood by its tradition as possessing a "divine element"—indeed one of the promises it involves is, as we shall be saying in this book again and again, *not* to make any such claim for it, as its Framers were careful not to do. And we will not entertain the suggestion that there is something somehow un- or non-reasonable about it—even if Burke, in some passages, seems inclined to edge us along in that direction.

c) The teaching is, quite simply, unintelligible as regards the relation between tradition and "change," the latter, as we have had occasion to notice before, being always a stumbling-block for Mr. Kirk. His creed teaches us that change is allowable if "slow"; here slowness disappears as the criterion, and we are taught, variously, that change is allowable if "in continuous train" or allowable, desirable even, if "beneficent," both criteria which Mr. Kirk would be wise to let disappear also, the first because it is uncongenial to the American tradition, the second because it is demonstrably tautological. Here again contemporary American conservatism needs a better teaching than Mr. Kirk is able to offer it—because, if I may put it so, he is relying on Burke for help with a problem, a very difficult one to be sure, over which Burke stumbled, too, and because, again if I may put it so, he has not got his problem stated in terms of the *American* tradition, or even in an American vocabulary. For the *American* tradition, stemming as it does from the *Federalist,* has a "built-in" solution to the problem, which we may put as follows: We are under contract, alike with our forefathers and our descendants, to perpetuate for the latter the heritage of tradition that we have received from the former. That tradition, however, is a tradition that, so to speak, *wills its own perfection,* unambiguously recognizes and welcomes change as the means by which that perfection is achieved, and includes *within* itself both a) the criteria, those of the Preamble of the Constitution, in the light of which proposals for further perfection are to be weighed, and b) procedures in accordance with which such proposals are accepted or rejected. The problem, *politically speaking,* is not properly a problem, and certainly not properly a stumbling-block, for contemporary American conservatives who look well to the sources of *their* tradition. And no teaching should be acceptable to them that treats it as a problem.

The teaching about the "open society."

Mr. Kirk does not address himself directly to the problem of the
open society; he speaks to us, rather, about "loyalty," which he prefers to construe in what we may call its philosophical sense, that in
which it is used in, *e.g.*, Royce's celebrated book, and *not* in the sense
which, as he condescendingly points out, was likely to be uppermost
in the minds of his readers at the time (1954, or perhaps 1953) he was
writing; that is, the sense in which it was then being used in the
phrase "loyalty [that is, internal security] program"; or perhaps we
should say: So Mr. Kirk insists, since I am less certain than Mr. Kirk
that those of us who at that time called the internal security program
the "loyalty" program were, as he puts it, "degrading" the word
loyalty (= leaving out of "loyalty," he says, the dimension, over and
above that of "fidelity," of "love"). But a) he does keep coming back,
in the course of his discussion, to such things as (p. 272) the "eagerness of legislatures and boards of regents in America to exact pledges
of conformity from civil servants and . . . teachers" ("so much lost
endeavor" for the most part, Kirk believes), and to (p. 274) "committees of Congress and of the state legislatures . . . busy . . . prying into
the opinions and conduct of various minorities," and b) does force
himself to square off to them, and, in doing so, does lay down a
teaching of sorts on the open society issue—which, on the showing
of this book, is one of the deepest issues that divide contemporary
American conservatives from their enemies the Liberals. The teaching is this:

An ordered society has a right, transcending the right of individuals to "follow their own humor," to protect its own existence. It
therefore has the right to "expect" that its "professors and teachers"
shall not "preach subversion" (p. 27 f.), to distinguish between "valuable criticism" and "irresponsible sedition," and to insist, upon pain
of inviting anarchy or tyranny, on the "very principle and necessity
of loyalty." It is, therefore, "pointless to ask whether legislatures have
a *right* to inquire into the loyalty of public servants and even private
persons"—"of course they have such a right" (p. 278-279); and not
only the "right," but also the "duty" (p. 280), because the "peril of
the present hour, when betrayal of scientific and military secrets may
mean national destruction, . . . has brought us face to face with the
grim nature of the problem of loyalty" *(ibid.),* and because "there is

something even more precious than absolute liberty, and that is absolute survival" *(ibid.).* In view, indeed, of the "menace of modern warfare," it is a "matter for congratulation that the American people and American legislators have been so moderate as they remain today." Indeed again, what "sustains the present demand for loyalty" is in point of fact a "conservative impulse"—an impulse on the part of the American people to "safeguard . . . a complex of rights and laws," and to "exact fidelity to certain prescriptive institutions and habits . . . : private property, liberty under law, a just distribution of political power, and a respect for individual personality" (p. 277). On the other hand, "sometimes the language and conduct of investigators has exceeded the bounds of decorum and even justice," so that this is an area in which we must be "jealous of our liberties" (p. 280). And, in any case, we must think of the "present interlude of loyalty checks . . . as a mere interim, however distasteful, between an era of doubt and an era of renewed faith"—in which, one gathers, the "loyalty checks," and the need for them, will disappear. Why? Because, if I read Mr. Kirk correctly, we shall have restored in our society those "qualities of loveliness, which encourage loyalty to a nation," (p. 290), which qualities—again if I read him correctly— have not of late fared well amongst us (p. 28, *et seq.*). "[We] will do well to suspect that there is something ailing with the heart of a society in which loyalty-investigations are a recurring phenomenon" (p. 292).

Now: let not the contemporary American conservative, especially the young contemporary American conservative who has turned to Mr. Kirk for instruction that will sustain him in his defense of the congressional investigating committees, of, indeed, the whole internal security program, against the never-ending demand of the Liberals that a stop be put to all that sort of thing—let him not, having at first got the impression that Mr. Kirk is himself going to attack the committees, heave a sigh of relief at the foregoing song-and-dance, and embrace *this* teaching of the Benevolent Sage of Mecosta. It is, let me assure him, a *false* teaching, which reflects at every point Mr. Kirk's ambivalence and hesitations on a matter on which there can, for conservatives who mean business about their conservatism, be no compromise, either in practice or in theory, with their opponents. And it is false for the following reasons:

First, the ground Kirk takes up in order to extend his tardy and reluctant blessing to the internal security program is exactly that to which the Liberals, back during Korean war days, finally *retreated*— in order to call off their direct attack on the program: We are up against a relentless and resourceful enemy, the World Communist movement, which is prepared to use against us, amongst other aggressive weapons, that of internal subversion; apparently that weapon can be turned only with such counter-weapons as the loyalty-program, legislative investigations, etc., which, accordingly, become necessary to our *survival* and, *qua* necessary but of course only insofar as necessary (wherefore henceforth we shall attack the program only indirectly, through the Courts), may go forward with our acquiescence. The tacit premise, shockingly immoral on the face of it, is that we are justified in doing whatever is called for us to survive; and the clear implication, where the argument is used in connection with the internal security program, is that the latter can be justified on no other grounds. Now: the argument from survival is, let us be clear, always and everywhere a *Liberal* argument; the Liberals, having nothing to die for, must survive *coûte que coûte,* must therefore go along with whatever appears to contribute to survival (including, as we shall see, a foreign policy that subordinates both honor and the national interest to the keeping of a tenuous, but presumably satisfactory from the standpoint of survival, peace). No conservative has any business being caught, dead even, using such an argument; the conservative's clear obligation is, rather, to *repudiate* the argument wherever, and in whatever form, it turns up. He will, by doing so, strengthen the case he can make out for the internal security program, and for the other conservative interests that are threatened by current Liberal interpolations of the First Amendment.

b) There is a second emphasis in the foregoing line of argument (and, on beyond that, still a third), which is difficult to square with his protestation, elsewhere in the book we are considering, that he and the Liberals are, so to speak, as oil and water, namely: the contention, half-explicit half tacit but certainly there, that if there are disloyal Americans we are ourselves, somehow, to blame; had we but made our country lovelier, our disloyal Americans would have loved it more, and would have been loyal Americans; there is, moreover, a happier time coming, off in the future, when having *made* our country lovelier we shall no longer have any loyalty problem, thus no longer have any need for the sort of thing associated with the internal security program. Have the Liberals been right, all along then, in insisting that society, not the criminal, is responsible for crime, when it occurs, and that, in any case, we can by manipulating the institutions of society so perfect the generality of men that crime will disappear? Or does Mr. Kirk see some significant difference between his line of argument about the crime of disloyalty and the Liberal line of argument about crime in general, between his version of the dogma of human perfectibility through institutions and the Liberal version. Nor is it any good to answer, on Mr. Kirk's behalf, that one can cite a thousand passages from his works that show he knows better. Of course one can, and of course he knows better—except where the issue of the open society comes into view. But with respect to that problem, which on the showing of this book is one of those on which the differences between our conservatives and our liberals are beyond compromise, Kirk has many of the stigmata of the unreconstructed Liberal, and, far from providing the kind of intellectual leadership the contemporary conservative movement needs, is sure to point young conservatives who turn to him for guidance in *exactly* the wrong direction.

c) So too with the third emphasis in Mr. Kirk's line of argument to which I wish to direct attention.

Conservatives, Mr. Kirk writes, regard "power" as a "dangerous thing"; they have, therefore, always sought to "hedge it about with strong distinctions," to "divide it among many groups and institutions," to see to it that "concentrated power may abide nowhere" (p. 251). Being "severely aware of the frailty of human nature," they have favored the checking and balancing of legislative, executive, and judicial authority, federalism (and presumably other devices) for restraining central authorities in favor of regional and local authorities, and—though one would have expected this to come first—the "prudent confinement of the state's sphere of action to a few well-defined objects" (p. 256); they have spurned the view that the passing over of power from kings and aristocrats to "the People" has changed matters in this regard; it is, indeed, the conservatives' "search after a just balance of authority" that has vouchsafed to us Americans, over the centuries, the "high degree of freedom and right" that we have enjoyed (pp. 256-257). All conservative voices here speak as one: Burke, in his struggle against the "unitary designs of George III" (p. 288); John Adams, in his *Defense of the Constitu-*

tions (p. 251); and the authors of the *Federalist,* "the most influential
work of all our political literature," with their insistence that justice
and liberty are safeguarded not so much by "any wisdom innate in
'the People'" as by "wise constitutions" (*ibid.*). The American conservative needs, therefore, to keep himself reminded that "power is
held in check by two influences: moral authority, or the dictates of
conscience, and *political authority, or the barrier of good laws*" (p.
259, italics added). And he needs, also, to recognize that processes
are afoot amongst us that, "unless conservatives begin to oppose
[them] effectively," are "liable to make an end of American society
as we know it" (*ibid.*)—processes that are "undermining every political and economic element of the old order" (p. 262): religious faith,
which "through its inculcation of humility and resignation has made
men ashamed of their appetite for power"; private property; and our
"constitutional provisions for the checking and balancing of political
authority" (p. 263), which may be so nullified by "judicial decisions
and legislative infringements"—not, mark you, through encroachment by the Executive, but through "judicial decisions and legislative infringements"—as to leave us with a "simple 'plebiscitary
democracy.'" And here, as a matter of program, the conservative
must not be afraid of public ridicule, must "be prepared for the role
of Don Quixote": "the further authority is removed from local communities, the less democratic it becomes" (p. 265); conservatives
must "stand firm" in favor of "states' rights," against centralization,
"against the conversion of representative government into plebiscitary absolutism."

Now: I shall be concerned throughout this book with the topics Mr.
Kirk touches upon in the statement just summarized; which is to say:
only at a much later point shall we have before us the materials that
would enable a full discussion of the statement's inadequacies from
the standpoint of the emergent conservative movement in the United
States; here, therefore, I shall do no more than place question-marks
beside certain emphases and certain "silences" about which I would
ask the reader, for the moment, to keep an open mind, as follows:

a) Processes are at work amongst us, says Mr. Kirk, that look to the
undermining of every *political and economic element of the old order*
and, as he goes on to say (p. 262), that are likely to remove the "moral
and institutional barriers" to the exercise of power that conservatives
deem indispensable. So far, so good; there are indeed such "forces"

at work amongst us: that which looks to the inauguration in the United States of a "plebiscitary democracy" is indeed one of those "forces"; those forces are, indeed, only too likely to prevail in the absence of effective conservative efforts to oppose them. But, if that is true, we stand in the presence of a *revolution,* already, on Mr. Kirk's own showing, far advanced, which it becomes the business of conservatives to *oppose at every point* with steps *not* "quixotic" but rather *infinitely and immediately practical*—first of all, that of identifying the *revolutionaries,* which, it will be observed, Mr. Kirk conspicuously fails to do, and secondly, that of bringing the revolutionaries' *entire program* into focus and exposing it *as* revolutionary, which Mr. Kirk's statement is certainly very far from doing. Put otherwise: Mr. Kirk's statement on power is the closest thing we have in the book before us to recognition on his part of that which, in these pages, we call the *Liberal Revolution.* But the theorist who can go so far without feeling impelled to go further (the chapter in which the statement appears tapers off into a homily on the dangers of concentrated power in international affairs, the effect of which is to link together, as instances of the "ferocious intoxication of power," the destruction of Hiroshima and the ambitions of World Communism!), is *not* the theorist contemporary American conservatism requires in its hour of need.

b) The tendency of Mr. Kirk's statement would be to commit contemporary American conservatism to a sort of "anti-power" *mystique* which, on the showing of this book, is characteristic of *Liberal* thought (and by no means merely Liberal thought about international affairs), and, worse still, to attribute some such *mystique* to the authors of the *Federalist.* It cannot be too often emphasized that the *Federalist,* to which indeed American conservatives cannot be too often referred, was *as understood by its authors,* a plea for, precisely, a *concentration of power* on the Eastern shores of this continent, that is, such concentration of power as they saw to be needed for the prosperity and happiness of the American people; that perhaps the most scathing single line of argument to be found in the *Federalist* is that which it directs against the superstition that the Constitution it defends possesses a built-in animus against the transfer of power from the states to the federal government; that the *Federalist,* perhaps more clearly than any other masterpiece of political philosophy, warns against the heresy, a constant temptation to American conservatives, that the tyrannical exercise of power can be prevented by a "wise constitution"; that, in any case, it was the *tyrannical* exercise of power, not the exercise of power as such, that the authors of the *Federalist* were concerned to prevent; and that their ultimate reliance, for this purpose, was upon the wisdom and virtue of the American people, whose "last say" on all questions concerning the use and extent of power in the American political system is permanently enshrined in Article V of the Constitution. The essence of the American political tradition, as we shall learn from the True Sage of Woodstock,[5] lies in the exclusion of political power itself from certain *spheres* of human activity, thus *not* in the "separation" or "division" of powers—in *limited government* as one face of the coin of which *freedom* is the other, thus not, I repeat, in any mystique about power in the spheres assigned, rightfully, *to* government. Yet Mr. Kirk's statement, by giving equal status to limitation of power, separation of power, and division of power, encourages just that *mystique,* and the dangers here for the contemporary conservative movement, which must learn to regard power as *morally neutral,* cannot be exaggerated. For one thing, as the Liberals are always there to remind us (and as Mr. Kirk seems to recognize *en passant*), power can be concentrated *economically* and *socially* as well as *politically;* and in the context of a mystique against power it is a short step from that discovery to the notion that it is the business of government, acting of course in the name of *equality,* to pulverize concentrations of power wherever and however they may arise, and thus, for conservatives, to an open alliance with the Liberals in Bobby Kennedy-type crusades on behalf of *un*limited government and, on beyond that, of the Liberal Revolution itself. (Conservatives must learn, about the Liberals, that which they already know about the Communists: that they are an intelligent and resourceful enemy, who can be counted on for correct judgments as to what will forward their Revolution; that, therefore, any enterprise, even "crushing Jimmy Hoffa," that allies Conservatives with them must have something wrong with it.)

Mr. Kirk is, of course, quite right in stressing the connection between true democracy and the local community, and, by implication, the conservative's deep concern for the good health and vigor of cities and towns and villages and countrysides in which people actually *live.* But that is one of those conservative interests which must be achieved, if ever it is to be achieved, through voluntary action which conservatives can only encourage through slow processes of education. In the present connection—*because* it is quixotic and not infinitely and immediately practical—it is sheer red herring.

c) Mr. Kirk recognizes only *two* ultimate "checks" on power: the "dictates" of conscience on the one hand, and "the barrier of good laws" (presumably the limitation, separation, and division of power by constitutional enactment) on the other, and, here too one gathers, he supposes himself to be repeating *Federalist* doctrine. But if "dictates of conscience" be intended here in its usual sense, which I believe it to be, then *Federalist* Number Ten, and, for that matter, the book as a whole *passim,* make it clear that the authors' ultimate reliance for their purpose (which was to check *not* power but *tyrannical* power, that is, the use of power for the invasion of natural rights) was on *neither* of these two things but upon a third, namely, what for lack of a better term we may call a "constitutional morality," or, in Rousseau's classic phrase, the laws engraved upon the hearts of the people. These it is that cause the people to maintain, by channeling their major energies into, a certain kind of society that we are now in the habit of calling "pluralist"; these it is that cause the people to *respect,* that is, neither undermine nor set aside, the general plan of government embodied in their Constitution; and it is well to remember, especially for conservatives to remember first, that if the people possess such a morality it is because *someone* has taught it to them, and, second, that the teaching of a constitutional morality is a continuous and never-ending task. There lies the *real* danger in conservative reliance upon the "Constitution," or even upon the Constitution plus "conscience," as sufficient safeguards against the tyrannical and unjust use of power; just to the extent that they permit themselves the luxury of such a reliance they are likely to neglect what must be their central task in this regard, namely, to see to it that the people *are* taught the constitutional morality handed down to them in the *Federalist*—or even, like Kirk, to forget that there is such a thing.

d) Mr. Kirk regards "plebiscitary democracy" as a distinct possibility on the American horizon, and one which conservatives should be concerned to prevent; but we are left wondering *both* what he means, and why he is so reluctant to satisfy our unavoidable curiosity. Is the emphasis on "democracy," with plebiscitary just thrown in like the first red in "red, red rose," the point being merely the tired old

Birchite slogan that ours is a "republic" not a "democracy"; or is it on plebiscitary, the point being that ours is a democracy, but a non-plebiscitary democracy, which may be on the point of becoming a plebiscitary one? One suspects, from what follows, that the emphasis is on "plebiscitary"; and we are led to comment: Ah! But there are two kinds of "plebiscitary democracy," which we may distinguish by calling one of them "French-type plebiscitary democracy" and the other "English-type plebiscitary democracy"; and they are, while perhaps equally objectionable from a traditional American point of view, as different as chalk and cheese. French-type plebiscitary democracy, with its roots in Bonapartism, is a device by which the French strongman, usually a general, assures himself the semblance of popular support by submitting his major policy or policies for ratification (always forthcoming, else the plebiscite is never held) by "the People"; it is, one might say, plebiscitary democracy *sensu stricto.* English-type plebiscitary democracy, by contrast, is a matter of conducting elections that eventuate in a choice by "the People" between the alternative "programs" of two disciplined, putatively "ideological," political parties, in conditions in which, usually, the results of the consultation cannot be foreseen: "the People" really *does* decide, and gives its "mandate" to one of the political groupings competing for its favor. Now: which of these two kinds of "plebiscitary democracy" is it that Mr. Kirk sees as a danger in the United States? Since, as he goes on to say, it is going to be a matter of an "executive . . . elected nominally *by the masses* but actually brought to office and kept there by the publicist and the manipulator, [and] compelled to make decisions for everyone," one suspects that it is the French-type he has in mind—which, if so, would represent another of the curious failures on Kirk's part to understand the Revolution which the Liberals are preparing under his very nose, and square off to it in the manner in which the intellectual leader and spokesman of contemporary American conservatism must square off to it. The Liberals are indeed bent on giving us plebiscitary democracy, English-type; with their usual clear-headedness, they know precisely where they must attack the American political system in order to convert it into a plebiscitary democracy, English-type; that attack must be fought off, year-in year-out, at each of those points, with the normal weapons of American politics; and the *least* the emergent conservative movement can expect of its spokesmen is that they should show an intelligent understanding of the necessary total conservative strategy required for the purpose. But Mr. Kirk fails conspicuously to pass this test.

e) Mr. Kirk's silence about the Executive, in the sentence in which he speaks of nullification of our "constitutional provisions for the checking and balancing of political authority," leaves one aghast. Especially since, as we have just seen, it is the Executive that he envisages as emerging victorious from the process of nullification.

We shall, curiously, find the Part-Time Sage of Ithaca[6] giving better advice to the conservative movement about the problem of power.

Notes

[1]Kirk, Russell. *The Conservative Mind* (Chicago: H. Regnery Co., 1953).

[2]Kirk is not easy to construe at this point. But I believe this is implicit in his language. [Kendall footnote]

[3]Clinton Rossiter.

[4]James Burnham.

[5]John Courtney Murray.

[6]Also Clinton Rossiter. See the next chapter (p. 59) for Kendall's explanation of his use of two titles for Mr. Rossiter.

The Part-Time Sage of Ithaca

The contemporary American conservative movement needs, on the showing of this book, to know far more than it does about the *past* of American conservatism—of *American* conservatism, the *Federalist* as over against Burke's *Reflections,* and of the *entire past* of American conservatism, including its immediate past as well as its more remote past; *and* to make some sharp and too-long postponed choices amongst the myriad, often-conflicting emphases of the various conservatisms, the various manifestations of resistance to the emergent Liberal revolution that have presented themselves in the course of American history. Put otherwise: *some* of the positions that American opponents of that revolution have adopted must go: this one because it is too sharp a departure from the wisdom of the Framers on a point so *fundamental* that it cannot be compromised; that one because it is "dated," and no longer relevant in the struggle against Liberalism; that one yonder because it flies in the face of an unambiguous and manifestly irreversible decision of the American people to move in this direction rather than that one; this one *or* that one because, all questions of fidelity to the Framers entirely to one side, they are clearly incompatible and cannot *both* be retained. Now: one of the paradoxes we are up against, given the present state of the literature of our topic, is that one of the most useful books we have, for the purpose just indicated, Clinton Rossiter's *Conservatism in America,*[1] is a book whose author pretty certainly never intended contemporary American conservatism any good, whose major counsels to contemporary American conservatism are, variously, prescriptions for self-betrayal and suicide, and whose major theses of an analytical character (to which we must give at least brief notice in the present chapter) are, demonstrably, incorrect—whether because tendentious politically or, as is usually the case, based on bad political theory. One would prefer, for all the latter reasons, to exclude it from consideration in these pages, but one cannot: Rossiter has done his homework, and done it mainly on American materials, about which he writes with affection and enthusiasm and in essentially American terms; any way you slice it, therefore, his book provides a sorely-needed counterbalance to the writings of Russell Kirk, and becomes, if only for that reason, a "must" item in the literature. Nor is that all: *one* way to slice it, at certain crucial points, is to shake the product of his homework loose from his tendentiousness and his bad political theory, and exploit it for sound conservative purposes, which is what I shall attempt to do in much of what follows (particularly with respect to his treatment of 19th century American conservatism). Another way to slice it is by coming to grips with some of its major errors and fallacies, and using them as springboards to a correct appraisal of the issues at stake. Still another is to seize upon the occasional point on which, on the showing of this book, he is right—even if for wrong reasons and, painful as it may be to confess our indebtedness to him, learn from him—as we shall do, for example, with his treatment of 19th century *laissez faire* conservatism, the best we shall find until we come to the implications, for contemporary American conservatism, of the teachings of the True Sage of Woodstock. That is why we call him the Part-time Sage—not, as he for the most part deserves, the Pseudo-Sage—of Ithaca, though as indicated we shall not overlook him in the latter, his vocational not his avocational, his work-a-day not his moonlighting, capacity.

a) Rossiter's version of *the conservative creed* bears marked similarity to Kirk's. According to Rossiter, whose propositions we "turn around," where necessary, in order to make them formally parallel to Kirk's, the Conservative believes:

1) That the nature of man is immutable but *mixed,* that is, capable of civilized behavior but potentially given to wickedness, unreason, and violence.

2) That men are equal in that each possesses a precious soul and an inviolable personality, but naturally unequal in other respects.

3) That liberty takes precedence over equality in the hierarchy of human values.

4) That social classes are both inevitable and necessary, so that "most attempts at levelling" are both foolish and futile.

5) That the good society needs an aristocracy, which both rules and serves.

6) That majority-rule is both fallible and potentially tyrannical.

7) That all forms of power (social, economic, and, most especially,

political), *because majority-rule is fallible and potentially tyrannical,* should be diffused and balanced.

8) That the "rights of man" are rights that a man *earns,* not rights that he has given to him.

9) That a man earns his rights by performing his duties, which include service, effort, obedience, cultivation of virtue, and self-restraint.

10) That the institution of private property is of the first importance, alike from the standpoint of liberty, order, and progress.

11) That inherited institutions, values, symbols, and rituals are indispensable to the good society, and sacred.

12) That religious feeling plays an essential role in the life of the individual, and organized religion an essential role in the life of society.

13) That human reason is fallible, and of limited reach.

14) That the mission of education is to civilize, discipline, and conserve.

15) That history, conceived as mysterious, tragic, but characterized also by grandeur, is the surest guide to wisdom and virtue.

16) That there are immutable principles of universal justice.

17) That the community, which is wondrous and divinely-ordained, takes precedence over the whims and rights of any individual, and that *therefore* both individualism and collectivism are to be rejected as means of reconciling liberty and authority.

18) That the marks of a good man are: reverence, contentment, sensitivity, patriotism, self-discipline, and the performance of duty.

19) That the marks of a good society are: stability, unity, equity, continuity and the confinement of change.

20) That the marks of a good government are: dignity, authority, legitimacy, justice, constitutionalism, the recognition of limits.

21) That Conservatism, as here defined, is absolutely necessary to the existence of civilization.

Such a creed, let us say at once, is a marked improvement over Kirk's (with which the reader will perhaps find it instructive to compare it, point by point), but shares with it certain basic faults, namely: It includes a number of points that clearly are *not* issues between conservatism and liberalism (because they are accepted by many if not most Liberals), that can be salvaged, for purposes of a conservative creed, only (as we have insisted with regard to similar emphases in Kirk's creed) by putting them forward as propositions whose *denial* conservatives can be counted on to resist, and that as they stand, give the creed overtones of a *moralism* that contemporary American conservatives will be well-advised to avoid. It is, like Kirk's, remote from the realities of the present major clashes between conservatism and liberalism, and it states badly, or prejudicially, some of the issues that in fact ought to be stressed in such a creed.

At the same time, it approaches nearly enough, in *some* of its emphases, to a correct statement of a conservative creed, to be worth reworking, as follows:

Item 21 (conservatism is necessary to civilization) must go out on grounds of triviality: it merely commits conservatives to conservatism on the one hand and to the probably not controversial proposition that civilization is a good thing. Item 18 must go (a good man is reverent, sensitive, patriotic, dutiful, etc.) as a piece of gratuitous moralism. Item 15 (the mystery, grandeur, and tragedy of history, and history as the "surest guide to wisdom and virtue") must go, along with Item 13 (human reason is fallible, and of "limited reach")—the first because it would reduce conservatism to one of the many forms of "historicism," which, along with relativism and positivism, it is the task of conservatives to oppose, the first *and* second (reason is fallible, etc.) because they deny the conservative commitment to *reason* as the surest guide to wisdom and virtue (some conservatives, to be sure, would place Revelation above reason as a guide, but my thesis is that they *must* not, *as* conservatives, press the point). (I do not suggest, of course, that the conservative regards reason as *in*fallible, merely that, for political and social purposes, that is where I understand him to place his bets.) Item 17 (the community takes precedence over the rights and whims of the individual) must go because it is the answer to a nonsense question, to which conservatives have no business giving any answer at all, the "choice" between the community and the individual being always the product of bad political theory. (Item 17 could, however, be salvaged by confining it to the notion: conservatism rejects both individualism and collectivism— not merely as a means of "reconciling" liberty and authority, which the conservative does *not* regard as in necessary conflict, but in and of themselves and on grounds of reason.) Item 3 (liberty takes precedence over equality, etc.) must go because, from the standpoint of American conservatism at least, the question of which takes precedence, liberty or equality, arises only on a tendentious, post-Lincolnian definition of "equality." (Item 3 could be salvaged by being made to read: Liberty takes precedence over egalitarian reforms; but that point would appear to be sufficiently taken care of in Item 4.) Item 9 (a man earns his rights by performing his duties, or, as the conservative would prefer to say, forfeits his rights by *not* performing his duties) must go, like Item 18, on grounds of gratuitous moralism. Item 11 (inherited institutions, etc., are indispensable) must go because it is a caricature of the conservative position, which as a matter of course cannot commit itself to the sacredness and indispensability of *all* inherited "institutions, values, symbols, rituals, etc.," or to the view that any criteria other than those of reasonableness are ultimately relevant in arriving at a judgment concerning the sacredness of *an* institution, "value," symbol, ritual. (The item can perhaps be salvaged by making it read: That the Conservative believes a *good* institution is rendered the *more* sacred by having been handed down from the forefathers.) Item 8 must go (but cf. Item 9) because it is simply *not* a conservative belief: conservatives believe that men are *endowed* with natural rights.

This leaves us with the items that must, in order to be acceptable as items of an *American* conservative creed, be restated:

Item 16 (there are immutable principles of universal justice), though unexceptionable as far as it goes, must be expanded to read: That there are principles of universal justice, which man discovers through *reason,* that is, through the procedures of *natural law speculation.* (Rossiter and Kirk are alike in their curious avoidance of the phrase "natural law," and, therefore, in failing to stress the conservative's commitment *to* natural law.) Item 19 urgently wants restatement in *American* terms, so that it will read as follows: The goals of *our* society should be "to form [an ever?] more perfect Union, establish Justice, insure domestic tranquility, provide for the general Welfare, and secure the blessings of Liberty to ourselves and our posterity"—that is, use the language of the Preamble to the Constitution of the United States (one hesitates to commit American conservatives to a general theory, applicable in other countries, as to what societies should be like). Item 20, similarly, must be made to read: That the best form of government for the *American* people is that stipulated in the Constitution of the United States, and explicated and justified in the *Federalist;* it is based, *inter alia,* on separation of powers, division of powers, limited power, and constitutionalism. Item 1 should read: That the nature of man is sufficiently constant to warrant certain firm propositions about him, namely that he is capable of both good and bad, both reasonableness and unreasonableness, both civility and barbarousness; sufficiently capable of good and reasonableness and civility to deserve the means to his self-protection, sufficiently capable of bad and unreasonableness and barbarism to warrant the separation and limitation of power that characterize the Constitution of the United States. (Why commit conservatism to the view that the nature of man is "immutable"?) Item 2 should read: That, despite the great and indisputable natural inequalities among them, all men *are* created equal, and are entitled in some respects but not in others to equal treatment; at the very least, all men have an equal claim to justice. Item 4 should be freed of any reference to "classes," which is and throughout the history of the tradition always has been regarded as inappropriate to the climate of American politics, and be made to read: That it is the business of government in the United States to promote a just not an equal distribution of rewards and privileges. Item 5 should be freed of any reference to "aristocracy," as also inappropriate to the climate of American politics, and made to read: That the people, in choosing the representatives who are to exercise the powers granted to office-holders under the Constitution, should seek the "best" men. Item 6, which more than any other is a caricature of the conservative position, should be freed of all suggestion of a special conservative animus against "majorities," and be made to read: That political power, no matter by whom exercised, is potentially tyrannical, that is, capable of injustice, that is, of invading natural rights, and should therefore be restrained. Item 7 should read: That because men are capable of injustice, that is, of invading each other's natural rights, the most desirable state of affairs—politically, socially, economically—is one in which power is diffused. Item 10 should read: That abrogation of the rights of property, save as this may be clearly necessary for the purposes set forth in the Preamble to the Constitution, is *theft,* and thus a violation of natural law. Item 12 should be freed of any reference to the role of religious feeling in the lives of individuals, which under the original interpretation of the First Amendment is *not* a proper concern of a conservative political movement in the United States, and be made to read: That organized religion plays a valuable role in the life of

American society, and should be regarded with favor even by those American conservatives who are not themselves believers. (Thus bringing the item in line, as we shall see, with Rossiter's own teaching concerning conservatism and religion.) Item 14 should read: That the proper function of American educational institutions, both public and private, is to inculcate upon their charges a belief in the *conservative* creed.

I make the following claim for the amended creed, as compared with Rossiter's: that it helps render intelligible, as his does not, the actual points of controversy in the continuing struggle between conservatism and liberalism in the United States.

b) *Conservatism and change.* Kirk, as we have seen, is at least tempted to make of attitude toward change *the* differentia between conservatism and radicalism-liberalism, and is saved from doing so, if saved at all, merely by his confusions as to what that attitude is. Rossiter has no comparable confusions to save him: conservatism is, for him, one point on a spectrum—leading from "revolutionary radicalism" through "radicalism" through "liberalism" through "conservatism" through "standpattism" through "reaction" to "revolutionary reaction"—of attitudes toward the "existing order" on the one hand and "change and reform" on the other. "Conservatism" is "discriminating defense of the existing order against change and reform." Conservatism's next-door neighbor, "liberalism," therefore, is a matter of "reasonable satisfaction" with the existing order, of determination *not* to "betray its ideals" or "undermine its institutions," but also of receptivity towards any "thoughtful plan to improve the lot of men," of optimism concerning the probable success of such plans, of, for the purposes of such plans, but *only* for the purposes of such plans, choosing "change over stability, experiment over continuity, the future [!] over the past [!]." Conservatives and liberals, by clear implication here and expressly elsewhere in the book, agree then on fundamentals, that is, on the "ideals" and typical "institutions" of the existing order; indeed every liberal is in considerable degree conservative, and every conservative, since his defense of the "existing order" is merely "discriminating" not absolute, is in considerable degree "liberal." At first blush, indeed, one gets the impression that Rossiter's conservatives and Rossiter's liberals don't disagree at all because they have nothing to disagree about ("no line separates one camp from the other, but somewhere between them stands a man who is at once the most liberal of conservatives and most conservative of liberals"). But there *is* a difference, which if we look hard enough we can finally detect: even in the presence of a "thoughtful plan to improve the lot of men," the conservative is pessimistic about its chances of success, prefers "stability over change, continuity over experiment, the past [!] over the future [!]." How silly it all is, even on the face of it, we may see by recognizing that it leads unavoidably to the conclusion: the conservative is pessimistic about change, the liberal optimistic, but somewhere between them stands a man who is the most pessimistic of optimists and the most optimistic of pessimists. His statement, in short, reduces *itself* to the absurd; it acquires meaning only in the light of his clear political purpose, namely to emasculate contemporary American conservatism by transforming it, through appropriate incantations, into liberalism.

There is, of course, no objection to Rossiter's setting up arbitrary definitions for such words as "conservatism" and "liberalism,", provided he gives due notice to his readers and provided, having set up the definitions, he subsequently sticks to them, and does not pretend to be using terms in their normal acceptations—just as, shall we say, there would be no objection to his calling the dimes in his son's piggy-bank dollars, provided he does not subsequently try to trade two of the resulting "dollars" for a parimutuel ticket. But these things, clearly, Rossiter is *not* prepared to do. His book is, for example, larded with quotations, indispensable for his argument, from the writings of men who know that what conservatives and liberals disagree about is, precisely, *fundamentals,* that the struggle between them is a struggle over the very destiny of these United States, and that the point at issue between them is *not* whether "changes and reforms" are likely to be successful—men, that is to say, who use the terms "conservatism" and "liberalism" even as my readers and I do. And this is perhaps as good a moment as any for disposing, once and for all, of all definitions of conservatism that equate it with one sort or another of negative attitude toward "change" *as such.* Or, to say that otherwise: for making it clear why conservatives, perhaps especially contemporary American conservatives, must not be understood as being somehow committed to keeping things as they are.

The relevant considerations are these:

A) "Conservatism"—any given conservatism—no doubt emerges,

in the first instance, as sheer opposition to change, any change, in whatever direction. In any *young* society or organization, that is to say, young enough to be finding itself confronted for the first time with members who have become dissatisfied with this or that aspect of its charter, its activities, its procedures, and wish to "change" it, there will be other members, whom there is no objection to speaking of as "the satisfied," who will *resist* the would-be reformers, and will, in doing so, make good an etymologically reasonable claim to be the society's "conservatives." That is the grain of truth in the notion that conservatism is opposition to change, which, accordingly, people come by quite honestly and naturally; and, if all societies and organizations were forever young, one could just leave it at that. But societies are *not* forever young, and once they have passed from childhood into adolescence or, worse still, from adolescence into maturity, the situation is by no means so simple, and for several fairly obvious reasons: First, the proponents of change may, in due course, have won on this or that point, so that their reform passes over into the "established order," in which case two possibilities present themselves. Either, on the one hand, the defeated "conservatives," refusing to accept their defeat with good grace, become "irredentists" on that point (that is, grit their teeth and say: we are going to *reverse* this change); or, on the other hand, the defeated "conservatives" swallow hard and, so to speak, "adopt" the reform, even though yesterday they may have been opposing it on the most "stridently" principled grounds. Now: whichever of these things happens, the kind of simplicity that, *e.g.,* Rossiter would like to have obtain in these matters goes out the window: in the one case we have the "conservatives" *proposing* change, in the other case we have the "conservatives" defending a different "established order" from that which they were defending yesterday—or, to face the new situation in *all* its horror, some of yesterday's conservatives may do the one and some the other and yet all of them, because agreed on all other matters, remain together in one and yet the same "movement." Moreover, the reformers may win again, and yet again and yet again, with the "conservatives" again going this way or that way or dividing over which way to go, and perhaps dividing along different lines than the time before. Evidently, at some point, the question "Who *are* the conservatives?" becomes frightfully complicated. In short, it is easy to say, when we are thinking of the time before Adam delved and we span, who the conservatives were and who the liberal (the serpent, of course); but after the Fall, it may be for the most part a matter of definition—as we may see most clearly, perhaps, by reminding ourselves that the "conservatives" in the Soviet Union today are the Communists, or perhaps even the allegedly defeated Stalinists, such as poor, poor Molotov, or poor, poor Malenkov.

B) Let us now make our model a little more complicated, by introducing, besides the dimension of "change," the two dimensions: that of the founding fathers, and what let us call the "principles," the constitutional morality, of the founding fathers, which is by no means necessarily based upon a teaching inimical to change, and may, indeed, be based upon a teaching that enjoins change in such and such a specified direction, or as may be required for achieving such and such a purpose or, in the jargon of our social sciences, "maximizing" such and such "a value," or good. And let us ask, Who *now,* who in a society with a *tradition* reaching back to the fathers and to the principles laid down by the fathers, who in this more complicated model are the conservatives? The question is, I think, easy to answer: the conservatives are the carriers of the principles of the fathers, the (within that society) *traditionalists,* who can be counted on to resist *not* "change" as such, but change in a direction contrary to or forbidden by the principles of the fathers, change the case for which involves an appeal to *new* principles. Not all organizations, not even all societies, perhaps, have "founders" in the sense intended; and not all societies that do trace themselves back to an act of "founding" possess, as a heritage from the founders, principles; but in one which does, we can make a kind of sense of the idea of conservatism that is impossible in other organizations and societies (in which attitude toward change as such does seem to be the only criterion we can use in defining conservatism), but do so only by adopting *fidelity to the principles of the founders* as the dimension to keep an eye on.

Having admitted the complication of "principles," several interesting possibilities, each involving a further complication of our model, suggest themselves: First, questions may arise, with the passing of time, as to the *meaning* of the principles of the founders, which may or may not have been so ambiguous as properly to give rise to such questions; and the day may come when the "conservatives" are being accused by their opponents of, for example, "misinterpreting" or "misconstruing" them, or are being told by those opponents that *they,* not the conservatives, are the "real" conservatives, the "true" heirs of the founders; or when, worse still, some of the founders are being played off against others of the founders, and disputes rage as to what founders were the "real" founders. At such a time, evidently, save as sound scholarship may adjudicate the issues, the idea of conservatism becomes beclouded by the same kind of indeterminacy that we encountered when we were using "attitude toward change" as our criterion, and we are tempted to say that the answer to the question "Who *now* are the conservatives" is, "It is anybody's guess."

Secondly, somewhere along the line an individual or group may attempt, with greater or lesser show of success, a *new act of founding,* intended to correct the original founders on this or that point on which, it is alleged, they were wrong, or ill-advised, or failed to think forward to some new situation that has presented itself. If the society has a constitution, for example, that constitution may be amended, in strict accordance with procedures laid down by the original founders, with or without the acquiescence of those who, hitherto, have deemed themselves the carriers of the tradition. Here, then, several possibilities present themselves: the new act of founding becomes generally accepted and is, so to speak, "absorbed into" the tradition —as at least seems to have happened with the Bill of Rights thrown up by the First Congress (though I shall have something more to say about that at a later point in this book), expelling that in the tradition with which it is uncongenial. Or the nation remains divided concerning the merits of the new act of founding, or—as seems to have happened with many of the clauses of the Fourteenth Amendment for nearly 100 years after its adoption—the new act of founding, failing to become effective, is subordinated to the original act of founding, and the tradition, save in outward appearance, remains unchanged. Now: in none of these cases do any difficult questions arise as to "Who are the Conservatives?": the Conservatives are those who cling to the principles of the Founders, either in their original form or as amended by general consent. But it is quite otherwise if we think forward to, *e.g.,* a moment when a dead-letter new act of founding picks up support and begins, or appears to begin, to become

effective, or, again, *e.g.,* when, confronted with the mounting consequences of a new act of founding, and finding them unpalatable, a
considerable group in the society appeals over the heads of the new
founders to the old, demanding a return, however tardy, to first
principles. Here all we can say, until the issue is somehow decided,
is that we are dealing with a society which is in full crisis: it is
uncertain about its tradition and, if we may borrow an anticipatory
phrase from the True Sage of Woodstock, is therefore confused even
about its own identity. *And* that the question, "Who are the Conservatives?" again, if the defenders of the new act of founding choose to
call themselves that, becomes indeterminate, though it could *perhaps*
be argued that those who demand a return to "first principles," to the
original act of founding, are the conservatives, and, similarly, that
where an older "tradition" and a newer "tradition" are in competition, it would be less confusing to speak of the older as *the* tradition.

Now: one of the theses of this book is: Abraham Lincoln and, in
considerable degree, the authors of the post-civil-war amendments,
attempted a new act of founding, involving concretely a startling
new interpretation of that principle of the founders which declares
that "All men are created equal"; that the real consequences of that
new act of founding could not become apparent until a great political
movement, built upon a demand for universal application of the
revised principle, gained sufficient power to begin to bring them
faith; and that the developing struggle between contemporary
American conservatism and the Liberal Revolution is, correctly understood, a struggle between those who are determined to "make
good" Abraham Lincoln's new act of founding on the one hand, and
those who demand, with greater clarity with each passing day, that
the new act of founding be set aside in favor of the principles of the
original founders. Of all that, more later.

The distinction between "conservatism" and "Conservatism." Rossiter describes his book as a "quest for understanding of American
conservatism" with a lower-case "c"—a study of "the principles that
have governed our *conservatives* in the past, that appear to govern
them in the present, and that ought to govern them in the future";
and it is, he believes, a quest that the "conservatives" who need to
know more than they do about the "nature, logic, and principles of
conservatism" ought themselves to undertake (p. 3). "[A] high-
minded *conservatism,"* he believes, "is America's most urgent need

for the years ahead." The "conservatism" of which he speaks is not, however, to be confused with "Conservatism" with an upper-case "c", which though it was a "major force in [American] politics and culture throughout the first half-century of the Republic" (pp. 17-18), and has "continued to appeal to a talented minority of thoughtful Americans (p. 18), yet "has no standing as a complete system of thought among any sizeable group in this country" (p. 18). "Conservatism" with an upper-case "c" is the "school of political thought" whose classical expression is Burke's *Reflections* and whose chief American spokesman has been John Adams. American "conservatism" is "conservative" not "Conservative"; in order to understand the former, however, we must first come to grips with the latter (p. 18)—to the exposition of which, accordingly, Rossiter devotes his Chapter I ("The Conservative Tradition"), which leads up to the creed we have examined above (pp. 61-62).

What exactly is the distinction between "Conservatism" and "conservatism"? Not, apparently, that between Burke on the one hand and even those Americans, Adams for example, who were "closest" to Burke—were *that* the distinction we should, on the showing of this book, have to welcome it, and adopt it as our very own. Not that, because "Conservatism" once "flourished" in the United States (p. 16)—was, indeed, "a major force in politics and culture throughout the first half-century of the Republic" (pp. 17-18). Adams, if I read Rossiter correctly, was a "Conservative" not a "conservative." It is not, either, the distinction between the Right-wing political theorists on the one hand and the Right-wing men of action on the other: there are "Conservatives of the tower," "Conservatives of the field," "Conservatives of the market-place," and "Conservatives of the Assembly" (p. 25). And it is not, finally, the distinction between such and such thinkers, including Burke but also thinkers other than Burke, whom we could identify by glancing at Rossiter's footnotes, and yet other thinkers of similar but not identical tendency—Rossiter does not document his discussion of "Conservatism," but rather goes exasperatingly on, "The Conservative this," "The Conservative that," page after page almost forever (pp. 16-98, *passim*). There are moments, moreover, when one wonders whether Rossiter himself understands the distinction, as when, having "proved" that "Conservatism" agrees with Liberalism on many points because

Burke was a Whig not a Tory (pp. 55-56), he can write: "And if Conservatism has turned more liberal over these hundred and fifty years, Liberalism has turned more conservative" (p. 56).

If the identity of Rossiter's "Conservatives" is shrouded in mystery, so too, it seems to me, is that of his "conservatives." They have, we are told, been for "at least a hundred years"—that is, since Lincoln?—the prisoner of "the American tradition" (which, of course, is a Liberal tradition) (p. 64), whereas formerly they were—what? "Conservatives"? Masters not prisoners of the American political tradition? We can only guess. There are, by contrast with "Conservative" principles, "conservative" principles (p. 71)—*e.g.,* "tradionalism" (p. 71), unity (p. 72), loyalty (p. 72), constitutionalism (p. 72)— all of which, however, as Rossiter sees at once, having got them down, must be "Conservative" principles, too (p. 73); indeed he would call them "Conservative" but that the American mind has displayed "contempt" for the Conservative faith, *e.g.,* again "religion and the higher law" *(ibid.),* which "resemble articles of the Conservative faith" but are, it seems, merely "conservative" *(ibid.).* Roger Williams, John Wise, and Benjamin Franklin were "conservatives [but not Conservatives] in many of their ideas and methods" (p. 86). The Puritan oligarchs, the conservative Whigs, and the American Tories, were "conservatives" (p. 101). The American revolution was "conservative" in "nature" (p. 105). Sometimes "conservatives" seem to be merely the "men on the Right" of American politics (p. 106). The framers of the Constitution were "conservatives" (p. 106), and the Constitution itself was a "triumph for conservatism" (p. 108). And the teaching of the *Federalist* papers is "authentic conservatism"— not, by clear implication, "Conservatism" (p. 109), though it is "flatly committed" to a "central proposition of the Conservative tradition" (p. 110); and, as if that were not by now confusing enough, we learn a moment later *(ibid.)* that "The *Federalist* is conservatism—we may fairly say Conservatism—at its finest and most constructive" (p. 110). The distinction, it becomes increasingly clear, is a distinction without a difference. Yet, if we read the two sentences that immediately follow that just quoted, we can see that Rossiter has in his hands the elements of a distinction that is, demonstrably, of the first importance for our subject-matter. In the *Federalist,* he goes on, there is "no talk of elites or a sharply-limited suffrage; there is no talk of men who are or can be angels. There is voiced throughout its pages the conditional hope that men who are properly educated, encouraged, informed, and checked can govern themselves wisely and well." He seems, indeed, on the point of saying that which, on the showing of this book, we should *like* to hear him say, namely: that Right-wing thought in America crosses, in the 1780's, perhaps we can even say during the Philadelphia Convention itself, a Great Divide; the *Federalist* is different from previous Right-wing thought in America, *different even from the previous thought of its own authors;* it is Right-wing thought taking its bearings in a new situation, where certain things have happened that are clearly irreversible, and that Conservatives, as realists, must try to make the best of, must cease to quarrel with. Here there is a distinction *with* a difference, since henceforth the gap between American conservatism and Burke— and, on beyond Burke, the other "Conservative" thinkers of the pre-democratic age—becomes, so to speak, official. It is not merely that the *Federalist* does not "talk of elites" or of "sharply-limited suffrage"; the big difference is that, in crossing the Divide, conservatism in America has adjourned *sine die* its quarrel with *democracy.* And if one were going to make Rossiter's distinction between Conservatism and conservatism make sense, that is how one would go about it: conservatism is Conservatism purged of its bias against genuine self-government, genuine democracy. But Rossiter, who for reasons of which we must speak later thinks of conservatism as inherently anti-democratic, is cut off from seeing it that way.

Let me, with all that in mind, now call out into the open an issue that we have, so to speak, been pushing forward throughout the foregoing pages, namely: By what criteria do we evaluate a creed that puts itself forward as *the* conservative creed—Kirk's, or Rossiter's, or, now, Rossiter's as revised by Kendall? By what warrant have I dared to say, in criticizing Rossiter's creed, this is a caricature, that is poorly stated, that yonder has no business in the creed at all, etc.? Or, more accurately, what are the objections to Rossiter's creed that I suppose my revised version able to meet? The main objection to Rossiter's, we are now in position to say, is that we are never told what conservatives where are supposed to have "believed" the items he includes; mine is not open to that objection because, to begin with, it is based on the *Federalist* and because, secondly, it is phrased with an eye to what, on the showing of this book, most American conservatives *must* have believed throughout the period since the *Federalist*. We shall speak more, later, of how we determine "what most conservatives must have believed" over the period in question, and of the extent to which, and the reasons for which, the principles involved turn out to be pretty much those of the *Federalist*.

Notes

[1]Rossiter, Clinton. *Conservatism in America* (New York, Knopf, 1955).

The True Sage of Woodstock

So far as I know, John Courtney Murray has never described himself—or been described by the spokesmen of contemporary American conservatism—as a Conservative; and I can imagine that neither
he nor they will thank me for describing him as one here: not he,
because he has given a wide berth to the contemporary conservative
movement in the United States; not they, because they give a wide
berth to the kind of problem that preoccupies Murray as a political
theorist, so that the question whether or not he is a conservative does
not, for them, arise. Murray is *the* contemporary theorist of the question, which *ought* of course to be central to conservative thinking,
What is it, in America, in *traditional* America, that we have the
obligation to conserve—a question, evidently, which we must answer
before the question, Is that which *is* traditional to America today so
endangered (apart from the military threat of World Communism) as
to require, in order to be conserved, any special effort on anybody's
part? And his answers to both questions are answers that contemporary American conservatives can ignore only at their peril.

Let us examine some of his teachings:[1]

a) The teaching on "consensus" and American "free" society.

Of two things, as the French say, one: *Either* we are still prepared
to take our stand with the authors of the Declaration of Independence and say: Our nation is founded on certain principles, which
we, the American people, grasp at least intuitively and sufficiently
understand. *Or* we are no longer prepared to say that, and this probably because we are no longer clear as to what the principles are.
Either the one, or the other; and if the latter *our peril, which is the
loss of our identity,* is great, since it may send us lumbering about the
world, lost and mad. For the necessary condition of self-identity and
self-confidence is self-understanding; and the foregoing—we have
principles, and do grasp them—is the only understanding of ourselves that we, as a people, have ever had.

There are, be it noted, two dimensions to the problem: the principles or as Murray calls them "the proposition," and the manner and
extent of our grasp of the proposition. We were, of course, once in

the habit of saying that they were "self-evident," but that, since there are other reasonable grounds for asserting a proposition, is not the key issue—is, in any case, posterior to the questions. Are we clear about the proposition itself—what words it is composed of, what those words mean precisely, what the proposition *in toto* actually affirms? About some of it, to be sure, most of us *are* fairly clear: the proposition states that we in America are a unique people, different therefore from other peoples, because uniquely free, because uniquely constituted as a *free society*. But how if we seek to define "free"? There, Murray clearly thinks we should begin to *disagree:* and the question arises, Can we have disagreement that close to the core of our understanding of ourselves, and still claim to know ourselves for what we are? That, stated in a preliminary fashion, is for Courtney Murray *the* question that American political philosophy must answer.

But, some will ask, what difference does it make if we do disagree? Is not disagreement in society, especially in *free* society, a symptom of good health? Is not disagreement free society's means of pursuing *truth,* and is not truth the most desirable of goods? One answer to such questions, easily confirmable in the course of a week-end at any well-stocked library, is that even those political theorists who set the greatest store by "debate" as the central ritual of free society, by the pitting against one another of conflicting views as miraculously productive of if not the truth then an ever-greater approximation to truth, still never dare to suggest that a society can thrive on *too much* disagreement; the "need for *consensus,* "the "need for agreement on essentials," even if the essentials reduce themselves to an "agreement to disagree," is a commonplace of contemporary democratic theory—so common a commonplace, indeed, that most democratic theorists are content merely to make their respective bows to it, and let it go at that; so that we have very little of what can properly be called a theory of consensus. Courtney Murray's answer to the question "What difference does it make?" however, is *not* the commonplace answer (though he would presumably have no quarrel with it). His answer, if I understand him correctly, is that consensus, consensus at the very least on *the* American proposition, is a *presupposition* of American free society, which, accordingly, ceases to be American free society when that presupposition is no longer valid.

Is consensus a presupposition of American free society? Or rather,

how, if the notion commends itself to our approval, would we go
about proving it—to ourselves, and to others? Murray's reasoning on
the point runs, rather surprisingly, as follows: Civilization—not, as we
would expect from the context, free society, but civilization—is
"formed by men *locked together in argument,*" in "dialogue," by
men who in virtue of their dialogue become a *political community.*

So much, he believes, is beyond dispute, and has been ever since
classic antiquity; and he will take it as his basic assumption, merely
restating it in language that he finds more congenial, namely, Political association has as its specifying note its *rational deliberative quality,* and depends for its cohesiveness on argument among men;
rational deliberation, argument, are what differentiates it from all
other forms of association. That does not mean, of course, that political association, the political community, is "purely rational": it is
determined in part by the fact that the raw material of which it is
made is *human nature,* which is not purely rational, in part by the
physical and historical soil from which it springs; it is sustained by
non-logical loyalties, and has ideals which it expresses in *legends,*
which, precisely because they "go beyond the facts," are vehicles of
truth; the materialisms of property and interest contribute to its cohesiveness. But its distinctive bond is "that exercise of reason which is
argument"; its climate is neither feral nor familial, but rather *forensic,*
and is "cool and dry, with the coolness and dryness that characterize
good argument among informed and responsible men; that climate
draws its "vital quality" from *civic friendship,* which is "a thing of
reason and intelligence, that men cultivate by imposing *discipline*
upon "passion, prejudice, and narrow self-interest." Ideally, indeed,
it should for these reasons have only one passion, "the passion for
justice," but even that passion finds its origin in "clear understanding
of what is due to the equal citizen from the [community], and what
is due from the citizens to the [community]," that is, in *intelligence.*
And it is the will to justice, so defined, that is the ground of that unity
of the community "which is called peace," and peace, in turn, is the
community's highest good, "the perfection of its civility."

The civil community, then, is "locked in argument," and the question unavoidably arises: About *what?* And Murray answers: About
three things: First, about those matters which are for the *public
advantage* and require a) *public decision,* and b) *governmental action* (such matters, he adds, originate in *facts,* which, however, must

be transformed into arguable issues before they can be rationally discussed). Second, about those affairs that are affairs of the *common-wealth,* some of which fall "in decisive part" *outside* the limited scope of government, cannot be settled though they may be affected by law, and transcend the necessities of the public order as public order—of these, he adds, the greatest is education, which includes the school system, the education of adult citizens in citizenship, and the advancement of knowledge by research. And third, about the *constitutional consensus,* whereby the "people" acquires its identity as a people and the society its sense of purpose in history. The consensus, he stresses, *is* constitutional, that is, tied up with the idea of *law,* and is something that the people *arrive* at, becoming a people in the act of so arriving, and arrive at "deliberatively, by the *methods of reason acting upon experience"* (italics added); it is made up of *truths,* of *basic knowledge,* of "elementary affirmations that reflect realities inherent in the order of existence." One of the characteristics of consensus is that it "occupies an established position in society"; another is that it *excludes opinions contrary to itself.* But it is also consensus that makes possible "all the rationalities and technicalities of constitutional and statutory law," and that "defines the larger aims" the society will pursue when and as it *acts.* And—returning now to the initial point—the public argument which is the differentia of political association is impossible in the absence of such a consensus to begin with, one moreover that is *really agreed to* among the people—or, to state the point negatively, is impossible where everything is in doubt, everything open to challenge. It is not true, as we are often told nowadays, that argument ends when agreement is reached; it is, rather, when agreement is reached that argument *begins,* becomes *possible.*

There are, let us pause to notice, some difficulties here: Murray began by asking, in effect, Why is consensus about a basic proposition necessary to *American* society conceived as a) free, and b) a unique historical realization? But that question suddenly disappears, or seems to at least, in favor of the quite different question, Why is consensus necessary to "civilization," to *civil* society, that is, just *any* civil society, or community, or "political association"? His answer to *that* question takes the general form, So it was understood by classic antiquity, and so everyone since has always agreed—which, first, might seem to want more "proving" than he gives himself the pains

to offer, and, second, to leave open the question, What does that have
to do with consensus as necessary to American civil society conceived as *free,* and as a *unique* historical realization? Why, in short,
have we substituted the word "civil" for the word "free"? Now: I do
not myself think these questions can be answered satisfactorily from
Murray's text (the difficulties are real, *not* merely apparent), but also
I do not think that any American, or at least any American conservative, has any business making issues of these questions, and for this
reason: *Whatever the merits of Murray's account of the origin and
character of civil communities in general, it is recognizable, even on
a schoolboy's knowledge of the Declaration of Independence, the
Philadelphia Convention, and the "ratifying conventions" in the several states, as a scrupulously accurate account of the origins and
original character of that American political society whose essentials
it is the business of conservatives to conserve.* And I propose, as an
exercise both interesting and profitable, to test it out, a point at a
time, from that angle: Question: Was American society "formed" by
"men locked in argument"? Answer: One could not imagine a better
description of the Congress that produced the Declaration of Independence, the Convention that produced the Constitution, the state
conventions that ratified it, and the First Congress that produced our
Bill of Rights. Question: Did the "argument" in those assemblies have
as its "specifying note" a "rational deliberative quality"? Answer:
The existing records leave no room for doubt on the point. Question:
Did the argument give "cohesiveness" to those assemblies? Answer:
The most vivid impression that one carries away from a perusal of the
records is that these were arguments that "got somewhere," that
drew the participants closer together hour by hour, day by day, that
progressively disposed of major points of disagreement, and so, as a
matter of course, contributed to their "cohesiveness." Question: Are
we to understand that the behavior of the delegates to these conventions was "purely rational"? Answer: No, that would be to claim that
the delegates were more than human, which none of them pretended
to be: they brought to the proceedings along with their capacity for
reasoned discourse, each his all-too-human share of "passion, prejudice, and narrow self-interest"; they were, again, men who had been
shaped by their respective environments, and by the history they
had lived and the history they had read and learned, and this also
gave to their deliberations a dimension that was by no means purely

rational; the society emergent from the deliberations was, still again, sustained at every point by loyalties, *local* in large part, of a demonstrably non-logical character, and by shared legends, by no means based upon "verifiable fact," but expressive of ideals passionately cherished; their cohesiveness was, finally, intensified—though also disrupted on occasion—by "materialisms of property and interest," by no means all of which could have been justified rationally. Question: Then how can you claim for the proceedings that their "specifying note" was their "rational deliberative quality"? Answer: Because the non-logical aspects we have just recognized were, in general, subordinated to a "distinctive bond," recognizably that of the "exercise of reason," which tied the delegates together. Question: How would you describe the *climate* of the deliberation? Answer: It was forensic, that is, not familial but also not feral; it was, for the rest, as you may see by sampling almost any page of the record, cool and dry, as the climate of discussion always is among men who are, as these men certainly were, "informed and responsible." Question: Men rarely exercise reason so persistently, and on so impressive a scale as you allege, unless motivated by a *passion* of some sort; what, as a student of the records, would you say to have been the driving passion of the delegates as they reasoned together? Was it, for example, a passion for justice? Answer: You must tell me first how *you* define justice. Question: Shall we, perhaps, define it as a matter of the community's giving to the equal citizen that which is due him from the community, and of the citizens' giving, each according to his capacity, to the community that which is due to it from them? Answer: Very well; but here I must give you a rather complicated answer, and in two parts. First, while the delegates spoke often of justice as the end they were trying to achieve, they spoke also of the protection of the "natural rights" of the future citizens, of the "happiness and prosperity" of the "people" that was coming into being. Now: all these may seem to *you* to be quite different things, but I must tell you that the delegates seem to have regarded them as the same thing— seem, that is, to have used these phrases almost interchangeably, thus tacitly assuming that if natural rights were made safe, that would *be* justice, and that if justice were done then the happiness and prosperity of the people would be assured. Certainly these things taken together were the driving passion of the delegates, and if we are willing to go along with the delegates in treating them as one and the same thing, then we can say that Yes, their driving passion seems to have been the passion for justice. Secondly, the problem that you pose, that of what is due from the citizens to the community and *vice versa,* certainly filled the delegates' minds as they reasoned together; and they seem to have spared no intellectual effort in their attempt to achieve clarity as to the solution of the problem.

What *does* lie at the core of the consensus that sustains the Congress, the Philadelphia Convention, the *Federalist,* and we must add now, the First Congress? It is, he insists, an agreed-upon *public philosophy,* stated in *propositional* form (*e.g.,* but only *e.g.,* all men are created equal), and propositional in *both* of the two senses of that ambiguous word "proposition": that of a *truth* that is *asserted* (as self-evident, as demonstrated, or as demonstrable); *and* that of an *intention* to be *realized,* an *operation* to be *performed* (as when we say: I propose to, etc.)—that, then, on the one hand, of a *doctrine,* and that, on the other, of a *project,* but claiming assent on grounds of reason. He will attempt, as he proceeds, to identify the content of the proposition; but sound methodology, as he understands it, requires that we should first be clear as to the *kind* of proposition it is and the kind of proposition it is not, and his theses here are, as I believe, theses of the first importance for the contemporary conservative movement, if it is to relate itself correctly to the origins of the tradition that it purports to cherish. These theses we may restate, with brief comments, as follows:

a) It was *not* the kind of proposition that is laid down as final, definitive, beyond revision, or incapable of further development. It was deemed to be, in language adopted earlier in this book, *dynamic, expansible, potentially explosive* even, like all else in America. Here, as very often elsewhere, Murray does not pause to document or demonstrate his point, but I think we can easily see what form the demonstration at least must take, namely: The proposition, when set down, represents merely a stage in a process of rational deliberation in the course of which men have *moved,* changed their *minds,* and *learned* something from their fellow deliberators. The propositions, *as* set down, even the self-evident ones because different things are self-evident to the same man or men at different stages of a reasoning process, are so to speak a report of the "findings of the deliberations" —to *date.* To treat them as definitive would have been inappropriate to, because a denial of, the very character of the reasoning process that has produced them, which is itself dynamic, potentially explosive. Men who place their bets on it cannot be "against change," and if they are conservatives, as the men we speak of certainly were, that was not in virtue of their being opposed to change *as such.* More simply: a proposition that is simultaneously asserted as doctrine and project *cannot* be regarded as definitive; the realization of the *project* must create new situations in which the doctrine must be re-examined. As Murray puts it: "it requires development on pain of decadence."

b) It was, taken together with the way in which it was asserted, the kind of proposition that commits its proposers on certain basic issues that we do not usually think of as "political." Here the heart of the matter is to be found (I borrow the phrase from another contemporary American sage) at the beginning of the beginning—in the words "We hold these truths," which, Murray thinks, wants, with its immediate sequel, more looking at than it normally gets (I would add: especially by conservatives). It is, so to speak, a goodbye kiss to a number of things which, however, we still have around: the tentativeness of the *positivist* (the truths are asserted as true, objectively true, thus excluding the view that the reason of man is incapable of discovering such truth); the simple-mindedness and anti-intellectualism of the *historicist* (the truths are the product of reason, not the reflection of a passing historical reality); the confusionism of the *relativist* (the truth are put forward as universal, excluding the idea that what is true depends on where one happens to be standing). Nor, warns Murray (and let the American conservative who is engaged in a flirtation with positivism, historicism or relativism, heed him well), can the proposition be shaken loose from the commitments of those goodbye kisses: deny those commitments, he says, pointing to the crystal-clear language of the beginning of the beginning, and "the American proposition is, I think, eviscerated at one stroke." Any attempt to set those commitments aside, or compromise them, to construe the proposition so that it does *not* begin "We hold these truths," is in the language of this book an attempt at a *new act of founding, revolutionary in character,* and conservatives will wish to examine carefully the *credentials* of the would-be new founders, which means above all putting to them the question: "In what sort of argument, with the rest of us, do you propose to lock yourselves before your new act of founding becomes official?" It is, on the showing of this book, a question that the carriers of the Liberal Revolution are ill-prepared, and little disposed, to answer in a satisfactory manner.

c) It is the kind of proposition whose ultimate depository was the public mind (p. 11), not a learned treatise or graven tablet; it was part of the "intuitive wisdom" by which the people lived (p. 12). Although the consensus about it was "arrived at," come to, in the course of rational deliberation, the content agreed to was in large part a patrimony, an "intellectual heritage." It asserted the "role of reason and logic in human affairs," but asserted it in continuity with Western constitutionalism over a long past, asserted it both as a present reality and as a *tradition.*

What, now, did the Proposition "hold"?

First, that God is "sovereign" over "nations as well as over individual men," thus also over *this* nation. This it held in sharp contradistinction to the Jacobin tradition, for which "religion is at best a purely private concern, a matter of personal devotion, quite irrelevant to public affairs" (p. 28), for which, therefore, "society" and "state" and "government" are by definition "agnostic or atheist," for which, finally, the "statesman as such cannot be a believer" ("his actions . . . are immune from any imperative . . . higher than the will of the people" [p. 29]). Murray presumably has in mind here, in the first instance, the reference to "the Creator" and to "Providence" in the Declaration of Independence, but he is able to cite also President Adams (1799), to the effect that "men . . . should, as a society, make acknowledgments of dependence and obligation to Him who hath endowed them with . . . [their] capacities" (p. 29); President Lincoln (1863), to the effect that the affairs of men and nations are under the "supreme authority and just government of Almighty God," and that nations like men have the duty to own "their dependence upon the overruling power of God" *(ibid.);* and four instances in which the Supreme Court has held, in one form of words or another, "We are a religious people whose institutions presuppose a Supreme Being." And, by way of confirming the point, he stresses the absence, throughout American history, of Jacobin-type "organized and militant atheism," and the difference in "content and purpose" between American secularism and continental (*i.e.,* European) laicism: American secularism "is clearly a dissent; it illustrates the existence of the American affirmation."

The point is a difficult one, and we shall return to it in discussing Murray's teaching on natural law (as content of the proposition), then again, more critically, in discussing his teaching on the First Amendment. For the moment, I content myself with observing: the evidence marshaled does not seem to establish the thesis in hand, though it does stand very much in the way of anyone who seeks to establish a contrary thesis—*e.g.*, that the Proposition calls for a wholly secular state.

Let us note, for future reference, that Murray's major reliance, in this connection, appears to be *not* on the documents (he does not cite the "Creator clause" of the Declaration), but on what we might call a "behavioral" type of argument: the American people have, even American agnostics have, to such and such an extent, *behaved* as if this were part of the Proposition. It is a type of argument we encounter all too seldom in the literature of this question, and one which we must learn to use more frequently. (I have myself used this kind of argument in questioning the existence of a "right" to freedom of speech in the American political system.)

Second (I vary Murray's order here), that government is limited by the will of the people it represents; the people are to adopt the Constitution (and any future Amendments); they are to share, through free-elections, representation, and rotation in office, in the enactment of laws; they are to be governed only by their own consent—really *governed*, yes, but under "the principle of consent [and] . . . the equally ancient principle of popular participation in rule" (pp. 33-34). Faith in the people, and not somebody else's faith in the people, not the faith in the people of somebody outside of and above the people, but faith in the people on the part of the people *itself*, faith in the people's sense of justice, in its capacity to understand at least (Murray says "especially") the moral problems involved in the broad issues government must decide, becomes here the heart of the matter—takes its place as one of those things the denial of which the consensus excludes as an idea "contrary to itself." (Murray seems to go further, and make the faith include faith in the capacity of the people to understand the broad issues themselves, and appears to see no difficulty in the fact that the American system has never submitted the broad issues themselves to popular decision; yet he recognizes that "it was not supposed that the people [even then] could master the technical aspects, etc.")

Murray sees, in this emphasis of the Proposition, affirmation of the principle ("inherent in the Great Tradition" the American people inherited): "the state is distinct from society and limited in its offices toward society" (p. 35); and at least seems to be saying, rather frighteningly, that the affirmation, though certainly present in the original American consensus, has disappeared from it: it has been "cancelled out by the rise of the modern omnicompetent society-state." And he also sees it in an American commitment to the "institution of *a* free speech and a free press" (italics added); and here, in view of his earlier statement that the consensus excludes ideas contrary to itself, we must attend carefully. He does *not*, we note at once, understand commitment to the institution of "a free speech" to involve commitment to the idea that "a man has a right to say what he thinks merely because he thinks it." Yet: "People who are called upon to obey have the right first to be heard" (p. 34). Is there a contradiction here? I do not, myself, happen to think so: the question "Who have a right to lock themselves in argument?" (to use Murray's own language), to enter the dialogue at all, is *not*, for all that we are often instructed to the contrary, the same question as "Should those locked in the argument enjoy freedom of speech?" The freedom of speech question remains after we have decided whether ideas contrary to the consensus shall or shall not be excluded, even when we have decided that question in the affirmative; and there is *no* inconsistency involved in a consensus which simultaneously excludes ideas *contrary* to itself *and* establishes the institutions of a free speech. Even after it has been decided to exclude ideas contrary to the consensus, even for the people to use government as an instrument for the exclusion of such ideas, the question remains: What shall be the relations between state and society, between government and people, with respect to the discussion, which must still go forward? And Murray sees in the Proposition the following clear answer: "The whole order of ideas in general was [to be] autonomous in the face of government; it was immune from political discipline . . ." Government was to be rendered "incompetent" in the field of opinion. Or again:

> Government submits itself to judgment by the truth of society; it is not itself a judge of the truth in society. Freedom of the means of communication whereby ideas are circulated and criticized, and the freedom of the academy (. . . the institutions

organized for the pursuit of truth and the perpetuation of the intellectual heritage of society) are immune from legal inhibition or government control (p. 35).

And Murray concludes: "This immunity is a civil right of the first order, essential to the American concept of a free people under a limited government."

For the "constitutional theory of the West," writes Murray, "the people are the living repository of a moral tradition," which enables them to know what is reasonable in the action of the state—in its laws, its public policies, its uses of force. The people consent because it is reasonable to consent to what, with some evidence, appears as reasonable. That moral tradition, he goes on, is the tradition of reason, the "ethic of natural law." Western constitutionalism itself is the product of that tradition, and in America at the end of the 18th century it was still strong enough to "give essential form to the American system of government," which, accordingly, was predicated on the view that "public policies borrow . . . their morality from the conscience of the people. Right policies, as well as due powers, derive from the consent of the governed." The people, that is to say, will remain—so it is assumed in the American system—sufficiently the carriers of "the ethic of natural law" to "judge, direct, correct" in a morally satisfactory manner. And the question arises (p. 291), Have the people fulfilled this expectation?—as do some other questions, for example: How would we, if we needed to know whether the natural law ethic remains alive, go about finding out? How do we know, even, that the ethic was alive in them at the beginning, and, in that case, alive *how*—as a matter of conscious and articulate profession of faith or belief, or alive merely in the sense that the judging, directing, and correcting they did at the beginning can be shown to reflect the ethic? As for the ethic's present status, might it be different with respect to a) the generality of men and women in the American population, and b) the "intellectuals"? To what exactly does a people that does possess the ethic "at least as a heritage" (Murray's phrase, and apparently his answer to the question as to how the people "held" the ethic in the beginnings) stand committed? If, as Murray certainly seems to believe, the hope for the future in America surely lies in the perpetuation (if it still be there) or renewal

(if it still be there, but in weakened form) or rebirth (if it is "dead")
of the natural law ethic, if, that is to say, a choice is to be made, either
of the natural law ethic or of this or that competing ethic, what are
those other possibilities? Now: Murray's teaching does not contain,
even by implication, an answer to all these questions, or an unambiguous answer even to all of those to which he addresses himself;
one can merely be fairly certain that he would be the first to agree
that all the questions do arise, perhaps even that they arise especially
for American conservatives, insofar as the latter think of themselves
as concerned with conserving the American tradition. We can only
follow him so far as, in the book before us, he has answered the
questions and, beyond that, either hold them in our minds as questions to which conservatives must find a satisfactory answer or—well,
strike out on our own, as, in what follows, I shall to some extent try
to do.

One of the questions to which Murray addresses himself most
directly is that as to the choice to be made, or the alternatives, other
than the natural law ethic or tradition, that so to speak lie before the
American people. These alternatives are, in Murray's view, three in
number, each of them, like the natural law ethic itself, involving a
particular view concerning the nature of man and, on beyond that,
concerning reality itself; two of them "Liberal" in a sense, but only
one of them, of which, however, Murray gives the best brief account
to be found anywhere in the literature, Liberal in the sense in which
I use the term in the phrase "Liberal Revolution."

There is, first, "Liberal individualism," the doctrine of "natural
rights" pure and simple (Murray distinguishes sharply between
"natural rights" and "natural right," whose "rights" are those of the
natural law ethic). Rights, in this view (which is often attributed,
erroneously, to the Framers of our Constitution), are indistinguishable from "material interests," whether those of "individuals or social
groups or nations," which are entitled to protection by positive law
backed up by governmental power. Society, in this view, is "atomis-
tic," and unambiguously organized "in terms of power relationships";
and the state, in this view, is an apparatus of compulsion (on behalf
of the protected interests or rights), without obligation toward or
concern with any "order of justice" (put otherwise: "justice," in such
a view, *is* the protection, and let the Heavens fall, of the "rights").
And the basic commitment, for this view, is always and necessarily

to *yesterday's status quo,* which produced *today's* statute book.

There is, secondly, the "Marxist concept of human rights, as based solely on social function, economic productivity." Here, as in the first view, the "ultimate reality" is the "material fact of power"—the power of the collectivity, however, not that of the component individuals and groups; alike society and state are based unabashedly on *force*; there is, accordingly, no such thing as a right vesting elsewhere than *in* the state, and no such thing as freedom other than freedom of the state; the individual *shares* in the state's freedom by pursuing the state's purpose. The basic commitment, on this view, is the *socialization* not merely (as some suppose) of man's work, but also of man's mind and man's will, to the mobilization of *all* energies for the realization of a "justice" conceived as the triumph, in a "classless" society that will know no exploitation, of collective man over nature.

Thirdly, we have "modern evolutionary scientific humanism," or as I should put it the ethic of the Liberal Revolution. Man, in this view, is *autonomous,* which is to say that he "transcends" nature but is not himself, so far as we can know anyway, transcended by anything, or anybody, neither by a law higher than his own positive law, nor by any Being or God to which he might stand subordinated. The view is, therefore, rationalistic, although, paradoxically, it by no means reduces man to reason: its "man" is a "total personality" which seeks, above all, an "ever-fuller life," a "totality of impulses" that includes some impulses that are by no means rational; and its passion is *not* the deductive argument that we have associated with rationalism in the past, but scientific method, understood as yielding up, at best, "provisional and partial hypotheses," all understood as subject to possible revision before today's sun sets (if set it does). It prides itself upon its sophistication about the category or dimension of "time," regarding everything, including therefore the rights of man and even nature and its laws, as the reverse of static, the reverse of "given once and for all." Its "nature" *evolves,* its law "emerges" in a process that is *not* one of *discovery* by man but of creation by man: man makes his "values" as he moves forward through time, makes also, therefore, the human rights that give his values legal expression—makes them as his "experience" teaches him to, teaches him that this or that right, for the moment at least, is "necessary" to *"fullness"* of life. Laws are merely instrumentalities, by which legislators and judges, looking to the "wants" of "society" in that time and that place, satisfy human desires (p. 323). (What other purposes, it can honestly ask, could a juristic order possibly have?) Its point of departure being the denial of transcendence, its criterion of truth being that of scientific method, its values *merely* "emergent," it can make room for no values that are absolute, no truths that are true; it is "at bottom an ethical relativism pure and simple." It is, therefore, openly at odds with what Murray has shown us to be one of the basic commitments of the traditional American consensus, which recognized

> an order of rights antecedent to the state ... These are the rights of the person, the family, the church, the associations men freely form for economic, cultural, social, and religious ends ... [It recognized also, as] implicit in the admission of the order of human rights, ... another order of right also antecedent to the state and *regulative of its public action* ... [The] democratic state serves both the ends of the human person ... and ... the ends of justice. As the servant of these ends, it has [itself] only a relative value. (pp. 325-326, italics added)

Yet those who opt for scientific humanism claim, variously, that it is the proper basis for democracy, and democracy the political expression of their philosophy; or, as I would prefer to put it for the purposes of this book, they are clearly determined to *reduce* democracy, of American democracy and its typical institutions such as the First Amendment, to that which you have left when you cut it off from all that the Framers regard as central to it. What do you have left? Something, according to Murray, rather surprising, namely, an absolute state, a state that cannot be other than absolute because it is, and hardly pretends to be other than, juridically omnipotent. For what you are up against here is the following "curious but inevitable paradox": deny the subordination of the state to higher law, free it in the name of ethical relativism from the *absolutes* of the Declaration of Independence, and *it*, the state, takes on as a matter of course the absoluteness that the older view attributed to the higher law and expressly denied to the state. Absoluteness, it would seem, must dwell somewhere; either you attribute it to the goods the state is to serve and thus deny it to the state, or you deny it to the goods and attribute it to the state. Each of the two views of the matter excludes the other; and, in the language of this book, if in a situation where the one view (that committed to the absolute rights and the relative state) has long prevailed, the attempt made to substitute the other (that committed to a relativistic view of rights and an absolutist view of the state) cannot be other than *revolutionary*. And, further in the language of this book, we stand here in the presence of the deepest issue that divides contemporary American conservatism from the Liberal Revolution. It is not without significance, Murray concludes in this area, that "evolutionary scientific humanism should be the favorite creed of our contemporary social engineers . . . And it seems that their inevitable temptation is to hasten the process of evolution by use of the resources of government." Once that temptation is yielded to, moreover, a further paradox supervenes: the absolute "wants" and the absolute state that ministers to those wants give us, instead of the "evolutionary process" that scientific humanism (that is, the Liberals) promises us, *men* who preside over the process, and preside over it *absolutely*.

> The "socially desirable objectives" are no longer "received" from society itself (as in the theory they should be); rather they are conceived in committee and imposed on society. The humanism ceases to evolve from below, and is directed from above; it remains scientific and becomes inhuman . . . The state tends to lose its character of servant, and assumes that of master.

This brings us to the fourth of Murray's alternatives, which, as we should expect, involves the reassertion (insofar as the assertion has lapsed among us) of the traditional barriers to the "expanding competence of the state"—that is, of

> the absoluteness of the order of human rights that stands irrevocably outside the sphere of state power, and the absoluteness of the order of justice that stands imperiously above the power of the state (p. 326).

[Mr. Kendall's essay was not completed beyond this point.—Ed.]

Notes

[1]Kendall's specific references in this chapter are to John Courtney Murray's book, *We Hold These Truths* (New York: Sheed and Ward, 1960).

Part II

A SELECTION OF
PUBLISHED ARTICLES
AND REVIEWS

The Majority Principle and the Scientific Elite

Those who—like Mr. Sidney Hook in a recent article in this review —call attention to that ambiguity in the term "democracy" which permits dictators to claim democratic sanctions for their regimes, have told only half the story. Even among those who would agree that "democracy" cannot be stretched to cover Mussolini's Italy and Hitler's Germany there are profound disagreements about what the word really means. Not disagreements about details; not disagreements about organizational devices; not disagreements as to the purposes to which the State should devote itself; but rather disagreements about the central problem of political theory: the residence of power within the State. It can be shown, I think, that between those who accept the majority principle as the differentia of democratic government, and those who repudiate it, a wider gulf is fixed than that which separates the latter from the defenders of Fascism.

By the majority principle I understand simply this: that in any decision-making group one half of the members, plus one, have a *right* to commit one half of the members, minus one, to any policy they see fit to support. For those who regard the word "right" as sicklied over with the pale cast of legal thought, the proposition may be changed to read: ". . . *ought* to be able to commit, etc . . ." The majority principle means, conversely, that those members of a decision-making group who are opposed to the policy of the majority *ought* to submit to that policy until such time as they can make themselves a majority. I emphasize the words *right* and *ought* because—and this is too often ignored by those who call themselves political scientists—any theory as to the proper residence of power in the State becomes, when stated in its simplest terms, an ethical imperative. It is stupid for men to argue about politics before they have settled their differences about morals.

Analyze the plain man's notions on democracy—as F.H. Bradley once analyzed his notions on morality—and you will find that they reduce themselves to something like the above statement of the majority principle. The plain man knows nothing of judicial review or separation of powers. He regards "civil rights" not as a condition but rather as a product of democratic government—like rural mail delivery or the police force. Mention universal suffrage to him and you will find that you have struck closer home. He will, for example, be displeased to learn that books are still being written to show that, since he cannot vote intelligently, he ought to be disfranchised.* But press him, and you will discover that his displeasure is tied up with the conviction that you can't find out what the majority wants without consulting everybody—which is another way of saying that universal suffrage is, for him, merely a corollary of the majority principle. That is why he will accept, without any sense of outrage, the notion that France and Switzerland can exclude women from the franchise and yet remain democracies—especially if you will remind him, as M. Rappard has done in a recent study of democratic government, that in those countries the women themselves make no complaint about their political disabilities.† For the plain man, the decision-making group is the entire community, and "democracy" is a word which describes those situations in which the majority of that group have their way about policy. If France and Switzerland choose to treat the family rather than the individual as the vote-counting unit, the plain man will have no quarrel with the arrangement. But his own behavior, through the nineteenth century, suggests that he feels otherwise about the exclusion of groups whose concurrence is clearly necessary for a majority verdict. He will not, for example, content himself with a franchise limited to the owners of property, or to the members of a particular church. What he expects from democracy is the automatic realization, in government and in law, of the wishes of the majority of the adult population.

Now: precisely the most interesting fact about the majority principle, as I have here defined it, is that some minds regard it as *obviously true*, and others regard it as *obviously false*. This is important because—in the language of a distinction once drawn by Lord Balfour —we waste our time when we seek for the *grounds* upon which a

*For example: *Political Institutions*. By E. M. Sait, New York: D. Appleton-Century, $4. *Anarchy or Hierarchy*. By Salvador de Madariaga. New York: Macmillan. $2.50
†*The Crisis of Democracy*. By William E. Rappard. Chicago: The University of Chicago Press. $2.50

man will defend a proposition which he treats as self-evident. If he could bring forward arguments in support of it—as Euclid was able to do for the theorems of his geometry—he would claim self-evidence for the arguments—as Euclid did for his axioms—and treat the proposition as derivative. The most you can hope to do for those beliefs which a man classifies as self-evident is to compile a history of how he came to believe them.

Because the majority principle is the kind of proposition for which self-evidence is claimed, it is one of the few propositions in political theory that we are justified in fighting about. Once we have agreed to accept it as a first principle of political action, we can reason together as to how to realize it in practice—and we can reason with some hope of convincing each other. Once we have agreed to abandon it, we can reason together about the proper method of choosing the minority to whom power should be entrusted. But we shall gain nothing by reasoning together about the majority principle itself, because the only reasons that can be urged for or against it are either (a) irrelevant, or (b) mere restatements of the principle or of its converse—reasons, that is to say, which assume the validity of the proposition they purport to prove. If, therefore, you and I disagree about the majority principle, we can either follow the example of Abraham and Lot, and go our separate ways, or that of Cain and Abel, and settle our difference in terms of thy blood or mine. For this, at least, is certain: if we remain in the same jurisdiction, the rules under which we live will be formulated either by the majority (*i.e.*, in accordance with the majority principle), or by some minority (*i.e.*, in contravention of the majority principle). There is no third possibility; and since the character of those rules will inevitably be a matter of profound concern to both of us, we shall not lack for issues about which to fight.

When, therefore, Mr. Herman Finer argues that the majority ought to have its way because in the long run it always does have its way, he not only writes bad history, but throws himself open to the graver charge of talking away from the problem at issue. He writes bad history because—as in Mexico in the days of D. Porfirio—today's majority may be long dead before today's dictatorship takes to its heels, and because there is no sort of guarantee that tomorrow's majority will agree, even in broad outline, with today's. He talks away from the problem at issue because there is no ethical imperative which bids us hasten the inevitable. Nor does Mr. Finer strengthen

his case when he tells us that power should be entrusted to the
majority because that which the majority is known to support commands "respect." Such respect no doubt makes for stability in government, but ethics is concerned neither with respect nor with
stability. The concern of ethics is with right, and she will not sell her
blessings so cleaply as Mr. Finer appears to suppose. Nor, finally, does
it help to insist that there is a presumption that the larger group will
possess a greater share of intelligence than any minority. Such a
presumption will exist only for those who believe in the majority
principle already. What Mr. Finer really means is that the majority
ought to have its way because it is right that it should. But that, of
course, is not a reason.

This, then, is the position: some amongst us build their political
philosophy upon the assumption that the last word in politics should
lie with the majority of the decision-making group. Some amongst us
build upon a denial of that assumption. The former are the true Left
of modern politics, and the latter are the true Right; and the man who
supposes that they may be reconciled through a friendly exchange
of arguments deceives himself with an idle fancy. We accept the
majority principle, or deny it, not because of the proofs we can offer
for it, but because we are the sort of people we happen to be. For the
same reason, if you like, that some amongst us think of the good
society as primarily urban and industrial, while others think of it as
primarily rural and agrarian.

If it be objected that such a view abandons politics to what Mr. C.
E. M. Joad calls the contemporary "cult of unreason," there are, I
think, two answers. First, that it does nothing of the kind. The first
step towards a rational treatment of any problem is to find out to what
extent it consists of elements which are irrational. This is especially
true in politics, where the propositions that men believe simply because they appear obvious are invariably the chief elements that we
must consider. Our task, once we have recognized these elements
and their essential irrationality, is to discover the most rational procedure for dealing with them—which is to assign to reason a role of
whose importance it can hardly complain. And second, that all the
evidence, whether we like it or not, appears to point in precisely the
direction I have indicated. Not only do men differ about the majority
principle in a way which places their disagreement beyond all hope
of rational reconciliation; we can see why, in a world organized as

ours is organized, they must differ in this way. If we cannot lay bare the rational grounds upon which their conflicting beliefs rest, at least we can see that the conflicts themselves are only what we should expect. We can, in Lord Balfour's phrase, see how each disputant came to believe what he believes. And we can satisfy ourselves that the existence of two schools of thought about the majority principle is an inevitable accompaniment of a society whose established religion—as Mr. Tawney has shown in a brilliant book—is the "religion of inequality." They are a part of the price we pay for the perpetuation of elites whose outlook is different from that of the remainder of the community. Men oppose majority rule because they know in advance that the views of the majority will not coincide with their own.

What I am here arguing is this: that the majority principle has necessary implications of which, in our social context, educated men must fight shy. I shall, in a later paragraph, attempt to show what those implications are, and why cultivated minds do by ordinary fight shy of them. For the moment, I content myself with calling attention to the results of this timidity as they have revealed themselves in the history of political theory:

(1) The majority principle has been, for the most part, neglected by professional political theorists. The academic political scientist has, indeed, accepted the phrase itself as part of his stock in trade; but he has never felt any obligation to formulate the ideas it represents or to seek out the arguments that might be urged in its favor. Even in England—a country whose political institutions give every evidence of deliberate adjustment to its requirements—political theorists have passed up the majority principle in favor of such doctrines as the divine right of kings, sovereignty, the right of revolution, etc.

(2) Where neglect has not been its portion, the majority principle has received abuse: abuse of a sort whose language and logic vary astonishingly little from century to century. It begins with the reminder that the *melior et sanior pars* of the community is, by definition, the smallest. The largest part is therefore the worst and the most unsound. Government by the largest part would therefore lead to intolerable consequences, the most shocking of which are listed seriatim. The inescapable conclusion is that government should be entrusted to an aristocracy of philosopher kings, or, *faute de mieux,*

to whatever minority happens to control it at the time of writing.

(3) Friends of the majority principle have been few indeed. Among our contemporaries, Mr. Finer speaks well of it in his *Theory and Practice of Modern Government,* and Mr. Harold Laski implies his allegiance at various points in his *The State in Theory and Practice;* even Mr. Finer, whose "authorities" are hardly less numerous than those of the indefatigable Grotius, marshals support in this connection only from Locke and Rousseau.

(4) American political theory, from the *Federalist Papers* to the day before yesterday, appears in this context as a nostalgic yearning after a definition of "democracy" that will somehow circumvent the implications of the majority principle. To exclude the majority principle from one's definition of "democracy" is, of course, to equate democracy with some form of minority rule; and since all are agreed that democracy cannot be the same thing as government by a minority, it follows that the sort of definition our political theorists have sought can be achieved only by chicanery. A Sisyphus whose stone simply can't be budged, the American political theorist has contented himself with creating and re-creating an optical illusion: a "democracy" in which ultimate power is entrusted to an unremovable judiciary. As spokesman for an elite which has never concerned itself with the aspirations and axioms of common men, he is kept at his task by an instinctive fear of what may happen when the illusion disappears. While the illusion lasts, there remains the hope that the common man will not withdraw his allegiance from the form of government which—under a constitution devised to meet the needs of eighteenth century property-owners—we have maintained in this country through the past one hundred and fifty years. Because he speaks only for an elite, his chief concepts—judicial review, separation of powers, "limited" government—remain to this day meaningless to the overwhelming majority of our citizens. That is why I have been able to argue, with particular reference to this country, that the opponents of the majority principle stand closer, in the amphitheater of modern politics, to the extreme right (*i.e.*, the defenders of Fascism) than to the friends of the majority principle. That is why, finally, two recently published books—Prof. Max Lerner's *It Is Later Than You Think** and Eduard Heimann's *Communism, Fascism or Democ-*

*New York: The Viking Press. $2.50.

racy†—will deserve a chapter all to themselves when the time comes for someone to write the definitive history of American political theory between 1776 and 1938; for both take a firm stand in favor of the majority principle.

"Foolishness repeated by thirty-six million mouths," Anatole France once wrote, "is none the less foolishness"; and when judged by the light it throws upon the qualms of educated men in the presence of the majority principle, this aphorism is not so trivial as you think. If there is anything upon which learned men see eye to eye as a matter of course, it is that foolishness remains foolishness even when underwritten by the majority of a decision-making group. They know that majorities cannot out of generosity repeal the law of gravitation; that they cannot for purposes of convenience reduce π from 3.1416 to 3; that they cannot out of envy make wise men over into fools or fools over into wise men; that they cannot out of pride impugn the validity of the evolutionary hypothesis. This is heady knowledge—too heady, perhaps, for so long as we have in our midst men who are prepared to credit a radio announcer's declaration that the Martians are about to attack us, we are likely to yield to its intoxication. And once that surrender has been made, we leap lightly from the knowledge that majorities cannot do these things to the belief that they are even now straining at the constitution in their eagerness to attempt them!

This, I suggest, is the point at which educated men break with the notion that the minority *ought* to accept the policies laid down by the majority. They see in the majority principle the implication that *the only right policy for a democratic government to follow is the policy desired by the majority.* They see in it the implication that the policy of the majority becomes the right policy simply by virtue of the votes cast in its favor—so that what is right today may be wrong tomorrow and right again the day after. They see in it the implication that the minority must be wrong no matter what policy it supports. And because they have been trained from early childhood to think in terms of other criteria of right and wrong, they shrink from these implications as from the ravings of an idiot.

Do such implications in fact flow from my definition of the majority principle? I think they do; but I think, too, that the comity of political

†New York: W.W. Norton & Co. $2.50.

discussion requires that they shall not be made to mean more than they actually say. You cannot, for example, deduce from an *ethical* judgment (and I have nowhere suggested that the majority principle is anything else) a canon of *scientific* proof (since the corollaries of any proposition, being merely different ways of saying the same thing, must belong to the same genus as the proposition itself).* Nor is it permitted, in "shaking" out the implications of a given proposition, to use the same word in two senses. And the corollaries which I have read out of the majority principle in the preceding paragraph are, I believe, harmless enough when they are construed in the light of these two rules of comity.

Let me explain. We begin with the majority principle, according to which it is right—*ethically* right—that the majority of a decision-making group shall have the power to commit the minority to its policy. From this it follows that the policy of the majority is the right policy—by which we mean simply that in a decision-making group which has agreed to govern itself in accordance with the majority principle, the adoption of any policy other than that of the majority would be ethically wrong. It follows, too, that the policy of the majority comes to be right, in this sense, at precisely the moment when it wins the support of the last voter needed to constitute a majority, and ceases to be right at precisely the moment when a majority can no longer be marshalled in its favor. It follows, finally, that a minority can never claim moral justification for an attempt to impose its policy upon a recalcitrant majority—not even when the minority can bring forward irrefragable proof that its policy is the wisest the group might adopt. None of these statements involved in any way the notion that the policy of the majority is necessarily "right in the scientific sense"—and so far as I have been able to learn no protagonist of the majority principle has ever defended such a doctrine. But if this is true, why should the majority principle offend the allergies of the cultivated?

I have already offered a partial answer to this question: while education remains the monopoly of a small minority who live in an economic and social context different from that of the majority, the educated may with every show of reason anticipate that the policies

---

*I here assume that the reader will accept without hesitation the statement that Science is not concerned with ends. For an admirable discussion of this point, see *The Science and Method of Politics,* by G.E.G. Catlin.

of the majority will be different from their own. They will, therefore, oppose these policies; and they will, out of logical consistency if not out of selfishness, avoid governmental forms likely to result in their adoption. But there is another—and, at this stage in my argument— a better reason: the educated in our time find it difficult to understand the word "right" in any sense other than the scientific sense. Policy is, for them, either right in the scientific sense or wrong in the scientific sense. Betrayed by those who, in Mr. Lionel Robbins' haunting phrase, "should have been their intellectual leaders," they have never learned that Science, cooped up as it is in the pigsty of Means, cannot see out over the broad acres of Ends. They have never learned that Science tells us not what things to do but how to do things. Thus they see nothing unreasonable in the hope that Science, which today sets the temper of their lives, shall tomorrow lay down directives for social policy. How shall they account for their negligence if, when the directives are at last formulated, they have permitted power to pass into the hands of the "nonscientific" majority?

The man who doubts that the typical modern intellectual does identify "right" with "right in the scientific sense," may easily satisfy himself on this point by consulting any of the great recent debates in this country about social policy. Shall the United States adopt a policy of isolation? Shall we add to the constitution an amendment requiring Congress to submit proposed declarations of war to popular vote? Shall we put a "floor" under wages and a "ceiling" over working hours? Clearly these are issues with regard to which the country must ultimately adopt a policy; clearly, too, those of us who believe in democratic government have every reason to congratulate themselves upon the fact that, with us, such issues are resolved only after full public discussion. Nor have I any wish to deny that such discussion should take cognizance of any relevant information which Science can supply. If, for example, Science can tell us whether or not a proposed policy is feasible, or whether the means envisaged by its proponents are likely to produce the results desired, we should give it a grateful hearing. If, again, Science can show us that a proposed policy is incompatible with other policies to which we stand committed, or demonstrate that a given course of action will prove more costly than its supporters suppose, we ought not only to listen, but also to recognize that in reaching our decisions we ignore such dicta at our peril. My point is that, when we have assembled all the information Science has to offer, someone must still reach a decision, and that this decision will be made in terms of the ethical and aesthetic *values* of those who are called upon to make the decision. My point is that though Science—in the hands of those who understand its uses—offers no pronouncements with regard to values, our leading publicists continue to talk as though it did. The effect of their debates is, therefore, to hide—from the debaters and listeners alike—the role of values in the formulation of social policy, and to perpetuate a situation in which political discussion is the monopoly of a scientific elite.

This is tantamount to saying that the claims of the majority principle cannot get a fair hearing from an educated minority whose real religion is Science. For what the proponents of the majority principle are really asking is, on the one hand, that we recognize the distinction between ends and means, and, on the other, that we repudiate the pretensions of Science to hegemony over ends. That hegemony may then be restored to Art and Religion, which can, for one thing, show sound title to it, and can, for another, offer us guarantees that it will be exercised *responsibly*. Art and Religion are, for the rest, activities in whose pursuit common men start even with those who regard themselves as their betters—since there is no correlation between the amount of scientific training a man has received and his capacity to deal effectively with aesthetic and moral problems. But to demand a "quarantine" against further aggression by Science is to seek a concession which the educated of our time cannot grant without denying the only meaning they have been able to read out of their experience.

On the Preservation of
Democracy for America

There is pretty general agreement, by this time, that the fifty-five gentlemen who assembled at Philadelphia in 1787 to "revise the Articles" were not very much interested in what we in our time call democracy. What they were interested in lies beyond the scope of this paper: Perhaps, as Mr. Beard would have us believe, they were chiefly concerned with protecting the selfish economic interests of their class. Perhaps, as the "nationalist" school of historical interpretation assure us, they were bent upon making good their dream of a united people, capable of occupying a place of honor and importance in what is euphemistically termed the family of nations. Perhaps, as Mr. Sait contends, we deceive ourselves when we look to them for a consciously formulated objective—since (as men who have "seen through" the farce of political "theory") we know that they gathered at Philadelphia because that was the only response which organisms like theirs could possibly make to the stimuli to which—during the preceding weeks and months—they had been subjected. Or perhaps, as the moralists insist, they were primarily concerned to build institutions which would enable the people on this side of the Atlantic to live the good life (as they conceived it). We do not, for our purposes here, have to make a choice between these conflicting hypotheses regarding the intentions of the Framers of the Constitution of the United States; but I hope the reader will agree that none of the evidence at our disposal suggests that they were inspired by an enthusiasm for those principles of equality and majority-rule and responsible government, which many of us associate with the democratic faith. I hope he will agree, too, that whatever the designs of the Framers may have been, American government is—150 years later—everything that an anti-democratic Constitutional Convention could have wished it to be.* For good or ill, political power has been

*I am well aware that there are definitions of democracy in the light of which this proposition must appear meaningless. I mean by democracy a form of political organization which lodges absolute power in the numerical majority of the adult population of the area which the organization is expected to serve. I therefore repudiate any

concentrated, from their day to ours, in the hands of an economic oligarchy which has, at every moment in our history, been as free from control by popular majorities as the most efficient of Oriental despots.

How has this miracle been accomplished? By what "inconceivable art" has a property-owning minority contrived—starting from scratch, mind you, in 1787—to impose its will upon a people who, during the preceding ten years, had shown a genius for self-government beyond anything the world had seen since the democratic period in Roman history? Or, to put the same question in another way, what strategy would an eighteenth-century Machiavelli have recommended to the Framers and their friends as the necessary course to follow if they wished to achieve such a miracle? However our political scientists may have failed us in other directions, they have provided us with a picture of contemporary American government from which we can, with some confidence, deduce an answer to this question; and I suggest that our answer would need to take some such form as the following: We are, you remember, listening to an eighteenth-century Machiavelli, advising the Framers of the Constitution on techniques for the permanent suppression of majority-rule democracy.†

"Your constitution," I think he might have said, "is admirably suited to your long-term purposes. You have, for example, been wise —eminently wise—taking refuge in ambiguity where frankness might have proved inconvenient. To have shown your hand completely at this time would have obliged you to forego the luxury of popular ratification; and your grandchildren, equally with yourselves, will be able to make good use of the fact that you did not forego it. Who, they will be able to ask, dares lift his voice against a constitution adopted by the free choice of the American people? You have been

definition of democracy which may, in some circumstances, make of it one and the same thing with minority-rule—any attempt, for example, to equate democracy with a particular set of "natural" rights, or with a particular conception of the proper limits of governmental action, or with a particular complex of putatively God-given political institutions. Democracy is, in a word, government which on the one hand is no respecter of persons (since it assigns equal voting power to all who live under its jurisdiction), and, on the other hand, government which always gives precedence to the wishes of majorities over those of minorities. That this definition leaves untouched an important aspect of the problem, will, I trust, be made sufficiently clear in the following paragraphs.

†Readers of *It Is Later Than You Think* will recognize my indebtedness to Mr. Lerner for the device employed here.

wise to require ratification by specially chosen conventions in the several states; for the members of the present state legislatures will not fail to see in, let us say, the obligation of contracts clause, an attempt to liquidate everything they understand by the phrase 'self-government.' The state governments must, of course, be liquidated—at least in their present form; for they embody principles which, in the nineteenth century, will be heralded the world over as indispensable to genuine popular government.

"You have acted wisely, again, in omitting a bill of rights—not because you don't want one, but because, by adopting one in the first Congress, you can both distract attention from your fantastically difficult amending process and create the illusion of a government genuinely responsive to popular will. You will, in the fullness of time, be able to make good use of that bill of rights; you will be able, by a magic which Alexander Hamilton will explain in one of the *Federalist Papers,* to change those amendments from 'popular triumphs' into so many chains with which to bind your subjects.

"You are to be congratulated upon the ingenious use you have made of old Montesquieu's doctrine of separation of powers. He thought of it, curiously enough, as a guarantee of liberty; but that was because he lacked *your* insight. In your hands, it has become a guarantee of the infinite perpetuation of the economic *status quo.* For your government is obviously incapable of concerted action for any purpose except war; and if you will only learn how to manipulate the symbol of Nationalism you may depend upon it that important economic issues will not be posed in time of war. From the same point of view, your Congress is admirable. If ever a popular majority were to capture the presidency and the lower house with a view to making drastic changes in the economic system, it would need at least two more years before it could capture the Senate—and no movement which has made promises to its supporters can survive a two-year delay. In your arrangements for selecting a president, you have, I predict, overestimated your ability to thrust aristocratic devices down the throats of a rebellious people. I therefore advise you to resign yourselves to the notion of a popularly elected Chief Executive; but you will, if you but keep your heads, be able to turn him also into an ally. Swallow your prejudices against the idea of political parties, then divide yourselves into two groups which, though in fundamental agreement upon such essentials as the sacredness of private property and the evil of uncontrolled democracy, will nevertheless be able to maintain a sham battle over trivialities. The electorate, if properly instructed by its betters, will never see that the parties are mere window-dressing, and it may be counted on to take great delight in the myth that it is permitted to decide great issues at election-time. You can, as time passes, use your control over the state governments (in whom you have wisely vested control over elections) and over the press to make it virtually impossible to start a third party; and if ever one should get started in spite of you—well, abandon one of the old ones and swamp the new one by joining it *en masse.* You may as well accept the idea that a limited electorate is not compatible with what will one day be called the modern temper; little by little you will find yourselves obliged to admit to the franchise the entire adult population—yes, absurd as it may seem, the entire adult population; and so broad a franchise has, beyond all question, its elements of danger. Add to that the fact that you will not be able to maintain, permanently, the indirect method of election which you have devised for your Senators, and you will see that your heirs, 150 years hence, may have plenty to worry about. But these difficulties need not prove insuperable, if you will play your cards wisely through the next fifty or sixty years. Attend carefully, and I will tell you what I mean:

"You must, first of all, move as quickly as possible to convert the Constitution into a *symbol.* Voters can be taught—by well-paid propagandists—to regard its essential principles as unchangeable; they can be taught to do all of their political and economic thinking within the assumptions which it affirms. Secondly, you must make the most of your constitution's indefiniteness regarding the powers of the judiciary. You will, during the years that lie just ahead, need to put your best talent into the Treasury Department; but your second best man ought to be put into the Supreme Court. Let him wait patiently for a case in which he can at the same moment decide an issue in a manner agreeable to the present President and the present Congress, *and* claim the power to declare a congressional statute unconstitutional. Neither the President nor Congress will complain, and you will thus establish a precedent which will serve you well in preventing legislation of a kind likely to prove expensive. Establish the power of the Supreme Court to pass upon the 'constitutionality' of legislation and you will create a situation in which the electorate will never know whom to blame for its failure to get the sort of legislation it wants. And, thirdly, you will have to do something about the impeachment clause—the one genuine blunder you have included in your constitution. Judicial 'review' will profit you nothing if a popularly elected Congress can impeach learned justices for insisting that the Constitution does not always mean what it says. Begin early, therefore, to sell the notion that the impeachment power does not extend to acts of a political character. Get that notion across and your justices will be virtually irremovable—and while even that does not take care of Congress' power to 'pack' the Court with new justices, you will discover techniques for dealing with that proposal when it is made. Meanwhile, such an interpretation of the impeachment clause will put the President, equally with the Supreme Court, beyond control by Congress. Among other things, that will enable him to give the country any foreign policy—pacific or warlike—that he sees fit. He will therefore be in a position to distract attention from domestic affairs whenever he has reason to believe that the populace is growing discontented with its lot.

"Finally, drive home the notion that a free press is indispensable not only to freedom and civilization but to life itself; for as technological development proceeds through the next century and a half a free press will come to mean a press that is 'free' only to yourselves and your servants. Keep control of the press and you will always be able to dictate the terms of the debates which, inevitably, accompany elections in any country whose real rulers regard themselves as obliged to maintain the pretense of popular government."

Such, I suggest, is the plan which an eighteenth-century Machiavelli might have laid before the Framers of the Constitution upon the completion of their work at Philadelphia. Whether our economic oligarchy ever consciously adopted it is not, I repeat, here in question —for my point is the simple one that American political institutions, even as we find them portrayed in a book of such patent anti-democratic bias as Ogg and Ray's ubiquitous *Introduction to American Government,* are today precisely what they would have been if such a strategy had been adopted. We owe a profound debt of gratitude to those publicists—J. Allen Smith and Louis Boudin were, here, the pioneers—who assembled, and forced upon American political science, the data which enable us to see, behind our present façade of theoretically free popular elections, the irresponsible authority of the tiny groups which actually control our country's destiny. Because these men did their work well any unprejudiced person who today takes the trouble to look into the problem will readily convince himself that our constitution, as it now operates, is as little congenial to majority-rule as it could possibly have become without abandoning the make-believe of democratic learnings.

For so much, I say, we owe to Smith and Boudin—as, also, to those who have continued their work—a profound debt of gratitude. Both these writers, however, seem to me to have reasoned from this conclusion regarding the undemocratic character of our constitution to a corollary which does not, in fact, flow from it—one which, as I hope to demonstrate in what follows, is essentially unsound. For both have, I think, given comfort to the notion that the failure of the movement for majority-rule democracy in the United States can be *explained* in terms of our undemocratic constitutional arrangements—that, therefore, all we have to do is to modify these arrangements in a democratic sense and we shall enter at once into full enjoyment of the benefits of majority-rule. Some such "axiom" has, I think, figured prominently in the thought of our majority-rule democrats ever since Smith gave it currency at the beginning of this century. In its least critical form it involves the extraordinary assertion that all that stands between the American people and majority-rule is our absurdly difficult amending process, which is thus regarded as a dyke which defends the other undemocratic features of our constitution against the raging seas of popular protest.*

My own view is that this whole approach to the problem of why we do not have majority-rule in the United States is root and branch wrong—and that its widespread acceptance has had a vicious effect upon our political life and our political thought. I propose to argue, in the first place, that it is based upon misapprehensions regarding the character of democracy as the latter has always been understood by its major exponents in the realm of political theory. I shall argue, secondly, that it is only when we fix our attention upon *local* government that we can provide ourselves with an adequate explanation of the failure of the American movement for majority-rule. And I shall,

---

*I disclaim here any suggestion that political institutions cannot operate as independent determinants of the course of historical development. It is not that dykes cannot hold back raging seas, but rather that there have been no raging seas to hold back. Smith and Boudin assume throughout that there have been.

thirdly, draw the obvious conclusion that those who would devote themselves to the preservation of American democracy must set aside their prejudices against the particularism of local government units (and, too, against the unparalleled dullness of local government literature) and hurl themselves, for the first time, into the attempt to build democracy where there is some hope of their succeeding.

My first point, then, is that in assuming the likelihood of a spontaneous irruption of democracy over so wide an area as the United States the Smith-Boudin theory of constitutional barriers to majority-rule involves itself in a basic error from which it might have been saved by closer attention to the teaching of the "great tradition" in democratic thought. For this tradition has always held, as a first principle, that democracy begins in the *small* group and spreads, if it spreads at all, outward—a proposition which either means nothing at all or embodies the warning that we have no right to look for democracy in the *large* group until we have first satisfied ourselves that the small groups of which it consists are democratic in character. It warns us that popular control over government is a technique which must be *learned;* that it can be learned only in connection with problems which not only affect us *vitally* (surely all the problems which we denominate "political" do that?) but also affect us intimately—in the sense that they are so close to us that we can hope to understand them; that, therefore, the technique must be mastered, in the first instance, in the neighborhood in which we actually live. It warns us, finally, that any inquiry into the reasons for the failure of the democratic movement in a large country ought to begin on the local government level—since in the absence of democratic habits on that level democracy could appear on the national level only by means of a miracle. It is this warning that the Smith-Boudin school seems to me to have ignored.

In reminding you that the democratic tradition thinks of democracy as spreading outward from the small group to the large one I have, you will notice, entered the proviso: if it spreads at all. We must now, however, take account of the fact that the great theoretical defenders of popular government—precisely the men whom we should expect to make the most extravagant claims for it—have always expressed profound skepticism regarding the possibility of extending it successfully beyond the confines of what we may, for convenience, call the neighborhood. When, therefore, George Sa-

bine dismisses Jean Jacques Rousseau's enthusiasm for the city-state
as an "anachronism," he really ought to add that pretty much everything Rousseau had to say about politics is an anachronism—and that
this is equally true of the overwhelming majority of democratic theorists. Of Rousseau it can be shown, I believe, that his enthusiasm for
the city-state was the core of his political teaching; and I should like
to summarize—before I proceed further with my argument—what I
conceive his position on this question to have been: You can, he
insists, take your choice between *government based upon force,* and
government based upon the general will; and if you choose the latter
you may as well face the fact that it can exist only where certain
definite conditions have been fulfilled. You must, above all, make sure
that a general will actually exists as between the persons to whom
your government is expected to minister—they must possess a *moi
commun,* a sense of common destiny sufficiently intense to bind
them to each other in what we today would call a genuine group or
community; a mere aggregate of individuals, brought together by
chance or by compulsion, will not therefore serve your purpose at all.
You must, secondly, make sure that the members of your group are
willing to accept, without reservation, the notion that decisions about
law and government are to be reached on a basis of absolute political
equality. You must, thirdly, make sure that there exists, on all sides,
a clear understanding that any policy adopted by the majority of the
group's members is to be accepted as the policy of the entire group.
In the absence of these three conditions, Rousseau argues, any government you may set up will be a government based upon force; and
since, for Rousseau, force is always morally irrelevant, this means that
such a government can never point to anything properly describable
as a duty to obey its commands.

Rousseau's critics have not, for the most part, seen fit to deal generously with this emphasis in his thought. It is easy to point out that,
in the state as we know it today, there is no such thing as Rousseau's
general will—that the general will can, accordingly, be written off as
a useless *abstraction.* It is easy to show that absolute political equality, of the sort Rousseau proposed, would in modern conditions lead
to disastrous results. And it is easy, finally, to demonstrate that no
right-thinking man could bring himself to entrust unlimited power in
the modern state to the "transient" majorities which assert themselves in popular elections. It is, I repeat, easy to do all of that, and

then to pass on to one's opening chapter on the nineteenth century, where one feels more at home. But the critic who takes this easy way out has, I believe, simply failed to come to grips with Rousseau— whose answer, on all these points, would surely have been: "Why, but of course! That is precisely what I was trying to say!" For Rousseau wrote as an intransigent enemy of the modern state; not in ignorance (as Mr. Sabine appears to suggest) that the stream of tendency in modern history was opposed to his solution of the problem of government, but as one convinced that men must either reverse that stream of tendency or resign themselves to an eternity in chains.

Rousseau's critics, in a word, have surpassed themselves in refuting claims which Rousseau would never have thought of making. Rousseau did not argue that wherever there is a government there is a *general will*, but rather that it is a mistake, from the ethical point of view, to attempt to set up a government where no general will exists. You do not, therefore, "refute" Rousseau by showing, as Laski has done, that it is nonsense to tell the man who is about to be hanged that the general will is "forcing" him "to be free"; for Rousseau's thesis is that there *is* no general will where men do not recognize that their government, in coercing them, does force them to be free. You do not "refute" Rousseau, either, by insisting that men, as we know them today, do not, when they cast their votes at election time, abstract from selfish considerations and support that which they believe likely to promote the general welfare; for Rousseau's clear answer will be, once again, that we are attempting government over too wide an area. "Cut down the size of the area," he would say, "until you have reached a group which is small and intimate enough to get at their problems in the way I have described. You may, subsequently, build back to larger groups and larger areas—but that should come only when men actually want it, when they have actually learned to think of themselves as members of the larger group in such a way as to fulfill the conditions necessary for government by the general will."*

As I have already suggested, Rousseau's insistence upon this point is by no means unique. Aristotle's argument that friendship is the only basis upon which you can build "constitutional" government, is, I think, simply another way of expressing the same idea. So, too, are

---

*I hope I have made it clear that these are not textual quotations from Rousseau, but rather attempts to summarize the full implications of his argument.

Laski's passionate pleas for "decentralization" in the modern state, and, also, his frequent emphases upon an atmosphere of "good will" as the only context in which peaceful decisions can be reached. So, too, is Herman Finer's *caveat* that majority-rule is impossible where the things upon which men agree are not more important to them than the things about which they disagree. So, too, is G. D. H. Cole's thesis that men owe no allegiance to governments toward which they feel no "loyalty." So, too, is R. M. MacIver's perception that a sense of "community" is always a necessary pre-condition of successful democratic government. So, too, is the proposition—ably defended by the Dutch jurist Krabbe—that just laws are assured only where a "common sense of right" has secured willing recognition of its supremacy. So, too, is Karl Marx's premise that genuine democracy can be conceived only in terms of the lodgment of power in *local* councils. It is, in short, an insistence common to all political thinkers who reason from the great democratic first principles of equality and majority-rule; for all of them are men who instinctively fight shy of "bigness" in politics, men who instinctively associate bigness with force, men who, I repeat, never doubted that *democracy begins in the small group* and spreads—if it spreads at all—*outward*.

To argue—as some writers have dared to do—that all this has been "changed" by modern developments in the sphere of communications is, I suspect, to miss the entire point which these theorists have sought to establish. Aristotle wished a citizenry small enough to sit within earshot of a single speaker not because the human voice, unaided by twentieth-century radio facilities, carries no further than it does—but because he thought that a group of people small enough to gather about a single speaker and hear him would be small enough to come to know each other well. The human voice is mentioned, in his formulation of this principle, only as a rough indication of the size of the sort of group of which he was thinking. Mutual understanding of the kind that grows out of lasting and intimate face-to-face relations between human beings was, for Aristotle as for Rousseau, the reality upon which to build a government for free men; and it is by no means evident that the essential character of that reality has been modified by the three R's of modern culture—the railroad, the radio, and the race with time. To suppose that it does is either to misconstrue Aristotle's word "friendship" or to commit yourself to the notion that, other things being equal, a radio announcer at station WJZ, or a Pullman conductor on the Twentieth Century Limited, ought to have more friends than Aristides the Just. Aristotle and Rousseau may have underestimated the area over which men can enter into relations of the sort they had in mind; but it would be difficult to show that that area is *necessarily* wider today than when they wrote.

I should not like to convey the impression that a grand array of "authorities" is the best possible defense of the view that we act foolishly when we look for majority-rule democracy in the absence of deeply-felt group relations between men; for the idea is, in fact, one which lends itself to demonstration of a peculiarly convincing kind. A full demonstration clearly lies beyond the scope of this essay; but we *can* pause long enough to examine what is, for me, the most interesting of its many facets: If democracy involves majority-rule, it involves also acceptance by the minority of all decisions behind which a majority can be rallied. We are, therefore, entitled to ask, What are the minimum conditions in which a minority can be depended upon to accept a majority decision which it views with genuine repugnance? If it acquiesces simply because the majority has at its disposition overwhelming *force,* then the situation does not satisfy the fundamental democratic slogan of *government by persuasion.* If, on the other hand, it acquiesces willingly, it is difficult to conceive of its doing so for any save one of the following three reasons. (1) It disagrees with the majority on the particular point at issue, but nevertheless shares with it long-term purposes which it does not choose to jeopardize by precipitating dissension. (2) It disagrees with the majority on the particular point at issue, but is so bound to it by personal ties of affection that secession is unthinkable. (3) In line with the old adage that we forgive that which we thoroughly understand, the minority is so familiar with the "causes" of the majority's decision that it accepts it as inevitable.

But all three of these reasons clearly presuppose group relations of a very special kind—and, more than that, relations which we should expect to arise most readily as between people who actually live together. In no case should we expect them to exist as between mere *aggregates* of individuals who have been brought together by chance or by compulsion.

I conclude from all this that those who have explained the failure of the democratic movement in the United States in terms of our undemocratic constitution should, at least, have considered the possibility that the people of this country are to this day a mere aggregate of individuals brought together by chance or by compulsion. I conclude that they should have considered the possibility that the United States covers too large an area to provide a congenial background for majority-rule. They should, finally, have asked themselves whether men were receiving, in their home communities, training in democratic habits and techniques of a kind likely to suggest the possibility of extending democracy over a wider area. Or—to put the same question in another way—was democratic government on the local level sufficiently healthy to supply the necessary nuclei for a nation-wide democratic movement? Is it sufficiently healthy for that purpose today? The answer to both questions must, I believe, be a round "No." The answer must be that while the Supreme Court, the United States Senate, and the American party-system have all found apologists sufficiently skilled in sophistry to demonstrate that they do somehow serve the purposes of democracy, nobody has ever dared to enter such a plea for our local governments. The answer must be, finally, that if we can arrive at a satisfactory explanation for the undemocratic character of our local governments we can with some confidence tell ourselves that we have discovered what the Smith-Boudin school cannot offer us: the real cause for the failure of our majority-rule democrats to influence the course of events in American politics.

What exactly do I mean by the round "No" with which I have answered our question about the health of democracy on the level of local government? I mean, first of all, that in local affairs we find no more than in national affairs a presumption that what government does is done by majority mandate. I mean that no matter where we turn for description of American local government in action, we find the story told in terms of boss and machine rule, financial corruption, nepotism, fixed elections, and popular indifference. I mean that here, to an even greater degree than in our federal government, we find the two unfailing symptoms of oligarchic political control: inequality before the law and regressive taxation. I mean, finally, that in local government we encounter a party system which does not even pay to democracy the courtesy of maintaining a sham battle about political principles. And all these are, for the rest, universally accepted truths about American local government. They add up, I suggest, to this: the democratic movement has somehow been prevented from taking root even in that area of our political life which should, on our showing, offer the most favorable conditions for the emergence of the group relations upon which democracy necessarily depends. American government is, therefore, government by coercion even in that area in which it is easiest to govern by persuasion.

Nor is the reason for all this so obscure as the custodians of our wisdom about local government would like us to believe. It is not true, that is to say, that the student of democracy requires an encyclopedic grasp of the facts and figures concerning local government as a preliminary to putting forward a theory as to why the American people do not govern themselves in their home towns—any more than we need to make ourselves authorities on anatomy before we can venture a theory as to why a man died whom we have seen swallowing a stiff three fingers of arsenic. For, just as the student of democracy knows that majority-rule is likeliest to emerge where conditions are friendliest to the formation of those group relations which we were discussing a moment ago, he knows, too, that majority-rule is an impossible adventure except where certain further conditions are scrupulously fulfilled. He knows, for example, that the democratic process can thrive only where it can become sufficiently interesting to compete for the attentions of men whose time is already mortgaged to other pursuits. He knows that it can become thus interesting only where it extends—at least potentially—to issues which are genuinely important. He knows, again, that the democratic process cannot be said to "extend" to an issue unless it involves a power to deal with it effectively and without interference from outside. He knows, finally, that popular majorities can be depended upon to provide responsible government only where formal political arrangements imply *unlimited* confidence in their capacity. And knowing all this, he needs only to glance at the institutional framework in which American local government operates in order to satisfy himself that it is here—and not in our federal constitution—that the fatal blows have been struck at the democratic movement. He will, I think, be inclined to content himself with the following scraps of information:

(1) That over most of the country local government is obliged to function within limits proposed by hand-me-down charters not subject to change by local majorities. (2) The taxing powers of our local government units are everywhere severely restricted—as also, because of the due-process clauses, are their powers of expropriation

and confiscation. (3) In all their functions, our local government units are ultimately subject to control by the larger political unit of which they form a part—that is, by the state.

More than this, I repeat, the student of democracy does not need to be told when he sets out in search of the cause of the undemocratic character of our local governments. Even if he can be shown, to return to my analogy, that there was a pathological condition in the left arm, he remains convinced that the man died of arsenic poisoning. That is why he grows impatient with the local government experts when they recite the virtues of the short-ballot, the city manager plan, and the merit system as correctives of our local governmental evils. Here—he tells himself—are the professional political scientists, up to their old game of prostituting democracy to efficiency. What our local governments need, from the democratic point of view, is a sufficient grant of power to make them *interesting;* and any other approach to the problem simply misses the point.

If all this is true—and this brings me to my third point—would not our Louis Boudins and our Max Lerners be well advised to transfer their attention from the federal to the local level of government? I cordially agree with them that the ultimate end is to shift power in this country from millionaires and their hirelings to the numerical majority of our citizens. I agree, too, that if that end is to be achieved it will ultimately involve getting rid of undemocratic political arrangements on the federal level. I submit, however, that in the last analysis such writers have nothing definite to propose to sympathetic readers of their books and articles. Suppose, for example, that that indispensable abstraction, the average man, reads Mr. Lerner's *It Is Later Than You Think*—a book in which local government is not, I believe, so much as mentioned. Suppose, further, that he is completely captivated by its point of view, and suddenly goes all out for majority-rule in politics and collectivism in economics. What, I wonder, does he do next? Does he not face this *impasse*—that the only governmental unit which lies within his reach has no power to act effectively along collectivist lines, while those governmental units which do have that power lie wholly beyond his reach? Anti-democratic writers have, in recent decades, made much of the fact that the average man in this country does not vote; and they have not hesitated to draw the impudent conclusion that he is an "irrational" fellow who shouldn't be permitted to vote anyhow. This is, I suggest, to overlook the possibility that the average man has a more rational grasp of the *impasse* described above than the political scientists who would like to disfranchise him. For if that *impasse* exists his vote is not, in point of fact, worth using—unless, of course, his cousin is a candidate for county assessor.

I am arguing, in short, that in the long run the quality of a democracy is to be judged by the facilities it offers to its individual citizens for exerting an independent influence upon the course of events. The democratic citizen will, to be sure, wish to vote when the time comes to make a decision; but the democratic faith is by no means exhausted by the old slogan of "one man, one vote." Before the vote occurs, he will wish an opportunity to help pose the question which the vote is to decide, and to win others to his way of thinking about that question. Tell him that all he needs to do, if he wants socialism, or free trade, or this policy or that one, is to marshal behind him one-half of the voters in the United States, plus one, or one-half of the voters in the state of Georgia, plus one, and you hold out a promise as empty as that in the old adage about catching a bird by putting salt on his tail. Tell him, on the other hand, that he can socialize the local motion picture monopoly the moment he can win over to his position a majority of the people in his home town, and you can begin at last —or, if you please, once again—to talk about self-government. Perhaps, of course, he will never get his majority; but he will at least have the satisfaction of knowing that he was not defeated before he made the effort. That satisfaction makes a big difference.

Bipartisanship and
Majority-Rule Democracy

The major purpose of this article is to answer the question, "What are the merits of bipartisanship in foreign policy as seen from the point of view of the majority-rule democrat?" But for reasons which will become clear, I shall be obliged to raise and try to answer two further questions, namely: (1) What is bipartisanship in foreign policy and (2) what hypothesis can we offer to explain the appearance and swift rise to popularity of this kind of proposal in this period of American history rather than in some previous period?

I

What is it, then, that the proponents of bipartisanship want? Mary Follett has written somewhere that we must maintain a sharp distinction between what a man *thinks* he is doing, what he *says* he is doing, and what he *is* doing. Following the applicable parts of her advice, I will try to distinguish here between what the proponents of bipartisanship say they want and the state of affairs it tends to bring about or perpetuate. The proponents of bipartisanship are honorable men and the question of distinguishing between what they want and what they say they want does not arise.

To find out what they say they want, let us call a few of the proponents to the witness box to speak for themselves. Mr. Ernest A. Gross, who was then Assistant Secretary of State for Congressional Relations, reads from a piece he wrote in the *Department of State Bulletin* in October 1949. "Bipartisan foreign policy exists," he tells us, "when there is a sustained sincere effort *to reach agreement on* objectives and on courses of action ... the end in view is to achieve agreement on a sound and publicly supported [foreign]policy ... [to] *make it* virtually impossible for 'momentous divisions' to occur in our foreign affairs ..."[1] Bipartisanship, then, is a state of affairs in which

[1]"What is a Bipartisan Foreign Policy?", *Department of State Bulletin*, XXI (October 3, 1949), 504-505. The *italics,* here and throughout the article are the writer's and are intended to direct the reader's attention to phrases that bear especially on the thesis presented.

we all (or perhaps only some of us?), make a sustained sincere effort to "reach agreement" on objectives and courses of action. And what the proponent of bipartisanship "objectives" says he wants is, presumably, to bring about that state of affairs. Is this a good idea, regardless of the extent of our disagreement? Mr. Gross has anticipated the question and is ready with his reply: "This is all the more necessary when serious differences of opinion exist within Congressional parties." Why is it a good idea? Because "national security demands that *continuity and consistency* [in foreign policy] survive changes in administration."[2]

We can dismiss Mr. Gross and place him in the general category of "not very helpful," but not until we give him an opportunity to say why he applies to it so strange a name (etymologically speaking) as "bipartisanship." "The evolution of a successful foreign policy is better assured if it is founded on the support of like-minded statesmen, whatever their party affiliation."[3] The reader can supply the missing step: since ours is a two-party system, the phrase "like-minded statesmen, whatever their party affiliation" equals "like-minded statesmen" of both parties. And a policy supported by such like-minded statesmen becomes a "bipartisan" foreign policy.

Listen next to Mr. Hamilton Fish Armstrong who is a little easier to follow. For him, bipartisanship "exists" where "political leaders . . . rule out partisan considerations *in trying to reach agreement* on basic national objectives [in foreign policy] . . ."[4] Since "partisan" might mean "of or pertaining to personal preferences" or "of or pertaining to party," Mr. Armstrong must be a little more precise. It appears that the reference of "partisan" must be to "party" for his point seems to be that where you have bipartisanship, "party leaders" do not "press differences to the point where the goal itself is brought into jeopardy."[5]

Mr. Armstrong will be a little more precise if we but concede him a distinction he wishes to draw between "basic objectives" and the "methods" for attaining them, and if we but grasp the point that bipartisanship is a modification of our "party system" which "normally requires that there be debate *both* as to objectives and as to

[2] *Ibid.*
[3] *Ibid.*
[4] "Foreign Policy and Party Politics," *The Atlantic,* April 1947.
[5] *Ibid.*

methods."[6] Mr. Armstrong—one wonders why—does not spell out the clear implication: under bipartisanship you do *something other than* debate both objectives and methods. (What you do will be explained later in interrogating Mr. Lippmann.) We may permit Mr. Armstrong one parting word as to why he favors bipartisanship. "It is," he says, "a healthy and perhaps necessary condition of American security [not only in wartime but] in normal times as well."

The next witness, Mr. Harold Laski, differs from the first two in that there is a visible connection between what he is describing and the manifest content of the word "bipartisanship." (Both Mr. Gross and Mr. Armstrong would have done better with "nonpartisanship.") "From the San Francisco Conference onwards," Mr. Laski explains, "American foreign policy has been made by the President in conjunction with a small body of advisers, chosen in part from Senators of *the* rival party . . ."[7] Or again, "The scale on which its power has compelled the abandonment of isolationism in the United States, has also made it necessary for the President to give to American foreign policy an institutional basis which *transcends the boundaries of the party he temporarily leads* . . . That means that no President can afford to repeat the mistake Woodrow Wilson made over the Treaty of Versailles . . . A bipartisan foreign policy [is now] imperative . . ."[8] In other words—and Mr. Laski is more specific than most writers on the subject—bipartisanship "exists" when the President associates with him, in the making of foreign policy, some leaders of the opposition party. This is, perhaps, as realistic a definition as we shall find.

Laski is equally realistic as to whether those leaders of the opposition party should regard their being associated with the President as an unmixed blessing. "An attempt to continue bipartisan relations when the President's party is in control of Congress *would tie the hands of the opposition,* to a degree that might easily *be fatal not only to its right to criticism, but also to its ability to pull over to its side an effective public opinion.*"[9] Mr. Laski—just this once, for he must not presume upon our generosity—goes into the category of "very helpful."

[6] *Ibid.*
[7] "The American President and Foreign Relations," *The Journal of Politics,* II (February 1949), 171-205.
[8] *Ibid.*
[9] *Ibid.*

Our next expert is Mr. Blair Bolles, a toiler in the vineyard of bipartisanship ever since 1943. What he says he wants now, and says we are well along toward having, is "systematic inter-party cooperation in dealing with foreign affairs."[10] He sees this as committing the party in power, or at least the President, to (a) soliciting the "opposition's" views on impending actions in international affairs, and (b) assigning members of the opposition as United States delegates to the United Nations and to certain diplomatic negotiations, and (c) soliciting opposition support for policy legislation sponsored by the party in power.

What good things does all this promise us? "If bipartisanship *engendered real unity and continuity* in policy, foreign governments would be able to predict the course the United States would follow in international relationships." [11] What obligation does bipartisanship impose upon the opposition party, correlative to the three obligations imposed upon the party in power? This he does not choose to answer directly. But in another context we get a hint. Mr. Bolles explains that bipartisanship has "suffered" up to the present time from a malady that he terms "limited territorial application," whereas it "probably should apply to the whole surface of the earth in order to achieve maximum effect."[12] Our policies with regard to the occupation of Japan, for example, as also our plans respecting Western Germany, have been formulated without participation by the Republicans. These policies and plans "are not bipartisan, *but Republicans refrain from discussing them.*" Again we must supply the missing step: what the Republicans don't understand is that it is *only* the policies and plans which are really and truly bipartisan that they are supposed to refrain from discussing.

We come at last to Mr. Lippmann who has done more than anyone else to create the aura of sanctity that now surrounds bipartisanship in foreign policy. We listen to him at a moment when he is trying to clear up any possible misunderstandings as to how far he is prepared to go with bipartisanship. Not that he is any less in favor of bipartisanship than he has always been: "It is evident that partisan politics should stop at the water's edge . . . National unity is essential in our

---

[10]"Bipartisanship in American Foreign Policy," *Foreign Policy Reports,* January 1, 1949.
[11]*Ibid.*
[12]*Ibid.*

main transactions with foreign powers . . ."[13] But Mr. Lippmann's candidate for the presidency, Mr. Thomas Dewey, had been raising questions about the disposition of the Italian colonies, and the high priests of bipartisanship had accused him of showing precisely the "partisan" interest in the suffrage of the American-Italian voters that we have been taught to regard as appropriate to our pre-bipartisan past. Mr. Lippmann, obligated to choose on this occasion between bipartisanship and Mr. Dewey, does not hesitate: he will have both and to this end he will redefine bipartisanship.

"The bipartisan understanding cannot be," he explains, ". . . an agreement to unite the parties by *ignoring differing views and suppressing debate* . . ."[14] What then is it? It is "an understanding to accept and abide faithfully by the decisions arrived at after prolonged and thorough debate"; it "covers" only "national commitments that have been settled by the normal constitutional processes of the American government." It "has never been meant"—and here we must arrive by inference at what *has* been meant—"that private consultation was to take the place of public debate in *determining* the great commitments of the country." The inference? Where bipartisanship does *not* extend, matters are still to be settled by public debate; where it *does* extend, they are settled by "private consultation." In short, Mr. Dewey, because of the nature of the subject he had in hand was right in rejecting "the idea that . . . American policy in . . . [an] *unsettled* field of foreign affairs can be determined privately and without public debate."

The reader will have to take this writer's word that the assembling of further quotes from the literature of bipartisanship would be unprofitable. We should only find slight variations in the themes that have already been illustrated in the foregoing paragraphs.

Definitions of bipartisanship vary to some extent from proponent to proponent, which is to say that there is something less than full agreement as to the character and/or geographical reference of the foreign policy decisions bipartisanship has been—or should be—extended to cover. There is something less than full agreement again as to what bipartisanship requires in the way of institutional implementation, and as to the reciprocal rights and duties it confers and imposes upon those concerned with foreign policy decisions. But we

[13] *New York Herald-Tribune,* August 24, 1948.
[14] *Ibid.*

must not leap to the conclusion that the writers whom I have been citing, and a host of other writers that might have been cited in their stead, are not enlisted in a common cause, or that they do not have a common body of doctrine. They are and they do have a common cause—at least to the extent of justifying the following comments:

1. All of them favor a fundamental and at least a partly accomplished revision of what we may call our traditional frontier treaty with regard to the making of foreign policy. ("Traditional frontier treaty" is a short expression for the sharing, among the President and the parties and the party leadership and the electorate, of powers and responsibilities in the field of foreign affairs.)

Few of the proponents of bipartisanship would accompany Joseph and Stewart Alsop to the length of describing bipartisanship as a "great, permanent constitutional amendment."[15] But none of them makes any secret of the alleged fact that it constitutes a sharp break with past practices in the making of foreign policy.

2. They are all demanding revision in one and the same direction, i.e., the incorporation in the frontier treaty of some set of rules or "understandings" that can be counted on to assure that one of two things shall happen in the United States: either (a) basic national objectives in foreign policy are always given such shape as to enjoy general support, or (b) general support is always forthcoming for current basic national objectives in foreign policy.

3. They all place an extremely high valuation upon something called "unity" or "agreement," at least upon "basic objectives" in the sphere of foreign affairs.

4. While they speak sometimes as if the desired unity or agreement were unity or agreement on the part of the electorate, their practical proposals always tend to fix attention upon the relation between the President and his party, on the one hand, and either (a) the other of the two great parties or (b) all or some of the Congressional leadership of the other of the two great parties—whereof the term "bipartisanship."

5. Their vocabulary does not appear to include such phrases as "the bureaucracy" or "the permanent officials in the Department of State"; i.e., they persistently ignore the impact of what it is now fashionable to call "the planners" in the formulation of foreign policy.

[15] *New York Herald-Tribune,* August 2, 1948.

6. They all use language (Mr. Gross' "to achieve agreement" is typical) that betrays the fact, and their knowledge of the fact, that the present situation in the United States is one of *disunity*, of *disagreement*, concerning basic objectives in foreign policy.

7. There appears to be no way in which the positive aspect of their proposals can be fully stated and defended without exposing a negative aspect to which none of them seems eager to draw attention: *Insofar as foreign policy is bipartisan, it is foreign policy arrived at via private consultation rather than via open debate*—or that, to put the same thing in another way, *the rules appropriate to bipartisanship automatically become "gag" rules as far as all-out discussion of the matters to which they are applied is concerned.* And the proponents of bipartisanship do not—I deliberately choose an unprejudicial form of words—give any evidence of the kind of distaste for this negative aspect that the majority-rule democrat *necessarily and as a matter of course* feels for it.

I wish space permitted full discussion of each of these points. Since it does not, I shall deal only in passing with 1, 2, 4, and 5, and fix attention primarily upon 3, 6, and 7.

II

The majority-rule democrat need have no quarrel with the pride of place assigned to "unity" or "agreement" in our writers' scale of values. The connection—inescapable, in his view—between majority-rule and democracy poses baffling problems both theoretical and practical save as majority-rule tries constantly to transform itself into unanimity-rule—save as the majority and its leaders sincerely seek to carry the minorities and their leaders along with them. Let us, then, have unity in foreign policy—if we can get it without sacrificing too much of too many of the other items in our scale of values. And let us not press, on this occasion at least, any objections the majority-rule democrat may have to all this preoccupation with unity in foreign policy rather than unity in public policy foreign *and* domestic.[16] But it cannot be overemphasized that unity is a large order in what my friend Dankwart Rustow calls a "low consensus society," i.e., a so-

[16]Cf. Harry S. Truman, as quoted in *The New York Herald-Tribune* on June 17, 1948, on the occasion of a speech in Emporia, Kansas: "Domestic issues can be fought out on the basis of their merits. The foreign policy of the United States must be the policy of the whole United States. . ."

ciety where for all that you may *want* unity what you *have* is disunity
—which is the kind of society that the proponents of bipartisanship
tacitly concede our society to be.[17] For failing a miracle of the kind
it would take in order to get Mr. James Burnham and Mr. Henry
Wallace mobilized behind one and the same set of basic national
objectives *vis-a-vis* the Soviet Union, you must in such a society
either:

(a) write off the achievement of unity as pie in the sky and
accept and live with the fact of disunity, inching forward toward your destiny in full awareness that some people are getting their way and others are not.

Or, if you are not prepared to do that,

(b) create, through one kind or another of optical illusion, an
appearance of unity sufficiently convincing to distract attention
from the fact of disunity.

And this, as I see it, is *the* issue between the majority-rule democrat
and the proponent of bipartisanship from which all other issues we
might draw between them are ultimately derivative. In the eyes of
the former, bipartisanship—in the present circumstances of American life—is precisely a formula for creating the appearance, the optical illusion, of a kind of unity that we know in our hearts (though we
may prefer to "repress" the knowledge) to be not only unachievable
but inconceivable.

The majority-rule democrat of course chooses the first horn of the
above dilemma: accept and live with the fact of disunity. He also
accepts the fact that nobody has ever yet discovered any democratic
alternative to majority-rule save that of the Palestinian *kibutzim*,
namely: postpone decisions (including what we may call the "decision by default" to carry on with existing policy) until you have talked
matters through to a to-all-intents-and-purposes unanimous sense of
the meeting. The majority-principle, or some version of the
unanimity principle, but on either showing the process of settling
"basic national objectives" in a democracy, is a matter of continuous
all-out public debate. This public debate *canvasses all the realistic*

[17]By speaking always of unity and agreement as something to be achieved.

alternatives and *ventilates all the arguments,* with the understanding that the ultimate decisions lie with *the electorate, which imposes
its preferences upon the President and the bureaucracy* through its
elected representatives in the Congress. The majority-rule democrat
can acquiesce in no other kind of frontier treaty among the elements
I have listed above.

I hasten to add that I should be the last to suggest that we have had
any such frontier treaty in America within the memory of living man.
To leave the reader with any such impression would be to encourage
him to miss the point about bipartisanship. The concept of bipartisanship can not be understood save as a recipe for preventing the canvass of all the alternatives and the ventilation of all the arguments by
the electorate. But it is *not* a new formula, *not* a modification of the
"normal operation of our party system." It is merely the American
political system as it applies to a particular aspect (foreign policy) of
the public, grown strangely aware of itself and strangely articulate
about itself.

The common inarticulate premise of the proponents of bipartisanship is, that in the absence of determined and ingenious efforts, the
disunity characteristic of American public opinion will bubble up in
the form of "momentous divisions" between our two great parties
whenever it is given something to get its teeth into. This conjures up
the awesome possibility, which as far as I know no proponent of
bipartisanship has yet dared to put into words: An election fought
over a clear-cut issue and resulting in a popular mandate that no one
could disobey without openly defying the great beast. Nothing, of
course, could be less realistic. The dissident, who might become the
nucleus around which opposition to current Presidential-State Department fiat might form, would need the voice of Stentor in order
to get himself heard above the roar of the State Department propaganda machine. He can, at the margin, always be discredited—on the
grounds that he is ignorant of information that it would not be in the
public interest for the President and the State Department to release
to those of us who are less burdened with responsibilities. If these
guarantees prove inadequate, he is up against the fact that any "momentous division" he contrives to bring about will be a momentous
division, not between the parties, but within his own party and not
the kind of momentous division that can be resolved by popular
mandate in the next election. Why? Because the political parties we

operate in America are the kind of political parties that, by definition, have hearts large enough to take in, accommodate, and neutralize *any* not-too-disreputable point of view about public policy. If the President is a knowing fellow—and this is the great tactical principle upon which the proponents of bipartisanship have stumbled—he will have "associated" with this policy (which our writers erroneously identify with that of the President's party) just that number of Vandenbergs he needs in order to create a presumption that the Tafts do not speak for the "opposition" party.

The American political system, in the very form in which it was handed down to us, embodies all the bias against majority-rule it needs in order to deny a police permit to the parade of imaginary horribles with which the proponents of bipartisanship are torturing themselves. It is America's great contribution to the theory of delivering nascent democratic processes stillborn; and those Republicans who, to Mr. Bolles' annoyance, kept right on not discussing, even when the rules of bipartisanship did not tell them to, were behaving just as the system requires them to. It seems highly improbable that that bias requires reworking, at this late moment, by Mr. Hamilton Fish Armstrong or the Brothers Alsop.

The majority-rule democrat will, then, have none of this latest addition to our vocabulary of honorific political terms,[18] regardless of which of the definitions canvassed above may become generally accepted. He will have none of it even in the relatively inoffensive form it takes in the skilled hands of Mr. Lippmann, who says he wants all foreign policy decisions fully discussed and debated. Mr. Lippmann limits the application of bipartisanship to a few major policies after the latter have been adopted, but not before he reveals that its effect is to keep issues from being raised. For the majority-rule democrat recognizes bipartisanship as an (conscious or unconscious) attempt on the part of its proponents to put into attractive language, and so reinforce, the most undemocratic features of our political system, namely, those that prevent it from producing real popular decisions on real issues. Nor is that all: the majority-rule democrat sees that the years of self-conscious bipartisanship, these years during which we have all been "for" bipartisanship (and, incidentally,

[18]Cf. Joseph and Stewart Alsop, *New York Herald-Tribune*, August 2, 1948: "A crypto-isolationist Republican leader urged making an issue of the Berlin crisis. 'But,' said Senator Vandenberg bluntly, 'that would be treason.' "

without having debated *its* merits either), have been years during which there has been less presumption than ever of any coincidence between current United States foreign policy and the will of the majority of the American electorate. He also sees that the men who have been stating the case for bipartisan foreign policy are, in the main, men who favor the particular foreign policy bipartisanship appears to have given us. And he suspects that all the fuss about bipartisanship is their tacit recognition that their foreign policy could not stand the test of competition in a free market for foreign policy ideas.

What is the majority-rule democrat's own formula over against that of the proponents of bipartisanship? The discovery of means for channeling into American foreign policy the native good sense of the American electorate.

Prolegomena to any Future Work
on Majority Rule

Although Herbert McClosky's "The Fallacy of Absolute Majority Rule"[1] was published in this journal as recently as November, 1949, it seems already to have been seized upon in certain quarters as the long-sought absolute weapon with which to bring the majoritarians to their knees.[2] So, at least, one judges from the comments on it that reach one these days via the grapevine of the political science profession. It seems, therefore, high time that some self-confessed supporter of "absolute" against "limited" majority rule stepped forward to explain how it happens that the majoritarian flag is still there, and why he supposes the advantage—despite this new development in offensive armament—still to lie with the defense.

Concretely, I shall attempt to show that (1) insofar as McClosky's article is an attack on a certain "theory of political obligation," it rests upon a fundamental misunderstanding of that "theory," in part because it violates the frontier that divides political theory from ethics; (2) the specific question to which McClosky addresses himself throughout most of the article is remote from the issue that has traditionally divided the majoritarians from the anti-majoritarians; (3) the principal dilemmas into which McClosky seeks to force the "absolute majoritarians" are false dilemmas; (4) McClosky's argument, when passed through the sieve of a sound methodology, tends rather to support than to undermine the majoritarian position; and (5) the standard of legitimacy to which McClosky commits himself is one that no democratic community could conceivably adopt—one that stamps him, furthermore, as more majoritarian on certain issues than the majoritarians themselves.

I propose to develop each of the above theses in that one of the following sections which bears the corresponding number.

---

[1] THE JOURNAL OF POLITICS, XI, No. 4 (November, 1949), pp. 637-654.
[2] Or, to vary the metaphor, as the earthly vessel in which the soul of the *Federalist Papers* is reincarnate.

I

McClosky's article is in part a critique of the "theory of absolute majority rule"—a "theory of political obligation" which, he tells us, is "not without support in the literature of political theory."[3] He summarizes this "theory" (he is using the word as a synonym for "creed") in a series of propositions,[4] to each of which, one gathers, an "absolute majoritarian"[5] is committed; and he cites in connection with it the names of H. Krabbe and J. Allen Smith,[6] each of whom certainly held a position that bears a strong family resemblance to that which McClosky attributes to them. Both of them contended, for example, that the highest authority in a democracy is (= should be)[7] the majority of its electorate.[8] They both held, again, that since the majority of the electorate should be the highest authority in a democracy, no "limits" can (= should be) placed upon its power.[9] The word "limits" denotes arrangements calculated to prevent the majority, e.g., by constitutional fiat, from doing certain things and has, I submit, no second or third possible meaning.[10] They both held, finally that democracy and majority rule are one and the same thing,[11] meaning, as I read them, not that democracy has no other differentiae (this being the meaning with which McClosky would like to saddle the majoritarians)[12] but that where you have limits placed on the power

[3] *Ibid.*, pp. 637-638.
[4] *Ibid.*, p. 638.
[5] This phrase, which I employ as a shorthand expression for "defender of the theory of absolute majority rule," is not present in the McClosky article.
[6] *Ibid.*, p. 638.
[7] See my comment below (fn. 30) on this point. Neither Krabbe nor Smith supposed himself to be describing existing democracies. Smith's book, indeed, is above all an insistence that existing constitutional limitations on the power of the majority be removed.
[8] The first proposition in McClosky's series (p. 638) reads: "(a) that a majority is, in a democracy, the highest authority, and its vote must therefore be final and absolutely binding." The words "of the electorate" in my text are supplied.
[9] McClosky's second proposition (p. 638) reads: "(b) being [*sic*] the highest authority, no limits can logically be placed upon its power." I purposely omit the word "logically" from my restatement. McClosky appears to mean by it merely that the majoritarians regard (b) as following from (a), which emphasis I have preserved.
[10] It is inconceivable that Krabbe or Smith would have taken exception to "limits" of the kind McClosky sees in Britain (pp. 652-653), i.e., limits built into the hearts and minds of the electorate themselves via a voluntarily accepted "social *ethos.*"
[11] McClosky's third proposition (p. 638) reads: "(c) that democracy and majority rule are, therefore, one and the same thing."
[12] "Democracy cannot," one of his demonstrations concludes (p. 653), "be defined as merely the rule of the majority."

of the majority you do not have democracy. So far, I say, majoritarians like Krabbe and Smith were certainly prepared to go with McClosky's "theory of absolute majority rule." But it is a far cry from these commitments to the further commitment involved in McClosky's proposition: "its [the majority's] vote must . . . be final and absolutely binding"[13]—if the words "final and absolutely binding" be read as McClosky's strategy tempts him to read them. This further commitment, as I hope to show, no majoritarian in his senses—certainly not Krabbe and Smith—would conceivably make.

The following observations should suffice to clear up McClosky's misunderstanding of the majoritarian (i.e., for our immediate purposes, Krabbe's and Smith's) position on this point. What McClosky evidently has in hand in his series of propositions is (as I have been intimating with my parenthetical "should be's") quite simply a *normative* definition of "democracy," which, however, does commit those who put it forward to the view that the last word (I avoid, for the moment, "final and absolutely binding") in a democracy should lie with the majority of the electorate (or, variously, that where the last word does not lie with the majority of the electorate you no longer, or do not yet, have a democracy). In a sense, therefore, the majoritarians do hold that the vote of the majority in a democracy is "final and absolutely binding,"[14] which is to say: they do refuse to contemplate machinery that would estop the majority even from, for example, voting a dictatorship into office, and do, as McClosky contends, claim for the majority the power even to abolish majority rule. For McClosky, however, whose initial statement of his problem[15] calls for majoritarians who will charge an anti-Communist minority in Italy to obey a majority-supported Communist dictatorship, this is not enough. He therefore permits himself to forget that the words "the vote of the majority must be final and absolutely binding" are part of a normative definition, and proceeds to attribute to them an independent meaning that Krabbe and Smith, on the face of it, could not possibly have intended; namely, that the minority is obligated to obey the majority even where democracy as they are defining it has disappeared.

[13]This is the second part of McClosky's (a) (p. 638). Note the shift from "is" in the first part to "must be" in the second; cf. fn. 5 above.
[14]Krabbe's phrase, however, is "binding" *tout court.* H. Krabbe, *The Modern Idea of the State* (New York, London: D. Appleton & Co., 1927), pp. 74-82.
[15]McClosky, *op. cit.,* p. 637.

Among the better known political theorists in the democratic tradition, the one who comes closest to saying what McClosky would have all the absolute majoritarians say in this connection is, curiously, that same Locke whom he makes over into something short of an absolute majoritarian. Locke, that is to say, does speak of the individual's "obligation . . . to submit to the determination of the majority, *and to be concluded by it.*"[16] It is only as we look further, for example, at what he says of "the common refuge which God hath provided for *all men* against force and violence,"[17] that we are able to see his precise meaning. For these words are Locke's reminder to us that each individual is capable of resisting—and fighting it out with—authority, as also that each individual has his own decision to make *(in the light presumably of his own ethics)* as to when what is being done to (and possibly around) him justifies resistance. Nor is there the slightest inconsistency between the two forms of words, as we may assure ourselves by raising the question: To what and what kind of query is Locke addressing himself in the one case and in the other? In the first case I take him (like Krabbe and Smith) to be answering a question that we should now phrase more or less as follows: To what method of making decisions does the individual member of a political society stand committed? (I am tempted to add: insofar as he is committed to that political society itself.) In the second case he is answering the very different question: What should the individual member of a political society do when the (written or unwritten) constitution of his political society has broken down?

Now the point to grasp about Krabbe and Smith and, I should say, recent and contemporary absolute majoritarians in general, is that they do not raise, and thus do not attempt to answer, the kind of question Locke is answering in the second case. Why? Because they are clearly questions that lie beyond the frontiers of political theory as we now define it, and are regarded as belonging to such other disciplines as ethics and theology. McClosky, in short, is not only abusing a normative definition; he is also attempting to get out of propositions distributed on the level of political theory the answer to what is clearly an ethical or theological question.

[16]John Locke, *Of Civil Government* (London: J. M. Dent and Sons, 1924), p. 165 (emphasis added).
[17]*Ibid.*, pp. 228-229 (emphasis added).

Here, then, is the majoritarians' answer to the hard bargain McClosky would like to drive with them that they either accept the thesis that the power of the majority in a democracy should be limited, or commit themselves to the view that democrats are bound to "recognize as legitimate the régimes that totalitarian parties may seek to establish in the name of the majority": This is a false dilemma. We, as political theorists, can say to the democrats in Italy: Where— and for so long as—you have a functioning democracy, the latter entails such and such obligations for its individual members, this being a question that properly arises in the course of defining a functioning democracy. We can say further to the democrats in Italy: The Italian democracy that has now been destroyed would have been a confidence game had it permitted the Communists to participate in elections while so stacking the cards as to prevent them, when they obtained a majority, from having their way with the statute book. And we can and must say to them: Do not try to persuade yourselves, or let others persuade you, that there is any democratic method by which, once the Communists had their majority, what has now happened could have been prevented; *for one of the hazards of democracy is that one's own side, even when one's own side is the side that wishes to maintain democracy, may lose.* But we cannot possibly say to them: Your obligations, now that your democracy has been destroyed, are such and such. For that would be to answer a question that does *not* properly arise in connection with our problem, and that does not belong to our discipline.

II

Let us assume, as McClosky himself clearly does, a community[18] and for the moment let us, again with McClosky, simplify matters by saying nothing about what sort of thing a community is save as we imply, by our examples,[19] that it is a modern nation-state. Let us assume, with McClosky, that our community is a community of political equals[20] or, as I should prefer to put it, that political equality is a value that it is determined to maintain. Let us also assume that a

[18]McClosky,. *op. cit.,* p. 642.
[19]Italy, Germany, United Kingdom, *et al.*
[20]McClosky, *op. cit.,* p. 639.

unanimous "will of the community" is "unlikely or impossible of attainment,"[21] or, as I should prefer to say, let us recognize that our community poses problems for political theory only insofar as there are differences of purpose or opinion within it that prevent it from arriving at a unanimous will, and so oblige it to content itself with a closest approximation to a unanimous will. And let us assume that our community, not wishing to leave to caprice the determination of the nearest possible approach to a unanimous will of the community, has adopted a set of rules, one of which is the majority principle.[22] For, though McClosky does not set all this forth in the form of assumptions, any careful reader will find all the foregoing premises present in his article, and will, I think, agree that they constitute the context in which he poses the problem with which he is attempting to deal.

What is that problem? Judging from the course his argument takes, it would have, I think, to be stated more or less as follows: There are, so to speak, two forms (or "interpretations") of the majority principle. One form can provide that the will of the majority shall be accepted as the closest possible approximation to the will of the community on any subject whatever and to any effect whatever. The other can provide that the will of the majority shall be accepted as the closest possible approximation to the will of the community *within limits set by certain other rules whose violation would prevent that free arriving at majorities which is taken for granted by the majority principle itself.*[23]

I have arrived at this statement by relying upon the implications

---

[21] *Ibid.,* p. 640.

[22] *Ibid.,* pp. 641-642. Opponents of majority rule will be well-advised, before adopting McClosky as their champion, to ponder well his assumption that (1) the community must make a choice between the majority principle and some principle that would entrust power to a minority (p. 641), and (2) any principle that would entrust power to a minority is excluded by the premise concerning political equality (p. 640). This hands the majoritarians, as on a salver, the two points on which they—I speak out of grim experience—usually meet the most stubborn resistance; namely, (1) is an *exhaustive* choice (the majoritarian expects to be told here that there is a third possibility: neither gets its way, and what prevails is *The Law*); and (2) the case against any form of minority rule is so overwhelming that *insofar as a choice must be made between them,* majority rule wins as a matter of course.

[23] McClosky clearly supposes himself, at the end of his article, to have established the case *for* the second form, but he has evidently done so only by stating a case *against* the first. His methodology imitates, in this particular, that of the Oriental despot who, having heard the first of the two poems entered in a poetry contest, forthwith awarded the prize to the second.

of the forms of words he elects to use. A statement more faithful to his own language would perhaps run as follows: What are we to say of the power that the majority, in the above premises, is to exercise? Is it "limited" or is it "absolute"?[24] His answer, to be sure, is that it is "limited" not "absolute."[25] My point, for the moment, is that he has modified the question we are accustomed to associate with what I have called elsewhere the "debate about majority-rule" so drastically that he can, and to a large extent does, answer it without revealing his own sympathies in that debate. Let no one suppose, for example, that because McClosky answers "limited" he goes ahead and enters a run-of-the-mill plea for requiring qualified majorities rather than bare majorities (many majoritarians would be more reluctant than he to extend to mere pluralities whatever blessings numerical preponderance has to confer)[26] or for a supreme court—armed with a bill of rights that forbids the majority to do certain things—to ride herd on that majority and see that it behaves, or for staggered elections and other devices calculated to delay or hinder the emergence of a clear majority will. Such pleas are nowhere to be found in his article.[27] And let no one, *per contra*, suppose that the absence of such pleas stamps McClosky as an opponent of such devices; for his reference to "specific constitutional limitations" and "institutional checks"[28] betrays no anxiety whatever on his part concerning the power which these notoriously place in the hands of minorities[29]—however difficult such unconcern may be to square with his argument against minority rule (pp. 639-641), or with his willingness to grant a majority unlimited powers over certain matters, e.g., property rights (p. 646) which existing bills of rights seek to place beyond the reach of majorities. I repeat my point: McClosky has—and by his answer tacitly recognizes that he has—stated his problem in a fashion that places him above the fray in which previous participants in the debate about majority rule have supposed themselves to be engaged. It is, of course, just possible that he has hit upon a more fruitful statement of the problem of majority rule than his predecessors ever arrived at. But it is also

[24] *Ibid.*, p. 641.

[25] *Ibid.*, pp. 646-647.

[26] He writes (*ibid.*, p. 369): "the agent attaining the *greatest* [not the greater] number of votes shall be empowered. . . ." (emphasis added).

[27] But cf. *ibid.*, p. 646: ". . . . the majority principle does not sanction freedom from any sort of *control*" (emphasis added).

[28] *Ibid.*, p. 652.

[29] *Ibid.*, pp. 639-641.

possible that he has stumbled into the worst of the methodological pitfalls that the problem of majority rule involves: namely, that of seizing upon a statement of the problem that ends you up talking about something other than the problem of majority rule.

Before attempting to decide which of the foregoing alternatives is correct, let us analyze the meanings attributed by McClosky to the "key" words in the proposition: "the power of the majority in a democracy is limited," in the proposition: the power of the majority in our community should be limited, in the proposition: the "legitimate" or "rightful" power of the majority is limited, or in the proposition: the legitimacy of the majority's power ceases when the latter exceeds certain limits.[30] The key words are evidently "limited" and "legitimate" (and their derivatives) and "democracy"—where, however, "democracy" appears to be merely a shorthand expression for a community in which the majority respects the rightful limitations upon its power, and "legitimate" merely that which may be predicated of a majority's power insofar as it is respecting these limitations. With regard to "limited" itself, however, the situation is by no means so simple; indeed, the air of plausibility that surrounds McClosky's argument can be attributed in large part to his shifting back and forth between different meanings of this word.

There are, as I see it, three possibilities here:

(1) "The power of the majority should be limited" *might* mean merely that there are some things that the majority ought not to do; or

(2) "The power of the majority should be limited" *might* mean that the (written or unwritten) constitution of our community should forbid certain actions by the majority; or

(3) "The power of the majority should be limited" *might* mean that the (written or unwritten) constitution of our community should embody institutional checks calculated to estop the majority when it attempts to do certain things—or, if you like, that the power to ride herd on the majority ought to be lodged in certain hands other than those of the majority.

---

[30]These propositions are intended merely as illustrations of the way in which McClosky uses the words in question. Let me add that I find no convincing grounds for supposing that when he moves from a "such-and-such-in-a-democracy-*is*" formulation to a "such-and-such-*should-be*" formulation to a "such-and-such-is-*legitimate*" formulation, he attaches any importance either to the direction in which or the distance over which he is moving—which is to say that the four propositions above would, on his showing, be merely different ways of saying the same thing.

These possibilities are not, to be sure, mutually exclusive, inasmuch as (2) in a manner of speaking presupposes (1), and (3), again in a manner of speaking, presupposes (2), but they are separable, in the sense that I can commit myself to (1) and still say no to (2), or to (2) and still say no to (3). Where on this ascending scale does McClosky take his stand? What he says about the situation in England ("the constitution can . . . be amended by mere statute," but "documents such as Magna Carta and the Bill of Rights of 1689 hold an honored place, even a *constitutional* status" [emphasis added]), to which he seems willing to extend his approval, places him—but does not pin him down—first at (1) and then at (2). The fact that he sidesteps certain questions that are inescapable at (2) or (3) (particularly the question: How are decisions to be made as to what the constitution is to forbid and/or what institutional checks are to be imposed?) suggests (1). Is it then (1), which makes of the proposition before us a truism? Hardly, since McClosky clearly supposes himself to be dealing with a controversial issue. Is it then (2)? No, because he does extend his apparent blessing to "institutional checks" (which to most readers, I suspect, will suggest the American constitution). Is it then (3)? No, or at least not a very confident yes, for, though he assures us that the majority cannot be trusted to delimit itself,[31] that the choice between majority rule and minority rule is an exhaustive choice, and that the objections to minority rule are overwhelming, he is silent about the kind of institutional checks he would favor.

I offer it as my opinion that McClosky's strategy calls for winning for the proposition "the power of the majority is limited" all the sympathy the reader is disposed to give it because of the self-evident proposition that there are things the majority ought not to do, while retaining at the same time whatever sympathy he might lose by using "limited" univocally in either of its other two senses, and facing the questions he would thus let himself in for. Coming to grips with his argument is not, then, a matter of deciding which of these three meanings he intends, but rather of recognizing that he intends now one and now the other.

III

McClosky's article is in part a defense of the thesis—an old dinner table favorite of the anti-majoritarians that I have never before seen

[31] *Ibid.*, pp. 652-653.

in print—that "absolute" majority rule is a contradiction in terms;[32] or, variously, that the power of the majority is "limited" under the majority principle because otherwise the majority would be free to destroy majority rule;[33] or, again, that since a majority rule system ceases to be a majority rule system when the majority principle is set aside, the majority can legitimately abrogate neither that principle nor certain rules presupposed in it;[34] or, yet again, that since the legitimacy of the majority's power derives from the majority principle, the majority cannot legitimately convey to "its" government, e.g., the power to place itself beyond criticism.[35] The grand axiom here is that it is in the very "nature" of a principle that it shall not destroy itself, i.e. that it shall be indefinitely self-perpetuating.[36]

Can we not phrase the reply the good people of our community might well make to the political theorist who, on this ground, forbids it to adopt "absolute" majority rule? *Why* precisely, they will ask, must we not adopt a rule concerning decision-making that is potentially self-destructive, that is, a rule authorizing the majority of us to dispose not only of our statute book but of our constitution itself? All democratic constitutions lodge the power to dispose of the statute book and, ultimately the constitution *somewhere*, so that this power can hardly be so fearsome a thing as you would like us to think. The problem a democratic community faces is, as it seems to us, merely that of deciding in what persons or group of persons amongst us our democratic values require us to lodge this power. There are, of course, several rules among which we may choose for this purpose (the unanimity principle, the principle of qualified majorities, the majority principle, etc.). Each of them, however, is *on the face of it* potentially self-destructive. The difficulty to which you call attention is not, therefore, peculiar to the rule placing this power in the hands of the majority of our electorate. It is, in any case, unavoidable.

Repudiation of McClosky's grand axiom becomes, as I see it, all the more urgent because of the use he seeks to make of it in connection with his argument concerning the Soviet Union and the Nazi dictatorship. Take your choice, he says in effect to the majoritarians: either

[32] *Ibid.*, p. 643.
[33] *Ibid.*, pp. 641-642.
[34] *Ibid.*, p. 643.
[35] *Ibid.*
[36] *Ibid.*

the majority principle does not leave the majority free to destroy majority rule, or we are left with no criterion by which to distinguish between a dictatorship able to point to a majority mandate on the one hand and a democracy on the other; either the power of the majority is "limited" or Nazi Germany would have had a democracy had the Nazis ever attained a majority vote—and by the same token the U.S.S.R. would be a democracy. Once again the appropriate answer leaps to the mind: Nonsense—if you are attempting to make of this an argument against "unlimited" majority rule. The Soviet Union is indeed *not* a democracy, *inter alia*,[37] because the majority principle has ceased to operate within it. A majority mandate for the Nazi dictatorship (which, significantly, it never got) would indeed *not* have made the Nazi dictatorship a democracy. But this is not to say that a Germany with unlimited majority rule would not have been a true democracy up to the point of its committing suicide. Much less it is to say that a Germany that imposed limitations upon the majority that would have prevented it from setting aside the majority principle (= *that would have permitted a minority to impose majority rule upon the majority*) would have been "more democratic" than one that did not. Even less is it to say (this being the conclusion into which McClosky would like to force the majoritarians) that such limitations should have been imposed. There is no connection between the premise and the desired conclusion.[38] *Democracy can commit suicide,* which is to say that the majority of the people operating a democratic system always have it within their power to kill it, if not otherwise then by withdrawing their allegiance from it, whatever their (written or unwritten) constitution may say on the point.[39] Nor does a political theory that boasts of "eschewing formalism" (p. 640) have any business ignoring, or tying to get around, this truth. Nor is that all; it is democracy's inherent capacity to commit suicide that

[37]But only *inter alia.* See below, Section V.
[38]I.e., I can agree that a democracy ceases to be a democracy when the majority destroys majority rule, without committing myself to the view that the majority should be other than free, before and up to and including the fact, to destroy majority rule. Similarly, I can concede that a free man should be imprisoned for his crime and still hold that the essence of his freedom is his capacity to get himself imprisoned (= destroy his freedom).
[39]Nor will the point hold water that, be the facts what they may, it *should* be otherwise in a democracy. No theory that would empower a minority to impose majority rule upon a reluctant majority can possibly be defended on democratic grounds.

makes the question of where it is to lodge the power to decide life-and-death matters so very urgent—which is why those of us whose bets are on majority rule hold that these matters, above all others, must be decided by majority rule procedures, rather than by one or another of the minority rule "checks" favored by some political theorists.

IV

"There can be nothing in the majority principle," writes McClosky, "that requires that the majority should have the power to destroy it. . . ."[40] We are, he insists, "bound not to recognize that an attempt by fifty-one per cent to relinquish their freedom can obligate the remaining forty-nine per cent to do likewise."[41] He proposes, he says, "to advance the empirical as well as the formal theoretical[42] considerations which lead to a rejection of majority power conceived as absolute."[43] When the majority principle ceases to prevail, he says finally, "the legitimate power of the majority must cease also."[44]

By way of simplifying the discussion I have largely withheld, in the preceding sections, a certain type of objection I might have urged against these and other comparable theses that McClosky puts forward; namely, the type of objection that runs in terms of methodological exceptions to his way of stating his problem.[45] It is with this type of objection that the present section is concerned.

But I should like to say first that McClosky is dealing, as through a glass darkly, with a problem whose importance for political theory cannot be overemphasized; it is one, furthermore, concerning which the area of agreement between him and the majoritarians is, I suspect, enormously greater than, given his misunderstanding of the majoritarian position, he perceives. No majoritarian needs cavil at the thing McClosky is trying to say when, for example, he insists that when the majority principle ceases to prevail the legitimate power

[40] *Ibid.*, p. 643.
[41] *Ibid.*, p. 654.
[42] It would be interesting to know on what McClosky understands the distinction between "theoretical" and "empirical" to turn. His "empirical" arguments (pp. 639-641) seem to me to assay at least fifty per cent pure theory.
[43] *Ibid.*, p. 638.
[44] *Ibid.*, p. 643.
[45] I have, however, anticipated such an objection by asking whether McClosky has not seized upon a statement of the problem of majority rule that ends him up talking about something else. I say "largely withheld" because the objection ventilated in Section I, i.e., to McClosky's confusion of political theory and ethics, is methodological.

of the majority must cease also. The majoritarian would merely put it in other words; namely, constituted authority in the community ceases to be legitimate when the majority principle ceases to prevail. So again with what I suppose McClosky to be trying to say when he pleads for "rejection of majority power conceived as absolute," where the majoritarian would say "rejection of the collective power of the community conceived as absolute." So too with the point really at issue in his insistence that fifty-one per cent cannot rightfully obligate forty-nine per cent to relinquish their freedom, where the majoritarian would say rather, that when a community ceases to be a community in which majorities are freely arrived at, the political obligations appropriate to democracy lapse. So finally with his thesis that the majority cannot, under the majority principle, rightfully destroy majority rule, which I take to be another way of saying that the majority surrenders its legitimate claim to the minority's obedience when it moves to destroy majority rule; the indicated restatements would be: the collective power in a democratic community cannot legitimately be used to destroy majority rule; when the collective power of the community is so used, the latter surrenders its claim to obedience.

But, some reader may protest, this is hair-splitting: your restatements are (I borrow the term from McClosky) "operationally" indistinguishable from the propositions they restate. By no means, for the following reasons:

The restatements differ from McClosky's propositions in that the problem on which they bear in what we may, taking a hint from Rousseau, call *the problem of the limits of the sovereign power of the community,* and in that they do not pretend to bear upon *the problem of the method by which the community is to make its decisions.* A full discussion of the problem on which they bear would evidently become, in the first instance, an attempt to identify and analyze the available alternatives as regards the standard of legitimacy by which this or that exercise of the community's collective power (this phrase also is Rousseau's) can be judged. Because political theory is itself value-free, the discussion would become at the margin an attempt to say what standard of legitimacy, given this or that value-premise (e.g., political equality) or set of value-premises (e.g., political equality, consent, etc.) is the appropriate one. We must not, to be sure, as political theorists, be under any illusions as to what we should have in the way of "results" if the time came when the problem might, insofar as political theory is capable of "solving" it, be regarded as "solved." At most, we should have a fund of "expert" advice that the political theorist in his cubicle might draw upon if and when some individual in some community asked him: At what point, given my own value-premises, does my community surrender such claim as it has to my obedience? Or, at most again, if and when some community asked him: What standard concerning the legitimacy of collective community action should we, given our value-premises, embody in our (written or unwritten) constitution? But, I hasten to repeat, this is an important problem, and a problem that, when correctly stated, is no less important for the majoritarians than for McClosky. I hasten to say also that insofar as McClosky is saying that there are irrefragable (theoretical and empirical) objections to any attempt to dispense with such a standard and still speak in terms of legitimacy, the majoritarian can whole-heartedly agree with him.

McClosky's propositions differ from the restatements in that they are attempts to pose the problem of the standard of legitimacy of community action in the language of the debate about majority rule. Take, for example, McClosky's question: Should the power of the majority be limited? It is either (1) a methodologically unsound version of the question: Should some method of making decisions other than the majority principle be brought into play when the majority attempts this or that type of action?—a question which he does not answer; or (2) a methodologically unsound version of the question: Should our community have a standard of legitimacy by which collective community action can be judged?—a question to which, I am saying, the majoritarian must, equally with McClosky, give an affirmative answer.

Sound methodology, I contend, calls for rigorous separation between the problem of the method of making community decisions (of which the problem of majority rule is, so to speak, a special case) and the problem of the standard of legitimacy; McClosky's propositions differ from the restatements in that they consistently violate this rule, with the unhappy result that we are left to figure out for ourselves when he is addressing himself to the one and when to the other, and we easily overlook the extent to which, insofar as he discusses the problem of the method of making community decisions, McClosky's position is a straight majoritarian position. For the task of political theory *vis-à-vis* the problem of the method of making community decisions, is, though distinct from, parallel to its task *vis-à-vis* that of the standard of legitimacy; it must identify and analyze and compare and contrast the alternative methods of making decisions among which a community must choose and, at the margin, must show which method is indicated on this or that value-premise or set of value-premises, i.e., it must confine itself to judgments regarding the relation between this or that value-premise (on whose validity it has, *qua* political theory, no means of pronouncing) and this or that method of decision-making. (The majoritarian is the man who finds the majority principle more congenial to his values than any other, but his finding on this point is, or should be, value-free.) It must, therefore, treat the majority principle as one of an indefinite number of alternative methods of decision-making that a community may use for the making of such decisions as it is going to make, just as, shall we say, economic theory treats the pricing "principle" as one of an indefinite number of alternative methods that an economy may use for deciding how to allocate its factors of production among those goods and services that it is going to produce. McClosky's thesis regarding the merits of the majority's (i.e., the community's) setting aside the traditional civil liberties has no more place in a discussion of the majority principle than a thesis regarding the merits of an economy's producing dum-dum bullets would have in a discussion of the pricing system.

I conclude therefore that McClosky consistently confuses the two problems, both when he is stating his question and when he is stating the theses with which he answers it. But there are parts of his *argument*[46] which are addressed to the problem of the method of community decision-making, i.e., to comparing and contrasting majority rule and minority rule; and, as I have already intimated, he reveals himself in these parts, where he is dealing with a *question bien posée*, to be a thorough-going majoritarian. He questions the infallibility of majorities? No doubt; but so, let me assure him, do the majoritarians—who, for the rest, willingly settle for the conclusion at which he arrives: "No better way is known to attain political accountability than to allow voters to select freely by whatever standards they deem important."[47]

[46] *Ibid.*, pp. 639-641, 648-651.
[47] *Ibid.*, p. 651. But cf. p. 652, where the same procedure is "superior *perhaps* to any other mechanism heretofore devised" (emphasis added).

There is a further difference, methodologically speaking, between McClosky's propositions and my restatements. The latter lead on, as the former (because addressed to a bogus problem) do not, to certain problems that, as I have suggested earlier, lie without McClosky's purview. For, once we are clear that what we are speculating about is the standard by which the exercise of collective power is to be judged (= the limits of sovereign power) we can hardly avoid going ahead, like Rousseau, to ask who is to decide what the standard means in this or that concrete instance, how it is to be adapted to changing circumstances, and, above all I should think, how the standard is to be changed when, for example, a significant number of people in the community have repudiated the value-premises to which the existing standard is appropriate. Rousseau, whose methodology is unexceptionable from the point of view expressed in this section, clearly sees that *one of the things a community has to decide and keep on deciding in order to function as a community is the question: What kind of collective action shall be regarded as* ultra vires? A community, that is to say, makes its own standard as it goes along; it will presumably be well-advised to adopt, for this purpose as for other purposes, the "best" of the methods of decision-making available to it. This Rousseau, for all his indecision about what method of making decisions is best,[48] recognizes, so that, insofar as he is a majoritarian at all, he would certainly have included decisions about the standard among the decisions to be arrived at by majority rule procedures. McClosky, by contrast, not only talks as if the standard could be settled for aye and ever and without regard to possible future changes in the community's, or a significant number of its citizens', value-premises, but also ignores the more immediate questions to which I have called attention: Who decides whether the standard is being respected? Who adapts the standard to changing circumstances? The majoritarians' answer to both these questions is: The majority. McClosky's answer we can only guess at; but for the reasons I have set forth in the preceding sub-section, it is difficult to see how he could refuse, in the pinch, to join forces with Krabbe and Smith.

[48]McClosky, who writes that I have made out Rousseau to be a supporter of "unrestricted majority rule," should look again at the relevant passages in my book. Cf. Willmoore Kendall, *John Locke and the Doctrine of Majority-Rule* (Urbana: The University of Illinois Press, 1941), p. 108, n. 64; p. 113, n. 4.

V

Let us turn now, abstracting from the objections I have urged in the preceding section, as also from the question of the status our standard of legitimacy is to enjoy (i.e., the question whether it is to be a permanent limitation upon the majority, or a standard to be adopted and applied and revised by the community via whatever method of decision-making it chooses to employ) to consider the particular standard that McClosky regards as appropriate to a democratic community.

McClosky arrives at his standard by the following steps: (a) since the determination of the closest approximation to the community will cannot be left to caprice, the community must have an arrangement or procedure, "known and agreed to by all," for determining it; (b) this calls for a "set of rules"; (c) the majority principle derives its legitimacy from this set of rules, whose own legitimacy evidently derives, in this same way, from the fact of its being known and agreed to by all. Now one of these rules, which as the source of the legitimacy of the majority's power cannot, according to McClosky, be at the disposal of the majority, is the rule that "the majority must be *freely-arrived-at,*" under which, indeed, all the other rules "can be subsumed." It, then, seems to be one generalized statement of McClosky's standard, as the rules enjoining respect for "the political rights traditionally associated with democratic thought and practice" are presumably another, and the rule that the majority must not destroy majority rule yet another.[49]

McClosky's detailed listing of the things the standard prohibits is precisely what we should expect from these generalized statements: The opportunity for individuals to form majorities and minorities must not be withdrawn; individuals must not be prevented from speaking and publishing and criticizing, assembling, and associating; individuals must not be prevented from casting their lot either with the government or the opposition, or from forming parties and participating in free elections; no government elected by the majority must be granted the power to prevent "even that same majority" from holding it accountable; and so on.[50]

Does the standard prohibit yet other things? McClosky is not very

[49]McClosky, *op. cit.,* pp. 642-643.
[50]*Ibid.,* p. 642.

clear about this. When he writes that "a majority . . . is limited . . . to the extent, *at least,* that it cannot abrogate the rules that authorize the power it can properly exercise"[51] we get the impression that there may be yet other limitations on the majority's power. But if we look then at the passage in which he reproves Locke for his failure to distinguish between the *"political freedoms,"* which "cannot be legitimately abridged," and the *"non-political freedoms,"* which can be,[52] we see that if the standard prohibits other things they must be this same kind of things, which is to say: "The principle of majority rule"—and here let the anti-majoritarian who has found comfort in McClosky's article hold on to his hat—*"recognizes no limitations on the power of the majority . . . except those that are essential to the attainment of freely-arrived-at-majorities and to the maintenance of political consent and accountability."*[53] What are some examples of the non-political freedoms? Freedoms, *if* you please, "like those often claimed for property" and—"religion"![54]

The majority to which McClosky is prepared to entrust "the exercise of power" over all matters save those that he defines as strictly political, thus presumably over all social and economic policy, is the self-same majority whose power over the political freedoms must be "limited" because "it is a mere arithmetical quality," an "arithmetical abstraction," "neither organic nor usually homogeneous,"[55] the self-same majority to which we can give "ultimate power to determine without limitation the very foundations of the polity" only by sacrificing "reality for formality."[56] On these trivial matters, in other words, we can trust the majority to delimit itself, and so can leave it free *inter alia* to set up extermination camps for Jewish children (not

[51]*Ibid.,* p. 643, end of 14 (emphasis added).

[52]*Ibid.,* p. 646.

[53]*Ibid.,* p. 647 (emphasis added). I deliberately omit the words "or its government" following "the power of the majority." McClosky's attempt to equate the power of the majority with the power of the government it elects (so that "to speak of a majority as being unlimited signifies *operationally* the grant of unlimited power to the minority that has gained access to the offices of government") warrants serious attention only to this extent: It illustrates the way in which his argument turns on him when he claims power for the majority over the "non-political" freedoms; it ends him up, *on his own showing,* claiming unlimited power over the "non-political" freedoms for the government of the day.

[54]*Ibid.,* p. 646.

[55]Cf. Kendall, *op. cit.,* p. 122, where it is argued that a democracy's days are numbered when the majority becomes "homogenous" in the sense McClosky evidently intends.

[56]All the quotations in this sentence are *ibid.,* pp. 648-649.

Jewish adults, because that would evidently prevent majorities from being freely-arrived-at by silencing some electors)—and, presumably, to obligate the minority to pay tax-monies with which to defray their expenses. We end up, in short, with a standard that assigns *a unique and exclusive value to the preservation of majority rule*. This seems to me to make McClosky more majoritarian than the majoritarians, who, if I know them would surely hold that there are other ways in which a "régime" can surrender its "claim on the loyalty of democrats"[57] than by destroying majority rule.

If the rule that "majorities must be *freely-arrived-at*" is indeed the supreme mandate, one wonders why the obligation to do nothing to *prevent* their being freely-arrived-at thus hogs the footlights at the expense of the obligation to take positive action to assure their being freely-arrived-at? Why, for example, should positive action against the Communist movement, which as McClosky recognizes looks precisely to future prevention of majorities being freely-arrived-at, not enjoy anyhow equal status with permitting all individuals, including presumably the Communists, to speak and publish, and so forth?

Does McClosky seriously believe that the "political rights traditionally associated with democratic thought and practice" are *that* much more important, from the standpoint of getting decisions freely-arrived-at, than a whole series of other rights that McClosky's majority (what with its free hand with respect to socio-economic policy) could extend or withdraw as it saw fit? Surely not. But if not, why must we attribute to the traditional political rights the special status McClosky claims for them?

Must we, along with the traditional political rights, marry the traditional interpretation of those rights as well? (McClosky of course authorizes the majority to "adopt regulations" concerning these rights; but this turns out to be subject to the proviso that the regulations must have the over-all result of securing the "conditions under which these rights may be equitably enjoyed,"[58] so the question remains: Must we marry all the traditional interpretation of the traditional political rights?) The traditional interpretation of the rights in question has, in the opinion of some of us, tended to ignore the axiom that rights are correlative to duties, i.e., it has tended to claim the traditional political rights for *everyone* (e.g., the present-day Commu-

[57] *Ibid.*, p. 653.
[58] *Ibid.*, p. 646, n. 11.

nist), whether or not he is performing the duties attaching to them. Does the standard then estop the community, or, as McClosky would put it, the majority, from denying the traditional political rights to those (e.g., once again, the present-day Communists) who are openly waging war upon the community? McClosky's language allows no room for doubt; it leaves the community impotent *vis-à-vis* its internal enemies.

McClosky, as I have pointed out at the beginning of Section II, is silent as to the sort of thing he supposes a community to be. It would, therefore, be unreasonable to expect his standard to take into account the majority's duty to maintain where it exists, and to restore where it is disappearing, the kind of consensus that, as some of us believe, no community can do without. It would be similarly unreasonable for us to expect from him any advice as to what happens when the majority's duty to maintain consensus conflicts with the negative demands of his standard. Yet for many of us who value, and value deeply, the traditional civil liberties, this is a problem with which any sense-making standard of legitimacy for a democracy must deal.

The elaboration of a sense-making standard by which the legitimacy of community action can be tested is no less important for the majoritarian than for McClosky. He would use the standard for one purpose (i.e., deciding what limitations to place on the majority beforehand), the majoritarians for another (i.e., deciding at what point constituted authority in a democratic community surrenders such claim to obedience as it ever has). Nor, as I see it, is there any reason to suppose that one and the same standard should not suffice for both purposes. But the foregoing considerations should make it clear that McClosky's standard is one that no democratic community could conceivably adopt.

The People Versus Socrates Revisited

The perplexities of the Athenian jury are our own problem.

My topic: Plato's teaching about "freedom" of thought and speech. My target: Liberal teaching about freedom of thought and speech, and the Liberal claim that it traces back somehow *to* Plato, to, concretely, the *Apology* and the *Crito*. My target, stated in other words: The freedom of thought and speech doctrine of J. S. Mill's *Essay on Liberty,* which let us call the simon-pure doctrine of freedom of thought and speech; and that sentence in Mill's *Essay,* "Mankind cannot be too often reminded that there was once a man named Socrates," etc., where the clear implication is: Keep yourself reminded of Socrates, and what happened to him as a result of limitations imposed upon freedom of thought and speech, and you will accept as a matter of course the thesis of Mill's *Essay,* namely: " . . . there ought to exist the fullest liberty of professing and discussing, as a matter of ethical conviction, any doctrine, however immoral it may be considered."

My thesis: Mankind should be reminded that there was once a man named Socrates, and another man named Plato who, out of a profound preoccupation with his execution, the events that led up to his execution, and the meaning of his execution, wrote about him; that there is in the *Apology* and the *Crito* a teaching that bears directly upon the problem of freedom of thought and expression; *but* that, as we steep ourselves in that teaching, and make it our own, we become less and less available to the appeal of "open society" doctrines like Mill's and, in our own day, Karl Popper's (who, however, unlike most opponents of the more-or-less-closed society, does *not* claim Socrates and Plato as allies). My own thesis restated: We have for several decades been hearing of the *Apology* and the *Crito* from writers who are themselves committed to Mill's position, who turn to them for reenforcement of the symbol that (as I believe) dominates their own thinking about freedom of thought and speech, and who (whether deliberately or carelessly let us not try to say) ignore in them such emphases as do not accord with what they are looking for.

What symbol? The symbol, of course, of Socrates the Bearer of the Word standing with unbowed head in the presence of his accusers and judges, who hold the Word in contempt; of the Servant of Truth being punished, murdered rather, for the truth that is in him; that of the Wise Man being sacrificed by fools who, had they but listened to him, would have been rescued from their folly. That symbol, I contend, lies at the root of the simon-pure doctrine, dominates the thinking of exponents of that doctrine, and, in any discussion of the merits of that doctrine, will be brought forward sooner or later as the "clincher" that resolves all freedom of thought and speech issues in favor of the Mill-Popper position. Mill, in a word, has had his way: we are forever being reminded and by men who, like Mill, spend their lives opposing Plato's teaching on all other problems (and do not, by ordinary, light candles at the altars of the ancients) that there was once a man named Socrates and a court named the Assembly, that Plato set down a record of the transaction between them in order to warn all future societes of the danger and wickedness of all such interferences with freedom of expression, and, I repeat, that that settles that. And my thesis, restated once more, becomes: That that symbol, though it can be pieced together out of elements that are indeed to be found in the *Apology* and the *Crito,* is *not* the symbol that emerges from close reading of those two documents. That Plato's own symbol, as it emerges both from the manifest content of the two documents (that is, from what Socrates actually says) and from that which, upon meditation, we find Plato the dramatist to be saying to us by his "handling" of the story, is infinitely more complex, and points us along toward a deeper meaning, oceans apart from the teaching of Mill's *Essay.*

Let us look first at the manifest content of the *Crito*: Socrates puts to his friend Crito, who has arranged for his escape and is urging him to flee, and then answers for him, a number of questions. Should we, in determining our conduct, concern ourselves about what "people", that is, the Many, will say, or only about the opinion of good men? Only about the latter. Is Crito correct in supposing that the Many must be feared because they can do the greatest evil? Certainly not: the Many can *not* do the greatest evil, because they are unable to make a man foolish; nor can they do the greatest good, because they are unable to make a man wise. By what, then, would a man be guided in determining his conduct? By *reason*—or, to be more precise, by that reason which, upon reflection, seems best. Are we ever entitled, because of the fortune of the moment, to drive a wedge between principle and conduct, or to abandon the rules regarding right and wrong that we have hitherto professed? No indeed. To whom, when we face a problem involving the just and the unjust, or good and evil, do we properly defer? Not to the Many, but to the one man who possesses understanding. Which is to be valued—life itself, life as such, or a good life, a life which is just and honorable? We should prefer a good life. Take the man whose reason tells him a certain course of action is right: should he be deterred from adopting that course of action by, for example, his duty to educate his children, or by what people will say of his friends' failure to rescue him from the consequences of that which he is about to do, or other suchlike considerations? By no means; all such considerations are, clearly, irrelevant to the choice he must make. Does a wrong action become less wrong because the agent is acting in response to wrong, or injustice? Doing wrong is always evil, always dishonorable.

These questions and answers, Socrates must be saying, are logically prior to any question that can be asked concerning the immediate issue—that is, whether he is to avail himself of the opportunity to escape ("Be persuaded by me," Crito pleads with him, "and do as I say."). Why logically prior? Because any answers Socrates can give to the question, "Shall he leave the prison against the will of the Athenians?" will be found to *presuppose* a set of answers to them; which is to say on the level of method, the level, I believe, on which Plato always wants most watching, that we must be clear in our minds about *ethics* before we can attempt anything in the way of a political decision.

Ethical inquiry is *prior to* and *different from* political inquiry— prior to and different from and, in consequence, certain to call for its own techniques and procedures as, in its turn, political inquiry, when we come to it, will involve *its* own techniques and procedures. Ethics, in a word, *before* politics, which is a subsequent inquiry, to be presided over by, to take its point of departure from, but in no circumstances to be confused with, ethics, and itself, in consequence, *ethically neutral though ethically committed.* Political inquiry, to put it a little differently (Plato says it, I think, somewhat more clearly in the *Republic*), is an intellectual adventure in which man engages when he already holds in his left hand a developed ethical and (we may now add) theological position, and wishes to hold in his right hand the answer to a certain range of questions (e.g., Shall Socrates avail himself of the opportunity to escape?) that are themselves always better stated, and better handled, if stated and handled in an ethically neutral manner. And the latter, I contend, normally involves for Plato the building of a *model,* itself I repeat ethically neutral, which when built enables the man who holds it in his right hand and a corpus of ethical and theological doctrine in his left hand, to dispose of that certain range of questions. Political inquiry, in fine, is an ethically neutral stage of the total inquiry that conduces from the raising of ethical and theological problems to, off at the end, ethically oriented political *decision.*

Let us, with all that in mind, follow Socrates through the political argument of the *Crito* to the decision *not* to escape, for only so can we fully understand the bearing of that decision, resting as it does equally on the ethical argument and the political argument, upon freedom of thought and speech. Let us, in a word, isolate the *political theory* of the *Crito,* which I see as involving the following steps:

One: No State can subsist in which individuals set aside legal rules. (We are not, be it noted, asking for the moment whether or not the State should subsist, but merely what is necessary to its subsistence.)

Two: One of the rules that must be observed (must not, that is to say, be set aside *if the State is to subsist*) is that according to which sentences must be carried out.

Three: For Socrates to escape would be to set aside the legal rule according to which sentences must be carried out.

Four: For Socrates to escape would be to overturn, to destroy, insofar as he is capable of doing so ("so far as in him lies"), the State.

Five: The citizen of the State owes his existence to the State's marriage laws, under which his parents begot him.

Six: As a matter of record, Socrates has never registered any complaint against *his* State's marriage laws.

Seven: The citizen owes his formation to the State's laws regulating the nurture and education of children.

Eight: As a matter of record, Socrates has registered no complaint against the laws regulating the nurture and education of children.

Nine: The citizen stands in the same relation to the Laws as the child to the father—not, that is to say, in the relation of an equal to an equal.

Ten: For the citizen to ask whether the Laws are treating him unjustly, and, having answered that question affirmatively, to contemplate doing to the Laws that which they are doing to him, and so destroy the Laws, is to upset the relation that exists, by definition, between them; the child, by definition, does not return the blow he receives from the father.

Eleven: Once the man of understanding grasps the relation between citizen and State, he sees that the citizen will endure in silence when the State punishes him, will follow when the State leads him into battle, and will obey when the State commands him.

Now: let us call that Phase One of the argument, and let us ask in passing, before proceeding to Phase Two, Is Socrates speaking of just any citizen of just any State? Or is he, as we might gather from the stress placed upon the fact that a certain individual named Socrates has never complained about certain particular laws of a particular State, speaking only of Athens, and certain citizens who have related themselves to Athens in a particular way? These are the questions— we shall not try to answer them for the moment—that the critics responsible for current misunderstandings of the *Crito* have always failed to ask, and we shall have to come back to them in due course. Now as to Phase Two:

One: The Laws of Athens say to the citizens as they come of age: You have seen the ways of our city. You know us well. If you do not like us, you may take your goods and go elsewhere.

Two: The citizen who opts to remain in Athens, once the Laws have addressed him in this manner, in the very act of doing so makes a *contract* with the Laws; he commits himself, through that contract, to obey the Laws, not destroy them; and if, later, he runs afoul of Athenian justice and administration, he is estopped from pleading that they are unjust.

Three: Socrates, upon coming of age, opted to remain in Athens; in doing so, he entered into a contract with the Laws of Athens; he is therefore estopped from arguing that Athenian justice and ad-

ministration are unjust; if he were to violate the law that requires
sentences to be duly executed, and so destroyed the State so far as
in him lay, he would be going back on a contract.

Four:—and here we must attend carefully: The Laws of Athens do
not "rudely impose" their commands; *the citizens, including Socrates, are given every opportunity, when they think the Laws to be in
error, of "convincing"* them.

Five: Socrates, more than most Athenians, has again and again
reaffirmed the contract in question: he never leaves town; he has
begotten children in Athens; he has, in the course of his trial, refused
a sentence of banishment, electing death in preference to exile; he
has, moreover, had seventy leisurely years during which, had he been
of a mind to, he might have called the contract into question.

Six: Socrates cannot evade the Laws without going back on his
pledged word.

There, in skeletonized and (as I see it) ethically neutral form is the
political theory argument of the *Crito.* It does not, be it noted, tell
Socrates what he ought to do—can tell him what to do only if, back
in that corpus of ethical and theological doctrine that he holds in his
left hand, there be a rule as to whether or not a man is obliged to keep
his pledged word. Let there be such a rule ("Thou shalt not violate
a contract"); let it be made to "preside over" the political theory
argument, and the decision not to escape follows as a matter of
course; the political theory argument has merely clarified the alternatives between which a choice must be made; and the choice can
never be better, however "good" the "will" of the chooser, than the
process by which the alternatives are clarified. To which let me
hasten to add: The argument does touch on what we today call the
freedom of speech issue, and in such fashion as to make it likely that,
off at the end, we shall find a teaching here about freedom of speech.
We must not, however, leap to any conclusion as to what that teaching is; and our next task must be to examine carefully the sentence
that makes it part of the argument. It reads as follows:

> thirdly, because he has made a covenant with us [that is, with
> the Laws of Athens] that he will duly obey our commands; and
> he neither obeys them *nor convinces us that our commands are
> unjust;* and we do not rudely impose them, but give him the

alternative of [either] obeying *or convincing us;*—that is what
we offer, and he does neither.

What, now, are we to make of that sentence? No more but also no
less, I think, than the following: It is an ethically neutral "empirical"
description of a state of affairs in a particular city named Athens. It
specifies the *extent* to which "freedom of speech" obtains in Athens.
It is, finally, integral to the argument—in the sense that, when we
attempt to visualize the model Socrates has constructed, the model
in terms of which, against the background of his ethics, Socrates is
to decide not to escape, we must, if we are to be faithful to the text,
include it as one of the model's *characteristics*. And the model, in
consequence, takes the following shape:

We have an indeterminate number of "citizens" in a "State" that
possesses "Laws", and the citizens stand over against the Laws in
certain relations, which it is the purpose of the model to depict.
There is, first, the relation of A who has been engendered by B to B
who has engendered him (the citizens are engendered by the Laws,
and the Laws engender the citizens). There is, second, the relation
of A who has been formed or educated by B to B who has formed and
educated him (the citizens are formed and educated by the Laws,
and the Laws form and educate the citizens). There is, third, the
relation between A who has entered into a contract with B and B who
is the other party to the contract (the citizens, in the first instance
upon reaching maturity and opting to remain within the city, and
every day thereafter by remaining, have contracted with the Laws
to obey them, and the Laws have contracted with them to exact
obedience from all citizens). And, fourth, there is the relation between A who is under contract to obey B *but* is in position to remon-
strate with B, to complain when he regards B's commands as unjust,
to "convince" B if he have arguments capable of convincing B, and
B who is under contract not, in this sense, to "impose" his commands
"rudely", to listen when A complains, to expose himself to being
"convinced"(the citizens are allowed to complain and try to convince, the Laws offer them always a choice between obeying *tout
court* and trying to "convince," though with the understanding that,
once having failed to "convince", the citizens are to obey).

That is the model, the full specification of Socrates' relatedness to
the Laws, which renders unavoidable, given Socrates' ethics, the

decision not to escape. The teaching of the *Crito*, taking the ethics and the political theory together, is not then(as we often hear) that all citizens are obligated to obey all States, but that given a certain kind of State, specified in the model, there is on the citizens' part a crystal-clear obligation to obey. One of the *minima* for that kind of state is, we now perceive, a certain "amount" of freedom of speech. By no stretch of the imagination, however, that amount of freedom of speech that is called for by the simon-pure doctrine; nor let any Liberal critic attempt to bring off any such argument as the following: Socrates is in fact *indicting* the Laws of Athens for having deprived him of the promised freedom to try to convince them. He was in the process of convincing them when he was brought to trial. The trial and the sentence have had the effect of silencing him. The freedom to convince appropriate to the model is therefore being denied to Socrates, and that is the point we are intended to grasp. Let not any Liberal critic, I say, try to bring off that argument, for the following reasons:

1) In order to bring it off, one would have to place an inordinate burden on the word "convince" in the passage I have quoted. Offering citizens the "alternative of obeying or convincing" is not the same thing as offering each citizen all the time he might like for the attempt to convince; and the most that can possibly be got out of the passage, evidently, is that each citizen is entitled to a "hearing" —to put forward his case fully, and be listened to, on at least one occasion. (Socrates, be it remembered, himself reminds us, for the rest, the fact that he has been pursuing the same line of argument, and been listened to, through several decades. Nor is it possible to point to any textual basis whatever for a supposed claim on Socrates' part that the Laws have not kept their promise to give him a hearing.)

2) In order to bring it off we should have to overburden the word "convince" in a second sense, namely: The talking that got Socrates into trouble did *not* have for its purpose the "convincing" of the Laws concerning the alleged injustice or wrongness of some particular command or commands; nor does Socrates at any point suggest or imply anything of the kind. On the contrary: he emphasizes that he has made no complaint, over the decades, either about the Laws or —if this be something different—Athenian justice and administration. And the most the Laws are committed to under the contract as stated, is to the hearing of pleas that their commands are unjust.

In a word: the most that can be squeezed out of the *Crito,* as the basis for a commitment to the simon-pure doctrine, is this: the Laws do offer the citizen an opportunity to obey or convince them, and this does constitute a further point in favor of obeying them, as also a further reason for loving Athens. Which is to say: that "amount" of freedom of speech which will enable the Laws to say, "We do not rudely impose ourselves; rather, we give each citizen a reasonable opportunity to convince us of any alleged injustice on our part"—that amount of freedom of speech, but by no means necessarily any greater amount, is one (but only one) of the goods the good society values, as maintenance of the right of emigration is another. And, in the context of any ethic that requires the performance of contracts, the State that vouchsafes to its citizens that amount of freedom of speech has a better claim to obedience than it would have if it denied them that amount. Nor does it follow that the greater the freedom the better the claim to obedience; that also would be to overburden the text.

We conclude: The *Crito* teaches that the good State, the State that deserves to be obeyed, places a high valuation upon a certain "amount" of freedom of speech. A high valuation, however, is not the same thing as a supreme valuation, which is what Mill demands. And, in any case, the "amount" of freedom of speech in question is evidently meagre by comparison with that required by the simon-pure doctrine. It involves a capacity on the part of the citizen not by any means to think and say whatever he pleases but rather merely to be heard—not necessarily *ad nauseam,* however, or with any prior guarantee that the State will not punish him for believing that which he says while being heard. For the State of the *Crito,* the State for which Socrates claims obedience off at the end, is, clearly, a State that strikes back at the dissident if, after hearing him, it decides that his dissidence is of such character or degree as to warrant punishment. It is, in a word, a State which, like our own when it takes action against the Communists, claims for itself the capacity to put its citizens on notice that they can embrace and communicate certain doctrines only at their own very considerable risk.

Let us return now to that symbol of the Bearer of the Word defying the Assembly, to my assertion that it "lies at the root" of the kind of thinking that produces the simon-pure doctrine of freedom of thought and speech, and to my further assertion that the genuine symbol, as it emerges from the drama given us by Plato, by no means lends itself to the uses to which the spurious one is forever being put by Liberal doctrinaires. First, however, a word about the latter:

The Liberal proclaims Truth to be his highest value. Press him, however, about his commitment to Truth, and you will find that it is a commitment not to Truth as, say, Milton would have understood that term, but rather to Truth as a shorthand expression for what the Liberal supposes to be the process by which Truth is arrived at, and to a certain view of the history of that process. The moment never comes, according to the Liberal, when man can pause in his search for Truth and say with any confidence: "This truth I know to be *valid*, and beyond possible revision in the light of the new discoveries of tomorrow or the day after." At most, for the Liberal, man progresses a little from time to time in what we may call an *asymptotic approach to Truth;* and the Liberal's mind is haunted with those situations in the past in which, as he believes, man failed to progress in that sense because an individual capable of achieving a nearer approach to Truth was martyred by a multitude. Push him a little harder, and you will discover that he can hardly conceive of a situation in which it is the other way 'round—that is, in which the multitude was "right" in this special sense of the word "right" , and the martyred individual "wrong." In the Liberal's history book, in a word, it is always Socrates and the Assembly, always Socrates who is "right" and the persecuting multitude that is wrong. Always, therefore, Socrates must be *saved,* retrospectively and prospectively, from the Assembly, which *ex hypothesi* brooks no disagreement with its "truths", and forever thirsts for the blood of those who presume to disagree with it. If Socrates is *not* saved, the next move forward in the asymptotic approach to Truth must await some happier occasion when he will be saved, when the Assembly is somehow prevented from spilling his blood, so that—and this is the main point—Socrates can *go on talking.* Snatching Socrates out of the jaws of the Assembly becomes, in consequence, *the* historical imperative for all who would love and serve the Truth. Nay, more: the problem "How order society?" reduces itself to the problem "How save Socrates—*any* Socrates— from the Assembly, that is, *any* Assembly?", and that, in turn, to the problem, "How make sure that no individual who wishes to say things certain to displease his neighbors will be silenced or, worse still, first be permitted to speak and then be punished for having dared to think that which he has said?" What Liberal doctrinaires propose is, in a word, a state of affairs in which all individuals can go on talking, indefinitely and with impunity, no matter how deeply convinced their neighbors may be that they ought to be silenced, or punished.

The position is, evidently, not without its difficulties: If the approach to Truth is indeed asymptotic at best, if indeed the moment never comes at which any particular truth can be asserted as valid, it would seem to follow that there are no Bearers of the Word. It would appear to follow, too, that the retrospective judgment, "Socrates was 'right' and the Assembly 'wrong'," is meaningless. Let us, however, not press such points. The difficulties disappear when we remind ourselves that there is for the Liberal one exception to the proposition that Truth always keeps one jump ahead of its pursuers, namely, the axiom "All questions are open questions," and that the Socrates of Liberal mythology is precisely an exponent of that axiom. In a word: All questions are open questions save the question whether all questions are open questions, which is—and always has been—a closed question; Socrates *believed* that; and sense can therefore be made of the assertion "Socrates was right and the Assembly, which believed that some questions are closed questions, was wrong." And my next task is to direct the reader's attention to what I have called the genuine symbol, as it emerges from the drama given us by Plato, and to do this by bringing together those emphases that the creators of the spurious symbol have ignored. Namely:

1) The Socrates of the *Apology* deliberately drives a wedge between himself and those who believe that Truth always keeps a jump ahead of us. His accusers, he says, "have scarcely spoken the Truth at all;" from *him*, he hastens to add, the Athenians "shall hear the whole truth." Precisely what is wrong, he insists, is that the Assemblymen have permitted purveyors of falsehoods to take possession of their minds; and precisely the grounds on which he demands to be heard and refuses to be silenced are that he has *exposed* the purveyors of falsehoods: "Their pretence of knowledge has been detected —*which is the truth!*"

2) Socrates thinks of himself as a man with numerous enemies, which is perhaps consistent with the spurious symbol; but these enemies are, early on at least, not so much the rank-and-file of his neighbors as the powerful and the influential. "I went," he relates, "to one who had the reputation of wisdom," and "I tried to explain to him

that he ... was not really wise; and the consequence was that he hated me, and his enmity was shared by several who were present and heard me." Socrates does not, however, mend his ways, as another man might have done with a view to avoiding a future clash in the bosom of his society: "Then I went to one man after another, becoming conscious of the enmity which I provoked, and it distressed and alarmed me."

3) Socrates well understands, again from an early moment, the process that will lead finally to his own execution—understands it, refuses to lift a finger in order to arrest it, becomes therefore the conscious creator of the state of affairs that leads to his death. (In Rousseau's phrase, he wills his own punishment not merely there at the end, when his neighbors attempt to force him to be free, but early days as well; that is, he wills the resentment that leads to the forcing.) "I made bitter enemies, and this will be my destruction if I am destroyed:... [The] envy and detraction of the world, which has been the death of many good men, and will probably be the death of many more; there is no danger of my being the last of them." Or again: " ... [Do] not be offended at my telling you the truth; for the truth is that no man who opposes you or any other crowd, and tries to prevent the unjust and illegal acts which are done in the state, will save his life."

4) Far from denying the charge that he has influenced the young men of the city, Socrates pleads himself guilty to it, and concedes that they have become bearers of the word he bears: " ... young men of the richer classes, who have most leisure, come about me of their own accord; they like to have the pretenders examined, and they often imitate me, and proceed to examine others." And, *mirabile dictu,* "then those who are examined by them are angry with me."

5) Socrates, better perhaps than any other commentator we have except Dr. Johnson, understands why societies cannot adopt, with respect to the propagation of opinions that it deems immoral, the policy that, centuries later, Mill is to enjoin upon them: "The good," he says, "do their neighbors good, and the evil do them evil." Or again: "If a man with whom I have to live is corrupted, ... I am very likely to be harmed by him."

6) Insofar as the issue at stake between Socrates and the Assembly concerns Truth, it concerns *religious* Truth not the jump-ahead-of-the-pursuer "scientific" truth of the Galileos (nor, I might add in

passing, is there any phenomenon of our day that wants more meditating about than the pains taken by our professors of philosophy to explain away the religious passages in the Dialogues of Plato). "[If] you say to me," he tells the Assembly, "if you say to me, Socrates, . . . you shall be let off, but upon one condition, that you are not to inquire and speculate in this way any more, and that if you are caught doing so again, you shall die—if this was the condition on which you let me go, I should reply: Men of Athens, I have the warmest affection for you; but I shall obey God rather than you, and while I have life and strength I shall never cease from the practice and teaching of philosophy." Nor, let us notice, is he willing for the issue between himself and the jurors to disappear from sight, to be "smoothed over": "[Are] you not ashamed of devoting yourself to acquiring the greatest amount of money and reputation, and caring so little about wisdom and truth and the greatest improvement of the soul, which you never regard at all? . . . [This] I shall do to everyone, . . . citizen and alien. But especially to the citizens, inasmuch as they are my brethren. For know that this is the command of God; and I believe that no greater good has ever happened in the State than my service to God. For I do nothing but go about persuading you all . . . not to take thought for your person or properties, but first and chiefly to care about the greatest improvement of the soul. . . .This is my teaching, and if this is a doctrine which corrupts the youth, I am a mischievous person." There are, in other words, teachers and teachers; some teachers are "mischievous"; and the question "What teachers are mischievous?" is (*pace* accepted opinion in our own day concerning academic "freedom") neither silly nor improper.

7) Socrates is no more willing to soften the issue at stake between himself and the Assembly that he is to "smooth things over": what he demands of the Athenians is not the correction of this or that particular wrong or injustice, but a drastic change in their entire way of life —a change, moreover, that cannot become a matter of "negotiation" or "compromise," because it is commanded by God. The Athenians must not "sin against God by condemning me, who am his gift to you . . . I . . . am a sort of gadfly . . . which God has attached to the State, and all day long and in all places am always fastening upon you, accusing and persuading and reproaching you." And again: "When I say that I am given to you by God, the proof of my mission is this: if I had been like other men, I should not have neglected all my own

concerns ... during all these years, and have been doing yours ... [that is], exhorting you to regard virtue." Still again: " . . . [This] duty of cross-examining other men has been imposed upon me by God, and has been signified to me by oracles, visions, and in every way in which the will of divine power was ever intimated to anyone. This is true, Athenians, and easy to test."

8) The Assembly does *not* think of itself as knowing all the answers: It listens patiently to Socrates as he pleads his case, finally decides his fate by a vote of 280 to 220. "Had thirty votes gone over to the other side," Socrates points out, "I should have been acquitted." In countering Meletus' proposal for a death sentence, Socrates "imprudently" and "arrogantly" (the adverbs are from Richard Livingstone, who writes out of deep animus against the Assembly) suggests that he be voted a reward—maintenance at the Prytaeneum no less. The Assembly might fairly have been expected to strike back at him for his "imprudence" and "arrogance", but the most Livingstone can permit himself to say is that "it was naturally annoyed, and the verdict of death was brought in by an increased majority." In the interval between the two votes, moreover, Socrates insists even more sharply than before upon the distance that separates him from his accusers, and from the minds his accusers have captured: " . . . [If] I tell you that [to hold my tongue] would be disobedience to God, and therefore that I cannot hold my tongue, you will not believe that I am serious; and if I say again that daily to discourse about virtue . . . is the greatest good of man, and that the unexamined life [that is, the life led by the jurors] is not worth living, you are still less likely to believe me."

9) Far from being just any individual refusing to be silenced by just any multitude, Plato's Socrates is "right" because the Word he bears is *true,* and is true because it is a *divine gift.* Plato's Assembly, similarly, is "wrong" because it rejects the Word, not because it refuses to declare all questions open questions. Socrates, indeed, is calling upon it to declare closed a whole series of questions that, by condemning him, it elected to leave open. Why? Because, as our excerpts show, the truth of which Socrates is the Bearer is *revealed truth,* and its acceptance as revealed truth would have placed it beyond challenge.

10) The drama Plato unfolds for us is, as it seems to me, projected upon two levels, and these must be sharply distinguished if we are

to comprehend the teaching he is urging upon us. We have, first, the compassionately told story of the failure of a divine mission—in which, I submit, the point being insisted upon by the dramatist is the sheer inevitability of the failure. Socrates possesses the truth of the soul, and *must* try to communicate it to his neighbors. His neighbors reject it, but at no point does Plato imply that they were capable of doing other than rejecting it, or that the chasm that divides them from Socrates could conceivably have been bridged. It is, to an astonishing degree, the same story as that of the Gospels, with the same teaching (whether we have it from the lips of the teacher or from those of the narrator is, evidently, a matter of indifference), "Forgive them,... for they know not what they do." And precisely what stamps the spurious symbol as spurious is that it is the creation and the tool of men who have *not* forgiven the Athenians. (Plato, who cannot know that the chasm between teacher and neighbor can be bridged by the Atonement, must—unlike the narrators of the Gospels—leave it at that.)

As for the second level of which I speak—the literature concerning the *Apology* seems to me, in general, to have overlooked the first and misunderstood the second—our dramatist is posing for us, as I read him, a problem of an entirely different character, namely: What, abstracting from our own knowledge of the divine character of Socrates' mission, was the issue at stake between Socrates and the Assembly as that issue must have appeared to the Assembly itself, and what does *political theory* have to learn from the Assembly's handling of that issue? Here, as in the *Crito*, Plato gives us a model, a paradigm of a constantly recurrent political decision that, if societies are to make it wisely, must be grasped on the level of ethically neutral political theory. And the model's *characteristics* are these:

1) Socrates, in the eyes of the Assemblymen, is a *revolutionary agitator*—not by any means the first they have ever had to deal with, and not by any means the last they will have to deal with. Socrates calls upon them to abandon their way of life, to cease concerning themselves with such trivialities as bread-winning and glory, and devote themselves to discourse about virtue.

2) Socrates rests his demand for a revolutionary change in the Athenians' way of life upon the most offensive grounds he could possibly have chosen: their present way of life is "not worth living."

3) Socrates, by way of driving home the worthlessness and point-lessness of the Athenians' way of life, strikes out at them on their most sensitive point, namely, their confidence in the men they most respect and admire: he seeks out these men and, with other Athenians looking on, proves—to his own satisfaction anyhow—that they possess neither of the two qualities the Athenians attribute to them, namely, wisdom and virtue.

4) Socrates surrounds himself with a group of young men who "imitate" him. How many? The Athenians cannot be sure. How do the young men imitate him? Precisely by insisting that the minds of the Athenians have been "captured" by "false teachers."

5) Socrates insists that he *has* to be a revolutionary agitator. There is an "inner voice" that leads him on. He is, as we have noted, acting under divine command, and would be guilty of disobedience to God if he did not call the Athenians' attention to the worthlessness of their way of life. The Athenians must, moreover, take his word for the divine character of his mission: when they demand of him a sign that he is a gift from God, all he can do is point to his poverty.

6) Socrates refuses to discuss any *modus vivendi* with the Athenians, even when they make clear to him that they are weary of being button-holed and "reproached"; it seems never to occur to him that he is hurting the Athenians' feelings, or being tiresome.

7) Socrates' teachings are incomprehensible to the Athenians; in order to grasp them, the Athenians would have to challenge all the axioms on which they have been brought up. Worse still, Socrates appears to equate any attempt to cling to their axioms with, simultaneously, viciousness and stupidity.

8) Socrates seems to be trying to make fools of the Athenians, to prove to them that the worse cause is the better.

There is the model, no detail of which, presumably, is there by accident: it catches up, paradigmatically, the situation of every society over against every revolutionary agitator; nor could there be better evidence of the poverty of post-Platonic political theory than the fact that it has received so little attention. It remains, I think, merely to ask what alternatives, in the sphere of political decision-making, it clarifies for us, what light it throws upon Plato's teaching, and, above all, what, in the context of it, we are to make of the implicit demand, on the part of those who traffic in the spurious not the genuine symbol of Socrates and the Assembly, that the Assembly permit Socrates to go on talking.

The Assemblymen have, clearly, three alternatives open to them. First, to silence Socrates, which they can do only if they are prepared to eliminate him if he refuses to be silenced (as refuse he must). Second, to proceed forthwith to make the changes in their way of life that Socrates the revolutionary agitator demands of them. Third, to "tolerate" him. Amongst these alternatives, as we know, they chose the first, and have been held in contempt ever since (by persons who deem themselves their intellectual and moral betters, and do not hesitate to sit in judgment upon them) for *not* having chosen the third, *but*, curiously as I see it, have been let off rather lightly for not having chosen the second. Why curiously? Because, with Plato's model in front of us, the comment that leaps to the mind is this: Save to the extent that the Athenians are prepared to contemplate the second alternative (that is, carry out the revolutionary changes Socrates demands), they can embrace the third alternative only by renouncing the only responsibilities they could conceivably recognize as *their* responsibilities. And for at least two reasons: First, to tolerate Socrates—remember those young men who imitate him—is to run the risk that the revolution that can now be prevented by deliberate choice shall, off in the future, take place because those who desire it are at last powerful enough to impose it, which is an eventuality whose acceptability had just as well be faced now as later, and second because, in any case, Socrates will not (*vide* the model) let the Athenians merely tolerate him. Because he is the revolutionary agitator *sans pur*, he will seize upon his toleration as a lever for bringing about his revolution, and *he* will at every moment translate our third alternative into an embryo of the second alternative.

It is, of course, with good reason that no-one calls upon the Athenians, retrospectively, to embrace the second alternative, and our model tells us why. The Athenians are running a *society*, which is the embodiment of a *way of life*, which in turn is the embodiment of the *goods* they cherish and the *beliefs* to which they stand committed. The question "What are *our* responsibilities?" can have no other meaning for them than "What must we do to preserve this society and its way of life, its goods, its axioms, its 'values'?" The most we can possibly ask of them, we who possesss a paradigmatic model of the way in which societies operate, is that they shall keep their minds a little open to proposals for this or that improvement in their way of life, this or that refinement that—Plato makes room for such refinements in the ideal state of the *Laws*—will enable their society's way of life to become, increasingly, itself at its very best. To ask of them, by contrast, that they jettison their way of life, that they carry out the revolution demanded of them by the revolutionary agitator, is to demand that they shall deliberately do that which they can only regard as irresponsible and immoral—something, moreover, that they will seriously consider doing only to the extent that their society has ceased, or is about to cease, to be a society.

Now: these same considerations, I contend, oblige the Athenians not only to refuse Socrates' program, but to refuse, also, to tolerate Socrates. They cannot tolerate him on the grounds that all questions are open questions because the very question at issue, whether their way of life is worth preserving, is for them a *closed* question, and became a closed question the moment the Athenians became a society. They cannot tolerate Socrates on the grounds that he is harmless because, for one thing, he has followers who may, if he keeps on talking, become more numerous tomorrow, and may become sufficiently numerous the day after tomorrow to take over, and destroy the Athenian way of life out of hand. For them to let Socrates go on talking, given his ability to fascinate youngsters who know no better than to be convinced by him, is to *court* that danger, and that is no less irresponsible and immoral than to carry out Socrates' revolution themselves. (They share with Socrates, as we have seen, at least one belief, namely: "if a man with whom I have to live is corrupted, . . . I am very likely to be harmed by him.") In a word: the Athenians can tell themselves Socrates is harmless only if they regard him as completely ineffective. And this, as the model tells us, they cannot possibly do. If, therefore, they fail to silence Socrates, they in effect endorse his revolution.

They elected not to do so. They rejected the (for you and me) noble alternative Socrates was urging upon them. If in doing so they turned their backs on God himself, we must learn to forgive them, and to keep ourselves reminded that they faithfully performed the duties attaching to their stations as they, necessarily, had to understand those duties. It would—so the model teaches us—be foolish, nay meaningless, to demand more of them than that. The way of life they sought to preserve was, for the rest, a valuable second best to the way of life Socrates wished them to adopt, and thus worth preserving, and, what is perhaps more in point, a realistic possibility, which Socrates' way of life was not. It had nurtured Socrates. It had nurtured Plato himself, and Crito, and the rest of the 220. Perhaps a second-best but eminently worthwhile task for political theory is to try to learn to build—and preserve—so good a city.

How to Read Milton's *"Areopagitica"*

Freedom, we have lately been reminded, is a "problem."[1] It is, moreover, a difficult problem, and one that is no less difficult to "solve" when, turning our attention away from what we may call freedom in general, we state it in terms of particular freedoms (*e.g.*, freedom of thought, freedom of speech, freedom of religion, *etc.*). Each of these turns out to be a problem, too, bearing no simple relation to the others, and likely to require *special* handling—different symbolization, vocabulary and theoretic procedures.[2] We may, for that reason, speak properly of a *literature* of the problem of freedom of thought and speech, one easy to identify in the sense that most scholars in the field of political theory, regardless of their views on that problem (if more than one view there be), would name the same list of "must" items dealing with the problem, and cite those items over and over again when they address themselves to the problem. All these items, we might add, are generally regarded as "pro" freedom of thought and speech (whether rightly or wrongly, we need not attempt to say here, except for that one of them that is the topic of the present article).[3] These items are: Plato's *Apology* and *Crito*, Locke's *Letters concerning Toleration*, Spinoza's brief

---

[1] See Walter Berns, *Freedom, Virtue, and the First Amendment* (Baton Rouge, 1955), *passim.* Professor Berns sometimes seems to forget that virtue also is "a problem."

[2] Mill, for example, when he turns to the topic of liberty of expression, drops the whole conceptual apparatus he has announced for his book, including that self-protection principle which, he has begun by telling us, is going to extricate us from all our difficulties concerning liberty in general. He proceeds to rest the case for freedom of expression on grounds so unexpected, in the premises, that one might question the propriety of his having included the relevant chapter, without apology, in one and the same book with the remaining chapters. For a curious attempt to have it both ways in this regard, see David Spitz, *Democracy and the Challenge to Power* (New York, 1958), where freedom of expression is assimilated to the other freedoms the author is concerned about (they are all good because they are part and parcel of "democracy," which is good in turn because it rests on consent, which is good for reasons that we are left to guess), but the familiar arguments from Mill, who certainly would not have been attracted by Spitz's, are brought in at the end—presumably to make assurance doubly sure.

[3] The openly "anti" freedom of thought and speech literature, of the modern period at least, is admittedly very small. My point, for the moment, is merely that books thought of as "anti" freedom of thought and speech (*e.g.*, a certain famous reply to Mill's *Essay*) have not received enough attention from recent scholarship to be classified as part of the literature in the sense intended.

discussion of the problem in the *Tractatus,* Milton's *Areopagitica* and, above all (in the two-fold sense that it is the item that comes most readily to mind, and that experts deem it the crowning achievement of the literature), Mill's *Essay on Liberty.*[4]

Now, the present article is written out of the conviction that at least one of these items, the *Areopagitica,* has got itself on the list only because people have not been reading it carefully; and that it is high time we did it justice by moving it across the line that divides the "pro" literature from the "anti"—to take its rightful place among the political treatises we have all been brought up to deplore and avoid. To that end, however, we shall need to have before us a statement of the "pro" position which, as the present writer understands it, is generally regarded as having "emerged" from the literature, and become the prevailing view among political theorists.

Brief Excursus on the Prevailing Doctrine

The major assertions involved in the contemporary doctrine concerning freedom of thought and speech (or freedom of thought and freedom of speech),[5] are that in the good—that is, progressive—society all questions, unless perhaps the question whether all questions are open questions, must be treated as open questions;[6] that in such a society there must be no orthodoxy (religious, political, social, economic), or, failing that, that everyone must act, at least in his public capacity, as if there were no orthodoxy; and, by implication, that there are a number of simple tests by which we can discover

[4]Leo Strauss' *Thoughts on Machiavelli* (Glencoe, 1959) gives to the defenders of freedom of thought and expression a surprising new ally, namely, Machiavelli himself. When the word gets around, the *Discourses* will no doubt be added to the list.

[5]There are formidable difficulties about this, especially in view of the current tendency, observable wherever the eye turns, to assume that freedom of thought will take care of itself if only freedom of speech be made safe, and so to treat freedom of thought and freedom of speech as reducible to a single freedom—which they clearly are not. Locke, as the present writer tries to show in another place, addresses himself to the problem of freedom of thought, and hardly seems aware that there *is* a problem of freedom of speech. Plato, by contrast, is clearly interested in both thought and expression, but should not lightly be accused of having been interested in "freedom" in any sense of that term likely to be intelligible to most readers of the current literature of the problem (or problems).

[6]I shall not, in this section, burden the reader with documentation. It is an attempt not to summarize a literature, but to catch up in a few paragraphs a climate of opinion with which we are all familiar.

whether a given society is living up to its obligation ("obligation" is the *mot juste*) to be a progressive society.

These tests may be fairly put in the form of a series of questions. Are the citizens of the society free to challenge any so-called truth, any received opinion, that they wish to challenge? Are they free, having challenged such a truth or such an opinion, to re-think it—first within their own minds, then aloud in the forum of public discussion? Are they free to "think things out for themselves," to reach their own conclusions in their own way, and thereafter to speak their minds, whether aloud or on paper, with a view to persuading others of the correctness of those conclusions? Are they *really* free to do these things—that is, are they so situated in fact as not to be blackmailed or goose-stepped into accepting this or that foreordained conclusion, and not to be placed at hopeless disadvantage when they seek to exercise their liberty to win others over to their point of view? Are there, for example, authorities (of whatever kind) who can in one way or another penalize a point of view whose tendency they dislike, and so—in Gerhart Niemeyer's felicitous phrase—give the "inside run" to points of view they find congenial?[7] If there are such authorities, the position asserts, then utterance is not really free, and soon thought will not be really free either.

Secondly, is there diversity—of opinion, of valuation, of *Weltanschauung*—among the citizens? Does the diversity *in fact* extend to a wide variety of matters? Are numerous points of view *in fact* represented in the forum of public discussion? If not, the position asserts, then the freedom extended to the citizens must be merely formal, and not real: universal agreement within a society, unless about trivial matters like the right of the road, is a sure sign that human spontaneity, which automatically expresses itself in conflicting points of view, is somehow being repressed—is, in any case, an unhealthy state of affairs in and of itself. (This is one of the points on which exponents of the position are most likely to cite the *Areopagitica*, which contains many phrases that do indeed seem to come in handy: a "muddy pool of conformity and tradition,"[8] for example; and "There be who

[7] See his "A Reappraisal of the Doctrine of Free Speech," *Thought*, XXV (June, 1950), 251-274, which, in my opinion, merits a place of honor beside Stephens' masterpiece.

[8] In preparing the present article I have used Professor George H. Sabine's convenient little *Areopagitica and Of Education* (New York, 1951), which is a turning-point in the publishing history of the essay (to say nothing of the history of our culture) because it recognizes that we are getting on to a moment when run-of-the-mine

... make it ... a calamity that any man dissents from their maxims ... [and] neither will hear with meekness nor can convince, yet all must be suppressed which is not found in their syntagma.")[9]

Exponents of the position are, let us notice finally, fully agreed as to its rationale: that is, that the "value" at stake is Truth and the process by which truths are arrived at. The search for truths, they hold, is a cooperative enterprise, in which by definition two heads are better than one, and three better than two, so that the more numerous the participants the better the chances of success, and, at the same time, it is an "on-going" enterprise (like an expanding imperialism, it is always discontented with its conquests to date, and is always, therefore, pushing forward into new territory or moving vigorously to consolidate territory already gained). And the search proceeds precisely by way of the *testing against one another of opposing positions,* that is, by way of *debate* between searchers who disagree—so that, in the nature of the case, it proceeds the more rapidly the more numerous the opposing positions being tested against one another, and the more vigorously these positions are pressed.

We never know, the position holds, what man or even what manner of man will, by striking out on a new path which everyone else regards as not worth exploring, make the next significant contribution to the search for truths. All would-be participants in the search are, therefore, to be welcomed, encouraged and, above all, listened to. And if, *per impossibile,* someone is to be excluded, let it never be on the grounds that the other searchers think he is wrong. For so long, indeed, as one lone human being takes issue with a so-called truth, the search with respect to that truth must go on, in recognition that the withholding of assent by that one human being establishes a presumption against that truth. Moreover, nothing that the participants suppose themselves to know at any given moment can be asserted more than tentatively, since even the propositions they to-day regard as least open to question may tomorrow have to be consigned to the dustbin. *Absolute* freedom of thought and *absolute* freedom of utterance[10] are both dictated by the very nature of the

undergraduates are ignorant of the language in which it is written. For purposes of citing the *Areopagitica,* however, I have adopted the simple procedure of numbering the paragraphs and referring the reader to them, not to pages (*e.g., Areopagitica,* 15th paragraph, becomes *A.,* 15).

[9]*A.,* 68.

[10]A venerable and learned friend takes vigorous exception to the use, in this context,

quest. Any interference with either defeats the latter's purpose, attenuates its pace, and impoverishes both the searcher interfered with and those who interfere with him (on behalf of some alleged truth that they would like to situate beyond challenge). The would-be interferer cannot be sure that his truth is true, cannot be sure even that he understands what his truth means, save as he subjects it to constant and never-ending testing and retesting.

At the roots of the position, then, lies a series of propositions about Truth, about the nature of the process by which Truth is discovered and about the rules to which truth-seekers must subordinate themselves lest they bring the process to a stop. These constitute what we may fairly call a *model* of the truth-seeking process; and for those who hold the position this model, demonstrably, is logically prior to the model of the free society on which they base their recommendations concerning freedom of thought and speech. Nay, more, the second model is constructed *in the precise image of the former,* so that the position presupposes a *methodological* premise; namely, that we may properly move, and move in a quite simplistic one-one manner, from a model of the truth-seeking process to a model of free society that we may with confidence urge upon our fellows. And the position as a whole, I contend, is no stronger than the case that can be made out for that (in my opinion, uncriticized) methodological premise.

Let me, in order to guard against any possible misunderstanding, restate the point: The prevailing position on freedom of thought and speech involves a series of recommendations as to how society ought to be organized. These recommendations are based upon a model of free society that, it is contended, any and all actual societies should be made to approximate. That model, in turn, presupposes a model of the truth-seeking process, which it reflects like a mirror. In order to criticize the position, then, we must raise the following questions, and in this order: Is its view of Truth and of the truth-seeking process

of the word "absolute," pointing out that Mill himself authorizes certain types of interference with liberty of expression. At the risk of appearing stubborn, I continue to assume that Mill meant what he said when he wrote: ". . . there ought to exist the *fullest* (that is, an unlimited?) liberty of professing and discussing, as a matter of ethical conviction, *any* doctrine, however immoral it may be considered" (italics indeed mine). Mill chose, curiously, to bury this passage in a footnote (it depends from the first paragraph of the celebrated second chapter of *On Liberty*), but it states admirably the conclusion to which his arguments in fact point. Those who do not like the conclusion should abandon the arguments.

one that a thoughtful man can accept? Assuming that it is, can we properly move from a model of the truth-seeking process to a model of free society, making of the latter a mere mechanical reproduction of the former? In doing so, to what tacit premise or premises do we, willy-nilly, commit ourselves?

The latter point, I contend, is the crucial one, and for this reason. *The* tacit premise to which the procedure commits us is that Truth is the *supreme* good of society, and the search for it society's central activity. In the absence of such a premise we have no explanation for taking the model of the truth-seeking process as our point of departure. To put it otherwise, the effect of the procedure is to subordinate all other goods in society to the quest for Truth (which the prevailing model certainly does)—that is, to overlook the patent fact that the good society is good because it is the custodian of many goods, all of which it seeks indeed to maximize, but each of which, alas, is of such character that it can sometimes be maximized only at the expense of the others, and none of which, accordingly, it can elevate to the status of an absolute value. And we have here, I contend further, the reason why actual societies never act upon the recommendations in which the position eventuates—and why proponents of the position spend their unhappy lives thinking up reasons to justify *their* not acting upon the recommendations themselves.

One final point. The procedure is, of course, all the more unwarranted if the relevant model of the truth-seeking process is itself at fault—as, in my opinion, that involved in the prevailing position demonstrably is. Even if we posit a community ready to make the quest for truth its supreme good (as, one likes to think, the communities that are the carriers of the various scholarly disciplines are always ready to do), and thus to act upon the recommendations, the latter would produce not truths, but sheer confusion. That is to say, the recommendations are a blueprint for bedlam, and the world would be a more pleasant (and a quieter) place to live in could they be recognized as that. And the reason, I contend, lies partly in the fallacies concerning the nature of Truth that are built into the first of its two models.

The *Areopagitica*

One thesis of the present article is that current misunderstandings of the *Areopagitica* are as the sands of the sea; and we may profitably pause, before entering upon the main body of the argument, to notice certain peculiarities about the work that partially explain the critics' failure to read it correctly.

(1) The *Areopagitica,* like many other masterworks of political philosophy, deals with, over and above the question with which it purports to deal, a wide range of other and far more important questions that are for the most part merely answered rather than posed. Indeed, the essay would hardly deserve our attention if it attempted nothing more ambitious than an answer to the question it most conspicuously asks. It puts itself forward as merely a reasoned plea for the repeal of a parliamentary order requiring prior censorship of books and pamphlets. Milton not only so describes it at the very beginning,[11] but again and again ties his argument back specifically to the issue of prior licensing. As he proceeds, however, the "answer" actually being offered broadens and deepens, mostly without warning to the reader moreover, to deal with the whole problem of liberty, especially intellectual liberty, in organizĕd society. (As to whether Milton intended *ab initio* to state a position on these broader questions and deliberately passed off an essay on liberty as a pamphlet on licensing, or found himself forced into the broader questions by the forward inertia of his argument, is an interesting side-issue that I shall not pursue.)[12] Now, Milton certainly answers the narrower question (as he promises to) in a manner congenial to what I have called above the prevailing contemporary doctrine; that is, he is "against" a particular interference with liberty of expression, namely, prior licensing of books and pamphlets, and thus to that extent "for" a "free" press. He even uses, with respect to that issue, lines of argument that do seem, to some extent, to anticipate those of Mill and his epigones. The hasty reader may, accordingly, stumble into either of two errors demonstrably fatal to an understanding of Milton's teaching. First, he may simply not notice that Milton, who certainly seems to state

[11]*A.,* 3, 4.
[12]But see *infra* (p. 456), the discussion of the verses quoted at the very beginning, close reading of which shows that Milton puts the reader on notice that he has something to say about issues far more important than that of prepublication licensing of books and pamphlets.

clearly enough the business he is about, is in fact dealing with broader problems and, therefore, have no reason to take into account the passages relating to them. In other words, he may read the essay selectively, and subsequently seek to infer from Milton's clear libertarian position on the narrower problem the position he should have adopted on the broader ones—would it not be natural to suppose that Milton would oppose the prohibiting of books *after* publication as well as before? Second, while noticing that the discussion addresses itself to the broader issues, he may, because of prior conditioning by the secondary sources, dismiss the passages that seem inconsistent with Milton's "known" position as *obiter dicta*. The very structure of the *Areopagitica*, in a word, invites misunderstanding by readers who are in haste.

(2) The essay abounds in passages, highly quotable because of their intoxicating rhetoric,[13] which when wrenched from context do indeed seem to commit Milton to the libertarian "side" on the freedom of thought and speech issue. Take, for instance, the familiar sentence: "Give me the liberty to know, to utter, and to argue freely, according to conscience, above all liberties."[14] Read it with the emphasis with which we are accustomed to read Patrick Henry's "Give me liberty or give me death," that is, with the stress on "give" and almost no stress on "me." Take the further small liberty of assuming that Milton means by "liberty" what Mill and his epigones mean by it, and Milton does indeed sound like a precocious early exponent of modern open-society doctrines. When the sentence is placed in context, however, it needs to be read with a quite different emphasis. I, Milton has just been saying in effect, am not a man to kick up a fuss about taxes and suchlike matters, which I am more than content to

---

[13]*Cf. A.*, 87: "... [It] would be no unequal distribution ... to suppress the suppressors themselves." *A.*, 86: where he pleads for "gentle meetings and gentle dismissions" with those who are allegedly in error, and asks why "we debate not and examine the matter thoroughly with liberal and frequent audience ... [No] man who hath tasted learning but will confess the many ways of profiting by those who, not contented with stale receipts, are able to ... set forth new positions ..." *A.*, 84: "[If] it come to prohibiting, there is not aught more likely to be prohibited than truth itself ..." *Cf. ibid.:* "And what do they tell us vainly of new opinions, when this very opinion of theirs, that none must be heard but whom they like, is the worst and newest opinion of all others ... ?" *A.*, 82, where he denounces a "gross conforming stupidity, a stark and dead congealment of 'wood and hay and stubble' forced and frozen together...." *A.*, 79, where we learn that it is "hurtful" and "unequal to suppress opinions for the newness or the unsuitableness to customary "acceptance..." *Cf. A.*, 61.
[14]*A.*, 78.

leave to others. That is, he is distinguishing between two kinds of men, himself and persons like himself, the learned, who are concerned with the quest for Truth, and those members of the community who become exercised over tax problems. It is in speaking for the former that he writes, "Give *me* [that is, us] the liberty [what I want for *myself*, what *I* am prepared to do battle for, is *my* liberty and that of other learned men] to know, to utter, and to argue freely, according to conscience" (italics added); and not necessarily, moreover, that of all learned men. Entirely apart, therefore, from any difficulties as to what Milton may have meant by "liberty" (the "according to conscience" is warning enough that difficulties there are), we see at once that this is not, like Patrick Henry's, a generalized plea regarding public policy concerning freedom of speech, but a particular demand put forward in a particular situation and, as we shall see, by no means necessarily libertarian in tendency.

(3) The *Areopagitica* is peculiarly susceptible to misunderstanding by the type of critic who repudiates the scholar's obligation to understand the past as it understood itself, and imposes upon it his own canons of logic. Take, for instance, the following familiar line of argument. Milton makes a strong plea for "toleration," as in the sentence: "Yet if all cannot be of one mind—as who looks they should be?—this doubtless [but note the reluctant "doubtless," and how our historicist's eye, if we have one, leaps over it] is more wholesome, more prudent, and more Christian: that many be tolerated rather than all compelled."[15] Milton, however, refuses to "follow through" with the idea, as witness his proceeding at once to specify what groups are not to be tolerated, and some that are to be "extirpate."[16] Why did Milton not see, as *we* do so clearly, that the very logic with which he supported his plea for that amount of toleration he did countenance must commit him to a still greater amount of toleration, and certainly to the toleration of Catholics? Similarly, why did Milton "stop" at prior censorship, when he should have seen that the arguments he uses are equally valid as applied to other types of censorship? The temptation to play that sort of game with the *Areopagitica* is very great, because the essay lends itself to the game; but yielding to the temptation can lead only to a perverse misreading of the text. For the critic who tries to understand Milton as Milton understood himself, it is easy to see where such critics go wrong. Milton con-

[15]*A.*, 83. This is another sentence that must be read in context.
[16]*Ibid.*

structs in the *Areopagitica,* as Mill does in the *Essay,* a model of the free society; but the essential meaning of that model is to be found in the fact that within it certain persons are *not* to be tolerated; that is, as we shall see later in detail, that the relevant population are to be in such full agreement about important things that, without the remotest danger to the goods they value, they can well afford to be "tolerant" of one another (to ask them to "tolerate" is to ask nothing of them except, in effect, that they tolerate themselves). The "principles" that should have "led Milton on" to demand a still broader toleration are simply not there. So, too, with the matter of prior censorship: the essence of the model lies in the fact that it involves appropriate means for preventing the free circulation from hand to hand of any published book of a malicious or harmful tendency, but at the same time seeks to stimulate the flow of books by releasing them from prior censorship; and the "inconsistency," or failure to "follow through," lies, in both cases, in Milton's having conceded perhaps more than we should expect him to to the open-society position, not in his not having conceded more than that. The fact that we do not like what the *Areopagitica* in fact says does not justify us in ignoring what it in fact says.

The Models (A)

Turning now to the critical schema we have outlined above, what, first, are Milton's views on our complex of issues concerning Truth?

Let us notice, to begin with, that he employs in the *Areopagitica* a number of metaphors about Truth (some his own inventions, some culled from literature with which he was familiar) that do seem to place him with the proponents of the open society. Concretely, the metaphors do stress the cooperative[17] and on-going character of the search for Truth,[18] and the dangers, from the standpoint of that search, of artificially-imposed unanimity. In what context, however, and for what purpose, let us not try to say until we have examined the metaphors.

Truth, Milton reminds us, is according to Divine Scriptures a

---

[17] *Cf. A.,* 71.
[18] *Cf. A.,* 85: "For such is the order of God's enlightening his church, to dispense and deal out by degrees his beam. . . . Neither is God appointed and confined, where and out of what place these his chosen shall be first heard to speak. . ."

"streaming fountain": its waters "sicken into a muddy pool of conformity and tradition" if they do not flow in a "perpetual progres-
sion."[19] Our "faith and knowledge," that is to say, "thrives by
exercise"; the man who does not keep a firm grasp upon the grounds
of his truths will find that the "very truth he holds becomes his
heresy."[20] Again: Truth is like light: we who possess it have good
reason to boast of it; but if we merely "stare" upon it, if we "look not
wisely" at it, if we use it not to "discover onward things more remote
from our knowledge," [21] it will smite us into "darkness." Those who
would have us look no further, those who are determined that the
"cruse of truth shall run no more oil," those who think "we are to
pitch our tent here, and have attained the utmost prospect of reformation," have stared at Zwingli's and Calvin's blaze so long that they
are "stark blind."[22] Moreover, we must bear all this in mind not only
within the church, but also where what is in question is the "rule of
life both economical and political";[23] not merely, that is to say, in
matters theological, but in matters pertaining to society and government as well.

Still again: Truth is a "virgin," who "once came into the world
... [in] a perfect shape, glorious to look upon"; she remained in the
world throughout the ministry of Jesus; then, after "He ascended,"
she fell victim to a "wicked race of deceivers," who "hewed her
lovely form into a thousand pieces and scattered them to the four
winds"; since when her "sad friends" have gone "up and down
gathering up limb after limb as they have found them." They have
not, however, yet found all the pieces, and will not find all of them
until the Second Coming of the Master, who will bring them all
together and "mould them into an immortal feature of loveliness and
perfection." Our task, meantime, is to "continue seeking," to "continue to do our obsequies to the torn body of our martyred saint"; and
none must be permitted to "forbid" and "disturb" the search[24]—as
they do who "think it a calamity that any man dissents from their
maxims";[25] they neither help "unite those dissevered pieces" nor

[19] *A.*, 59.
[20] *Ibid.*
[21] *A.*, 67.
[22] *Ibid.* The two preceding quotations are from *A.*, 58 and *A.*, 65 respectively.
[23] *A.*, 67.
[24] *A.*, 66.
[25] *A.*, 68.

permit others to do so. We must always be "closing up truth to truth as we find it," in the knowledge that the body of Truth is "homogeneal and proportional," and that the truths we close up one to another will finally fit together.[26] That is the "golden rule in theology as well as arithmetic," because it "makes up the best harmony"—as contrasted with the "outward union of cold and neutral, and inwardly divided minds."[27] We must become a "knowing people, a nation of prophets and sages"; and what is wanted for that is "pens and heads . . . sitting by their studious lamps, musing, searching, revolving new notions and ideas, . . . others as fast reading, trying all things, assenting to the force of reason and convincement."[28] For "Where there is much desire to learn," there is of necessity "much arguing, much writing, many opinions; for opinion in good men is but knowledge in the making."[29]

Finally: God Himself it is who stirs up the "earnest and zealous thirst after knowledge and understanding."[30] All that prevents us from uniting together in "one general and brotherly search after truth" is that we do not exercise a "little forbearance of one another, and some grain of charity";[31] that in our attempts at "crowding free consciences and Christian liberties into canons and precepts of men" we forget that the temple of the Lord is built by making "many schisms and many dissections . . . in the quarry and in the timber," by having "some cutting, some squaring the marble, others hewing the cedars."[32] For when the stones have been laid "artfully together," they cannot be "united into a continuity," since they are not "all of one form." The perfection of the finished work will rather consist precisely in its "goodly and graceful symmetry," which arises out of "many moderate varieties and brotherly dissimilitudes that are not vastly disproportional."[33] Let us, then, be "more wise in spiritual architecture," and Moses may see his "glorious wish" fulfilled: not merely seventy elders but "all the Lord's people . . . become prophets."[34] They are wrong who fear that "divisions and subdivisions will

[26] *Ibid.*
[27] *Ibid.*
[28] *A.*, 71.
[29] *A.*, 72.
[30] *Ibid.*
[31] *Ibid.*
[32] *A.*, 73.
[33] *Ibid.*
[34] *A.*, 74.

undo us."[35] Especially wrong is the "adversary," those "malicious applauders of our differences," who tell themselves that "when we have branched [ourselves] . . . into small enough parties," they will have their hour. They do not know the "firm root out of which we all grow," and "will not beware"—not until "our small divided maniples" cut through at "every angle of [their] . . . unwieldy brigade."[36]

The Models (B)

We have conceded that the above metaphors do—we may add now, *at first glance*—seem to range Milton on the side of the exponents of open-society doctrines. Our next task, then, as that way of putting it implies, is to take notice of the fact that when looked at a second time, and in abstraction from what we have been brought up to expect to find in the *Areopagitica,* they do nothing of the kind.

For example, Milton indeed says that our truths become heresies if we fail to keep a firm grasp upon them, and Mill no doubt picked up the idea from the *Areopagitica.* But in Milton's hands, as he reveals to us by one turn of phrase after another, it has a very different meaning from that which Mill is to impose upon it. Milton, our second glance shows us, is clearly committed to the view that our major concern is with *our* truths, those which we possess already, opposed to which there are heresies, that is, *untruths,* which we speak of as untrue not merely because they conflict with what we happen to think (that edges over in the direction of relativism, of which there is not a whisper in Milton), but because they conflict with Truth itself. Our truths, moreover, are to be preserved,[37] which is to warn us that the function of the model Milton is developing is by no means merely that of discovering new truths, but also, and at least equally, that of enabling us to cling fast to old ones, and to keep the latter alive and strong.

Milton does indeed tell us that we are not to content ourselves with the old truths—that is, that we can stare too long at the "blaze" of Calvin and Zwingli. But his language makes it clear that what we are

[35] *Ibid.*
[36] *Ibid.*
[37] *A.,* 57: "This Order . . . will be a stepdame to Truth; and first, by disenabling us to the maintenance of what *is known already"* (italics added).

urged not to stare upon too long really is, for him, a "blaze," a "light," which we are to use confidently as we go about the discovery of things that lie beyond our present knowledge; so that there is no whiff of a suggestion that the blaze may turn out to have been an optical illusion, the light to have been darkness. It is to Mill,[38] and not to Milton, that we must go for the notion that our whole present corpus of knowledge may well turn out to be erroneous. For Milton, the search for Truth is a "searching what we know not by what we know";[39] the model maintains a neat balance between the preserving of what we know and the discovery of what we know not; insofar as it subordinates the one to the other it subordinates the latter to the former (as we shall see more clearly below).

Milton does indeed remind us that the friends of the virgin Truth, who go about gathering up limb after dissevered limb, have not found all of them yet. But if we are expecting to be told that the dissevered limbs already brought together may not really be limbs at all, or that, worse still, they may be the limbs not of the virgin Truth but of some nameless young woman whose morals were no better than they ought to have been, Milton can only disappoint us; the notion is not present, even by implication. Further, Milton clearly believes that "we" possessed the entire body of Truth during Jesus' incarnation; and we are obliged to notice that Truth is associated in Milton's mind mainly with religious truths (when he wishes to call to mind other kinds of truth, he puts their names to them—as in the phrase, which we have already noticed, "the rule of life both economical and political," or his references to "arithmetic"), and also, that he deems Revelation to be the major and most authoritative source of such truths. Here again we are oceans apart from Mill, and from the positivistic scientists who are forever citing him.

Our task, Milton indeed insists, is to close up truth to truth wherever we may find it, and to do so unceasingly, indefatigably. But (we

---

[38]Mill does indeed conduct part of his discussion on the assumption that the received opinion, that which might serve as the grounds on which another and different opinion is to be suppressed, is correct—that is, the truth. Careful examination will show, however, that the assumption is an assumption *arguendo;* the received opinion's being true is merely one of three theoretical possibilities that would-be suppressers in the name of truth must, on their own showing, take into account: the received opinion is true, it is partly-true partly-false, it is untrue. He is prepared to show that in each case nothing is to be gained by suppressing a novel opinion; but he seems to me quite careful not to commit himself to the view that there are in fact situations where the received opinion is "the Truth."

[39]*A.,* 68.

repeat ourselves, but the metaphors are themselves repetitious) it is clear that the truths that he would have us close up one to another are "true" truths (the idea is by no means that of closing up tentative hypothesis to tentative hypothesis)—capable of elaboration, certainly, but as far as they go true, and not destined to be set aside. Similarly, he would indeed have us be suspicious of the outward union of inwardly divided minds, and we are indeed tempted to detect here an appeal for the kind of "diversity" for which Mill is to plead—and the more when our eye falls upon that sentence about the necessity for much arguing, much writing, many opinions. But our second glance will enable us to notice the numerous warnings that we are in a realm of discourse entirely different from Mill's; God Himself—and when Milton says "God" he leaves us in no doubt that he means God, a God upon whom he *believes*—stirs up the much arguing, the much writing, the many opinions, for purposes that are His Own; and, in any case, the "many" opinions that accompany the desire to learn are, we see now, many in the sense of numerous rather than many in the sense of widely-divergent (for all that it seems "natural" to some of us to understand the phrase in the second sense). Milton's concern, it becomes clear, is with the crowding of free *consciences* and *Christian* liberties, not *free* consciences and Christian *liberties* (which is how we tried at first to read it)—that is, for men who think and act out of conscience, which is to say, for Christians. Finally, the arguing turns out to be arguing amongst men who do not disagree profoundly with one another (as we shall notice again and again); the many opinions, which are the blocks that are to be combined together in the symmetry of the house of God, do differ from one another, but we perceive now that the difference is a matter —again we have merely to shift the emphasis—of *moderate* varieties, not moderate *varieties,* of *brotherly* dissimilitudes, not brotherly *dissimilitudes* and that Milton has driven the point home by adding "not vastly disproportional." We do not overburden the passage when we attribute to Milton the view, which evidently is *not* Mill's, that the search for truth thrives best in situations of *consensus,* that is, where the participants are like-minded men. And, finally, we notice now that what prevents us from uniting in "one general and brotherly search after truth" is that we do not exercise a *little* forbearance of one another, and *some* grain of charity.

We shall fail to grasp the true character of Milton's model of the

Truth-seeking process unless we raise questions about the persons he has in mind when he speaks of "we" (we are tempted to read the "we" as shorthand for "mankind," which it is sometimes, but by no means always). For one thing, the *Areopagitica* is above all a message addressed by an Englishman to compatriots of his, so that "we" as often as not means "we here in England," "we Englishmen"[40]—that is, Milton plus his addressees, so that often where he seems to be paying tribute to the discussion process as such, the praise is in fact intended for the discussion process as he sees it going forward in England. This means that the model has "in it" a whole series of tacit or near-tacit assumptions about the character, the mutual related-nesses, the traditions and the qualities of the "people" in whose bosom the search for Truth goes forward. Or, to put the point differently, we must ask, in connection with such passages as those in which we find the words "much arguing, much writing, many opinions," or the words "opinion is . . . only knowledge in the making," or the words "pens and heads" musing beside "studious lamps," whether Milton, like Mill, means us to understand: Let *any* people that would be a "knowing people," and possess Truth, devote itself to intensive and unlimited debate, or rather, Given a society made up of men of a certain type (with, we can safely add, such and such traditions),[41] the search for Truth will profit from intensive and unlimited debate. It seems clear to me that we torture the passages in question when we seek in them, as we do well-nigh instinctively, a meaning akin to that of the *Essay* (where the "Given a society made up of men of a certain type" is precisely what is most conspicuously lacking). The emphasis, then, as our second glance reveals, is less on the "much arguing, *etc.*" than on the identity and quality—the *goodness*—of the arguers;[42] and whatever Milton is urging about the vir-

[40]*A.*, 69: "Lords and Commons of England, consider what nation it is whereof ye are . . . ; acute to invent, subtle and sinewy to discourse, not beneath the reach of any point the highest that human capacity can soar to. Therefore the studies of learning in her deepest sciences have been so ancient and so eminent . . ." *Cf. A.*, 72: ". . . a nation so pliant and so prone to seek after knowledge." *Cf. A.*, 50: with its proud reference to the "invention, the art, the wit, the grave and solid judgment which is in England. . . ."

[41]*Cf. A.*, 78: "That *our* hearts are now more capacious, *our* thoughts more erected to the search and expectation of greatest and exactest things, is the issue of your own virtue propagated in us" (italics added). (The "Give me the liberty to know" passage soon follows.) *Cf. A.*, 14: ". . . *our* English, the language of men ever famous and foremost in the achievements of liberty" (italics added).

[42]Thus the "opinion is . . . but knowledge in the making" turns out to read "opinion

tues of "free expression," it is misapplied when extended to situations in which the presuppositions he has in mind are not fulfilled.[43]

In the second place (a similar but different point), if we would understand the *Areopagitica* we must not beg the question, What persons, even within the society embodying his presuppositions, does Milton think of as actually participating in the quest for truth? Does his model, like Mill's, abstract from or ignore the differences in quality among the individual members of the society, and in consequence, anticipate the democratical and egalitarian tendency of the Mill model? Mill's one lone dissenter, who must be convinced before the question on which he dissents can properly be regarded as closed (and then only until another dissenter turns up), and who contributes to the search for Truth by the mere fact of his dissenting, is, clearly, just anybody not a minor or an idiot; there is no test of intellectual or moral excellence that he must meet in order to be taken into account. When Milton speaks of the "whole people, or the greater part, more than at other times taken up with the study of highest and most important matters to be reformed . . ., reasoning, reading, inventing, discoursing, even to a rarity and admiration, things not discoursed or written of," we do seem (leaving aside the above question as to what kind of "people" we are speaking about) to be standing in the presence of an idea not unlike Mill's. (So, too, when we read "not only our seventy elders but all the Lord's people become prophets.")[44]

Our answer here must be that to overlook the *aristocratic* character of Milton's conception of the Truth-seeking process is to ignore one of the major emphases of the essay, one moreover that is driven home to us at the very beginning. The lines from Euripides that precede Milton's opening sentence read:

in good men is but knowledge in the making" (italics added), the Mill-trained eye having slipped over the "in good men."

[43]Including, of course, the presuppositions as to the persons excluded from the debate, because of which, as noted elsewhere, the debate is really not unlimited at all. Milton was highly knowledgeable about the relation between policy recommendations and their presuppositions, as witness: "Plato . . . fed his fancy with making many edicts to his airy burgomasters . . . [He] seems to tolerate no kind of learning but by unalterable decree . . . [But] Plato meant this law peculiarly to that commonwealth which he had imagined, and to no other. . . . [He] knew that this licensing of poems had reference and dependence to many other provisoes there set down in his fancied republic . . . [The course he recommends], taken apart from those other collateral injunctions, must needs be vain and fruitless" (*A.*, 33).

[44]*A.*, 74.

This is true liberty, when free-born men,
Having to advise the public, may speak free,
Which he who can, and will, deserves high praise;
Who neither can nor will, may hold his peace;
What can be juster in a State than this?

Here also, to be sure, we are beset by very considerable temptations: (a) To let the eye skip the words "having to advise the public"
and read "This is true liberty, when free-born men . . . may speak
free"—which we must not do, since the words "having to advise the
public" are strictly *defining* (*i.e.*, they tell us *what* free-born men in
the justest State may speak free). (b) To fail to read closely the following two verses, which, strictly construed, establish a distinction, logically prior to what they assert, between two types of free-born men:
first, those who "can, and will [advise the public]," and second, those
who "neither can nor will [advise the public]"—which "reads out"
for us the dichotomy implicit in the defining phrase "having to advise
the public." (c) To overlook the *asymmetry* of what the two verses
end up asserting, which is that men of the first type "deserve high
praise" (as why should they not, since they "can" advise, that is, are
capable of advising, and "will," that is, are men who are willing to
shoulder the responsibilities that go with their liberty?); and that men
of the second type, who "neither can nor will," "may" hold their
peace—where the absence of the symmetrical "does not deserve
high praise" or "deserves contempt" (which is what we should have
expected) rather emphasizes than obscures this point; as the absence
of "may not hold his peace" (which is what we should have expected
if we had read the verses backwards) rather emphasizes than obscures *that* point. The assertion, in other words, is far more complex
than, at first glance, it appears to be, and it becomes: We have true
liberty, and the maximum of relevant justice, where those who have
something to say that is worth hearing *both* are in position to "speak
free" and actually do so, thus deserving (and being recognized as
deserving) high praise, and where those who do *not* have something
to say both do not deserve (and are recognized as not deserving) high
praise, and "may" remain silent. Nor must we permit the irony of the
"may" to elude us (we seldom think of a man's being *permitted* to
hold his peace as a liberty; and, in any case, it is only those who have
nothing to say that, according to the verses, possess it); and if we take

the irony into account we may fairly understand: *"do* hold their peace." In short, we look in vain for the democratical-egalitarian assertion (which our secondary sources would dispose us to expect) that those who cannot (are not capable) and those who will not (some of whom perhaps *are* capable) are entitled to speak freely. The "true liberty" in question is that of an aristocracy, whose excellence is *both* intellectual and moral.[45] (d) To fail to notice the implicit distinction between "true liberty," which we have just seen to be as much a matter of limitations and responsibilities as of absence of limitations, and false liberty, *and* the manner in which it is "picked up" and developed in the peroration. "True liberty" there becomes that "utmost bound of civil liberty" which "wise men look for";[46] Milton is suggesting what that "utmost bound" in fact is;[47] and we must not permit our over-weaning interest in the answer he seems to offer to obscure the nature of the question, its presuppositions and the way in which they color the answer. We have that "utmost bound," he assures us, where "complaints [but remember from whom] are freely heard, deeply considered, and speedily reformed." Wise men, the form of the question teaches us, do not seek *more* liberty than is consistent with "true liberty"—that is, for the implication is surely present, more liberty than they can have and still have liberty at all. There is an "utmost bound" beyond which liberty cannot be pushed without the pushing of it becoming folly: so that *the* question to ask about liberty is, in the first instance, How much? (along with, we repeat, For whom?). And the question does color the answer: "Complaints" does not estop questions about what complaints; "freely heard" does not estop further questions as to how freely; nor does "deeply considered" estop further questions as to how much time should be devoted to the considering, nor "speedily

[45]I have not attempted to go into the question whether the Greek original warrants this construction, since we have here the rare case where what matters is precisely the translation—the more certainly since the translation is Milton's own. See John Milton, *Prose Works* (London, 1839), Vol. I, "Introductory Review," where Robert Fletcher writes: ". . . the motto is taken from [Milton's] . . . favourite Euripides, and happily translated by himself." It is a matter of more than passing interest that the Everyman edition, whose introduction is cited *infra*, unaccountably *omits* the motto.

[46]*A.,* 2.

[47]*Cf.* Boswell's *Life of Johnson* (Oxford, 1931), p. 422: "He went with me, one Sunday, to hear my old Master, Gregory Sharpe, preach at the Temple. In the prefatory prayer, Sharpe ranted about *Liberty,* as a blessing most fervently to be implored, and its continuance prayed for. Johnson observed, that our *liberty* was in no sort of danger:—he would have done much better, to pray against our *licentiousness.*"

reformed" further questions as to how speedily and what we are to mean by "reformed." Milton, in his first two pages, does all that properly needs to be done to seal us off from the major fallacies of the *Essay on Liberty.* And to read him otherwise is to misread him.

Milton moves, then, from aristocratic premises: that the distinction between good men and bad men is knowable, meaningful and applicable in human affairs; that theorizing about liberty must as a matter of course be rooted in that distinction (and in the conception of goodness itself that it presupposes); that liberty (unless the liberty of publishing pamphlets and books without prior censorship, and perhaps not even that liberty) is for good men and not for bad men. All the apparently democratical and egalitarian emphases in the essay must be read in the light of those premises; and when so read, as it seems to me, prove to be entirely consistent with them. Thus, the passages in question turn out to contain no suggestion that "the [whole] people, or the greater part,"[48] as contrasted with "learning and learned men," might play an independent and creative role in the search for Truth. The role of the former in the model is that of *learners,* who, because they have been well-taught by their proper teachers,[49] can now be trusted, within the limits we shall soon be noticing, to choose their own reading-matter.[50] Where the *pursuit* of Truth is foremost in Milton's mind, the emphasis is invariably, as it should be, upon scholarship and scholars; and we may be sure that Milton, no more than Burke after him, would have wished to put ordinary men, even in England, to trade upon their private stock of reason. Those who "can, and will" become, in due course, "the free and ingenious sort, of such as evidently were born to study and love learning for itself, not for lucre or any other end but the service of God and of truth, and perhaps that lasting fame and perpetuity

---

[48] *A.,* 75.

[49] *Cf. A.,* 29: ". . . the learned (from whom to the common people whatever is heretical . . . may quickly be conveyed). . . ." *Cf. A.,* 87, the reference to "teaching the people to see day." And *cf. A.,* 42, with its reference to a "man above the common measure, both studious, learned, and judicious."

[50] *Cf.* p. 456 *supra,* where it might be argued that the presence of the word "inventing" in the list of things ("disputing, reading, [*etc.*]") destroys the point. But *cf.* the following paragraph (*A.,* 76), where the "people" are spoken of as merely bestowing *attention* on the "solidest and sublimest points of controversy and new invention." The two passages are not necessarily inconsistent: a "whole people" can "invent" through the good offices of that "part of them" that is capable of inventing.

of praise which God and good men have consented shall be the reward of those whose published labors advance the good of mankind."[51]

The Models (C)

We come now to certain frequently-quoted passages, apparently highly inconvenient to the thesis of the present article, that seem to throw Milton's weight behind the curious notion that History is somehow on the side of Truth, that in a free "market of ideas" good money can be counted upon, in accordance with a Gresham's Law in reverse, to drive out bad, and that interference in the market on behalf of Truth is certain to be self-defeating.[52] ". . . [Who] knows not," Milton certainly demands, "that Truth is strong next to the Almighty? She needs no policies, nor stratagems, nor licensings to make her victorious"—the latter being, rather, "the shifts and the defenses that error uses against her power."[53] We must, therefore, "give her . . . room, and . . . not bind her when she sleeps, for then she speaks not

[51]*A.*, 45. He is not, he makes clear, concerned about the liberty of the "mercenary crew of false pretenders to learning"; and there is one passage in which he seems to imply that scholars may properly be asked to "win their spurs" before entering upon the full liberty of their calling: ". . . if . . . no years, no industry, *no former proof of his abilities,* can bring him to that state of maturity as not to be still mistrusted and suspected . . ." (*A.*, 46; italics added). *Cf.* especially, *A.*, 86, with its reference to "those whom God hath fitted for the special use of these times with eminent and ample gifts." Others (that is, such others as are being tolerated at all) seem to be present for these to sharpen their wits on (*cf. A.*, 84: ". . . [God] raises to his own work men of rare abilities and more than common industry, not only to look back and revise what hath been taught heretofore, but to gain further and go on some new enlightened steps in the discovery of truth"). *Cf.* also, *A.*, 71, where he appeals to the "general instinct of holy and devout men, as they daily and solemnly express their thoughts"; *A.*, 57, with its emphasis on "learned and religious men"; and *A.*, 63, where the implicit plea for freedom is for a "man judicious, learned, and of a conscience," and for those "whose business and profession it is to be the champions of truth." *Cf.* finally, *A.*, 55, with its reference to "those who had prepared their minds and studies above *the vulgar pitch,* to advance truth in others and from others to entertain it . . ." (italics added), and *A.*, 47, with its question: "And how can a man teach with authority, which is the life of teaching, [*etc.*] . . .?" its sarcastic reference to the "pupil-teacher" (a meaningless notion unless there be such a thing as a "teacher-pupil"), and the phrase, "what is vulgarly received already."

[52]There is a difficulty here: Mill expressly disclaims any such notion, and recognizes that persecution is sometimes successful. Despite the disclaimer, however, Mill's position is one of great optimism as to how truth *will* fare in the free market; and the very frequency with which his epigones quote the Milton passages we are about to notice testifies to the fact that some such notion is implicit in the prevailing doctrine.

[53]*A.*, 81.

true, ... [and] turns herself into all shapes except her own."[54] Stranger still, "Let ... [Truth] and Falsehood grapple; who ever knew Truth put to the worse in a free and open encounter?"[55] Or: "Her confuting is the best and surest suppressing."[56]

These passages constitute a problem of a quite different order from that of the apparently libertarian passages we have considered above; *i.e.*, they cannot be disposed of simply by reading them with a different emphasis, or by restoring them to their immediate context; they do appear to add up to a plea for an "open society"; and they do not merely appear in the *Areopagitica* but bear upon their face the evidence that Milton channeled into them the very best of his unequaled rhetorical skills. What, since the *Areopagitica* really advocates quite drastic limitations upon the free market of ideas, are we to make of them? Must we conclude that Milton indeed believed that which they appear to say, and failed to grasp their seemingly unavoidable implications—that is, that Milton was "inconsistent" if, having written them, he did *not* go ahead and adopt a position like Mill's? And that, accordingly, the *Areopagitica* is indeed the remote source of the "prevailing doctrine"?

The issue is worth restating in the following generalized terms: What are we to do when we have before us a book clearly written to support such and such readily-identifiable conclusions, in which, nevertheless, we find passages that, on the face of them, militate against those conclusions? Our minimum obligation, I suggest—one does not lightly plead a writer of Milton's stature guilty of contradicting himself in so brief an essay[57]—is to ask ourselves whether the trouble perhaps lies in ourselves. We are required to go back to the text and see what happens when we try to read the apparently peccant passages in the light of and as colored by the major argument (not, in fairness to the author, the other way 'round). When, in other words, we give to the words in the peccant passages *meanings appropriate to the major argument*[58]—which, in the *Areopagitica*, is that

[54] *Ibid.*
[55] *A.*, 80.
[56] *Ibid. Cf. A.*, 31: "Truth, ... when she gets a free and willing hand, opens herself faster than the pace of method and discourse can overtake her."
[57] Another easy way out of the difficulty, which we shall also avoid, would be to point out that Milton shows himself to know better: "revolutions of ages do not oft recover the loss of a rejected truth, for want of which whole nations fare the worse" (*A.*, 6).
[58] The full force of the point can best be grasped with reference to the crucial "I mean not tolerated" passage (*A.*, 83). Milton can write: "... it is not possible for men to sever the wheat from the tares, the good fish from the other fry; that must be the

there is an "utmost bound" of liberty that wise men seek, and that a free society is *not* an open society.

"[Truth] needs no policies, nor stratagems"? We do indeed have a difficulty, if we assume that "policies or stratagems" includes the common-sense measures a society adopts in order to protect and perpetuate the truths it believes itself to embody, but the difficulty disappears if we are generous enough to let Milton have a distinction between these measures and "policies or stratagems." We must "give ... [Truth] room, and ... not bind her when she sleeps"? The difficulty is again of our own making: the words "give Truth room" by no means estop the question, How much room?, or exclude the particular answer to that question the essay provides; nor do the words "not bind her when she sleeps" estop the question whether, *e.g.*, the suppressing of malicious books, to which Milton certainly had no objection,[59] is or is not a "binding" of Truth. "Let . . . [Truth] and Falsehood grapple?" ". . . [Who] ever knew Truth put to the worse in a free and open encounter?" But the sentence does *not* say, Let Truth and Falsehood grapple in just any set of circumstances, among just any kind of people—that is, it leaves Milton entirely free to raise and answer in his own way the question, In what circumstances, among what kind of people, can Truth and Falsehood in fact grapple? As for "free and open encounter," the interesting questions, as Milton is there to teach us, arise only when we ask what *is* a "free and open encounter"—*how* free and *how* open can the encounter be and remain "free" and "open," that is, remain an encounter in which Truth can grapple with Falsehood, and tell itself with confidence that it will not be "put to worse"? Besides which, the whole series of passages takes on a different meaning when we remind ourselves that Milton, unlike those who today cite the passages in question, supposed himself to know what *is* the Truth—so that "Truth," for him,

angels' ministry at the end of mortal things. Yet if all cannot be of one mind—as who looks they should be?—this doubtless is more wholesome, more prudent, that all should be tolerated rather than all compelled." And go on to say in the same paragraph: "I mean not tolerated popery and open superstition, [*etc.*]". To speak of "contradiction" or "inconsistency" here obviously will not do, unless we go further and assume we are dealing with a writer who is feeble-minded. We have learned to read the *Areopagitica* only when we can read this passage and *not* find in it any inconsistency. *Cf. A.*, 82: "How many other things might be tolerated in peace and left to conscience, had we but charity, and were it not the chief stronghold of our hypocrisy to be ever judging one another!" "We" here is clearly shorthand for "we who agree on fundamentals." "Fundamentals" is Milton's own term *(ibid.)*.

[59]But see below, pp. 465-471.

is shorthand for "our Truth," and the purpose of the "grappling" is, quite simply, the confuting of error, not the finding out what *is true*.[60] We have, I repeat, indeed been creating the difficulties for ourselves; concretely, by reading into phrases like "free and open encounter" a meaning that we could have learned only from Mill, and that Milton could not possibly have intended. For the model of free society which emerges in the course of Milton's argument, and which is full of what Mill would regard as "policies and stratagems," *is* the "free and open encounter" of which he speaks.

The Models (D)

The *Areopagitica,* correctly read, is on one side a plea for the removal, within a certain kind of society, of a particular restriction upon freedom of expression—that is, the prior censorship of books and pamphlets. On another side it is an impassioned defense of a *status quo*[61] which, save in that one regard, Milton is clearly ready to identify with "true liberty," which he clearly regards with great satisfaction, and which (as already intimated) is *presupposed* in his demand for a press free from prior censorship. The contention that he uses arguments against prior censorship that should have "led him on" to advocate an open society like Mill's, or that are in any case applicable to all forms of censorship, is, therefore, nonsensical; for his purpose in advocating that degree of openness involved in freeing books and pamphlets from prior censorship is merely to eliminate, from a society the essence of which is that from a Millian point of view it is "closed," what he regards as an absurdity.

As he proceeds, Milton reveals for us and praises the major characteristics of the kind of society of which he approves, and these we may fairly speak of as constituting the model of free society as Milton understood it. Those major characteristics are:

(1) It is a society that regards itself as founded upon *religious truth*—as not only living under God for a purpose that is His, not merely its own, but as especially favored by God,[62] and as having in conse-

---

[60] *Cf. A.,* 65: "[We] are to send our thanks ... to Heaven, louder than most nations, for that great measure of truth which we enjoy, especially in those main points at issue between us and the Pope. ..."

[61] *Cf. A.,* 78. Also *A.,* 75, 76.

[62] *Cf. A.,* 2, where he argues that if we have regained our "liberty . . . , it will be

quence an obligation to protect and propagate a certain corpus of religious doctrine.[63] As intimated above, its highest good (as we should have expected Milton to say if we had not been taught to misread the *Areopagitica*), is not "the pursuit of truth" in the Mill sense, but the living and propagation of an expanding revealed religion.

(2) It is a *homogeneous* society, in which very far from there being a cult of diversity there are *at most* "neighboring differences, or rather indifferences, on some point of doctrine or discipline"; it is, moreover, a homogeneous society because it *wills* itself to be homogeneous, that is, because, though "tolerant," it does *not* tolerate "popery and open superstition" ("it"—not "they," but "it"—should be "extirpate," because "it extirpates all religions and civil supremacies"); nor does it tolerate "that which is impious or evil absolutely, either against faith or manners."[64] (Milton does not tell us what he means by "extirpate"; perhaps he would have contented himself with banishing the papists.) The *big* issues concerning doctrine and discipline, those between Protestants and Catholics, are regarded as closed—that is, not as proper topics for discussion. And the society Milton approves of, because founded on an initial act of intolerance and exclusion, is appropriately closed too.

(3) It is a structured, that is, *hierarchical,* society, where "honor . . . [is] done . . . to men who [profess] . . . the study of wisdom and eloquence" so that they are heard "gladly and with great respect";[65] that is, where the "common people" know their place over against their intellectual and moral betters.

attributed first, as is most due, to the strong assistance of God, our deliverer."

[63] *Cf. A.*, 70, where he argues that but for the "prelates," the "glory of reforming all our neighbors had been ours."

[64] *A.*, 83. That, he goes on, "no law can possibly permit that intends not to outlaw itself." To put it otherwise: the whole position rests upon a distinction between that which does and that which does not "interrupt the unity of spirit," between "neighboring differences" and differences that are *not* "neighboring"; and we do not dispose of the point by saying that subsequent experience has proved Milton wrong as to whether the differences between Protestants and Catholics are "neighboring" in the sense intended (especially as subsequent experience is not over yet). The teaching: unity of spirit is a precondition of our free society, and of the discussion process that goes forward within it. For the present writer, what subsequent experience shows is that the discussion process does break down where such unity of spirit is absent. *Cf. A.*, 79, where Milton cites Lord Brooke as teaching that we must "hear with patience and humility those, however they be miscalled, that desire to live purely, in such a use of God's ordinances as the best guidance of their consciences gives them, though in *some* disconformity to ourselves" (italics mine).

[65] *A.*, 4.

(4) It is a society that thinks of itself as both entitled and obligated to see to it that both "church and commonwealth . . . have a vigilant eye how books demean themselves as well as men; and thereafter to confine, imprison, and do sharpest judgment on them."[66] ". . . [If] they be found mischievous and libelous, the fire and the executioner will be the timeliest and the most effectual remedy that man's prevention can use."[67] And: ". . . [If] . . . [any man's intellectual offspring] be proved a monster, who denies that it was justly burnt or sunk into the sea?"[68]

Is it, then, a society which, though it is to have no *prior* censorship of books and pamphlets, will maintain arrangements for suppressing them after publication? That, certainly, is what at first glance the passages seem to suggest; it is also what many of our critics, while pointing out that many of Milton's arguments against prior censorship are *prima facie* equally good arguments against any censorship at all, have accused him of advocating, or at least being prepared to contemplate, and so of having been blind to the implications of his own argument. There are, however, at least two reasons, over and above the patent applicability to posterior censorship of some of the arguments, especially the strongest ones, against prior censorship, why we should fight shy of any such reading of the *Areopagitica,* namely: (a) The fact that Milton, who here as elsewhere is nothing if not prolix, and is if anything too attentive to detail, at no point gives us any hint as to the machinery that a free society might establish for confining and imprisoning and doing sharp judgment on "mischievous" books; and (b), the presence within the *Areopagitica* of lines of argument clearly intended to prove that we do great hurt, alike from the standpoint of virtue and from that of Truth, when we forbid our fellows access to *any* book on the grounds that it is heretical or of malicious tendency. Worse yet, as he develops these arguments, he repeatedly lets the prior censorship issue slip through his fingers altogether (though as noted above he "ties back" to it with great frequency),[69] and develops them precisely as arguments against cen-

---

[66]*A.,* 6.
[67]*A.,* 88.
[68]*A.,* 15.
[69]*Cf. A.,* 5, where in a single sentence he moves from the *prior* censorship issue ("the inventors of it be those whom ye will be loath to own") to the broad issue of "what is to be thought in general of reading," then back to the prior censorship issue. By no means all the arguments against prior censorship, we may notice, are simultaneously

sorship *tout court;* and if in the context of those arguments, which
we must now pause to notice, Milton was prepared to contemplate
post-publication censorship, we do indeed stand in the presence of
an intellectual blunder about which we are entitled to speak condescendingly.

The major arguments of this character are the following (he is
answering the question whether "books, *whatever sort they be,*"[70]
"promiscuously read,"[71] do more "benefit . . . or harm"):[72]

" 'To the pure all things are pure'; . . . all kind of knowledge
whether of good or evil; the knowledge cannot defile, nor consequently the books, if the will and conscience be not defiled."[73]
". . . [Best] books to a naughty mind are not unapplicable to occasions of evil."[74] "[Bad] books . . . to a discreet and judicious reader
serve in many respects to discover, to confute, to forewarn,
and to illustrate."[75] ". . . [All] opinions, yea, errors, known, read,
and collated, are of main service and assistance toward the speedy
attainment of what is truest." God "left arbitrary the dieting and
repasting of our minds; as wherein every mature man might have
to exercise his own leading capacity."[76] God "uses not to capti-
vate under a perpetual childhood of prescription, but trusts [man]
. . . with the gift of reason to be his own chooser." ". . . [The] knowledge of good is [deeply] . . . involved and interwoven with the

arguments against posterior censorship: *e.g.,* the argument that the best and wisest
commonwealths of the past, Athens (*A.,* 7), Sparta (*A.,* 8), Rome (*A.,* 9, 10, 11, 12) had
no prior censorship ("books were as freely admitted as any other birth; no envious Juno
sat cross-legged over . . . [their] nativity . . ."). The evidence cited regarding the best
and wisest commonwealths shows that they *did* do sharp judgment on books: Athens
on writings that were either "blasphemous or atheistical"; Sparta on compositions in
a higher strain than their own soldierly ballads and roundels; Rome on "libelous books
and authors," and that which was "impiously written against their esteemed gods"
(although "not so often bad as good books were silenced"). The Christian emperors
"prohibited, or burnt" the "books of those whom they took to be grand heretics," and
interdicted "heathen authors" who wrote "plain invectives against Christianity" (*A.,*
11). Prior censorship, Milton concludes, was invented by the "most anti-christian
council and the most tyrannous inquisition that ever inquired" (*A.,* 15), by the "falsest
seducers and oppressors," and precisely to "obstruct and hinder the first approach to
reformation" (*A.,* 16), though he later accuses Plato of having invented the idea (*A.,*
33).
   [70] *A.,* 16, (italics added).
   [71] *A.,* 25.
   [72] *A.,* 16.
   [73] *A.,* 20.
   [74] *Ibid.*
   [75] *Ibid.*
   [76] *A.,* 21.

knowledge of evil . . ."[77] He that can apprehend and consider vice with all her baits and seeming pleasures, and yet abstain, and yet distinguish, and yet prefer that which is truly better, is the true wayfaring Christian."[78] And, the strongest statement of them all: "Since therefore the knowledge and survey of vice is in this world so necessary to the constituting of human virtue, and the scanning of error to the confirmation of truth, how can we more safely and with less danger scout into the regions of sin and falsity than by reading all manner of tractates, and hearing all manner of reason?"[79]

Moreover: If we start "removing" or "prohibiting" books, for fear that "infection . . . may spread," the first book to go must be the Bible, which "oftimes relates blasphemy not nicely, [and] . . . describes the carnal sense of wicked men not unelegantly . . ."[80] ". . . [Those] books . . . which are likeliest to taint both life and doctrine . . . cannot be suppressed without the fall of learning and of all ability in disputation . . ."[81] ". . . [A] wise man . . . can gather gold out of the drossiest volume, and . . . a fool will be a fool with the best book . . ."[82] So that "there is no reason . . . [to] deprive a wise man of any advantage to his wisdom, while we seek to restrain from a fool that which being restrained will be no hindrance to his folly."[83] "[Evil] manners are as perfectly learned without books a thousand other ways which cannot be stopped . . ."[84] To some men, books containing "vice and error"[85] are not "temptations nor vanities, but useful drugs and materials wherewith to temper and compose effective and strong medicines . . . The rest, as children and childish men, who have not the art to . . . prepare these working minerals, well may be *exhorted to forbear,* but hindered forcibly they cannot be . . ."[86] It is pointless to suppress books unless we are to take "equal [care] to regulate all other things of like aptness to corrupt the mind . . ."[87] "They are not skillful considerers of human things, who imagine to remove sin by removing

[77] *A.,* 23.
[78] *A.,* 24.
[79] *A.,* 25.
[80] *A.,* 26.
[81] *A.,* 29.
[82] *A.,* 30.
[83] *Ibid.*
[84] *A.,* 29.
[85] *A.,* 30.
[86] *A.,* 31 (italics added).
[87] *A.,* 34.

the matter of sin ..."[88] "... [How] much we thus expel of sin, so much we expel of virtue."[89] "Why should we then affect a rigor contrary to the manner of God and nature, by abridging or scanting those means, which books freely permitted are, both to the trial of virtue and the exercise of truth?"[90]

Why, indeed? But how then can any book ever be justly burnt, and why should church and commonwealth keep a vigilant eye on how books behave themselves, to confine and imprison and do sharpest judgment upon them? And if that last, will not church and common-wealth each need twenty imprisoners and confiners, who would be open to the same objections as twenty licensers? To which the an-swer is, we are again making the difficulties for ourselves; the intel-lectual blunder is ours, not Milton's, and in making it we are blinding ourselves to Milton's teaching, which emerges clearly enough when we cease to patronize him.

Let us, in order to clarify the matter, speak of the principle in-volved in the passages cited at the beginning of this section as the "book-burning principle," and state that principle, in the context of the foregoing arguments, as follows: There *are* good books and there *are* bad books, books that teach good and books that teach evil, books that teach truth and books that teach error. A society that denies these distinctions, which are correlative to the distinctions between good and evil and truth and falsehood themselves, *or* that, while recognizing them, denies itself the capacity to intervene when and how it sees fit to prevent the harm that bad books can on occasion do, is *no* society. Now: we start out from the fact that Milton asserts the book-burning principle, deems it axiomatic ("who denies?"), and puts it forward as an integral part of his teaching; but he in effect adds (by mentioning no machinery, and, as we have just seen, by arguing plainly that there must be none, if by machinery we mean a censor-ship), to our great surprise: But no book-burners! To which *we* reply, out of our superior wisdom: Either book-burners, or no book-burning principle; you must choose. To which Milton rejoins: I refuse to choose; I shall have the book-burning principle, and no book-burners; the connection between the two exists only in your own minds. If we

[88] *A.*, 37.
[89] *A.*, 38.
[90] *Ibid.*

have book-burners, then our society loses the benefits that bad books, properly used, can confer. If we do not have the book-burning principle, we place ourselves at the mercy of the harm that bad books, improperly used, and good ones, too, can on occasion do. Society can afford neither of these luxuries.

Anyone who steeps himself in the two sets of passages—that enunciating the book-burning principle and that which states the case against censorship—can imagine Milton's going on to say (a little impatiently, perhaps): The crucial passage for understanding my position is that in which I speak of "children and childish men," and say that "they may be exhorted to forbear, but hindered forcibly they cannot be." Now: either the "children and childish men," when they are "exhorted to forbear," *do* forbear, or they do not. If they do forbear, society will have "burnt" the book in question far more effectually than ever it would have burnt it through the good offices of any twenty book-burners,[91] and with none of the adverse effects that (as I point out) those good offices would have produced. But note that the exhorting to forbear—an exhorting by society's proper teachers to their proper pupils—presupposes the book-burning principle: an insistence upon the validity of the distinction between good and bad books, and on the necessity of taking appropriate action, on occasion, with respect to bad ones. My main point is that the appropriate action is never, or almost never, coercive; or, to put it a little differently, that the solution to the problem of how to use good and bad books lies in the channeling of both into the hands of those who will use them properly, and in the keeping of both out of the hands of those who will misuse them. As for the machinery, the healthy

---

[91]Those to whom this point seems far-fetched might set out tomorrow, anywhere in Europe, to try to purchase a copy of that book which is by common consent the *worst* book of our age, namely *Mein Kampf* (of which a few years ago there existed millions of copies). Having failed to find one, they may then ask themselves: Who did the burning, and burning of what kind?

It must be emphasized, however, that Milton's position would not exclude, or even discourage, all government intervention with the sale and distribution of literature; on the contrary. But it stands as a warning, wholesome in my view, that such intervention does not get at the real problem (the necessity for it is evidence that the proper relatedness between society's proper teachers and society's proper learners has broken down), that it is in the nature of the case clumsy and full of dangers, and in any case (as suggested by Milton's analogy) actions against books and pamphlets should be assimilated to actions against persons who have allegedly committed crimes or misdemeanors.

society, in and of itself, in virtue of its spontaneous and voluntary hierarchical relations, is itself a great machine for the continuous sifting of books and ideas, for distinguishing the good ones from the bad ones, and for "burning" the bad ones in the sense that I hope I have now made clear. Thus, to go back, if the childish men do *not* forbear, the difficulty will be found to lie in the relatedness between society's proper teachers (who must then learn to be better teachers) and society's proper pupils (who must be taught to be better-behaved).[92]

Here, then, as elsewhere, we find that when Milton's teaching coincides with modern open-society doctrines (as it certainly does with regard to coercive censorship, prior and posterior), what we have is at most a recommendation for a largely-closed society that, within itself, will and can afford to *act like an open society*, but precisely because it does not assert the opposite of the book-burning principle (the distinction between good and bad books is meaningless, society has no business taking any action with respect to bad books). It is as if Milton had anticipated, and written for, an age when the censorship issue would be torn loose from the only presuppositions[93] upon which it can be discussed.

(5) It is a society which deems itself entitled and obligated to inculcate in its members "positive" notions concerning the good and the true—that is, a society based upon "those unwritten or at least unconstraining laws of *virtuous education, religious and civil nurture,* which Plato . . . mentions as the bonds and ligaments of the commonwealth. . . ; these they be which will bear chief sway in such matters as . . . [censorship], . . . when all licensing will be easily eluded."[94] And Milton's teaching becomes: the censorship issue arises only where free society fails to discharge its educational responsibilities, which involve the converse of the book-burning principle (the insistence on the distinction between good books and bad books, and on the need for appropriate action on behalf of the teachings of the good books).

---

[92]See R. G. Collingwood, *The New Leviathan* (Oxford, 1945), *passim,* for a full discussion, in terms of an analogy between "parents" and "nursery," of the relation in question. *Cf.* again, *A.,* 87, with its reference to "teaching the people to see day."
[93]Again see *A.,* 33, for Milton's own warning that proposals in politics are inseparable from their presuppositions.
[94]*A.,* 36 (italics added.)

The Relation, if any, Between the Models
and the Generalized Teaching

It remains to inquire (1) where Milton seems to stand on the methodological issue we have posed above, and (2) whether we are entitled to ascribe to Milton any teaching whatever, with respect to freedom of thought and utterance, on the level of generality on which Mill's recommendations are projected.

(1) I hope to have shown that Milton does develop a model of the Truth-seeking process, and how different it is from (and how much more likely to commend itself to those who value Truth than) Mill's. I hope to have shown also that Milton develops, as he goes along, a model of free society, which also differs profoundly from that of Mill. I hope to have made clear, finally, the extent to which the model of free society involved in the "prevailing doctrine" is derivative from, and subordinate to, its model of the Truth-seeking process: the requirements of the Truth-seeking process, it argues, being such and such, society must be organized thus and thus, this may be done and that may not be done—the effect being, as I have indicated, to posit the pursuit of Truth, new truths especially, as free society's *summum bonum.* And we are now asking, Are the Milton models related to one another in this manner?

I find no passages in the *Areopagitica* that might support an affirmative answer to this question. Milton is indeed concerned about Truth, both the preservation and the pursuit of it; he does indeed show that the process by which Truth is preserved and expanded thrives best in the absence of formal restraints upon intellectual liberty; he does indeed argue that free society should not impose such restraints. But (as I have implied frequently above) the sequence of ideas in Milton is always the reverse of that in Mill; his thought about the character of free society is clearly prior to and independent of his thought about the preservation and pursuit of Truth; insofar as either model is subordinated to the other (which for the most part neither is, Milton's problem being precisely that of how to accommodate the two models *to one another),* it is the model of the Truth-seeking process that is subordinated to that of free society. To put it otherwise, Milton's point is always precisely that his kind of intellectual freedom will serve the *purposes of society,* especially the Reformation; and it is not too much to say that he would have made no sense of Mill's procedure at all. Concretely, he is not prepared (though on Mill's procedure he would have to be) to move from his arguments concerning intellectual freedom to a re-opening of either of the two questions the essay answers most flatly, namely: What is the status within our free society of the Reformation? (Milton's answer, in effect: It is *a public truth*, an *orthodoxy*, which free society as a matter of course places beyond question, and conceives of itself as serving.) And what is the status within free society of those who deny or flout that orthodoxy? (Milton's answer: They have no status within free society; having been "extirpate," they are not even present, and so pose no problems.) That is, it does no good to argue: Milton *should* have seen that, *e.g.*, spokesmen for "popery and open superstition" could play with respect to the "proving all things," the same role as bad books, or, *e.g.*, that all arguments for treating all questions as open questions, for proving all things, in the republic of learning,[95] are equally valid arguments for a *society* that treats all questions as open questions. This, for Milton, is to reverse the proper order of business, and misconceive the relation between the republic of learning, which like all else in free society is subordinated to certain public truths, and to free society itself.

(2) This brings us to our second remaining question, which we may now put thus: Are we to understand Milton as teaching, then, that in all societies everywhere the dominant group is entitled to proclaim its truths as the public orthodoxy, to which all things, including the republic of learning, may properly be subordinated; that just as we here in England are entitled, before we begin "proving all things" together, to eliminate all unbrotherly dissimilitudes, so, *e.g.*, in Spain the bearers of "popery and open superstition" are entitled to "extirpate" those who disagree with them on "important points"? Is Milton, like Mill, prepared—once we follow him to the deepest and most prior levels of his political thought—to assert that which we find him teaching (eliminate unbrotherly dissimilitudes, then eschew restraints on intellectual freedom) as a general prescription for organized society? The answer is, of course, in the negative (though we might conceivably extract from him a generalized teaching concerning the unprofitability of reasonable discourse among men whose differences are "vastly disproportional"). That would be to mistake

[95]Which is not to concede that Milton goes so far, even with respect to the republic of learning.

his entire animus: For the reason why "we" are entitled to extirpate Papists is that we are right and they are wrong, that God has revealed Himself to *us,* not to them, and that we must be about Our Father's business.[96] That is the context in which the problems of politics and intellectual freedom arise for Milton; and he does not pursue those problems in the *Areopagitica* beyond the point of asking what "we"[97] should do about them.[98] One feels confident, indeed, that had Milton faced the question: What should societies toward which "the love of Heaven ... is [less] propitious and propending"[99] than towards us, *do* about politics and intellectual freedom?, he would have given an answer analogous to Voltaire's about how to found a religion: First you get yourselves the Reformation. That is why all the attempts to make of Milton (who on the crucial issues is the soul of intolerance)[100] the remote source of modern doctrines of toleration and the open society,[101] must proceed by ignoring not only certain crucial passages but the very sequence of ideas in the essay, and must, like the "exploit of that gallant man who thought to pound up the crows by shutting his park gate,"[102] fail.

[96]*A., passim;* in order to document the statement we should be obliged to cite half the paragraphs in the essay.

[97]Meaning (at most) those countries that possess the Reformation.

[98]Perhaps the nearest he comes to a generalized teaching about politics is in those themes of the *Areopagitica* that have received the least attention from the critics; that is, the teaching about the book-burning principle, and that concerning the "utmost bound of freedom." But we do not easily imagine Milton recommending that the works of John Knox be burnt in Spain.

[99]*A.,* 70.

[100]We are not concerned here, of course, with the merits of the issues between Milton and those whom he would not tolerate.

[101]*Cf.* C. E. Vaughan, "Introduction," in Ernest Rhys (ed.) *Areopagitica* (London, 1927): "It has sometimes been regretted that the only one of Milton's prose works [now] widely read ... should be that which enforces a commonplace so universally accepted as that of toleration."

[102]*A.,* 29.

The Two Majorities

[Reprinted from *Midwest Journal of Political Science*, Vol. IV, No. 4, Nov., 1960, by permission of the Wayne State University Press.]

My point of departure: the tension between Executive and Legislature on the federal level of the American political system. My preliminary thesis: that the character and meaning of that tension, as also its role in the formation of American policy, has been too little examined during the period in which the tension has been at its highest; that the explanations of the tension that are, so to speak, "in the air," do not in fact explain it, but rather tend to lead us away from a correct explanation—and, by the same token, away from a correct understanding of our recent political history; that the entire matter, once we have the elements of a correct explanation in hand, opens up a rich field for investigation by our "behaviorists," hitherto unexplored because (in part at least) of the latter's lack of interest in what politics is really about.[1]

First, then, as to the character of the tension:

A. The tension between our "national" Executive and our "national" Legislature, though as suggested above it varies in "height" from time to time, and at one moment seemed to have disappeared altogether, has in recent decades been a characteristic feature of our politics.

B. The tension typically arises in the context of an attempt or expressed wish on the part of the Executive to "do" something that a majority of one or both houses is inclined to oppose. Typically, that

---

[1]This is almost, but not quite, the same point as that involved in the frequently-repeated charge that the behaviorists spend their time (and a great deal of money) studying the trivial and the obvious, a charge too often put forward by writers who are something less than ready with an answer to the question, "What *is* important?" My point is less that the reader of our behavioral literature finds himself asking, "So what?" (though indeed he does), than that he finds himself asking (to quote Professor Rogow), "What happened to the great issues?" The behaviorists go on and on as if the latter did not exist.

is to say, we have an Executive *proposal,* which now successfully, now unsuccessfully, a large number of legislators seek to disallow, either as a whole or in part.[2]

C. The tension is peculiarly associated with certain readily identifiable areas of public policy; and in these areas it is both continuing and predictable.[3] Those that come most readily to mind (we shall ask later what they have in common) are:

1. The Legislature tends to be "nervous" about "internal security." The Executive tends to become active on behalf of internal security only under insistent pressure from Congress; it (the bureaucracy probably more than the President and his official family) here tends to reflect what is regarded as enlightened opinion[4] in the universities and among the nation's intellectuals in general.

2. The Congress adheres unabashedly to the "pork barrel" practices for which it is so often denounced; it tends to equate the national interest, at least where domestic economic policies are concerned, with the totality of the interest of our four-hundred-odd congressional districts.[5] The Executive regards "pork barrel" measures as "selfish" and "particular," and does what it can, through pressure and maneuver, to forestall them; it appeals frequently to a national interest that is allegedly different from and superior to the interests of the constituencies.

3. The Legislature tends to be "protectionist" as regards external trade policy. The Executive, again reflecting what is regarded as

[2]A distinction that is indispensable for a clear grasp of the problem. We may call it the distinction between "whether to?" and "how much?" And failure to keep it in mind often results, as I shall argue below, in our seeing Executive "victories" where there are in fact Executive defeats.

[3]We shall have something to say below about what we might call the "latent but always-present tension" in certain other areas of public policy, where the Executive would like to do such and such, but because of Professor Friedrich's "law of anticipated reactions" does not dare even to formulate a "proposal." Much of what we hear about the so-called "decline" or "eclipse" or "fall" of Congress becomes less convincing when we take into account the matters in which Congress always gets it way because the Executive, much as it would *like* to do such and such, is not sufficiently romantic even to attempt it.

[4]No implication is intended, at this point, as to whether the opinion *is* enlightened, as that question is inappropriate to our immediate purposes.

[5]Cf., *The Federalist,* ed. Edward Mead Earle ("The Modern Library" [New York: Random House, n.d.]), No. 64: ". . . the government must be a weak one indeed if it should forget that the good of the whole can only be promoted by advancing the good of each of the parts or members which compose the whole." All subsequent citations to *The Federalist* are by number of the relevant paper.

enlightened opinion among intellectuals, tends to favor ever greater steps in the direction of "free trade," and acceptance by the United States of a general responsibility for the good health of the world economy.

4. The Legislature (again a similar but not identical point) tends to "drag its feet" on foreign aid programs, unless these promise a demonstrably *military* "pay-off." The Executive seems to be deeply committed to the idea of foreign aid programs as the appropriate means for gaining American objectives that are not exclusively, or even primarily, military.[6]

5. The Congress (though we must speak here with greater caution than has been necessary above because the relevant tension expresses itself in a different and less readily visible way) does not, by its actions at least, reflect what is regarded as enlightened opinion among intellectuals on the complex of issues related to the integration of the southern schools, withholding all action that might ease the Executive's path in the matter. The Executive stands ready to enforce the ruling in the Brown case, and seems unconcerned about the difficulty of pointing to any sort of popular mandate for it.

6. The Legislature insists upon perpetuating the general type of immigration policy we have had in recent decades. The Executive would apparently like to bring our immigration legislation under, so to speak, the all-men-are-created-equal clause of the Declaration of Independence.

7. The Legislature is, in general, jealous concerning the level of the national debt, and thus about government spending; it clings, in principle at least, to traditional notions about sound government finance. The Executive, at least the vast majority of the permanent civil servants (who are, as is well known, in position to bring notable pressures to bear even upon a President who would like to side with Congress), appears to have moved to what we may call a Keynesian position about the national debt and year-to-year spending.

8. The Legislature tends to be "bullish" about the size of the United States Air Force and, in general, about military expenditure as opposed to expenditures for "welfare." The Executive, though no simple statement is in order about its policies, continuously resists congressional pressure on both points.

[6]It perhaps gives to "military objectives" a wider and looser meaning than the congressmen are willing to accept.

9. The Legislature tends to be "nationalistic," that is, to be oriented to the "conscience" of its constituents rather than the "conscience of mankind." The Executive tends to be "internationally minded," that is, to subordinate its policies in many areas to certain "principles" concerning the maintenance of a certain kind of international order.

10. The Legislature appears to have no quarrel with Right-wing dictatorships; it tends to favor policies with respect to them based rather upon expediency than upon commitment to democratic forms of government. The Executive, despite the tendentious charges we often hear to the contrary, is disposed to hold governments not based upon free elections at arm's length.

11. The Executive[7] tends to favor each and every component of the current program (the product of what is generally regarded as enlightened opinion among political scientists at our universities) for transforming the American political system into a *plebiscitary* political system, capable of producing and carrying through *popular mandates*. These components, so well known as to require only the briefest mention, are: Remake our major political parties in such fashion that their programs, when laid before the American people in presidential elections, will present them with "genuine" "choices" concerning policy, and that candidates for office within each party will stand committed to their party's program. (The major public spokesmen for such a reform are the chairmen of the national committees, one of whom is of course the appointee of the President.) Get rid of the Senate filibuster, as also of the seniority principle in congressional committees (which do indeed make it possible for little bands of willful men to "frustrate" alleged majority mandates). Iron out inequalities of representation in Congress, since these, theoretically at least, are capable of substituting the will of a minority for that of the majority. (Although it is perhaps difficult to attribute any policy on the latter two components to the White House itself, anyone who has himself been a permanent civil servant knows that in the executive departments the animosity against the filibuster, the seniority principle, and the alleged "over-representation" of rural folk and white southerners is both intense and deeply-rooted.) Further assure equal representation, and thus genuine majority mandates, by enact-

[7]For the sake of simplicity of exposition, I here reverse the previous order, and speak first of the Executive.

ing ever stronger "civil rights" legislation calculated to prevent the white southerners from disfranchising or intimidating potential Negro voters, and by putting the Justice Department permanently into the business of enforcing the "strengthened" civil rights. (The extreme "proposals" here do normally originate with senators and congressmen, but it will hardly be disputed that the White House is consistently on the side of the proponents, and consistently disappointed by Congress' final reply, from session to session, to the question "How much?") "Streamline" the executive branch of government, so as to transform it into a ready and homogeneous instrument that the President, backed up by his "disciplined" majority in Congress, can use effectively in carrying out his mandate, and so as to "concentrate" power and make it more "responsible" (by getting rid of the independent agencies, and eliminating the duplication and competition between agencies that perform the same or very similar tasks). Finally, glorify and enhance the office of President, and try to make of presidential elections the central ritual of American politics—so that, even if the desired reform of the party system cannot be achieved at once, a newly-elected President with a popular majority will be able to plead, against a recalcitrant Congress, that *his* mandate must prevail.

Congress seldom shows itself available to any such line of argument, and off-year congresses like to remind presidents, in the most forceful manner possible, that the system has rituals other than that of the presidential election. For the rest, it resists the entire program with cool determination. With respect to the party system, it is clearly wedded to our traditional system of decentralized parties of a non-"ideological" and non-programmatic character. With respect to mandates, it clearly continues to regard the American system as that which, as I contend below, its Framers intended it to be—that is, one in which the final decisions upon at least the important determinations of policy are hammered out, in accordance with "the republican principle," in a deliberative assembly made up of uninstructed representatives, chosen by their neighbors because they are the "virtuous" men; thus as a system which has no place for mandates. As for the filibuster and the committee chairmen, it clearly regards as their peculiar virtue that which the Executive and its aggrandizers within the bureaucracy and out among the nation's intellectuals regard as their peculiar vice, namely, that they *are* capable of frustrating an alleged majority mandate. With respect to "streamlining" the executive branch of government, it appears to yield to proposals in this sense only when it has convinced *itself* that further resistance is an invasion of presidential prerogatives rooted in the same consitution from which it derives its own; it clearly clings to the traditional view, again that of the Framers themselves, that power should *not* be concentrated, but rather (since a most efficient Executive might well come to be the most efficient against the liberties of the people) shared out in such fashion that ambition may counter ambition. With respect to civil liberties, it clearly cherishes the notion that the Tenth Amendment has not been repealed, and that, accordingly, there is room in the American system for differences in civil liberties from state to state and even, within a state, for differences in civil liberties from differently situated person to differently situated person. With respect to the aggrandizement of the office of president and the glorification of presidential elections, it again takes its stand with the tradition and the Framers: there is no room in the American system for a presidential office so aggrandized as to be able itself to determine how much farther the aggrandizement shall go; the ultimate decisions on that point must be made not by the President but by *itself,* in the course of the continuing dialectic between its members and their constituents; plebiscitary presidential elections cannot become the central ritual of our system without destroying the system.

II

What general statements—of a sort that might throw light on their meaning in the American political system—may we venture to make about these areas of tension?[8]

---

[8]I do not forget that the areas of tension are also areas of tension *within* both houses of Congress, where the Executive always, when the big issues are "up," has considerable support, and sometimes "wins" (or at least seems to). It would be interesting, though not relevant to the purposes of the present paper, to study the incidence of the tensions within Congress (as revealed, e.g., in voting, about which we have a rich and growing literature), particularly with a view to discovering whether there is a discernible "trend" in this regard. As also whether there is any relation, of the kind my analysis below would lead us to expect, between the character of an M. C.'s constituency and the "side" he takes in these matters. One imagines that the tensions are also repeated within the bosom of the Executive. But we must not get in the habit of permitting our sophistication about such matters to obscure for us the fact that "Congress" acts finally as *an* institution, whose "behavior" as an institution can and for some purposes must be observed without regard to its internal divisions.

At least, I believe these:

A. They all involve matters of policy which, by comparison with those involved in areas where tension is *not* evident and predictable, bear very nearly indeed upon the central destiny of the United States —on the kind of society it is going to become ("open" or relatively "closed," egalitarian and redistributive or shot through and through with great differences in reward and privilege, a "welfare state" society or a "capitalist" society); on the form of government the United States is to have (much the same as that intended by the Framers, or one tailored to the specifications of democratic ideology); or on our relatedness to the outside world on points that, we are often told, nearly affect the central destiny of mankind itself. They are all areas, therefore, in which we should *expect* disagreement and thus tension in a heterogeneous society like ours (though by no means necessarily, I hasten to add, tension between its Legislature and its Executive—not, at least, for any reason that leaps readily to the eye).

B. They are areas in which the Executive (as I have already intimated) is able, with good show of reason, to put itself forward on any particular issue as the spokesman for either *lofty and enlightened principle* or still undiffused professional *expertise,* or both. The Executive tends, that is to say, to have the nation's ministers and publicists with it on "peace," the nation's professors and moralizers with it on desegregation, the nation's economists with it on fiscal policy and redistribution, the nation's political scientists with it on political reform and civil rights, etc. To put it otherwise, Congress at least *appears,* in all the areas in question, to be holding out for either the repudiation or evasion of the moral imperatives that the nation's proper teachers urge upon us, or the assertion of an invincibly ignorant "layman's" opinion on topics that are demonstrably "professional" or "expert" in character, or both. The Executive is *for* world government, *for* the outlawing of war, *for* unselfishness in our relations with the outside world, *for* the brotherhood of man, *for* majority-rule, *for* progress, *for* generosity toward the weak and lowly, *for* freedom of thought and speech, *for* equality, *for* the spreading of the benefits of modern civilization to "underdeveloped" lands, *for* science and the "scientific outlook," *for* civil rights; apparently it is its being *for* these things that somehow runs it afoul of Congress in the areas in question; and it is difficult to avoid the impression that

Congress is somehow *against* these things, and against them because wedded to bigotry, to selfishness both at home and abroad, to oppression, to the use of force, to minority rule, to outmoded notions in science. Because the Executive so clearly represents high principle and knowledge, the conclusion is well nigh irresistible that Congress represents low principle (or, *qui est pire,* no principle at all), reaction, and unintelligence, and does so in full knowledge that the President (both he and his opponent having, in the latest election, asserted the same high principles and the same generally enlightened outlook)[9] has not merely a majority mandate but a virtually unanimous mandate to go ahead and act upon high principle.

C. They are areas that, for the most part, do not lend themselves to what is fashionably called "polyarchical bargaining." For example, the internal security policies that Congress has in recent years imposed upon the Executive have been in no sense the result of protracted negotiations among groups, conducted with an eye to leaving no group too unhappy; so, too, with the policy that it imposes (by inaction) with regard to the desegregation of the southern schools, and that which it imposes (by action) concerning immigration and the armed forces. To put it otherwise, the policy problems involved are by their very nature problems about which everybody can't have a little bit of his way, because either we move in *this* direction (which some of us want to do) or in *that* direction (which others of us want to do); and the line Congress takes with respect to them seems to be determined much as, before Bentley and Herring and Truman and Latham and Dahl, we fondly supposed all policy lines to be determined—that is, by the *judgment* of individuals obliged to choose between more or less clearly understood *alternatives,* and obliged ultimately to choose in terms of such notions as they may have of justice and the public weal.

D. They are areas—though we come now to a more delicate kind of point—in which, little as we may like to think so and however infrequently we may admit it to ourselves, Congress pretty consistently gets its way; indeed the widespread impression to the contrary seems to me the strangest optical illusion of our politics, and worth dwelling upon for a moment: the question actually at issue becomes, quite simply, whether in recent decades (since, say, 1933) the "liber-

[9]See below, pp. 342-44.

als"—for, as intimated repeatedly above, the tension between Executive and Legislature is normally a liberal-conservative tension—have or have not been "winning"; and I contend that the reason both liberals and conservatives tend (as they do) to answer that question in the affirmative is that we are all in the habit of leaving out of account two dimensions of the problem that are indispensable to clear thinking about it, and that we may express as follows:

First, we cannot answer the question without somehow "ranking" political issues in order of "importance"—without, for example, distinguishing at least between those issues that are "most important," those that are "important" but not most important, those that are "relatively unimportant," and those that are "not important at all"—meaning here by "important" and "unimportant" merely that which the liberals and conservatives themselves deem important or unimportant. In the context of such a ranking we readily see that "winning" in our politics is a matter of getting your way on the matters that are most important to you, not getting defeated too often on those that are merely important to you, and taking your big defeats on those that are relatively unimportant to you or not important at all. Take for instance that liberal "victory" of the period in question that comes most readily to mind: the creation and maintenance of the Tennessee Valley Authority. Everyone familiar with the politics of the period knows that the TVA enthusiasts intended TVA to be the first of a *series* of "authorities," which would have the effect of shifting the entire American economy away from "capitalism" and "free private enterprise." That was what the liberals wanted, and that was what the conservatives, if they meant business, had to prevent; that was what was "most important," against the background of which the creation and maintenance of a single TVA (one, moreover, that men could support out of no animus whatever against private enterprise) was at most "unimportant"; and, once we put the question, "Who won?" in *those* terms, and remind ourselves where the White House and the bureaucracy stood, we are obliged to give an answer quite different from that which we are in the habit of giving: The Executive got its TVA in particular, but Congress put a stop to TVA's in general (nor is there any issue so dead in America today as that of "socialism").

Secondly, there is the dimension we have mentioned briefly above, that of the things that the Executive would like to propose but has the good sense not to because of its certain foreknowledge of the impossibility of getting the proposals through Congress, it being here that Congress *most* consistently gets its way, and without anyone's noticing it.[10] James Burnham is quite right in arguing that the capacity to say "No" to the Executive is the essence of congressional power;[11] but he exaggerates the infrequency with which Congress does say "No," partly by ignoring the "No's" that Congress does not have to say for the reason just given, and partly by failing to distinguish between the "No's" that are "most important" to the Congress itself and those that are not.

To summarize: The areas of tension are typically "most important" areas in which this or that application of high principle desired by the Executive gets short shrift from enough congressmen and senators to prevent it, or at least to prevent it on anything like the *scale* desired by the Executive. And in these areas the Congress normally "wins," "high principle" seemingly going by the board. Nor would it be easy to show—and thus brings us to the nub of the matter—that the tensions are less acute, or produce a notably different result, during the two-year periods that *precede* presidential elections than during the two-year periods that *follow* them, which if it were true might enable us to argue that the tensions arise because of *shifts* of opinion in the electorate; or that they relate particularly to the two-thirds of the senators who, after any biennial election, are "hold-overs." And, that being the case, we are obliged, as I have already intimated, to confront an unexplained mystery of our politics, namely: the fact that *one and the same electorate maintains in Washington, year after year, a President devoted to high principle and enlightenment, and a Congress that gives short shrift to both;* that, even at one and the same election, they elect to the White House a man devoted to the application of high principle to most important

---

[10]Let anyone who doubts the point (a) poll his liberal acquaintances on the question, is it proper for non-believers in America to be taxed for the support of churches and synagogues (which they certainly are so long as churches and synagogues are exempted from taxation)? and, (b) ask himself what would happen in Congress if the Treasury Department were to propose removal of the exemption. There is no greater symbol of Executive-Legislative tension than the fact that the sessions of both houses open with prayer, whereas we cannot imagine a prayer at the beginning of a meeting of, say, an interdepartmental committee of bureaucrats.

[11]Cf., James Burnham, *Congress and the American Tradition* (Chicago: Henry Regnery Co., 1959), p. 278.

problems of national policy, and to the Hill men who consistently frustrate him. More concretely: the voters give an apparent majority mandate to the president to apply principles "x, y, and z," and a simultaneous (demonstrable) majority-mandate[12] to the Congress to keep him from applying them. And the question arises, why, at the end of a newly-elected President's first two years, do the voters not "punish" the congressmen? Are the voters simply "irrational"? Our political science has, it seems to me, no adequate or convincing answer to these (and many kindred) questions.

III

What *is* "in the air" in American political science (to return now to the hint thrown out above) because of which my statement of the problem of executive-legislative tension sounds unfamiliar—not to say "against the grain"? Not, I think, any doctrines that clash head-on with such a statement on the ground that it appears to move in a direction that might be "pro-Congress"; that would be true only if contemporary American political science were "anti-Congress," which, I, for one, do not believe to be the case[13] (besides which the statement is *not*, up to this point, "pro-Congress"). Not either, I think, any specific doctrine or doctrines concerning executive-legislative tensions as such; for though contemporary American political science is certainly not unaware of the tensions (it might, at most, be accused of sweeping them now and then under the rug, contrary to the rules of tidy housekeeping), it seems safe to say that there is no prevailing "theory" of the problem. The answer to our question lies rather, I believe, in this: there are *overtones* in the statement, perhaps even *implications*, that simply do not "fit in" with what we are accustomed, these days, to say or assume, and hear others say and assume, not about legislative-executive tensions, but about some very different matters, namely, elections, majority rule, and the comparative "representativeness," from the standpoint of "democratic theory," of the Executive and the Legislature. And perhaps the best way to bring the relevant issues out into the open is to fix attention on what we *are* accustomed to hear said and assumed about these matters.

[12]Unless we want to argue that Congress does *not* have a majority mandate. See below my reasons for thinking such a position untenable.

[13]There is, of course, an "anti-Congress" literature, but there is also an enormous literature that is friendly to Congress.

I propose to use for this purpose Robert A. Dahl's celebrated Walgreen lectures,[14] which precisely because they are *not* "anti-Congress" (are, rather, the handiwork of one of our major and most dispassionate experts on Congress) have the more to teach us about the problem in hand. The lectures seem to me to show that we are accustomed now to assume (if not to say), and to hear it assumed, that when we speak of "democratic theory," of majority rule in the United States, we can for the most part simply ignore Congress and congressional elections. This is nowhere *asserted* in the *Preface*, but I submit to anyone familiar with it *both* that such a tacit premise is present throughout its argument, which goes on and on as if our presidential elections were not merely the *central* ritual of our politics but also the *sole* ritual, and that Dahl's procedure in the matter seems, in the present atmosphere, perfectly natural.

But let us think for a moment about that tacit premise, and the resultant tacit exclusion of executive-legislative tension as a problem for democratic theory (Dahl, I think I am safe in saying, nowhere in the *Preface* refers to it).[15] To put the premise a little differently: the majority-rule problem in America *is* the problem of the presidential elections; either the majority rules through the presidential elections (which Dahl thinks it does not), or it does not rule at all; a book about majority rule in America does not, in consequence, need to concern itself at any point with the possibility that fascinated the authors of *The Federalist*, namely, that of the "republican principle" as working precisely through the election of members to the two houses of Congress. And the *effect* of that premise, whether intended or not, is to deny legitimacy, from the standpoint of "democratic theory," alike to Congress as a formulator of policy, and to the elections that produce Congress as expressions of majority "preferences"; that is, to deny the relevance of those elections to the problem to which the authors of *The Federalist* regarded them as *most* relevant, i. e., the problem of majority rule in America.[16] Nor is the reason for the

[14]Robert A. Dahl, *Preface to Democratic Theory* (Chicago: University of Chicago Press, 1956).

[15]The function of his Congress, in the *Preface* anyhow, is that of "legitimizing basic decisions by some process of *assent*" (italics added), and of registering pressures in the process he likes to call "polyarchical bargaining." See respectively pp. 136, 145.

[16]Cf., *The Federalist*, No. 54: "Under the proposed Constitution, the federal acts ... will depend merely on the majority of votes in the federal legislature. ..." Cf., No. 21: "The natural cure for an ill-administration, in a popular or representative constitution, is a change of men"—through, of course, elections. Cf. also No. 44: If Congress

premise difficult to discover: for Dahl, and for the atmosphere of
which his book may fairly be regarded as an accurate summary,
Congress, especially the lower house, is a stronghold of entrenched
minorities,[17] and in any case is, and was always intended to be, a
barrier to majority rule, not an *instrument* of majority rule.[18] It is
bicameral; its members are chosen in elections deliberately staggered to prevent waves of popular enthusiasm from transmitting
themselves directly to its floors; it "overrepresents" rural and agricultural areas and interests; many of its members are elected in constituencies where civil liberties, including even the liberty to vote, are
poorly protected, so that the fortunate candidate can often speak
only for a minority of his constituents; and as the decades have
passed it has developed internal procedures—especially the filibuster and the seniority principle in the choice of committee chairman—that frequently operate to defeat the will of the majority even
of its own members;[19] it reflects, in a word, the anti-democratic,
anti-majority-rule bias of the Framers, who notoriously distrusted
human nature (because of their commitment to certain psychological
axioms).[20]

Now the doctrine just summarized is so deeply imbedded in our
literature that it may seem an act of perversity to try, at this late a
moment, to call it into question (as the overtones and implications of
my discussion in I and II certainly do). The present writer is convinced, however, that a whole series of misunderstandings,[21] partly
about the Framers and partly about majority rule, have crept into our
thinking about the matter, and that these have disposed us to beg a
number of questions that it is high time we reopened. The Framers,
we are being told, distrusted the "people," cherished a profound
animus against majority rule, and were careful to write "barriers" to
majority rule into their constitution. But here, as it seems to me, the

were to ". . . misconstrue or enlarge any . . . power vested in them . . . in the last resort
a remedy must be obtained from the people, who can, by the election [in elections
where the candidate who gets the largest number of votes wins?] of more faithful
representatives, annul the acts of the usurpers."

[17]Dahl, *op. cit.*, p. 142.

[18]*Ibid.*, p. 14. I am sure Professor Dahl will not object to my mentioning that the
point about civil liberties, although not present in his book, he has pressed upon me
in private conversation.

[19]*Ibid.*, p. 15.

[20]*Ibid.*, p. 8.

[21]To which I must plead myself guilty of having contributed, particularly in my *John
Locke and the Doctrine of Majority-Rule* (Urbana: University of Illinois Press, 1941).

following peculiar thing has happened. Taught as we are by decades of political theory whose creators have been increasingly committed to the idea of majority mandates arising out of plebiscitary elections, we tend to forget that that alternative, not having been invented yet, was *not* in the mind of the Framers at all; which is to say, we end up accusing the Framers of trying to prevent something they had never even heard of,[22] and so cut ourselves off from the possibility of understanding their intention. Above all we forget that what the Framers (let us follow the fashion and accept *The Federalist* as a good enough place to go to find out what they thought) were above all concerned to prevent was the *states'* going their separate ways, their becoming an "infinity of little, jealous, clashing, tumultuous commonwealths,"[23] so that there would *be* no union in which the question of majority rule could arise. The "majority rule" they feared was the unlimited majority rule within the several states that would, they thought, result from disintegration of the union; and we are misreading most of the relevant passages if we read them in any other sense. We take an even greater liberty, moreover, when we sire off on the Framers the (largely uncriticized) premise that the proper remedy for the evils of some form of majority rule is as a matter of course non-majoritarian. No one knew better than they that the claim of the majority to have its way in a "republican" (or "free") government cannot be successfully denied;[24] indeed what most amazes one upon rereading *The Federalist,* in the context of the literature with which we have been deluged since J. Allen Smith, is precisely the degree of their *commitment* to the majority principle,[25] and their respect and affection for

[22]This is not to deny that the "barriers" do, as it turns out, operate to prevent a plebiscitary system. My point is they were not, and could not, have been intended to, but also that a plebiscitary system is not the only possible majority-rule system.

[23]*The Federalist,* No. 9.

[24]Cf., *ibid.,* No. 58: ". . . the fundamental principle of free government would be reversed. It would no longer be the majority that would rule. . . ." Cf., No. 22, with its reference to the fundamental maxim of republican government as being: that the "sense of the majority shall prevail." Cf., *ibid.:* ". . . two thirds of the people of America could not long be persuaded . . . to submit their interests to the management and disposal of one third." Compare Dahl, *op. cit.,* pp. 34, 35, where after citing various strong pro-majority-rule statements, from political philosophers, he concludes that they are all "clearly at odds with the Madisonian view." Note that one of the statements, curiously, is from Jefferson, whom Dahl immediately describes as a "Madisonian."

[25]See preceding note. The point has been obscured by our habit of reading the numerous passages that insist on ultimate control by the "people" on the assumption, impossible in my opinion to document, that the authors of *The Federalist* thought they

the "people" whose political problem they were attempting to "solve."[26] Their concern, throughout, is that of *achieving* popular control over government, not that of *preventing* it.[27] That they thought to do by leaving the "people" of the new nation organized in a particular way,[28] that is, in constituencies which would return senators and congressmen, and by inculcating in that people a constitutional morality that would make of the relevant elections a quest for the "virtuous" men[29]—the latter to come to the capital, normally, without "instructions" (in the sense of that term—not the only possible sense—that we are most familiar with). These virtuous men were to *deliberate* about such problems as seemed to them to require attention and, off at the end, make decisions by majority vote; and, as *The Federalist* necessarily conceived it, the majority votes so arrived at would, because each of the virtuous men would have behind him a majority vote back in his constituency, represent a popular majority. (My guess, based on long meditation about the relevant passages, is that they hoped the deliberation would be of such character that the votes would seldom be "close," so that the popular majority represented would be overwhelming.) That, with one exception, is the only federal popular majority of which Madison and Hamilton were thinking—the exception being the popular majority bent on taking steps adverse to natural rights,[30] that is, to justice.

had discovered some way to have matters decided by the people in elections, *without* having them decided by a majority of the people. See following note.

[26]Cf., *ibid.*, No. 14: "I submit to you, my fellow-citizens, these considerations, in full confidence that the good sense which has so often marked your decisions will allow them due weight and effect. . . . Hearken not to the unnatural voice which tells you that the people of America . . . can no longer continue the mutual guardians of their mutual happiness. . . . Is it not the glory of the people of America [that they have heeded] . . . the suggestions of their own good sense, the knowledge of their own situation, and the lessons of their own experience?" Such passages abound in *The Federalist.*

[27]Cf., *ibid.*, No. 40: ". . . the Constitution . . . ought . . . to be embraced, if it be calculated to accomplish the views and happiness of the people of America." Cf., No. 46: ". . . the ultimate authority . . . resides in the people alone. . . ."

[28]Cf., *ibid.*, No. 39: "Were the people regarded . . . as forming one nation, the will of the *majority of the whole people* . . . would bind the majority . . . and the will of the majority must be determined either by a comparison of the individual votes, or by considering the will of the majority of the States. . . . Neither of these rules has been adopted." (Italics added).

[29]Cf., *ibid.*, No. 57. The chosen are to be those "whose merit may recommend [them] to . . . esteem and confidence. . . . Cf., No. 64, with its reference to assemblies made up of "the most enlightened and respectable citizens" who will elect people "distinguished by their abilities and virtue. . . ."

[30]*I.e.*, a majority "faction." See *ibid.*, No. 10, *passim.*

What they seem to have been thinking of here, however, and took measures (though not drastic ones)[31] to prevent, was precisely *not,* I repeat, an electoral majority acting through a plebiscitarily-chosen president, but rather a demagogically-led movement that might sweep through the constituencies and bring pressure to bear upon the congressmen; nor must we permit our own emancipation, because of which we know that the difference between unjust steps and just ones is merely a matter of opinion, to blind us to the implied distinction between a popular majority as such and a popular majority determined to commit an injustice. Madison and Hamilton not only thought they knew what they meant, but *did* know what they meant, when they used such language;[32] and we err greatly when we confuse their animus against the popular majority bent on injustice with an animus against the popular majority, the majority of the people, as such.

Ah, someone will object, but you have conceded that the measures they took operate equally against both; the Framers, that is to say, made it just as difficult for a popular majority as such, even a popular majority bent upon *just* measures, to capture the Congress, and use it for its purposes, as for an "unjust" majority. But here again we must hold things in their proper perspective—by keeping ourselves reminded that Madison did not think the measures we have in mind (staggered elections and bicameralism in particular) would constitute much of a barrier to either. As Dahl himself points out, Madison placed his sole reliance against the popular movement that snowballs through the constituencies in the hope that the constituencies would, because of the growth and development of the nation, become so numerous, so widely flung, and so diverse as to make it impossible to bring people together into the kind of popular movement he feared, which is one point. But there are several other dimensions to the thought implicit in *The Federalist* on this matter. There is, first, the constitutional morality suggested in the doctrine concerning the vir-

---

[31] Indeed, Madison clearly believed *(ibid.)* that nothing could be done *constitutionally* to block a majority "faction."

[32] That is, when they distinguished between just and unjust, and measures adverse to the rights of others and measures not adverse to them. Cf., *ibid.:* ". . . measures are too often decided, not according to the rules of justice and the rights of the minor party, but by the superior force of an interested and overbearing majority." Cf., Dahl, *op. cit.,* p. 29, where he illustrates the gulf between himself and the Madisonians by writing "good" and "bad," the implication being, I take it, that the distinction is operationally meaningless.

tuous men; these being, by definition, men bent upon justice, constituency elections turning upon the identification of virtuous men would, on the face of them, constitute a major barrier to a popular movement bent upon injustice,[33] *but not to a widespread popular movement demanding something just.*[34] There is, second, the fact that the constitution, being a constitution that limits governmental power, might fairly be expected to bear more heavily upon the prospects of an unjust movement, which as Madison must have known is of the two the more likely to run afoul of the relevant limitations, than on a just one. And there is, thirdly, the fact that so long as the system works as Madison intended it to, bicameralism and staggered elections themselves might be expected to bear more heavily upon an unjust movement than upon a just one: they constitute a "barrier," as far as Congress is concerned, only to the extent that the hold-over senators and the congressmen from constituencies not yet captured by the spreading popular movement *resist* the relevant popular pressures—which they are most likely to do by *debate* in the course of deliberation, and can do most effectively precisely when they are able to wrap themselves in the mantle of justice (which by definition they cannot do if the popular movement is itself bent upon justice). In fine: once we grant the distinction between a popular majority in the constituencies bent upon injustice and a popular movement bent upon something just, grant it with all the literalness with which it was intended, there remains no reason to attribute to Madison, or to the constitution he defended, any animus against popular majorities (as such) having their way. He simply wanted, I repeat, the majority to be articulated and counted in a certain way, and had confidence that so long as it was it would produce just results. And we must, if we are to bring the whole problem into proper focus, recognize that the Madisonian majority, articulated through and counted within the constituencies, is still present in the American political system; which is to say that we must learn to think in terms of what we may call *two* popular majorities, the congressional and the presidential, and that we must accept, as an unavoidable problem for American politi-

---

[33]Cf., *ibid.*, No. 51: "... a coalition of a majority ... could seldom take place [except on] principles ... of justice and the general good."

[34]Cf., *ibid.*, No. 57, where it is argued that a political constitution should aim at obtaining for "rulers men who possess most wisdom to discern, and most virtue to pursue, the common good of the society"—and taking the "most effectual precautions for keeping them virtuous. ..."

cal theory, the problem of the respective merits of the two (and must not, like Professor Dahl, talk as if one of them did not exist). What is at stake when there is tension between Congress and President is *not* the majority principle (the "Rule," Dahl calls it), but rather the question of where and how we are to apply it.

IV

What we are always dealing with in the American system is, on the present showing, Two Majorities, two *numerical* majorities,[35] *each* of which can, by pointing to the Rule, claim what Dahl calls the "last say," and each of which merits the attention of that part of "democratic theory" that deals with the problem of majority rule. The moment this is conceded, moreover, the problem of executive-legislative tensions begins to appear in the light in which it is presented above.

As for the merits of the respective claims of the two majorities, I content myself here with the following observations:

A. One of the two majorities, the presidential, has (as I have intimated) been *engrafted* on our political system: it was not intended by the Framers, not even present to their minds as something to be "frustrated" and have "barriers" put in its way. It is, in other words, insofar as we can satisfy ourselves that it exists *qua* majority and eventuates in "mandates," something new in our politics, something therefore whose appropriateness to the spirit and machinery of our system may fairly be regarded as still open to question. (I hope I shall not be understood to mean that its newness necessarily establishes a presumption against it.)

B. Professor Dahl, for all his fascination with presidential elections, is himself the author of the most brilliant demonstration we have (or could ask for) that nothing properly describable as a majority mandate, sanctioned by the Rule, emerges from a presidential election.[36] Indeed, one way of stating the question concerning the merits of the respective claims of the two majorities is, Is the congressional majority open to the same objections, from the standpoint of the

---

[35]But cf., Burnham, *op. cit.,* p. 316 (and the preceding discussion) for a different view of the two majorities. Burnham, of course, follows Calhoun.

[36]Dahl, *op. cit.,* pp. 124-131.

Rule, that Dahl brings so tellingly against the presidential? If not, we should be obliged to view with suspicion Dahl's contention that, there *being* no majority in America, the majority cannot rule (so that we can stop worrying about majority tyranny).[37]

C. It is interesting to notice some of the claims that Madison (were we, like Professor Dahl, to go so to speak to his assistance) might be imagined as making for *his* majority "mandate" that, as Dahl demonstrates, cannot be made for the side that gets the more votes in a presidential election:

1. It does not stand or fall with the possibility of proving that the voters who are its ultimate sanction voted for the same man because they endorse the same policies; the other, as Dahl admirably shows, does.[38] It is *heterogeneous* by definition, and is supposed to be, was intended to be, heterogeneous; it cannot, indeed, accomplish without being heterogeneous its intended purpose, which is the ultimate arriving at policy decisions through a process of deliberation among virtuous men representing potentially conflicting and in any case different "values" and interests.

2. It is at least potentially *continuous* in its relation to the voters, whereas, as Dahl shows, the presidential sanction is *discontinuous*[39] (his majority speaks, insofar as it speaks at all, then promptly disappears), and potentially therefore *simultaneous* with the policy decisions in which it eventuates. Indeed, the major difference between Madison and Dahl as theorists of majority-rule is precisely that Dahl clearly cannot, or at least does not, imagine a popular majority-rule system as working through any process other than that of elections, which, as he himself sees, are in the nature of the case discontinuous and prior to actual policy decisions. Madison, on the other hand, is not in the first place all that preoccupied with elections, and ends up describing a majority-rule process rich in possibilities (as we all know) for what we may, with Burnham, call a continuing dialectical relationship between the virtuous men and their constituents, though

[37] *Ibid.*, p. 25, and Chap. V, *passim.* It might be pointed out that Dahl has difficulty deciding just how to phrase the point; "rarely, if ever," does not say the same thing as "rarely," and "ruling on matters of specific policy" does not say the same thing as "ruling."
[38] *Ibid.*, pp. 127-129.
[39] *Ibid.*, p. 130.

one which by no means necessarily takes the form of the member of Congress "keeping his ear to the ground" and seeking to carry out automatically the "will" of a majority of his constituents; he is himself a part *of* his constituency, potentially "representative" in the special sense of reacting to policy problems just as his constituents *would* were they present, and also informed (which, of course, they often are not); besides which the dialectic, as Madison could hardly have failed to realize, may take the form of actually *thinking* with them, whether by communication back and forth or in the course of visits back home.[40] Finally, as again Madison certainly knew, the member of Congress will, if normally ambitious, wish to be reelected, and will not willingly become a party to policy decisions that, when they come to the attention of his constituents, will seem to them foolish or outrageous; which means that he must ask himself continuously how at least his general course of behavior is *ultimately* going to go down at home.

3. In two senses, it does not need to be, and Madison did not expect it to be, "positive" in the way that a writer like Dahl assumes a mandate must be if it is to be really a mandate.[41] First, it is as likely to express itself in prohibitions and "vetoes" as in imperatives. And second, the popular command involved is basically, as Madison conceived it, a command to help produce *just* policy decisions in a certain manner, and normally does not presuppose a positive mandatory relation with respect to particular matters.

4. It is a mandate that emerges from a process that was always intended to emphasize specifically *moral* considerations, e.g., the kind of considerations involved in deciding who are the virtuous men. To put the point otherwise: it is a process that was originally conceived in terms of a moral theory of politics, where the theorists of the presidential mandate tend, to say the least, to a certain relativism about morals (which is why they can end up insisting that this and this must be done because the majority demands it *tout court*). Its emphasis, therefore, is on the ability of the people, i.e., at least a majority of the people, to make sound judgments regarding the virtue

---

[40]The essence of *Federalist* thought here is that of a "deliberate sense of the community" (meaning by community, surely, not less than a majority?) formed as problems arise and get themselves discussed in the Congress and out over the nation, and by no means necessarily expressing itself always through elections.

[41]*Ibid.*, pp. 129, 131.

of their neighbors, not on the ability of the people to deliberate on matters of policy. (Dahl leaves us in no doubt about its inability to do the latter.)

V

The above considerations seem to me not only to throw light on the respective claims of the Two Majorities, but also to show why (assuming that the older of the two continues to function much as Madison intended it to, which I do believe to be the case) we have no cause to be astonished at the fact of executive-legislative tension in our system: since there is no reason *a priori* to expect the virtuous men to be attracted as a matter of course to the proposals put forward by the Executive (with whatever claim to a "majority mandate" for them); at least, that is to say, we see how such tension *might* occur. But there are some further considerations that seem to me to show why it *must* occur, and at the same time to throw light on how each of us should go about making up his mind as to which of the two to support. These are:

A. The essentially *aristocratic* character of the electoral process that produces the older of the majorities as over against the essentially *democratic* character of the electoral process that produces the newer (despite the fact that the electors are in the two cases the same men and women). A moment's reflection will reveal at least one reason for that aristocratic character: although the constituencies and states differ greatly in this regard, they all nevertheless approximate, in a way in which the national constituency cannot do, to *structured communities,* involving more or less endless series of face-to-face hierarchical relations among individuals—of superordination and subordination, of capacity to influence or subject to pressure and susceptibility to being influenced or subjected to pressure, of authority and obedience, of economic power and economic dependence, of prestige enjoyed and respect tendered, etc., that are patently relevant to the choice of a congressman or senator in a way that they are not relevant to the choice of a president. In the election of the member of Congress, a community faithful to the constitutional morality of *The Federalist* makes a decision about whom to send forward as its most virtuous man, a decision which is the more important, and which it accordingly takes the more seriously, because the community knows that it can have little effect on a presidential election (i.e., its most direct means of defending its own interests and "values" is by sending the right senator or representative to Washington, and sending the right one becomes therefore a matter of sending a man who will represent the hierarchical relations in which those interests and values are articulated). In the congressional election, therefore, the "heat" can and will go on, if there is a powerful community "value" or interest at stake in the choice among available candidates; so that although the voters vote as nominal "equals" (one man, one vote) they do so under pressures that are quite unlikely to be brought to bear on their "equal" voting for President (especially as the powerful and influential in the community are normally unable to estimate accurately, for reasons we shall notice below, the probable impact of the presidential candidates upon their interests and "values," whereas they *can* do so with the candidates for the legislature). This state of affairs is reflected in the notorious fact that congressmen and senators, when they phone home to consult, are more likely, other things being equal, to phone bank presidents than plumbers, bishops than deacons, editors than rank-and-file newspaper readers, school superintendents than schoolmarms—and would be very foolish if they were not more likely to. And the unavoidable result is that the men chosen are likely to be far more "conservative," far more dedicated to the "status quo," than the candidate whom the same community on the same day helps elect President (or, to anticipate, than the candidate whom the same community on the same day helps defeat for President); and the chances of their disagreeing with that candidate a few months later on "most important" and "important" questions are, on the face of it, excellent. So that we have at least one built-in reason for *expecting* executive-legislative tension.

B. The difference in the discussion process as we see it go forward in the constituencies and the discussion process as we see it go forward in the national forum. This is partly a matter of the point just made (that the constituency is to a far greater extent a structured community), and partly a matter (not quite the same thing) of the sheer difference in *size* between the local constituency and the nation—or, as I should prefer to put it, of the kind of considerations that led that remarkable "empirical" political theorist, J.-J. Rousseau, to declare, at a crucial point in *Du contrat social,* that there is more wisdom in small bands of Swiss peasants gathered around oak trees to conduct their affairs than, so to speak, in all the governments of Europe. One of the questions that that sentence necessarily poses, when we examine it carefully, and that which leads on to what I believe to be a correct interpretation of it, is whether it intends a tribute (which the attribution of wisdom certainly was for Rousseau), (1) to the Swiss, or (2) to peasants, or (3) to peasants who are also Swiss, or (4) to small groups of persons caught up in a certain kind of discussion situation. The context, I suggest, leaves no doubt that the correct answer here is (4): Rousseau certainly thought highly of the Swiss, but not so highly as to claim any sort of monopoly of wisdom for them; he also thought highly of peasants, because of their simplicity of life (if you like—which I don't—because of their closer approximation to the "noble savage"), but precisely *not* because of their native wisdom in the sense intended here, which evidently has to do with wise decisions concerning public affairs; by the same token, as we know from the *Julie,* he thought highly of Swiss peasants in particular, but not so highly as to permit himself the claim that the small bands, merely *because* made up of Swiss peasants, are the repositories of wisdom. The emphasis, in other words, is upon the "small bands," the fact that each embraces only a *small number* of individuals, and on the fact of that small number being gathered to dispatch the public business of a small community—the Swiss peasants and the oak tree being simply the symbol, the example, that comes most readily to Rousseau's mind. So we are led on to ask, what difference or differences does Rousseau think he sees between their "deliberation" and other kinds of deliberation? We can, I think, answer with some confidence. First, there is a presumption that each small band is talking about *something,* not *nothing.* Second, there is a presumption, because of each band's relatedness to the community whose affairs it is dispatching, that its members are reasonably well-informed about the *something* they are talking about—the implication being (it is caught up and developed in the *Government of Poland*) that, as a discussion group increases in number and a constituency in size, there is greater and greater danger that the persons concerned will find themselves talking about *nothing,* not *something,* and will also find themselves talking about situations and problems that are too large, too complicated, for them to understand. Wise deliberation—the point recurs again and again in Rousseau's political writings—occurs only where people are discussing problems that they can, so to speak, "get outside of," and where the participants in the discussion are not so numerous as to give scope to the gifts of the orator and the rhetorician.

Now: evidently a congressional or senatorial constituency is *not* a small band gathered around an oak tree; but also nothing can be more certain than that the national constituency in America long ago became so large and complex that, even were there candidates who themselves understood it (which is doubtful), the audiences to which they must address themselves do not understand it, cannot even visualize it. Yet we have engrafted upon our constitution an additional electoral process that *forces* discussion of "national" problems in the national constituency; that obliges candidates to "go to the people" and court votes; and that, for the reason just mentioned, makes it necessary for them to avoid talking about something and leaves them no alternative but to talk about nothing—that is (for this is always the most convenient way of talking about nothing), to talk about high—or at least high-sounding—principle, without application to any concrete situation or problem. Add to this the fact that the candidates, hard put to it to produce in a few weeks enough speeches to see them through the campaign, must enlist the assistance of speech-writers, who come as a matter of course from the intellectual community we have frequently mentioned above, and things—*inter alia,* the sheer impossibility of saying, after a presidential election, what "issues" it has decided—begin to fall into place. There are no issues, because both candidates for the most part merely repeat, as they swing from whistle-stop to whistle-stop and television studio to television studio, the policy platitudes that constitute the table-talk in our faculty clubs: no one, not even the most skilled textual analyst, can tease out of the speeches any dependable clue as to what difference it will actually make which of the two is elected; it seems probable, indeed, that the candidates themselves, unless one of them be a White House incumbent, do not know what use they would make of the vast powers of the presidency. And the inevitable result, as intimated above, is that what you get out of the presidential election is what amounts to a *unanimous* mandate for the principles *both* candidates have been enunciating, which is to say: the presidential election not only permits the electorate, but virtually *obliges* it, to overestimate its dedication to the pleasant-sounding maxims that have been poured into its ears. Even did the electorate *not* deceive itself on this point, moreover, it has no way to arrest the process: it must vote for one of the two candidates, and tacitly commit itself, whether it likes it or not, to what they have been saying.

We now stand in the presence, I believe, of the decisive explanation of executive-legislative tension in the American political system, and the decisive clue to its meaning. Elections for congressmen, and up to now at least most elections for senator, do not and cannot follow the pattern just outlined. With rare exceptions, for one thing, the relevant campaigns are *not* running debates between the candidates, and thus do not offer them the temptation to raise each other's ante in the matter of principle. For another thing, principle is for the most part *not* what gets talked about, but rather realities, problems, the potential benefits and potential costs (and for whom?) of doing this rather than that, and in a context where the principles that are applied are those (very different we may be sure from those of the presidential candidates) upon which the constituents are actually accustomed to act. The talk generated by the campaign, much of it at least, is in small groups made up of persons involved in the actual face-to-face situations we spoke of earlier, and is, therefore, *not* wholly dissimilar to that of those peasants under the oak tree. So that, insofar as the presidential election encourages the electorate to overestimate its dedication to moral principle, the congressional election encourages them, nay, obliges them, to take a more realistic view of themselves, and to send forth a candidate who will represent, and act in terms of, that more realistic view. By remaining pretty much what the Framers intended them to be, in other words, the congressional elections, in the context of the engrafted presidential election, provide a highly necessary corrective against the bias toward quixotism inherent in our presidential elections; they add the indispensable ingredient of Sancho Panzism, of *not liking* to be tossed up in a blanket even for high principle, and of *liking* to see a meal or two ahead even if the crusade for justice has to bide a little. And it is well they do; the alternative would be national policies based upon a wholly false picture of the sacrifices the electorate are prepared to make for the lofty objectives held up to them by presidential aspirants. And executive-legislative tension is the means by which the corrective works itself out.

If the foregoing analysis is correct, the tension between Executive and Legislative has a deeper meaning—one which, however, begins to emerge only when we challenge the notion that the "high principle" represented by the President and the bureaucracy is indeed high principle, and that the long run task is to somehow "educate" the congressmen, and out beyond the congressmen the electorate, to acceptance of it. That meaning has to do with the dangerous gap that yawns between high principle as it is understood in the intellectual community (which makes its influence felt through the President and the bureaucracy) and high principle as it is understood by the remainder of the population (which makes its influence felt through the Congress). To put it differently: the deeper meaning emerges when we abandon the fiction (which I have employed above for purposes of exposition) that we have on the one hand an Executive devoted to high principle, and a Legislature whose majority simply refuse to live up to it, and confront the possibility that what we have is in fact two *conceptions* of high principle about which reasonable men may legitimately differ. Whilst we maintain the fiction, the task we must perform is indeed that of "educating" the congressmen, and, off beyond them, the electorate, "up" to acceptance of high principle; once we abandon it, the task *might* become that of helping the congressmen to "educate" the intellectual community "up" to acceptance of the principles that underlie congressional resistance to executive proposals. In the one case (whilst we maintain the fiction), discussion is unnecessary; in the other case (where we recognize that what we stand over against is two sharply differing conceptions of the destiny and perfection of America and of mankind, each of which conceivably has something to be said for it), discussion is indispensable; and in order to decide, as individuals, whom to support when executive-legislative tension arises, we must reopen (that is, cease to treat as closed), reopen in a context of mutual good faith and respect, the deepest issues between American conservatism and American liberalism. Reopen them, and, I repeat, discuss them; which we are much out of the habit of doing.

Subversion in the Twentieth Century

A COMMITTEE *of the Congress as conspicuous as the House Committee on Un-American Activities must, to justify its flamboyant experience, represent a serious answer, however imperfect, to a peculiar need of our time. The questions are whether subversion by the Communists is a large or a small matter. Is the commonweal affected by the success, or lack of it, of the concerted agitations of the enemy? In espionage? In the subversion of public opinion? Can one actually point to decisive steps taken by the Government of the United States in a direction contrary to its own best interests, which might not have been taken but for the influence of Communist propaganda upon our affairs? Can we, in the last analysis, distinguish between the internal and the external threat, or are the two, considering the compression of global affairs, indistinguishable?*

My purpose in this chapter is to discuss the role of subversion in the struggle in which we are presently engaged, to single out some successful ventures in the subversion of American policy and to argue the continued relevance to the national defense effort of an organization with the powers of a Congressional committee, a broad mandate, and a continuing curiosity about the operations of the Communist movement.

The twentieth century is called, rightly, an age of revolution. It is, by that token, also an age of subversion, which frequently precedes successful revolution.

One meaning of subversion is the overturning or overthrowing of existing governments or institutions. Another and more prevalent meaning is the undermining of a people's allegiance or faith in its institutions, which is often the precondition for the overthrow of those institutions.

Western democracy, resting as it does upon a moral consensus, the free exchange of ideas, and the understanding that one set of ideas prevails over another by a process of reasoned discussion, is poorly equipped to deal with the new (i.e., Communist) type of subversion. Communist subversion, let us note at once, is not a simple thing. Its mechanics and pace vary, most particularly with changes in the growth and allocation of Soviet military power. Invariably, however, subversion takes place in three stages. First comes the corruption of accepted ideas, and the substitution for them of views consonant with Communist objectives (we may call this the stage of intellectual and spiritual infiltration, and say of it that it demands, of those who would prevent or forestall it, notably more, in the way of sophistication and resourcefulness, than either of the other stages). Second comes a stage during which the Communists seek to manipulate the policies of the target government in such fashion as to favor Communist goals. Finally comes the stage of overt individual and collective action (espionage, sabotage, insurrection, etc.), under Communist guidance or direction.

The Bolsheviks, seizing power in Russia in 1917, began at once, against the day when the world situation might become more propitious, to ready themselves for expansion. They created a world-wide network of Communist Parties, and initiated a massive domestic training program for future collaborators in other countries, including the United States. The idea was to exploit any visible weakness in the enemy's regime or institutions, and to drive home invidious comparisons with Soviet society. This requires, simultaneously, the exaggeration of the enemy's faults and the exaggeration of Soviet virtues. The recognition of such propaganda themes by the leaders of the free world and their constituencies is, therefore, necessary to the proper ordering of anti-subversion policy. Ideally, it should be the intellectuals and the press of the free world that spot, and quash, the incipient themes of Communist propaganda. Actually, however, it is difficult for them, even assuming their willingness to undertake the task, to cope fully with this responsibility, most particularly because they do not have the power to compel testimony. You and I may know it is the intention of the Communist Party to foster internal dissent by exaggerating the misery of the Southern Negroes, or inducing a state of tension between white and Negro; and we may proclaim the fact, based on a projection of our knowledge of Soviet techniques and on impressionistic evidence garnered from the activities of the Party here. But our case is made much more forceful when a Congressional committee reveals, let us say, that thousands upon thousands of dollars were spent during such and such a period on false and exaggerated propaganda; that Negroes' houses were burned down by Communists as an act of provocation; that John Jones and Harry Smith traveled last year to Moscow, and were lectured to there by Ivan Ivanovitch on the techniques for increasing racial strife.

In 1928, the Communists announced their first Five-Year Plan, and pointed to it as proof that they had not only genuine insight into the political future, but also a concept of industrial and economic development destined to bring a new world into being. By their good fortune, this first massive venture in state planning began almost simultaneously with the Great Depression in the principal target countries, so that the Five-Year Plan could fall far short of its announced objectives and still be passed off as a "success." Thus: the capitalist economies were "stagnating," while the Soviet economy was blazing trails into a future in which stagnation would be unknown and unthinkable. These contentions beguiled many people. They might have beguiled far fewer if competent testimony had been published comparing, say, the lot of the depression-ridden American farmer and that of the liberated kulak.

Many impatient Western intellectuals accepted the Soviet Union as the model of future economic and social relations, so much so that not even the bloody purges of the late thirties could disturb their image of a "decadent" capitalism projected against the background of a "progressive" Communism. The "locomotive of history" charged forward, with many of them safely aboard.

Hitler attacked Russia; the United States joined with Russia—and, in the passion of our embrace, Russia seemed to us a fine catch. "Harry [Hopkins] says that Stalin doesn't want anything but security for his country, and I think that if I give him everything I possibly can, and ask for nothing in return, *noblesse oblige,* he won't try to annex anything and will work with me for a world of democracy and peace."* Thus the President of the United States, who four years before had denounced the House Committee on Un-American Activities which, *noblesse oblige,* had labored to inform the country, and its President, of some of the enduring truths about the Communist movement.

Or consider the "bring-the-boys-home" campaign. Obviously it

*William C. Bullitt, quoting from a conversation with F.D.R. *Life,* August 30, 1948, p. 94.

was not the Communists who kindled the desire of American mothers and wives to bring their men home. But a national policy uninfected by Communist misrepresentations, while not loving the boys less, would not have dismantled our military machine at a moment when it alone could have checked the Communist irruption into eastern Europe and southeast Asia.

And so on, through the tragic years.

Successful subversion is, I repeat, a matter of bringing about a fundamental change in a people's attitude toward its society and its government, and Communist subversion has raised to a high degree of perfection techniques for speeding up and directing the process by which a people moves from one set of attitudes to another. It has developed an instrument appropriate to these techniques; namely, the Communist Party. Its task is to locate and aggravate conflict within the target society, to pit elements of that society against one another, and to promote crises as a means of affecting governmental policy, even far in advance of the moment for any future attempt to seize governmental power. And we possess now a rich literature about the structure, the strategy, and the tactics of the Communist Party.

The Party, seeking always to block action hostile to the Soviet Union and to induce action favorable to its purposes, lets no opportunity go by to enlist the assistance of non-Communists who want something that will in any way contribute to these purposes. The announced objective of the satellite organization may be anything you like, but it will always be found to have a bearing, however hidden, on Soviet foreign policy.

The Principal Targets of Communist Subversion

The Communists describe themselves as a party of and for the masses. Many persons have, therefore, supposed that the unique and final aim of their operations is to indoctrinate everyone with Marxist-Leninist beliefs. Nothing could be further from the truth. Communism is an elite movement. It seeks to subvert actual or potential members of the ruling groups within the target country, and these in turn will gain control of and dominate the masses. Even in Communism's motherland—the Soviet Union—only some three or four per cent of the population is deemed qualified to belong to the Communist Party, and take part in controlling and influencing the development of Soviet society.

Communism considers as most available for its purposes men and women who feel superior to their own society, its institutions, its accepted values. Rebecca West made this point convincingly in her book, *The Meaning of Treason,** which describes the Canadian atomic spy ring that was uncovered by the defection of Igor Gouzenko, the Soviet cipher clerk. The ring's members apparently cherished none of the ordinary moral obligations toward their Canadian society, and therefore "felt no qualms whatsoever, but great pride and pleasure, in handing over to the representative of the Soviet Union any information required of them, no matter how brutally this treachery might conflict with their duty to their employers, public or private, or what dangers it might bring down on their fellow countrymen."

The Communists are forever on the lookout for men and women who have repudiated traditional sentiments of patriotism toward the society that has nurtured them. The liberal societies of the West, say the Communists in framing their appeals to foreigners for help, are smashing themselves on the shoals of their own contradictions, but subversion can hasten the progress that leads to the inevitable final disaster. That being the case, the "duty" to subvert stands, paradoxically, high in the scale of Communist "moral" obligations. That is why the Communists, although determinists, often behave more like believers in indeterminacy, in free human agency, than we who actually profess belief in it.

The enlisted agents of Communist subversion, then, have always been numerically few, however great their impact upon events. The few must in turn lead the many. The Communists know that takes time, and are prepared to think and plan in terms of a carefully orchestrated campaign of subversion that may take many years to complete. Ideally, as they recognize, they must shift the mind of an entire people from one set of convictions to another, and this calls for seizing upon particular issues as they arise, and so handling them as to cause key groups to accept current Marxist interpretations of "objective, scientific truth." Above all, it calls for convincing everyone,

*Rebecca West, *The Meaning of Treason* (New York: Viking, 1947).

everywhere, that like it or not the Communist system is riding a wave that must and will wash upon the shore of complete victory, while its enemy, the West, is slated for final and ignominious defeat. That explains why the Communists concentrate first on the elite group of the country they seek to subvert. It molds and sets public opinion, so that anything cast upon its waters is indeed likely to come back a hundredfold. First the writers, the scientists, the professors, the teachers, the artists. If they can be brought around, they can be counted on to force all other doors, and so carry Communist influence into all walks of life. These are simple truths, but they are still widely ignored for all that the House Committee on Un-American Activities has copiously documented them, and communicated them to many Americans. What a pity we did not know, in 1944 when we might have averted catastrophe, as much about Soviet Far Eastern policy as many Americans now know, thanks in large part to HUAC, about Soviet "peace" campaigns.

After the Russian victory at Stalingrad in June 1943, nobody could doubt that the Allied coalition would win the war. Stalin therefore turned his attention to the task of advancing the post-war position of Communism, preferably at the expense of, or if necessary in direct opposition to, the interests of his Western comrades-in-arms; and, as we should expect from the above, he reached first for the weapon of subversion, turning it upon the United States. The two most pressing goals of the resulting campaign were (a) to shift United States policy from support of the Nationalist Government of China over to acquiescence in a Communist take-over in that country, and (b) to obtain, by whatever means but in any case quickly, America's atomic secrets. The first of these, the shift of American policy from active support to betrayal of the Nationalist Government of China, called for a sustained effort over a long period: co-ordinated actions, propaganda, above all the planting of elaborate misinformation in numerous diplomatic and political forums throughout the world.

Within the United States itself, these tasks were entrusted to three groups: First, the Communist Party, which during the period of our wartime alliance with the Soviet Union had been highly influential in the circles that distribute news and form public opinion, and whose influence was to outlive the shooting war by several years. The Party, with membership at an unprecedented peak and with a wide variety of influential fronts at its disposal, could, at the end of the war, deeply affect American thinking when and as it needed to. Second, a number of Communist dupes who held high posts in certain strategic areas within the government of the United States: Alger Hiss, for instance, who became the first General Secretary of the United Nations; Harry Dexter White, who was Undersecretary of the Treasury; and Lawrence Duggan of the State Department. Third, the Institute of Pacific Relations, which was to prove a remarkably effective instrument for the purpose in hand. The IPR's role in the molding of United States Far Eastern policy is, no doubt, today generally forgotten. That is a pity—and it would repay anyone's time to review the detailed hearings of the Senate Internal Security Subcommittee from July 1951 to June 1952 (the task might well have fallen to HUAC) covering the IPR's activities. What the IPR did by way of promoting the interests of the Soviet Union in the United States, and bringing American Far Eastern policy in line with Communist objectives, is a model of the USSR's *modus operandi* in these matters. Only by understanding how it worked can we hope to learn how to prevent a repetition of the entire episode, or to ferret out less ambitious and less concentrated attempts to accomplish similar objectives—as, for example, in Latin America or the Near East.

The IPR found room in its organization not merely for a wide range of Communist sympathizers and dupes, but for Communist espionage agents as well—Michael Greenberg, for example, a British-born Communist who in 1941 became managing editor of IPR's *Pacific Affairs*. (By 1942, Greenberg was the proud occupant of an office in the White House.) IPR's reliance on persons with Communist affiliations who also had close ties with the State Department is fully documented in the IPR hearings.*

The IPR was in considerable part responsible for the proposal, finally put forward by the United States, that Chiang Kai-shek form a United Front coalition government with the Communists. Chiang, to be sure, knew from the first that the coalition in question would be only a first stage in an eventual Communist take-over of China: he resisted the proposal at every turn, and only under constant pressure from Washington officials, who were in turn being prodded by IPR, was he induced to yield, little by little, on first one point of substance, then another. During the celebrated China civil war truce engi-

---

Institute of Pacific Relations, Report of the Senate Committee on the Judiciary, 82nd Congress, 2d Session.

neered by Ambassador George Marshall, for example, Chiang found himself stripped of nearly all forms of military assistance (he was refused ammunition for the very weapons the United States had placed in his hands). "I was informed by the Chinese Government officials that they had ceased to receive war equipment manufactured in the United States," General Chennault subsequently testified. "When I inquired why, they said that General Marshall had forbidden its shipment from American-held islands and from the United States."* The Chinese Communists, of course, made the most of the truce—to build up their army with equipment that the Soviets had captured from the Japanese-Manchurian army and turned over to them.

We must not oversimplify or exaggerate: a number of forces had to be combined in order for the Communists to win in China. But it was the IPR that accomplished the first essential victory, which was to pull the wool over the eyes of Washington officials, and enable the Communist strategy of conquest in China to develop until it was too late to do anything about it. Nor is there any doubt that the IPR operation was masterminded from the Kremlin itself and, at the same time, effectively supported by the simple technique of keeping up the appearance of correct and formal diplomatic relations with the Nationalists, while at the same time directly encouraging and covertly aiding the Chinese Communists.

Above all, it was the IPR that invented—and put across—the convenient myth that the Chinese Communists under Mao Tse-tung were not really Communists, but "agrarian reformers," dedicated to the ideal of genuine democracy for China. Anything to discredit Chiang Kai-shek in American eyes; and, as we know, the final result was a Washington policy that contributed to Chiang's ultimate defeat on the mainland. Even as early as November 1945, Secretary of State James F. Byrnes was saying, "The wise course would be to try to force the Chinese government and the Chinese Communists to get together on a compromise basis, perhaps telling Generalissimo Chiang Kai-shek that we will stop the aid to his government unless he goes along with this."** But the main point is this: A systematic and diversified campaign of subversion finally persuaded the United States

*Hearings on the Institute of Pacific Relations, testimony of General Claire Lee Chennault, May 29, 1952.
***The Forrestal Diaries* (New York: Viking, 1951), pp. 1-3.

Government to accept, in general, the Communist position about China as the basis for its own policy decisions.

If the evidence regarding the IPR is compelling, so is the evidence concerning the group of American, British, and Canadian scientists who handed the secrets of the atomic bomb over to our avowed enemy. We are, to be sure, told that their largesse was of little use to the Russians, since the latter would have discovered the same atomic secrets anyway, perhaps even at just as early a moment. But the available data point to the opposite conclusion. The report of the Royal Canadian Commission, published June 27, 1946, sets forth the findings of an exhaustive inquiry into the matter, and leaves no room for doubt that the Communist spy ring in question operated successfully over a long period not only in Canada, but in the United States and Great Britain as well. "It is clear," states the report, "that the information sought was considered of the greatest importance by the Russian espionage leaders, and that alone might be a fair test on the question of value.... [much] secret and valuable information was handed over, some of it is so secret still that it can be referred to only obliquely and with the greatest care, and this is especially so in the case of certain secret information shared by Canada, the United Kingdom, and the United States."† Dr. Allan Nunn May, whom Rebecca West described as "one of a close corporation of the most inconvenient kind of traitors any community ever had to fear," never specified the amount of information he handed over, but he did say that it was more comprehensive than that to be found in the authoritative Smyth report,* which was not published until considerably later. Thus M. Rubenstein, no doubt accurately informed of the successes of his country's spy rings, could write, in 1947, "The secret of the atom bomb has long ceased to be a secret, and America's temporary monopoly of the atomic weapon is becoming a thing of the past."** Klaus Emil Fuchs, who was convicted for his participation in atomic espionage in Great Britain in 1950; Ethel and Julius Rosen-

†Report of the Royal Commission, p. 616.
*H. D. Smyth, *Atomic Energy for Military Purposes* (Princeton University Press, 1945). This book was authorized for release in August 1945, and is the official report on the development of the atomic bomb. The work was prepared at the request of Major General Leslie R. Groves, U. S. Army.
**New Times, M. Rubenstein (No. 50, December 10, 1947), "A New Sect of the Atomic Religion," p. 7.

berg, who were sentenced to death in 1951 for parallel espionage as a result of the testimony given against them by Ethel Rosenberg's brother, David Greenglass—they and their fellow conspirators did incalculable harm to American—and Western—interests. Soviet nuclear technology gained, in consequence, not less than three years, and possibly as many as four. It is unlikely Stalin would have initiated the Korean aggression (cost: 157,000 casualties) if the United States had still possessed an atomic monopoly.

Nor is that all the experience we have of how the Soviet Union has used scientists as instruments of subversion. Scientists have prestige as well as secrets. As we have watched the USSR build atomic weapons that they could not have built without personnel in the Manhattan project, we have also watched the USSR conduct a world-wide campaign, to a considerable extent through the medium of the world's scientists, to paralyze America's development of its nuclear potentiality by the cessation of tests. It is unlikely that a sophisticated student of Communist technique—e.g., someone who is familiar with, and has absorbed the meaning of, the hearings of the House Committee on Un-American Activities—would have walked into the trap set by the Soviet Union in the fall of 1958 (when we were persuaded, without assurances of any kind, that the Russians would do likewise) to cease testing; and unlikely that, in the absence of pressures built up by the engines of Communist propaganda all over the globe, "World Opinion" should have succeeded in disarming President Eisenhower.

Semantic Subversion

Another distinctively Soviet method of undermining a people's political ideas and institutions is through what we may call "semantic subversion"—that is, seeking to obfuscate and destroy the stable meaning of the words men use in communicating with one another in the process of arriving at political choices. Consider what has been done to "democracy," "peace," "war," "neutralism," "imperialism," "capitalism," "socialism," "colonialism." All these have been co-opted by the Communist slogan mongers for their special uses. They will never, in our time, regain their pristine meaning.

The first victims of semantic subversion, as originally practiced by the Bolsheviks, were paradoxically not the bourgeois or capitalist elements of the West, but the socialists. Ever since Lenin, the Communists have claimed that *their* movement, and their movement alone, looks to genuine socialism (wherefor the "bastion" of Bolshevik Communism is officially called the "Union of *Socialist* Soviet Republics"). This word juggling has, moreover, worked: by unfurling the banner of Western parliamentary socialism as if it were their very own, the Communists have been able to carry with them a great number of European intellectuals and workers who venerate the principles of socialism much as we Americans treasure the Bill of Rights.

The Communists, like many other observers, had foreseen that the State would play in modern industrial society a vastly more important role than in the agrarian societies of the past. The fact that the modern liberal is in some degree a "statist" has, accordingly, contributed to the success of the Communist masquerade. The Communist concept of the State, since it is totally totalitarian, does differ fundamentally from that of the typical liberal. But the Communists have been able to identify themselves conspicuously with liberal programs, which they have wished to do, partly, to distract attention from the illiberalism of their own conduct when in power. Their duplicity can best be appreciated when one compares simultaneously events on the two sides of the Iron Curtain. Behind the Curtain, successive big brothers have used force, internal propaganda, or organized social compulsion to ensure compliance with their will. Yet outside of their own domain, they continue to pose as progressive; that is, as liberals and democrats. The "dialectic" makes understandable their working of both sides of the street; but it is their own skill that enables them to do so with such effect. Thus the Communists advocate general and universal disarmament—and practice cold-blooded nuclear blackmail; they support wars of national liberation —and reject historical nationalism once they have themselves acquired power; they put themselves forward as champions of peaceful coexistence—and engage in permanent war. And these are the three issues that are likely to dominate the Cold War in the years ahead. Let us, then, glance at the concepts the Communists are sure to use in their attempt to subvert the free world's resistance.

The Nuclear Trap

The Soviet exploitation of the nuclear weapons issue has been intensified *pari passu* with the increases in the USSR's nuclear stockpiles. Prior to their acquisition of their first nuclear device, the Soviets' sole objective was to see to it that the United States should never employ nuclear weapons as a defense against Communist expansion —as witness Molotov's 1946 proposal that the United Nations establish a control commission to execute the U.N. decision to prohibit the use of atomic energy for military purposes, and the Soviets' concurrent rejection of the United States offer (the "Baruch plan") to place America's atomic secrets in the custody of an international organization. Though clearly terrified at the thought that the United States might use nuclear weapons against Soviet power, their domestic propaganda simultaneously (a) pooh-poohed such weapons as ineffective, and (b) applauded the Western scientists who were asserting that atomic weapons, once brought into play, would destroy the human race. Typical of such Communist double-talk was Molotov's statement to the General Assembly on December 14, 1946:

> The honor and conscience of the freedom-loving peoples demand that the atomic bomb be outlawed, for the United Nations will never assume the responsibility for any plans to use atomic energy for the purpose of wholesale destruction of people, and in general use it to the detriment of mankind.

Once, however, the Communists had acquired their first atomic bomb, and with increased emphasis after they had added hydrogen weapons, they moved promptly to a different position—that of the champions of nuclear disarmament *and* the principal practitioners of nuclear blackmail. Apart from a temporary heresy on the part of Malenkov (according to which nuclear weapons might be destructive to both Communist and capitalist societies), the Communists have never since abandoned their thesis that revolutionary conquest of the world cannot be accomplished without some application of violence —although (they add) if nonviolent techniques are applied successfully, the amount of violence required in a specific situation may be reduced. And they have repeatedly implied that their system, based as it is on a high degree of discipline, can absorb a nuclear attack better than any capitalist nation.

It has become increasingly evident in the course of the vain and endless East-West negotiations on arms control that the fundamental barrier to real agreement is ideological. Any effective system of arms control requires an effective inspection system, which the Communists cannot and will not accept. Accordingly, by Soviet logic, the demand for arms-control measures must be made into an important ideological and propaganda weapon. Thus they reason: If the West ever accepts, on a permanent basis, any degree whatever of arms control or test-banning, it will, in doing so, increase the relative strength of the Communist powers. Khrushchev has never proposed demobilization of his political warfare machine, for the obvious reason that the Kremlin can never give up its role as direct organizer, and spiritual preceptor, of world revolution. Khrushchev has openly asserted, as recently as January 1961, that he intends to use arms negotiations as a means of undermining Western military power, especially the United States'. Notwithstanding, the influence of the Unilateralists grows.

Lord Bertrand Russell's slogan, BETTER RED THAN DEAD, superordinates survival over any other value. Mr. Adlai Stevenson has noted the phenomenon. "Millions of persons," he said in a speech on May 23, 1961, "appear to be groping for new ethical guidelines as if they had never before been traced, or as if the old ones were no longer relevant. This seems to me curious, and I wonder if we can trace this uneasiness and search for a new ethic to the nuclear power-balance between East and West. Certainly, men everywhere are now living under a shadow of fear as horrendous universal implications of nuclear holocaust become more apparent."

Mr. Stevenson would, however, limit the casual connection to the nuclear aspect of the struggle; that is, to fear. But this is not the only possibility and, in the United States (where people in general have remained remarkably calm in the teeth of authoritative pronouncements concerning the horror of nuclear war), perhaps not the most interesting one. Some observers, for example, speak of a crisis in the soul of Western man himself that long antedates the discovery of atomic weapons—a crisis whose "causes" are to be sought not in external historical events, where Mr. Stevenson seeks them, but in the autonomous realm of the spirit itself; a crisis, indeed, that far from being caused by the struggle between East and West, itself produced that struggle.

Our struggle against the collaborationists and pacifists is no less urgent than our struggle against Communism itself, and the Bertrand Russells are not so different, in the pinch, from those Western statesmen who, while they do not speak as the Russells speak, often act much as the Russells wish them to act. It remains true, nuclear weapons or no nuclear weapons, that "where there is no vision the people perish"; and, conversely, that where there *is* vision, the people must be prepared to sacrifice life in defense of it. Russia's leaders appear to understand this better than ours: they encourage and foster nihilism and defeatism among other people but do no such thing at home. Perverted though their values are, from a sane Western point of view, the Russian leaders do not permit those values to be challenged from within the USSR, and punish draconically all who so much as hint at the possibility of defeat or abdication. One cannot imagine *On the Beach*, for all that it has done to weaken the will to resist in the West, being shown at Soviet movie palaces* which, we may be sure, are reserved for morality plays that inculcate the virtue of *courage*, as that virtue was once understood in the West. As for ourselves, the correct answer to the Russell slogan is always the battle cry that Russell was surely paraphrasing: "It is better to die on your feet than to live on your knees."

The Strategy of National Liberation

Communist strategy seems to be relying, in the sixties, on "wars of national liberation" much as, in the thirties, it relied on the "Democratic Popular Front"; and importantly situated men and women in the West seem as little able to see through the one as the other. The politically deluded fail adequately to understand (a) that the Russians use their support for colonial peoples merely as a cloak for Communist expansion, and (b) that the West is not simply anticolonial, but *suicidally* anticolonial. Wars of national liberation, Khrushchev assures us, are "just," thus "justified . . . [and also] inevitable, for the

*At the instance of the American producers, who designed world-wide simultaneous premieres, the film was shown once only, to Soviet film workers, at their own Domkino Theater, presumably to satisfy a professional curiosity.

colonialists do not fully bestow independence on the peoples. The peoples win freedom and independence only through struggle, including armed struggle."† Among such wars of national liberation, Khrushchev cites the Communist take-over in North Vietnam, the uprising of the Arab people against the French in Algeria, and Castro's seizure of Cuba, which he describes as "an uprising against a tyrannical regime, backed by U. S. imperalism." Such wars, he continues, will go on as long as imperalism exists, and "the Communists support just wars of this kind wholeheartedly and without reservations. . . . [They] march in the van of the people fighting for liberation."

The doctrinal basis for current Communist strategy in this area was laid down in Lenin's book, *Imperialism, The Last Stage of Democracy.* Marx, Lenin contended, had been wrong in thinking that declining capitalist profits must plunge the workers of the advanced countries into ever-growing poverty. Marx had overlooked a second possibility, namely: the profits brought into the industrial countries through their exploitation of the colonial areas. These might temporarily avert the decline and so postpone the (ultimately unavoidable, of course) pauperization of the workers. But this siphoning off of the colonial people's wealth, despite its beneficent results in one direction, comes with a hidden price: the bourgeoisie, by maintaining and living off a feudalistic system, signs its own death warrant. The execution of that death warrant is a major Communist responsibility, which must be discharged if the workers are to be led into the new world of plenty and freedom. The proletariat must take over the erstwhile task of the bourgeoisie—as Lenin put it, must carry through the "bourgeois-democratic revolution," which has now been translated into the "National Liberal Democratic Revolution," with which the Communists spearheaded their entrance into the former colonial areas. In general, however, the Communist line on this topic has changed little in the past forty years, as witness almost any Communist pronouncement on the colonial countries. This, for instance from *New Times,* August 23, 1953: "[The people of the colonial countries] are not inclined to reconcile themselves any longer to the colonial system which robs and exploits them in the interest of a few 'advanced' capitalist countries."

†Nikita S. Khrushchev, address, January 6, 1961.

The important thing to grasp here is the bearing of national liberation on the strategic interests of the USSR. The latter's strategy calls for the splintering of the non-Communist world into units, each too weak to defend itself, and too demoralized to combine with other units in the general defense. But for that, national liberation would be an extremely dangerous game for the USSR to play, since if the American doctrine of "self-determination of peoples" were to be strictly applied the world over, the USSR would fall instantly apart into a great number of independent nations. And the same goes, of course, for Red China.

The process of Communist subversion through support of movements for national liberation will, predictably, go on at an accelerated pace, and for many years, in Asia, Africa, the Middle East, and Latin America. And national liberation will continue to serve the Communists in any number of ways. It will unite the active nationalist elements in the colonial areas and in the "unadvanced" independent countries, and urge upon these elements extreme action. Thus the Communists will hope simultaneously to make friends among the backward countries, which in due course they will the more easily communize, and to weaken the "colonial" powers, who happen to be the USSR's probable enemies in any future war. And national liberation will provide the Soviet propaganda mills with an endless supply of grist: All social ills in the colonies and former colonies have their nests in imperialist exploitation, and can be indefinitely and profitably exploited for propaganda purposes. "Throw the imperialists out" becomes an appropriate propaganda slogan everywhere, good not only until the imperialists are thrown out, but also until the last reminder of their earlier presence has been snuffed out. (If, after they go, political chaos and economic stagnation ensue, the imperialists can still be blamed for both.) If, as is alas all too likely, the expelled imperialists get a case of bad conscience and offer to help, they can be denounced for trying to get back in and re-establish "colonialism"; they must be rebuffed, and the case for rebuffing them also makes good propaganda, since what just man wishes to see them "perpetuate . . . oppression . . . by foreign capital"?*

New Times, No. 33, August 5, 1953, editorial, p. 3.

The Lure of "Peaceful Coexistence"

We turn now to "peaceful coexistence" as a technique of Communist subversion.

The Communists invented the term "peaceful coexistence"—along with its twin sister "relaxation of tensions"—to describe a peculiarly deceptive transitory phase of their struggle for world power. The purpose, put in its crudest terms, has been to persuade non-Communist leaders everywhere that "coexistence" with Communism is now the only course open to the free world. And here, as with the other techniques, we can measure the effectiveness of the stratagem by asking ourselves how many people all over the world believe that Communism, like the poor, will always be with us, and must be lived with on terms that it chooses to dictate. To ask the question is to answer it, and to shudder at what the answer implies. And here, as with their other techniques, we can understand what is involved by keeping attention fixed on the totality of the Communists' behavior. That will enable us to see that the term means to the Communists exactly the opposite of what, on other lips, it might seem to say.

Peaceful coexistence is neither "peaceful" (it calls for peacefulness from only one side in the world struggle, always for unlimited aggression by the other side) nor "coexistence" (only the Communists are intended to keep on existing). Once again the "dialectic." Herewith four expressions of it,* each contributing a dimension in our understanding: (1) "It does not at all follow from the fact that we stand for peaceful coexistence and economic competition with capitalism, that the struggle against bourgeoisie ideology, against bourgeoisie survivals, can be relaxed." (2) "The only correct and reasonable principle of international relations is the principle of peaceful coexistence of states with different social systems advanced by Lenin and further elaborated in the Moscow declaration and in the peace manifesto of 1957. . . . [But] the slogan of the fight for peace by no means contradicts the slogan of the fight for Communism. The two go hand in hand. . . ." (3) "Peaceful coexistence promotes the growth of the forces of progress. . . . In the capitalist countries it facilitates the work of the Communist parties and other progressive organizations. . . ."

*The first is incorporated into a statement issued by the 20th Congress of the CPUSSR, the remaining three are by Khrushchev in his January 6, 1961, speech, *op. cit.*

And (4) "The policy of peaceful coexistence is, then, as far as its social content is concerned, a form of intense economic, political, and ideological struggle between the proletariat and the aggressive forces of imperialism in the world arena."

In short: "Kindly put your pistols away, because we are going to shoot you with ours."

"Coexistence" is a temporary phase of Communist strategy, though we may not hear the last of it for many years. What the Communists intend is to go on nibbling up the countries located in the power vacuums of Asia and Africa, and to refrain from direct attack on the West for so long as suits their purposes. The West must not, according to the rules of "peaceful coexistence," do anything so "unpeaceful" as, for example, actually to block Communist infiltration into the free world. The West must write off millions who are already Communist slaves, and it must look on, unmoving if not unmoved, as new areas are led to the slaughter. The rules are simple, and the West has merely to abide by them to remain safe from war.

The Balance Sheet

The United States and the other Western democracies have not shown much skill in waging the "war called peace." Yet the nature of Communist subversion, as we have insisted, changes over the years only in detail; what varies is merely its intensity. Its invariable purpose is to promote confusion in the ranks, and even the high command, of the free world, to paralyze our action, and to twist policy in a direction favorable to the Communists' interests and designs. As a tool of the Soviet state, subversion marches hand in hand with Soviet military and political power. Both operate within a moral framework that was succinctly defined by Radio Moscow some years ago: "At the root of Communist morality, said Lenin, lies the struggle for the consolidation, for the completion, of Communism. Therefore, from the point of view of Communist morality, only those acts are moral which contribute to the building up of a new Communist society."

Communist subversion strikes first, and most energetically, most craftily, at our capacity to *judge*, to choose rationally, to opt for the course that is "right" in the twofold sense that it reflects true morality and that it takes genuine reality into full account. The Communists know that no one, individual or nation, can choose rationally unless, to begin with, he knows—knows and remembers—that some things are "better" than others, and which things are better and which worse. They know, too, that no one, individual or nation, can choose rationally unless he or it sees reality clear and sees it whole. Wherever, then, there is today confusion amongst us, whether about moral principle or about the true character of the situation we face, we are well advised to ask whether, or to what extent, it is the result of a deliberate Communist-subversive effort to create it. Confusion amongst us there certainly is, of both kinds, and more certainly than at any earlier moment in our history. And these, I submit, are urgent matters, of proper concern to a Congress charged with the common defense.

Take, for instance, the existence within our ranks of the three schools of thought: (1) that which agonizes over the internal Communist threat to our security, but seems blissfully unaware of any external threat; (2) that which is willing to devote unlimited resources to meeting the external threat, but dismisses the existence of an internal one; and (3) that which concentrates exclusively on social and economic problems, for the solution of which it will contemplate any sacrifice, however great, but gives no thought to Communism's threat to our own security, internal or external.

This is not a matter of healthy democratic disagreement about policy. It can be explained only on the grounds that there are those among us who are either unable to recognize reality, or unable to refer it to what we have always regarded as acceptable moral concepts—or both. It is analogous not to the momentary indecision of the troubled but clearheaded man, but the successive phases of euphoria and depression in the schizophrenic. Some of us are terribly wrong on the foregoing issues and, all too probably, because Communist subversion, working diligently in all corners of the world, under every guise, taking advantage of every situation, has successfully changed the appearance of reality. Is there an internal Communist threat? Is there an external threat? Should we act vigorously against any and all threats? These questions are surely capable of being soberly investigated and soberly decided; yet the continuing debate about them seems to get nowhere.

On Monday, June 5, 1961, the Supreme Court upheld the Internal

Security Act of 1950, which requires the Communist Party in this country to register as the agent of a foreign power. The Court upheld the requirement in question, as also the further requirement that the Party divulge its membership, by citing the Party's secret and conspiratorial character and its domination by the Soviet Union, as established over the years by Congressional investigations. Overnight the nation's leading newspaper hit back: "The sustaining of the Smith Act's membership clause ... could only serve again to divert public attention to the virtually nonexistent internal Communist threat. The real Communist challenge is from abroad."*

There is sufficient evidence by now to demonstrate the ultimate impossibility, in the age of subversion, of distinguishing clearly between the "external" and the "internal" threat. Is it an "external" or "internal" victory of the Communists when the President of the United States is moved (by the euphoria following the "relaxation of tensions" period after Stalin's death) to say, as Mr. Eisenhower did in Geneva in 1955: "I believe the Soviet Union wants peace every bit as much as we do"? How much of a hand did Soviet propaganda have in the planting of that hallucination in the mind of the principal leader of the West? Was the resulting imbalance in American foreign policy, which accepted the Spirit of Geneva as the new cornerstone, "externally" or "internally" induced? And as for espionage, how many spies does it take to put sand in the machinery? What did Martin and Mitchell, who disappeared from their jobs with the National Security Council in the spring of 1960, to surface a month later in Moscow, tell the Russians? Did they take along, as is widely suspected, the vita information on the U-2's? Did they, in a word, make possible the Soviets' apprehension of the U-2, and thereby change the course of history?

In the few weeks before and after the *Times'* blasé dismissal of the internal threat, the Government of Israel was shaken by the exposure of Israel Baer (it is as though Bernard Baruch had been shown to be a Communist spy), the Government of England by the exposure of George Blake, Henry Houghton, Peter and Helen Kroger (alias Morris and Lola Cohen, both Americans), Gordon Arnold Lonsdale, and Ethel Elizabeth Gee. Meanwhile, the United States was wrestling with the problems posed by its most recently apprehended spies: Dr.

---

* The New York Times, editorial, June 7, 1961.

Robert Soblen, Irvin C. Scarbeck, and Miroslav Nacualec and Karel Hlasmy.

The Congress of the United States has shown wisdom in creating machinery to investigate and expose the nature and scope of Communist subversion in the United States. Communist subversion, as we have said, seeks to twist U.S. policy in the direction of Communist designs. This is done by bringing one or more U. S. officials to make, wittingly or unwittingly, decisions that forward Soviet objectives. So much is obvious. It is less obvious that no governing group, no Administration, is ever eager to recognize that one of its trusted officials, even one not highly situated, has played into the Communists' hands. Its instinct for political self-preservation naturally disposes it to defend any suspected employee against such a charge even, as we know, when the adverse evidence is overwhelming. The Executive, in short, cannot be counted on to police itself in this regard, which means that either someone else polices it, or that it goes unpoliced. Under our form of government Congress has the power necessary for such work—has, indeed, broadly interpreted, a constitutional duty not only to oversee the execution of policy, but to inquire into the pressures that go into the formulation of policy—whether pressures by monopolists, or pressures by Communists. Many instances of Communist-tilted decision making would never have come to light but for Congressional scrutiny of decisions and decision makers. And had they not come to light, officials sympathetic to Communism might, with impunity, have gone right on serving Soviet interests. Examples are legion: the one-sided advantages frequently given the Soviets in the Cultural Exchange Program; the sale of wheat to the USSR at bargain prices during the height of the 1961 Berlin crisis; the semi-official status of Owen Lattimore in Outer Mongolia during an intensive campaign, and his attempt, fortunately aborted, to rush recognition of that Soviet satellite. For a knowledge of this kind of thing, Congress relies mainly on the Committee, and will, predictably, continue to do so, since the Committee's function is bound to be more important as the pace of the Cold War is stepped up. "The showdown with the Communist world conspiracy is on," writes Eric Sevareid in the *New York Post* (July 9, 1961). "We have entered the final stage of the long struggle to determine if we can hold our world position short of a great war. We are in that stage because Khrushchev has decided we are. He will act accordingly, which will force us to act accordingly—if we can clear our heads."

Towards a Definition
of *"Conservatism"*

(with George W. Carey)

The words "conservatism" and "conservative" are employed with respect to a wide variety of subject-matters, have taken on a rich variety of meanings, and pose problems of definition that have frequently given rise to heated controversy. Men have, for example, called themselves (or been called) conservative in religion, conservative in art, science, or even in a craft, conservative in a game or sport. Within each subject-matter, moreover, men have meant demonstrably different things by conservative; some have laid down rigorous definitions, and others definitions so vague as to be virtually useless. Some writers have insisted, in consequence, that conservatism and conservative have ceased to have any fixed meaning whatever, and should henceforth be used only "positivistically," that is, to denote movements or parties that in fact call themselves conservative; and other writers have demanded that the terms be abandoned altogether.[1]

With this background, no useful purpose would be served by attempting here a new, rigid definition of conservatism or conservative. Rather, we shall seek (a) to articulate the basic human situation out of which the terms conservative and conservatism first arose; (b) to indicate, with reference to this basic human situation, the sources of the seemingly endless confusion and complexity concerning the meaning of conservatism; (c) to illustrate concretely how our approach helps answer certain recurrent and important questions concerning the past and present status of conservatism in the United

---

[1] Governor Rockefeller writes: "We all know that, in any serious historical sense, these terms [liberal and conservative] have lost all meaning. The use of such artificial labels, in political debate, merely distorts the issue and confuses the citizen. It substitutes the slogan for thought, the false label for the serious goal." *The Future of Federalism* (Cambridge: Harvard University Press, 1962), p. 21. Governor Rockefeller undoubtedly has a point as regards the present confusion; but we hope to have shown that the terms in question remain indispensable.

States and Great Britain; and (d) to set forth certain conclusions which our survey seems to warrant for understanding the status of conservatism in the American and British contexts.

I

A society or community is marked by a series of complex interrelationships among individuals. At one level there is interaction *within* numerous sub-systems or groups within the society: we observe daily that individuals interact, either competitively or cooperatively, in any number of functional areas such as politics, sports, religion, arts, crafts, sciences, etc. At still another level, there is interaction *among* the groups within the society: for example, athletic teams compete with each other, political parties in a democratic system compete for votes in order to gain control of government, and various economic and social groups within the society engage in an endless process of struggle and cooperation with one another.

In this context, three phenomena necessarily present themselves: First, there arise practices, beliefs, ideas, standards of judgment or rules which to a large extent prescribe the permissible form of interaction among individuals and groups. The degree to which rules governing interaction are formally prescribed, of course, varies. In the conduct of a political campaign, for instance, there are relatively fewer written rules than, say, for competition between baseball teams. Nevertheless, there appears to be a universal need for rules and norms; without them there would be no patterns of expectation among individuals within the society, and without patterns of expectation both orderly competition and cooperation among individuals would be virtually impossible.

A second phenomenon that presents itself we may put as follows: certain norms, values, practices, rules, standards of judgment come, little by little, over a period of time, to be regarded as more or less "established," that is, to be accepted as a "heritage" from the past. Individuals, in most instances, through various agencies such as the family, church, school, learn and absorb the elements of the heritage as they grow up in society, without questioning or critically examining them.

Third, the heritage from the past, no matter how carefully guarded, reveals itself as subject to *change and innovation*. The change and innovation may be unintended; that is, not consciously sought by any of the members of society or groups within society. A "technological" "advance" may have the unanticipated effect of rendering obsolete a series of prescriptions and may also necessitate the development of new rules, values and norms of behavior for the regulation of interaction between individuals and groups. Or changes may be the long-term cumulative result of what, at any given point in the past, were imperceptible modifications of existing rules or norms. In either case, the participants in the social situation cannot be said to have intended or willed such changes.

Of greater importance for our present purposes, however, is intentional or deliberate change. In any given society, there are individuals, either within a given group or acting as a group, who advocate changes and innovations in the heritage. So, too, there are those who resist or fight such changes. As this constitutes a recurrent phenomenon within society, terms or words develop to describe those who seek change and those who resist change. In the languages of modern Europe such words as "progressive," "liberal," "radical," or "modernist" denote the former and the words "conservatism" and "conservative" denote the latter. It is not surprising, therefore, to find that most current definitions of conservatism stress resistance to change as its most fundamental and prominent characteristic. However, as the subsequent section will indicate, the phenomena in question are too complex to be caught up in a single term, and we readily see why the term conservative has come to be the subject of controversy and confusion.

II

In order to clarify and better understand the varied uses of the word conservative, we must take into account at least the following difficulties:

1. Because the clash between the proponents and resisters of change and innovation is certain to occur in all manner of groups and activities, there emerge as a matter of course in any society numerous particular "conservatisms," each with as good a claim to the description as the next. Nor is that all: since in any grouping or activity different persons may resist different changes and innovations, or resist change and innovation because of attachment to different as-

pects of the heritage from the past, we must not be surprised to find more than one particular conservatism in one and the same grouping or activity. We can, therefore, see why the term conservative is used with great frequency, and other than univocally, in everyday discourse. Moreover, we should note that, as the terms can be legitimately used to describe resistance to change in any group, it often refers to controversies that have little significance for the entire society.

2. There is a *dynamic* dimension to most social relationships that further complicates our use of the word conservative. Change and innovation do occur, even if the resisters appear to have their way, so that as time passes the heritage from the past comes to include elements that are merely heritage from the *recent* past; and we perceive a further reason for the multiplication of particular conservatisms. For some individuals will accept the newly admitted elements, and proceed to resist any attempt to alter them in the name of further progress; others, yesterday's conservatives, may refuse to accept them and demand that they be eliminated (that is, that "we turn back the clock"). Both positions are, clearly conservative positions, but with the hitherto unnoticed complication that some of our "conservatives" now differ with progressives not as to whether there shall be change and innovation, but as to the direction it shall take.

3. Particular conservatisms are likely to multiply over still another set of issues, having to do with the question whether—and, if so, to what extent—conservatives see themselves as called upon to *develop* the "tradition" or "orthodoxy" they have received from their forebears, or, contrariwise, to hand it down to their descendants without modification or elaboration. Some demonstrably conservative utterances certainly treat tradition or orthodoxy as if its "goodness" were exclusively a matter of its "oldness," as if that which is ancient were good merely because it is ancient, and as if that which is new or "modern" were bad merely because it is new. Others tend to emphasize the "goodness" of their tradition or orthodoxy, point to its antiquity as merely attesting to that goodness and recognize, accordingly, an obligation to nurture it and cause it to "grow." Only the former, properly speaking, fall under those definitions of conservatism that equate it with opposition to change and innovation; the latter, far from simply resisting change and innovation, often become its most ardent proponents and, as intimated above, clash with

progressives over the direction in which modifications shall occur and the "principles" that are to govern them. Thus, we can speak of *static* conservatives and *developmental* conservatives.

4. Conservative resistance may in certain circumstances (for example, in a society or organization or activity that at an earlier moment has passed under more or less complete control by progressive changers and innovators), express itself in the desire to overthrow the *status quo* and the tradition or orthodoxy to which it points as its justification. The conservative may, that is to say, regard himself as the defender of a tradition or orthodoxy which, though it has been reduced to a mere remnant, he continues to insist upon as *the* tradition or *the* orthodoxy appropriate to that organization or activity.

5. The progressive in a given society, organization, or activity, as noted above, may achieve a complete triumph and, as appears to have happened in Russia in the years following 1917, may impose an entirely new set of institutions, practices, beliefs, standards of judgment, etc. Then, the new system having been consolidated, the progressives may themselves begin to play a conservative role, resisting proposals looking to change and innovation that come simultaneously from new progressives and from the former conservatives. We thus arrive at the theoretical possibility of a conservative political movement dedicated to, for example, the preservation of Communism.

We conclude: (a) The multiplicity of meanings caught up in the terms conservatism and conservative reflect genuine complexities in the historical phenomena to which the terms refer. (b) The terms may reasonably be applied to all the many forms that, as noted above, the struggle on behalf of a tradition or orthodoxy may take. And (c) the terms nevertheless continue to be useful in discourse, though only to the extent that we make clear, in any particular discussion, which of their many possible meanings we intend.[2]

[2]We feel there are distinct advantages to be derived from our approach to an understanding of conservatism. Clinton Rossiter in his *Conservatism in America* (New York: Alfred A. Knopf, 1956) finds it necessary to speak of four types of conservatism: "temperamental," "possessive," "practical," and "philosophical." Russell Kirk in *A Program for Conservatives* (Chicago: Henry Regnery and Co., 1954) writes of the "conservatism of desolation" and the "conservatism of mediocrity," both of which he feels are not "genuine" or "real" conservatisms. Our approach eliminates the need for such classifications and disputes. In our framework Rossiter's "possessive" conservative is one who resists changes in his environment that would lead to a diminution of his status, reputation, or power. The "conservatism of desolation," which Kirk speaks of, is one that resists changes that would result in further loss of "individualism." Both

III

With an understanding of the basic human situation which gave rise to such terms as conservative, progressive, liberal, and radical—and of the complexities involved in the use of these terms in a "going" social system—we are in a better position to comprehend and evaluate the nature and character of conservatism in the United States and Great Britain. We will in the following discussion confine our attention to the sphere of *politics*, which is the commonest referent of the terms conservatism and conservative.

From the foregoing discussion it is clear that we need some reference point in assessing the nature and incidence of conservatism in the United States and England. That is, even though we confine ourselves to the general area of political conservatism, there are even here several conservatisms, each with its own orthodoxy or tradition that it seeks to preserve or advance. Consequently, our assessment of conservatism in these countries will vary, depending upon which particular conservatism we fix attention upon. We propose to take as our referent the conservatism of Edmund Burke since he is, by fairly common consent, regarded as the "father" of modern conservatism.

Burke's leading work, *Reflections on the Revolution in France,* was an attempt (a) to state the character, purposes, and predictable results of the French Revolution as a venture in deliberate change and innovation, (b) to isolate the major issues at stake between the Revolution and the traditional political and social order that, in Burke's view, must be maintained in England and salvaged in France, and (c) to articulate the underlying principles of that traditional political and social order. Here it must suffice to notice some of the major issues that book draws which, not merely in England and France but all over Europe and in the United States as well, seem to remain the great divide between conservatives and progressives throughout the ensuing decades, as follows:

1. The issue between the *principle of consent* in politics, according to which good law and good policy in the State are merely that to which the "people" agree, and the *principle of morality,* which

Rossiter's and Kirk's formulations are, in any case, open to the objection that they are *temporary* and *local* in reference. That is, at any given time and place, such conservatisms may or may not be present. Thus these formulations are of limited utility for cross-cultural or historical studies of conservatism.

insists that a law or policy is to be judged good or bad according as it does or does not measure up to an objective "standard" ("It is with the greatest difficulty that I am able to separate policy from justice. Justice itself is the great standing policy of civil society, and any eminent departure from it . . . lies under the suspicion of being no policy at all"[3]). 2. That between the *principle of equality*, which claims for each man an equal share in political power, and the *principle of hierarchy*, which would assign a greater share of political power to those who are most capable of providing wise and good government (". . . the will of the many," Burke wrote, "and their interest, must often differ. . . ."[4]). 3. That between the *doctrine of the "rights of man,"* according to which, as Burke understood it, all men have an "equal right" to "equal things," which, in turn, may be precisely defined in "declarations" or "bills" of rights, and the *principle of convention,* according to which the rights of man are "incapable of definition,"[5] "vary with times and circumstances,"[6] and are determined, for each individual, by "the fundamental laws of [his] country, . . . whose merits are confirmed by the solid test of long experience. . . ."[7] ("The restraints on men," Burke wrote, "as well as their liberties, are to be reckoned among their rights."[8]) 4. That between the *democracy of the living,* which authorizes each generation in a nation's history to remake laws and institutions in accordance with its own preferences and beliefs, and the *democracy of the dead* (the phrase is not Burke's but G. K. Chesterton's), according to which laws and institutions are, as Burke held, "an *entailed inheritance* derived to us from our forefathers, and to be transmitted to our posterity. . . ."[9] 5. That between what we might call today the *principle of redistribution,* which would require the state, in the interest of "equality," to prevent undue concentrations of wealth, and the *principle of property and inheritance,* under which the "power of

[3]Edmund Burke, *Reflections on the Revolution in France* (New York: The Liberal Arts Press, 1955), p. 180. We do not want to enter the growing controversy concerning the status of natural law in Burke's philosophy. On this point see: Peter Stanlis, *Edmund Burke and the Natural Law* (Ann Arbor: University of Michigan Press, 1958) and Leo Strauss, *Natural Right and History* (Chicago: University of Chicago Press, 1953), pp. 294-323.
[4]Burke, *Ibid.,* p. 59.
[5]*Ibid.,* p. 71.
[6]*Ibid.,* p. 69.
[7]*Ibid.,* p. 66.
[8]*Ibid.,* p. 69.
[9]*Ibid.,* p. 37.

perpetuating our property in our families is . . . that which tends the most to the perpetuation of society itself "[10] (. . . we [in England] have never dreamt," wrote Burke, "that parliaments had any right whatever to violate property, [or] to overrule prescription. . . ."[11]). And again: "The characteristic essence of property . . . is to be *unequal.* The great masses [of property] . . . must be put out of the possibility of danger."[12] 6. That between *atheism,* which Burke identified with what we have come to call "relativism" or "skepticism" (the French Revolutionaries, he wrote, "tolerate· all opinions" because they "think [no opinion] to be of estimation"[13]), and *"true religion."* ("All persons possessing any portion of power," Burke held, "ought [to understand] that they act in trust, and that they are to account for their conduct in that trust to the one great Master, Author, and Founder of society."[14])

Certain characteristics of Burkean conservatism merit special attention in light of our previous discussion. Burke certainly regarded the principles he was enunciating as a "heritage from the past," which no single generation of the British people was entitled to modify or set aside. But, we must be careful to note, Burke was a *developmental,* not a *static,* conservative. That is, he fought valiantly against his conservative contemporaries who wished merely to preserve the heritage rather than, as he put it, "preserve and improve" it in the interest of an expanding justice and ever-greater well-being for the country as a whole. Thus it was not at all inconsistent for Burke to support the American colonists against London, since they were

[10] *Ibid.,* p. 58.
[11] *Ibid.,* p. 175.
[12] *Ibid.,* p. 58.
[13] *Ibid.,* p. 173.
[14] *Ibid.,* p. 106. This statement of Burkean principles differs in important particulars from the statements of other commentators. See, for example, Chapter Two of Russell Kirk's *The Conservative Mind* (Chicago: Henry Regnery and Co., 1953). In our view, Burke's principle of the "peccant part" merely places a question mark beside the right of any generation of a nation's citizens to set aside the prescriptions of the past; in the very nature of the case, it ends up asserting that each generation must make the relevant decision for itself. Moreover, we do not equate the principle of hierarchy with inequalities based solely on birth. Rather, we feel, the principle is best interpreted as justifying inequalities among individuals on various grounds consistent with the principle of morality.

In constructing our statement of Burkean principles we have been careful to focus attention on those areas where Burke, himself, perceived the greatest threats to the tradition. In so doing, we are guarding against the charge that we have merely abstracted from Burke's theory those principles that fit *our* conception of "true or "genuine" conservatism.

seeking to overthrow a *status quo* that drastically departed from the tradition to which they had been accustomed as Englishmen. Or, to take another example, in the famous trial of Warren Hastings, Burke supported principles of colonial administration that many regarded as not merely novel but revolutionary. To understand this, however, we must recall that the controversy did not revolve around the issue of change itself but, rather, the direction of change. Here also Burke was seeking change in existing policies in order to advance those enduring principles that he deemed to be the *true* "heritage of the past."

The major controversies surrounding Burke and his relevance to contemporary English politics stem from the developmental character of his conservatism. Certainly, there is always room for controversy about what constitutes, in any given historical context, an "improvement" on the heritage of the past. In an important sense, Burke himself seems to have opened the door to the long series of "concessions" by which British conservatism has, now by espousing the cause of reform itself, now by accepting reforms forced upon it by political opponents, moved to a position in present-day politics that, according to some observers, is difficult to distinguish from that of its major opponent, the British Labor Party. Some progressivist historians have, indeed, claimed Burke as their very own, denying that he was a conservative at all.[15]

Consequently, in assessing the current status of conservatism in Great Britain, certain questions arise: Did Burke draw the lines, in a manner valid for the entire subsequent period, marking the position that British conservatives have in fact defended against the forces of modernism? Or, have British conservatives yielded principled position after principled position in order to "go along with the times," so that Burke's issues are no longer real issues between conservatives and their opponents? As Section II (above) indicates, our answers to these questions will depend on what elements of Burke's heritage we take into our purview. If, for example, we concentrate solely upon organized British conservatism, i.e., British conservatism as represented by the Conservative Party, and the specific matters of policy on which it appears to have moved furthest from Burke, we should probably conclude that conservatives have moved sharply in the

[15]For an excellent survey of these progressivist claims see Peter Stanlis, "The Basis of Burke's Political Conservatism," 5 *Modern Age* 263 (Summer, 1961).

direction of both "Tory Democracy" and "Tory Socialism." The Conservative Party under Disraeli and his successors has not only accepted but often led the way in reforms, especially extensions of the suffrage, calculated to broaden the base of, and intensify, popular control over government, and in yet other reforms calculated to mitigate the alleged abuses of unrestricted private capitalism, to redistribute wealth and income, and to provide "social services" for the masses of the British people.

On the other hand, we are likely to come to a markedly different answer if we focus our attention on the resistance of British society to the major trends associated with the French Revolution. That is, if we use *all* of Burke's principles in our assessment, we should probably conclude that Burke's principles are not only relevant but continue to be accepted as genuine prescriptions by the bulk of English society. For example, millions of Britons still cling to Burke's views on an established church, on the religious basis of society, on the hereditary and prescriptive character of the British constitution, including the British monarchy, on the rights of man, and most crucially, perhaps, on what we have called above the "principle of morality," according to which there are objective standards of right and wrong in politics to which electoral majorities, no less than kings and magnates, must subordinate their wishes and appetites.[16] We might well conclude, using Burke's entire range of principles, that those matters that lay closest to Burke's heart have in large part been prevented, up to now in Britain, from entering the sphere of political controversy at all.[17] And even in those areas where the Conservative

[16]For confirmation of this point note the reaction of the British public to the Profumo scandal. There is room for intelligent speculation about whether the French public reaction would have been nearly so sharp under similar circumstances.

[17]In this connection, we must be careful to distinguish between the arena of actual political controversy and the logomachies of savants and *littérateurs.* If one focuses his attention on the relevant literature he will find that not only have Burkean principles been the subject of debate but that they have, to a large extent, been rejected. Thus Russell Kirk can write: "By and large, radical thinkers have won the day. For a century and a half, conservatives have yielded ground in a manner which, except for occasionally successful rear-guard actions, must be described as a rout." See Kirk, *The Conservative Mind,* p. 4. This may be and probably is a valid judgment, if taken as merely literary history; it is an absurd exaggeration if intended as a judgment about modern politics.

Such gaps between the fortunes of what let us call "literary conservatism" and conservatism as actually given in political reality are not uncommon. Samuel Stouffer's *Communism, Conformity and Civil Liberties* (New York: Doubleday and Co., 1955) shows very clearly that conservative (that is, antiliberal) attitudes toward freedom of

Party's concessions appear to have been the greatest, namely, those relating to economic measures of a redistributive or "welfarist" character (inheritance taxes, use of the income tax for the purpose of bringing about ever-greater economic equality, nationalization of industry, the complete abandonment of private capitalism, etc.), Britain remains divided between those who would subject the whole of British life to the egalitarian and modernist principles against which Burke inveighed, and those who, in the name of traditional principles, continue to resist, and by no means always unsuccessfully.

If anything, the nature and status of American conservatism is even more complex and controversial. There is, of course, the crucial question of whether the principles of Burkean conservatism are applicable to, or appropriate for, the American context. On this point some have insisted that American institutions, environment, traditions, development, and problems have been so dissimilar from those of England that Burke's principles are of limited utility for identifying legitimate American conservatives.[18] Yet there are peculiarities in the American tradition which make it virtually impossible to discover a comprehensive, systematic, and indigenous conservative theory which would serve this function. First, the United States has produced few systematic political philosophers, so that it is hardly surprising that there has been no American counterpart of Burke.[19] As a consequence, there has not been, in the American tradition, any systematic articulation of generally recognized conservative principles that apply specifically to the American context. Part of the reason for this may be that rapid social and economic change were characteristic of the American experience from the very beginning and, along with them, general acceptance of rapid social and economic change as necessary and desirable. At no time, therefore, up

speech have, out in the general population of the United States, suffered no such eclipse as that which has overtaken them in the groves of Academe (where visibility is notably lower).

[18]Writes Clinton Rossiter: "... American conservatism must be judged by American standards, the standards of a country that has been big, new, diversified, successful, and non-feudal, a country in which Liberalism has been the common faith and middle-class democracy the common practice." *Op. cit.*, p. 129. We should note, however, that the United States has not declared its independence from Western Civilization, whose traditions and principles are presumably still relevant to a final judgment on American conservatism.

[19]For an imaginative discussion of possible reasons for this lack of systematic and comprehensive theory, see Daniel Boôrstin, *The Genius of American Politics* (Chicago: University of Chicago Press, 1953).

to a recent date at least, has there been in America an "old order," with more or less settled "tradition," that men have thought of themselves as called upon to preserve, or even to "preserve and improve," or that other men, in any significant numbers, have been determined to "reform" or "destroy." To a great extent, Americans appear to have moved over the decades to their present political, economic, and social arrangements with tacit agreement on all sides that everything, including the American "tradition," must grow and develop, and that no one possesses a reliable model of the most desirable outcome of American growth and development.

Second, issues have arisen, to be sure, and have been fought out and decided, but they have tended to be narrow (that is, to concern this or that small part of the political or economic system) and ephemeral (as with the controversy over the Bank at the time of Andrew Jackson, and that over "Free Silver" in the 1890's); more often than not, both "sides" have thought of themselves as defending the "tradition" (the definition of which, accordingly, has itself often been a topic of controversy); and the usual result, even in so bitter a struggle as that over slavery, has been that the institution or policy favored by the victors on a given issue has been at once absorbed into and made a part of the "tradition."

Third, while it is true that there is what can be considered an American tradition (namely that which is embodied in the Declaration of Independence, the Constitution, and the *Federalist*), there has been and is wide-spread disagreement about what this tradition actually means. Further, there is debate as to whether the principles contained in this heritage are to be interpreted in a "static" or "developmental" manner. In the Civil War, for example, the Southerners no doubt felt that they were waging a conservative battle against both a revolutionary interpretation of the Constitution and the "All men are created equal" clause of the Declaration of Independence. Yet, Lincoln has gained increasing recognition, in some quarters, as the leading conservative statesman and political thinker of nineteenth century America, on the grounds that he truly interpreted and advanced the heritage bequeathed to us by the Founding Fathers. In a similar vein, contemporary debates concerning the First Amendment and how its provisions are to be interpreted, are marked, on both sides, by appeals to the intention and purposes of its authors.

In the absence of norms, standards or principles which are, on all sides, generally accepted as the heritage from the past, there is, in America, unavoidably, endless controversy surrounding the efforts to distinguish conservatives from progressives. Even more, in the absence of generally-recognized standards by which to identify conservatism and progressivism, it is always difficult in America to say where significant clashes have taken place, and are taking place, between the two camps. For these reasons, no doubt, many have found it both necessary and profitable to try to apply the Burkean principles to the American context. And, if we approach the American phenomena in terms of the political issues that have become sharp in recent decades, using Burkean conservatism as our criteria, the following issues would seem to divide conservatives from progressives:

1. Conservative belief in a decision-making system with a division of powers and diffusion of authority, with intermediate institutions through which the popular will is refined and interpreted *versus* the progressives' desire to remake American institutions to conform with models of plebiscitary democracy in which the majority could rule directly and with a minimum of delay. The conservative, consistently with Burke's prescription, resists efforts intended to advance a conception of political equality that would give to a majority, through periodic elections, the power to make substantive policy decisions. Hence the conservative opposes progressive reforms, such as a "responsible" and "disciplined" two party system, that would have the effect of centralizing authority and eliminating separation of powers and the elaborate checks and balances provided by the Framers. Still more, the conservative favors those devices in the present system that check and divide the power of the national majority, such as federalism, a bicameral legislature, equal representation of the States in the Senate and, among others, the existing procedure for amending the Constitution. Thus, by this standard we may speak of the authors of *The Federalist* as conservatives not only because they set forth and explicated the norms that modern conservatives defend against progressive attack, but also because their beliefs are much more closely akin to those of Burke than to those articulated in the French Revolution.

2. The issue raised by conservative resistance to egalitarianism, that is, the use of the power of government for the redistribution of income, for the "equalization" of "opportunity," and for the provi-

sion of "social services" calculated to benefit the poor at (so conservatives allege) the "expense" of the well-to-do. On this issue the conservatives include the few American voices out of the past, Alexander Hamilton's especially, who have spoken out boldly in favor of "natural aristocracy," unequal wealth, and unequal privilege, together with, more recently, those of opponents of such measures as the progressive income-tax, inheritance taxes intended to prevent the perpetuation of large concentrations of wealth, minimum wage laws, social security, etc.

3. The issue posed by conservative attachment to the "rights of property," which has gradually transformed itself, over the decades, into that of the status of "free enterprise," or "capitalism"; and the American conservatives now become those, especially certain justices of the United States Supreme Court and certain Senators and Representatives, who have resisted the trend toward government intervention in the economic order.

On these issues there have always been American conservatives who have stayed quite close to Burkean conservatism, which, accordingly, has perhaps fared better in the United States than in Britain —a statement that takes on added force if we include within our purview certain other issues that have never yet entered the arena of political controversy in the United States, especially: (a) that of the prescriptive binding force of the first nine Amendments to the Constitution and, beyond those amendments, of a "higher law" upon legislative majorities; and (b) that of the propriety, despite current interpretations of the First Amendment, of a whole series of practices having to do with the status of religion in America (e.g., the references to the United States as a "Christian nation" in Presidential addresses, the exemption of churches and synagogues from property taxes, the maintenance of chaplains in the Armed Forces), where the prevailing American view seems to parallel Burke's sentiments concerning the "principle of morality," the religious basis of society, and the dangers of atheism.

One thing is certain: The French Revolution, as Burke understood it, has yet to occur in *either* Britain or the United States, though it has always had its proponents in both countries. In the decisive dimension, the "Burkeans," British and American, have had their way.

IV

From our discussion thus far, it is not difficult to see why controversy and confusion have surrounded discussions of conservatism in the United States and England. We may now add: because the *basic* division between conservatives and progressives turns upon issues concerning political, economic, and social equality, both in the United States and in Great Britain, acknowledged conservatives of the Burkean school are joined by others, distinctly non-Burkeans, in resisting movements or policies which would lead to greater equality. One can, as we noted in Section II (above), correctly classify these non-Burkean resisters as conservatives, at least on this issue. But, if and when other issues, such as, for example, the religious practices and policies of the society or the government arise in public debate, these same non-Burkeans do *not* align themselves with the Burkean conservatives. Thus, from issue to issue, we can expect shifting alliances of conservatives. This process in itself causes confusion, for individuals who on one set of issues are seemingly united in their resistance to change or in their attempt to reestablish past practices, will divide into various "camps" when still another set of issues arises. As a consequence, trying to formulate in theoretical terms a "common denominator" among those who have been united at any one time in resistance to change is a complex, if not impossible, task.

Clearly, as we have emphasized in our brief survey, a systematic analysis of conservatism is not possible unless there is some referent which constitutes a standard to which existing "conservative" policies can be compared. As our discussion in Section II (above) shows, any number of standards could legitimately be used for this purpose, and this in itself becomes a further source of controversy and confusion. Such a standard, as we have indicated, will be related in some way to the processes and direction of change within a society. Yet we feel there are certain distinct advantages in using Burke's principles as a standard. They are, for one thing, the most comprehensive and encompassing. That is, they identify a wide range of issues that have, in fact, at different times, produced conflict between acknowledged progressives and conservatives within the American and British societies. More than this, the Burkean principles are capable of "encompassing" less comprehensive conservatisms that have fought the forces of progressivism on a more limited basis. And when the principles of Burkean conservatism are used to distinguish conservatives from progressives, the results are generally in accord with commonly-held opinions. As we noted in speaking of American history, for example, the Federalists, when we use Burke's principles as our measure, fall into the conservative camp, a classification which will hardly surprise anyone but does illustrate the applicability of Burkean principles to the American context. If we add to these considerations, (a) the fact of the growing recognition, in recent scholarship, that modern conservatism somehow echoes Burke, in both the United States and England, and (b) the fact that there is no American theorist who approaches Burke in comprehensiveness and who might therefore be a suitable substitute for Burke in analyzing conservatism in the American context, the case for using Burkean principles as our standard becomes even stronger.

Even using the Burkean principles set forth in Section III (above), there are still problems. First, as we have indicated, Burke was a developmental conservative and hence we can expect controversy even among Burke's followers about what movements, reforms, or theories do or do not serve to advance and promote these principles at any given time or place. Secondly, analysts have reason to differ about whether all these principles are of equal importance, or whether some should be more highly cherished than others; and the resulting judgments will, clearly, affect the estimates of different judges as to the status of conservatism in the United States and England. If, for example, one places the issue of egalitarianism before all others, one will, no doubt, at least in the English context, see a decline in conservative belief and influence.

We should note, finally, that Burke's principles provide only in "strategic" terms the basis of conflict between American conservatives and progressives. Contemporary American debates about majority rule and political equality, for instance, often center on such questions as the nature of federalism, proper Executive-Congressional relations, the role and function of the Supreme Court, and the organization of political parties. While on these issues many conservatives base their positions on Burke's prescriptions, the subsequent debate, in large part, is conducted in distinctly non-Burkean terms. Burke's principles, then, serve only the function of determining the position his adherents will take toward specific proposals.

For these reasons, even if Burke's conservatism does become a more generally acknowledged and accepted standard, we hardly anticipate controversy about the past and present status of conservatism in the United States and England to abate. However, we may indulge the hope that the areas of disagreement will be more sharply defined, and that the debate will be conducted with increasing clarity and precision.

Dialogues in Americanism

A Debate Between
James MacGregor Burns
and
Willmoore Kendall

"Resolved: The deadlock in Washington is to be deplored."

Opening Statement by Willmoore Kendall

I confess that Mr. Burns leaves me worried about whether we're to have a debate here. I've listened with fascination as he attempts to state the issues between liberals and conservatives (as he understands them), but with all the more fascination because I happen to be an avid fan of Mr. Burns and his writing. And I've heard him say very little that I would have expected him to say. Let me, at the risk of spoiling this occasion for everyone, say that I, at least, am not the kind of conservative who moves from the axiom, "the more government the less freedom." Neither am I the kind of conservative that has a net preference for local and state action rather than federal government action. I'm equally willing with Mr. Burns to let these questions be decided on their merits. What concerns me, and what I would have expected Mr. Burns to be concerned about (though I well know the difficulty of setting forth so complex a position as his in a mere twenty-five minutes), is how we are *going to make decisions* here in America about the kind of problem that lies so heavily upon Mr. Burns's heart.

In my opening remarks, therefore, I am going to try to come to Mr. Burns's assistance and get us a debate—by drawing not merely upon the speech he has just made, but upon my vast knowledge of his writings. And I will try to get a quarrel going between what I regard as the Burns position as set forth in his books, and the Kendall position as set forth in mine. (Mostly—let me say at this point—I concede Mr. Burns's major points in his opening remarks.)

Mr. Burns has, as we see him here and in his books, two complaints: first, that Washington is a place where nothing happens; second, that nothing happens when nothing happens in Washington. To put it a little differently: first, there is "deadlock" in Washington, and second, that deadlock is more than flesh—well, more than Mr. Burns's flesh—can bear. Something ought to be done—*must* be done as Mr. Burns argues in book after book—to end the deadlock and to prevent similar deadlocks in the future.

Let us dispose, initially, of his first complaint—that there is "deadlock" in Washington. Now on the *factual* side, let me say at once that I have very little quarrel with Mr. Burns here. Congress does indeed —month after month, session after session, decade after decade— refuse in general to pass the legislative proposals rained upon it from the White House. Mr. Burns wants to call that state of affairs "deadlock," and the congressional stance that produces it "obstructionism." And I say, Let us be generous with Mr. Burns and try to bring out into the open, and understand, why this curious use of language commends itself to him; and, happily, we do not have to go very far afield in order to find parallels that will help us to understand.

Take, for instance, the thief who attempts repeatedly to burgle a certain house, and cannot do so because the double bolt on the door foils his best burgling techniques. From the thief's point of view, from the thief's family's point of view, even from the point of view (which brings us back to Mr. Burns) of the thief's mouthpiece, the owner of the house (who put the double bolt on the door) is indeed an obstructionist. And the state of affairs between the thief and the owner of the house (all those well-laid plans, all gone aft-a-gley!) is indeed deadlock. More, we should be guilty of lack of *empathy* if we did not understand why they (the thief, the thief's family, the thief's mouthpiece—Mr. Burns) latch onto words like "deadlock" and "obstructionism." We can understand the curious use of language, yet I hope still keep on using language correctly ourselves and still keep ourselves reminded of how to put it in English, namely: from the standpoint of law and order, from the standpoint of justice, the owner of the house is a citizen rightfully defending his property—not an "obstructionist." The state of affairs between him and the thief is the

successful prevention of burglary, not "deadlock"; and the thief is—
well, a thief.

Or again: from the standpoint of, say the anti-social monster who
would like to see the towns in the valley inundated, who would like
to see the population of the valley drowned—from the standpoint of
any such anti-social monster, I say, the dam that holds back the
waters is obstructionist and the state of affairs between the dam and
the waters is that of deadlock. We will waste our time arguing with
him about his use of words. Our task is, rather, to recognize (despite
the verbal mist he surrounds himself with) that he and ourselves are
looking at one and the same state of affairs: the dam does indeed hold
back the waters, mercifully sparing the towns and people of the
valley; we simply put it differently: what he calls deadlock we call the
successful protection of the valley against floods; what he calls obstructionism we call the civilized control of potentially dangerous
natural forces; where he deplores, we reverently say, Thank God!
And no, my point is *not* that "it all depends on the point of view";
I will not, I trust, be suspected of any such relativism. Precisely not:
my point is that there is a *right* use of words and a *wrong* use of
words; that the way the thief and the anti-social monster in the valley
use words is (though understandable) *wrong*. And our use of words,
as I have just illustrated it, is *right*.

So, too, with the way my distinguished opponent uses words. He
and his friends (to paraphrase a hero of his) think not of what they
can do *for* America, but only of what they can do *to* America. He and
his friends have (for the purpose of doing things *to* America) a *program* (the thing Mr. Burns seems most concerned to talk about here)
which they are *determined* to carry out (so determined, as some of
Mr. Burns's friends like to say these days, that they "will not take no
for an answer"). They are determined to carry it out because, firstly,
being the sort of people they are, and given the sort of thing over
which their hearts go pit-a-pat, they *like* that kind of program. So
much is understandable. But there is a second reason, which is: they
believe, or say they believe, their program would contribute to the
happiness and well-being of the American people (which is perhaps
less understandable).

Now because of the queer quirk in the process by which we elect
our presidents, Mr. Burns and his friends—let's begin now to call
them by their right name, which is "the liberals"—normally dominate the White House (or, if you like, are always able to put a liberal

in the White House, who goes into the White House with their program already in his pocket. The liberal just leaving the White House has another copy in his pocket as he goes out the door—just in case he'll be coming back some day). The new President sends their program, bit by bit, bill by bill, over to one of his flunkies in Congress, who, one by one, drops the bills into the hopper. Congress then proceeds—the one with one bill, the other with another bill—either to sit on the bills until adjournment or, if the President is able to force a showdown, to vote them down, or if not vote them down then pass them in such emasculated form that the liberals protest (quite properly) that they are not *their* bills, their program, at all. Congress, of course, sits on the bills, or votes the bills down, or emasculates the bills, because it is opposed to anyone's *doing* to America what the bills propose to do; because it believes the bills would accomplish *not* the happiness and well-being of the American people but the misery and degradation of the American people; because, in a word, the program, bill by bill, is an assault on the congressmen's most strongly held convictions, an affront to their deepest loyalties and beliefs, an outrage to their conception of the destiny of America. Congress hurls the bills back into the teeth of the President and the liberals in the same manner, and in much the same mood, in which a self-respecting nation would hurl back the advance columns of an invading army.

Mr. Burns wants to call that "deadlock." The majority of Congress, naturally enough, want to call it protecting the country against the extremist proposals of the liberal intellectuals. Mr. Burns wants to call Congress "obstructionist." We, the people, who biennium after biennium elect a Congress that *will do just what Mr. Burns says Congress does,* think of it as defending our way of life against those who would undermine and destroy it. Mr. Burns and his friends want to call the Congress that strikes the President's program down a "do-nothing" Congress. We, the people, who elect and re-elect such a Congress—elect and re-elect such a Congress with what Mr. Burns must deem *monotonous* reiteration—think that such a Congress, far from doing nothing, does a very great deal: it does *just* what we send it to Washington to do.

Yet (as I have intimated all along) we must not quarrel with Mr. Burns merely about words: he is saying nothing that cannot be translated out of the tortured jargon of liberalese into plain English. What he means is that Congress won't do what he and his friends *want* Congress to do and (despite his strange use of language) we can, I repeat, understand him—nay, must understand him, because he is "a problem" (a problem, moreover, that we the people who elect the Congress must learn, somehow, to deal with). And we may count ourselves fortunate to have Mr. Burns for a whole evening under our microscope, where we can hope to find out what makes him tick.

What more can we say to Mr. Burns—what more is conceivably *worth* saying to Mr. Burns—about his complaint that nothing happens in Washington, that there is a deadlock? At least, I think, this (though in order to say it we are going to have, this time, to ask him to do the translating, because I do not know how to say it in liberalese): Mr. Burns likes to talk about deadlock, about obstructionism in Washington, because, I submit, he does not want to face political reality—political reality as it is given to us in contemporary America. Mr. Burns likes to talk about deadlock and obstructionism because that implies that the *trouble* is in Washington—that is, in the nation's political *machinery*, about which Mr. Burns usually writes—in the nation's political institutions and practices, where it may lend itself to solution along the kind of lines that have always fascinated minds like Mr. Burns's (along lines, that is to say, of political *gadgetry*).

Give Mr. Burns and his friends a free hand with our political machinery (and I hope he will tell us a little more about his plans in that connection), let them do a little tinkering with it, and everything (so Mr. Burns and his friends like to think) will come out all right! All of which is to say, Mr. Burns and his friends will then get their way in American politics: the White House program will be adopted, and all good things will be added unto us. And I do think it worth saying to Mr. Burns, You mistake your problem. You are treating a surface manifestation of your problem for the problem itself. *We* understand why you are hurting, but you yourself do not understand what is hurting you. The deadlock, if you still insist on calling it that, is not in Washington, but out in the country; and yes, I repeat, I do think that is worth spelling out for Mr. Burns here on the very threshold of our debate.

What is political reality in contemporary America? Mr. Burns says, Political reality in America is our faulty *political* machinery [and again I urge him to come to that central theme of his in his reply], which keeps my friends and me from getting our program adopted. I say, Political reality in America is that we Americans disagree profoundly on the *merits* of that program. Mr. Burns says, Ah! But the program is *good;* it alone will enable America to live up to the imperatives of the age [I cite Chapter one of his recent book] to fulfill its historic destiny. And I say, But exactly what we Americans disagree about, on the deepest level, is what the imperatives of the age are and what *is* the historic destiny of America. But, Mr. Burns will reply (a little disingenuously, perhaps), How could people possibly disagree about things like *that?* Is it not *obvious* that we must carry out the civil rights program? That we must wage and win the war against poverty? That we must broaden and deepen social security? That we must learn to coexist peacefully with World Communism? That we must get the federal government busy solving our transportation and urbanization problems? And so on down the line? And I answer, patiently, No, no, Mr. Burns, *none* of that is obvious; the things you mention are, if I may put it so, the bones of contention. But, Mr. Burns asks (for at last I have captured his attention!), How can *that* be? And I answer, Well, look; what it amounts to is: some of us here in America are liberals, whose hearts do go pit-a-pat over the program you sketch. And some of us are conservatives, who dislike the program very much. Then Mr. Burns, who at least in his writings tends to avoid those words "liberal" and "conservative" that we suddenly find him using tonight, asks (a little incredulously perhaps), What's *that* got to do with it? And I answer, Well Mr. Burns, to begin with, just this: some of us think there are vastly *more* conservatives in America than there are liberals, and that political reality in America (what you call "deadlock") merely reflects a failure on the part of the liberals to plead their case successfully before the tribunal of public opinion.

It is here, let us pause to note, that the automatic response we can expect from Mr. Burns becomes most interesting: We have *not* failed to plead our case successfully, he will say. We have all the best arguments on our side—as witness our strength in the nation's academic community, among the nation's top columnists and television and radio commentators, on the editorial pages of the nation's leading newspapers; on foreign policy, we have on our side the great experts on international relations and Communism; on fiscal and tax policy and on welfare legislation we have with us the great names in economics; on civil rights, we have with us the bulk of the nation's clergy and the great names in constitutional law (including of course the learned justices of the Supreme Court); on reapportionment, on enfranchisement of the southern Negroes, on Congress, we have with us *en masse* the nation's political scientists. How can you say that we have not pled our case successfully before the tribunal of public opinion? And I answer, Not good enough, Mr. Burns; all you prove is that the liberals plead their case successfully *with one another!;* that you find each other *infinitely* persuasive (which I never doubted for a moment).

My point is that you have failed to persuade—I take the phrase from a great political philosopher—the "generality of men amongst us"; that you have failed to create a consensus in favor of your program; that, so far as we know, the liberals are still a small minority in the American community; that—to come back—the deadlock you *should* be worried about occurs out in the cities and towns and villages and farms of America, out among the American people themselves. And that deadlock has got to be stated in terms something like this: the militant minoritarian liberalism for which you speak has run up against a blank wall of conservative opposition; it is *not* just Congress that rejects your program, it is *we the people* as articulated through the Constitution that *we* ordain and establish. It is *we* who reject your program; and you, Mr. Burns, you and your friends, are clearly powerless—powerless at least under the existing rules—to do anything about it! Political reality in America is that the liberals don't have the votes. More, the liberals, finding themselves called on at last to explain why liberal solutions don't work, are fresh out of ways to enlist new voters. The liberal program, to put the matter in its simplest terms, lacks sex appeal. And let any reader of this debate who doubts that go to what learned folk like Mr. Burns and myself call the *locus classicus*—namely, the pages of Mr. Burns's recent book, in which he tells of his own unsuccessful race for Congress. Mr. Burns appears to have persuaded everyone in his constituency except . . . well, the generality of the voters. He does not need *me* to explain to him the political reality the liberals are up against. In order to get the picture he has only to go call on his neighbors.

But let us pass on to Mr. Burns's second complaint: nothing happens when nothing happens in Washington. Mr. Burns deplores the fact that nothing happens in Washington—the fact, that is, that Congress consistently bids the President (if I may put it so) to go roll his hoop. And Mr. Burns thinks that when nothing happens in Washington, something ought to happen about it, something ought to be done about it (a question, I say, to which he returns in book after book). He has strongly-held and carefully-worked-out ideas as to what ought to be done; and it is of the first importance that we should grasp the real bearing of what he has said repeatedly he wants us to do about it.

Since he and his friends *cannot* win under the existing rules, he asks us to *change* the rules so that he and his friends *can* win. Indeed, if we were to translate his basic proposal into the language of, say, basketball, it would run something like this: Our team loses all the time, and clearly has no prospects of winning in the future. But that is because the existing rules confer overwhelming advantages on our opponents; and I'm here, I, Mr. Burns, am here, to tell you where exactly in the existing rules the bias occurs. The trouble, clearly, is this whole business of having the baskets at the two ends of the court the same size. Let us forthwith double the size of the basket at one end of the court, and make the basket at the other end of the court exactly the size of the basketball. And let it always be understood that we liberals play toward the end of the court that has the larger basket. Things'd be different from *then* on!

Things would indeed be different from then on. I agree completely with Mr. Burns (though without taking back what I have said earlier) that the adoption of certain gadgets would improve the prospects of the liberal program and the prospects therefore of breaking the deadlock in Washington. Redraw the lines that demarcate our congressional districts, so as to give city folk more representatives—and the liberals will, no doubt, pick up a few Congressional seats. Abolish the seniority principle in congressional committees, abolish the filibuster—and you will, no doubt, weaken the hold we conservatives have on the easiest method for frustrating the President. Go still further, if you like, and eliminate somehow those troublesome midterm elections that Mr. Burns and his friends worry so much about —and again, things will look up for the liberals. Though not to an extent that I for one would lose any sleep over. The baskets at the two ends of the court, as far as I'm concerned, would still be the same size, and the conservatives would still win the big games. But that is because I have not yet mentioned what we may call Mr. Burns's Special Gadget (as set forth in his latest book).

Nobody, I venture, knows better than Mr. Burns that the modest changes in the rules that I've mentioned up to now—the modest changes proposed by Mr. Burns's predecessors in the attack on the American political system—won't turn the trick. Won't, that is to say, dish the conservatives. But Mr. Burns has left his predecessors so far behind in this regard that when he looks back over his shoulder he can't even see them. *They* proposed, as *the* means of cutting the

Gordian knot, what they called the responsible party system: let our two parties become, respectively, a Conservative Party and a Liberal Party; let them, at election time, offer the American people a genuine choice between competing sets of policies; let the people, in their quadrennial elections, themselves decide the destiny of America; let us end the White House-Congress stalemate by putting both President and Congress under one and the same freely-arrived-at popular mandate. Mr. Burns, I repeat, is not to be confused with those earlier, Casper Milquetoast would-be reformers of the American political system. Mr. Burns, fed as he is on the red beef of Machiavellism, proposes nothing less than a *coup d'état*—and, along with it, an ingenious scheme for bringing it off:

Let the liberals—he calls them the Presidential Democrats and the Presidential Republicans, but we have no difficulty identifying them —conspire together to capture *both* parties. Let us have, instead of a Liberal Party and a Conservative Party, *two* liberal parties (each of which will offer the electorate only liberal candidates). Let us, in effect, remake all our elections in the image of our presidential elections, so that no matter how a man votes, he will vote (or at least seem to vote) for the liberal program. That is Mr. Burns's proposal for ending the anti-liberal bias of the existing rules; and I have, by way of conclusion, three small things to say about it.

First, the very shape of his proposal concedes my main point here this evening: the liberals have failed to plead their case successfully before the tribunal of public opinion.

Second, the proposal, on the face of it, justifies the claim I have made in the language of basketball: what Mr. Burns *really* deplores is the baskets being the same size for both his team and his opponents.

Third, the proposal runs hard up against what I like to call the Dilemma of the Little Gingerbread Boy. The Little Gingerbread Boy, you remember, couldn't run 'til he got hot, and couldn't get hot until he ran. And Mr. Burns's proposal—which stripped of irrelevancies is a proposal for eliminating from our system what he calls the one-party congressional constituency, the congressional constituency constantly dominated by a single one of our political parties—is up against that same difficulty. Before you can eliminate the one-party congressional district, you must eliminate the one-party congressional district, and you can't do *that* because of the one-party congressional district.

In short, there are no short-cuts that will get Mr. Burns and his friends their program. Like it or not, they are going to have to do it the hard way—by persuading the American people (the American people moreover acting not by mere majority vote but by consensus) to adopt the program as their own. I do not—I hasten to add—exclude the possibility that the liberals may, in the long run, accomplish that miracle of persuasion. But in the long run, as Lord Keynes is there to remind us, we are all dead.

Rebuttal:

Now we're getting somewhere!

But two quick points. First, let Mr. Burns not try to confuse the issue into which I am attempting to draw him, by pointing to the literary weeklies and fortnightlies and monthlies that profess to speak for American conservatives. Mr. Burns very well knows from my book that *my* conservatives are the voting majority of the Congress which is not today and has never been properly confused with those end-of-the-nineteenth-century Supreme Court justices who talked all manner of natural law foolishness and thus attempted to frustrate the Congress of the United States.

Second, let Mr. Burns not confuse things by pretending to summon me back to the historical bases of conservatism in America. The historical bases of conservatism in America have to do with the American political system, and not with the content of the decisions that that political system produces. As I understand it—as Madison and Hamilton understood it—the sky has always been the limit about the content of those decisions, provided the proponents of the several decisions won their victory within the rules of the system as they were originally laid down in the Constitution and in the Federalist papers. Mr. Burns is just as interesting to me as I to him. He is the liberal of liberals because it is he who challenges us conservatives *on our political system itself.* It is he who says that it is a bad political system; he who has the most ingenious plan for remaking it.

Having said that let me get really down to business. In my opening remarks I spoke of Mr. Burns as constituting for the rest of us "a problem" that we must learn somehow to deal with, and we have now got him on record in his rebuttal as the kind of "problem" I see him as being. I also took the liberty, you will remember, of referring to his

Machiavellism. And now that we have the second speech of his tingling in our ears, I perhaps owe it to you—if only in the hope of driving our discussion to the deepest level of disagreement between Mr. Burns and me—to say why I deem him a problem and what I mean when I describe him as a Machiavellian. Mr. Burns is a problem, because—let me lay it on the line—of his blind devotion to (and I might add his peculiar understanding of) what we political scientists call the majority principle—and I am now speaking to Mr. Burns directly on his accusation about "the numbers game."

Think back over what he has said explicitly; think back even more carefully over what he has tacitly assumed, tacitly taken for granted, and you will see that I do him no injustice when I speak of his blind devotion to the principle of majority rule. And he's now about to try to convince you that I also am blindly devoted to it.

Mr. Burns, I submit, is absolutely committed to the following proposition about how we should govern ourselves here in America: in a democracy, he confidently believes, the majority has a *right* to call the turns about policy. Democracy, that is to say, *is* majority rule —his very words of a few moments ago. In a democracy, the outvoted minority has therefore (we must understand) a duty to accept and to obey the policy directives of the majority. *The* problem in a democracy is (as it has always been for Mr. Burns in his books) to *get* yourself your majority and then get on with whatever jobs you have mobilized your majority for. (Mr. Burns's picture of Jefferson in his last book is highly relevant in this connection.)

Whether the outvoted minority is going to *like* your policy directives, whether the outvoted minority *can* accept those policy directives and continue to find political life tolerable, whether or not the outvoted minority will in fact *obey* your policy directives—these are questions that a man like Mr. Burns feels no need to discuss or even raise with himself. The majority principle, the right of the majority to have its way, the duty of the minority to obey (for example, the duty of the white Southerners to obey the policy directives of the civil rights program, if and when it is enacted)—these things figure in Mr. Burns's political philosophy and in that of his friends as, quite simply, Higher Dogma, as self-evident truth that requires no demonstration or justification, as the This Is It Boys of American democracy.

If that is not what Mr. Burns believes, I call upon him to tell us in the course of this debate what it is he believes that is recognizably different from that. While, if it *is* what he believes, I call upon this audience to agree with me that Mr. Burns is indeed "a problem." For Mr. Burns's Higher Dogma is, I contend, novel doctrine in our democracy—so novel, I contend, that most of us cannot hear it stated, cannot hear it put into words, without shuddering.

Mr. Burns's understanding of majority rule is not, I contend, the American understanding of majority rule. The American understanding of majority rule is: yes, the majority decides; the numbers are taken, they are counted; in a sense the numbers do prevail, in a sense it is a numbers game. Concretely however, the majority of our *elected representatives* decide, *not* the majority of the electorate—but decide, in any case, subject to two clearly understood provisos:

First, the majority decides precisely with an eye to whether or not the minority *will* obey, can be counted upon to obey—with an eye, therefore, to the necessity of carrying the minority with it. And second, that we Americans are for some purposes, but only some, a nation capable of making decisions by majority rule, and for other purposes not a nation (Mr. Burns will recognize that I am merely reading him the basic doctrine of the tradition of the Federalist papers)—not a nation—but a federation of states in which majority rule has no status and no meaning. We have no tradition here in America for the kind of majority rule that is prepared to say to the minority (as Mr. Burns would not, I think, hesitate to say to the white Southerners on civil rights, or on the seniority principle), You are going to obey our policy directives *because* we are the majority. You are going to obey because if you do *not* obey, we are going to *make* you obey.

We have, I repeat, no tradition in America for that kind of majority rule. And anyone who *talks* that kind of majority rule in America becomes by that very fact "a problem." Why? Because that kind of majority rule won't go down in America. Because the preconditions for that kind of majority rule are not present in America. And because the man who talks that kind of majority rule in America is consciously or unconsciously preparing the inevitable breakdown of the American political system.

The American political system is not and never has been a system for the automatic acceptance of majority mandates by the minority. It is not and never has been a system for the large-scale coercion of the minority (which is what at *every* point Mr. Burns's program is going to require). Under the American political system *the majority bides its time until it can act by consensus* (which is ultimately the *opposite* of the numbers game)—that is, in conditions where it can reasonably expect the minority to go along. And I say, There is grave question whether the American political system can digest a Mr. Burns, who is simply not interested in consensus.

So too with my point about Mr. Burns's Machiavellism—for, let me hasten to say, I use the term Machiavellism in its strict technical meaning among political scientists (without, of course, any implication that Mr. Burns is particularly wicked or particularly unscrupulous, by comparison with the rest; only more ingenious than most of us). My point is quite simply that Mr. Burns, like Machiavelli, *is in full rebellion against the whole political tradition to which he was born.* Mr. Burns, like Machiavelli, refuses to subordinate himself to the norms of political discourse as his fellow citizens understand it. Mr. Burns, like Machiavelli, stands forth before his fellow citizens not merely with novel proposals, but also with a new kind of political thought—a new kind of political thought that they, his fellow citizens, can only find *shocking* once they begin to understand it. For Mr. Burns's quarrel with the American political system is in the last analysis, first (and again I refer to his books), that it is not a good system for translating the will of the majority (which he equates with the will of the people) into action. And second, that it is not a good system for getting the government to do things for the people.

Now, at the risk of sort of pulling the rug out from under Mr. Burns in this debate, I am going to concede *both points.* It is *not* a good system for translating popular will into action. It is *not* a good system for getting government to do things for the people. If what we want in America is a system for translating popular will into action, and for getting things done for the people, then the system ought indeed to be reformed along the lines Mr. Burns proposes.

But, as Mr. Burns well knows off at the back of his mind, the system was *never* intended for translating popular will into action, or for getting government to do things for the people. And if Mr. Burns is sincere in summoning me back to the tradition, he would have to expect me to adopt just the position that I am adopting. Our system was devised by men who feared and disliked *above all things* the operation in politics of sheer, naked will (men therefore who were not given to using language like "the will of the people"). It was devised for purposes that had nothing to do with simplistic formulae like "the will of the people" or "government doing things for the people." It was devised to bring about amongst us a more perfect union, thus not to divide us into majority and minority. To assure us the blessings of liberty, thus not to keep us busy coercing one another. Above all: to achieve the ends of justice, thus not to effectuate the will of any group amongst us, but rather to reconcile the conflicting claims of *different* wills amongst us. It was devised to effectuate not the will of the people, but rather, as *The Federalist* puts it, the deliberate sense of the community, the *whole* community, as to what ought to be done, what policies ought to be adopted.

Most of us, I believe, still think that these are the right purposes for our political system to have. And we still think, therefore, that it is the best political system we could possibly have. That is why, after fifty years of attacking the system for its alleged anti-majoritarian bias, Mr. Burns and his friends have got, well, exactly nowhere as regards the acceptance by the American people of their proposals—which begin with J. Allen Smith and flow directly in a straight line right to Mr. Burns. That is why we Americans will look askance at anyone (even so persuasive an advocate as Mr. Burns) who seeks to give our system a Machiavellian twist in the direction of the sheer naked will of the majority.

Conclusion:

Before beginning my summary, I'd like to pose two quick questions to Mr. Burns—in the hope that he will touch upon them in his own final summary. I would like to ask him, as a political theorist, about his characteristic doctrine—the notion that any American majority is ipso facto a moderate majority. I follow that in connection with the Eisenhower majority. I follow it in connection with the Goldwater majority. I do not see how it could possibly be true of any future *liberal* majority, since it seems to me that within the spectrum of American public opinion, the liberal proposals are precisely *extremist proposals*—extremist proposals on the face of them—which explains the general character of the sort of quarrel they kick up amongst us.

The second question I'd like to ask is, I would like a little more clarification of his peculiar distinction between things the majority

has a right to do and things that it doesn't. First, I would like to know
the source of the distinction (or whether it is merely an arbitrary
distinction Mr. Burns imposes upon the majority principle). Secondly,
how does he explain that civil rights turns up, so to speak, on both
sides of the equation? With one side of his mouth Mr. Burns tells us
[in the question period—Ed.] that the majority must not touch civil
rights and that he hopes that the Supreme Court will police them if
they try to. With the other side of his mouth he is clearly hoping for
a majority action for the civil rights bills. So he is hardly excluding
civil rights from the general sphere of the majority, and he leaves me
quite confused.

As for my summary, it, happily, can be very brief. Ever since I first
learned of this debate, I have sort of looked forward to it as a peculiar
debate. In an ordinary debate, one supposes, the two principals at
least go through the motions of trying to persuade each other, trying
to transform each other into converts. (Or failing that, at least each
principal tries to pick up a convert or two out in the audience.) Not
so tonight. Mr. Burns and I—engaged as we are in exactly the same
racket—have been eying each other across a chasm for lo these many
years. Neither of us, I suppose, thought to coax the other over to his
side of the chasm here, or even much expected that the chasm would
be particularly narrowed in the course of our exchange.

What we did hope, I like to think, was that we would get our
respective positions out on the table where both ourselves and the
audience could look at them more clearly than we've been able to in
the past—with each party coming perhaps to *understand* each other
a little better (not only the other party's position, but also understand
its own position a little better). What I did hope, too, was that we
would see to it that both positions in the course of the debate got
sharply delineated, so that the audience could see clearly what
choices a man is actually making when he takes sides on the issues
that divide conservatives and liberals.

That hope, I believe, has been abundantly realized in the course
of the evening. The issues do seem to me to be out on the table
(particularly those about the future of the American political system)
where we can understand *why they are issues* and where, better still,
we can see that they are *indeed* issues—that is, questions on which
there are indeed two sides, and where each side is capable at least
of a certain amount of reasoned argument in its favor.

I'm willing to content myself in this final summary with merely listing the big questions as they seem to me to have emerged in the course of the debate—with the hope that the audience will go away prepared to pursue them further *as issues*, to seek new evidence bearing upon them, to discuss them further so that one day we can hope to see them decided by a genuine American consensus.

Here then are the issues as I understand them here at the end of the evening:

First, do the liberals, as they often pretend, have a majority out in the country? Or am I right in saying that they remain a mere minority? Put otherwise, have the liberals, as I allege, failed to plead their case successfully before the tribunal of American public opinion? Second, are the current liberal proposals for the reform of the American political system (especially Mr. Burns's proposals) dictated by desperation—by a desperate desire to change the rules obviously in favor of the liberals, by a determination to stack the cards in favor of a future liberal victory? Are such proposals, as I contend, liberal attempts to sidestep the responsibility of building a genuine consensus behind the liberal program? Third, does Mr. Burns, as I allege, have a new and dangerous conception of majority rule? And would that conception, because it cannot carry with it the outvoted minority, lead inevitably to a breakdown of the American political system as I have suggested—that is, to the disappearance from amongst us of our most treasured possession, which is government by discussion? Fourth, are we ready, we Americans, to abandon the Federalist dream of governing ourselves by consensus, of governing ourselves by way of arriving (through deliberation, not mere matching of strength at the polls) at a "deliberate sense" of the whole community? Are we prepared, we Americans, to shift the basis of our political system over to reliance on the sheer, naked will of the majority?

Those, then, are the questions I'd like the audience to think further about in the months and years ahead. And if Mr. Burns and myself have helped draw the issues more sharply—helped perhaps to illuminate them a little—I for one shall remember the evening as, well, a happy occasion.

Deadlock

———✒———

James MacGregor Burns' *The Deadlock of Democracy* (Prentice-Hall, $5.95) is (1) a new kind of political history of the United States, (2) a *Summa* of five decades of political science literature hostile to the American political system, (3) a new proposal for remaking the system so as to eliminate its alleged vices, and (4) over all, an initial venture in a new kind of American political theory. It is brilliantly and entertainingly written, and based upon a depth of knowledge and an analytical skill far beyond those of the system's previous detractors (none of whom was any great shakes on either score). It is, therefore, likely to be around for a long while, and to exercise great influence upon the Liberal constituency at which it is clearly directed. Let me take up, *seriatim*, each of the four aspects of this major event in American political science.

1) *A new kind of political history of the United States.* In the beginning was the "Madisonian model" of American government and politics, which prevailed from 1789 until 1801. The model was built on the two-fold idea that the "accumulation of powers ... in the same hands . . . may justly be pronounced the very definition of tyranny," and "Ambition must be made to counteract ambition." Its "central aim" was to "stop people from turning easily to government for help," and to give minorities power to prevent "the majority from acting through government." Its essence lay not so much in separation of powers, limitation of power, and federalism (though all of these are prominent characteristics of the model), as in the facilities it offered to politicians "to collect groups of followers and to build positions of power," in the proliferation of offices not only on the national level but also in the states, counties, and localities—and, worse still, in a parallel proliferation of "clusters of aspirants and their circles of supporters." Its basic mechanism was "interlocking gears of government, each one responding to different thrusts originating in different groups of the electorate." On the federal level, the model tended to exaggerate the one great defect (according to Burns) of the Philadelphia Constitution, which lay in its failure to provide for a

strong presidency. It accordingly led to policy-decisions based on "coalition, compromise, and consensus," at the expense of "leadership, vigor, speed, and effective and comprehensive national action." It did provide "flexibility, accessibility, and representativeness," but at a terrible price.

In the beginning, then, was the "Madisonian model"; after it, with the rise of the Republican Party through the 1790's and, at the end, the election of Jefferson, came the "Jeffersonian model." It arose in response to the personality and strategy of a great party *leader*, whose first qualification was that he was determined to put to good use what we may call the "majority-rule potential" of the Philadelphia Constitution—that is, the fact that that Constitution, as such, does *not* oppose any effective barrier to the winning and exercise of power by the spokesman for a popular majority. The leader must, accordingly, mobilize behind himself (as Jefferson did) a genuine popular majority—partly by "competing," through organization and policy-proposals with sex-appeal, for the support of voters already on the rolls, partly by enfranchising new voters and "getting their bodies" out on election day. He must—how else would he attract enough voters from the opposing party to build his majority?— *"rise above principle* in order to win [the] election; as, once in office, he must *cut through the separation-of-powers apparatus* to [take] over the three branches of government," then proceed to "govern rather [!] freely and vigorously" with his "broad mandate" (italics added). Thus the Jeffersonian model eliminated, for the moment, the veto on national policy that the Madisonian model had placed in the hands of each and every major "group" in the country. Whatever action might be called for was legitimized *ipso facto* by enjoying the support of a "simple majority of the people." Was the Jeffersonian model built, then, on a tacit denial of the need for limiting power in a democracy, for guarding against tyranny? No, indeed—which brings us to one of the key passages in *Deadlock*: "Majority rule in a big, diverse nation must be moderate. No majority party can cater to the demands of any extremist group . . . [without antagonizing] the great 'middle groups' . . . A democratic people embodies its own safeguards in . . . the great variety of sections and groups and classes and opinions stitched into the fabric of society and thus into the majority's coalition . . . [Neither] major party could abuse any major interest without . . . [alienating] moderate voters holding the balance of power." (Apparently, then, the Jeffersonian model, equally with the Madisonian model, gives a veto to each major group? Burns, curiously, does not see the difficulty.)

Now: The "Madisonian model," with the "heavy price of delay and devitalization," has remained the norm of American government and politics. The Jeffersonian model, when it has reappeared over the decades, has always proved *ephemeral*—has (as I would put it) always soon run afoul of the fact that the "Madisonians" built too well for any competing model ever to have much of a lease on life. The leader either fails to hold his popular majority together (one possibility), or he fails to get his legislation through Congress (another possibility.) Unable to govern *without* getting his legislation through Congress, which calls for a Madisonian "strategy" (that is, wheeling and dealing over in Congress), he is forced to opt for the latter. And as he does so American politics descends from the level of epic poetry appropriate to a Jefferson, a TR, a Wilson, an FDR, to the level of dull prose appropriate to the two Tafts, to the late Representative Treadwell (Burns' pet peeve), to the "do-nothing Congress." American politics, normally, is the Sleeping Beauty, who can only lie abed until awakened by the kiss of a Young Prince who has wrapped himself in the mantle of the Popular Majority. And, in Burns' hands, the political history of the United States becomes above all the history of the alternation of these two models—or, more narrowly, the history of the precise moments when the prosaic but wayward Dr. Jekyll is transformed into the heroic but virtuous Mr. Hyde, and vice versa.

Professor Burns' colleagues, out in the reviews and over the faculty-club luncheon-tables, have been and will continue to be hard on him about his history—on the (I think) irrelevant grounds that, in detail, he is wrong about "what happened" in American political history (this alleged fact is unsubstantiated; he says nothing of that, or that yonder, which is surely part of the story). These critics simply fail, I think, to grasp the character of his enterprise, which is, I repeat, a new kind of American political history. It is, in Eric Voegelin's phrase, *paradigmatic* history not mere *pragmatic* history, the history of America's political past as it *should* be remembered by men for whom it has a meaning, and not just any old meaning but this meaning rather than that meaning—men, accordingly, for whom America has this destiny rather than that one. As Burns indicates by the dreamy, "once-upon-a-time" mood of his opening account of Madison and Jefferson, his political history is a venture in *myth-making,* and his colleagues are wasting their time when they attempt to set him right on the "facts." A myth does not set forth facts; it teaches a lesson. It should be judged good or bad according as the lesson it teaches comes through clear or unclear, and according as that lesson is valid or invalid, beneficent or dangerous. I happen to think the lesson Burns' myth teaches is invalid and dangerous. But it is the right myth for teaching that lesson, and our literature is the richer for it.

2) A *"Summa" of the attack on the American political system.* The attack on the American political system begins with J. Allen Smith's *The Spirit of American Government* in 1912, and burgeons in the course of the Liberal onslaught on the Supreme Court during the New Deal. In due course it enlists under its banners the overwhelming majority of American political scientists. It seems, despite ancient wisdom to the effect that no such thing is possible, to have been created *ex nihilo:* no one appears to have turned up an American intellectual ancestor for Smith (he has, to be sure, clear affinities with Chartism, but that was in another time and in another country and, anyhow, there is no proof that Smith ever knew the wench). From its beginning in Smith's hands, the attack already possesses its characteristic features—an understanding of "political equality" that must eventuate in a demand for universal suffrage; emphasis on the *will* of the people as opposed to that "deliberate sense" of the people that the author of the *Federalist* sought to midwife; dogmatic insistence on the "right" of the majority of the people to call the turns in public policy; glorification of elections (*not* deliberation in the bosom of a representative assembly) as the central ritual of American politics; all-out condemnation, therefore, of all those features of the American political system that render difficult or even postpone the translation of majority preference into governmental policy. After Smith, it remains for the attackers (a) to work out the details of a program for transforming the American political system into the new "image" of democracy (which now holds undisputed sway in our intellectual circles), (b) to expand the attack into an onslaught on American political parties, (c) to identify an ever more powerful Presidency as the logical rallying-point for the attackers, and Congress as *the* enemy, and (d) to learn to accept the once "anti-democratic," and thus inimical, Supreme Court as an ally. All that, to be sure, takes some doing—takes, in Milton's phrase, many "pens and heads" mus-

ing beside "studious lamps" over a long period. Smith's "compact" attack, as Voegelin would put it, is "differentiated" into several attacks, each of which becomes the business of a group of specialists who concern themselves with one or another of the system's vulnerabilities, and each of which produces a mountain of books and articles with which, in a pinch, one might dam the Mississippi at New Orleans. Small wonder, particularly in view of the attack's scanty theoretical basis, if as the decades pass its strategy becomes untidy. Small wonder, again, that its literature has long needed an Angelic Doctor to synthesize it, to pull things together, to eliminate the false starts and the irrelevancies, to smooth out inconsistencies—to provide, in brief, the *Summa* to which the faithful, without pausing to read all those books and articles, can turn for the straight poop. *Deadlock,* for the literature of the attack on the American political system, is just that *Summa.* And, like any good *Summa,* in the act of becoming a *Summa* it becomes more than a *Summa,* by giving new direction to the whole enterprise. Above all, by abandoning hopeless emphases in the position, and replacing them with hopeful ones. Burns does, for the Liberal attack, precisely that.

3) *A new proposal for remaking the American political system.* The attackers' central difficulty, where the author of the new *Summa* takes over, is the classic difficulty of the Little Gingerbread Boy, who can't get hot 'til he runs and can't run 'til he gets hot. Fifty years have passed since Smith published, yet the system, the system with all its anti-majoritarian, anti-egalitarian bias is, damn it, still there. The attackers have, to this day, gained none of the objectives for which they have been fighting: realignment of the parties into a system of "responsible" parties; enfranchisement of the Southern Negroes; the translation of American elections into plebiscites over policy; abolition of the "seniority" system in congressional committees; unhorsing the hated Rules Committee in the House of Representatives; "reapportionment" to terminate "rural overrepresentation" in Congress. The case for each of these good things has, to be sure, been proved over and over again. But the "addressee" of all the relevant flood of reasoned argument, the American people, has paid no attention— either it likes the system as it is, or it is too "apathetic," too indifferent, to accept and act upon the proposals for remaking it. So, for a long time, the attackers have merely been spinning their wheels, saying the same things over and over again, talking only to each other

—louder and louder perhaps as times goes by, but entirely without effect upon the supposed audience. They have, indeed, been too busy talking to each other to pause to ask why they are not getting anywhere. Their tacit premise (unexceptionable, no doubt, in a democracy) is that continued reliance upon "debate," upon public discussion, is the only course open to them—so that, win or lose, they must follow it to the end. Burns breaks with the literature he synthesizes by quietly giving up—so quietly indeed that nobody seems to have noticed—on the attackers' entire strategy-to-date. It is, he tacitly confesses, a "no-win" strategy. The problem narrows, for him, down to how to get the Little Gingerbread Boy hot. He thinks he sees a way to do it, and the real significance of *Deadlock* (apart from my point 4 below) is to be sought in his breathtaking new proposal for heating up the Little Gingerbread Boy.

The "Madisonian model," Burns argues, has ended us up with not the two political parties of our textbook lore, but four: The Presidential Democrats, the Presidential Republicans, the Congressional Democrats, and the Congressional Republicans. The Presidential Democrats and the Presidential Republicans have much the same foreign and domestic program (roughly speaking, the Kennedy program), and are at one in preferring the "Jeffersonian model" to the Madisonian. The Congressional Democrats and the Congressional Republicans oppose the program, and are in position, through session after session, to block it; both, moreover, are prepared to fight to the death to preserve the "Madisonian model." Thus "deadlock"—deadlock that cannot be broken by the plead-your-case strategy-to-date of the attackers, because within the present legal and institutional framework of American politics every attempt to break it is, and will continue to be, frustrated by the one-party congressional constituencies that perpetuate control of the House in the hands of the "leadership." The traditional "attacker" solution to this problem is: Let the American people divide off into two "meaningful" parties, a Liberal and a Conservative Party, that will present "genuine" alternatives to the electorate, produce a "mandate" that must be carried out, and give us a President and Congress that will see eye to eye. Burns, I say, sees that all that gets us nowhere. Something new—not the less new because it is the oldest and perhaps ultimately the only truly Machiavellian strategy in politics—is called for, namely, what amounts to a *coup d'etat.* Let the Presidential Democrats and the Presidential

Republicans *not* merge in a new party, forcing the Congressionals into a second. Let them rather, connive briefly for the single purpose of over-throwing the going system (that is, carrying out the institutional program of the attackers, especially breaking the back of the one-party district), and, into the bargain, capture *both* parties, which would henceforth "compete" with one another for the honor of carrying out the program of the "Presidentials." Professor Burns' device will fetch you, not the *one* Liberal party of the "responsible"-partyites' dreams, but *two* Liberal parties (Burns, for reasons at which one can only guess, avoids the term "Liberal" and "Conservative"). Like that of the young man from Moline, it can be concave or convex as needed, and so fit both the Democrats or the Republicans. Burns' demonstration that the thing can't be brought off any other way (though hidden in the interstices of his analysis of the dilemma Roosevelt and Eisenhower found themselves up against when they were tempted by the idea of building a "responsible" party) is, I submit, devastating. And never mind that it can't be brought off Burns' way, either. Never mind that he offers a merely "intellectual," or "theoretical," solution to a practically insoluble problem, namely, how to get the program of the Liberals adopted despite popular attachment to the "Madisonian model" and to anti- or non-Liberal policy directives. Burns is at least talking about something, or, if not that, has at least stopped talking about the nothing of the "responsible party system" advocates. His proposal is, clearly, born of desperation, and becomes a tacit confession that the Liberals cannot win, cannot even hope to win, whilst the Conservatives among the electorate are offered some kind—any kind—of alternative to Liberalism.

4) *A new kind of political theory for America.* If Burns' proposal is (as I have argued) startlingly novel, it is still less novel than his mode of argument. His predecessors in the attack on the American political system have, for all their hostility to the "Madisonian model," stayed largely within the traditional assumptions of American political discourse: the "Madisonian model" is bad, and must be replaced, because it *misrepresents* the American people, stands between the American people and public policies *representative* of (to use Publius' term) their "deliberate sense." The attackers' avowed purpose was to perfect our machinery for canvassing the alternatives in public policy, and for referring them to the standards set forth in the preamble of the Constitution, all without any attempt, at least any attempt

that met the eye, to foreclose any alternative, to stack the cards in favor of this alternative rather than that one, to substitute for the deliberate sense of the people the *will* of any particular group. The attackers indeed wanted to change the rules, but were, like Publius, willing to let the game, a game whose outcome could not be foreknown, be played out under the changed rules. The changed rules, they were there to argue, would be better rules than the old ones, because they would provide a better test for the competing teams. The attackers, even if the "solution" they put forward was new and unfamiliar, had in hand an old and familiar problem. Not so Burns, to whom I believe I do no injustice when I say that the problem to which he addresses himself is, quite simply, this: Some of us are committed to such and such policies, such and such a program, for the American Republic. We are determined that these policies shall be effectuated, and the question arises, What will have to be done to our political institutions and practices in order to break the "deadlock" that keeps them from being effectuated? What is *really* new in Burns, then, is on the one hand the problem to which he reduces American political theory, and on the other hand his repudiation, no less flat and unambiguous than that of Machiavelli himself, of the whole range of concerns, principles (witness his reference to principles in the above citation) and above all inhibitions handed down to him from the past. The nation's political regime is, for Burns, the *ancilla* of a set of policies that he and his friends have declared good. Let the Liberal program prevail, and *ruat coelum!*

Jefferson and Civil Liberties:
The Darker Side

———♪———

Reprinted from the *Stanford Law Review*, Volume 16, No. 3, May, 1964.
© 1964 by the Board of Trustees of the Leland Stanford Junior
University.

Jefferson and Civil Liberties: The Darker Side. By Leonard W.
Levy. Cambridge: Harvard University Press. 1963. xv+225 pages.
$4.50.

In *The Legacy of Suppression,* the book to which the one under
review is a sequel, Leonard Levy wrote,

> This has been a difficult book to write. . . . [T]he facts have
> dictated conclusions that violate my predilections and clash
> with the accepted version of history. But . . . my views as a
> scholar do not depend on my civic convictions nor [*sic*] on
> historical convention. . . . [T]he past must be taken on its own
> terms.[1]

"I would be delighted," he added, "if this book were proved to be
wrong"[2]—as, we may safely add for him, would a great many other
people who share Professor Levy's "predilections" and are in the
habit of resolving certain great issues of our time by appealing mainly
to the "historical convention" he has in mind.

Those predilections are, roughly speaking, those that we have,
with gross historical inaccuracy, come to associate with the name of
Mr. Justice Hugo Black, to whose line of dissents in first amendment
cases we are indeed indebted for their most recent and most vigorous
articulation. They are predilections as to the policy a self-governing
people ought to adopt concerning the so-called "basic" individual
"freedoms" or "rights"—freedom of speech, press, petition and assembly, conscience, and above all perhaps, though seldom mentioned, freedom of thought. To use Popper's phrase, they are

[1]Levy, The Legacy of Suppression viii (1960).
[2]*Id.* at xi.

predilections in favor of an "open society"—a society in which there is no legal or governmental interference with the "free market" in ideas, no legal or governmental barrier to unrestricted liberty of choice by the citizens among all conceivable alternatives in religion, politics, morals, and indeed all areas of possible controversy. They are predilections that our generation should, in strict justice, associate with Alexander Meikeljohn who, in their specific application to constitutional problems in the United States, was the first writer to urge them upon us and who, more I think than any other writer including Zechariah Chafee, Jr., is responsible for their current regnancy among American intellectuals. They are, finally, predilections with which we are sufficiently familiar to be able to say with some confidence that the major types of argument by which they can be supported intellectually are the following:

First, the argument that there is an unanswerable "pure" case for these predilections to be found in the literature of political philosophy, especially in the writings of John Stuart Mill—the appeal to the authority of what Professor Levy calls "libertarian theory" from Milton to the present day.[3] Secondly, the argument that the constitutional rules appropriate to these predilections are presupposed in the very idea of self-government—the appeal to the "necessity" of the logic of democracy (which, for convenience, I distinguish from the appeal to philosophical authority in order to set it apart from the argument to be found in Mill). Thirdly, the argument that all questions as to these predilections are settled for us by the "plain language" of the first amendment: "Congress shall make no law. . . ." that abridges the freedoms in question—the appeal to the authority of the Constitution. Fourthly, the argument that the plain language of the first amendment reflects the settled convictions and thus the intention of the "Framers" and, beyond that, of the generation of Americans who ratified the Constitution—the appeal to the authoritative wisdom of the founding fathers.

These four types of argument constitute the American brief for the open society. It is well that we should have all four in mind before we consider those "conclusions" that made the first of Professor Levy's two books so "difficult" to write because they "violated" his

[3]As Levy says, "the case for civil liberties is so powerfully grounded in political philosophy's wisest principles, as well as the wisest policies drawn from experience, that it need not be anchored to the past." *Id.* at 4.

predilections and the conclusions, for him equally unpalatable, to which he has been driven in his new book. For once the two books are digested by the scholarly community, the relative status of the four arguments can never again be what it was when Professor Levy took pen in hand. Levy completely, definitely explodes the fourth argument (appeal to the Framers) and gives to the third argument (appeal to the plain meaning of the first amendment) a wholly new cast that will cause it to figure less prominently in future than in past discussions. Thus he places in the forefront of the debate the arguments (the appeal to the logic of democracy and the appeal to political philosophy) of which in the past we have, to our misfortune I think, heard least. Defenders of the open society and of policies that will move the United States in the direction of becoming an open society will find themselves obliged in the future to argue these questions on their merits, that is, on the level of political philosophy. One can, I think, imagine no more wholesome development in our public debate.

We must, therefore, attend carefully to at least the major conclusions to which Professor Levy found himself driven in *The Legacy of Suppression.*

Levy states that the question as to the intention of the Framers and of the generation that ratified the constitutional rule that "Congress shall make no law . . . abridging the freedom of speech, or of the press" boils down to whether they intended to abolish the common law of seditious libel.[4] There is no evidence of any such intention on the part of any member of the Constitutional Convention or of the First Congress, which drafted the Bill of Rights.[5] At least freedom of speech had in America "prior to the First Amendment or even later" little or no history either *"as a concept or a practice."*[6] It was a "concept without basis in everyday experience and nearly unknown to legal and constitutional history or [even] to libertarian thought";[7] and to the extent it was known, it referred to the immunity of the *legislator* for utterances made in his official capacity, not to immunity of private individuals.[8] Nor was the situation notably different in

---

[4]See *id.* at 1, where Levy initially states the accepted proposition that the Framers intended to abolish seditious libel but then challenges its validity.
[5]See *id.* at 4-5.
[6]*Id.* at 5. (Emphasis added.)
[7]*Ibid.*
[8]*Id.* at 5-6.

regard to freedom of the press, which meant at most freedom from "prior restraints" on publication. "One might publish without a license, but he did so at the peril of being punished for libel";[9] "any comment about the government which could be construed to have the bad tendency of lowering it in the public's esteem or of disturbing the peace was seditious libel, subjecting the speaker or writer to public prosecution."[10] Nor is there any doubt that "the presence of punishment afterwards, for 'bad sentiments,' oral or published, had an effect similar to a law authorizing previous restraints."[11] So it had been in England, and so it was, despite historical convention, in colonial America: "The persistent image of colonial America as a society in which freedom of expression was cherished is an hallucination of sentiment...."[12] "The American people simply did not understand that freedom of thought and expression means equal freedom for the other fellow, especially the one with hated ideas."[13] The most "dreaded and active instrument of suppression," moreover, was "that acclaimed bastion of the people's liberties, the popularly-elected Assembly";[14] "the law of seditious libel . . . was enforced ... chiefly by the provincial legislatures..., secondly by the executive officers in concert with the upper houses, and lastly, a poor third, by the common law courts."[15]

> Any words, written, printed, or spoken, which were imagined to have a tendency of impeaching an Assembly's behavior, questioning its authority, derogating from its honor, affronting its dignity, or defaming its members, individually or together, were regarded as a seditious scandal against the government, punishable as a breach of privilege.[16]

"None of the available evidence ... [for any of the colonies] suggests that freedom of speech or press existed before the revolutionary controversy,"[17] as witness the treatment meted out to the American

[9] *Id.* at 9.
[10] *Id.* at 10.
[11] *Id.* at 15.
[12] *Id.* at 18.
[13] *Ibid.*
[14] *Id.* at 20.
[15] *Ibid.*
[16] *Id.* at 21.
[17] *Id.* at 63.

Tories[18]—"Yankee Doodle's Liberty Boys vociferously claimed for themselves . . . [a] right of free expression which they denied their opponents."[19] In the words of one writer of the pre-Revolutionary period, "Political liberty consists in freedom of speech, so far as the laws of a community will permit, and no farther: all beyond is criminal, and tends to the destruction of Liberty itself."[20] Nor is there any "known evidence proving that any American prior to 1798—that late —thought otherwise."[21]

> Animadversion was regarded as subversion. Any verbal attack on government officials or policies which might be deemed an affront to the authority or honor of the legislature was subject to a power of repression from which not all the writs precious to the liberty of the subject could effect a rescue.[22]

In short, the "people" whose representatives wrote and who themselves ratified the first amendment, with its apparent guarantees of freedom of expression, had no tradition of free speech or a free press, no statesmen who were urging the need for these guarantees, and no political philosophers who had made out a case for them.

The first amendment "happened" where and when it could not possibly have happened, except to the extent we repeal the axiom that nothing is ever created out of nothing. How we are to explain the first amendment brings us to a second, and still more breathtaking, set of Professor Levy's conclusions. Levy notes that the remote source of the first amendment freedom of expression clauses appears to be a provision of Pennsylvania's first constitution, adopted in 1776, "that *the people* have a right to freedom of speech, and of writing, and of publishing their sentiments; therefore freedom of the press ought not to be restrained."[23] But it is not true, as historical convention would have us believe, that the first amendment merely bumped up to the federal level speech and press guarantees that were already familiar features in the state constitutions—twelve states had left speech entirely unprotected and four had provided no

[18]See *ibid.*
[19]*Id.* at 64.
[20]*Id.* at 68-69.
[21]*Id.* at 68.
[22]*Id.* at 86.
[23]*Id.* at 183. (Emphasis added.)

constitutional protection for freedom of the press.[24] Worse still, "The history of Pennsylvania . . . shows that the only one of the original states to protect constitutionally both speech and press *did not intend to abandon the common law of seditious libel."*[25] The same thing appears to be true of the eight states that protected the press:

> There is no evidence to show that . . . [the term "freedom of press"] was not used in its prevailing common-law or Blackstonian sense to mean a guarantee against previous restraints *and a subjection to subsequent restraints for licentious or seditious abuse.*[26]

The guarantees probably meant, to those who wrote them, "the right of unrestricted discussion of public affairs," but it was clearly understood "that discussion *was* unrestricted if there was a guarantee against previous restraint."[27] The "freedom" toward which the Constitution-makers were groping was a "freedom to write, print, or utter anything that was *temperate, accurate, well-intentioned, and that fell short of what a court or the community might deem seditious or libelous.* "[28] Benjamin Franklin put the idea very well when he wrote that, if freedom of the press meant " 'the Liberty of discussing the Propriety of Public Measures and Political opinions, let us have as much of it as you please'. . . . [but] as to writers who affront the government's reputation 'we should, in moderation, content ourselves with tarring and feathering and tossing them in a blanket.' "[29] He further felt that verbal criticisms of the government must be "guided by moderation, truth, and good motives."[30] As for the political theory of the pre-first amendment period, such as that reflected in the famed Cushing-Adams correspondence,[31] the only break one finds in the direction of Professor Levy's "predilections" is the two-fold insistence that "truth should be a defense against a charge of criminal utterance" and that juries "should decide whether the

[24] *Id.* at 184-85.
[25] *Id.* at 185. (Emphasis added.)
[26] *Ibid.* (Emphasis added.)
[27] *Id.* at 186. (Emphasis added.)
[28] *Ibid.* (Emphasis added.)
[29] *Id.* at 186-87.
[30] *Id.* at 187-88.
[31] See *id.* at 192-96.

defendant's words were criminal."[32] Neither Cushing nor Adams had broken with the idea that falsehoods and scandals against the government should be punished, as Cushing put it, "with becoming rigour."[33] In due course, Adams as President was to sign the Sedition Act of 1798 and "eagerly" urge its enforcement; Cushing as Associate Justice of the Supreme Court was to preside over some of the trials and to charge juries on the statute's constitutionality.[34] Moreover, Cushing and Adams wrote as *reformers,* far ahead of the constitutional law of the period.[35] We need not be surprised, then, when we find nobody challenging James Wilson's contention at the Pennsylvania ratifying convention that the Constitution would leave the common law of seditious libel in force.[36] There are thus no grounds for Zechariah Chafee's often quoted statement that the authors of the first amendment "intended to wipe out the common law of sedition, and make further prosecutions for criticism of the government, without any incitement to law-breaking, forever impossible in the United States of America."[37] With one very minor exception, "from the time of the revolutionary controversy through the ratification of the first amendment," one finds no statement to the effect that the doctrine of seditious libel is incompatible with liberty.[38] What one does find "indicates the contrary proposition."[39] Finally, as some persons will learn to their surprise, no book or pamphlet was available to the authors of the first amendment that urged any such novel doctrine.[40] Nor can it be argued, as we often hear, that the first amendment guarantees were rendered necessary by the famous "recommendations" with which the ratifying states accompanied their respective acts of ratification: none of the first nine states to ratify recommended guarantees of freedom of speech or press,[41] and while three other states did make recommendations along these lines, there is no rea-

---

[32] *Id.* at 196.

[33] *Id.* at 198.

[34] *Ibid.* The weakness of the protection derived from the Cushing-Adams concept of freedom of the press is demonstrated by the fact that "only one Sedition Act jury returned a verdict of acquittal." *Id.* at 199.

[35] *Id.* at 200.

[36] *Id.* at 202.

[37] CHAFEE, FREE SPEECH IN THE UNITED STATES 21 (1948) (quoted in LEVY, THE LEGACY OF SUPPRESSION 213-14 (1960)).

[38] LEVY, THE LEGACY OF SUPPRESSION 214 (1960).

[39] *Ibid.*

[40] See *id.* at 88-125.

[41] *Id.* at 217-18.

son to attribute to them an intention to supersede the law of seditious libel.[42] We begin to see the answer to the question, "How did the first amendment guarantees of free speech and free press happen when and where they did?" If what we are talking about are *guarantees* of *free* expression to the individual citizen, they did not happen at all. *Pace* Mr. Justice Black, the first-amendment support for Professor Levy's "predilections" has been brought off by mirrors. Both terms, as used in the first amendment, were understood as having their common-law meaning and *only* that meaning, because there is no other meaning they could have had for the persons concerned. Moreover, even had they had another meaning, one tending in an "open society" direction, the fact would remain that the first amendment "offered against *state* violation no protection whatever to speech and press, or to religion."[43] As I like to put it in classroom lectures, what the first amendment in fact does is to declare suppression a monopoly of the state governments. Nor can there be any question of making the amendment look better in these respects by appeal to the relevant congressional debate. It was "unclear and apathetic; ambiguity, brevity, and imprecision of thought characterize the comments of the few members who spoke. It is doubtful that the House understood the debate, or cared deeply about its outcome. . . ."[44] "To assume the existence of a general, latitudinarian understanding [of the speech and press guarantees] that veered substantially from the common-law definition is incredible. . . ."[45] "Not even the Anti-Federalists offered the argument that the clause on speech and press was unsatisfactory because insufficiently protective."[46] The Anti-Federalists, the primitive source of the demand for "amendments guaranteeing individual rights,"[47] disliked Madison's Bill of Rights, including the guarantees here in question, the moment they saw it and switched sides on the Bill of Rights issue.[48] We can now understand why they disliked it— why, for instance, Burke of South Carolina denounced the guarantees as "little better than whip-syllabub, frothy and full of wind, formed only to please the palate; . . . we have done nothing but lose our

---

[42]See *id.* at 218-21.
[43]*Id.* at 223. (Emphasis added.)
[44]*Id.* at 224.
[45]*Id.* at 225.
[46]*Ibid.*
[47]*Id.* at 226.
[48]See *id.* at 227-28.

time. . . . ."[49] The events surrounding ratification of the amendment leave matters unchanged: their history "indicates no passion on the part of anyone to grind underfoot the common law. . . . Indeed, the history of the framing and ratification of the First Amendment scarcely manifests a passion on the part of anyone connected with the process."[50]

Professor Levy's conclusions should, as they become known to scholars in the field of constitutional law, put an end to appeals to the intention of the Framers of the first amendment by proponents of open-society doctrines. And Professor Levy's book should also end appeals to the "plain meaning" of the language of the first amendment, save on the part of those who are prepared to wrest it unabashedly out of its historical context: its plain meaning for the men who wrote it and the men who ratified it was precisely *not* the meaning it now seems to have because history has played strange tricks with the *usage* of the terms "freedom of speech" and "freedom of the press." The best Professor Levy can do to salvage it is to say that its Framers "formulated its language in words of such breadth . . . that *we* have been able to breathe a liberality of meaning *into* it in keeping with the ideals of our expanding democracy,"[51] which gives the show away as regards "plain meaning" as a libertarian edict. The "rights" vouchsafed by the plain meaning of the first amendment were the very reverse of "absolute," to use Mr. Justice Black's phrase, and belong rather in the same category with the right to swim guaranteed in the celebrated rule of jurisprudence: "Yes, yes, my darling daughter; hang your clothes on a hickory limb, but don't go near the water." Mr. Justice Black therefore must, on pain of being declared either an ideologist or a careless scholar, change his line of argument in first-amendment cases.[52]

[49] *Id.* at 228.

[50] *Id.* at 233.

[51] *Id.* at xii. (Emphasis added.)

[52] There are, let me add, three further difficulties about the whole matter to which Professor Levy's leanings in political philosophy blind him—difficulties that the present writer will deal with in a book now in progress. There is—as witness the word "people" in the above reference to Pennsylvania's 1776 Constitution, where the "right" to freedom of speech would seem to inhere not in individuals but in the *populus*—grave doubt whether the men responsible for the "plain language" were yet thinking at all in terms of "rights," automatically extensible to all individuals. There is also grave doubt that anyone except Madison and Jefferson was yet thinking of rights as enforceable by the courts against Congress. Finally, the Supreme Court has yet to attempt to enforce the first amendment against Congress, which *might* mean that it does not think it can.

In dispelling one mystery, how the first amendment could have happened when and where it did, Professor Levy raises another: where and when and how then *did* his predilections, the predilections in favor of a legally open society, originate in America? Still another mystery is when and where the first attempt occurred in America to defend the libertarian position philosophically. To the first of these two questions his answer, on the "where" and "when," is: with Jefferson and the "Jeffersonians," in the course of the controversy over the Sedition Act ot 1798; and on the "how": in a manner that is highly "suspect" (from, one supposes, the standpoint of political philosophy). "Had any of . . . [the Jeffersonians] declared at any time before 1791 . . . some of the opinions they formed in *the party battle* of 1798-1800," their later statements might be accepted at face value; but none of them meets this test.[53] "Not a single Federalist in the United States is known to have opposed the constitutionality of the Sedition Act. . . . Every Democratic-Republican with the exception of James Sullivan believed it to be unconstitutional."[54] The predilections were born in the ardors of a struggle for power by some "outs," in the form of promising arguments to be used against some "ins," and should be taken *cum grano salis*. This is especially true since "many of the Jeffersonians, *most notably Jefferson himself,* behaved when in power in ways that belied their fine libertarian sentiments of 1798."[55]

Jefferson and Civil Liberties: The Darker Side, which is to all intents and purposes a lengthy appendix to *The Legacy of Suppression,* is a detailed account of the fall from libertarian grace that accompanied the Jeffersonians' rise to power. It, too, must have been a "difficult book to write"; indeed Professor Levy's mood is not unlike that of a devoted husband reading aloud a private investigator's report on how his errant wife spends her afternoons. Unlike *Legacy,* therefore, *Jefferson* tends to be iterative and tiresome; few readers will—or ought to—wish to stay the course, the more since Levy early establishes the overall point his data are capable of supporting. Jefferson did, from the standpoint of Professor Levy's predilections, have a "darker" side. He went into office with heavy commitments to maintain civil liberties; one could piece together, out of the quotes strewn through the book, a veritable libertarian credo. However, he

[53]*Id.* at 247. (Emphasis added.)
[54]*Id.* at 246.
[55]*Id.* at 247. (Emphasis added.)

did, while in office, appear to act on the principle that no government should permit qualms about individual rights to get in the way of its policies. He *did,* although he was in part responsible for the adoption of a Bill of Rights that would presumably limit the power of the federal government by, for example, forbidding unreasonable searches and seizures, make constant use of such searches and seizures in enforcing his embargo legislation and even persuaded his Democratic Congress to authorize them, "the most repressive and unconstitutional legislation ever enacted by Congress in time of peace."[56] He had, on countless occasions, testified to his belief in freedom of the press, yet in power "he experimented with censorship and condoned the prosecution of his critics."[57] In 1783 he had wished to forbid the Virginia Legislature the power "to pass any bill of attainder,"[58] but he lived to argue that "legislative outlawry and attainder was justifiable . . . when a person charged with a crime withdrew from justice or resisted it."[59] So on down through all the articles of the credo: "Practices once reprehended by Jefferson as shocking betrayals of natural and constitutional rights suddenly seemed innocent, even necessary and salutary, when the government was in his hands."[60] He "tended to stretch his political powers as he stretched his mind in intellectual matters, leaving his conscience behind. . . ."[61] "In Jefferson's case power produced a myopia that permitted bills of rights to be seen only dimly."[62]

How, Professor Levy asks all along the way, are we to judge "the foremost [libertarian] spokesman of his generation" when we find him behaving in this manner? And his answer is that we are to pronounce a verdict of "culpable."[63] I agree, as I agree also with Professor Levy's contention that "Jefferson's experience . . . has particular relevance to the problems of the 1960's, a decade in which expediency seems often to demand a sacrifice of rights."[64] Culpable, yes—but of which of the two possible charges: (1) Knowing the right yet doing the wrong—that is, failing to "live up," while in the office

[56] P. 139.
[57] P. 19.
[58] P. 41.
[59] P. 39.
[60] Pp. 162-63.
[61] P. 166.
[62] P. x.
[63] P. xi.
[64] P. viii.

of President, to the pronouncements previously handed down from his study; or (2) having handed down pronouncements from his study that turned out, when put to the test, to have been ill-considered— pronouncements, if you like, that were insufficiently grounded in political philosophy and especially that chapter of political philosophy that teaches us to leave room when we make pronouncements for the possible future claims of prudential considerations? For Professor Levy, who though he chides Jefferson with overconfidence in his "rightness" is "certain that he is absolutely right"[65] on all questions concerning civil liberties, the choice between the two charges is easy: he will take the first every time and will unhesitatingly sweep aside Jefferson's now tacit, now explicit, insistence that the conduct Levy retrospectively demands of him would involve constant betrayal of the responsibilities of his office. For me the choice is not easy[66]—it is, indeed, possible only because I look behind Jefferson's commitments to the *assertions* involved and find them bad political philosophy because they violate Madison's wise injunction against "absolute restrictions in cases that are doubtful, or where emergencies may overrule them." But since bad political philosophy is a greater crime than "talking one way and acting another,"[67] I must in the end find Jefferson even more "culpable" than Levy thinks him to be; and by the same token I must find Professor Levy "culpable" too—for approaching all these questions with a dogmatism, an apodictic certainty, that cuts him off from the very possibility of political philosophy. This he does, moreover, at the moment, when having deprived his fellow-libertarians of the appeal to the Framers and the appeal to the plain text of the first amendment, both they and he have no place to go *except* to political philosophy. Were he ever to develop one iota of doubt about the correctness of the libertarian "position" or even a little familiarity with the writings of its critics,[68] a whole new world would be opened to him and, because of his great intellectual gifts, to us all.

In conclusion, as to the second of Professor Levy's mysteries and his "solution" to it, it *is* possible to say when and where a case for the libertarian position first emerges in America, and one of the

[65]P. 163.
[66]I do recognize that something is to be said for a statesman's acting in office as he has led people to expect.
[67]P. x.
[68]Even James Fitzjames Stephen is not mentioned in his survey of the literature.

virtues of *Legacy,* indeed a major "breakthrough" for which we shall remain forever in debt to that book, is that it settles the question once and for all. Louis Wortman, a New York lawyer, published in 1800 a book entitled *A Treatise Concerning Political Inquiry, and the Liberty of the Press* that establishes itself, even in Levy's brief exegesis of its argument,[69] as the great neglected American masterpiece on freedom of expression and as, therefore, *the* book to which the libertarians will be well advised to go for ammunition when they begin to argue questions concerning civil liberties on their merits. "It is . . . ," says Professor Levy, "the book Jefferson did not write but should have."[70] I would pay it even higher praise: it is a book Jefferson could not have written even if he had tried and the book John Stuart Mill later tried to write but did not write as well.[71] Stephen would have had with Wortman's *Treatise* no Roman holiday of the kind he indulged in with Mill's *Essay;* the *Treatise,* indeed, would present a real challenge to any nonlibertarian critic. If Levy deprives his coreligionaries of a couple of old and jaded lines of argument, he gives them a new hero. And they have everything to gain and nothing to lose from this redistribution of assets.

[69]See LEVY, THE LEGACY OF SUPPRESSION 283-90 (1960).
[70]*Id.* at 283.
[71]Wortman, it may be noted, preceded Mill by several decades.

The Bill of Rights &
American Freedom

Let me begin by setting down a few easily confirmable but perhaps not very well-known facts:

I

1. The Convention that drew up the Constitution of the United States voted down unanimously a proposal (by Colonel Mason) that the Constitution be made to include a declaration or bill of the natural rights of man.

2. Proposals for such a declaration or bill of rights became, in short order, the major rallying points in the several States for opponents of ratification of the Philadelphia Constitution.

3. In the controversy over ratification, as it went forward in the so-called ratifying conventions, no clear distinction was drawn by the opponents of ratification between the two issues: (a) Will the new Federal government be "too powerful" in the sense that it will threaten the integrity and sovereignty of the *States?* and (b) Will it be "too powerful" in the sense that it will threaten the natural rights of the *individual citizens of the States?*

To put it otherwise: We know that a very considerable percentage of the opponents of ratification were primarily concerned about what was going to happen to the States in the new Federal union. This is the objection to ratification that is uppermost in the minds of the authors of the *Federalist,* so that Hamilton's attack on the very idea of a bill of rights appears at a relatively late date in the series, too late to affect the controversy. But *this* animus, which would have produced a demand not for a bill of individual rights but for something roughly equivalent to the Tenth Amendment—some barrier to the expansion of Federal power at the expense of State power—never expresses itself very clearly in the course of the controversy, somehow gets absorbed into the demand for guarantees of individual rights.

Here is one of the curiosities of the whole business; one might have
expected, for example, a concerted attack by the States'-rights men
on the "necessary and proper" clause, which was—one is tempted to
say "obviously"—*the* threat in the Constitution to the powers of the
States. But the major rallying point of opponents of ratification
becomes, I repeat, and becomes at an early date, the demand for
guarantees of personal liberty; they apparently do not see that a bill
of individual rights will in no way, or at least no direct way, protect
the "sovereignty" of the States. I leave to one side, as unresearchable,
the "cynical" explanation, namely: that those who opposed ratification out of concern for the States embraced the bill of individual
rights in the fond hope of saving the States by defeating the Constitution altogether. The Federalists often made this charge, which we
may call the "phony issue" charge. But I do not see how, even if it
were true, it could possibly be substantiated; that is, I see no scholarly
alternative to taking the participants in the controversy at their word
and assuming that the bill-of-rights men wanted what they are
reputed to have got, namely, a bill of rights.

4. The controversy was in many respects a curious one; properly
speaking, perhaps, we should not speak of *a* controversy but of the
several controversies in the several States: neither the Federalists nor
the anti-Federalists ever threw up anything much in the way of a
union-wide organization; the Federalists in each state merely took on
their local anti-Federalists. (Let me stress the point, because it will
assume considerable importance in a few minutes.) Letters and documents were exchanged; strategies were no doubt affected, within a
given State, by influences coming from outside; but that was about
it. Another curiosity is that the controversies were not (to some extent
no doubt for the reason just mentioned) over *the* Bill of Rights, but
rather over *a* bill of rights, which nobody ever took the trouble to
draw up, so that what the controversies were in fact over was Bill of
Rights X, where X, as in algebra, was an unknown. This, too, will
assume importance below, so let me stress it: Madison, when he
finally came up tails on the issue, had an extremely free hand in
preparing the first draft.

5. It is *not true,* though many historians would like us to think so,
that nobody bothered to draw up a draft because "everybody knew"
what provisions the future bill of rights, if incorporated in or added
to the Constitution, would "have" to contain; this remained a great

uncertainty right down to the moment when *the* Bill of Rights was finally voted in the First Congress. Or rather let me respond to the stirrings of scholarly caution and say: Everybody perhaps knew certain things it would contain, namely, the common-law rights that do in fact make up the bulk of *the* Bill of Rights. Indeed I have come to the conclusion that if a draft *had* been prepared and adopted by a nation-wide anti-Federalist organization, and *if* that draft had limited itself to the common-law rights, there need have been no controversies. The Federalists would have said, would have *had* to say, "Ah! If *that* is all you mean, let us by all means have your bill of rights." They were not going to take the public position that they wished the new government to have the power to make unreasonable searches and seizures, or to force witnesses to testify against themselves, or to try accused persons a second time for one and the same offense.

To put it still otherwise: *if* a draft had been prepared, and *if* it had confined itself to the substance of Amendments II through X, the only point on which the Federalists might have felt tempted to take exception was that of jury trials in civil cases. The Framers had had their reasons, rather honorable ones in point of fact, for excluding civil cases from the guarantee of jury trial in the Constitution, and their animus on that matter might well have perpetuated itself, in the hearts of the Federalists, into the hypothetical situation I envisage.

But *that* solution was out of the question, we can see in retrospect, for two reasons: First, the anti-Federalists, as we learn from the so-called "recommendatory" amendments that went forward to the First Congress from the ratifying conventions, were not of one mind even as to which of the II-X rights were "essential"; such rights appear in the most remarkably spotty fashion in the recommendatory amendments. But, second, and this brings us closer to the heart of the matter, there was the grave and potentially divisive matter—potentially divisive as between the two sides *and* potentially divisive on each side—of what rights (apart perhaps from freedom of petition and of peaceable assembly) should "go in" relating to the area we today identify with the First Amendment.

Even if *arguendo* we were to concede the point, Yes, there was consensus concerning the substance of Amendments II-X, no one could possibly argue, for reasons to which I shall give due attention a little later, that there was consensus or potential consensus about the provisions of Amendment I. To put this otherwise: I now feel

sure, after careful study of the documents and long meditation, that
(a) the anxieties that led the Federalists to oppose a bill of rights must
have related *mainly* to what the framers of the future Bill of Rights
might do in what we may now begin to call the Hugo Black area and
(b) the fervor of the anti-Federalists for a bill of rights can be explained only in terms of their determination that it must say this or
that in the Hugo Black area. But I stress again: one must not think of
the anti-Federalists as agreed about what a bill of rights should say
in that area. (Many were concerned exclusively with what it should
say about *religious* freedom, but even these meant different things
by religious freedom. Many were concerned mainly about freedom
of the press.) To which I must now add: This is above all the area in
which debate was never joined between the Federalists and anti-
Federalists; nearly everyone, as one reads the records, seems to be
avoiding the problem, precisely, perhaps, because it *is* so controversial. For the Federalists it is easier just to oppose a bill of rights, and
so postpone the problem. For the anti-Federalists it is easier, if I may
put it so, just to raise hell in favor of this or that provision that *must*
"go in." The "fight" is analogous to one between two men, each
convinced that the other threatens something sacred in his existence,
groping blindly for one another in a pitch-dark cellar, but each avoiding contact when he senses the other's approach.

At the risk of stating it over-graphically, I offer the following thesis:
The First Amendment had already become, long before it was ever
written, *the* potentially—I am tempted to say unavoidably—explosive problem of the American Republic. With only minor exceptions
(such as whether wire tapping is an unreasonable search or seizure
or whether the self-incrimination provision of Amendment V extends
to the House Un-American Activities Committee), the problem of the
Bill of Rights and American freedom is and has been, ever since
Mason made his motion at Philadelphia, the problem of the First
Amendment and American freedom. Perhaps someone will say I
should have entitled this essay "The First Amendment and American
Freedom." But I couldn't: the controversies, articulately, were over
a bill of rights, and we must start out from there.

6. There is some little talk in the literature on the Bill of Rights
about the First Congress having "had" to enact such a bill because,
variously, it was under what amounted to a "mandate" from the state
ratifying conventions to do so; or the Federalists had in those conven-

tions "committed themselves," that is, promised, to go along on the bill-of-rights issue; or (those considerations apart) there was overwhelming popular pressure, too insistent for the Congress to ignore, in favor of such a bill. None of the three notions, however, will hold water. The sentiment in favor of a bill of rights in the ratifying conventions was, in each case, a *minority* sentiment; in no case were the bill-of-rights men able (though they tried) to make the ratification voted conditional on subsequent adoption of a bill of rights; they just plain got licked all the way along the line. The Federalists, in case after case, "conceded" on the matter of "recommendatory amendments"—that is, they agreed that ratification should go forward with proposals for amendments that the First Congress might take under advisement; but one gets the strong impression that the Federalists in each convention are "conceding" not because they have to, but in the hope that the majority in the final vote shall be as large as possible, thus giving the new Constitution a broader basis of support than it would otherwise have had.

The main points to grasp are (a) that no one was in position to speak for the Federalists union-wide and (b) that, in any case, the ratifying conventions, even assuming the concessions in question to be properly speaking additive, were not in position to lay down a "mandate" to the First Congress, which would evidently be responsible to its constituents not to the conventions. The most that the conventions could do was what they did, namely, make recommendations. The majority in each case, having won on ratification *and* against conditionality (ratification to be conditional on the holding of a second convention, on the subsequent adoption of such and such amendments, on the adoption of a bill of rights), simply agreed to send along to the First Congress recommendations reflecting the views of the minority.

As for the third point, alleged popular pressure on the First Congress, the proofs are even less convincing; the anti-bill-of-rights men won the elections hands down, and so completely dominated the First Congress. Apart from the elections there existed, of course, no avenue through which such pressure could make itself felt effectively and convincingly. And, finally, nothing could be clearer to us, as we read the history of the First Congress, than this: if such pressure existed, only Madison seems to have been much aware of it or anything properly describable as sensitive to it.

Madison's problem, from the beginning, is to get attention—even a modicum of attention—from his fellow legislators to the bill-of-rights matter; *they* think there is vastly more important business to transact; in the parlance of a later era, they "stall," "drag their feet." But let me not overstate the point; there *is* satisfactory evidence of widespread minority sentiment in favor of some sort of step to assure "separation" of "church" and "state," to assure "freedom of conscience." And Madison had *promised* his own constituents in Virginia that he would try to get them a bill of rights. But that is all you can get out of the account of the matter by Rutland, who is not uneager to make the adoption of the Bill look as "democratic" as possible. I conclude: no Federalist commitment, no mandate, no overwhelming popular pressure. We cannot hope to understand what happened until we get these false notions out of our heads. The problem narrows down, in an astonishing manner, to Madison. He is indeed the "father" of the Bill of Rights, and doubly so because he begat it on the body of so reluctant a mother.

7. Back now to the "controversies" in the ratifying conventions. Astonishingly little attention has been paid to the Federalist case against a bill of rights, though the arguments they used—now on the floor of the conventions, now in the public print, above all of course in the *Federalist*—are perhaps not unworthy of attention. Permit me, in the briefest possible manner, to summarize them, and then, also briefly, to attempt the rather unorthodox exercise of listing a few arguments they *might* have used if (to repeat my earlier language) the issue had ever got joined and they had seen themselves obliged to pull out all the stops. The overt arguments were:

a. A bill of rights is unnecessary; the new government is a government of merely delegated powers, could not possibly do the things a bill of rights would forbid it to do.

b. A bill of rights would be ineffective, unenforceable; so, the Federalists argued, bills of rights had proven themselves to be in the States, even in that great primitive mother of American bills of rights, the State of Virginia. The barriers a bill of rights imposes are, in Madison's classic phrase, "parchment barriers"; the legislature will, in a given situation, go ahead and do, *pace* the bill of rights, what seems to be called for. Only Madison and Jefferson were sufficiently prescient to envisage possible enforcement by the courts, and they did not press the point. Hamilton's discussion of unenforceability in the *Federalist* shows clearly that, whatever dreams he may have dreamed about judicial review, *he* was not thinking of future clashes between the Supreme Court and Congress over the rights to be embalmed in a bill of rights; there is not a whiff of such a suggestion in No. 84.

c. As a limitation on the powers of the new Federal government, a bill of rights would be self-defeating; it would have the effect of expanding not diminishing them. As Hamilton puts it, in effect, in No. 84, to tell the new Federal government that it must not impair freedom of the press is to create a presumption, not present in the Constitution as it came from Philadelphia, that its power somehow does extend to such matters; erect the dam, so to speak, and the water of Federal power will flow right up to it, where otherwise it would remain right back where the fifty-five at Philadelphia had left it.

This time, however, I cannot proceed without a word or two of comment: That argument, even in Hamilton's hands, would be on the face of it disingenuous without the "necessary and proper" clause, with which Hamilton was presumably familiar. The new government was, notoriously, to act directly on the citizens; it would in due course, to go no further, be called upon to wage war; Hamilton and his fellow citizens had just had some experience of the impossibility of waging war, even under a constitution without a "necessary and proper" clause, without curbing freedom of the press. Did he really believe that in some future war the sort of dam he was opposing would *pull* Federal power harder than the "necessary and proper" clause would *push* it? It is one of the misfortunes of the whole matter that the anti-Federalists were not sufficiently adroit to smoke Hamilton out, force him to face the real problem.

On the other hand, viewing the argument from the point of vantage of 1963, what a piece of prediction! I say prediction, not prophecy, because it proceeds in terms of *analysis,* and the shrewdness of the analysis is surely validated by the accuracy of the prediction. For have things not fallen out *just* as Hamilton said they would? As Hugo Black never wearies of pointing out, and Alexander Meikeljohn before him, Federal power has indeed flowed down to the dam of the First Amendment freedoms. Owing largely perhaps to the kind and capable ministrations of the United States Supreme Court, the question long ago ceased to be "Can the Federal government abridge freedom of speech, press, association, assembly, petition, etc.?", since everybody knows the answer to that question is, "Yes, it can, and does, and in the opinion apparently of most of us *must.*" Rather the question is: "In what circumstances? Clear and present danger? The existence of a proper governmental interest that must be 'balanced' against our interest in enforcing the First Amendment?" I don't say it wouldn't have happened that way anyhow under the "necessary and proper" clause (though it might, mercifully, have done so without the verbal and logical saltimbankery of the decisions that make Mr. Justice Black so furious); I do say that Hamilton had himself quite a point and that we should be proud of him for it.

d. No bill of rights should be adopted because natural rights are as safe as you can make them in the hands of the people acting through their elected representatives; you can trust the people and—this overlaps, of course, the "parchment barriers" argument—in point of fact have no alernative *but* to do so. As Rousseau had put it a while before, if the people wills to do itself harm, who is to say it nay? But let us speak only of an overlap; the two points are distinct, and those who have been brought up on J. Allen Smith and his epigones may find it difficult to grasp at first that it was the Federalists not the anti-Federalists who used the "democratic" argument, the put-your-confidence-in-the-people argument, in the controversies over a bill of rights. And the argument is already prefigured in the way the *habeas corpus* provision of the Philadelphia Constitution is worded. No attempt is made to place *habeas corpus* once and for all beyond the power of Congress; rather circumstances are frankly envisaged when the "public safety" may require suspension of the right.

A pretty convincing case, in the opinion of this writer, and, insofar as convincing, let me add, as convincing a case for repealing the First Amendment as ever it was against adopting it. Yet one suspects, as one canvasses it, that it does not reveal very fully the Federalist state of mind on the bill-of-rights issue. So I now ask, how then, without injustice to Federalist political thought as we know it across the decades, can we round it out? What arguments can we add? At the risk of appearing impudent, I am going to attempt to add a few as the Federalist spokesmen *might* have put them:

a. The anti-Federalists, beginning with Colonel Mason and his statement on the floor at Philadelphia that a committee could draw up a list of the natural rights of men in "three hours," show a "temper" that is inappropriate to the genius of the Constitution drawn up at Philadelphia (and defended in the *Federalist*). That Constitution envisages the *self*-government of America by the "deliberate sense of the community," which must extend, *inter alia*, to the making of decisions from situation to situation and moment to moment as to what is called for by the purposes set forth in the Preamble. No, no, no; the issue is *not* whether men have natural rights or whether those rights should be respected by government; the issue is whether our generation, by contrast with scores of preceding generations that were also deeply committed to the idea of natural rights, has any particular reason for claiming that it can now make a "list" of them and, having done so, seek to impose them, forever and a day, on future generations. The issue is not whether men have natural rights, but whether those rights can at any moment be specified once and for all.

We might make an exception here of the common-law rights—which, however, precisely do not, in detail, have their origin in a list that some person or persons sat down and "drew up"; they have been hammered out in the courts of law over long centuries and reflect the accumulated experience of the English-speaking peoples with the vexed question of how to prevent miscarriages of justice. Probably we confuse matters by calling them "natural rights" at all. In any case, we suspect you, having seen these recommendatory amendments of yours, of wishing to go far beyond—how far, nobody knows—a mere statement of the common-law rights. We suspect you of wishing to venture where the wisest of our ancestors (none of whom ever attempted to draw up a "list") have feared to tread; there is even talk among you—not much, but enough to give us pause—of writing into your bill of rights something new and unheard-of called "freedom of speech," of writing it in as a right which government must in *no* circumstances abridge. Well, we do not think such a right is ultimately compatible with orderly government, much less with *free* orderly government. Gentlemen, let us be sensible!

b. We are not clear as to the status your bill of rights would enjoy if we did adopt it. You speak of "amendments," to be accomplished under the procedures laid down in Article V. But the Article V procedures envisage amendments that, once ratified, will enjoy *equal* status with the main body of the Constitution, and it may be that is what you seriously intend. That, however, is going to raise some very serious problems to which, honestly, you do not seem to have given much thought. There's the whole question of how and by whom your bill of rights is to be enforced the day Congress, or Congress and the President, or Congress and the President and the Federal Courts wish to set aside this provision or that one. It is hardly too much to say that if you are going to expect equal status for your bill of rights, equal with the main body of the Constitution, you are going to have to do more than just tack on a bill of rights; you are going to have to get back into the main body of the Constitution and reword it so as to take care of the enforcement problem. Otherwise you are going to create a great confusion of responsibilities; over here the Constitution will seem to say that the deliberate sense of the community, as expressed through the republican principle of majority rule, is to prevail; over there the Constitution will seem to say, No, there are these and these absolutes that the deliberate sense of the community must stay inside of, must deem itself bound by, and let the chips fall where they may. The system looks to us, with all candor, downright unworkable; either your bill of rights will, as a barrier on the power of Congress, become a dead letter, unenforceable on the face of it, or machinery is going to have to be developed *for* enforcing it. And we cannot imagine what shape that machinery might take.

c. We have still another anxiety about all this. It now seems likely that the main body of the Constitution will go into effect backed up by a very high degree of consensus. That, we believe, is good; we as a nation made it clear as long ago as the Declaration of Independence that we believe in government by the consent of the people. Now, let us concede, *arguendo,* that you could embody the common-law rights in a series of amendments, perhaps even embody in such an amendment the provision some of you speak of about reserving to the States all powers not expressly delegated, and still hope for a high degree of consensus. Such provisions might well be *self*-enforcing, and so get you around the enforcement problem we mentioned a moment ago; because all Americans believe in these guarantees, there is good reason to suppose they would be respected. But once you go beyond that—to freedom of speech, or freedom of press, or freedom of conscience—we doubt whether forms of words could be devised that would command any general agreement. Look at the wide variation in the State bills of rights in this area. To put it otherwise: once, in your listing of rights, you go beyond the common-law rights, you kiss good-bye to the sanction of tradition; as a people we *have* no tradition of free speech, or free press, or freedom of conscience—not even a tradition of having no established church. Gentlemen, you wish to launch us on uncharted seas, and we will have none of it!

d. To go back to the status of your future bill of rights, perhaps you do not, if only because of the apparently insoluble enforcement problem, intend it to have equal status with the main body of the Constitution. It is well-known, for instance, that the Virginia Declaration of Rights is not regarded as part of the constitution of that State but rather as—how shall we put it—a statement of ideals that the citizens are understood to entertain in common but know not to be immediately applicable. Well, if that is the sort of thing you have in mind, we shrink from the idea of your using amendments to the Constitution as your vehicle. The Constitution is intended to be a *law*, the supreme law of the land; it is not a proper locus for high principles that we might get around to applying, if all goes well, at some moment in the indefinite future. If Congress, when the "public safety" requires, or in the interests of justice or liberty, is to set the Constitution, or any one of its provisions, aside as it sees fit, that is to undermine the very notion of law, to encourage disrespect for law, And that, Gentlemen, as you surely know, no nation can do with impunity. Or, failing that, it is to encourage verbal games, with which you persuade yourselves that you are not really violating the law although it is obvious that you are, not really setting aside the principle when you clearly are setting it aside. And no nation can do that with impunity, either.

8. One thing is certain and cannot be overemphasized: At no point in the struggle over a bill of rights, and so far as I have been able to learn at no point in that First Congress which enacted the Bill of Rights, was the question "up" whether the American society of the future was to be, should be an "open society." The rights the future bill of rights would embody, the guarantees it would vouchsafe, were to be rights and guarantees against merely the new Federal government. Paradoxically, the anti-Federalists would have been the last to wish for them any broader scope than that. The anti-Federalists were States'-rights men, not prepared to put the new Federal government into the business of enforcing such rights and guarantees against the

State governments, or to alter in any significant way a state of affairs which we may define roughly as follows: the quality and intimate detail of the ordinary citizen's freedom would be determined, through an indefinite future, by the laws and policies and actions of the governments of the several States. The anti-Federalist talk of a bill of rights that would embody those natural rights that man "holds back" from "government"—and there was a great deal of such talk —represents, from this point of view, an unfortunate confusion. It suggests that the anti-Federalists were somewhat confused themselves, and it is an inexhaustible source of quotes by which our own contemporaries confuse the meaning which, at its problematical maximum, the Bill of Rights and, most especially, of course, the First Amendment, could have had for *anybody*, Federalist or anti-Federalist, at the time of its enactment. But of that, more in a moment.

9. Finally, the procedures that brought the First Congress into existence were, from first to last, in accordance with the "republican principle"—were, that is to say, "majoritarian," and not characterized by majority submission to minority dictation or blackmail. That is true not merely of the elections that actually produced the First Congress, which involved no sort of flirtation with the so-called unanimity principle; and not merely of the post-electoral situation, in which apparently it was clearly understood on all hands that the Federalists—or as John Roche prefers to call them, the Constitutionalists—having won their majority, would rightfully dominate the scene in the new "national" legislature. It is true also of the State ratifying conventions, where the final decision went by majority vote (one State, I believe, did require an extraordinary majority, but that is still not the unanimity principle). It is true, finally, of the Philadelphia Convention, where, apart from "withdrawees" like Yates and Lansing, the minority, once it saw that further talk was futile and that it was outvoted, "went along" with the majority—the one exception here being the Great Compromise between the large and small States, where, according to Roche, Madison had the votes but decided not to press his advantage lest the Convention go to pieces. There the minority was able to prevent a majority decision that it disliked, but not—even Roche does not claim that—to "dictate," merely to force an accommodation. (Even within the State delegations—witness poor Alexander Hamilton—decisions as to how to cast delegation votes went by the majority principle.)

II

So much, I say, is not very well-known but easily confirmable fact, all of it, I believe, sorely necessary for any approach to my central topic, which is:

Justice Black assures us, with three Justices already concurring, that the Founders of the American Republic intended the First Amendment freedoms to be "absolute"; that is, intended that they should not be set aside in any circumstances whatever; that, therefore, any infringement of those freedoms, on this ground or that, militates towards a drastic change in the basic character of the American Republic. Is he or is he not talking "good" history?

Put otherwise: Did the First Amendment, as passed by Congress and ratified by the States, declare the American Republic an "open society" and put in motion machinery that would make it an "open society"? Put still otherwise: Can we properly argue, as Justice Black does, from the "plain language" of the First Amendment to the "intentions" of the majority that voted it in the First Congress and the majorities that ratified it?

These are questions, I believe that can only be answered by recurring to facts that are even less well-known than those I have been canvassing and that are, in the nature of the case, far more difficult to confirm, partly because we do not by any means have at our disposal the data we should like to have and partly because the data we do have are, many of them, open perhaps to different interpretations. For the key questions become, in my view: First, what are we to make of Madison's course in the matter? And second, what significance are we to attach to the favorable vote he finally midwifed for his Bill of Rights out of his fellow M.C.'s?

I do not, obviously, pretend to "settle" either of these questions in this essay. But I do hope to show that there are great difficulties about Black's position in the matter. (He himself, for the most part at least, contents himself with consulting, apart from the "plain language" of the First Amendment, secondary sources.) And I hope to show that these difficulties are sufficiently great to suggest that the whole Black and Co. interpretation of the intention of the Founders is, quite simply, a *myth,* rooted ultimately in the airy fancies of J. S. Mill (who somewhat postdates the Founders). The two questions are, let me say by way of further preliminary, simultaneous, and I shall not take them

up *seriatim,* but shall proceed rather by pointing to certain considerations that would, I have concluded from my researches, have to be
taken into account in order for them to be answered fully and definitively.

Item. The story, as I have already intimated, narrows down in an
astonishing manner to Madison (just as the Bill of Rights problem,
again as I have already intimated, almost narrows down to the First
Amendment, or if you like the First and the Tenth Amendments;
almost but not quite, because of a little-noticed dimension that I shall
speak of below). Madison is the *sine qua non,* the necessary, though
not of course sufficient, condition of the Bill of Rights as we have it.
The accounts, whose authors are *not* eager to convey that impression,
leave one convinced that (a) if Madison, over against the indifference
and delaying tactics of his fellow Congressmen, had given up on a bill
of rights, the First Congress would not have sent one forward to the
States, and (b) those constituents of his in Virginia, to whom he had
made his famous promise to work for a bill of rights (in order to defeat
James Monroe for his House seat), would at an early moment have
had to agree that he had done on its behalf all that could in good
conscience be demanded of him. Yet he persevered and in the end
—Rutland's chronological account of the relevant legislative events
is punctuated by the word "finally"—won.

The question arises: Why? Not, one gathers, because he had
changed his mind with respect to the major Federalist arguments
against a bill of rights. Not only is the *Federalist* to be handed down
to posterity, with his signature, as an *anti*-bill-of-rights book, but also
Madison is to take steps later to make sure that his role in writing it
is not underestimated (he remains, to go no further, the source of the
contemptuous term "parchment barriers"). The most he is willing to
commit himself to, even off at the end, is in effect: A bill of rights will
(as I have put it earlier) do no harm—or, to use now his exact phrase,
would not "endanger the beauty of the Government in any one
important feature, even in the eyes of its most sanguine admirers."
It is characteristic of the "debate" to which we owe our Bill of Rights
that no one effectively calls upon him to say why, to square his new
position on the matter with his old one, to meet the Federalist arguments against.

Yet an answer to our "Why?" does emerge, even from relatively
stingy accounts of the matter, and, as far as it takes us (which is *not*

all the way), we can be fairly sure of it, namely: somewhere along the line Madison changes the *état de la question,* ceases, if I may put it so, to be interested in the merits of a bill of rights and becomes interested primarily in the merits of *passing* a bill of rights. A single sentence of his seems to put that much in the clear: the proposed Amendments will make *"the Constitution better in the eyes of those who are opposed to it,* without weakening its frame or abridging its usefulness, in the judgment of those who are attached to it [;] . . . we act the part of wise and liberal men who make such alterations as will produce that effect." Madison, in other words, takes it into his head that the new Constitution must have behind it, to all intents and purposes, a 100 per cent consensus; that the last opponent and objector must be silenced; and that he is prepared to pay, and persuade others to pay (as he proceeds to do), whatever price be necessary for accomplishing that objective. And that is the argument with which he appears to have fetched the necessary majorities in House and Senate—that plus the tacit inducement: pass my Bill of Rights and I'll leave you in peace.

He calls on his Federalist friends (never mind that he is already in the process of crossing the floor of the House; they are still his friends, else he would never have got those majorities) to change the rules of the constitutional game, at the very moment when they have won a clear victory under them. He calls on them to set aside that "republican principle" of majority rule that has, from first to last, governed the proceedings up to now, and to move suddenly for unanimity *on the terms of the defeated minority*—that is, by giving the minority its way not merely on the first of the two big issues that have been at stake (a bill of rights) but on the second as well (whether something further should be done to "nail down" State "sovereignty").

The question of the *merits* of a bill of rights promptly goes under water and has not, so far as I have been able to learn, surfaced until today. The Federalist M.C.'s, though they must have been well-schooled in the Federalist arguments, seem to have dismissed them overnight, so to speak, from their minds. Unlike the King of France, they had *fought* their troops up the hill, not merely marched them; but like the King of France, they were content to march them down again. Why? —which plunges us (pending a great deal of research on just that point, which does *not* seem to have engaged the fancy of our historians), into the realm of the truly speculative. I shall content myself with saying merely this: Concede everything you like to Madison's "prestige," which was undoubtedly great. Concede everything you like, too, to the point that Madison's fellow-M.C.'s could get him off their backs only by going along with him on the bill-of-rights issue (the brevity, peremptoriness even, of the sessions devoted to the Bill of Rights does suggest that the Congressmen and Senators were eager to get on with other things). But the mind does not rest satisfied with these answers and is, therefore, driven to seek another.

The two possibilities that seem to cry up at you are (a) Madison's fellow Congressmen themselves suddenly changed their minds on the merits of a bill of rights, which seems improbable, or (b) Madison must have been mighty convincing in the cloakrooms, not only on the consensus point but also on the point that the Bill of Rights would not "endanger the beauty of the Government," would not "weaken its frame or abridge its usefulness." Now, we find ourselves wondering, *did* he argue these points? What did he mean by them? And once again, I think, the possibilities are confined to a fairly narrow range. Either he argued (a) that the Bill of Rights, in the absence in the Constitution of any effective means of enforcement, would remain a dead letter save to the extent that the representatives of the people —ultimately, of course, Congress—chose *to enforce it upon themselves;* or (b) that the Federal judiciary would in due course put forward a claim to "guardianship" of the Bill of Rights *and make it good* (that is, that the other two branches would in fact acquiesce in that claim, and permit the judiciary to have the "last say" as to what the Bill of Rights forbids and what the Bill of Rights allows); or (c) that the Bill of Rights was of such a character that—the people over the decades, the future congressmen, presidents, and judges being all, or in their generality, of one and the same mind about such matters— no troublesome problems would ever arise.

No fourth possibility, it seems to me, presents itself. Of the three before us I offer it as my opinion that (b) the judiciary, with Congress and the Executive acquiescing, will enforce the guarantees, can safely be eliminated, just plain on the grounds that had this been Madison's rationale it would have kicked up enough fuss for us to have heard about it. As for (c), that, after all, these are matters on which we all agree and are sure to keep on agreeing, one can imagine Madison's having used it with great effect as regards the Second, Third, Fourth, Fifth, Sixth, Seventh, and Eighth Amendments as we now know them; also as regards the Ninth; conceivably, even, if we may suppose both him and his listeners to have forgotten all about the "necessary and proper" clause, as regards the Tenth; but not as regards the First.

Returning now to our distinction between *a* bill of rights and *the* Bill of Rights, it seems safe to say that Madison had a remarkably "free hand" as to what "went in," and what didn't, what sources to draw on, and what "status" the bill he introduced would, so to speak, seem to claim for itself. At one point, we are told, he receives congratulations from a friend for the excellent choice he has made among the myriad proposals that had come in from the several ratifying conventions for guarantees of rights over against the new government. He drew heavily, we are told further and more frequently, on the original Virginia Declaration of Rights. But the first of these notions must be sacrificed to Occam's razor; except for the one nearly incredible "surprise" in his original draft, it seems to be a culling from a single document and, to come to the second notion, *not* from the original Virginia Declaration of Rights but from the recommendatory amendments sent forward by the ratifying convention in Virginia (though it might well be argued that *its* authors drew heavily on the original Virginia Declaration). Those recommendations, or rather the document in which they are embodied, is from the standpoint of modern constitutional theory a very curious affair, and for two reasons that are of considerable interest for our purposes.

First, it urges numerous guarantees for the future bill of rights that are, on the face of them, already taken care of in the *main body* of the Constitution (the guarantees, for example, that the military shall be subordinate to the civil, that legislative and executive officers shall from time to time return to their private stations); one keeps asking oneself as one reads it: "Have the authors not taken the trouble to read the Constitution they propose to amend?" and asks oneself, at the margin, "Do they or do they not take this business seriously?" (Madison, in any case, eliminates all that sort of thing out of hand; if there are objections from Virginia he can make the obvious, and unanswerable, answer.) But secondly, the document is made up, like the original Virginia Declaration, of statements of "principle," statements as to what "ought" to be done and "ought" not to be done, as contrasted with "rules of law." Both points seem to me to have an important bearing upon our topic, because they suggest that the people Madison was putatively trying hardest to please, the opponents of the Constitution in his own State of Virginia, got in Madison's draft, on one side at least, rather *more* than less than their thinking on the matter to date prompted them to ask for.

Madison does two things out of hand that have, perhaps, been insufficiently noticed. First, he confines his draft (apart from Amendments IX and X) to matters appropriate to a bill of rights as, say, Mr. Justice Black understands a bill of rights, thus *already* setting his draft apart from any "mere" statement of principles analogous to the original Virginia Declaration. But second, he transforms each provision that he adopts into a rule of law; that is, into unambiguously mandatory (as Austin would put it) *commands*. Both, evidently, were things that would have *had* to be done in order for subsequent claims as to the status of the Bill of Rights, as a series of genuine and enforceable limitations on the power of Congress, to make any sense; yet neither change seems to have been hauled out into the open for discussion, or even mentioned. No one, that is to say, seems to have noticed that the bill was so stated as to be enforce*able* and as, therefore, to invite some thought about *how* it was to be enforced. Indeed, the complaints from Virginia, when they come in, are complaints to the effect that Madison's bill did not go far enough towards guaranteeing natural rights! Add to that what I have just called Madison's Big Surprise, namely, inclusion in his draft of a provision that would have forbidden the *States* to infringe trial by jury in criminal cases, or the rights of conscience, or freedom of speech or of the press, and we begin to see the complexity of the question. What *was* Madison up to? (Of course that provision was, as Madison must have known it would be, duly struck out in the Senate; on Madison's own showing, the idea of a bill was to please the objecting minority, who were above all anti-consolidators, anti-centralizers, States' righters.)

But it is the *First* Amendment that really wants looking at from the standpoint of the Virginia recommendations. Here the Virginian text had read: (a) "That the people have a right to freedom of speech, and of writing and publishing their sentiments, *but* [my italics] the freedom of the press [the very "freedom" on which Hamilton sets his sights in Number 84] is one of the great bulwarks of liberty and ought not to be violated"; (b) "That the people have a right peaceably to assemble together, or to instruct their Representatives; and that every freeman has a right to petition or apply to the legislative for the redress of grievances"; and, finally, (c) "That religion" [promptly defined, if you please, as the "duty we owe to our Creator"] and "the manner of discharging it can be directed only by reason and conviction, not by force or violence, and therefore all men have an equal, natural, and unalienable right to the free exercise of religion according to dictates of conscience, and that no particular religious sect ought to be favored or established by Law in preference to others."

The evolution under these topics is indeed interesting to watch. The draft that goes to the Senate moves from the verbose principle on religious freedom that I have just quoted to virtually the form of guarantee we presumably live under: "Congress"—but note the shift, characteristic only and for no obvious reason of the First as contrasted with the remaining Amendments—"Congress shall make no law establishing Religion [not "a religion" but "Religion"] or prohibiting the free exercise thereof, nor shall the free rights of Conscience be infringed." "Free rights of Conscience" disappears before the final draft, never to be heard of again (though some such guarantee had been recommended by *several* States); "no law establishing Religion" becomes "no law respecting an establishment of religion," and "the equal, natural and unalienable right to the free exercise of religion" becomes a prohibition against "prohibiting the free exercise [of religion]...." The Virginia provision "That the people have a right to freedom of speech, and of writing and publishing their sentiments, etc." becomes first "The freedom of speech, and of the press ... shall not be infringed" and then, in the Bill of Rights itself, "Congress shall make no law ... abridging freedom of speech, or of the press"—again with the new emphasis on Congress, and the small shift from "infringe" to "abridge." As for the right of assembly, it moves from "the people have a right to peaceably assemble together" to, first, "the right of the people peaceably to assemble, and consult for their common good, shall not be infringed," to "Congress shall make no law ... abridging ... the right of the people peaceably to assemble." And, finally, we move from "That every freeman has a right to petition or apply to the legislative for redress of grievances" to, in the House draft, "Congress shall make no law ... abridging ... the right of the people ... to petition the Government for a redress of grievances."

Madison, except for narrowing it down to what *Congress* "shall not" do, merely pares and gives the "sound of law" to the Virginia text. The qualifying phrases disappear. The effect achieved is one of

austere simplicity, but by the time he has done—remember, we are
concerned primarily with how he could have persuaded the Federalists to vote for it—we are, so to speak, a long way from Virginia, yet
not so far from Virginia that the men of Virginia can take much
exception. And, *pace* Mr. Justice Black, what has suffered most, as far
as the "plain language" of the First Amendment is concerned, is
precisely what all the argument was about, namely, "rights," of
which, indeed, according to the "plain language," we are left with
only two, the right of peaceable assembly and the right to petition
for redress of grievances. The "right to freedom of speech, and of
writing and publishing their sentiments," is gone, and we have only
that Congress shall make no law abridging *the* freedom of speech; the
idea that "the freedom of the press is one of the great bulwarks of
liberty" is gone, for we have only that "Congress shall make no law
abridging *the* freedom of the press." The "equal, natural and unalienable right to the free exercise of religion" is gone (along with, we
might notice, the notion that the "Religion" whose "free exercise"
the Congress must not "prohibit" is a "duty" we "owe to our Creator"), and we have only "Congress shall make no law prohibiting the
free exercise of religion"; most particularly, the "according to the
dictates of conscience" is gone ("freedom of conscience," incidentally, had turned up in several of the sets of recommendations from
the State ratifying conventions, and the House draft speaks specifically of "the rights of Conscience" as one of the things that are not
to be "infringed"). Finally, the most curious change of all, the Virginia pronouncement that "no particular religious sect or society
ought to be favored or established by law in preference to others"
becomes simply "Congress shall make no law *respecting* an establishment of religion." [My emphasis]

All very minor changes, you say, and why all the fuss? I answer,
Yes, minor in the sense that Madison, final draft in hand, can reasonably say to his constituents in Virginia: "I got you what you asked for."
Or, if you like, minor in the sense that the Virginians, if they look hard
enough, can "see" in the First Amendment what they had been
demanding. But not minor at all from the standpoint of Justice Black's
question, which is whether the First Amendment embodies a decision to make the United States an open society, and not, we may I
think be fairly sure, as regards picking up Federalist votes in Congress and out in the future process of ratification. For to begin with,

we see that, translated into the language and concepts of the time, what the First Amendment in effect does (through the emphasis on Congress) is to recognize laws respecting an establishment of religion, or prohibiting the free exercise thereof, or abridging the freedom of speech or of the press, or abridging the right of the people to assemble peaceably and petition for redress of grievances as a *monopoly of the State governments;* that is, what it precisely does *not* do is to "take a stand" on the matters Mr. Justice Black now sees as being at stake in it. Not only is no "right" to freedom of speech asserted, rather it is also expressly avoided; no right to freedom of the press is asserted, rather it is expressly avoided; no right to the free exercise of religion, no "rights of conscience" are asserted, rather they are expressly avoided; no right to live in a land where no religious sect or society is favored or established by law in preference to another is asserted, but rather expressly avoided.

All that is left in the way of "rights," I repeat, are peaceable assembly and petition for the redress of grievances, both of which, we may note in passing, were traditional, both to a greater or less extent recognized by the common law, *unlike* any supposed right to free speech or nonestablishment or free exercise of religion. Read in the context of the times and of the document from which they were midwifed, in fine, the major provisions of the First Amendment are conspicuous precisely for the *absence* of overtones to the effect that the "freedoms" involved are "rights" and so, in Black's favorite phrase, "absolute." They are merely the Tenth Amendment (and the basic theory of the Constitution) restated in terms of speech, press, and religion, and Madison can indeed say, by the time he has done, that they will not mar the beauty of the frame of government devised at Philadelphia, that, in the language I have imagined his using, they are so worded that they are certain, as limitations on the power of Congress, to remain dead letters. Why, in view of their "plain language" after Madison has done, should any Federalist vote against them? Do they not leave the content of the freedom of speech and press and exercise of religion to be determined as, according to the *Federalist,* they ought and must be determined, namely, by the deliberate sense of the community, which must be expressed through that very Congress which the Amendment forbids to abridge them? And Madison drives the point home, one might say, by simultaneously forcing his fellow Congressmen through the (surely predictable) symbolic step of eliminating a provision that would have forbidden the States to infringe trial by jury, the rights of conscience, the freedom of speech, or the freedom of the press.

Two further points, and *I* shall have done.

First, unpleasant as it may be for some of us to contemplate, Madison has turned out, *operatively speaking,* to be quite right (though only because, as we have seen, the First Amendment does *not* say what it might have said) about the Bill of Rights not doing any "injury" to the "beauty" of the Philadelphia frame of government—as, incidentally, all those Federalist arguments against a bill of rights may be seen, in retrospect, to have been pretty good political theory. Nearly two centuries have passed since the ink dried on Madison's Bill of Rights, but the showdown that he and Jefferson expected and that his recasting of the Virginia document seemed to invite—the showdown between a Congress bent on invading a natural right and a Federal court system, armed with a declaration of rights elevated to the status of enforceable law, saying (as what else can it do given the "plain language") "No" to it—has yet to occur in the area that, as all Americans know and seem always to have known, is the dangerous one, namely, that of the First Amendment. *To this day, the Supreme Court has never declared an enactment of the Congress of the United States unconstitutional on grounds of the First Admentment.*

Opinions may, to be sure, differ as to whether "natural rights" have thrived or suffered in consequence; that is, as to whether "natural rights" would, as the Federalists insisted, be safer with the people, which is where the Philadelphia Constitution left them, than they could be made by any alternative scheme the bill-of-rights men might end up devising. But Madison's Bill of Rights, correctly read (as I believe myself to have read it here) and read as we as a people have in fact ended up reading it, also leaves the natural rights, in the areas that Justice Black correctly regards as crucial, subject to the general Federalist principles that the deliberate sense of the American community is to be trusted, and that any attempt to put parchment barriers in its way will as a matter of course be ineffective. That is perhaps not the American political system as we describe it in our civics textbooks or our Fourth of July orations; it is certainly not the American system as, for example, Jellinek describes it and has taught other Europeans to describe it; but it is the American political system as it has worked to date, and it is high time we begin to recognize it as that. Again as Rousseau put it long before the Federalists put forward their arguments: If the people wills to do itself hurt—or, we may safely add, good either—who is to say it nay? And the answer, for the American system, would appear to be: in the crucial area, nobody.

American Conservatism and the "Prayer" Decisions

"Children Still Pray in School." "Massachusetts town defies the Supreme Court." So the title and sub-title of a spread in a recent issue of *Life* magazine;[1] and the accompanying text and photographs amply justify both headings: The school board of North Brookfield, Mass., the text relates, finds itself confronted with (1) a 137-year-old state law that requires prayers in the public schools, (2) three widely-publicized Supreme Court decisions that seem to imply that that statute is unconstitutional, and (3) a State Attorney General's ruling to the effect that the 137-year-old statute is indeed null and void in consequence of the Supreme Court decisions.[2] The school board has deliberated and voted no less than four times on the question "Whom —what law—shall we obey?"; and on each of these occasions it has decided to obey the state legislature, and so disobey—defy, if you like—the Supreme Court and the Attorney General. North Brookfield's 3,616 residents, the text continues, mostly agree with the school board: among 418 students at North Brookfield's high school, only 17 (reflecting, perhaps, the views of their parents) have been willing to sign a petition demanding reversal of the school board's decision. ("You're against *God,*" the more vocal of the non-signers tell the lad circulating the petition.) Classes in North Brookfield's schools "still" begin—not "keep right on" beginning but *"still"* begin (by analogy, one supposes, with "the flag was still there")—with *viva voce* reading of a verse from the Bible and recitation of the Lord's Prayer. And there are some fascinating quotes which are not the less revealing, I think, because they clearly come from the "extremists" in the controversy: "We," says Board Member William Boyd, "will challenge and defy the world movement toward atheism." "This is Massachusetts, the cradle of liberty," says Board Member Lawrence Delude, "...here is where the first shots are going to be fired"—shots, one gathers, that are intended to be "heard 'round the world," *inter alia* in Moscow, Peking, and Washington; Boyd and Delude are conscious not merely of making history, but of making it on a stage that is neither merely local nor merely national. Against them they have William Smith and Joseph Durkin: "It's futile," says Smith, "to continue challenging the Supreme Court decision." "They"—Durkin observes of the Board's victorious majority—"are for God, for prayer, and they're *simple*. . . . The whole thing should never involve your feeling about prayer. That's not an issue. The law is the issue." North Brookfield's stand, Smith and Durkin ominously insist, "makes us look like Governor Wallace." We look further and find, presiding over the whole spread (as we should expect?), a photograph of 10-year-old Ellen Waydaka, head bowed, hands clasped reverently on her desk, hair and eyes whose brunette quality may or may not have ultramontane associations for most of *Life's* readers, and the chilling pronouncement by the editors of *Life:* "Around the country *thousands* of school children"—I'd guess millions, but never mind—"[are] starting their day the same way. . . . Several states are openly disobeying the ruling and, even in states that officially comply, some schools still continue prayer."

Life, to be sure, chose to subordinate its spread on North Brookfield to a grand exposé of "The Bobby Baker Bombshell." But I confidently predict that history will longer remember, symbolically at least, the events in North Brookfield than those in Baker's motel. I propose, therefore, to take the crisis in North Brookfield (for surely it is a crisis) as my point of departure for this article. The events there hold in deposit, force upon our attention even in *Life's* account, the crucial aspects of the problem I want to explore. And these events seem to me to warrant at least the following preliminary comments:

1. North Brookfield is divided—angrily divided—on the issue of religious observances in its public schools—which, day before yesterday, the people of North Brookfield had never thought of as conceivably becoming an issue. For, day before yesterday, an objector to North Brookfield's long-established custom of beginning the school-day with a verse from the Bible and the Lord's Prayer would have been told in effect: "Look, your youngsters aren't required to participate; they are not even required to be present; the rest of us, which is to say pretty nearly all of us, deem it a religious duty to see to it that our youngsters begin their day in school as we began our day in school—that is, with a reminder that God exists, that we are His creatures, rightfully subject to His will. Moreover, North Brookfield is not peculiar about this: the same thing happens all over Massachu-

setts, and what's more always did; besides which, state law—the same state law that requires us to maintain public schools and authorizes us to collect taxes for their support—*requires* it to happen. Do you expect us to change our way of doing things just because you and a few other people don't happen to like it?" And if the objector had answered: "It isn't a matter of what I happen to like; I take my stand on the Constitution, which prohibits the 'establishment of religion' in the United States," he would have been told: "Your understanding of the establishment clause is not ours; it certainly does not prohibit religious observances in the public schools." The objector, in short, would have been told that he did not have a leg to stand on, and that would have ended the discussion. Day before yesterday, I repeat, no issue could have arisen in North Brookfield over the topic. If the town is in crisis, it is in crisis because of a disturbance that has come from *outside*. From, concretely, three unprecedented and wholly unexpected decisions by the United States Supreme Court.

2. North Brookfield's crisis is indeed a crisis, a crisis moreover of the worst kind that can possibly overtake a political community. Its citizens face a problem from which, in Lenin's wonderful phrase, "there is no way out." Why? Already divided against itself, North Brookfield faces a future in which the wedge that has been driven between its majority and its minority must as time passes be driven deeper and deeper, forcing majority and minority ever further—ever more angrily—apart. That fact cries up at us even out of *Life's* meager data, which oblige us to say: Blessed no doubt are the peace-makers, but in North Brookfield, alas, they have no role to play. The issue that has arisen there cannot be side-stepped, cannot even be postponed; either the schoolday does begin with Bible-reading and prayer, or it doesn't; either the watchword is to be, "Out, out brief prayer," as the minority demands, or established custom will prevail, as the majority is clearly determined it shall. There is no middle course between Yes, having prayers in school, and No, not having prayers in school, no chance of what Mary Follett used to call the "integrated solution" (which so disposes matters that everybody gets his way and ends up happy). Middle courses have been excluded by the manner in which the issue has been drawn—first by the Supreme Court, later, now, by the spokesmen for the two "parties" in North Brookfield. "You are against God," cries one party, "And what's more, freedom is at stake!"—from which, in America, it is always a brief step to "Give us

liberty or give us death!" "We are a government of laws not of men," cries the other party, "and the law says there shall be no religious observances in the public schools; you, sirs, are against the law, and the law, cost what it may, must be enforced." Each position, be it noted, is essentially *theological*—I shall substitute another word for "theological" later, but for the moment let it stand—basing itself ultimately upon high principle of the kind that *eo ispo* places itself beyond discussion and beyond compromise. Ineluctably, therefore, the anger generated by the dispute must take on increasingly the mood and quality of *odium theologicum* ("I've got my P.T.A. members," says Mrs. Richard Walther, a substitute teacher at North Brookfield high school. "We call them minutemen . . . This is like the Revolution all over again."). In brief: North Brookfield cannot, even if *per impossibile* it brings to bear upon the controversy all the resources of imagination and good will that it has at its disposal, *cannot* resolve its crisis—any more than a man can chew a morsel of beefsteak by describing an arc with his upper teeth. Nobody from now on, nobody in sight anyhow, can restore peace except the United States Supreme Court itself. And it can do so only by restoring the *status quo ante*—which, I suppose, nobody thinks it is going to do.

3. We, say in effect the two dissident school board members, are going to "look like Governor Wallace." Indeed they are going to look like Governor Wallace, to begin with for the same reason that Governor Wallace looks like Governor Wallace: certain strategically-situated persons—among them, off at the end, no doubt, the President himself—are going to see to it that they do. Nay, more. The suggested analogy with Governor Wallace will stand on more legs than the Board dissidents may have had in mind: some North Brookfield, somewhere (which, in what state, of course doesn't matter), is indeed slated to play, in the working out of the prayer decisions, the role of Little Rock in the working out of the school desegregation decision. One day some district court will—will, because under the Supreme Court ruling in the "prayer" cases, it must—*order* the school board in some North Brookfield to abolish religious observances in the schools for which it is legally responsible. At that point, to be sure, the story may take any of several turnings—of which none, however, is going to improve matters in North Brookfield: The school board, its members, like Governor Barnett, not wishing to go to jail and pay an out-size fine for contempt of court, will surely order its

teachers to discontinue the Bible-reading and the recitation of the Lord's Prayer, may even put teeth in the order by promising to fire any teacher who refuses to go along. That will keep the school board members out of jail, but (a) the teachers must now choose between "defying" the school board and "defying" the State legislature, besides which (b) unless North Brookfield is a mighty peculiar American town, which up to now it gives no evidence of being, the school board's reversal of its earlier stand is *just* what it will take to harden the majority's *odium theologicum* into sullen, we-won't-take-No-for-an-answer determination—to have religious observances in the schools or bust. The teachers obey the school board? The youngsters, with a little coaching at home, can recite the 23rd Psalm and lead themselves in prayer; and, to quote Harry Truman, The Buck Stops Here. We are still a government of laws not of men? Then the parents stand in contempt of court—and must not the law, with them as with Governor Barnett, have its pound of flesh? And the question forthwith becomes, How many parents can the federal marshals of the district accommodate in their jails, especially as the pray-in-school-or-bust movement has by now snowballed—who can doubt that it will have?—into neighboring towns? Legally, remember, it is no longer merely a question just of praying or not praying in school, but of obedience or non-obedience to a command from a federal court, of the sanctity of the law and of legal process, of order against anarchy no less. Yet the prayers in school do remain the crucial dimension, and I defy any reader of this article to come up with the dodge by which the White House that sent troops to Little Rock and Oxford can now—without looking so foolish that it must go back and undo Little Rock and Oxford, which would not be easy—refuse to send troops to North Brookfield. And *then*—the imagination balks, but we must proceed—the question becomes, What can a soldier with a fixed bayonet do to Ellen Waydaka? Force her hands apart? Hold her head erect by main force? Seal her lips with adhesive tape? Very well; but once the federal troops are withdrawn, the prayers—for the movement will by now have become a crusade—will start all over again. A caricature, you say? I answer: Little Rock was a caricature, and the White House, nowadays, is normally occupied by a specialist in caricature. (To be sure, we have it on the high authority of Walter Berns that "There is reason to believe that federal marshals will not be ordered to swoop down upon the nation's schoolrooms and arrest teachers leading their children in daily prayer."[3] But Professor Berns is silent as to his reasons for this judgment; and who would have guessed in, say, 1950 that federal authorities would one day escort Negro students into Central High School, or serve as bodyguards for a Senior at Ole Miss?) I repeat: the dissident school board members are on solid ground when they point up the analogy between the controversy over desegregation of the public schools and that over—if I may coin a phrase—their *deorisonation*.

4. The issue that has been drawn in North Brookfield is one on which no Liberal—unless an occasional odd-ball like Bishop Pike— will have any difficulty "taking sides," or any difficulty saying why he takes the side he takes. What is in question, for him, is what I have called in a recent book the Liberal Revolution,[4] which is to say the wave of the future. The majority in North Brookfield, as the Liberal sees it, is impudently resisting the Liberal Revolution, just as the White Southerners are impudently resisting it. Both must, quite simply, be prevailed upon to abandon the positions they have adopted —preferably of course by persuasion (that is, by instruction in the principles of democracy); if not by persuasion then by legal fiat, at the margin and if necessary, by coercion. The North Brookfield majority, as the Liberal sees it further, just isn't with it: the First Amendment prohibits any and every Congressional enactment "respecting an establishment of religion"; the Fourteenth Amendment "extends" that prohibition to the state legislatures, and to state agencies like the school board of North Brookfield; the Supreme Court has now spelled the prohibition out in, so to speak, words of one syllable, which it becomes the business of the citizens of North Brookfield to cognize, to take to heart, and to obey. For them to refuse to obey is tantamount to their declaring war on American democracy, which for present purposes at least we may take as the Highest Good, and having declared war they may fairly expect to be treated like enemies. Send troops to North Brookfield to enforce a court order implementing the Supreme Court ruling? If we must, we will. Freedom of conscience is just as necessary to democracy as freedom from racial discrimination, and both just as necessary as freedom of speech and press, freedom of assembly, and freedom to petition. I repeat: North Brookfield's crisis poses no problems for which the Liberals are less than fully prepared, both as regards where, politically, they are going, and why, doctrinally, that is where they ought to go. Nor could

the North Brookfield crisis take any turn for which the Liberals would not have a ready strategy and a carefully worked out doctrinal justification.

Not so, however, with the Liberals' putative opponents, the Conservatives. Many of them could not say for sure whose side they are on in North Brookfield; some, I venture, would side, however reluctantly, with the dissidents on the school board (some because they too believe in the absolute "wall of separation" between Church and State, some because they too are not about to encourage disobedience to orders emanating from federal courts, some because they think, here as with "Civil Rights," that any battle that might once have been worth fighting against this aspect of the Liberal Revolution is already lost, so that there's nothing for it now but an orderly retreat from yesterday's Conservative positions). If, moreover, as I do suppose to be true, most would side with the North Brookfield majority, the reasons they would give for doing so would vary greatly from individual to individual. And if, as I suppose also to be true, many would say "Look, the problem can't be decided in North Brookfield," and "The question is what we are going to do *nationally,*" these again would disagree as to what ought to be done nationally. To put it otherwise: the prayer decision has caught the Conservatives intellectually unprepared—just as, in 1954, the school desegregation decision caught them unprepared intellectually; and just as, hard after the turn of the century, the Liberal attack on the American Political System—beginning as it did with the publication of J. Allen Smith's *Spirit of American Government*—caught them unprepared intellectually.[5] American Conservatism, one is tempted to say, seems to be in the *business* of being unprepared intellectually for the next thrust of the Liberal Revolution; the Conservatives never do their homework until after they have flunked the exam. If the resistance to the Liberal Revolution had been left up to them, the Revolution would be over and the American Red Widow (a Red Grass-Widow, no doubt, automated on top of that) would have settled matters for the Conservative intellectuals, once and for all. Certainly most of the effective resistance to the Revolution, up to now, has come precisely at the intellectual level of the majority in North Brookfield—at, if you please, the level appropriate to the North Brookfield slogan: "You're against *God,*" to planting your feet in the mud and saying to the enemy, "You shall advance no further," but *not* appropriate to the elaboration and implementation of Conservative solutions. Such solutions, and the necessary prior penetration of problems, as they arise, through skillful and realistic analysis, only the Conservative intellectuals can provide—they, moreover, only if they are good at their job. And that they will never be until, like the Liberal intellectuals, they have developed a theoretical base from which, carrying their rank and file with them, they can strike right to the heart of each issue as it presents itself, and promptly identify the Conservative strategy called for. We have Brent Bozell's word for it that fifty—yes, fifty—proposals for constitutional amendments, all inspired by the prayer decision, now lie before Congress (none of them, I might add, with a Chinaman's chance of reaching the floor of either House). Moreover—handily enough for purposes of my present point—the thesis of the Bozell article to which I refer is that *no* constitutional amendment is needed at all![6] We are a movement—assuming that is that we are a movement—rent not merely by divided counsels, but also by sharply conflicting views of political reality and, above all, of the American political system itself, and the proper role of Conservatives with respect to its proper functioning, its good health, and its preservation. The condition of our learned literature, moreover, offers little hope of our ceasing, any time soon, to be that kind of movement.

Now: We shall not move, in this article, from intellectual unpreparedness to intellectual preparedness. But we might, just might, take a step or two in the right direction; and I have, to that end, the following theses to propose:

A) We Conservatives must stop frittering away our energies in *argument* with the Supreme Court—whether about the intention of the Framers of the Constitution and the First Amendment[7] (and we may now add the Fourteenth Amendment) or about the "clear meaning" of the words "Congress shall make no law respecting an establishment of religion, or prohibiting the free exercise thereof," and "equal protection of the laws," and "due process of law." Concretely, we must withdraw from the great current debate on the so-called "broad" interpretation versus the so-called "narrow" interpretation of the "establishment" clause I have just quoted, which debate let me explain briefly as follows: According to the "narrow" interpretation, we are committed under the First Amendment merely to a policy of government neutrality over against the numerous religious groups into which we are divided: government action must not tend to strengthen the hand of the Baptists against the Methodists, or that of the Protestants against the Catholics, or that of the Christians against the Jews, or that of the "Judeo-Christians" against Mohammedanism or Bahai. According to the broad interpretation, by contrast, our commitment goes much further: government must be neutral over against all possible states of conscience or belief (including, one supposes, cannibalism provided you don't actually eat anybody, and certainly including the Black Mass, provided it be celebrated behind closed doors and so without offense to public standards of decency); governmental action must be of such character as not even to strengthen the hand of religion against irreligion. I am not saying, of course, that it is a matter of indifference which of these two views prevails (assuming for the moment that one of them is to prevail), or that the Conservatives who are doing battle on behalf of the "narrow" interpretation are incorrect in preferring it to the broad interpretation: Let the broad interpretation prevail and, as Leonard Levy puts it in a brilliant statement of the Liberal position,[8] "even government aid that is impartially and equitably administered to all religious groups is barred by the First Amendment." Let the broad interpretation prevail, and not merely Bible-reading and prayers in the public schools have to go: released-time programs must go, too, along with Christmas plays and public *crèches* and even religious songs; so must invocations and benedictions at school graduation exercises; so—to bump the problem up to another level—must chaplains in the Armed Forces and, one supposes, in Congress; so must the words "In God We Trust" from the nation's coinage; so must—above all perhaps— the exemption of the property and income of religious groups from taxation (which certainly does have the effect of forcing the irreligious to help propagate the superstitions of the religious). Somewhere along that line, I suppose, any American Conservative except perhaps R. P. Oliver[9] is going to begin to feel misgivings about our famous "wall of separation," and come out against the First Amendment so construed; and, as I have already said, in my opinion rightly, as far as he goes. On the narrow interpretation, by contrast, all the goods I have named, if goods they be, would be safe, which I am prepared to assume they ought to be. My quarrel, then, is not with the *animus* of the Conservative defenders of the narrow interpretation; I merely call upon them, in the first instance, to stop "argue-

barguing" with the Supreme Court about which of the two interpretations the First Congress intended and, short of that, which of the
two interpretations the actual language of the First Amendment adds
up to. This for a number of reasons that, in so brief an article, I can
hardly do more than adumbrate in the following summary manner:
(a) There is no reason to suppose that the Supreme Court is ever
affected by such arguing, or even listens to it; the inertia of the
Supreme Court is a forward inertia, and always in the direction of the
Liberal Revolution. (b) If the purpose of the arguing be to appeal over
the heads of the Supreme Court justices to public opinion, the advocates of the narrow interpretation are indeed frittering away their
energies: Mr. Dooley to the contrary notwithstanding, the Supreme
Court precisely does *not* follow the election returns; besides which
—look again at North Brookfield—there is *no* reason to suppose, up
to now anyhow, that public opinion is other than basically sound on
the First Amendment issue. (c) The argument, insofar as it turns on
the intention of the Framers of the First Amendment and the clear
meaning of the establishment clause is—how curious that no Conservative publicist has ever stepped forward to say so!—in its present
phase a silly argument, and silly on the very face of it. For in its
present phase *all* that is in question is what our 50 *states* (and their
subordinate agencies) can or cannot do under the First Amendment,
which is a matter about which the Framers of the First Amendment,
directed as it is exclusively at Congress ("Congress," it reads, "shall
make no law," etc.), certainly had no discoverable intent; about
which, therefore, the language of the First Amendment certainly has
no meaning *sensu stricto* except this meaning: the States are free,
under the Constitution of the United States, to do exactly what they
please "respecting an establishment of religion" and about "prohibiting the free exercise thereof." The question of possible limitations
upon the power of the states in this area was, quite simply, not "up."
(Except, we may pause to notice, in the mind of Madison, who indeed
included in the original draft of the Bill of Rights a provision that
would have extended the "Bill of Rights" limitations upon the power
of the Federal government to the states; but the First Congress made
short shrift of that.) (d) The energies that Conservative publicists
fritter away on the current argument ought to be channeled into
another kind of argument altogether, namely: What policy *should* we
adopt—we the people of the United States, that is to say—with re-

spect to the problems that have arisen amongst us under the general
heading: "church and state, government and religion"? For as Conservatives, that is, as disciples of Publius, what we should want above
all is that the relevant questions shall be decided by the "deliberate
sense of the community"—and the deliberate sense of the community *not* about the intent of the Founders (it was, above all, that we
should *govern* ourselves, and so prove to mankind that self-government is *possible*); and not, Talmudically, about the meaning of verbal
formulae penned by the dead hand of the past, but about the *merits*
of the competing policy alternatives amongst which we, as a self-
governing people, are obliged to choose. Which is to say: about the
appropriateness of competing policies to our conception of ourselves
as a people, to our historic destiny as *we* understand it, to our settled
views as to the nature of the good society. That is the argument into
which we ought, I say, to be channeling our energies—that and the
further argument, What is it we are going to have to do to the American political system in order that (look again at North Brookfield) the
deliberate sense of the community *shall* prevail, as, generally, we
believe it to have prevailed always in the not-too-remote past. Those,
I say, are the kinds of questions into which Conservative publicists
should be pouring their energies. Yet—so it seems to me, as a student
of the relevant literature—it is an argument that nobody amongst us
seems to be conducting except John Courtney Murray. (His *We Hold
These Truths* should, in my opinion, be the take-off point for all future
Conservative discussion of the establishment problem.)

So much for my first thesis—we must stop arguing with the Supreme Court—and the reasons I offer in its support.

B) My second thesis, which I believe reaches to the remote source
of Conservative helplessness and indecision in these matters, is this:

*We must seek a way out of the apparently exhaustive dilemma:
Either give the Supreme Court its head* (even if giving it its head leads
to North Brookfield—and Birmingham), or *strike at the whole business of judicial review.* I assume here, correctly I think, that what
keeps Conservatives from taking sides (and all of us the same side)
in North Brookfield is—I have intimated as much above—that we see
no way to take the side to which we are instinctively drawn without
ourselves defying the Supreme Court and, off at the end, not merely
questioning its power under the Constitution to set itself up as a
legislature but also deciding to try to eliminate that power from the

American political system. I assume also that the reasons for which we hesitate to strike at the Supreme Court, hesitate even to think of striking at the Supreme Court, are sound. For one thing, they have behind them a tradition that reaches as far back as *Marbury v. Madison* and *The Federalist.* For another, the explicit case for judicial review, as urged by Marshall and Publius, is a case well nigh impossible to answer in the Conservative idiom. We judge, and with good reason, that judicial review is the chief institutional barrier that ultimately protects us against (as I like to call it) the *plebiscitary potential* in our Constitution, that is, its potential for transforming itself into something very like the British Constitution. Nor is that all. The Conservative intellectuals must never forget that those good folk of North Brookfield, who are today defying the Supreme Court, are *their* constituents, and only too likely to turn against them the day they set out to "do something" about judicial review (it was, remember, they, precisely they, who rose in their fury against FDR's Court-packing plan). And, all that apart, it is by no means certain that the American political system, insofar as it is *federal,* would be workable without judicial review at least of the acts of the states and of state agencies (which, not judicial review of acts of Congress, is the kind of judicial review that has precipitated the "Civil Rights" crisis and the "prayer"-decision crisis). At the present moment, to be sure, the temptation to strike at judicial review is indeed very great. The Court hardly keeps up even the pretense, these days, that it is not legislating. Instead of merely postponing governmental action until there exists a deliberate sense of the community, which was its traditional practice, it today situates itself far out ahead of that deliberate sense. Very far from moving to blur divisions amongst us that might undermine civil peace, it has taken to creating divisions where yesterday there were none, and then, as it seems, does what it can to aggravate them. Its decision in the *Nelson* case (though that, of course, involves the other, the Congressional aspect of judicial review) involved a kind of judicial aggression of which, so far as I know, it had never before been guilty.[10] Smaller wonder, then, that we shall soon hold in our hands an important Conservative book—the first, I think—that will summon us, in the name of the good health of the American political system, to take any steps that may be required now in order to *curb* the Court.[11] Our dilemma, in consequence, is a painful one. That indeed is *why* we argue-bargue with the Court: the alternatives to argue-barguing—giving the Court its head, curbing the Court—we find too horrible to contemplate. Now: we must, I say, stop the argue-barguing, because it is the political equivalent of the sin of Onan. But we must also, I am saying, hit upon a means of escaping between the horns of our Supreme Court dilemma, and confer upon the making good of the escape the very highest priority in the American Conservative movement. Nor, once you put it that way, can there, I think, be any doubt where we have to go: We must recognize that the cancer that threatens not merely the good health but the very survival of the American political system is not judicial review (which unlike a cancer confers great goods upon the body politic); it is those clauses of the Fourteenth Amendment—*equal protection of the laws* and *due process*—that, as we see now, make of it an invitation to the Supreme Court to tamper, in the teeth of the Tenth Amendment, with our traditional division of powers between the federal and state governments. But for those clauses (they were of course never intended for the purpose for which they are being used, but let us not insist on that: to do so belongs under our general heading of arguing with the Supreme Court), the Court could not have catapulted itself into either the school-desegregation decision or the deorisonation decision. Those clauses, I repeat, are the cancer, and so the point at which we must apply the knife, which we can do in any one of several ways: Repeal the Fourteenth Amendment as a whole, telling ourselves—as with good conscience we can—that the purposes for which it was enacted were long since accomplished (it lay dormant through the decades that divided the Reconstruction crisis from the Gitlow case, which was the case in which the Supreme Court first took it into its head to extend the so-called Bill of Rights limitations on the federal government to the states). Or, short of repealing the Amendment as a whole, amend it so as to get rid of the offending clauses. Neither of these things, I think, need be particularly difficult to do if we set out to mobilize, behind repeal or amendment, the resentments engendered by the desegregation, deorisonation, and apportionment decisions (making the most we can, of course, of the procedural irregularities that were involved in the adoption of the Fourteenth Amendment to begin with). Or, if repeal or amendment seems too big a job, let us then call upon Congress (where, unlike the Supreme Court, we *are* listened to) to clarify the Fourteenth Amendment (as the Supreme Court has itself, on occasion, invited it to do)

—clarify it, of course, in the direction to which I have just been pointing. Or, finally, let us call upon Congress to remove the offending clauses from the appellate jurisdiction of the Supreme Court— over which, so far as we know to date, it has complete control.

It does not much matter, I think, which of these alternative means we adopt for achieving the desired proximate end, which is to leave judicial review untouched while exercising *our* rightful control over the Constitution of which the Supreme Court is the guardian—which means we use, I repeat, does not matter, *provided* we get it through our heads that the present situation, alike in North Brookfield and in Birmingham and in Austin, is intolerable; that *no* less drastic remedy can meet the test of Conservative principle; and that we, as Conservatives, have *no* reason to suppose our political resources inadequate for bringing it off (whether by legislative enactment or by amending the Constitution). To which let me add: a campaign to draw the teeth of the Fourteenth Amendment would give us something to do in life, which apart from our pipedream of a committed Conservative in the White House is exactly what we have never had. I reiterate: *We must escape between the horns of the dilemma:* suffer the Supreme Court, curb the Supreme Court; and soon, for in these matters time presses and, as Cabell's Jurgen remarks, in pressing sets us an admirable example.

C) We must learn—and having learned make the most of it—to distinguish between the *legality* of a decision handed down by the Supreme Court and the *prudence* of such a decision. Then, if argue with the Supreme Court we must, we must learn to confine our part in the debate to the *prudential* area. And no, I by no means agree, from the point of view of Conservative doctrine and strategy, that this distinction is "jesuitical," or a distinction without a difference. Challenge the *legality* of a Supreme Court ruling based upon its interpretation of the language of the Constitution, and you get yourself into an argument that is (a) endless, and (b) impossible to win. Challenge the *prudence* of such a Supreme Court ruling, or at least of its enforcement within the foreseeable future, and you situate yourself upon different and altogether more promising ground. This for a number of reasons: The claim of the Supreme Court to the last say as to the *meaning* of a constitutional provision, as I have already noticed, is pretty well unanswerable in terms of our traditional constitutional theory—and legally unanswerable altogether. Attack it, and you attack an aspect of our political system that, to go no further, now has behind it nigh onto two centuries of prescription. Attack it, and you must not only meet the case for judicial review as worked out by Hamilton and Marshall, but meet it to the satisfaction of your neighbors (who, as one of the dissenters on the North Brookfield school board reminds us, are pretty sure to be "simple"). The case for the Supreme Court's last say on the meaning of the Constitution is on the same footing, like it or not, as the case for papal infallibility within the Roman Catholic Church. And from all this it follows that one enters an argument with the Supreme Court about legality before, so to speak, a packed jury. On the other hand, no one, so far as I know, has ever worked out a case for deeming the Supreme Court infallible in the realm of prudence, or for supposing the American political system unworkable unless the Supreme Court have the last word on whether, given the current lay of sentiment and opinion in the American community, immediate enforcement of this or that inspired ruling by the Court would be so destructive of civil peace, so certain to produce those divisions among the people that threaten the whole process of government by the deliberate sense of the community, so likely to eventuate in bloodshed, or, as in North Brookfield, in impossible situations, as to be (I deliberately use Dwight Eisenhower's magic phrase) "unthinkable." The Supreme Court has a right, nay a duty, to say what, in a given case, the Constitution *means*, and thus to the inside track in an argument about its meaning. It does not have the right and duty to add to its rulings, as further constitutional doctrine, *ruat coelum*—which as matters stand, with the President apparently having accepted a general cost-what-it-may obligation to enforce all federal court orders in any conditions anywhere, and Congress a similar obligation to keep hands off, is *just* what it does in effect add to its rulings. "Let the Heavens fall!" But this, I contend, is under the Preamble to the Constitution ("in order to form a more perfect Union," it says) impossible constitutional doctrine in America, once it is brought skillfully out into the open where you can get at it. But back to my distinction: I hazard the guess that the reluctance of the Congress to resort to its control over the appellate jurisdiction of the Court as a means of sidestepping an unacceptable Court ruling—it has, I think, resorted to it only twice—may be a matter of Congress' seeing no way to resort to it, on a given ruling, without seeming to question the Supreme

Court's last say on the *law*. Let Congress, I say, taught by Conservative publicists, learn to assert its own last say about what will go down in the American community, along with its own final responsibility, together with the President but *not* the Supreme Court, for the maintenance of civil peace. The Supreme Court, remote as it is from the brute facts of American life, is not in a strong position for talking back in an argument about what is prudent (in strict theory, indeed, it is not even supposed to take prudential consideration into account in handing down its decisions). And it would be terrible to think that the responsibility for confining governmental action within the bounds of prudence lies nowhere in the American political system.

D) One thesis more, and I shall have done. I have spoken above of restoring the *status quo ante* in North Brookfield, that is, the *status quo* that obtained before the New York Regents' case, and with the apparent implication that everybody is clear what that *status quo ante* is. I have also spoken above of a choice between the so-called "narrow" interpretation of the establishment clause and the new "broad" interpretation, with the apparent implication that the choice between them is an exhaustive choice. In both instances, let me say now, I was merely postponing problems; and I owe it to my readers, in conclusion now, to meet those problems head on. As regards the *status quo ante*—the relation between church and state, religion and government, before the Engel case—I must make the two-fold point: First, there *was*, generally speaking, no particular *status quo ante;* and second, insofar as there was a particular *status quo ante* it was *not* what we commonly pretend it to have been. As regards the choice between narrow interpretation and broad interpretation, that choice is not exhaustive at all—and is not likely to be in our time. Here, let me emphasize, is one of those matters in America that one can see clearly only with a carefully-cultivated *innocent* eye, an eye whose owner has *deliberately* removed from it the blinders of constitutional myth and often-repeated, never-challenged verbal formulae, so that it actually sees that which is actually "given" to it by reality—a rare gift, I happen to think, among students of politics. Now: The First Amendment, we are in the habit of telling ourselves, establishes a "wall of separation" between church and state, between religion and government, that it is the agreed business alike of Congress, the State, and at the margin the Supreme Court to maintain. To which I answer: that is an Old Wives' Tale, from which, if we are to make sense of our affairs, we must speedily emancipate ourselves. In point of fact, the wall of separation in America has always been as full of holes as a kitchen sieve. This is not, moreover, wonderful; the religion clauses of the First Amendment (which are the only verbal formulation we have of our wall of separation) went into our constitutional law, and similar clauses have gone into our state constitutions, not as a matter of high principle, not as a sacred presupposition of freedom, but (as Father Murray has shown, though I deliberately use unpriestly language)[12] as a *deal*—a *deal* rendered necessarily by the fact that we are a people divided not only pluralistically (Father Murray's point) but *spottily* (my point over and beyond his) amongst a wide variety of religious persuasions. We the people have always known that the absence of any wall of separation at all must lead to the undermining of civil peace; but we have always known also that a complete wall of separation is out of the question. The deal—my understanding of it differs from Father Murray's—was a deal, so to speak, for having it both ways about civil peace on the one hand and a little-not-too-much penetration of the governmental sphere by religion—both ways, if you like, about on the one hand the wall of separation (in the absence of such a wall, civil peace will be broken because some religious people will seek too great a penetration of the civil order, and other people will resent it) and on the other hand that minimum of religious penetration of the civil order that you cannot, in America, begrudge religious people without, as in North Brookfield, breaking civil peace. The American answer to the problem of having it both ways here, the *traditional* American answer, which to our misfortune we have all too rarely tried to put into words, has been this: Maintain a wall; celebrate it in myth and song even as the Great Wall of China was celebrated in myth and song; celebrate it, indeed, as a wall that cannot and must not be breached. But let the wall be *porous;* and if now and then here or there, some moisture seeps through from one side of the wall to the other, that is, from religion to government (though not the other way 'round), use some common sense, of which we expect you to have some, in deciding how excited to get about it. Americans carry that answer, I like to think, not so much in their minds as (in Lincoln Steffen's phrase about T. R.) in their hips; they apply it to their affairs, if I may put it so, instinctively, and without need of assistance from their intellectual betters. Thus the chapels, maintained at public expense, in our service academies; thus cadets required by law to turn up in them on Saturday or Sunday, or explain why not; thus church organizations testifying before Congressional committees (which, as Peter Drucker has pointed out, would not be tolerated for a moment in any country deadly serious about the "wall of separation"); thus a score of yet other Congressional acts of defiance against the "clear" language of the First Amendment, and thus the systematic tacit acquiescences of the Supreme Court in all these acts of defiance; thus, *most* especially, the continuing phenomenon of religious observances in the public schools throughout our history and pretty much all over the land. (I give it as my educated guess that the biggest surprise of the Engel decision, for most Americans, must have been the discovery that the public schools *are* "state" or "government" at all; *who*, they might well ask, were they, like their intellectual betters, a little more articulate, who ever *heard* of such a thing?) The public schools of America, as we all know off at the back of our minds, were originally established in America with a legal mandate to foil the Old Deceiver Satan by providing religious and moral instruction for the young; nor, except spottily (in the big cities especially, of course) has the average American ever ceased for one moment to expect them to perform that function; nor, over most of the country, have the public schools ever stopped performing it in some fashion or other—often, to be sure, half-heartedly, often formalistically only, often with the religion so purged of doctrinal or sectarian content as to be hardly recognizable as religion, but still in a manner oceans apart from the genuine neutrality toward religion, or even enmity towards religion, that is characteristic of, say, our great secular universities. There are exceptions? No doubt; indeed the point I am leading up to could hardly stand if there were not some exceptions. For my point is going to be: Insofar as there has been a general rule, it has been: go ahead with your religious observances in the public schools, *provided* you keep the peace. But that is only another way of saying there has been *no* general rule except, surprising as it may be to see it down in black and white, this rule: let the local community decide: in favor of virtual exclusion of religious observances if you like (as in California), in favor of a wee little bit of religious observances (that, one gathers, was the decision in New York, with the well-nigh meaningless Regents' prayer), in favor of quite a bit of religious observances (as in, say, Massachusetts or Connecticut). Let the local community decide, but on the tacit condition that it recognize and live up to its local responsibility for keeping the peace, for not having people at each others' throats. Our history in this matter, moreover, as I proudly believe, has been an impressive one.

The real significance and danger of the "prayer" decisions lies, then, precisely in the attempt to lay down a general rule on religious observances in the schools where formerly there was none—and to accomplish this by setting aside a universally understood (if never articulated) general rule on another matter, namely: Let the people of the local community work the matter out, as part of their general problems of living together on their little portion of American real estate.

That way of slicing it, so familiar to us that it is difficult to put into words, had certain very great advantages as compared with any alternative way of slicing it—advantages, we must now notice, tied up with the relevant rules, commandments even, that have, I believe, been generally observed in our local communities. These are:

> I. Thou shalt not be *doctrinaire* about religious observances in the public schools (that is, thou shalt assert no high principles, allegedly governing this matter, that thou placest beyond discussion or negotiation). (Doctrinaire, of course, is the word I promised to substitute for "theological"; and now I have kept my promise.)
> II. Thou shalt keep thy sense of humor (on pain of being laughed at and, ultimately, laughed out of town).[13]
> III. Thou shalt bear in mind, in the course of thy face-to-face negotiations with thy neighbors on this matter, that tomorrow thou must live neighbors with them.

These three commandments, like the Ten, are parts of one and the same *ethos,* and are for that reason members one of another. Not being doctrinaire makes for greater neighborliness, as neighborliness knocks the edges off the tendency to be doctrinaire. Both neighborliness and the avoidance of doctrinairism increase the chances of people keeping their sense of humor, as sense of humor cements neighborliness and wears down, still a little further, the tendency to be doctrinaire. The fact that the relevant negotiations are and must be conducted face-to-face, and are presided over by the necessity of living together tomorrow, sets a stage on which alike neighborliness, sense of humor, and the avoidance of doctrinairism can thrive like the green bay tree. Are we going to permit the Supreme Court to uproot them, in the name of spurious and novel doctrine?[13] If not, then let us get busy and amend the Fourteenth Amendment.

Notes

[1] *Life,* November 8, 1963.

[2] *School District of Abingdon Township v. Schempp, Murray v. Curlett* (83 Supreme Court 1560, 10 Lawyer's Ed. 2nd. 844, 1963). *Engel v. Vitale* (370 U.S. 421, 82 Supreme Court 1261, 8 Lawyer's Ed. 2nd. 601, 1962).

[3] Walter Berns, "School Prayers and 'Religious Warfare'," *National Review,* April 23, 1963, pp. 315-318.

[4] Willmoore Kendall, *The Conservative Affirmation* (Chicago: Henry Regnery Co., 1963), Chapter I, *passim.*

[5] J. Allen Smith, *The Spirit of American Government* (New York: The Macmillan Co., 1912).

[6] L. Brent Bozell, "Saving Our Children From God," *National Review,* July 16, 1963, pp. 19-22.

[7] For a skillful though in my opinion wrongheaded explication of this issue, see Leonard W. Levy, "School Prayers and the Founding Fathers," *Commentary* 34, 225-230.

[8] *Ibid.*

[9] R. P. Oliver, "Conservatism and Reality," *Modern Age,* Fall 1961, pp. 397-406.

[10] *Pennsylvania v. Nelson* (350 U.S. 497, 1956)

[11] This book, by L. Brent Bozell, will be published in 1965 by Henry Regnery Co.

[12] John Courtney Murray, *We Hold These Truths* (New York: Sheed and Ward, 1960), Chapter II.

[13] How far people quickly go—in the direction of doctrinairism and loss of sense of humor—emerges clearly in the following Letter to the Editor from the complainant in the Maryland "prayer" case: "I am the Maryland Atheist, Sirs: I am a principal in one of the cases now pending before the Supreme Court concerning the reading of the Bible and prayer recitation in the public schools.

"The Atheist's position (I am that Maryland Atheist you mentioned) is one arrived at after considerable study, cogitation and inner search. It is a position which is founded in science, in reason and in a love for fellow man, rather than in a love for God.

"We find the Bible to be nauseating, historically inaccurate, replete with the ravings of madmen. We find God to be sadistic, brutal, and a representation of hatred, vengeance. We find the Lord's Prayer to be that muttered by worms, groveling for meager existence in a traumatic, paranoid world.

"This is not appropriate untouchable dicta to be forced on adult or child. The business of the public schools, where attendance is compulsory, is to prepare children to face the problems on earth, not to prepare for heaven—which is a delusional dream of the unsophisticated minds of the ill-educated clergy.

"Fortunately, we atheists can seek legal remedy through our Constitution, which was written by deists (not Christians) who had *enough* of religion and wanted to grow toward freedom from it, not enslavement in it.

"Signed, Madalyn Murray, Baltimore, Maryland."

Equality and the American Political Tradition

"Every Frenchman," Charles de Gaulle has written somewhere, "wants a special privilege or two; that is how he expresses his passion for Equality." "Every American," I suppose an equally cynical observer here in the United States might say, "wants a right or two that he is by no means willing to concede to everybody else; that is how the American expresses *his* passion for Equality." The tacit premise in each case—that of the Frenchman who seeks special privileges, that of the American who denies to others rights that he claims for himself—must go something like this: The Frenchman, the American, has an official "commitment" to equality that he "handles" by paying it lip-service but refusing to live up to it; or, if you like, Both the Frenchman and the American publicly profess equality as a political ideal, but violate that ideal in the detail of their day-to-day living. Now: in the case of the Frenchman, at least, the official commitment, or public profession, is clear enough: the French Revolution did indeed do its mischief under the slogan "Liberty, Equality, Fraternity"; and, throughout French history, the slogan has been conspicuously displayed in French public places, vociferously iterated in French political discourse. If the Frenchman doesn't live up to the slogan, including its middle term, "Equality," he is indeed the man of divided counsels, the schizoid of the de Gaulle epigram; we are entitled to think poorly of him. But what about the American: is the epigram correct in suggesting that the American who wants the exercise of a couple of rights that he "brazenly" denies to others also has a public commitment to equality? Is he also refusing to live up to a political ideal to which he nevertheless pays lip-service, and to which his forefathers have paid lip-service before him? Is he also schizoid? I think the prevailing scholarly answer to these questions is, Yes, he has the same official commitment to equality as the Frenchman and, no less than the Frenchman, knows perfectly well that he does. Ask for proof that this is true, and quick as a flash you will be told about the findings of the team that produced Gunnar Myrdal's

American Dilemma. The team, in order to get on with their study of race relations in the United States (but, of course, especially in the South), wanted to know not merely, How do Americans actually behave in race relations? They wanted to know also, How do Americans think—or say they think—they ought to behave? To this end they put to their respondents in effect the question, What political ideals do you as an American believe in? And wherever they turned, even in the benighted South, they were told (quite usefully, it happens, for the purpose in hand), We believe in Liberty and Equality: the American political Creed is Liberty and Equality. Nor, since Myrdal published his book, do I recall any piece of writing in which that finding has been called into question. The American, we are constantly told, does have a public commitment to equality that— purely aside from the fact that he ought to anyway—he ought to live up to because it *is* his public commitment. And if he doesn't live up to it, he is in the same boat with the Frenchman: we are entitled to think poorly of him. (As, if we are Liberal, we certainly will.)

The Myrdal finding has, for the rest, a certain surface plausibility. The Declaration of Independence, we are reminded, does, indeed, say, as plain as the nose on your face, "All men are created equal," and does indeed sound as if it meant something should be done about it. We Americans, we are reminded, did indeed fight *our* Revolution under the Declaration, so that equality, here as in France, is indeed a slogan over which our hearts go—or ought to go—pit-a-pat. Never mind that you don't see it about quite as much as in France. Never mind, even, that the major egalitarian movement of our time in America, the Civil Rights movement, pins to its banners the slogan "Freedom," *not* "Equality." Never mind, either, that the word order in the Myrdal finding is suspiciously French—"Liberty, Equality," not, as in the Declaration of Independence, "Equality, Liberty." Never mind anything. Both the Declaration of Independence and Gunnar Myrdal say we are committed to equality as a political goal, so committed we are.

Now: as will have been guessed already, I have—or have begun to have—some doubts about all that, and I propose to ventilate those doubts in this article. Craving the reader's forbearance, however, I am going to come at them in a rather roundabout way and begin my argument with a thesis, or statement, that may seem rather far afield, namely, a thesis or statement about the United States Supreme Court.

There is shaping up amongst us—amongst Us the people of the United States—a series of *problems* relating to the *powers* of the Supreme Court. (I was tempted to write: an *issue* concerning the powers of the Supreme Court; but I am glad I didn't, since I believe the best hope for all of us is that the problems I speak of shan't ever turn into an issue, properly speaking, with lines sharply drawn, positions deeply entrenched, compromise or temporizing solutions irrevocably renounced; the problems I write of have *not* yet become an issue, and I celebrate the fact.) I repeat: there are problems shaping up amongst us about the powers of the Supreme Court, and these problems are sufficiently urgent to enable us to say: Every educated American ought to know what those problems are, how far they have already developed as problems, and what we can conclude, in a brief article like this one, as to their meaning as problems. It is, let me say, a complicated business, which I as a specialist can only try to make as simple as possible; and it will perhaps help if I begin by making about them a few observations that, taken one by one, can be kept reasonably free of complexities and technicalities.

First, the problems that are now shaping up about the powers of the Supreme Court are, as bones of contention, *new* problems: which is to say, we must not confuse them with, for example, the problem about the powers of the Supreme Court that arose under the New Deal. Then the issue—and it *was* an issue—had to do with the traditional power of the Supreme Court to take in its hand an enactment of the congress, scrutinize it, and, if the learned justices saw fit, declare it null and void, or unconstitutional. The problems now shaping up, we must be clear, have nothing to do with that issue; there is, at the moment, no clash between the Supreme Court and Congress, at least not overtly. And, to put it the other way around, the age of the New Deal, the age of the late Franklin Delano Roosevelt, knew nothing of the problems, the problems relating to the powers of the Supreme Court, that are now shaping up; and we must, I repeat, be clear about that, lest the problems slip through our fingers.

Second, the problems I speak of are not—not yet, anyhow—of such character as to make of the Supreme Court itself an issue (though Liberals sometimes try to state the problems in a way that *would* make it an issue). Nothing has happened up to now that is likely to put Conservatives into the business of trying to abolish the Supreme Court, or of trying to revise its role in the American constitutional system. It is not, in short, that we have entered upon a period when the Conservatives are anti-Supreme Court, the Liberals pro-Supreme Court, and may the best man win. To put it that way is to misunderstand what the fight is really over.

Third, the problems—the problems that are "up," or at least shaping up, as contrasted with the potential problems, the ones that may begin to shape up later—have to do (this much, happily, *is* simple) with a single clause in the Fourteenth Amendment to the Constitution of the United States, namely, the clause concerning the equal protection of the laws—and that clause's equally famous sister, the "due process clause," which frequently comes up also, but comes up merely as the more convenient formula, as the lawyers see it, for achieving the objectives of the equal protection clause. Or, to make it just a little more complicated, the problems have to do with the relation of those two clauses to the Tenth Amendment to the Constitution of the United States. And here, I *must* go into a little history —about the Tenth Amendment, the Fourteenth Amendment, *and,* most particularly, the *idea* of equality (which is the key word in the whole business) in the American political tradition.

The roots of the American political tradition—so we are told, anyhow, by the official custodians of our national lore—lie in two great documents, the Declaration of Independence and the Philadelphia Constitution. The two documents were, as you know, written within a few brief—brief, but of course, crowded—years of one another, and by representatives of one and the same people, that is, of We (or, watching our grammar, Us) the people of the United States; and, that being the case, we have always liked to tell ourselves, We the people of the United States, that the two documents say more or less the same sort of thing—as, having been written so close together by *our* representatives, why shouldn't they? And yet—it gives me no pleasure to point it out—and yet, the most casual look at the two documents reveals that on one important point they do not say the same thing at all, or, if you like, that on one important point one of the two documents is eloquent and emphatic, the other, if I may put it so, tight-lipped and uncommunicative. Concretely: the Declaration of Independence puts forth, as one of the truths we the people hold as "self-evident," the proposition: All men are created equal. It puts that proposition forward, indeed, as the very *first* of the truths we hold, and seems, therefore, to put it forward as *the* truth, along with the truth about certain natural rights, that is to be planted at the very heart of the American political experience. Not, I hasten to add, that anyone appears to have been very clear as to what it *meant* to declare all men created equal; no doubt the words, even at the moment they were uttered, meant different things to different persons, even to different persons among those immediately concerned. To some the words no doubt meant merely that all men were created equal in the eyes of God. To some they no doubt meant merely that all men were created with an equal claim to justice under the existing law. For some they no doubt expressed the hope, though merely the hope, that the republic about to be formed would be that land, the first land of all lands ever and anywhere, in which men would *become* equal, that is, achieve the equality of which humble and disadvantaged men have often dreamt dreams that other men have called Utopian. To some the words no doubt meant merely the hope that America would be a land in which men would be anyhow more equal than elsewhere —a land in which *in*equalities among men would be less glaring, less intimately related to what we fashionably call the accident of birth, less likely to be handed down to, say, the third and fourth generations. To some the words no doubt meant the hope that the new republic would be one in which men—well, white men, and male men only, not female men, for no one had yet thought of going in for that sort of thing—would cast equal votes in at least some elections for public office. To some they *may* have meant—that is all I can say because I find no evidence of it—the hope that America would be a land in which government, political authority, would take steps to *make* men equal—we cannot exclude the possibility, and must mention it because that is what the words have come, in the fullness of time, to mean to some amongst us, some even of the most learned amongst us.

But whatever the words may have meant to whomever, there are two things we may assert with some finality: first, that the Framers of the Philadelphia Constitution, by contrast with the Declaration, did not so much as mention the topic of equality in the new instrument of government—not even in the Preamble, where, remember, they pause to list the purposes (a more perfect union, the blessings of liberty, justice, etc.) for which We the people ordain and establish the Constitution, and where, if nowhere else, one might have expected them to recall that first proposition of the Declaration under which and for which, remember, they had just fought a great war; and second, that Publius, when he came to write the *Federalist*— which, we are told, is also one of the documents in which the American political tradition is rooted—has a way, if I may put it so, of clamming up whenever (as does sometimes happen) the topic of equality heaves into sight. And perhaps we can add, third, that when Madison, during the First Session of Congress, penned the Bill of Rights, he also failed to mention equality, and this despite the fact that the model he certainly had before him—the Virginia Declaration of Rights—begins with at least a courtly *bow* to equality. Let us, if you like, be cautious, and not make too much of all this: the fact stands that the only place you can go, among our so-called basic documents, to find equality placed high among the "values" of Us, the people of the United States, is the Declaration of Independence. Nor is it, I think, quite good enough to say: The Constitution, the Federalist, the Bill of Rights *naturally* did not have to say anything about equality; it was already there, as part of our political Credo, in the Declaration. Our Founding Fathers were *not*, I insist, all *that* reluctant to say things a second time. We can, rather, hardly avoid the conclusion that the Constitution, the Federalist, and the Bill of Rights conspicuously *avoid* any commitment on the point of equality— beyond, of course, the tacit commitment to the equal right of all men, under the existing laws, to equal and just treatment in the courts of law. But note that I say "under the *existing* laws." There is in the three post-Declaration documents no suggestion, as maybe there is maybe there isn't in the Declaration of Independence, that the existing laws ought to be made over, so to speak, in the *image* of equality. That idea, if it was ever there at all, promptly disappears after the Declaration of Independence, and does not appear again, in the American political tradition, until, to say the least, a much later date —perhaps, but only perhaps, in the Fourteenth Amendment (which was, as we know, adopted soon after the Civil War); I think not until certain Supreme Court cases that are the source of the problems I spoke of at the beginning, and that, I repeat, I believe, or fear, to be shaping up.

Now: what about the Fourteenth Amendment? Did it bring the promise of equality—that *promise* of equality for the citizens of our

Republic that some people see in the Declaration of Independence —did the Fourteenth Amendment bring the promise of equality back within the central meaning of our political experience? Certainly it restored the *word* "equal" to our political vocabulary; certainly it guarantees to all, and apparently in as plain language as anyone could ask for, the "equal" protection of the laws. But here, as so often happens in our constitutional law, the plain language, upon examination, proves not to be plain at all, and for a reason I have already anticipated, namely: the equal protection clause of the Fourteenth Amendment does not tell us, will never tell us no matter how hard we squeeze it, which of *two* things it actually means, and we must be very clear as to what those two things are. It might mean *first*, as the reader is already prepared to hear me say, that all are to have the equal protection of the *existing* laws, which *existing* laws may involve any amount you like of *in*equality, of *un*equal treatment, of *un*equal rights and privileges. Or it might mean *second* that, if I may put it so (I think no one ever has before), all are entitled to laws that in fact *give* equal protection to each. Now: if it means the first of these things, then all it calls for is the impartial enforcement of existing laws—existing laws, we must add, however unjust or inequitable those laws may be. If it means the second, it can of course become a standard—nay, *the* standard—by which existing laws may be tested and—where they fail to meet the test—set aside. In the first case, the laws would continue, after the Fourteenth Amendment as before, to be made—equal or unequal, equitable or inequitable, just or unjust— exclusively by the Congress and by the state legislatures, according to *their* lights. A man might, armed with the Fourteenth Amendment, go into the courts and demand the protection to which the existing laws, as made by Congress and the State legislatures, entitle him. But he could *never* go into the courts and say: "I demand that this law be set aside, be declared unconstitutional, because it is the kind of law that in and of itself gives unequal protection to different citizens." In the second case—that is, if the Fourteenth Amendment means that all are entitled to laws that in fact *give* equal protection to each—Congress and the State legislatures no longer have the last word about the existing laws: if those laws fail to meet the test of equal protection then the courts are entitled to strike them down, and to keep on striking them down until we have laws that, in the courts' view, do give equal protection. In the first case—that is, if the

Fourteenth Amendment merely guarantees the equal protection of the existing laws—the promise of equality in the Declaration of Independence remains just where it was before the Fourteenth Amendment was adopted, which is to say: pretty much nowhere among our public commitments. In the second case—that is, if the Fourteenth Amendment guarantees laws that will in fact provide equal protection—the equal protection clause becomes, as of the moment of its adoption, a summons to a legal revolution—and, necessarily, a legal revolution that must ultimately be presided over by the Supreme Court. So I can now repeat my question in a new and, I think, more manageable form: Does the Fourteenth Amendment call for the equal protection of existing laws? Or does it call for revising existing laws until they confer equal protection? And if I have dwelt long and teacherishly over the point, it is for a very good reason, namely: until one grasps these two possible meanings of the Fourteenth Amendment, one cannot hope to understand the problems that are shaping up in the United States about the Supreme Court—about, most particularly, the prayer decisions, and about so-called reapportionment.

Now: perhaps my one claim to uniqueness among students of the Fourteenth Amendment is that I do not believe the issue as to which of the two meanings is the "correct" one will ever be settled by appeal to the document itself. A pretty good case, to be sure, can be made out for each, but also neither case is such that it is likely to satisfy the proponents of the other. When the Supreme Court points to the plain language of the Fourteenth Amendment and says, The Mississippi ruling that keeps James Meredith from enrolling at Ole Miss denies James Meredith the equal protection of the laws, and is therefore unconstitutional because it violates the Fourteenth Amendment, it does have on its side—well, the plain language of the Fourteenth Amendment, which appears to guarantee to James Meredith *the* equal protection of the laws. And when Governor Ross Barnett answers that the Supreme Court is misinterpreting the Fourteenth Amendment, he also has some things to point to. He can, for instance, point to the fact—an incontestable fact by the way—that the very session of Congress that enacted the Fourteenth Amendment established a segregated school in the District of Columbia—which is to say: if the Fourteenth Amendment has the meaning the Supreme Court says it has, so that it prohibits segregated schools, the authors of the Amendment didn't know that that was what it meant, which is surprising to say the least. Governor Barnett can also point to the speeches made by the state legislators in the process of ratifying the Fourteenth Amendment. Here, also, we find no evidence that the men who added the Fourteenth Amendment to our constitutional law contemplated a legal revolution presided over by the Supreme Court. And Governor Barnett can, finally, point to the fact—again an incontestable fact—that the Supreme Court itself, for decades and decades after the Fourteenth Amendment went into effect, leaned almost entirely toward the view that it guaranteed only the equal protection of existing laws—which is to say, Governor Barnett has behind him the Supreme Court's own long-pull tradition. But don't —because I state his points vigorously—understand me to be saying that Governor Barnett wins the argument. *My* point is that the argument, when conducted in those terms—and who ever heard of it being conducted in any other terms?—is inconclusive, and always will be. We shall never—never, never—be able to answer the question, What is the *true, intended* meaning of the Fourteenth Amendment? to everybody's satisfaction.

Let me round out that picture—that picture of the background of the problems that are shaping up—by bringing into it the Tenth Amendment as well—the Tenth Amendment, and the implicit principle of the Philadelphia Constitution that the Tenth Amendment merely restates. The Philadelphia Constitution, which, as we all know, was formed by the *representatives* of the original thirteen states—the Philadelphia Constitution assigned certain powers and functions of government to a newly-created *federal* government (the conduct of foreign affairs, for example, the national defense, the regulation of interstate commerce, etc.); but by clear implication it left all other powers and functions of government precisely where they had been before the Philadelphia Constitution was adopted, that is, with the states themselves. One of these powers, pretty clearly, one certainly reserved to the states, was the control of the suffrage; the making of decisions as to who in the United States may vote. Another such power, again pretty clearly, was the control of education—that is, the making of decisions about our public schools: what kind of education they are to provide, what persons shall attend what schools, etc. Still another such power, another of those powers reserved to the states, was the whole business of making decisions about the relation between church and state—or, as I like to put it, between religion and politics: whether to have an established religion, whether to bring religion into the public schools or keep it out of the public schools, etc. Yet another such power, a power clearly reserved to the states, was the control of districting—the drawing of the lines that form the districts in which Congressmen, and State Senators, and State representatives, are elected—the power to decide, therefore, (to use the fashionable jargon) whether our legislatures, national and state, are to be "rural-dominated," or "urban-dominated," or so devised as to give both country-folk and city-folk a fair shake. Let's tick them off again—the four powers we have mentioned that were clearly reserved to the states, since they are part and parcel of our business here: the control of the suffrage, the control of education, the handling of problems of Church and State, and the control of legislative districts. At least these four powers, according to the Philadelphia Constitution, were to be *monopolies* of the states and their governments; at least these four things the state governments were to go ahead and run just as they would have had there been no federal government; at least these four things the new federal government was to keep its hand *off* of; at least these four things, therefore, the Supreme Court was to keep *its* hands off of, because the Supreme Court is an agency of the federal government, and what the federal government cannot touch the Supreme Court presumably cannot touch. That, if I may put it so, was the original *deal* between the states and the federal government; nothing, I hasten to add, sacred about it, nothing that couldn't be revised as time went on, but still: the original deal, as written into the Philadelphia Constitution, and as clearly understood on all sides.

Now: the Tenth Amendment, which as I have intimated we have *got* to bring into our picture, merely hammers down that original deal: Some powers and functions, it says in effect, are entrusted to the federal government; all remaining powers, including, of course, those four we have mentioned, are reserved to the states, that is, to the state governments, and to the people of the states, who presumably control the state governments just as We the people of the United States control the federal government. It says in effect: The deal's a deal: for some purposes we are going to be a nation, and have uniform laws and regulations all over the country; for other purposes we are going to remain separate states—thirteen of them, or fifteen of them, or forty-four or forty-eight or fifty—and have different laws and regulations within these separate states. The deal's a deal, the Tenth Amendment says in effect, and can only be revised by the same solemn process by which it, the deal, came into effect. The deal's a deal, and can only be revised by Us, the people of the United States —which means, under the Philadelphia Constitution: the deal can be revised only by constitutional amendment, or, failing that, by congressional action under the "necessary and proper" clause. Powers can indeed, it says in effect, be moved across the line—powers now exercised by the states can indeed be assigned to the federal government—but only by a solemn act of Us the people of the United States acting through those instruments of government that are most intimately ours.

Now: put all that, all I have just said about the Tenth Amendment, put all that together with what I said above about the Fourteenth Amendment—put the two together and you will see where we have to come out: if the equal protection clause of the Fourteenth Amendment means merely that all are entitled to the impartial application of existing laws, then the original deal between states and federal government is still on; since there has been no constitutional amendment revising the deal, then the suffrage, education, religion, legislative districting all remain on the side of the line that belongs to the states. But if the equal protection and due process clauses of the Fourteenth Amendment mean that the laws must be revised and reinterpreted so as to in fact *give* equal protection to all, then the deal is off. If the two clauses mean that the laws must *give* equal protection to all, then any state enactment, or policy, or practice, that discriminates in favor of some persons and so against other persons, becomes the business of the Supreme Court—and so the business of the federal government. The Tenth Amendment line—between powers entrusted to the federal government and powers reserved to the states —loses all of its meaning as a line. Or, to put the matter in its most dramatic terms: if the Fourteenth Amendment means that the laws must give equal protection to all, then the Fourteenth Amendment *repeals* the Tenth Amendment. For the Tenth Amendment either gives equal protection or doesn't give equal protection, and if it does not give equal protection then, according to the Fourteenth Amendment, it is, to that extent, void. And that consequence may properly be recognized, under our constitutional system by the United States Supreme Court. And we are at last in position to talk business about the problems I speak of as shaping up as really major problems—in particular, civil liberties, desegregation, and over-representation—and to fix attention on and explain what is making them major problems, namely: that the American Conservatives are resisting Supreme Court innovations under all three headings. The problems are, I am saying, major problems because the Conservatives are dragging their feet in all three areas, and because the Liberals are unwilling to acquiesce in their doing so.

The Conservatives *do* drag their feet.—Let the Liberals take note that I concede the point.—When a Conservative reads in his newspaper that nearly ninety percent of the Southern schools are still segregated, and that the rate at which Southern schools are being desegregated is tapering off, he does not—unlike the Liberal—feel moved to condemnation of the White Southerners for their allegedly wicked ways. When the Conservative learns, once again, that hundreds of thousands of Southern Negroes are denied the vote, he feels no stirring in his heart to go teach those Southerners a lesson about democracy. When the Conservative finds himself up against proof that the kids in the public schools of Middletown, Connecticut—which is ninety percent Catholic—recite "Hail Marys" in the classrooms and even in the corridors, he does *not* feel that liberty has died in America—any more than he feels that liberty has died in America when he learns that the public schools of the State of California are conducted just as they would be if California were populated exclusively by atheists and agnostics. And when the Liberal hammers the Conservative over the head with the awful fact that the good folk of New Haven and Hartford—again I speak of Connecticut, because I have lived there most of the time for many years—do not have the voice in the state legislature to which their numbers might seem to entitle them—when the Liberal hammers the Conservative over the head with that awful fact, I say, he feels no temptation to order a couple of divisions of the U.S. Army to Connecticut, to restore its republican form of government. I repeat: I concede the point that the Conservatives drag their feet on what are fashionably called civil liberties, equal representation, desegregation. I shall, indeed, go further and concede another point, namely: the Conservative will not feel differently about these matters, *basically* at least will not feel differently about them, when he learns that a federal court has ordered the public schools of Middletown to *stop* reciting Hail Marys, and that the court order is being *defied*. Not, of course, that he likes a situation where court orders are being defied: he does not. But he sees more things to be involved than just a court order. And he values some of those things equally with the sanctity of court orders.

Finally—though this is a point I make rather than concede—Conservatives are likely to continue to drag their feet on these matters for a long time off in the future. The Liberal may not like that. He may think it shocking. He may—I often think he does—hate the Conservative for it. But he had best get it through his head that those are the facts of life, and he had better, for the sake of his ulcers, get ready to live with them for quite a while. For if he doesn't, he simply doesn't understand American politics in their present phase, and, worse still, doesn't understand the *main* fact about even himself, namely: he is no Joshua. Joshua commanded the sun and the stars to stand still and they obeyed him. But when that would-be Joshua the American Liberal commands the sun and stars to stand still, they do not obey, and are not likely to begin to obey tomorrow or the next day. The Liberal's struggle for what he calls civil liberties, if he ever wins it, is going to be won in only one way, which is by *persuasion*—that is, by persuading the Conservatives, who are I believe the overwhelming majority of Us the people of the United States, over to his point of view. Not by court orders. Not by ordering federal troops to Little Rock, or Oxford, or Birmingham. But by *convincing* the Conservatives. And that, let me assure him, is going to take some doing.

Why is it going to take some doing? Well, let me, by way of summary, go back over the political science of the matter as I have laid it out.

All the current hullaballoo about civil liberties, about desegregation, about redistricting on a one-man-one-vote basis, is, I am saying, the result of one thing, namely: the Supreme Court decided, a few years ago, to revise its own traditional interpretation of the Fourteenth Amendment. From now on, it said in effect, the Fourteenth Amendment is going to require not equal protection under existing laws, but the revision of existing laws so that they will give equal protection. And the effect of that change of mind and heart on the part of the Supreme Court was, quite simply, this: it put the Supreme Court into the business of upsetting the deal—the deal between the federal government and the states—written into the Philadelphia Constitution and the Tenth Amendment. The Conservative, however —and my hope for this article is that it will help to make him better understood—the Conservative was brought up to believe that that deal can be altered only by Us the people acting through the amendment process of the Philadelphia Constitution, or, in a pinch, by a consensus of Us the people acting through Congress under the necessary and proper clause. He *still* regards the suffrage, the relations between Church and State, the drawing of lines for legislative district, education—he *still* regards these things as the business exclusively of the states, as not, therefore, the business of the federal government, and not, therefore, the business of the Supreme Court. He still regards the equal protection and due process clauses of the Fourteenth Amendment as guarantees merely of impartial enforcement of existing laws. He still does not want to help silence Hail Marys in the State of Connecticut, because he still does not want Connecticut to be interfering in the affairs of *his* state. That is the Conservative state of mind—the American political tradition—with regard to the issues involved in recent Supreme Court innovations. And I repeat to the Liberals: Do not underestimate the Conservative politically. There is a lot of him, must be a lot of him because he is pretty certainly the overwhelming majority of the American people. And what I referred to as the problems that are shaping up I can now nail down as follows: about the future—the future of civil liberties, of desegregation, etc.—there are as I see it two possibilities: either the Liberals—and I make no distinction, for this purpose, between the Liberals and the Supreme Court—either the Liberals pull in their horns and decide to do it the hard way, that is, by persuading Us the American people over to their point of view; or, second, the Liberals will continue their present strategy, which is to attempt—from a mere minority position in American politics—to impose the new interpretation by sheer fiat of the Supreme Court. Either first, I say, the Liberals and the Supreme Court pull in their horns and let us get back to deciding these matters by public debate, or, second, we face a future of more Oxfords, more prayer decisions, more interference by the Supreme Court with the electoral and districting practices of the states—with more hard feelings, more use of federal troops against American citizens, more attempts to bring about social revolution by court order. Either the one or the other. And I, as a Conservative, hope for the first—the Supreme Court pulling in its horns—but fear, because of the fanaticism of the contemporary Liberal, the second.

The Civil Rights Movement and the Coming Constitutional Crisis

My topic* commits me to: First, a prediction—that the American constitutional system will within the foreseeable future enter upon a period of crisis. And second, a statement, not predictive, but analytical, as to which of the dynamic forces in our politics seems most likely, given what we know of American political movements and our constitutional system, to precipitate such a crisis.

The subject of the Civil Rights Movement is one of great delicacy, one about which people on both sides easily get their dander up, and are tempted from an early moment in any discussion to say: Your position is outrageous, illegitimate in American politics, incapable of being defended morally or intellectually. From that, of course, it is a brief step to denunciation and name-calling—neither of which is likely to contribute much to our understanding of what is happening to us. I should like, therefore, to place on record three disclaimers that I hope will be taken on good faith.

I.

First, I have no thesis to argue, one way or the other, as to the merits of the Civil Rights Movement as such. The demands put forward by the leaders of this Movement, demands for the early acknowledgment of certain hitherto-unacknowledged claims to rights, are treated here as having the selfsame footing as any other claims to unacknowledged rights by any sector of the American public—the same footing, for example, as my claim to my unacknowledged right to a recognizably tough anti-Soviet foreign policy, or Madalyn Murray's claim to her unacknowledged right to live in a country that does not exempt church property from taxation. It is the proper business of the American political system to adjudicate such claims to rights —as the proper business of an American political scientist is to look

*This essay was read before the annual meeting of the Southern Political Science Association, held at Durham, North Carolina, on November 14, 1964.

to the good health of our arrangements for adjudicating them, and to try to see to it, at the very minimum, that we do not jettison one set of arrangements until we have worked out an alternative set that we can adopt with confidence. It may or may not be too much to add: the American political scientist will perform that proper business of his the better if he holds himself aloof, *qua* political scientist, from the concrete questions as to what currently-unacknowledged claims to rights "ought" to be forthwith acknowledged. I shall attempt to do just this in the present paper. In any case, I have no axe to grind as to the merits of the claims to unacknowledged rights that are the essence of the Civil Rights Movement.

Secondly, when I refer to a "coming constitutional crisis," that is, of an imminent breakdown of the constitutional system under which we Americans have governed ourselves for nigh onto two centuries, I do not associate myself with what I like to call the Tenth Amend-mentite anxieties recently set forth in a volume of learned essays, possibly the most important volume on federalism that we have had in a long time, by James Jackson Kilpatrick and Russell Kirk.[1] In other words, I have no case to plead for any particular division of powers between the federal government and the states. On the contrary: For my money, it is also part of the proper business of the American constitutional system to decide when powers reserved to the states and the people shall be moved "across the line" and be exercised henceforth, in whole or in part—by the federal government, or, if I may be permitted a moment of fancifulness, *vice versa;* and there is no chapter of my favorite book *The Federalist* that I like better than that in which Hamilton speaks with scorn of the idea that the revolution was fought, and that the union was being founded, to perpetuate a given set of governmental powers in the hands of the states.[2] For me, as a political scientist, the sky's the limit, both as regards the acknowledgment of hitherto-unacknowledged claims to rights and as regards the so-called "erosion" of "states' rights"—*provided,* I repeat, we do not stumble into a constitutional crisis that I believe no one seriously intends or desires. I do hold that the preservation in America of government by discussion—by, as I shall be calling it, government by consensus—is to be preferred at all times to the immediate acknowledgment of any set of hitherto-unacknowledged

---

[1] See *A Nation of States,* ed. by Herbert Storing (Chicago: Rand McNally, 1964).
[2] *The Federalist,* No. 45.

rights, or the immediate stepping-up to the federal level of any particular power hitherto reserved to the states. But that bias does not
conceal another either against the Civil Rights Movement or in favor
of the present division of powers between the federal government
and the states.

Finally, it is no part of my purpose in this paper to urge any supposed prescriptive claims upon us of what I shall call our "traditional
arrangements," traditional *qua* traditional, for making decisions on
such important matters as the acknowledging of hitherto-unacknowledged claims to rights, or the transferring of powers from the province of the states to the province of the federal government. As I see
it, a third part of the proper business of our constitutional system, as
Article V of the Constitution makes clear, is the making of new
decisions, as and when these are called for, concerning the procedures we are to follow in making decisions. I do hold that our traditional arrangements for making decisions were good arrangements,
and view with suspicion all current proposals for changing them.
But I do so *not* on the grounds that they are traditional, that is, old.
Furthermore, I do hold that the changing of our arrangements for
making decisions is the gravest part of our system's proper business.
But that is merely to say that we should not change them in ignorance
of the case that can be made out for them, or in favor of arrangements
the case for which is a poorer case.

II.

My thesis, concretely, is this: That we are moving rapidly in the
direction of a constitutional crisis comparable to and graver than that
which precipitated the Civil War—"comparable to," because like the
pre-Civil War crisis it will take the form of a breakdown of govern-
ment-by-discussion, "graver than" the Civil War crisis because it will
pit neighbor against neighbor rather than section against section; and
that the crisis is most likely to be triggered by the claims to hitherto-
unacknowledged rights represented by the Civil Rights Movement.
I do not, however, exclude the possibility that the crisis will be
triggered by some other dynamic force in our politics—for example,
that which looks to what I call the "deorisonation" of the public

schools, or that which looks to the enthronement of the One-Man-One-Equal-Vote principle in our arrangements for apportioning legislative seats. Neither do I exclude—though I shall not be able to say much about it here—the possibility that each of the three dynamic forces, desegregation, deorisonation, and reapportionment, will reinforce the crisis-producing potential of each of the other two, so that the crisis will be triggered by all three together, or any two of them together.

What do I mean by the Civil Rights Movement? I mean by it, quite simply, what the leaders of that movement say *they* mean by it: the movement on behalf of meaningful equality for the American Negro both in the North and in the South—or, if you like, the movement to eliminate from American life, at least but not necessarily only to the extent that this can be done by the exercise of governmental power, all forms of discrimination against American Negroes because of their race. To say that, however, is merely to identify the movement's goal, which is an old and familiar policy-alternative in our politics, and which does not explain, or even begin to explain, the movement's crisis-producing potential. That goal, one might say, had been for many decades a topic for low-key, marginal debate amongst Americans before the Civil Rights Movement, as we know it today, made of itself one of the great dynamic forces in our public life. Nor can we explain its crisis-producing potential by saying merely that that goal has now embodied itself in a movement, with a large and apparently devoted following, and with eloquent and forceful spokesmen who mean business; our politics has known and "handled" many such movements, and will, no doubt, know and "handle" many more in the future. If the Civil Rights Movement has set some of us to wondering whether it also can be "handled," short of a breakdown of the American constitutional system, that must be because it has characteristics that we have not yet mentioned, that set it apart from other contemporary movements—characteristics, however, that we had best learn about from the movement's spokesmen themselves, from the movement's own statements on, if I may put it so, the level of self-understanding, of self-definition. What, then, do we know about the movement, over and above its goal and the fact that it is a full-fledged and serious movement, that we can readily document from its own pronouncements? Three things, at least.

III.

First, it is a movement that understands itself as a "revolution," as —for I can attach no other meaning to the phrase, which as I understand it is put forward as precisely *not* a metaphor—a demand for revolutionary changes in the American way of life. Second, it understands itself as a movement that "will not take No for an answer:" the changes it demands *must*, it tells us, be effectuated in the near future, because—and I do not believe this is a misrepresentation of the spirit of the relevant declarations—it proposes to keep the price of withholding them higher than the American public, or that part of it that is dragging its heels, will find itself willing to pay. Third, the movement understands itself as one demanding changes that, while revolutionary *sensu stricto,* are nevertheless called for by long-standing commitments of the American people—changes, that is to say, that have in the past been promised and re-promised but consistently withheld.[3]

These three statements move, let us notice, from the rhetorically novel and unfamiliar in the direction of the rhetorically commonplace—as we can see by asking ourselves, with respect to each, What parallels suggest themselves out of the history of the political movements in the American past? As for the first—that the movement is a revolution, in the strict sense that it demands revolutionary changes in the American way of life—*no* parallel comes immediately to mind: We have in America no experience of political movements—at least of political movements that get off the ground—that label their objectives as "revolutionary." The word "revolution" does not come lightly to American political lips or fall pleasantly on American political ears: American political movements have, in any case, seemed to avoid it, just as American scholarship has attempted, even with the Revolution that brought us into existence as a nation, to play down its revolutionary character (were our ancestors not asserting merely the traditional rights of Englishmen? was not George III the real revolutionary?). Our "revolutions," the Jacksonian, the Rooseveltian, have been called such, in general *retrospectively,* and by persons not in-

---

[3]In, specifically, the "all-men-are-created-equal" clause of the Declaration of Independence, and the "equal protection" and "due process" clauses of the Fourteenth Amendment.

volved in them, rather than contemporaneously and by their leaders. As for the second statement: Two movements in our history come at once to mind, so that we feel that we are at least treading ground that our feet have known before: the Suffragettes and the Prohibitionists —both of them models that must have figured prominently in the minds of the Civil Rights leaders—did make it clear to the American people that they would not take "No" for an answer, even if not taking "No" for an answer meant recourse to "means" that some persons might regard as coercive or violent. As for the third statement (we demand only that longstanding promises be kept): the Jeffersonians, the Jacksonians, the Abolitionists, the Suffragettes (though not, I suppose, the Prohibitionists), perhaps even the Progressives, understood themselves as pressing that kind of plea: they were, they insisted, demanding nothing new in "idea," nothing indeed that was really arguable on the level of accepted principle as opposed to that of expediency, nothing that we the American people had not always understood that we must, one of these days, get around to doing.

Now this nation has shown a remarkable capacity for absorbing movements that, with some show of reason, call upon us merely to keep long-standing promises; no such movement, unless it has added to its self-understanding the notion that it will not take No for an answer, has ever led to a constitutional crisis (although one movement that did *both* did lead to such a crisis, though not necessarily, of course, for that reason; it may have done so because the changes demanded were revolutionary, though it did not describe itself, or think of itself, as a revolution). We have shown a lesser capacity to absorb, without constitutional crisis, the political movement that will not take "No" for an answer. As for our capacity to absorb a movement that demands a revolution in our way of life, we may say of it either that that capacity is untested, or that the one time we were called on to meet the test we failed to do so (this according to whether we think of the changes demanded by the Abolitionists as revolutionary or not). I have, in any case, said enough to pose the problem in political theory to which I have been leading up: What are the chances of a self-styled revolutionary movement's gaining its objectives without precipitating a constitutional crisis? What are the pre-conditions for such success? And, are those conditions met in the case of the Civil Rights Movement?

IV.

The founding fathers well knew that movements would arise, under the constitutional system they were creating, that would demand drastic changes in our way of life. That is the tacit premise of Article V, which lays down a set of rules for effectuating changes that cannot, within existing constitutional law, be effectuated by mere legislation. It is also the tacit premise of *Federalist* 10, which for present purposes might be described as an oblique discussion of the general problem—oblique because that is not the problem explicitly posed—of how movements advocating drastic change can be handled in a constitutional system. One might go so far as to say that it is the tacit premise of the *Federalist Papers* as a whole, and that the *Federalist Papers* as a whole lay down one possible solution to the problem: the form of stipulation that movements looking to drastic change—e.g., movements looking to the acknowledgment of hitherto-unacknowledged claims to rights—must, so to speak, wait in the ante-room of our constitutional law until it is the deliberate sense of the community that they should be admitted to the inner sanctum. How does the deliberate sense of the community express itself? The *Federalist Papers* seem to me to provide three (or perhaps only two, since the third may be said to reduce itself to the second) alternative answers to that question: That "sense" may express itself (though presumably within limits set by the Constitution) through a consensus among the three branches of the federal government. It may express itself, in case of deadlock among the three branches, through—for there can be no doubt where, in the view of the authors of the *Federalist,* the "last say" here lies—the voice of the people speaking through popular elections—that is, *imposing* consensus on the three branches by electing officials, legislative and executive, who will bring it about. Opinions differ as to where, exactly, that leaves the matter—as to whether, for example, it leaves a House and a Senate elected by the people free to impose consensus by using the weapons that the Constitution placed in Congress' hands in order to force a recalcitrant President or a recalcitrant Supreme Court into line. That, happily or unhappily, is a question that has been little explored in our political literature.[4] What is remarkable, in any case, is that the whole business

[4]The notable exception: Charles Hyneman, *The Supreme Court on Trial* (New York: Atherton Press, 1963), *passim.*

appears to have worked, over the decades and in general, much as the authors of the *Federalist* intended: Movements looking to drastic change, over the long pull, have indeed waited in the ante-room until they were sanctioned either by a constitutional amendment or by consensus among the three branches. And until a fairly recent date, at least, we have had no experience in this country—apart perhaps from that resulting from the Civil War—of drastic change, through the processes of government, that has been effectuated in the teeth of strong and sustained opposition from any of the three branches, or from the constituency (the three branches *are* presumed, let us remember, to have different constituencies) of any of the three branches. That is not to say that drastic changes have not occurred: they have. But—again apart from the Civil War and again with the proviso: until a fairly recent date—the proponents of such changes appear to have been content to cool their heels until a consensus, expressed either through the amending process or through the concurrence of the three branches, has swung behind, or at least into acquiescence with, what they were proposing. That, no doubt, helps explain why we also have little or no experience of the phenomenon of "irredentism" with respect to major changes—only Prohibition comes to mind as an example of a drastic change that has left us, as a political legacy, any considerable and determined constituency bent on repeal of the relevant statute or amendment. That, then, is our traditional way of handling the problem of drastic change— of acknowledging hitherto unacknowledged claims to right that, once acknowledged, require profound alterations in people's behavior.

Now Publius, as we all know, puts the "case" for such arrangements, the case for making important decisions in the way just indicated, in terms—no longer fashionable, of course—of preventing the "invasion" of "natural rights" by *majority* "factions"—and that case, presumably, was accepted (by that American people who are the "addressee" of *The Federalist*) on those same natural rights grounds. Insofar as Publius' arrangements have been challenged, the relevant challenge has come from two quarters: From persons who regard our traditional arrangements as incompatible with the principle of majority-rule and would like to bring them into line with that principle, and from, more recently, persons who are prepared, at least in certain circumstances, to contemplate changes—decreed either in the name of principles allegedly embodied in our constitutional law or in the name of the higher conscience of the American people—by judicial fiat. Neither challenge, of course, is put forward in the natural rights language of the Fathers—the only language, apart from that of the naked appeal to tradition as such, in which our traditional arrangements for drastic change by consensus only have been defended. We have, in consequence—there being no currently intelligible brief for the affirmative—very little, to date, in the way of meaningful debate between those who resolve to retain the traditional arrangements, on the one hand, and those who would like to see them go by the board in favor of either majority-rule, or judicial fiat, or some combination of majority-rule and judicial fiat (in favor, that is, of some changes by judicial fiat when, though desirable, they cannot be brought about through the elective branches, and other changes by the will of the popular majority). Defenders and opponents of the traditional arrangements have been moving, since the attack on them began, on different levels of discourse, never establishing contact with one another. And the moment is long overdue when we must ask: Can the traditional arrangements be defended on any level of discourse other than natural rights? I think they can, and that we can profitably pause to ask what shape such a defense—for example, on the level of prudence—would take.

The defense might well run more or less as follows. Let us take as our point of departure the *purposes* of our constitutional system as set forth in the Preamble of the Constitution. These are: to form a more perfect union; to establish justice (not, we gather, a matter exclusively of setting up courts of law, which is the business of Article III; the system, we gather, is to attempt to "do" justice); to insure domestic tranquillity (that is, the civil peace, including, one understands, the whole "business" of "civility," the conduct of government without arbitraments by force—the conduct of government, therefore, by discussion); to promote the "general welfare"; and to "secure the Blessings of Liberty." Does the Preamble "assume" that these objectives will never get in one another's way, never conflict? There is no reason to think so. All we can say is that it gives us no help on the question of the priority among these objectives if they do come into conflict, in what order are they to be sacrificed? The objectives appear, at least, to enjoy equal status; the apparent intention, one might argue, at most, is that no one of the purposes shall ever be totally sacrificed to any other or any others. (The Preamble, be it noted in passing, is strangely but for present purposes conveniently silent about natural rights, as also, about "equality"—conveniently because it might be argued, in terms that *are* currently fashionable, that these terms are not "operational.") Some of us, of course, may boggle a little at "justice" and "liberty" and perhaps even "general welfare," on the grounds that these terms may mean different things to different people, i.e., they are not "operational."[5] But, that difficulty to one side for the moment, our original statement stands: The Constitution gives us the objectives the system is to serve and, by the same token, the standards by which the system's performance is to be evaluated. And a prudential defense of our traditional arrangements would presumably show that they are the arrangements most likely to gain these objectives.

V.

What about "justice" and "liberty" and the "general welfare" which, as we have just reminded ourselves, do mean different things to different persons? Is each of the participants in the system to expect it to conform to his notions of "justice," of "liberty," of "general welfare"? No one who examines the full text of the Constitution, or who has made himself at all familiar with the thinking of the Framers, could suppose *that* to be the intention. About justice, about liberty, about the general welfare, they well know, it is clearly impossible that all should have their way all the time (though all or most might, perhaps, agree on union, domestic tranquillity, and the common defense); the document, on the face of it, contemplates a continuing situation in which some will feel that "justice" is *not* being done, whether to themselves or to others with whom they choose to "side"; in which some will feel that some participants in the system are not only less free, less blessed with liberty, not merely than they would like to be but also than they "should" be—in which some will feel that there are statutes on the books that pretend to promote the general welfare but do not do so. The only answer to the questions "What *is* justice?" and "What *is* liberty?" and "What *is* the general

[5]See Robert A. Dahl, *A Preface to Democratic Theory* (Chicago: University of Chicago Press, 1956), Chapter 1.

welfare?" that you can get out of the document is this: We had best
not try to nail these things down, or, for that matter, the other three
objectives—insofar as their meaning might become a bone of contention. We must content ourselves, in this constitution, with sketching
out the *procedures* by which, from moment to moment, we shall
determine the *laws* that we, given these purposes, are to live under
pending future determinations as to changes, or innovations, to be
made in those laws. "Justice," from moment to moment under the
system, will have to be that amount of "justice" that you get under
existing laws (though there can be no objection, of course, to each
participant's appealing to *his* notion of "Justice," in some more exalted sense of that term, and using it, in his own mind, as a standard
by which to evaluate the laws with a view to proposing that they be
changed). So too with "liberty": "Liberty," from moment to moment,
will have to mean that amount of "liberty" (or "freedom") that the
laws, as legislated under the system, provide for. So, finally, with the
"general welfare." That, moreover, is what, in practice, "justice" and
"liberty" and the "general welfare" *have* meant, over the decades
under our constitutional system—down at least to a fairly recent date;
the general understanding has been that that is how it has to be under
a constitutional system; and that general understanding, one can
safely say, has itself been a part of our traditional arrangements.
There is, under the system, no objection to, rather every encouragement for, a man's attempting to get the existing laws changed in the
direction of a higher "justice," or a greater "liberty," or a higher
standard of "welfare." But short of the law's *being* changed a man
must not, so the understanding has always run, I think, attempt to
improvise, attempt to substitute his conception of "justice" and "liberty" and the "general welfare" for that embodied in the existing
laws. Some will ask themselves, indeed, how anyone with notions of
his own about "justice" and "liberty" and the "general welfare" ever
brought himself, as most Americans did at the beginning and have
continued to do, to enter into such an understanding. And that question becomes the more urgent when one considers that the Constitution itself, the Constitution as it came to us from Philadelphia, even
the Constitution as amended by the Bill of Rights, is far from clear
as to how future changes in the existing laws are, in fact, to be made,
as to what procedures exactly are to govern such changes.

VI.

What do I mean by that? Just this: We have never, for purposes of effectuating drastic legal changes in this country, governed ourselves according to the Philadelphia Constitution, but rather according to an *unwritten* constitution whose major effects have been (a) to repeal what might be called the "plebiscitary potential" of the Philadelphia Constitution, mainly by (b) outlawing the weapons with which the Congress could easily have turned it into a straight "congressional supremacy" Constitution. The Philadelphia Constitution precisely does *not* solve the problem of *Federalist 10* (as *Federalist 10* itself concedes), precisely does *not* place effective barriers in the way of the majority "factions" that Publius fears. It does indeed "divide" power among the three branches (let us, to keep it simple, waive any possible objections to current doctrine according to which it does provide for "judicial review"), and so among a number of constituencies (those of the President, the Senate, the House, and the Judiciary respectively). It does stagger the filling of the offices for which it provides. It does, perhaps, presuppose the *extra*-constitutional safeguards to which *Federalist 10* directs our attention (diversity—in ideas, in loyalties, in interests, etc., and an "extensive republic"), and these do, perhaps, tend to discourage majority factions. But if we look a second time we see that the constitutional barriers are in fact barriers only to what we may fairly call an ephemeral and therefore frivolous majority faction. If my faction has a majority out in the country, and if I can hold it together that long, I can capture a majority of the House within two years, a majority of the Senate plus the Presidency in four years, and a majority of the Supreme Court so soon as either (a) enough justices die off, and so make room for appointees sympathetic to the designs of my majority faction, or (b) my majority faction decides to juggle the Supreme Court's appellate jurisdiction or to pack the Court. Four, or five, or six years, may to the impatient seem rather a long time to wait for the "justice" or "liberty" or "general welfare" that their majority faction proposes to confer upon the nation, but it is still something short of an eternity, short even of the time through which political movements have been known to perdure. Under the Philadelphia Constitution I can, if I hold my majority together, make of the election two years hence and four years hence a popular plebiscite, and if I can win those elections, as *ex hypothesi,* I certainly can, I can capture the whole Philadelphia machinery of government and work my will with it—as far, that is, as the actual language of the Constitution is concerned. Nor is it any answer here to say: All the same, that has never happened. That might be because no majority faction in our history has been other than ephemeral, and so frivolous. Or it might be because, as a people, we have imposed upon ourselves rules and procedures, in Strauss' phrase modes and orders, over and above those provided for by the plain language from Philadelphia, and so prevented any showdown between the majority and any considerable and determined minority. It might be that somewhere along the line "We the People" tacitly incorporated into our constitutional system the idea, very difficult to be sure to pin down and put into words, of government by *consensus;* that is, a general understanding that majorities, whether popular or congressional, shall use their formal power over the Philadelphia machinery subject to the limitation: No drastic changes without the acquiescence of the "generality of men" out in the country; no drastic changes that will leave us a legacy of irreden-tism; no drastic changes, above all, that given the present lay of opinion out in the country will involve, at the implementation stage, any considerable amount of coercion. Where the idea could have come from, how it could have translated itself into an effective consti-tutional morality presiding over the Philadelphia machinery, how it could have communicated itself from generation to generation of Americans—all these are good questions (and, I might add, neglected ones). Perhaps it radiated out from the *symbol* of the Philadelphia Convention itself, which left in its wake only the handful of Bill of Rights irredentists, and certainly registered a consensus through a unanimous vote of the delegation. Perhaps it acquired its status by Madison's great gesture concerning the Bill of Rights itself, when he persuaded the Federalist majority in the First Congress that they must adopt a Bill of Rights and so bring aboard the Masonite irreden-tists. Perhaps it derives from *The Federalist* itself—which, as it would be easy to show, is from the first to last a plea against "bare majority" determinations. The record, in any case, certainly points to the exis-tence of such an understanding; apart from the Civil War crisis that record is a brilliant demonstration of how to run a republic free from irredentism, and unfamiliar with legislation that can be enforced only

at the point of a gun. Paradoxical as it may seem, the idea of transforming our traditional arrangements into straight majority-rule (as
set forth, e.g., by James MacGregor Burns in his recent book)[6] is itself
now "revolutionary," in the sense in which I am using that term in
this paper, and revolutionary *because* it would return us to the plain
language of the Philadelphia Constitution (much as, according to the
Civil Rights leaders, their "revolution" would return us to the plain
language of the Declaration of Independence, of the Bill of Rights,
and of the Fourteenth Amendment).

Have our traditional arrangements for making, or refusing to make,
drastic changes given to our constitutional system a decided "conservative" bias? I see no way to deny it. The idea of consensus has
indeed placed well-nigh unsurmountable short—and middle—term
obstacles in the path of those amongst us who have wished to use the
power of government for effectuating major reshufflings of legal
rights and duties and major shifts of powers from the state to the
federal government. (Meaning what by "major?" Just this: anything
and everything that considerable numbers of people deem major.)
The system has, by the same token (since it has been by no means
a system committed to perpetuation of the *status quo*), relied for the
accomplishment of major changes in the pattern of our existence
primarily upon the capacity of individuals, families, neighborhoods,
etc., to accept new ideas and translate them into reality by their own
actions (which, to say the very least, the system leaves them remarkably free to do). That is how (to go no further) the two great "defeats"
of the conservatives of which we hear so much from Clinton Rossiter,[7] "industrialization" and "urbanization," have been brought
about: industrialization is simply the term we apply to an endless
series of free individual decisions to produce things with machines
instead of by hand, and urbanization the term we apply to an endless
series of individual and family decisions to move from the farms and
the small towns into cities. What always loses is indeed the *status quo;*
and the American way of life, as we are also forever being reminded,
is indeed the proof positive that that is true. So it is; the *status quo*

[6]James MacGregor Burns, *The Deadlock of Democracy* (Englewood Cliffs, N. J.:
Prentice-Hall, 1963), *passim.*
[7]Clinton Rossiter, *Conservatism in America* (New York: Alfred A. Knopf, 1956),
Chapter I.

always does lose, but under our constitutional system it has rarely done so through changes governmentally-introduced. And our question, restated, becomes, Is there anything to be said, entirely apart from those natural rights that figured so prominently in the minds of those who devised our traditional arrangements, for giving to a constitutional system dedicated to the purposes set forth in the Preamble, this kind of conservative bias? And if there is something to be said for it, does it have a bearing upon our topic? I think the answer to both questions is Yes.

VII.

The system's conservative bias, its bias against governmentally-induced drastic change, is dictated by obvious considerations of prudence. And for the following reasons:

(a) Governmentally-induced drastic change tends to take the form, I repeat, of legal acknowledgment of hitherto unacknowledged claims to rights (even shifts of power from the state to the federal government involve such an acknowledgment). After such a change has been legislated and has gone onto the books, then, certain individuals find themselves possessed, as a matter of law, of a right or rights that, prior to the new enactment, they did not have. Each of us knows, however, at least somewhere off at the back of his mind, that the selfsame enactment that confers the new *rights* on such and such individuals also confers upon certain other individuals new *duties*—duties, moreover, that may require them to adopt wholly new patterns of behavior that they have been reluctant to adopt (which, to put the matter in its simplest terms, is one of the reasons why the enactment went onto the books yesterday rather than the day before yesterday, when its supporters were too few to gain access to the books). Now just to the extent that the enactment does confer new rights, it is by definition capable of encountering resistance from those upon whom it imposes new duties. Claimants to hitherto-unacknowledged rights may, with the zeal of advocacy upon them, forget or overlook that; legislators forget or overlook it at their peril.

(b) Every society, for the reasons just mentioned, has a built-in conservative bias against governmentally-induced drastic change: To the extent that those reluctant to perform the new duties are numerous, the very principle of economy of effort will, other things being equal, stay the legislator's hand. Each recalcitrant looms on the horizon as a potential source of resistance, defiance even, for the proposed enactment; if it does come to resistance, the recalcitrants must be brought into line by the imposition of penalties; the penalties, in order to be effective, must be enforced; and the more recalcitrants there are, the greater the coercive force that must be brought to bear. Governments, to be sure, differ greatly in the coercive force at their disposal, and in their willingness to use it. But the consideration we now have before us places an upper limit or ceiling on any government's capacity to acknowledge hitherto-unacknowledged rights— and a ceiling, we may add, that is necessarily lower in the presence of a more revolutionary, higher in the presence of a less revolutionary, demand for new rights. That is a basic fact about politics that is well known to political philosophers as different as Plato and Machiavelli—to Plato, who tells us that if we wish to establish a truly new regime, a truly new way of life, we had best rid ourselves of all members of society of teenage and over; to Machiavelli, who tells us that the prince who wishes to establish totally new modes and orders must begin by destroying everything.[8] Nor, once we give thought to the matter, is the fact here in question at all surprising, at least whilst the family persists as society's basic institution for the formulation of the young. The men and women produced by most families will, other things being equal, regard the existing "deal" as to rights and duties as, so to speak, part of the nature of things, much like the topography. To the extent that they are other than downright discontented, they will regard it as also good. To the extent that they are other than temerarious, their caution will dispose them to view with suspicion any proposed change whose consequences are less than readily foreseeable. To the extent that they are less than bundles of energy, they will, out of sheer inertia, shrink from the idea of shouldering new duties—even from that of exercising new rights.[9] To the extent that they are less than saints, they will be unwilling to perform those duties out of sheer devotion to the moral law. To the extent that they are unimaginative, and not given to speculation, they will be unavailable to the moral "case" for the proposed change. All this

[8]Niccolo Machiavelli, *The Discourses*, Book I, Chapters 25-26.
[9]Though we are the most opinion-polled people in the world, no data appears to be available as to the incidence of support for the Civil Rights Movement among American Negroes.

poses great problems for claimants to hitherto unacknowledged rights, who—though the *status quo* does indeed always lose—can for the most part expect to see, and do see, their claims refused.

(c) The foregoing applies, and applies *a fortiori*, to the extent that decisions as to governmental acknowledgment of hitherto-unacknowledged rights are subject to popular pressure, direct or indirect —that is, to the extent that the decision-making process is "democratic." The conservative bias that is characteristic of every society, for all the reasons just noted, is rooted in the masses of the people; and where the masses of the people themselves pass on the new claims to rights that conservative bias has a maximum opportunity to express itself in flat refusals to change the existing "deal" on rights and duties—even, I repeat, where the masses of the people are alleged to be the prospective beneficiaries of the new rights (genuinely popular revolutions are, therefore, among history's rarest phenomena). To the extent that the system is democratic, in short, the potential resisters get in their "say" *before* the government's attempt to force them to perform the duties correlative to the new rights. And we may add: That society that gives itself a decision-making process that neutralizes or sidesteps its built-in conservative bias, so that enactments requiring the large-scale performance of hitherto-unperformed duties can get onto the statute-books *without* prior approval by the masses of the population, is, other things being equal, headed for crisis—save as the government has at its disposal the coercive force that will be needed in order to exact compliance and, what is more, be prepared to use it.

(d) All the foregoing (as I have already suggested) applies with the greater force, the more revolutionary the claims of the claimants to hitherto-unacknowledged rights—that is, to which the new enactment will in fact require large numbers of persons to behave in unaccustomed ways that they would not have adopted spontaneously.

(e) Back to *The Federalist:* There are indeed considerations of prudence, nonetheless urgent because long forgotten, that justify the peculiar reading imposed on the Philadelphia Constitution, and explicitly defended in the name of natural rights, by Publius—that point, that is to say, to government by the deliberate sense of the community, and so to the postponement of govermentally-imposed drastic change until the relevant enactment can go onto the books with the acquiescence not of a mere majority but of the "generality" of the citizens. If the new republic is to move toward an ever-higher realization of justice and liberty (on whatever definition of these goods) *in a context of domestic tranquillity,* it must hold to a minimum the imposition upon its citizens of new duties that will be performed only at the point of bayonets or—the contemporary equivalent of that—at the point of an order by a federal court that, if defied, will bring in the troops. Publius therefore takes a dim view of legislation that goes on the books with the support or acquiescence of the bare majority, though he is well aware that, at the margin, the bare majority, popular or legislative, *can* force the issue. One might say that the ultimate addressee of his plea for government by consensus *is* the majority, popular or legislative, and that what he calls upon to do is to bide its time, even after winning, until it has behind it a genuine consensus. He does not wish to see the new central government go into the business of imposing new legislation that, on the face of it, requires coercive enforcement upon any considerable number of people out in the population. For large-scale coercive enforcement of the law is, to go no further, itself likely to prove inconsistent with domestic tranquillity; and the fact that Publius does not put it quite that way does not warrant our supposing that the thought was absent from his mind. The essence of Publius' proposals, in any case, is the hard discipline it would impose upon claimants to hitherto-unacknowledged claims to rights: They must, as I have put it above, cool their heels in the ante-room of our basic law until they are admitted to the inner sanctum by a consensus. And, in general (let me say it once more), under our constitutional system, that is what they have done, so that we have no experience of enactments looking to drastic change in the patterns of day-to-day behavior of any very considerable minority, except the Eighteenth Amendment. And in that case, very significantly for purposes of the present paper, what happened was, quite simply, this: In the pinch, the task of coercing the recalcitrant minority seemed too big to attempt on any level of genuine seriousness. The conservative bias that the Eighteenth Amendent had attempted to foil thus ended up working its way, and today there is nothing so dead amongst us as the Prohibition Movement.

VIII.

How much need I do by way of spelling all that out in terms of the Civil Rights movement? Perhaps the following will suffice.

First: Two of the three points that the Civil Rights movement seems most concerned to make about itself—that it demands a social revolution, that it will not take "No" for an answer—seem, in the context of the foregoing arguments, to bear upon their very face the promise of a constitutional crisis. Unlike most of the political movements of which we have experience in this country, the Civil Rights Movement does not gloss over, but rather emphasizes, the fact that the changes it contemplates are *drastic* changes, that the unacknowledged rights whose recognition it demands have, as their correlatives, unaccustomed duties that a very considerable number of Americans are less than eager to perform—nor will anyone with experience of American life as it is actually lived be likely to contest the point. Add to that the insistence "We will not take 'No' for an answer," and the problem the movement poses for the American constitutional system begins, any way you look at it, to take on frightening proportions. Translated into the language of the basic argument of this paper, it becomes: "We will *not* wait in the ante-room of our constitutional law until a consensus has formed behind us," or, if you like: "We demand the immediate enactment into law of our claims to hitherto-unacknowledged rights, and we propose to make a very considerable nuisance of ourselves until they are enacted into law." I have already noted that such a stance on the part of a political movement is not without precedent in our history (to repeat: the Abolitionists, the Suffragettes, the Prohibitionists, were, all of them, movements that would not take "No" for an answer). What *is* without precedent, at least among previous movements that did *not* lead to constitutional crisis, is, I repeat, the joining together, in one and the same movement, of the "We-will-not-take-'No'-for-an-answer" and demands that are deemed revolutionary even by those who put them forward. The Abolitionists we may leave to one side: that movement *did* lead to a constitutional crisis, and to arbitrament by force rather than discussion. That leaves the Suffragettes and the Prohibitionists as precedents upon which to rest present hopes that a constitutional crisis can be avoided. The Prohibition precedent as we have seen, is not encouraging, since what the Prohibitionists ended up doing was to precipitate an unprecedented surge of open defiance of law and of domestic intranquillity, plus into the bargain to defeat their own purposes, and make of the cocktail party an American institution hardly less basic than the family and the church. There remain only the Suffragettes, who did get their way, and did so without much in the way of enforcement at bayonet-point. But several differences between the Civil Rights Movement and the Women's Suffrage Movement force themselves on our attention: The future subjects of the new rights were a far more numerous sector (over half) of the total population than are the American Negroes. And the duties correlative to the new rights called not so much for performance on the part of the defeated minority as for forbearance—that is, for not obstructing women on their way to the polls to exercise the new rights.

IX.

Is the Civil Rights Movement the less likely to precipitate a constitutional crisis because it understands that the rights whose acknowledgment it demands are called for by long-standing commitments of the American people?—or because a strong case can be made out for them in morality? I doubt it. The very existence of the long-standing commitments, as interpreted by the Civil Rights leaders, is in the first place open to doubt, and will hardly, within the foreseeable future, cease to be a hotly-disputed issue. The Civil Rights leaders' reading of the "all-men-are-created-equal" clause of the Declaration of Independence and of the "equal protection" and "due-process" clauses of the Fourteenth Amendment is only one of the possible readings of those three clauses, and perhaps *not* the reading you come out with if you go behind the plain language, as by long-settled custom we do go back of the plain language of controversial clauses, to the "intention" of their authors and ratifiers. To that we must add the fact that the status of those clauses, their status, that is, as promises or commitments binding upon the descendents of their authors and ratifiers, is something less than readily demonstrable under the clear meaning of Article V, which leaves subsequent generations free to repudiate any such supposed commitment that "we" may undertake to make on their behalf. Even, moreover, if we assume that the Civil Rights leaders and their sympathizers are going to come up with unanswerable debaters' arguments both on the meaning of the

clauses and on their status as promises, it is I should think notorious
that the conservative bias of the generality of men cannot be depended upon to yield—or even to take cognizance of—unanswerable
debaters' arguments. So too with the case that can be made out in
morality, above all in Christian ethics, for the rights that the Civil
Rights leaders propose to write into law. What it ends up proving,
always, is that discrimination is immoral and/or sinful, not that it
should be made illegal. Beyond the argument about morality and
Christian ethics, which itself is perhaps not yet over, there lies a
further argument about the relationship between the moral order and
the political order, about the advisability, from the standpoint of
political prudence, of warring upon immorality and sin by declaring
them criminal. And on all these issues, the Civil Rights leaders are up
against the difficulty that the better case—better in logic and justice
—does not necessarily win in public debate.

   Another, similar question: Is a constitutional crisis the less likely
because the Negroes are not alone in their current demand for recognition of hitherto-unacknowledged rights for Negroes, because they
have behind them (as they undoubtedly do) a considerable percentage of the nation's leading newspapers and journals of opinion and
of its leading publicists—along with the prevailing ideology, which
is Liberalism, and, by the same token, a considerable percentage of
the nation's teachers, churchmen, and social-workers, plus the millions of Americans whose views, naturally enough since they hear no
other ideology defended in public, reflect the prevailing ideology?
Is a crisis the less likely because they also have behind them, beyond
any doubt or question, a safe majority of the United States Supreme
Court, and the White House? Is it not fairly certain, one might indeed
ask, that the opposition to the Civil Rights Movement has now been
routed, that the struggle is to all intents and purposes over, that the
whole argument of this paper falls before the patent *facts* of contemporary American politics? Is it not fairly certain that what lies ahead
is simply the quiet enactment into law of the Civil Rights Movement's
objectives? Finally, is not the Civil Rights Act of 1964 the final answer to any talk about constitutional crisis? That is a powerful argument, and I have, you may be sure, had it in mind at every moment
as I have composed the present paper. It is also, however, an argument that is no stronger than its recognizably weakest link, which is
the point about the Civil Rights Act of 1964. The Civil Rights Act of

1964 *was* the product of a consensus in the true *Federalist* sense of the term, a product of what I have called here our traditional arrangements for deciding what hitherto-unacknowledged rights to recognize. *But precisely for that reason*—so my answer to the argument must run—*its bearing upon the topic we have in hand is perhaps the opposite of what many of us have been believing,* and points rather *towards* constitutional crisis than away from it. Perhaps I can put the point best by venturing another prediction, namely this: The Civil Rights Act of 1964 will, once the dust has cleared, prove to have been a major defeat and perhaps the *decisive* defeat for the Civil Rights Movement, and this for a number of reasons that seem to me overwhelming. Just to the extent that the Act was important (which the argument before us assumed it to have been), what it did *constitutionally,* was to move the Civil Rights problem out of the White House, out of the Supreme Court Building, out of the streets, and into the jurisdiction of the Congress of the United States (which is, notoriously, the constitutional stronghold of the nation's conservative bias), and thus to shore up the idea that the recognition of hitherto-unacknowledged claims to rights is the business not of bare majorities in America but of the deliberate sense of the community. The salient fact about the Civil Rights Act of 1964, the fact which the optimists among us would do well to ponder, the fact that will become painfully clear even to the most optimistic in the next few months, is that it confronted the Civil Rights leaders' demand for a revolution with the "No" that they will not take for an answer. Its impact will, to go no further, be felt almost exclusively in the South; even there, it will affect the lot of the masses of the Negroes marginally at the very most; and, in its handling both of Mrs. Murphy's boardinghouse and jury trials in contempt of court cases, it bears on its very face the marks of the built-in Conservative bias to which I referred earlier. The real problems of the American Negro, as set forth for example in Mr. Whitney M. Young Jr.'s current plea for a "Marshall Plan," the Act does not touch, or even pretend to touch. The Act will, to be sure, prove different from previous expressions of the American consensus in that it *will* leave behind it great pockets of irredentism; but the irredentists will, predictably, be not the "losers" but the "victors" in the legislative battle that produced it. And, as may well be quite evident, the Civil Rights problem, with the electoral "truce" over, will be back in aggravated form on the front pages of our newspapers.

X.

The gravity of the situation can best be brought home, it seems to me, by asking, in conclusion, What things might happen, within the foreseeable future, that would prevent a constitutional crisis? They are, I think, easy to identify: First, the Civil Rights Movement might step down its demands to a level that would be something less than "revolutionary." Second, the Civil Rights Movement might, while maintaining the level of its demands, abandon the slogan, "We will not take 'No' for an answer"—that is, signify its willingness to wait for a consensus to form around its demands. Third, there might occur, and occur soon enough, that change of heart and conscience, on the part of the potential resisters, that we hear of from men as different as Martin Luther King, Jr. and Barry Goldwater. Fourth, "We the people" might decide to "repeal" the unwritten constitution that bids political movements advocating drastic change to await a consensus, and so make way for enactment of the Civil Rights program by the bare numerical majority that it might hope to marshal behind it within the foreseeable future—"We the people" might, that is, at long last adopt the majority principle as a part of our constitutional law, accepting, all of us (for this would be necessary), a clear obligation to obey the majority when we are outvoted and/or to let the majority use such coercive force as may be needed to eliminate pockets of resistance. Or, lastly, ways might be found to accomplish the revolution by a series of fiats by the United States Supreme Court. If the Court can command state legislatures to reapportion their seats, and to appropriate funds for counsel for defendants in state trials, can it not also command Congress to appropriate funds for Mr. Young's Marshall Plan? I, at least, fail to see why not.

Of the above alternatives the first two—the stepping-down of the level of the demands, the renunciation of the slogan "We will not take 'No' for an answer"—would seem to be excluded by the very urgency of the considerations that have brought the Civil Rights Movement into existence as the kind of movement it is. The third— the change of heart and conscience—is precisely the kind of development that occurs only over the long pull, and can hardly come soon enough to avert the crisis. The fourth—outright adoption of the majority principle for great national decisions—is again not likely to take place overnight. The fifth—accomplishment of the Revolution by Supreme Court fiat—will hardly begin to look probable short of the moment when the South ceases to defy the ruling in the Brown case. And there is, as I see it, no sixth alternative.

How to Read Richard Weaver: Philosopher of "We the (Virtuous) People"

"Richard M. Weaver of Chicago (but a devoted son of Western North Carolina) . . . [bespeaks] a Conservatism that owes much to Plato but perhaps even more to a 'complete disenchantment' with the presumptuousness and vulgarity of Liberalism . . . [His] recent writings have become increasingly concerned with the debasing effects of 'mass plutocracy.' " So Clinton Rossiter in the revised version of his *Conservatism in America.*[1]

Weaver—so Rossiter a few pages later—"must . . . be given a very special place in the intellectual history of the American Right" because he, among others, has "belabored Liberalism in season and out."[2] Weaver is the "spiritual heir" of Donald Davidson, fighting—how "sincerely" Rossiter is at a loss to decide—for the "embattled [sic] cause of southern agrarianism."[3] Again: Weaver is a man "quick with the timeless truths of Conservatism" (though no quicker with these truths, Rossiter adds, than many of his Liberal opponents), and one of several readily-recognizable "voices of the Right" which, "for

---

[1] *Conservatism in America: The Thankless Persuasion* (New York: Vintage Books, 1962, p. 223-4.) There are 10-page references to Weaver in the revised version, as against only four in the original version (Knopf, 1956)—one of which points us to a list of major "items" in the "literature of American Conservatism," which includes Weaver's *Ideas Have Consequences* (Chicago: University of Chicago Press, 1948), and *The Ethics of Rhetoric* (Chicago: Henry Regnery and Co., 1953); one which cites some of his early writings of the Southern Agrarians, esp. his essay in *Southern Renascence: The Literature of the Modern South* (Baltimore: John Hopkins University Press, 1953), a third that links him with Peter Viereck (!), Russell Kirk, Francis G. Wilson, John Hallowell, and Thomas I. Cook (!), *et al.*, who allegedly belong together because of their "outspoken distaste for the excesses, vulgarities, and dislocations of the industrial way of life," their "deep-seated antipathy toward the undiluted Jeffersonian tradition," their "emphasis on our European and English heritage," and their *"peculiar affection for Burke* and John Adams, but not Hamilton . . ." (italics added). The revised version contains 20-page references to Russell Kirk, and a two-page summary of his "political theory."

[2] *Ibid.,* p. 226. What months of the year, one wonders, has Rossiter set aside as the "season" for "belaboring" Liberals?

[3] *Ibid.,* p. 231.

the first time in many years," are now becoming audible. Weaver—
so Rossiter in the following chapter[4]—is again a Southern Agrarian,
whom Rossiter calls upon to decide whether to "abdicate responsibility for the future of the American republic" or help teach American
Conservatism that it must "enlist and serve the interests of American
business." Then, finally: Weaver, now suddenly linked with Russell
Kirk, Anthony Harrigan, and Gerhart Niemeyer, because of his "contempt" for Liberalism, is one of the only "real" Conservatives "now
writing in America"—"too real," indeed, because "they find themselves in a state of all-out war with Liberalism—and thus, in fact, with
the American tradition," "reckless, imprudent, and [therefore] *'un-
conservative'*."[5]

No, my point is not, or at least not primarily, my usual one, namely,
that Rossiter doesn't know what he is talking about.[6] But rather that
Richard Weaver was, even for so skilled a labeller as Rossiter, a hard
man to stick a label on, and for some reason or reasons other than that,
Picasso-like, he went through "periods" (he was, from his very beginnings in the Southern coterie reviews, all of one piece), and that, as
I have put it in a footnote, *one* of those reasons is that lines are not
easy to draw among contemporary Conservative intellectuals: relevant categories, relevant in the sense that they result from asking
questions that bring to light the real *differentiae* of the writers involved, apparently do not exist. Even M. Morton Auerbach, who
unlike Rossiter sounds as if he had actually read the books he speaks
of, has trouble classifying Weaver, just as Rossiter does. He does not,
to be sure, commit the (in part anachronistic) error of making Weaver

---

[4] *Ibid.*, p. 252.

[5] *Ibid.*, p. 262 (italics added). Cf. Fn. 1 above, and note, *in re* Rossiter's linkings, that
Weaver is now *contrasted* with a list that includes his former companions Viereck and
Hallowell. (Despite the incomprehensible linking of Weaver and Kirk, who are as
different as chalk and cheese, it is only fair to note that Rossiter's categories have
improved in neatness between p. 223 and p. 262, which may or may not indicate that
Rossiter has begun to understand where the lines need to be drawn among contemporary Right-wing intellectuals in America.
As for the words in italics: If Professor Rossiter will write out on a piece of coarse
sandpaper any sentence Weaver ever wrote that is "contemptuous," "reckless," or
"imprudent," and send it to me, I'll eat it in the presence of reliable witnesses. The
works of Weaver the writer are informed throughout by the gentleness, courtesy, and
moderation that were the outstanding characteristics of Weaver the man.
Note (ibid., p. 288) that Weaver reappears as a professional Southerner (because of
his "The Regime of the South," *National Review*, March 14, 1959).

[6] I have developed that point sufficiently in my *The Conservative Affirmation*
(Chicago: Henry Regnery Co., 1963), pp. 159.

a Southern Agrarian, as distinguished from a writer *on* Southern agrarianism, but even he still cannot resist the temptation to tar him a little with the Southern Agrarian brush. Among the many statements Weaver made about the Southern Agrarians, the one Auerbach chooses to emphasize, accordingly, is that to the effect that they asserted the "timeless moral values"—with, of course, the unavoidable implication that, in morals and, one supposes, politics, they were in some special sense Weaver's forebears.[7] Again: Weaver bases his "Conservatism" on "tradition" (what tradition Auerbach does not tell us), which according to Auerbach, is a matter of Weaver's ultimate reliance on "values" that are, like those of any other ideologist, "intuitive": tradition alone enables "men to live . . . together harmoniously over an extent of time."[8] "Communal harmony," the "absence" (by which Auerbach of course understands *total* absence, so that Weaver begins to emerge as an authoritarian) of "conflict and ten-

[7]Weaver did write his (unfortunately unpublished) Ph.D. dissertation, on the intellectual history of the ante-bellum South, under the then Southern Agrarian Cleanth Brooks, and did, as suggested in the text, produce a sizable literature on the Southern Agrarians: *Shenandoah*, Summer, 1952, pp. 3-10; *Sewanee Review*, Autumn, 1950; and an essay in *Southern Renascence (ut supera)*. But even the most casual reader of that literature will see at once, Weaver writes mainly *as a literary historian and critic, without immediate political intent*, and, in any case, as an outsider—as witness the following key passage, of great significance for the present article, from the essay cited by Auerbach: ". . . The nation as a whole welcomed [*I'll Take My Stand*] . . . That is because *the nation* as a whole wishes the South to speak, and wishes it to speak *in character*. . . . Despite *our* excitement over differences, *our* pain over invidious comparisons, and our resentment of suspected superiorities, *we* desire, as long as *we* are in possession of our rational faculty, to hear an expression of the other point of view. That is a guarantee of *our* freedom and a necessity for *our* development" (italics, except for *"in character,"* added). The connection between the *"nation as a whole,"* (for which, as I argue below, Weaver always thought and prayed and spoke) and the *"our," "our," "we," "we,"* is inescapable. The Southern Agrarians were, on one side, a movement with politico-economic objectives: they were, for example, distributivists, much under the influence, in their economic ideas, of Chesterton and Belloc, thus militantly, and by no means merely romantically, anti-capitalist, as Weaver certainly was not; and the presence in the book here discussed of an important chapter justifying the rationality of arbitraments by war is difficult to explain save as a sermon-in-retrospect, delivered from a *national* pulpit, on the professional Southerners' tendency to keep the War between the States alive as a political issue, and on the overtones of irredentism that were always present in Southern Agrarian pronouncements. (My most vivid recollection of my first meeting with Richard Weaver is the expression on his face when I referred to him, as apparently no one had ever done before, as a "political theorist"—a term which, as I have implied above, I do not dispense freely. I was, of course, using the term "political" in a sense that is no longer fashionable, but the beginning of wisdom about these matters is to understand that most of what passes today for "political" literature is written by men who are not interested in politics at all.)

[8]Richard Weaver, *Ideas Have Consequences*, p. 19, *apud* Auerbach, *The Conservative Illusion* (New York: Columbia Univ. Press, 1959), p. 137.

sion,"[9] is Weaver's "primary concept"; Weaver seems to believe indeed, that "any tradition" (that is, any tradition whatever) is a Conservative tradition, and thus, by implication, a tradition a Conservative must defend.[10] Still again: Auerbach follows Rossiter in making of Weaver a "Platonic Conservative," by which he turns out to mean not that Weaver wished to build Plato's *Republic* on earth, as Auerbach's[11] earlier discussion might appear to suggest, but rather that Weaver believed that our troubles began when "the Middle Ages" surrendered "Platonism" in favor of "the easier ethic [!] of Aristotle." Again (and not, as we shall see, a bad point) Weaver, unlike Kirk (again not a bad point), is on the optimistic side about the possibility of "restoring lost ideals," though only through "teaching poetry and precise dialectical definition in the schools."[12] Again (a little difficult to follow, but let us always be patient with Auerbach): In 1953 Weaver wrote a further book, *The Ethics of Rhetoric*, in which he seems, says Auerbach, less "pessimistic" than in the earlier one (in which, as we have just seen, he was "hopeful of restoring lost ideals," *i.e.* optimistic), and in which—at last we begin to get somewhere—he argues (with Auerbach's approval) that Edmund Burke's frequent arguments from "mere traditionalism" were without meaning as long as Burke did not "abstract the essence of the traditions he was defending," which begins to make it sound as if Weaver, after all, did not, despite Auerbach's earlier statement, defend just any old tradition.[13] Burke, we find Weaver saying in the pages to which Auerbach refers us, argues "from circumstance." Burke tells us, to be sure, that "he is going to give equal consideration to circumstance and to ideals (or principles)"—which, Weaver is there to assure us, cannot be done, because the man who attempts it finds himself,

[9]Auerbach, *op. cit.*, p. 137. Auerbach relies in this discussion entirely on Weaver's first book, which is the least "political" of his works (in the sense I am giving to that word in this article), and the least mature. When I say that Weaver is all of one piece, I do not mean, of course, that he did not develop over the years.

[10]*Ibid.*

[11]*Ibid.*, p. 154, This is surely a misreading of *Ideas Have Consequences*, whose thesis is that the "long process of degeneration" (Auerbach's phrase, and Weaver did believe that things out in the world have got worse and worse) is to be laid at the door of *nominalism*. Any quarrel the mature Weaver would have had with Aristotle's ethics would, surely, have been pressed on *Christian* grounds.

[12]*Ibid.*, pp. 154-5. The reference is to *Ideas Have Consequences*, pp. 166-67, 187.

[13]*Ibid.*, p. 155. Auerbach notes that this got Weaver into an argument with Kirk, and adds, gleefully (p. 156), that there are "ideological cleavages even within the ranks of reactionary Conservatism." To which I would add: The half has never yet been told.

inevitably, following circumstance not principle; the "argument from circumstance," is "philosophically appropriate for the Liberal," and "is very far from being conservative."[14] More: a man's method of argument is a "truer index" to "his beliefs than his explicit profession of principles." And, in the sequel, Weaver scores Burke as a preacher of a "gospel of *precedent* and gradualism" (italics added), as, in the end, a man who bases his argument for prescription *merely* on the grounds that it is backed up by precedent, merely on the grounds that it is old. Weaver concluded, Auerbach himself concludes, that "Burke should not be a model for Conservatism at all." Auerbach's treatment of Weaver, as I had encouraged the reader to expect, is a considerable improvement on Rossiter's, if only because he sees that Weaver's repudiation of Burke is somehow significant, even though the reason it is significant escapes him.[15] I repeat my point: The categories for classifying Right-wing intellectuals in America do not exist, or, if they do, are unknown at least to the major Liberal writers on these matters. And I begin to lead up to my further point: Weaver just may be unique, so that even if the relevant categories did exist he would not fit into any of them. The Rossiter-Auerbach Weaver cannot, in any case, appear other than an outrage in the eyes of any real "studier" (I borrow the phrase from my hero Locke) of Weaver's thought.

Weaver, apart from (for the most part scanty) reviews of his books as they have appeared, has been little written about by his fellow-Right-wing intellectuals. Or, to put it more precisely, he was much eulogized but seldom if ever subjected to analysis and, what is more important, seldom if ever really listened to. The last claim that could be made for him, for example, would be that he has impressed his influence upon or swayed the minds of the present-day high-priests of Conservatism in America.[16] This is perhaps partly a matter of their

---

[14] *Ethics of Rhetoric,* p. 58, *et seq.*

[15] Had he written: Weaver concluded that "Burke should not be the model for *American* Conservatism" he would have been hitting the nail on the head—*i.e.,* showing an incipient understanding of where the lines must be drawn among our contemporary Conservative intellectuals, and opening up the way for an understanding of Weaver.

[16] As witness *National Review's* 23 March 1965 editorial on Selma, with its nice impartiality between Governor Wallace and his attempt to "maintain Alabama as an enclave of racial stability," and Dr. Martin Luther King and his use of the "methods and arts of modern psycho-political warfare ... to move public opinion ... in his chosen direction." It is not easy to imagine Richard Weaver writing an angry "letter to the editor"; but the editorial in question, which could never have been written by anyone

being too busy writing their own books to read each others', but only partly; among them also, the questions have not been raised that would lead to the drawing of significant lines[17]; among them, too, the stereotype of Weaver as somehow a spokesman for the South has continued to pop up with surprising frequency; there, more perhaps even than on the Left, Weaver has tended to be thought of as a writer mainly on "cultural" and "literary" matters, and not as a political theorist—or, if as a political theorist, as one concerned with answering the Right-wing intellectuals' question of questions, "What is Conservatism?" (as distinguished from the question "What is *American* Conservatism?"); there, too, what I call Weaver's uniqueness, and the qualities in him that made him unique, have gone un-noticed.[18] Thus Russell Kirk, the publisher's unhappy choice to write the Foreword to Weaver's posthumous *Visions of Order,* lets the essential Weaver slip through his fingers about as clumsily as Rossiter and Auerbach. Here, too, Weaver's "view" is "Platonic" (though Weaver spends several pages of this very book scolding Socrates, who is said to have been greatly loved and admired by Plato). Here too we might easily get the impression that Weaver, in the decisive dimension, was a johnny-come-lately Southern Agrarian. Here too we are struck by the failure to try to dig down and identify the deep differences that in fact divide our Conservatives, and "place" Weaver with respect to them. Mr. Kirk's main purpose, indeed, seems to be to make Weaver sound, apart from certain purely personal idiosyncrasies, like "one of the boys" in the exalted Right-wing circles in which Kirk himself

who had begun to grasp the essence of Weaver's teaching, would certainly have fetched one from him. His letter would, of course, have driven the discussion to a higher level, but nothing could be more certain than that he would have defended Selma, and would have done so on identifiably *non-Southern* grounds. It is perhaps in point that Weaver, though a regular contributor to *National Review* in its early years, wrote for it less and less as the magazine found its stride.

[17]A major effort is under way, indeed, to prove that no such lines can be drawn. See Frank Meyer's introductory chapter in *What Is Conservatism?"* (New York: Holt, Rinehart and Winston, 1964), and the review of that book by Vincent Miller, *Modern Age,* Fall, 1964, pp. 416-417.

[18]The writer who has, though tacitly, noticed Weaver's uniqueness is, curiously, Ronald Hamowy. Weaver, who was certainly grist for Hamowy's mill for purposes of his vicious attack on the "Neo-Conservatives" (*Modern Age,* Fall, 1964, pp. 350-359), is not mentioned, though the two must often have brushed shoulders on the Chicago campus. I might add that Weaver's vogue among the libertarians and "individualists," who seemed to adore him, is the proof positive of how little understood Weaver was. Had they ever found him out for the kind of scoundrel he really was, they would—in some manner consistent with the free market, of course—have torn him limb-from-limb.

normally moves when he emerges from Mecosta—like, if I may put it so without seeming impudent, a sort of alter-ego of Mr. Kirk's: a deplorer of pretty much everything on the horizon, a "despiser" of everything modern, a man who thought of himself as "speaking to a Remnant," above all a trafficker, again like Kirk himself, in *Weltan-schauüngen*, grand style, who when he writes that "we" have been "stumbling down the path of Avernus," that "we" have been "distorting rhetoric" and so "subverting the high old order" of "our civilization and our human dignity," means "we" of the West, and thinks of his redemptive mission as an act to be performed on a world-wide stage.[19] More: Kirk even attempts (I anticipate a little a major argument to which I am leading up) to transform Weaver into "one of the boys" *(ut supra)* in a more intimate dimension, namely, that of his day-to-day way of life. Finding himself in an uncongenial "climate of opinion," we are told, Weaver "withdrew much of the time to the fastnesses of his solitary reflections" (*i.e.*, to his equivalent of Mecosta).[20] After Mr. Kirk has done, only one drop of quicksilver remains in hand; but it, as far as it goes, is a precious one, and in justice to Mr. Kirk, I have saved it for the end: "*Order . . . was Weaver's* austere passion: the inner order of the soul, the outer order of society."[21]

I conclude: Everybody appears to be hard put to it to "classify" Richard Weaver, or to say what he was up to without, pretty soon, sticking his foot in his mouth.

[19]There was indeed something of this emphasis in *Ideas Have Consequences*, and there are flashes of it in the later works, even that here under review. But as I argue in the text, to stress this aspect of Weaver is indeed to let the essential Weaver slip through your fingers.

[20]As a friend who frequently visited Weaver at Chicago, I must record my impression that Kirk is "factually" wrong on the whole point. Weaver always seemed to me to be happy in his work at Chicago, to hold his colleagues there in high esteem, to be taking an active part in the day-to-day life of the University and, what would presumably shock Mr. Kirk most, to love Chicago. He lived, by choice, a tidy distance from the campus, in order to give himself the pleasure of the daily walk to and fro (each day, he boasted, by a different route) through its streets. As for Weaver's alleged "withdrawal" to the "fastnesses of his solitary reflections," an accurate statement, readily intelligible to persons who have spent their lives close to universities, would run: Weaver was a professional scholar, who worked hard at his business, and preferred—like many other scholars, many even who find the prevailing intellectual climate congenial—to work at home rather than in the office. I might add that Weaver ate his meals for the most part at the University cafeteria, at the mercy of students who might wish to descend on him—an unlikely choice for the kind of "recluse" Kirk tries to make him.

[21]Richard M. Weaver, *Visions of Order* (Baton Rouge: Louisiana State Univ. Press, 1964), p. ix.

To the reader who wishes to object at this point, "This is supposed to be an essay, and you are not getting anywhere," I answer: "Ah! But I *am*." *All* the above has been necessary for the business I have in hand, namely: To explain to the readers of this essay (whom I think of as the Conservative intellectual spokesmen of that morrow when the "false teachers" who produce most contemporary Right-wing literature will have been shunted aside) why Richard Weaver's *Visions of Order*, it and it alone among American Conservative books, is the one that they must place on their shelves beside *The Federalist*, and confer on it, as on *The Federalist*, the political equivalent of biblical status. For the danger (because of the confusion about where Weaver stands among the thinkers with whom, erroneously, his name tends to get itself associated) is that it is *Visions of Order* that will get shunted aside. (Certainly no review has appeared to date that might conceivably prevent that from happening.) Now it is only after we have asked the questions that expose the significant groupings on the Right, and drawn the necessary lines, that we can distinguish the true from the false teachers, and assign to Richard Weaver the pride of place that he deserves, and so avoid that danger.

What are the questions that want asking? I think they are these.

a) Who have, who have not, fallen for the Liberal lie of the past 40 or 50 years, according to which the American political tradition is a tradition of "individual rights," of rights that because "individual" end up (they always do, because there's no stopping on this downward slope) rights that are equal from individual to individual and thus for all individuals, of, therefore, equality as the ultimate destiny of the American Republic? The answer to the question "Who have?" would be too painful to contemplate. The answer to the question "Who have not?" is: Only Richard Weaver, who never had so much as a flirtation with an individual right.

b) Who have, who have not, fallen for latter-day Right-wing *ideology* according to which government is "evil" as such, and "freedom" over against government, especially the wicked brand of government known as "big government," is good as such—though the authors of *The Federalist*, in which our political tradition has its roots, repudiated both these notions? Those who have: Pretty much every celebrity you can name among Right-wing intellectuals. But not Richard Weaver, who was steeped in *The Federalist* and its thought, and did not lightly accept new-fangled notions.

c) Who have, who have not, fallen for the propaganda-line—it comes at you from *both* the Left and the latter-day Right, where it derives from De Tocqueville—according to which the forces of the Left, the egalitarians and the levellers, are going to win in any case, so that "we Conservatives" are fighting, at best, a rear-guard action? (Has not the history of the past two centuries been one of continuous defeat for the followers of Burke by the followers of Rousseau?)[22] As I have written in an unpublished book dealing with Russell Kirk, Frank Meyer, *et al.*, the favorite battle-cry of the contemporary American intellectual Right is: "We are losing! We are losing! But in how noble, how fine, how glorious a cause!" I find no trace of any such pessimism in the mature writings of Richard Weaver. Nor, for reasons I am about to note, is this a matter, as Kirk suggests in his Foreword, of Weaver having refused to "despair," of his having dared to "hope." Weaver simply believed that if we of the Right only use our heads, we have the strength and the resources with which to win.

d) Who do, who do not, conceive of Right-wing victory in America, and thus of the immediate Right-wing task in America, in terms of storming American public opinion from *without*, of *conquering* the hearts and minds of an essentially hostile because already Left-wing *people*, ready always to sell its votes to the highest bidder?[23] Again the answer is too horrible to contemplate. But Richard Weaver addresses himself to the American people through his pupils of course, as an *insider*, avuncularly lovingly, that is, in the tone of a wise uncle seeking to emancipate those of the nephews who may have fallen under the influence of "false teachers." (The pessimistic,

[22] Cf. Russell Kirk, *The Conservative Mind* (Chicago: Henry Regnery Company, 1953), pp. 3-10, and pretty much any issue of *National Review*, esp. those that appeared hard upon the 1964 elections. Cf. Kendall, *op. cit.*, Chapter One.

[23] Again I must mention *National Review*, whose picture of American voting-behavior is almost as purely a "pork chops" picture as, say, that of Hubert Horatio Humphrey's. And, for the amusement of the curious, let me add—here in a footnote because the matter is perhaps too delicate to haul out into the full light of day in the text—the following speculation: On the basis of the data available to me, I deem it not impossible that there is a high correlation between, on the one hand, having been born and brought up a WASP, a White Anglo-Saxon Protestant in America, a member of an established "ruling-class" in American society, with a feeling not only of "belonging" but of being, by inheritance so to speak, a "part-owner" of America, on the one hand, and refusing to accept the "conquest" conception of the political future of the American Right on the other. For the further amusement of the curious let me recommend study of the evolving masthead of *National Review*, with an eye to the incidence, among early active participants in the magazine who have fallen by the wayside, of persons who were either born WASPs or, like Willi Schlamm, were born and brought up in a foreign land (but still not in either of the major American ghettoes).

storming-from-outside overtones of the Goldwater campaign are, in this context, too obvious to dwell upon. No wonder Goldwater lost!) Weaver always writes reverently of America and the American people, with never a doubt of their ultimate soundness, good judgment, uprightness, and good faith.[24]

e) Who do, who do not—a point akin to (d), but by no means the same point—share with the Founders of the American Republic the belief that the Republic's destiny will in fact be decided by the *discussion-process;* that therefore writing good, well-argued books matters not merely for its own sake, but because (Keynes has said it better than anyone else) what ultimately sways events is books; that, though the "world of the intellect" does go crazy now and then, as it has certainly done both in America and in the West-in-general in recent decades, the law that obtains in the world of the intellect remains the precise opposite of Gresham's Law: good books drive out bad, and the debate is won finally by those who, in their books, prove themselves *right.* It is a difficult faith to keep alive in the evil days in the world of the intellect, when writing and publishing good books —witness the fate of *e.g.,* Leo Strauss' *Machiavelli*[25] and Harry V. Jaffa's *Crisis*[26]—seems hardly less futile than dropping pebbles in a bottomless well. Yet the Strausses and Voegelins and Jaffas and Weavers continue to ply their trade, and produce books that breathe confidence, a confidence that the apt pupil will quickly learn to recognize and value: that the ultimate effect of their books will be to purge the intellectual climate of ideology, and to restore true philosophy to its rightful place of honor and *influence.* This, of all the issues I mention, is certainly that which cuts deepest; for it is precisely the confidence I speak of here that is lacking in the "mainstream" of contemporary Conservative writing,[27] so that the latter is shot through and through

[24]Perhaps, or perhaps not, in point: Weaver normally spent his summers, throughout the years I knew him, with his mother in Weaverville, North Carolina, dividing his time between gardening and his scholarly pursuits, and permitting himself no "vacation" in the usual sense of that term. The one time I ever heard of his taking a vacation, he bought himself (for the first time I think) an automobile, fetched his "Mamma" (he was the only American intellectual I ever knew who didn't regard the advance from "Mamma" to "Mother" as a necessary part of growing up), and made the grand tour —of the United States of America. If he ever set foot outside his beloved America, he never mentioned the fact in our conversations, though it is not impossible that he did so at Niagara Falls or El Paso, in the course of that One Big Trip.

[25]*Thoughts on Machiavelli* (Glencoe, Illinois: The Free Press, 1958).

[26]*Crisis of the House Divided* (New York: Doubleday, 1959).

[27]Because of the acceptance, on all sides, of the "inevitability" of a Leftist victory.

with a fundamental, though gracefully-concealed, anti-intellectual-ism.

f) Who do, and who do not, earn their living by (or, if they inherited that, devote the bulk of their working-time to) being Conservative intellectuals—or, if you like, who are, who are not, "professional" Right-wingers? Again the point is a delicate one, but it cannot be side-stepped: much of the quality and the importance of Richard Weaver's thoughts about the deepest issues in our politics is intimately tied up with the fact that, like Hamilton and Madison, he had, and wrote from, a *locus standi* in American life as somebody in particular with a particular function to perform in American society. No hurler of thunderbolts from Olympus (or from the ski-resorts in Switzerland) he: he was first and foremost a "working" school-teacher, with a job to do *within* one of America's basic institutions, whose first thoughts were always, in Bradley's pungent phrase, of his "station and its duties"; and he philosophizes about politics in that capacity (which is one of the many reasons why those who try to read him as simply another of the high-priests, who are sermonizers not teachers, will never understand him).

g) Who does, who does not, mean by the American Tradition that which he in his wisdom happens to like about the American past— but rather that which Americans, Americans from their very beginnings at Plymouth Rock and Jamestown,[28] have *made* the American Tradition, especially the American Political Tradition, by actually living it, which leads on to the further question, Who does, who does not, mean by American Conservatism the *assertion, protection,* and *perfection* of that tradition as the kind of thing it is? This is the point at which the "Burke business" becomes relevant, the point that explains why the issue between the Burke "cultists" and the non-Burke cultists is another of the deepest-cutting issues on the American Right.

h) Who are, who are not, in one sense or another, darlings of the Liberal Establishment, invited to appear on its television programs, called to lecture far and wide at its universities, reviewed in its newspapers and magazines, privileged to debate with its major spokesmen in its vast auditoriums? The Liberals, who know a thing or two about the business *they* are in, have a "little list" of their

[28]Long before Burke.

favorite Conservatives and, of course, their "little list" of Conservatives whom they would not touch with a ten-foot pole. (Also, presumably, their well-pondered though of course secret criteria for choosing the former, at which we can only guess: X, though he does make those Conservative noises, really agrees with us on the fundamentals, in the long run means us no harm, is, therefore, a man we can do business with? Y, though he too makes Conservative noises, is so out of touch with reality that we can make mincemeat of him? Z, though indeed a Conservative, says such silly things that he in fact forwards *our* cause? And old A, though he does write those savage attacks on our foreign policy in *National Review,* is he, down deep in his heart really any more eager than we to force a showdown with the USSR? Is he not, therefore, really one of us?) Here Weaver is perhaps less lonely on his side of the line than in the previous cases (one thinks at once of Frank Meyer, of Brent Bozell, of yet others of the high-priests); What is certain, and a further proof that Weaver was indeed a "real" American Conservative, is that the Liberal Establishment avoided him like the plague because he was clearly out to do 'em in the eye.

I conclude: Richard Weaver's "uniqueness" lies in part in the fact that he, and he alone, falls on the (for me) "right" side, from the standpoint of true American Conservatism, of each of the lines I have drawn. But it is a matter, mainly and far more importantly, of the unique manner in which he has performed, in *Visions of Order,* a unique task.

"We the people," according to our basic constitutional theory, "ordain and establish" the Constitution for certain *purposes:* among others, to establish *justice,* to promote the *general welfare,* to secure the *blessings of liberty* for ourselves *and our posterity.* In doing so, that is, in the act of writing and ratifying the Constitution, "we" constitute ourselves a "people" (which we may or may not have been prior to the writing and ratification). And, by speaking of "our" posterity declare our intention to *remain* a "people," with such and such "machinery" of government, to which "we" assign certain coercive functions, the necessity of whose performance "we" assert by assigning them to the government, to which, however, we do not assign certain other functions, not necessarily less necessary in our minds, and not necessarily less coercive, which "we" tacitly declare "our" intention to perform "ourselves," *i.e.* in "our" capacity as a "people" (*e.g.*, providing for the education of the young, building and supporting churches, growing "our" food, making arrangements for "our" transportation—all of which, and many others, we might have assigned to "our" government but did not). "We" also indicate, by the purposes "we" in the act of constituting ourselves a "people" choose to emphasize over and above the two-so-to-speak clearly indispensable ones (providing for our defense, maintaining the civil peace) what *kind* of "people" we think of ourselves as being and intend to keep on being, *i.e.* a "people" dedicated to "justice," the "common good," and "liberty," and dedicated to these goods with respect *both* to the functions "we" assign to "our" government and the functions "we" propose to perform in "our" capacity as a "people." If there is, at the time, any question in "our" minds as to whether we will in fact remain that kind of people, any thought in "our" minds as to who is to see to it that "we" do remain that kind of people,[29] "we" in constituting ourselves say nothing about it, unless by implication this: seeing to it that we remain a people dedicated to justice, the common good, and liberty, is *not* one of the functions that "we" assign to "our" government. If there be a problem here, "we" do not face it head-on.

Let the reader hold all that still, and let us approach the matter along another path. In the course of ratifying "our" Constitution, "we, the people" tacitly adopt a book, directed to us precisely in our capacity as a "people," entitled *The Federalist.* That book—so we are assured by our major contemporary authority on its contents—[30] "interprets" the Constitution for us, and spells out certain rules and principles, not explicit in the Constitution, the observance of which, according to the book's author Publius, will help "us"[31] to see to it that no "branch" of our government shall monopolize the functions "we" have assigned to the government, and divided among three "branches." *The Federalist* does not, however, concern itself exclusively with problems of government, that is, with the kind of govern-

---

[29]The thought at the back of "our" minds may have been: "our" churches will see to it.

[30]See Martin Diamond, "The Federalist," *apud, History of Political Philosophy,* edited by Leo Strauss and Joseph Cropsey (Chicago: Rand, McNally and Company, 1963).

[31]Yes, "help." Publius makes no greater claim, either for the Constitution or for the rules he spells out.

ment we are going to have. Publius knows only too well that the problem of actually doing justice, promoting the common good, and insuring the blessings of liberty cannot be solved on the governmental "level"; that, in a word, it depends somehow on the kind of "people," or "society" we are going to be; and Federalist 10 does raise, however obliquely, the question to which I have led up in the preceding paragraph, and has something—not much, but something —to say by way of an answer to the question. "We, the people" must add to the three optional purposes we have noted above a fourth, namely, the prevention of "tyranny," by which Publius means the use of government, by a *majority* of "we, the people," for effectuating measures "adverse to the rights of other citizens, or to the permanent and aggregate interests of the community." "Our" machinery of government, Publius sees, *is* subject to capture by a popular majority, and does, for all its built-in guarantees against tyranny, lend itself, once captured, to the uses of tyranny (as he defined it). The solution, if one there be, must be sought "out there" among "we, the people," in society, in, as I put it a moment ago, the "kind" of "people" we are going to be.

Publius is, however, strangely stingy with his recommendations ("we" must be a "people" spread over a large territory, "we" must be a "people" characterized by diversity), and strangely reluctant to open up, really open up, the problem he is skirting the edges of. I say "strangely" because he shows, in many a scattered passage, that he knows the shape at least of the correct answer to the problem: The machinery of government will help; diversity will help; spreading the "people" over a large territory will help; but in the end *nothing* will prevent tyranny, since the machinery of government is open to capture by a popular majority, except that "we, the people" shall be virtuous, that is, to go no further, dedicated in our hearts to justice, to the common good, to liberty, and to the prevention (the renunciation on "our" own part) of tyrannical measures; that is, which brings us back to where we were at the end of the preceding paragraph, a certain kind of "people." The question, however, and for whatever reasons Publius chooses to ignore it, cries up at you throughout the argument of *The Federalist:* if all depends ultimately on the virtue of the "people," how—unless we are to take it for granted that that will just take care of itself—are the "people" to be kept "virtuous"? And this, translated into the language of our basic constitutional theory, becomes the question "How are 'we, the people' to keep 'ourselves' virtuous?" *Bref:* There is a "missing section" of *The Federalist,* in which *that* question, the question as to how "we the people" shall *order* "ourselves" so as to remain virtuous, and become ever more virtuous. Worse still: "we, the people" have been only too ready to conclude, from the fact that Publius left out the section in which he might have discussed the ordering of society, of "we, the people" *qua* "virtuous people," that no such section was needed, and, even the best of us, to focus our thinking on the range of problems to which Publius did address himself.[32]

My claim: At last we have, in Richard Weaver's posthumous *Visions of Order,*[33] that missing section of *The Federalist.* No matter that Weaver nowhere posed, in so many words, the question "How shall 'we, the people' be kept virtuous?"[34] No matter, either, whether he "consciously" set himself the task of answering that question, although, once you begin to look at his mature essays from this standpoint you will, so unerringly "on target" each of them is, find it difficult to suppose that he had not done so. No matter, finally, that he elects to state himself in terms of "culture," "rhetoric," etc.— never, that is to say, openly assumes the rôle of political philosopher, of philosopher of the order of society (modest man that he was, he would have deemed open assumption of that rôle pretentious). Just, provisionally, take my word for it that each of his essays takes on new and deeper meaning when read as a partial answer to the question as I have posed it for him, and that the essays taken together do add up to an answer to the question, which you—like the high priests of contemporary American Conservatism, who as I have intimated repeatedly would be providing us a very different kind of leadership had they attended to the teachings of Richard Weaver—will do well to lay in your heart and ponder. Then go read—nay, *live with*—the book, until you have made its contents your own. It will prepare you, as no other book, not *even The Federalist* will prepare you, for your future encounters with the protagonists of the Liberal Revolution,

[32]Not so the worst of us, the Jeffersons and the Deweys, who *have* addressed themselves to the range of problems that would have been discussed in the missing section, though with a new twist: How can the virtue of the people, as Publius would have understood it, be undermined?

[33]And in the other miscellaneous essays of the mature Weaver.

[34]One of the first things I learned from R. G. Collingwood, when I was his tutee at Oxford, is that it is a rare philosopher who can state clearly the question he ends up answering.

above all by teaching you how to drive the debate to a deeper level than that on which our present spokesmen are engaging the Liberals.

How shall the people be kept virtuous? Weaver answers—though here I can only indicate in the briefest manner, the general outline of his reply—only through a self-chosen "select minority"[35] who assume responsibility for people's *culture,* in which its virtue must be rooted—for, therefore, understanding what needs a culture must satisfy if the people are to adopt it and live it as their own, for, therefore, keeping alive and healthy a culture that will satisfy those needs, and for disseminating it among the several members of the people, each according to his capacity for receiving it. It must, as part of the culture it disseminates, teach the people those lessons that the people must learn if they are to operate a society in which a sound and healthy culture is possible. It must teach them, for example, the *value,* the value for their own sake, of that diversity which Publius showed to be necessary for the prevention of tyranny. It must teach people the value, for the people themselves including those who had the short end of the stick, of distinction of rank and status in society, and the unwisdom of making such distinctions wholly dependent upon "functions performed." It must teach them the correctness of the Christian picture of man, of, that is, Christian anthropology, and so render them proof against all forms of "reductionism" (in order to be virtuous, the people must suppose themselves capable of virtue, which, to the extent that they think of man as an animal, they will not do). It must itself be clear as to the respective roles in a healthy culture of "dialectic" and "rhetoric,"[36] that is, between pure, "abstract" propositional reasoning as in science or economic theory, and the task of relating the results of such reasoning to the "existential world," in which facts must be "treated with a sympathy" and "historical understanding and appreciation" that are, as they should be, foreign to the "dialectical process".[37] It must not permit the culture

[35]The phrase is from José Ortega y Gasset, *The Revolt of the Masses.*

[36]Weaver gave his best efforts over many years to wrestling with this problem, which he believed to be the most difficult problem any culture must face, as also the problem with which we in America have dealt least successfully. *Visions of Order* contains his most sophisticated treatment of the problem.

[37]This is the aspect of Weaver's thought for which the libertarians would never have forgiven him had they grasped it. Weaver's favorite examples of "dialectic" gone wild are taken from science, but all that he says in this regard would apply equally to those who seek to implement conclusions arrived at *via* abstract reasoning about "the market," without mediation by techniques appropriate to rhetoric, in the living flesh of

of which it is custodian to become contemptuous of, or hostile to, the "arts of persuasion," which alone can "move men in the direction of a goal." It must keep alive within itself, and develop in the people, "historical memory," *i.e.,* knowledge of their own traditions—lest, in ignorance of them, they forget, like madmen, what and who they are.

But enough. I warned you that I could at most suggest, not summarize, the contents of *Visions of Order.*

The Liberals, according to Weaver, are by definition, so to speak, incapable of supplying a "select minority" that can build a healthy culture, and so keep the people virtuous (wherefore, on Publius' logic, a people led by Liberals must become tyrannical). The task to which Weaver's teaching points us, therefore, a task that only Conservatives can perform, and they, of course, only if they understand its nature and the means by which it can be peformed—which our "name" Conservative spokesmen, believing as they do that the people is already corrupt, and innocent as they are of proposals even for restoring its virtue, clearly do not. But the existence of Weaver's book enables us, I repeat, to indulge the hope their successors, nurtured on a less narrow view of politics and especially Conservative politics, will be men of another stamp.

a going society. Nor is that all: Weaver spells out at great length the presuppositions of the healthy, need-satisfying culture, but economic freedom (though Weaver was "for" it on other grounds) is certainly not one of them. One can hardly imagine Weaver losing a night's sleep over the size of the GNP.

How to Read "The Federalist"

(with George W. Carey)

The book you are about to read is, by common consent among scholars and publicists, the third in point of time of the four "basic documents" of the American political tradition: the Declaration of Independence, the Constitution itself, *The Federalist*, the Bill of Rights. No one putting forward a "list" of the documents that deserve that status would be likely to omit it, and so far as we know no one has ever seriously contended that similar status should be accorded to any fifth or sixth document. Put otherwise: *The Federalist* is a "must" for anyone who seeks an "intellectual" understanding of our tradition and of the political system under which we have governed ourselves, happily and well some of us would say, for nigh onto two hundred years. The first thing we want to say, then, in the Introduction to this new printing of the book is this: We cannot too strongly urge upon the reader, who for reasons we shall be speaking of in a moment is not unlikely to be reading it (actually reading *it*, as opposed to this or that one of its "papers" that turns up in an anthology) for the first time, his obligation—yes obligation—to linger over its every paragraph, turn over and over in his mind its every idea, steep himself in it, master it, and make it his own. And this equally whether he is a defender of the political system produced by the four "basic documents" or a critic of the system, determined to "reform" it along "more democratic" lines, and so bring it abreast of the prevailing political ideas of our time: political equality, majority rule, and individual rights. In either role, he will speak and act out of ignorance insofar as *The Federalist* is not part of his intellectual baggage.

But why, the reader may well ask, save as a matter of just knowing American history, should that be true? Were my college or university teachers not correct in telling me that *The Federalist* is not "serious" political philosophy? That it is not really a "book" at all, but a hodge-

podge of articles, hastily written at that and by three different authors, all busy with other matters and not in very close touch with one
another, for newspapers? That, far from being serious political philosophy, it is first and foremost a venture in what we today call "political
propaganda," whose overriding purpose was, quite simply, to persuade the reluctant peoples of the thirteen states to accept and ratify
the Constitution written at Philadelphia, and so form a Union? That,
insofar as it is anything more than mere political propaganda, it is a
mere "schoolteacherish" expounding of the several articles of the
Constitution, which goes on and on for several hundred pages, saying
nothing much that one cannot, on one's own, dig out of the text of
the Constitution itself? That, in any case, ours is a "changing Constitution," a "growing Constitution," which constantly adapts itself to
"new" problems, "new" situations, "new" needs, "new" ideas that
have won acceptance by the American people—so that no brief for
or commentary on the Constitution written so long ago could have
the contemporary relevance and importance that you attribute to
The Federalist? Does the "book" you ask us to "steep" ourselves in
really belong in that list of "basic documents," save in the sense that
the Constitution probably wouldn't have been ratified but for the
skillful propaganda job it accomplished? Has it not been included in
the list (by what you call the "common consent of scholars and publicists") by, so to speak, courtesy, because of the influence it exerted
at a crucial moment in our history, but only for that reason? Well,
these are good questions and, given the intellectual climate at our
universities, which unavoidably trickles down into the high schools
and out into the forum of public discussion, natural questions for the
reader to ask as he weighs our statement of *The Federalist's* claim to
his attention. So we shall take them up, one at a time (though not in
that order), and, as we hope, dispose of them to the reader's satisfaction.

Is The Federalist *a hodge-podge of "hastily"-written ventures in
"mere" journalism?*

On two points, no argument: (a) most of the pieces of which it is
composed (not all of them) were indeed first published in newspapers, and (b) the pieces were indeed composed in a remarkably brief
period of time. But to concede these two points is by no means to
concede that they are "mere" journalism, and so beneath our notice
as political philosophy. To write quickly is by no means the same

thing as to write "hastily" (think of the Gettysburg Address!): that depends, in any given instance, on, first, the amount and quality of the thinking, about the topic in hand, that the writer who writes quickly has done, and, second, his just plain ability to write well under pressure of time. Now: nothing can be more certain than that the authors (but see below about "authors") of *The Federalist* had thought long and hard about the major problems (again see below) to which the book, as opposed to the individual pieces, addresses itself; that all three had been deeply involved in the most important affairs of the emergent Republic over many, many years—came, therefore, to this venture in "quick" writing with a kind of preparation that must have made it impossible for them to write about those affairs in a way properly describable as "hasty"; and that each of them brought to the task in hand very considerable intellectual and literary abilities. The query which we are answering is, in other words, question-begging, and the problem as to the status of *The Federalist* as political philosophy is *not* to be decided in terms of its having been published first in newspapers (newspapers were the *only* medium through which the authors could have got across their teaching in the time available), or in terms of the book's having been executed in less time than, say, Locke's *Second Treatise on Civil Government* (in which, let us say in passing, it is easier to discover flaws of the kind we associate with "haste" than ever it would be in *The Federalist*). Let the reader, at the very least, dismiss these two irrelevancies from his mind before he tackles the book—if only because, as we can assure him out of a considerable knowledge of the relevant literature, those who have dismissed *The Federalist* as "journalistic" and "hasty" tend to be quite stingy with citations of chapter and verse to support their thesis. So, too, with the charge that *The Federalist* is a hodge-podge: true though it be that it originally appeared as articles in newspapers, and that it was written in a few months, it is a *book*, executed with loving care and based (as, for example, Locke's *Second Treatise*, at least on the face of it, certainly is *not*) on a well-thought-out plan.

Is The Federalist *primarily a venture in "propaganda," with the over-riding intention of getting the Constitution ratified?*

Here, again, we can make some concessions to the objector whom we are answering and still, we believe, dispose of the main point he seeks to make. *The Federalist* is, certainly, on one level, *"polemical"* in character—that is, it is the affirmative "side" of a "debate" (with the opponents and critics of the proposed new Constitution), addressed to the "judges" in the debate, the people of America, in the hope of rallying doubters to the support of the "Federalist" cause. Its polemical hand, moreover, is not always gentle: at numerous junctures, for example, it calls into question the good faith of the "negative" in the debate, as also its knowledgeability and good sense; frequently, it "hits hard," in a fashion more likely to knock the opponent out than to show him up as a poor boxer. It is, if you like, a book manifestly intended, *inter alia,* to "influence" "events," by moving people's hearts and minds in a desired direction; and if all books written with that purpose in view, if, in other words, that is what you mean by "propaganda," then *The Federalist,* along with many of the masterpieces of political philosophy, is indeed "propaganda." So much by way of concessions. But again our reply is, the query is itself question-begging, because it presupposes that the authors, and their allies, wrote out of a genuine fear that the new Constitution would be rejected. That, however, is a highly questionable assumption, and those who have given currency to the idea that adoption of the Constitution was a "near thing," so that swift and perhaps even desperate *démarches* by its supporters were called for, have, to date, offered us extremely little documentation of their thesis; besides which, as far as *The Federalist* is concerned, their chronology is all wrong. By the time any significant number of the pieces that make up *The Federalist* had appeared, ratification of the Constitution was, legally and constitutionally speaking, already "in the bag": ratification, by the number of states required by the Constitution in order for it to go into effect, was already assured, though two "indispensable" states, both to be sure states in which there was more, and more vocal opposition to the Constitution than elsewhere, Virginia and New York, had not yet acted. The authors of *The Federalist* may well, then, have been hoping to influence the outcome in those two states, though to concede that is by no means to concede that they believed that either might actually fail to ratify. (Another possibility: though already sure of a majority in both, they wished to increase the *size* of the relevant majorities.) And, in any event, it is certainly not to concede that the "overriding" purpose of their book was "propagandistic" even to this limited extent. Though nominally addressed to the People of New York, the authors, as the reader will quickly see if he keeps his weather eye peeled, are writing for and to the people of *all* the states, that is, to the American people *as a whole*—who as we have noted had, in effect, already ratified, and for large numbers of whom, therefore, ratification was no longer an issue. Why? We offer it as our opinion, based upon long study of the text and long meditation, that their primary purpose on the level here in question, was to make sure that the peoples of the several states, in ratifying, fully understood what exactly they were committing themselves to, what exactly they were doing. And as our further opinion that the correct adjective to apply to a book with such a purpose is "educational," not "propagandistic," pedagogical, *not*, in the pejorative sense of the term, primarily polemical at all. Indeed, one of the most valuable themes that weaves in and out of the book's argument is provided by the numerous passages that, taken together, lay down what amounts to a set of rules, an *ethos*, as to how public discussion, worthy of gentlemen, should be conducted by a sober, intelligent, and intellectually honest self-governing people. The opponents of the Constitution, *The Federalist* insists, constantly violate these rules and should, for that reason alone were other reasons lacking, be disregarded. One might say that the rules in question were the rules that had been observed in the deliberations of the Constitutional Convention itself. One might say, also, that what we mean by "propaganda" today is precisely public utterance that violates the ethos those rules embody. And if that is what we mean by it, *The Federalist*, taken as a whole, is oceans apart from propaganda.

Does the fact that The Federalist *had three different authors, not in very close touch with one another, detract from the book's claim to our attention?*

The Federalist is indeed the product of three different pens: That of Alexander Hamilton, who initiated the project and, in general, master-minded the pro-Constitution forces through the period between Philadelphia and the ratification by his home state of New York. That of James Madison, a Virginian, who wrote the two most famous of the single papers (Federalist 10, Federalist 51). That of John Jay, who wrote the key pieces on the "advantages" of union in the remarkable first section of the book (see below), but early withdrew from active participation because of illness. The reader will wish to know at least this much about these men. Only one of them, Madison, had played a conspicuous role in the actual writing of the Constitution the book defends and explicates. (Hamilton, though a delegate, was a minority voice in the delegation from his state, had, therefore, strictly speaking, no vote, and frequently absented himself from the proceedings; Jay was not a delegate at all.) All three were graduates of distinguished institutions of higher learning: Hamilton and Jay of King's College (Columbia), Madison of Princeton. Hamilton, a man of great talent and energy, had by the age of 30 made himself an outstanding figure in the New York bar; during the Revolutionary War, still in his early twenties, had held critically important posts, both staff and line, under Washington's command; was destined to be the Secretary of the Treasury in the first Cabinet under the new Constitution, and the great issue-drawer of the Washington administration; had, as a lad of 17, before the Revolution, already been writing lengthy and sophisticated tracts in defense of the colonies. Jay, the oldest and perhaps, at the time *The Federalist* was written, the best-known of the three, was also a prominent New York lawyer; had played a leading role in the governmental affairs of his state just before and during the war, especially in connection with the administration of the loyalty oath; had been Secretary of Foreign Affairs for a time under the Articles of Confederation, so that the Treaty of Peace with Britain (1783) had been the product of negotiations he had conducted; was destined to be the first Justice of the Supreme Court. Madison, a man of remarkably broad "scholarly" interests, had served conspicuously in the Continental Congress; had perhaps given more, and deeper, thought to the form a future "Union" constitution ought to take than any other delegate to the Convention at the time it assembled, so that while it is perhaps an exaggeration to speak of him as the "Father of the Constitution," it is not too much to say that he has a better claim to that title than any single rival claimant; he was destined to be an influential member of the First Congress, where he wrote and "floor-managed" the Bill of Rights (of which he was the "Father" in the strictest sense of the term, and perhaps also the "Mother").

All of that the reader should be told before reading the book, lest he accuse the writers of this Introduction of having withheld information to which (as he can prove by pointing to the Introductions of countless editions of *The Federalist*) he is entitled. All of that, we say, he should be told, in order to take notice of it, and then, if we dare say so, promptly forget. *The Federalist* is written in the first person singular, and signed "Publius"—which is to say, it is not only put forward as the product of a single pen, but in a very special sense, the critical sense, *is* the work of a single pen. That pen, to be sure, we now know to have passed from hand to hand among three able writers, but three able writers each of whom, by entering into the project, at least tacitly agreed, for purposes of the project, to contribute not in his individual, personal capacity, but in a *role*—that is, as "Publius." Though it is now fashionable, in the successive editions of *The Federalist,* to "assign" the respective papers to one or another of the three "authors," the reader will enjoy the book more, and profit more from it, if he ignores these designations and substitutes for them, in his mind, the original signature "Publius." This for several reasons: (1) He will improve his chances of understanding the book as the people to whom it was addressed understood it, and as the authors intended it to be understood. For the fact that "Publius" was a man with three heads—thus, also the identity of those heads—was not known to the first generation that read him (not until 1802 was it revealed in America—ten years later, curiously, than in France— that "Publius" was Hamilton plus Madison plus Jay). (2) He will improve his chances of understanding the book, period. For one thing, he will be able to approach each individual paper, as the original readers could, without his opinions concerning the author getting "between" him and the argument. (One of the three "authors," Hamilton, has, of course, had a "bad press" over the decades, even amongst conservatives, many of whom do not lightly forgive him for his views on governmental "interference" with the economy; and his name, at the head of a paper, is not unlikely to get the reader's back up—in a way that "Publius" would not.) For another thing, to think of each of the individual papers as the handiwork of the particular writer we now know (to our misfortune, the present writers would say) to have written it is, quite simply, to misunderstand the character of "Publius' " enterprise, and thus to misunderstand the book. Let us put it this way: Precisely the point about *The Federalist,* precisely the point which, once grasped, opens it up to our understanding, is that it is a re-enactment, in miniature, of the *miracle* of the Philadelphia convention itself—the miracle that produced a document which (a) reflected accurately the deepest convictions of nobody present as to the shape it should have taken, and to which, nevertheless, (b) nearly everybody present (we must never forget Mason) was prepared to give his all-out support. The Constitution was made possible, one might say, first and foremost because in the course of its proceedings the individual delegates became increasingly willing to "write off" their own pet ideas, to subordinate their personal preferences, to the overriding necessity of arriving at a *consensus.* Put otherwise, and we consciously paraphrase a famous passage from perhaps the most famous of modern ventures in political philosophy: The Constitution became possible because, increasingly, the delegates were willing to ask themselves not "What do *I*, personally, think the Constitution ought to be?" but rather "How *much* of what I think can I insist on with any hope of getting others to go along with me?" and "How *much* of what we can all get together on is there any hope of getting accepted by the American people?" (Not, as that famous book puts it, "What do I will?", but "What is the general will?") *The Federalist,* we are saying, re-enacts that political miracle—as, we would add, with the exception of the tragic years that produced the Civil War, American political life has re-enacted it over and over again ever since—and eventuates in a public act that became possible only because the authors were prepared to submerge their individual personalities, their individual political philosophies, in the common enterprise. Hamilton precisely does not write as Hamilton, but as "Publius," that is, as a collaborator of Madison and Jay, in writing the book that is needed to continue the work of the Convention by helping to get the Constitution ratified, to make sure (as we have put it above) that the American people, in ratifying it, understand what they are doing, and, lastly, to accomplish still another purpose to which we shall allude below. Thus the question—a great favorite among writers of Introductions to *The Federalist*—"Was Hamilton 'sincere' in his contributions to the book?"—is of all silly questions perhaps the silliest. The man Hamilton, the man Madison, the man Jay—each of them, as he writes assuming the mantle of Publius, is, in the very nature of the case, in no position to shoot the works with his pet notions about politics. He must, as he writes this or that piece that is to go into the book, ask himself: "Will my two collaborators go along with this?" The "contradictions" between what "Hamilton" wrote in *The Federalist* and what he wrote elsewhere are, therefore, neither here nor there; and it is sad that so much American "scholarship," which might have been employed for better purposes, should have gone into exposing such contradictions. *The Federalist* must be read as the common ground on which Hamilton, Madison, and Jay could meet in defense of the proposed Constitution—as the consensus, between Hamilton, Madison, and Jay, as to what did need to be said at that moment in order to assure the destiny of the United States of America. The whole business as to the authorship of the individual papers, which has been the topic of a major controversy in American letters, is, then, a red herring, which the reader had best dismiss as a red herring before he begins to read the book.

Is The Federalist, *if not mere propaganda, a mere "schoolteacherish" explication of the Philadelphia Constitution?*

Of all the questions we are raising in this Introduction, this is the easiest to answer, and to answer with a flat "No, indeed!" The Philadelphia Constitution, the Constitution submitted by the Convention for ratification by the American people, is, to put the matter in its simplest terms, not one but many constitutions—a crossroads, from which, once having situated itself there, the people of America might have moved in any of several directions, might have moved (as, to our sorrow, we rediscover every now and then) to this or that one of many alternative political systems under which we might have governed ourselves. The point is not, as the present writers well know, an easy one to grasp—which is why we implore the reader, *inter·alia,* to re-read, and re-read carefully, the Philadelphia Constitution, *the Constitution without the Bill of Rights,* before he plunges into the book he is about to read. Not easy to grasp, we say, and for two reasons: First, because it is now difficult for even the most knowledgeable reader to read the Philadelphia Constitution with an "innocent eye"; he is in the habit of thinking of the Constitution as the Constitution *plus* the Bill of Rights, and is likely, therefore, as he reads *The Federalist,* to forget from page to page that the Constitution it purports to explicate is precisely a Constitution that has no Bill of Rights. (More: as the reader will discover, perhaps to his horror, *The Federalist* is *opposed* to a Bill of Rights, to the whole idea of a Bill of Rights—as, by unanimous vote, the Philadelphia Convention declared itself to be opposed to one.) Second, because of the influence of *The Federalist* itself, which expounds a single one of the numerous alternative "readings" of the Constitution, but precisely that one which we, for good reason (the question of a Bill of Rights apart), are in the habit of "seeing" in it. The Philadelphia Constitution, for example—read it with a deliberately cultivated innocent eye and you will see that for yourself—does *not* provide for a government of three "equal and coordinate" branches, though it also does not exclude the possibility of one. The Philadelphia Constitution does *not* provide "judicial review" of statutes enacted by the Congress and signed by the President, but also does not exclude the possibility of it. The Philadelphia Constitution appears, on the face of it, to be an invitation to a political system in which Congress shall be hardly less "powerful" than the Parliament of Great Britain: nothing in the text, for example, forbids Congress to use the impeachment power, or the power of the "purse," to force the President and the Supreme Court to subordinate themselves to *its* will, but it does not demand that the invitation be accepted. The Philadelphia Constitution does *not* provide for, but also does not forbid, a "plebiscitary" political system—that is, one in which the great decisions about legislation and public policy shall be made by the electorate, choosing between alternative "programs" at the polls and thus giving a "mandate" to its new Congress and its new President. The choice amongst such possibilities as these the Constitution leaves up to the good (or bad) sense of the American people, whom it thus leaves "free" to give itself, and give itself *constitutionally,* any one of a wide variety of political systems. Now: "Publius" has, first, his own "special" way of reading the Constitution, and, second, a great wish to persuade the American people not only to choose *his* reading over all alternative readings, but to convince itself that no other reading is so much as possible. But let us postpone further development of this point until we raise, and attempt to answer, our next question. Suffice it to say, for the moment, that you will not understand *The Federalist* unless you bear in mind that, on one side at least, it is an attempt, oceans apart from mere "school-teacherish" explication of the Constitution, to impose upon that constitution a particular meaning that is present in it *only* potentially.

Is The Federalist a *"basic document" of the American political tradition?*

We have already answered this question by implication, but let us now spell the answer out. "Publius' " attempt to impose a particular reading upon the Philadelphia Constitution has been so successful that one is tempted to say: The Constitution expounded in *The Federalist*—because it has, in its crucial dimensions, only one not several meanings and points forward to only one not several possible political systems—is not really the Philadelphia Constitution at all. One is tempted, indeed, to say that we should in strict propriety distinguish between the Philadelphia Constitution and what we might fairly call "*The Federalist* Constitution," and, further, that it is under the latter, the Philadelphia Constitution as refined by "Publius," and refined so daringly as to make of *The Federalist* a further and drastic step in constitution-building, that we have lived and governed ourselves since 1789. The Philadelphia Constitution, as we have already noted, leaves the door wide open to "legislative supremacy," and places in the hands of Congress "weapons" that make of it a "coordinate" but *not* equal, a coordinate but *superior* branch of the Federal government, in position, whenever it sees fit to do so, to bring the other two branches to their knees. In "Publius'" Constitution, by contrast, so little is said about those weapons as, in effect, to spirit them away; and we have yet to witness the spectacle of Congress' impeaching a President because it dislikes, *e.g.*, his foreign policy, or of Congress' "packing" the Supreme Court in order to force the reversal of a Supreme Court decision it finds abhorrent. The Philadelphia Constitution contents itself with saying that the judicial power shall be vested in a Supreme Court—which, as our good friend Brent Bozell has conclusively demonstrated in a book soon to be published, certainly did not mean to the men who wrote those words that the Supreme Court can and shall refuse to enforce, or declare null and void, legislative acts that it deems "unconstitutional." "Publius'" Constitution, by contrast, reads those words in the Philadelphia Constitution as meaning precisely that; and it is "Publius'" meaning, not the Philadelphia meaning, that Americans, through long habituation, now see in them—so that our political system is often described as one not of "legislative supremacy" but of "*judicial* supremacy." The Philadelphia Constitution says—the point is similar to but not identical with that which we have made about legislative supremacy— nothing about "separation of powers." "Publius," by contrast, makes of "separation of powers," of the notion, to put it briefly, that it is "unconstitutional" for any one of the three branches to "encroach" upon the powers and prerogatives of the other two, *the* basic doctrine of the Constitution; and, lo and behold, we teach our children, from an early moment in their educaton, that "separation of powers" lies at the very heart of our constitutional theory. The Philadelphia Constitution, with certain minor exceptions, leaves a bare majority of the two houses of Congress free to attribute to itself the full powers of Congress, and work its will without regard to the views of the minority. "Publius," though he perhaps never goes so far as to suggest that a bare majority of the two houses of Congress can *not,* under the Constitution, arrogate to itself the plenitude of congressional power, teaches throughout *The Federalist* the doctrine that legislation under the Constitution should reflect the "deliberate sense" not of the majority of the American people but of the American people as a whole, and it is "Publius' " teaching, not the plain language of the Philadelphia Constitution, that we have, in general, taken to heart and lived by: the congressional majority in the United States does not, and does not think itself entitled to, ram legislation through without consulting the views and wishes of the congressional minority (so that the normal legislative act is in America, and always has been, a "deal" hammered out, in the course of lengthy deliberation and negotiation, between majority and minority, and by no means the act that the majority, had it consulted only its own views and wishes, would have put on the statute book). The Philadelphia Constitution is, as we have suggested above, potentially an "invitation" to the American people to govern itself by plebiscitary *mandates*—that is, to insist, in the conduct of its elections, that these be fought over sharply drawn "policy" issues, so that the real policy decisions get themselves made by the electorate (Congress and the President being reduced, so to speak, to the ministerial role of carrying out popular mandates). "Publius" teaches us that the American people should elect to Congress the "best" and "wisest" men, not the men whose policies they happen to approve of; even if he does not come out and say so, he clearly contemplates elections that are *not* plebiscitary in character, elections that precisely do not ventilate, and so submit for decision by the people themselves, the great choices among policy alternatives; and, as the reader hardly needs to be told, nothing is so rare in America as an election, whether of a new Congress or a new President or both, that produces a clear-cut popular decision about public policy, and the word "mandate," in its British sense, is not, even today, part of our political vocabulary. (Though there are those amongst us who would like, by "reforming" our political system in a plebiscitary, that is allegedly "more democratic" direction, to make it that.) The Philadelphia Constitution leaves the American people and their representatives free to make what use they like of Article V, that is, of the amending process, and might well have made of our politics a sort of permanent constitutional convention. "Publius," by contrast, convinced as he is of the need for a *stable* constitution and fighting shy (as we have already seen him do) of "great debates" calculated to produce decisions by the people, teaches the unwisdom of frequent use of the amending power; and no one would, we think (so infrequently have we resorted to the amending process), deny that "Publius'" teaching is to all intents and purposes a part of our "real" Constitution. (The latter reads, in effect: the power to amend the Constitution shall be used sparingly.) Finally—again a point similar to but not identical with one we have already made—the Philadelphia Constitution in no wise discourages, save perhaps by its provision for staggered elections, overnight action by Congress on great controversial issues, on, for example, proposals for drastic social or economic "change" that might, if enacted, require for their enforcement large-scale coercion. "Publius," given the lengths to which he "pushes" his characteristic doctrines of "separation of powers" and "judicial review," teaches by implication that the proponents of drastic change in America, even if they have a majority out in the country, must (as one of the present writers has put it in a recent essay) cool their heels in the ante-room of our politics until they can achieve a consensus among the three branches and so, since the branches represent different constituencies out among the people, a popular consensus as well; and, as the essay just mentioned argues (rightly, we think), we have no experience in America, apart from the Civil War, of governmentally imposed social or economic change that has called for large-scale enforcement by bayonets. "Publius'" Constitution, that is to say, has a built-in "conservative" bias that is not readily discernible in the Philadelphia Constitution.

We conclude: to omit *The Federalist* from the list of "basic documents" of the American political system would be to leave unaccounted for, on the documentary level, many of the major features of that system. Or, to put the point a little differently: much of the teaching of *The Federalist*, through tacit ratification by the American people, has assumed a status that it would be foolish to call other than "constitutional."

Is The Federalist *nevertheless "dated"—that is, no longer so "relevant" as to warrant the claim we have made for it at the beginning of this Introduction?*

Again the question is one to which we have already, at least by clear implication, given an answer, but one which, especially in an Introduction to an edition of *The Federalist* to be distributed by the Conservative Book Club, wants spelling out and driving home. Increasingly, over the past sixty-odd years, the American political system has been under attack from Liberal quarters, is under attack today in college classrooms presided over by the typical American political scientist, on the grounds that it is fundamentally "undemocratic." More: the Liberals have a carefully worked-out program for "reforming" that system. We must, the Liberals insist, provide ourselves with a new kind of political parties, capable of presenting to the electorate at election time a clear choice between competing "ideologies" and competing policy alternatives, and so turn our elections into plebiscites that will lay bare the genuine "will of the people." We must see to it that every President goes into office with a mandate to carry out certain policies, and with a congressional majority pledged to give him unquestioning support in doing so. We must get rid of those features of our political system—staggered elections, the "seniority principle" in our congressional committees, the filibuster, etc.—that prevent the immediate translation of the will of the majority into legislation. We must infuse into the system, by whatever means necessary, the principle of "one man, one equal vote"—must, especially, "reapportion" our legislative assemblies, alike on the federal level and that of the states, in a fashion consonant with that principle. We must free the Supreme Court from the outmoded notion that it is somehow bound by the plain language of the Constitution, and learn to think of it as, literally, the "conscience" of the nation, bound by nothing save the requirements of lofty moral principle. We must increase the powers of the President. We must, above all, impose upon the system a clearly understood new purpose, namely, that of making our citizens increasingly "equal." Now: the reader of this Introduction will hardly need to be told that the Liberal attack in question is an attack not so much on the Philadelphia Constitution as, to recur to the distinction we have drawn above, on "Publius' " Constitution; and *The Federalist*, though it will not, as Mr. Russell Kirk has lately accused one of the present writers of believing, "solve all our problems," remains *the* book to which conservatives must go to learn the "case" for, the "philosophy" that underlies, those features of the American political system that the Liberals dislike and wish to abolish. It remains, above all, the book to which conservatives must go in order to learn how to wrest from the hands of the Liberals their most effective weapon, namely, the charge that our traditional political system is "undemocratic." Precisely the claims that "Publius" makes, and substantiates, for the system—let us emphasize the point, on the off-chance that the reader may begin to read *The Federalist* under the impression that "Publius" is against democracy—are, first, that it is a *democratic* republic, because it provides for self-government (or, in Lincoln's phrase, government by the people) with justice, and, second, that any democratic republic constructed along other lines will prove unworkable because it will lead, automatically, to "tryanny" (which "Publius" understood to be the very negation of self-government and thus of true democracy). We must learn, we conservatives, that the issue is *not* whether the American system is or is not "democratic," but which of two competing definitions of "democracy"—that which equates it with government by the "deliberate sense" of the people, acting through their elected representatives, and that which equates it with direct majority rule and equality—should prevail, and, in doing so, learn to expose the falseness of the Liberal's claim that the reforms he proposes can properly be defended in the name of democracy. Here again, *The Federalist* remains the book to go to for instruction, as, also, for reenforcement of our will to realize the destiny which "Publius" holds up to the American people as their destiny, namely: to demonstrate to all mankind that self-government—self-government with justice, of course—is *possible.* That, again, of course, is precisely the destiny that the Liberals, by equating justice with equality and thus rendering it meaningless, are calling upon us to reject; let *them* have their head, and we shall speedily have the "tyranny" that *The Federalist* teaches us how to avoid. Let the conservative, then (we will not urge the point again on the Liberal, who will not read the book anyway), accept "his obligation—yes, obligation"—to linger over "Publius'" every paragraph, turn over and over in his mind "Publius'" every idea, steep himself in "Publius'" book, master it, and make it his own.

John Locke Revisited

Let me begin with a little contemporary "intellectual history": My generation of political theorists in America—the generation that "did" the Ph. D. before World War II—was brought up on George Sabine's *A History of Political Theory*.[1] Preparing for the Ph. D. examination in political theory was, indeed, merely a matter of "sweating up" Sabine. At examination time, the typical question— e.g., "What was Machiavelli's contribution to political theory?"—was shorthand for the question: "How much of Sabine's chapter on Machiavelli has entered into and formed part of your intellectual baggage?" And you could pretty confidently answer the question on the tacit premise: Give 'em Sabine and you can't go wrong. In other words: Machiavelli was what Sabine said about Machiavelli.

That, I take it, is no longer the case. Out over most of the country, one likes to think that, and in political science literature in general, Sabine's *History* no longer enjoys biblical status. Ph. D. candidates are now expected, in some places at least, to go and actually read the original texts—besides which there is today an enormous monographic literature dealing with the individual political philosophers, and the Ph. D. candidate is supposed to have a nodding acquaintance with at least some of it.

Now, if we were to take the Leo Strauss-Joseph Cropsey *History of Political Philosophy*[2] as representative of the present situation in political theory scholarship, with its publication date (1963) as one base, and the publication date of Sabine (1937) as another, then the latter might be traced as the end of one "age" or "epoch" and 1963 as the end of another, and one might speak of the "distance traversed" between Sabine and Strauss-Cropsey. My topic, "John Locke Revisited," might then be construed as follows: Let us adopt 1963, the publication date of Strauss-Cropsey, as our point of departure, and go back to 1937, to Sabine's *A History of Political Theory*, thus "revisiting" Sabine's Locke, and then go on to ask, "What has hap-

[1](New York: Henry Holt and Co., 1937).
[2](Chicago: Rand, McNally and Co., 1963).

pened in the course of 26 years, to George Sabine's Locke."[3] By "revisiting" Locke we shall, then, mean going first to look at Sabine's Locke and then stopping, on the way back home, for some further visits—e.g., with my own *John Locke and the Doctrine of Majority-Rule*, Leo Strauss' *Natural Right and History,* and Peter Laslett's introduction to his critical edition of *Locke's Two Treatises of Government.*[4]

First, then, Sabine's Locke who, as we should expect, is a "son of his times." He wrote the *Second Treatise* "with the avowed purpose

[3] A couple of things that have happened, let us notice *en passant* for what they are worth, are given away by the titles of the two books to which I refer: Sabine writes *"A History,"* and Strauss and Cropsey write "History of." Sabine puts us on warning that his is only one of many possible "histories of;" his will be Sabine's history, that is, it will tell about how the history of political theory looked from Sabine's place and times, conditioned as Sabine was by *his* circumstances, *his Weltanschauung,* his point of view. Strauss and Cropsey write "History of"—by which we understand *"The History"* of, and no foolishness if you please about this being only one of a wide variety of possible histories, each shaped by its time and place. Strauss and Cropsey would not, of course, exclude the possibility that their book contains errors, errors of interpretation or even errors of fact, that need to be corrected, in *the* "definitive" history; but there is only *one* history, and that is the *correct* one, which is the one at which we in this book are making an attempt. And we must note, secondly, the shift in the title from "political theory" to "political philosophy"—again a tacit criticism of Sabine, who probably should have called his book. "A History of Political Theories," or even "A History of Political Ideologies," since for Sabine all political theories are what Strauss and Cropsey would call ideologies. Sabine would deem the question "Is this political theory 'true'?" a nonsensical question (as he makes abundantly clear in his Introduction). Not so Strauss and Cropsey: theirs is a book about the search for *truths* about politics, *the* truth about politics. They tacitly put us on warning that they make a sharp distinction between political philosophers, who seek truth, and political ideologists, who seek to make their readers "feel good." The term "theory," analogous for their purposes to ideology, especially since most of what passes for political theory in America these days *is* ideology, goes by the board. We are indeed in a different age.

[4] This leaves out two "visits" that I should have liked us to make, and that we certainly should have made had we been able to allow more time for the trip, namely: with Cox's Locke, which would have taken us into Locke and international law and international relations; and MacPherson's Locke, which would have taken us into Locke and the theory of property. No "slight" is intended for either critic: alike Richard M. Cox's *Locke on War and Peace* (Oxford: Clarendon Press, 1960) and C. B. MacPherson's *The Political Theory of Possessive Individualism* (Oxford: Clarendon Press, 1962) are extremely important books, and will, predictably, have a lasting impact upon Locke literature. Both, however, come latish in the story of what has happened to Sabine's Locke. And while Laslett comes latish, too, he happens to be a very good place to land for purposes of looking back over the distance travelled. I would have been only too glad to exclude Kendall 1941's Locke, and not merely for the obvious reasons of modesty and decorum. But he is for historical reasons a necessary stop on the trip; and I promise to be—watch and see if I am not—*very* severe on him. Between my *John Locke and the Doctrine of Majority-Rule* (Urbana: Univ. of Illinois Press, 1941), and the present article, I have published nothing on Locke, or the Locke literature.

of defending the Revolution [of 1688]", and "refuting" Hobbes—
whom he had to refute if he was to vindicate the "theory of constitutional government." Sabine, of course, would not himself touch a
"value-judgment" with a ten-foot pole; but the reader will not miss
the point: Hobbes was the bad guy, Locke the good guy. Sabine's
Locke, however, is also the pupil of Hooker, and through Hooker of
the "long tradition of medieval political thought, back to Saint
Thomas [with its insistence on] . . . the reality of moral restraints on
power . . . and the subordination of government to law . . ." Sabine's
Locke, in short, set out to refute Hobbes "upon lines suggested by
Hooker," though he "did not assume the full obligation thus laid upon
him."[5] Locke got hung up between the "medieval tradition," in
which governmental power is limited by moral law, and in which
"the corporate or social reality of the community" is taken for
granted, and the view of that same Hobbes he was trying to refute:
that the community as such has no existence "save in the cooperation
of its members, which cooperation is always due *to advantages enjoyed by its members individually. . . .*" Now, says Sabine: "If Locke
could have adopted either of those two points of view and rejected
the other, he would have been more consistent than he was." Naturally, however, "the circumstances under which he wrote required
him to adopt both." In any case, adopting both was a task that "exceeded Locke's powers." Locke *had* to adopt a "large part of
Hobbes' premises . . . [A] theory of society in terms of individual
interests was in Locke's day a foregone conclusion." Why? Because
"the whole drift of the theory of natural law was in this direction"
(italics added)—that is, toward interpreting natural law as a claim to
"innate, indefeasible rights inherent in each individual." On one
side, therefore, Locke's political theory was *not* less "egoistic" than
that of the "bad guy" Hobbes: "Both government and society exist
[according to Locke] to preserve the individual's rights, and the
indefeasibility of such rights as a limitation on the authority of both."
Again: "In one part of Locke's theory . . . the individual and his rights
figure as ultimate principles; in another society itself plays this part."
Both, for Sabine's Locke, are "absolutes," which is to say: Sabine's
Locke has more absolutes, one more anyhow, than a political theorist
can permit himself. Locke has one foot in the medieval world, where

[5]Attend carefully: we are about to hear a Cornell professor give a lesson in logic to
one of the key figures in modern political philosophy.

there are moral rules to which the positive laws of government must conform, and one foot in the modern world, where each individual has, as attributes born with him, "natural rights" that are indefeasible claims on both society and government. Society and government exist to protect these rights; society does not create them and dares not, except within narrow limits, even regulate them. Locke did not, to be sure, follow Hobbes and base his theory on the individual's right of self-preservation,[6] but he and Hobbes together did bequeath to their heirs the presumption that individual self-interest "is clear and compelling" while the public interest is "thin and unsubstantial." And Locke—Sabine's Locke, that is—did "put up a body of innate, indefeasible rights which . . . stand as bars to prevent interference with the liberty and property of private persons."

Having made the point that Locke is simultaneously a spokesman for "the old theory of natural law" *and* a spokesman for indefeasible natural rights, and having made the point that the two positions are incompatible, Sabine shifts suddenly to the view that Locke is not really a spokesman for traditional natural law at all. What Locke did was to change the meaning of the term "natural law",[7] and make it a law that itself confers indefeasible rights. This appears to dispose of the alleged contradiction between Locke the spokesman of natural law and Locke the spokesman of individual rights, but at the same time makes nonsense of the view that Locke has one foot planted side by side with that of Saint Thomas. According to Sabine, a moment later, Locke expounds a natural law that enjoins the common good but is ready to assume that "preservation of . . . [the] common good and protection of private rights . . . come to the same thing." Sabine's Locke begins, then, to be something of a mystery, though not for Sabine. Sabine never doubts that he understands Locke better than Locke could possibly have understood himself. Locke, Sabine is thus able to conclude, seems not "to have been aware how greatly his own theory of natural rights [*sic*, since in Sabine's context we should expect "natural law"] differed from the older versions. . . ."

Sabine's Locke "derives society from the consent of its members": "Civil power can have no right except as this is derived from the individual right of each man to protect himself and his property."[8]

---

[6]But *ut infra*, n. 7.

[7]Without, Sabine cannot resist adding, "knowing it," though he, Sabine, knows it.

[8]Sabine does not explain why this does not commit Locke, like Hobbes, to a right of self-preservation.

"The individual resigns his natural right to the community . . . ;" but, as we should now expect, "this surrender [is] . . . conditional against both society and government." Society itself is obliged to secure everyone's property—that is, the individual's right to "life, liberty and estate." Yet Sabine's Locke holds that the "consent by which each person agrees with others to form a community obligates him to submit to the majority." Thus Locke has no answer to the question that arises from these premises: "What if the majority invades, or fails to protect, those indefeasible individual rights?" Sabine sees the difficulty ("it is no better for . . . [the individual] to be deprived of his rights by a majority than by a simple tyrant"); but the point Sabine is most concerned to make, it seems, is that Locke did not see it: "apparently it did not occur to Locke that a majority could be tyrannical," and that Locke has it "both ways" about individual rights and majority-rule.

The "importance" of the political philosophy of Locke lies, for Sabine, in its impact on "the political thought of America and France which culminated in the great revolutions of the end of the eighteenth century," where "Locke's defense of . . . inalienable rights . . . had [its] . . . full effect." Sabine does not tell us whether he regards Locke as the philosophical father of the American Revolution or whether he repudiates that view, which was in his day (and perhaps remains) widely current among scholars.

This brings us to Kendall 1941's *John Locke and the Doctrine of Majority-Rule*—about which let me put forward at once my reasons for referring to it. Kendall 1941 breaks sharply with the traditional interpretation of Locke that Sabine summarizes, *and* with the prevailing methods of scholarship in political theory that Sabine represents. Kendall writes with Sabine's Locke in front of him—or, if you like, Sabine's Locke "expanded" to include current doctrines about the relation between Locke and the Founding Fathers (which Sabine, for some reason he does not explain, skimps).

Kendall's own method, a "universal confrontation of the text," as he calls it, demands, in principle at least, that we accept no sentence or paragraph from the *Second Treatise* as Locke's "teaching" without first laying it beside every other sentence in the treatise, and attempt to face any problem, regarding the interpretation of that sentence or paragraph, posed by the presence within the text of those other sentences. His exclusive concern is with the text, which he accuses his predecessors of having read on the assumption that it will yield up its meaning to a hasty reader.[9] He writes, moreover, out of a kind of respect or even reverence for Locke that earlier commentators have, he alleges, denied to him: Kendall gives Locke no lessons in logic, does not think of himself as having scored a point when he runs down a verbal "contradiction" or "inconsistency" in Locke, certainly does not suppose himself capable of seeing contradictions and inconsistencies that Locke himself was not clever enough to see. Any contradictions or inconsistencies he finds pose, rather, problems for Kendall 1941. He himself writes out of a profound consciousness of, in Leo Strauss' phrase, the "difference in *rank*" between himself and Locke, so that no question of patronizing Locke can possibly arise in his mind. Kendall is uninterested in Locke as the "son of his times," and judges the "historical background" of the *Second Treatise,* and Locke's biographical data, as irrelevant to the interpretation of the book. He denies that such a book could have been written to "justify" the Glorious Revolution, that it is a *livre de circonstance* as contrasted with a venture in "pure" political theory, and even suggests that the book was written *before* the Glorious Revolution occurred. Kendall 1941 never doubts that the *Treatise* has a single, unambiguous meaning—if only one has the wit to find it. The idom did not yet exist that would have enabled Kendall 1941 to say: "Let us try to understand Locke as Locke understood himself"[10]—the nearest he can come to that, tutored as he has been by R. G. Collingwood and converted as he is to Collingwood's logic, is to say: "Let's find out, above all, what *question* the book is asking, the problem to which it addresses itself first and foremost; let us try first to grasp that question, then to find out what the author's overall answer to the question actually is. Let us, in a word, not make the mistake of trying to get answers to the question out of parts of the book that turn out to have no bearing either upon the question or upon the answer." In brief: Kendall 1941 makes a sharp *methodological* break with his predecessors and calls into question the latter's entire conception of political theory scholar-

[9]It is, he believes, a book that wants months and months, or even years and years, of poring over.
[10]Also a recurrent and typical phrase in Strauss' writings.

ship. Not surprisingly, therefore, he comes up with a "new" Locke, hitherto unknown to literature.

For purposes of explication, Kendall 1941's Locke is best projected against the background of Sabine's Locke which Kendall challenges on at least the following major points:

(a) While not yet sure enough of himself to say, "Let's stop all the foolishness, and admit to ourselves that on the really crucial issues Locke is a Hobbesian, a fairly docile pupil of Hobbes," Kendall 1941 does do this: He writes a big question mark beside the prevailing view of the "relation" between Hobbes and Locke. Kendall 1941 is much more impressed with the similarities between Locke's teaching and Hobbes' than with the dissimilarities; his Locke is by no means a "good guy," to be set against Hobbes; he is, rather, an "embroiderer" on Hobbes.

(b) Kendall 1941 repudiates both horns of the dilemma on which Sabine seeks to impale Locke: Kendall's Locke is neither a bridge, moored on Hooker, "connecting" Locke with the great tradition of natural law political thought, nor a spokesman for natural law as a "claim" to innate, indefeasible rights inherent in each individual. On the first of these points Kendall 1941 is by no means as clear as Kendall 1965 could wish him to have been. Perhaps the most one can say is that he is skeptical when Locke professes his indebtedness to the "judicious Hooker," and when Locke seeks to pass off his "law of nature," which man is "under" in the "state of nature," as traditional natural law. Kendall 1941 at least sees that Locke's account of the "law of nature" is full of difficulties, and that these had *not* been present in the traditional natural law teachings. Kendall's Locke, concretely, cannot be pinned down on the question "What rights does the law of nature actually confer, what duties does the law of nature actually impose, on the denizens of the 'state of nature?' " Rather, Kendall's Locke has several accounts of the law of nature, and unabashedly uses one or another of them in accordance with what he is attempting to prove or establish. Kendall 1941 is, in any case, clear about at least two things. First, that the "trouble" with Locke's account of the "law of nature" is somehow tied up with Locke's insistence on "natural man's" right (and duty) to "preserve himself," which Kendall 1941 does identify as Hobbesian doctrine, *not* traditional natural law doctrine. Second, that this Hobbesian doctrine is impossible to square with the apparently traditional elements in Locke's law-of-nature teaching. Kendall, moreover, does manage to explicate all this without accusing Locke himself of being "confused:" he sees that, whatever the case may be with Locke's law-of-nature teaching, all of it except the right of self-preservation disappears into thin air at the crucial moment (when the contract is made), and never again affects matters. Men in the state of nature, according to Kendall's Locke, "emerge" from the state of nature *not* because they have a *right* to preserve themselves and to elect freely the means for preserving themselves; they come into civil society because they see it as a "good deal," a "profitable transaction;" and Kendall's Locke must, therefore, just as Hobbes must, prove to our satisfaction that the deal, as he explains it, is one into which a right-of-self-preservation man would conceivably enter on selfish grounds. Kendall's Locke is, when the chips are down, pretty straight Hobbes: the denizens of Locke's civil society have, "operationally" speaking, no "indefeasible" or "inherent" or "natural" or "inalienable" rights; to suppose them to have such rights is to overlook the character of the "deal" they make when they emerge from the state of nature *into* civil society, and the character of the arrangements under which they live *in* civil society. For their "rights" in civil society are merely *the rights that are conferred by the majority,* and withdrawn at its pleasure—or worse still, by the legislature in which the majority, perhaps a majority long dead, has chosen to repose its trust. The majority or the majority's government, moreover, *creates* those rights and their correlative duties; it is not only under no obligation to make those rights and duties congruent with the rights and duties of the state of nature (i.e., of the law of nature), but it is also free to set completely aside any supposed "standards" of right and wrong laid down by the law of nature. Perhaps it is not too much to say that Kendall 1941 is the first critic to treat Locke's political society as a "model," which we must recognize in terms of its explicit *characteristica,* and must learn to *visualize* in order to be able to answer the question, "How, actually, does this model work? In what position does the individual caught in it find himself regarding any inherent rights and duties he may, taught by the early pages of Locke's *Treatise,* suppose himself to have?"

(c) Kendall 1941's Locke, amusingly enough in the eyes of Kendall 1965, *could* not have been the remote philosophical source of the

ideas of the American Revolutionaries and of the Framers of the
Constitution of the United States, because Kendall's Locke is, as we
have noted, *not* the philosopher of individual rights. Kendall 1941,
in other words, accepts the then-prevailing view of the nature of the
American Revolution, of the Philadelphia Constitution, of the Bill of
Rights, and so of the American political tradition in general. The
remote philosophical source of that tradition, the "teacher" of the
Founding Fathers, must be a spokesman for unalienable individual
rights; his name, therefore, cannot be John Locke, who is the philosopher of majority-rule authoritarianism—of which, Kendall 1941 joins
others in assuming, there is not a whisper of in the American political
tradition. Kendall 1941, in short, challenges the whole dominant
view of Locke's relation to the American political tradition, but does
so on grounds that Kendall 1965 would classify as fifty per cent dead
wrong: on the grounds that Locke was not the philosopher of inalienable rights, which is the fifty per cent that Kendall 1965 would
classify as correct, and on the grounds that the Framers were concerned about inalienable rights, which is the fifty per cent that Kendall 1965 would classify as dead wrong.

(d) Kendall's Locke differs from Sabine's Locke and other previous
Lockes also in this: he joins hands with Hobbes in shifting the attention of political philosophy away from questions about the proper
content of the laws enforced in political society to questions concerning the proper *source* of those laws.[11] Locke's individual member of
society is duty-bound to obey every law of the legislature in which
the majority has placed its trust, and because, and only because, it
emanates from that source. No one can relieve him of this duty except
a revolutionary majority, by withdrawal of its "trust" from the existing legislature and replacement of that legislature with another.[12]

Now Strauss' Locke, about whom we learn mainly by consulting his
Natural Right and History.[13]

Strauss, breaking even more sharply than Kendall with the tradi-

[11]The "source-content" distinction, unknown to Kendall 1941, is Bertrand de Jouvenel's.

[12]I deliberately postpone any mention of Kendall 1941's curious chapter called
"The Latent Premise," (a) because what I have to say about it can best be said in
connection with Strauss' Locke and Laslett's, but also (b) because Kendall 1965 views
that chapter with some embarrassment and, being only human, likes to postpone that
which is embarrassing as long as possible.

[13](Chicago: Univ. of Chicago Press, 1953), pp. 202-251.

tional interpretations of Locke's teaching, concentrates on Locke's doctrine of property (it is "almost literally the central part of his teaching, [and] ... certainly its most characteristic part"). Like Kendall, however,[14] he distinguishes sharply between Locke's teaching as to how things do and should work in Locke's state of nature and how things do and should work within Locke's civil society. Like Kendall again, he stresses the apparent incompatibility between Locke's "law of nature," as it obtains in the "state of nature," with its apparent emphasis on men's duties to one another,[15] and that which Locke puts forward as just and rightful in the commonwealth. Like Kendall finally, he holds, in a very different manner however, that Locke's apparent teaching about men's natural duties in the state of nature for all practical purposes vanishes into thin air at the crucial moment, that is, the moment at which men "enter" into civil society—or, more specifically, that what men "have" at the end of the state of nature, whatever Locke may have said earlier about duties, is merely the *right* of self-preservation; that it is this right which is solely responsible for their entering the commonwealth; and that, in consequence, it reigns supreme *within* the commonwealth.

In the state of nature, according to Strauss' Locke, a man owns that with which he has mixed his labor, but under severe limitations, dictated by justice and right under the law of nature, which are concerned mainly with how *much* he can own. Ownership as such, the natural, pre-commonwealth "right" to property, is "a corollary of the fundamental right of self-preservation, which involves the right to everything necessary for self-preservation" (e.g., the right to the "pursuit of happiness"). Among the severe limitations are these: natural man must not take away the property of others ("harming others, is against the natural law"); he must appropriate no more than that which is "necessary and useful for self-preservation," or at least potentially useful (that is, capable of being bartered for that which is useful); he must not take (from the "common") more than he can use before it spoils ("the terrors of the natural law," Strauss writes, "no longer [that is, do not, like those of traditional natural law] strike the covetous, but the waster"). In appropriating things by his labor, natu-

---

[14]No suggestion is intended that Strauss could have been influenced by Kendall's book.
[15]And, thus its apparent similarity, on some points, to traditional natural law teachings.

ral man must think exclusively of the prevention of waste; he does not have to think of "other human beings," since the watchword is, Strauss adds, "every man for himself." And, like Kendall, when he deals with Locke's several versions of the law of nature, Strauss is content to let Locke have it both ways, without taking him to task for it: natural man *both* must not harm others, and does not have to take into account the welfare of others. He is, however, very sure which teaching Locke "really" means: In "the poverty of the first ages of the world," Strauss' "real" Locke assures us, the "original law of nature . . . permitted unconcern for the need of other human beings."

Within "civil society," in any case, a new "form" of the "law of nature" replaces, for Strauss' Locke, the "original law of nature." Within civil society almost everything has already been appropriated: there is no longer a "common" from which men can "remove" things by mixing their labor with them. Logically, as Strauss points out, we might now fondly expect Locke to demand in civil society—in the name of "not harming others"—even more severe restrictions on appropriation and accumulation than in the state of nature, "lest the poor be straitened." But not so: "In civil society, the right of appropriation is completely freed from . . . shackles," the reason being that *money* has now been introduced, and has "revolutionized property." "Man in civil society"—such is the new decree of "natural law"—and this means according to the moral law, —"may acquire as much property of every kind . . . as he pleases; and . . . in every manner permitted by the positive law. . . ." Why? Because such unlimited accumulation "is conducive to the common good, . . . or the temporal prosperity of society." The day laborer, even if he is in extreme want, has no right to complain about having lost his right to mix his labor with the common: "the exercise of all the rights and privileges of the state of nature would give him less" than he has out of his "subsistence" wage. "Far from being impoverished by the emancipation of acquisitiveness, the poor are enriched by it." That emancipation, in short, is *the* cause of the *plenty* that is the distinguishing feature of civil society, where "[unlimited] appropriation without concern for the need of others is true charity." The "plenty" in question, like property in the state of nature, is indeed the product of labor, of work; and men in civil society, like men in the state of nature, indeed perform their labor for the purpose of satisfying wants that are, *ipso facto,* "selfish." But the "wants" present in civil society are something very different from the selfish want, characteristic of

the state of nature, for that which is necessary for *mere* self-preservation. Man in civil society wants *more* than he "needs," and he does
so because his views have been "enlarged," transformed in the direction of insatiability, by "the few men of larger views," the small
portion of mankind that are truly "rational"—that is, in Ortega's
phrase, by a "select minority." These must and do "take the lead"
and somehow force the overwhelming majority, the "lazy and incon-
siderate," to work for more than they need "against their will . . .
[though] for their own good. The "rational" minority thus become the
true benefactors of mankind, greater benefactors by far than "those
who give alms to the poor." The "common" disappears (because the
industrious minority have acquired ownership of it), and this indeed
creates a "scarcity" that obliges the lazy to "work much harder than
they otherwise would," but at the same time to improve "their [own]
condition by improving the condition of all." What prevents the
industrious and rational few from lapsing into "drowsy laziness,"
when they have all they want to meet their own enlarged needs?
Strauss' Locke's answer is, once more: the existence of *money*—of
which, Locke thinks, no man ever has enough. And the whole process, the continued "enlargement" of man's wants, the continued
quest, by the industrious and rational, is enabled to go on and on.
Strauss' Locke thus emerges as the prophet of a public policy whose
chief norms are the "spirit of capitalism," i.e., unlimited capitalist
accumulation, the maximization of production, and the indefinite
encouragement and glorification of science and technology.[16]

There emerges, up to this point, no necessary incompatibility between Strauss and Kendall 1941's Locke, though they are very different Lockes. One might say that Strauss and Kendall 1941 merely
seize on different portions of the *Second Treatise* as the "characteristic"[17] part of Locke's teaching: Strauss on the doctrine of property,
Kendall 1941 on the doctrine of majority-rule; and one is tempted to
add that each, because of the extensive evidence he marshals, presents a Locke future critics will, predictably, find it difficult to eliminate from the literature.[18] Each writes in greater or lesser awareness

[16]Of which, Kendall 1965 would add, the "rational and industrious" also never have
enough.
[17]I avoid the "central" in Strauss' phrase, because "central" is for Strauss a term of
art, with a special meaning.
[18]Not, to judge from developments in the literature to date, that anyone will ever
necessarily make the attempt. Several critics have taken exception, sometimes vigorous exception, to both Strauss' Locke and Kendall's Locke. But none has yielded to

of the existence in the *Second Treatise* of the other's Locke, but does not hesitate to subordinate the other to his own.[19] In any case, both Strauss' "real" Locke and Kendall's "real" Locke build unabashedly not on duties, but on the *right* to self-preservation.

Strauss' and Kendall's Lockes *are*, nevertheless, incompatible at the margin, though it is to the next portion of Strauss' argument that we must go in order first, to grasp the issue between Strauss and Kendall, and second, to appreciate the superiority of Strauss' Locke to Kendall's, whatever the merits of that issue. We shall then be in position third, to make plain the extent to which the main point both Strauss and Kendall are making, in large part tacitly, is one and the same point.

the temptation to try to meet the respective "cases" on their merits. *Ut infra.*

[19]This statement requires qualifications of a kind that would certainly overburden the text of the present paper. Strauss (pp. 232-233) writes, on the issue raised by Kendall 1941's Locke: "Locke ... [teaches] that wherever 'the people,' or 'the community,' *i.e., the majority,* have placed the *supreme* power, they still retain 'a *supreme* power to remove or alter' the established government, *i.e.,* they still retain a right of revolution. But this power (which is normally dormant) *does not qualify the subjection of the individual to the community or society* [i.e., the majority?]. On the contrary, ... Hobbes stresses more strongly than does Locke the individual's right to resist society or the government [*i.e.,* to make a martyr of himself in the name of his "rights?"] whenever his self-preservation is endangered" (italics added). Thus far, at least, Strauss would seem to be very much aware of the existence of Kendall 1941's Locke. The sequel, however, somewhat beclouds the matter (p. 233): "[Locke's] ... mighty leviathan, as he had constructed it, offered a greater guarantee of the individual's self-preservation than Hobbes' Leviathan. The individual's right of resistance to organized society, which Hobbes had stressed and Locke does not deny, is [to be sure] an ineffectual guaranty for the individual's self-preservation. ... [The] only effective guaranty for the rights of the individual is that *society* be so constructed as to be incapable of oppressing its members: only *a society or a government* thus constructed is ... in accordance with natural law. ... According to Locke, the best institutional safeguards for the rights of individuals are supplied by a constitution that, in practically all domestic matters, strictly subordinates the executive power ... to law, and ultimately to a well-defined legislative assembly. The legislative assembly must be limited to the making of laws ...; its members must be elected by the people ...; the electoral system must take account of both numbers and wealth" (italics added). Kendall 1941 would reply that this fails to meet the issue, which is whether there is any passage in the *Treatise* upon which an individual might base a claim to a right to resist a "non-dormant" majority; that Strauss' transition from "society" to "a society or a government" seems unwarranted, since Locke has nothing to say, in the dimension here relevant, on the question as to how *society,* as distinguished from government, should be *"constructed;"* and that even what Locke says as to how *government* should be constructed has, like his views on unlimited accumulation *(ut infra),* the "political" status of, at most, a recommendation. I find in Locke, just as I find in Article V of the U. S. Constitution, no limit on the power of the majority to set up any form of government that meets its fancy, and thereby to withdraw any and every supposed individual right.

When I say that Kendall 1941 is "aware" of the existence of Strauss' Locke, I do not suggest that Kendall 1941 understood him very well.

Strauss' Locke holds that *the* end of government is "the peace, the safety, and public good of the people," that "peace and safety" are the indispensable conditions of *plenty* (this Strauss abundantly documents), that "the public good of the people is identical with plenty;" that *the* end of government is, therefore, in the last analysis, plenty, and that plenty requires the emancipation of acquisitiveness. From all this it follows that *the* end of civil society (as distinguished from government?) is "the preservation of property" (Locke's language)— not, Strauss adds at once, of "each man's small property," but of "dynamic property," or the wide-open path to acquiring of property, which alone can produce ever-expanding plenty. "Men enter society," Strauss' Locke believes, "in order not so much to preserve as to enlarge their possessions": property ante-dates civil society, and even civil property, according to Strauss' Locke, "property owned on the basis of positive law," is "in the decisive respect *independent* of civil society" (italics added). Civil society "merely creates the conditions under which the individuals can pursue their productive-acquisitive activity without obstruction;" and while Strauss goes no further, he would not, I think, hesitate to take the unavoidable next step: Political power, the power of government, *does not extend to the obstruction of productive-acquisitive activity.* It cannot, in other words, invade the individual's right to acquire, which is the civil equivalent of the individual's pre-civil-society right to self-preservation. Locke's civil government is, therefore, on Strauss' showing, a *limited* government, and individuals do have rights "against" it. We come finally, then, to a sharp clash between Strauss' Locke and Kendall 1941's Locke. Strauss' Locke emancipates acquisitiveness; Kendall 1941's Locke emancipates majority rule. Strauss' Locke emancipates the South African diamond-mine-owners; Kendall's Locke emancipates the Bantu majority which, one day soon (all too soon, Kendall 1965 would say) will expropriate the mine-owners and, if it feels like it, kill them off too. For Kendall 1941 (echoed by Kendall 1965) would ask Strauss: What if the present legislature, dedicated to non-obstruction and inequality and installed by an earlier majority, passes laws that the people, having changed their sentiments, now deem incompatible with the public good—laws that, because they defend the Rockefellers against the "straitened laborers" or, in more fashionable language, the "impoverished workers," involve in the eyes of the majority the use of force by the government without right, and so create a state of war between the government and the popular majority? Does not Locke assure the majority, in no uncertain terms, that they are entitled to declare the government outlaw, overthrow it, and then install a government that is to their own liking? Can the "public good," according to Locke, ever be other than what the popular majority choose, in their wisdom, to regard as the public good? Where, in Locke's teaching, can the individual Rockefeller turn for protection of his "right to acquire" against a mobilized egalitarian majority? Kendall 1965 sees no answer that Strauss' Locke can give here to Kendall 1941's Locke.

That would not, however, be Kendall 1965's last word on the topic, since the last word would run in terms more like the following. Strauss has certainly shown, beyond any possibility of refutation, that Locke's *recommendation* to civil society is: No obstruction of the right to acquire, no measures against any resulting inequalities; plenty is civil society's proper supreme good, and any interference with the right to acquire, to discover, to invent, since it will reduce plenty, is *ipso facto* bad. Strauss does demonstrate that no other recommendation could be consistent with the right of self-preservation, which is indeed absolute. But according to Kendall 1941's Locke, we must distinguish between the policy-recommendation to which that right leads, and what Locke puts forward on the level of principles of political right, and recognize that the policy recommendation will be carried out only so long as the majority of the people share Locke's views, and not only value plenty above all other things, but also believe that plenty can be "maximized" only by *not* obstructing the right to acquire. The right of self-preservation, in Locke's logic, leads *both* to unlimited acquisition as good policy and to unlimited majority-rule as an ultimate principle of political right.

Is Kendall 1965, after all, "scoring" off Locke by showing, in the Sabine-manner, that Locke "contradicts" himself, is "inconsistent" and is a poorer logician than Kendall 1965—i.e., patronizing Locke? Not at all. Kendall 1965 argues: The "trouble" lies not in Locke's logic, but in the right of self-preservation itself, the selfish "interest" of the individual, as the point of departure for all typical modern political "philosophies." One of the tests a "point of departure" must meet is, *"Does* it lead to contradictory conclusions?" *If* it does, then there is something wrong with it as a "point of departure," and we ought to give it up, instead of merely savoring the inconsistencies to which it leads. Classical political philosophy, which never so much as toyed with any such point of departure, led to neither unlimited acquisition nor to majority-rule, and thus to no such contradictions, which is perhaps as good a reason as we need for returning to classical political philosophy. Kendall 1965 would add: Whatever the incompatibility between Strauss' Locke and Kendall 1941's Locke, between Locke the prophet of plenty and Locke the majoritarian, the modern world (perhaps because it is itself not very good at logic) has accepted *both*, just as Locke did. Both Strauss' Locke and Kendall 1941's Locke have "triumphed." The modern world believes in *both* the indefinite maximization of production and plenty *and* in majority-rule. There is indeed an inconsistency, but the modern world has been able to "absorb" it; both the maximization of plenty and majority-rule ride high in the political theory of our contemporary intellectuals.

The chief point to grasp about Strauss' Locke is that he is a *revolutionary* against both the biblical tradition and the great tradition in political philosophy. His real ancestor in political thought, as we learn in a more recent work by Strauss[20], is Machiavelli, who is the first political thinker to justify unlimited acquisition. Like Machiavelli, Locke seeks to emancipate his pupils (and the "modern" world he envisages) from the "bad" traditions of the past, necessitating first, a shift of emphasis from natural duties or obligations to natural *rights*, and second, enthronement of the *individual* as the "center and origin of the moral world"—or, making man, as distinguished from the proper *end* of man, the center of origin. The first thinker to put the matter in those terms is, of course, Hobbes; but Locke, according to Strauss, far from being a "refuter" of Hobbes, an anti-Hobbesian, is here *more* Hobbesian than Hobbes. Each—Machiavelli, Hobbes, Locke—is in his generation the architect of modern political theory; and Locke, from Strauss' perspective, is the most "advanced" modern of the three. Hobbes, according to Strauss, had not broken sufficiently with "nature" to be really "free" of classical philosophy; and it is Locke who becomes the first to cut man off from nature completely, to make of nature, including man's own nature, something hostile and "irrational" to be conquered by science and technology,

[20]Leo Strauss, *Thoughts on Machiavelli* (Glencoe, Ill.: Free Press, 1958).

to "make . . . man, not nature, the work of man and not the gift of nature," the "origin of almost everything valuable," and to insist that man "owes almost everything valuable to his own [unaided] effort." After Locke, man need no longer "obey" nature or "imitate" nature; "self-reliance and creativity" are to be, henceforth, the "marks of human nobility." "Man is effectively emancipated" from nature's bonds, and the "individual is emancipated from . . . [all] social bonds" that do not rest ultimately on consent—that is, the individual's consent.[21] The world replaces the "rule of nature" by the "rule of convention." "From now on, nature furnishes only the worthless materials . . . ; the forms are supplied . . . by man's free creation." Locke thus completes the murder of political philosophy, which has never since raised its head. The way is cleared for ideology—for "theory" in Sabine's sense—because philosophy, what I shall call repeatedly below the norms of philosophical discourses, now ceases to matter. And philosophy is the only antidote to the power of ideology.

As indicated earlier, Kendall 1941, viewed in the light of subsequent developments in the literature, was baffled by, first, Locke's putting forward several versions of the law of nature, none of which truly reflects traditional natural-law teachings, and second, the impossibility of squaring Locke's commitment to justice and to objective moral standards with his willingness, within civil society, to make of the majority the ultimate arbiter of both. Regarding the first of these points, Kendall 1941 merely demonstrates the impossibility of extracting from Locke's discussion of the "law of nature" an intelligible account of men's mutual rights and duties in the state of nature, and lets it go at that. As regards the second, the best Kendall 1941 can do is to suggest the *possibility*—only that, Kendall 1965 would insist—that Locke wrote on the tacit ("latent," he called it) premise that the majority of men in any civil society can be counted upon to act justly, and with due respect to objective standards of right and wrong. This was an attempt on Kendall's part not so much to "rescue" Locke the "good guy" from the charge that he is a majority-rule

[21]Strauss is certainly correct about this, which is yet another point on which Locke has "triumphed"—in the sense that the prevailing political theory of the present day accepts Locke's view of the matter. But this makes it only the more surprising that Locke, as Kendall 1941 shows him to do, finally reduces individual consent, the consent of all individuals and thus of each individual, to the consent of the majority. Here, too, our prevailing political theory follows Locke: It stresses individual consent as the basis of legitimacy, but "absorbs" it into the consent of the majority.

authoritarian, as to indicate what Locke would have had to do in order to "rescue" himself, namely: Make the premise in question explicit and, *per impossibile,* defend it philosophically. One might possibly claim that Kendall 1941 is on the verge of a "breakthrough" about the relation between Locke's teaching about the law of nature as it obtains in the state of nature and Locke's teaching about civil society; that he sees that there is something "sour" about the former, namely: it appears to be the traditional teaching, or it at least contains apparently traditional elements; it appears to (as Strauss will put it later) "impose perfect duties on man as man," but ends up not really doing so; and finally, Locke appears to write as a believer in Christianity, but puts forward a solution to his problem that, clearly, is not affected by his religious beliefs. Kendall cannot, however, make the breakthrough, because it has never so much as occurred to him that a serious writer on politics would indulge in "hanky-panky." For example, engage in "secret writing", i.e., write statements into a book that he not only does not really mean, but even as good as tells the reader that he has not really meant them. Or, again for example, pay lip-service to widely-accepted traditional notions, and subsequently as good as say that the lip-service is just that. Or, for still another, write a book deliberately devised to communicate different things to different kinds of persons.[22] Strauss' Locke is "superior" to all previous Lockes, and to all future Lockes that may be put forward by critics who refuse to treat the *Second Treatise* as other than a venture in "secret writing," because Strauss has demonstrated—that many parts of Locke's argument must be treated as something other than candid statements of Locke's real intention, put there for a *strategic* purpose, and by a strategist who is quite willing to employ, *inter alia,* deception.

The important event in the history of Locke literature between 1937 and 1963, I believe, has been Strauss' exposure of Locke's discussion of the "law of nature" as a venture in secret writing—i.e., as a "revolutionary" teaching camouflaged in biblical and traditional-natural-law language, now to make it more palatable to persons with delicate taste-buds, now to conceal its revolutionary character from

---

[22]Put otherwise: conceal his real intention for all save a select few of his readers, or include in his book statements that are there only to mislead the general reader. Not yet having read Strauss, Kendall writes out of an innocence that renders him incapable of dealing with the *Treatise.*

persons in positions to deal roughly with revolutionaries. Strauss'
Locke, far from being a "son of his times," is their very "step-son,"[23]
seeking to pass himself off, in certain quarters, as a full-fledged member of the family.

Strauss lends himself less, perhaps, than any writer of our times to
condensation or summary. All one can hope to do here is indicate the
main points established in his breath-taking statement on Locke's
"law of nature."

(a) Locke, as previous critics had conceded, is a "cautious" writer;
but these critics have, thinks Strauss, overlooked the possibility that
the best interpreter of Locke's "caution" is Locke himself. Locke's
own idea of caution, as revealed in certain passages of *The Reasonableness of Christianity,* makes of it (as Strauss himself does) a kind
of "noble fear." In a political writer, such fear obliges him to "state
the case for the good cause [i.e., the cause he deems good] in a
manner which could be expected to create general good will toward
the cause." That, Strauss shows, is just what Locke did; though certainly the spokesman for a revolutionary cause, he "took every advantage of his partial agreement with Hooker [and tradition teachings]
. . . [and] . . . avoided the inconveniences which might have been
caused by his partial disagreement with Hooker [and traditional
teachings] by being practically silent about it." Again: ". . . [Legiti-
mate] caution is perfectly compatible with going along with the herd
in one's professions or with using ambiguous language *or with so
involving one's sense that one cannot easily be understood"* (italics
added).

(b) Careful reading of the *Second Treatise* leads unavoidably to the
conclusion that, as Strauss puts it, Locke recognized *no* "law of nature in the proper sense of the term," and certainly not (as he pretends) Hooker's law of nature. To begin with, Locke's "law of nature"
(Locke does, of course, use the term, and pays lip-service to it) is
inseparable from his doctrine of the "state of nature," which is pure
Hobbes (there is not a trace of a "state of nature" in Hooker). Similarly, for all of Locke's talk about the "state of nature" as one of
"peace, goodwill, mutual assistance, etc.," where men have profound
moral obligations to one another, Locke, Strauss shows in due course,

[23]I take the phrase from Strauss' *Thoughts on Machiavelli.*

"demolishes" that picture of the state of nature and replaces it with another, which is the one on which he proceeds to build. The state of nature emerges finally as one of "mutual grievances, injuries and wrongs," in which "strife and troubles ... [are] endless," a state "full of fears and continual dangers"—again almost pure Hobbes. There *cannot* be a law of nature, properly speaking, in the state of nature because, for one thing, in order for it to be a *law* in the state of nature, it would have to have sanctions, which it does not have. Locke explicitly rejects the traditional view that these sanctions can be provided by "the judgment of the conscience which is the judgment of God" —"conscience" is "nothing else than our own opinion"; because, for another thing, if it were law, its execution could not be left, as in the state of nature it clearly is, to the whim of each individual; and because, finally, it cannot be a law unless it is promulgated, which in the state of nature it is not.

(c) What does obtain in the state of nature is simply the desire for happiness which Locke does not hesitate to claim as an "absolute" right, i.e., the status of a right without correlative duties, and so a kind of right unknown to the tradition against which Locke rebels. That right is, nevertheless, itself a derivative right: happiness presupposes *life;* "the desire for life [therefore] takes precedence over the desire for happiness," and the "right of self-preservation" becomes, accordingly, the "most fundamental of all rights." Still again, almost pure Hobbes.

(d) Since *the* fundamental right is the right of self-preservation, "all social or governmental powers" must be based on it, must be derived from "powers which by nature belong to ... individuals." And the contract upon which society and government rest is, of necessity, a contract among individuals concerned primarily with their self-preservation.

Strauss' Locke, whom we have now "visited," is, I repeat, "superior" to all previous Lockes, because he is the product of scholarly procedures in the absence of which all books like *The Second Treatise* (and there are many like them) must remain impenetrable mysteries. Strauss' interpretation of Locke's "law of nature,"[24] in short, excels

[24]Locke puts forward several versions of the law of nature? Kendall is baffled? He can think of no other explanation than that Locke is hesitating as to which to marry.

all other interpretations in this: it can *explain* the presence of, and so "fit in," each and every passage that a hostile critic might bring forward as inconvenient, and can do so without merely dismissing them as inconsistencies. The "inconvenient" passages are not, on Strauss' showing, inconvenient at all; they are there for a purpose, a *strategic*[25] purpose, one moreover that, in its execution, can meet the supreme test for a strategic purpose: it succeeds. For Locke *did* succeed in getting across his message, and building it into the very fibre of the modern world; and he did so precisely by eschewing the "unqualified frankness" that might have "hindered" his "noble" cause, or exposed Locke himself to persecution, or "endangered the public peace."

I come now to my point that there is an area of at least tacit agreement between Strauss and Kendall, in a more decisive dimension than that of the issue between them, that quite overshadows their possible "quarrel" over that issue. That area of agreement, let me say briefly, has to do with the question concerning the philosoph-

[25]Again in order not to overburden the text, I compress in a footnote what I understand to be Strauss' picture of what let me call Locke's strategic situation, *i.e.,* the situation over against which he needed to think in strategic terms. The traditional, that is, the generally accepted teaching was: There *is* a natural law, which imposes perfect duties on man as man; it is identical with "the law of reason," is, indeed, "plain and intelligible to all rational creatures;" it is also a "declaration of the will of God," the very "voice of God" in man, the *law* of God, and the law of God not only in fact, but in the future sense that it is *known* to be the law of God. Only through obedience to this law, which is promulgated both by reason and by revelation, can man act morally (it was first made known in its entirety through revelation, was then confirmed by reason). Now: Locke, as a cautious man *(ut supra)* is not prepared to challenge this traditional teaching openly, but is prepared to direct attention to the following "difficulty" in it: "Unassisted reason" is "sufficient for leading to men's happiness;" it is by no means necessary, in order to explain his writing the kind of book he wrote, to assume either that he doubted the possibility of demonstrating revelation, or that he doubted that the New Testament expresses "in the most perfect manner the entire law of reason." The point is, rather, that "solid demonstrations" along lines based on Scripture would not necessarily seem "solid" to all his readers (most especially, one can imagine Strauss adding, the readers he was most eager to fetch for the "noble cause."). "He must have been aware of the fact that a political teaching based on Scripture would not be universally admitted"—if only because of the already considerable incidence of deists; as he must also have been aware (Kendall would add) that an open break with the traditional teaching, especially at the beginning of this book, would bring him quickly into the disrepute that had already overtaken those "justly decried" authors, Hobbes and Spinoza (Locke's own phrase, *apud* Strauss). Put otherwise: since the political teaching independent of Scriptures that he wishes to convey will be *ipso facto* repugnant to those who accept the traditional teaching, save as he wins their confidence and puts them off guard, his most promising potential pupils are precisely those who would not attend to an argument based on Scripture. We see not only why Locke must engage in hanky-panky, but also why he chooses the mode of hanky-panky that Strauss exposes.

ical status of "the right of self-preservation" as a point of departure for any inquiry into men's rights and duties in civil society. I believe Strauss to be saying, and *know* Kendall (even Kendall 1941) to be saying, between the lines: The so-called right of self-preservation, upon which Locke builds his entire politics, is nonsensical—because it is evolutionary not only over against the traditional teachings of philosophy, but against philosophy itself. It *has* no status philosophically. Its status is ideological, not philosophical. The proposition that asserts it is born out of defiance of the norms of philosophical discourse, because it claims a right that has *no* correlative duties. Philosophy *knows* no such right; it is incapable of knowing any such right. To put it otherwise, right-of-self-preservation political theories are *all* ideological, and recognizable as such because they owe their survival, in large part, to their habit of stealing terms from philosophy, giving them without due warning a new and philosophically illegitimate meaning, and using them to mobilize for *political* purposes the respect and reverence that philosophy, using them in their *correct* meaning, has won for them (as the Communists use words like "freedom," "justice," etc.). The proposition that asserts the right to self-preservation is adopted by those who appeal to it *not* because of the cause that can be made out for it philosophically, but because of its potential value as a weapon. And make no mistake about it: the "right of self-preservation" is *the* weapon that the modern politics has used for the overthrow of the traditional politics.

Kendall and Strauss (Kendall believes) are saying between the lines: The ideological character of the right of self-preservation is "given away" by the very form of the argument that Locke, again following Hobbes, uses to support it. What that argument boils down to, alike in Locke and Hobbes and their successors, is merely this: People, as we observe them, do desire life, and for the most part appear to desire it above *all* other things. People are "like that," whether because God made them so, or Nature made them so, or Environment made them so; that is why they *behave* as they do; to suppose otherwise is to blind yourself to reality, to kid yourself. People behave as they do, that is to say, putting self-preservation first, because they *cannot* behave otherwise; and since they cannot behave otherwise than they do, they "ought" to behave as they do, and so have a "right" to behave as they do. Because of the philosophically illegitimate transition from "men as they are" to "men as they *ought* to be" to "men as they have a right to be," the entire argument proclaims, I say, its defiance of the norms of philosophical discourse.

It is the right of self-preservation that leads on (logically enough, once granted the point of departure) to the contemporary doctrine of consent as the sole basis of legitimate government (if I have a right to preserve myself, I can be bound to that which is potentially dangerous only by my own consent). It leads on, too, to the doctrine according to which the protection and "implementation" of "individual rights" as inherent in all individuals, and thus equal from individual to individual, is the be-all and end-all of governmental purpose, and to the doctrine of majority-rule (must not the greater number of "consents" triumph over the lesser, if consent be the essence of legitimacy?). Nor does any of these derivate doctrines ever divest itself of the purely ideological character of the premise from which they flow.

Finally, Laslett's Locke, which is mainly a matter of pp. 79-120 of the "introduction" to his critical edition of *Two Treatises of Government.*[26] I say "mainly" because the Laslett edition will be of lasting importance for reasons wholly independent of the "success" or "failure", in the eyes of future critics, of his (if I may put it so) "last ditch" rescue operation for the "good" Locke. First, Because of Laslett's dogged and skillful work with the manuscripts we now possess for the first time—astonishing as that may seem—a dependable text of the *Second Treatise*[27] (Laslett's scolding to political theory scholars for their carelessness about texts is one of the truly exciting moments in his book). Second, because of Laslett, we now *know* (he has placed the matter beyond dispute) that the *editio princeps* of the *Second Treatise* is not, as scholars have always assumed, the first edition, with which Locke was completely dissatisfied, but the seventh; that the title *Second Treatise* (though Laslett retains it) is a misnomer—it was in fact written *before* the *First Treatise;* that, as Kendall 1941 had guessed (but only guessed), the *Second Treatise* was written well before the Glorious Revolution. Third, Laslett has given us a rich

[26](Cambridge: Cambridge Univ. Press, 1960.)
[27]The Laslett text, accordingly, differs at many points from that which we have been using in our classrooms. I have, however, "checked out" the modifications and concluded that none of the existing interpretations of the *Second Treatise* would have come out differently had the author had before him the perfected Laslett text.

Locke bibliography, which, we may be sure, Locke scholars will treasure for many decades.

We can hit only the high spots of "Laslett's Locke," which I feel are these:

(a) Laslett sweeps aside completely any and all doubts cast by Strauss and Kendall 1941 upon Locke's commitment both to natural law and to theism. Locke's "initial position," upon which he builds his entire political philosophy, is that men "do not own themselves, they do not dispose of themselves, they are the workmanship of God. They are his servants, sent into the world on his business. . . ." (p. 92). Now, God has not "given any man, or any order of men, superiority over other men . . ." *(ibid.) Therefore,* men, everywhere are born "free" and "equal." Free how (since "absolute freedom has no meaning" [*ibid.*])? Free, answers Laslett's Locke, within the "bounds set by the law of nature," which "limits" man's "natural freedom" (p. 93), and is an expression of God's will" *(ibid.).* "God's positive direction is known to all of us through our reason" (p. 94), which, in Locke's own phrase, is "the Voice of God in man." Reason "promulgates to us the law of nature and it is our reason which makes us free" (p. 94). Reason and its dictates are "given by God to be the rule betwixt man and man." All, Laslett concludes, quite "traditional": it "goes back beyond Christianity to the Stoics and Aristotle." Strauss' "revolutionary" Locke is thus disposed of—without, we may note, any necessity of coming to grips with Strauss' argument, of which, let me say in passing, Laslett never shows any real comprehension whatever.

(b) Laslett now moves very fast: *Because* "reason" is the rule "betwixt man and man," and is the "mode of cooperation between man and man" (p. 95), therefore "any man who behaves unreasonably," especially any man who "seeks to get anyone else into his power," is "to that extent an animal" and, "becomes liable to be destroyed by the injured person and the rest of mankind" (Locke's wording throughout the quoted passages). ". . . The basis of political life is the rule of the rational man over his irrational fellows" (p. 96), though what this does to the "freedom" and "equality" with which presumably the irrational, like the rational, were presumably born, Laslett does not pause to explain. "Government" becomes possible because "everyone . . . has the Executive Power of the Law of Nature"; everyone has "the right to punish [the offender]" (again Locke's phrasing throughout) against that law, and so "vindicate the rule of reason." "We may ... [exercise this right] individually, but [also] we *may and must* cooperate with other individuals against [the trespasser]" (p. 96).[28] The right of governing, and the power to govern, is a "fundamental, *individual,* natural right and power, set alongside that of *preserving oneself and the best of mankind" (ibid.).*[29] Nor does Laslett hesitate to add: *"The whole of Locke's political theory is now in view, even the concept of trust and the separation of powers"* (p. 97).[30]

(c) How does Laslett answer the Strauss-Kendall objection that at the decisive moment (that of entering political society) *all* that the negotiators of the compact have left, out of all the above, is the right of self-preservation (i.e., *no* duties)—and that, in any case, even when he has on his law-of-nature hat, Locke always subordinates the duty to preserve "mankind" to the duty to preserve oneself?[31] Two answers are possible here: First, he doesn't meet it; and second, insofar as he seems to meet it, he does so by legerdemain. He is *not* unaware of the problem, as witness his statement (p. 97): *"All the characteristics of men, and the relationship between them, which we have discussed so far belong to the state of nature."*[32] The state of nature, however, is men "living together according to reason without a common superior on earth, in mutual assistance, peace, goodwill and preservation."[33] *That* "is the universal background against which government is to be understood" (p. 99); it "tells us what government is and what it does by showing what it is not and what it does not do," and "even makes it possible to distinguish proper forms of government from improper ones" (p. 99); the "absolute monarch" is in

[28]Italics added. Laslett thus attempts to make it a duty—what else could he mean by "must"?—to "enter" civil society *(Ut infra.).*

[29]Italics added. How the right of the collectivity to "govern" could be an "individual" right, Laslett does not tell us. Note that in a single sentence he has brushed aside the difficulties to which Kendall 1941 directs attention by stressing the multiplicity of Locke's "accounts" of the "law of nature." He does conclude (p. 97, *n.*) that Locke is a "very unconventional natural-law writer, much more so than Hobbes."

[30]Italics added.

[31]It does seem to me that Strauss and Kendall 1941 read Locke in much the same way on this point. Laslett conceded the second point when he speaks of "the right and duty of every man to preserve himself and *everybody as much as possible"* (p. 97, italics added)—i.e., presumably, as much as is possible consistently with his *self*-preservation.

[32]Italics added.

[33]Thus ignoring all the passages inconvenient to this reading, and the whole of Strauss' argument, summarized above, to the effect that Locke's state of nature, off at the end, is about as Hobbesian as Hobbes' own.

a "state of nature" *vis à vis* his people, because he substitutes his force and will for the "rule of reason clothed in natural law" *(ibid.).* "The state of nature is already social and political . . . [and the] state of society never completely transcends the state of nature; the contrast is never complete" *(ibid.).* [34] Yet a moment later, when *he* speaks of the decisive moment at which the state of society is created, he seems, for the moment anyhow, to decide *not* to challenge the Strauss-Kendall interpretation: ". . . [Where] the question arises why it should be that men ever do proceed from a state of nature to a state of society, he suddenly departs from *all* his predecessors, classical and medieval" (p. 99). [35] This would seem to justify Strauss' contention that Locke is a "revolutionary": Mankind has a right to the "goods of nature," which right derives from first, the Scriptures, second, man's rationality, and third, the fundamental law of self-preservation. From this it follows that "every man has a *Property* in his own person," and "the Labour of his Body, and the Work of his Hands," are his (in both cases, the language is Locke's). This leads to the emergence of *private property,* which unlike money in the state of society, does *not* arise from "common consent." *"In fact"*—and we begin to think Laslett is now going to adopt Strauss' account—"men were led to leave the state of nature" for one "great and chief end," namely: the *"Preservation of their Property,"* where "their," taken in context, *must* mean *individual* property, and the "motive" does become, as Strauss and Kendall insist, wholly selfish (*i.e.,* a matter of *individual self-preservation).* [36] Again: ". . . [It] is through the theory of property that men can proceed from the abstract world of liberty and equality based on their relationship with God and natural law, to the concrete world of political liberty guaranteed by political arrangements" (p. 102). [37] Locke was prepared "to allow material property . . . to stand for many or all of the abstract rights of the individual." [38]

[34] Which is to pass over all the passages in which Locke insists upon the contract and, *inter alia,* the irrevocability of the contract, plus the fact that the people, when they "resist," are in a "state of war" not a "state of nature" with the government they are deposing.

[35] Italics added.

[36] P. 101. Laslett notes that Locke sometimes defines "property" as including "Lives, Liberties, and Estates." But these also, surely, are individual. *Cf.* Laslett, p. 102: ". . . property to Locke seems to symbolize rights [individual rights, surely] in their concrete form. . . ."

[37] To paraphrase Alice, the two worlds do begin to sound "differenter and differenter," though earlier the one "never transcends the other."

[38] Which rights, Laslett emphasizes however, are precisely the rights that, according

But Laslett, bent as he is on rescuing the "good" Locke, cannot follow Strauss very far: ". . . [It] is gratuitous to turn Locke's doctrine of property into the classic doctrine of the 'spirit of capitalism' . . ." (p. 103). What men do when they establish governments is to "set up" what Laslett is pleased to call "conscious, cooperative control" *(ibid.),* the essence of which is that "the Laws *regulate* the right of property."[39] While "it would be extremely difficult to argue that [Locke] had any sort of doctrine in mind which we should call socialist" (pp. 103-104), we must not ignore that word "regulate:" ". . . [The] magistrate *can* appoint ways of *transferring property from one man to another,* and *make what property laws they like,* provided they are equitable" (page 104).[40] When Strauss, like MacPherson (whom Laslett deems more "exact" and "subtle" than Strauss), tries to make Locke a "crypto-capitalist," he can do so only by a "reading of Lockeian texts which is so arbitrary and so *concerned to discover a 'real' meaning,* that it is quite unacceptable . . ." (p. 105).[41] The pronouncement with which Laslett concludes this discussion—"If we are prepared to deal with historical texts in such a way, we can prove just what we like from them" (p. 105)—seems to me applicable not to Strauss but to Laslett himself. Not only does Laslett pick and choose his passages from the "text;" by pooh-poohing the whole idea of a "real meaning," he makes nonsense of the whole business of Locke scholarship.

Laslett's Locke, then, is a bold challenge to Strauss' Locke, and one that Laslett brings off only by cutting himself off entirely from the duty of "universal confrontation of the text," in the act of joining himself with Sabine in yet another respect: Laslett's Locke, like Sabine's, is "incomplete" "inadequate," "confused," etc. (p. 105). As I said at the beginning of the present discussion, one answer to the question, "How does Laslett meet the Strauss-Kendall argument that Locke bases society exclusively on the right of self-preservation?" is: he does not meet it at all.

to Locke, a man *can* "alienate" to civil society *(ibid.).*

[39]Italics added. The reference is to *Second Treatise,* 50.

[40]Italics added. Yet he has just conceded that Locke's object seems to have been to guarantee secure and quiet possession, however large the estate *(ibid.).*

[41]Italics added. One might comment that the use of the word "arbitrary" about a reading, without demonstration or evidence, might in some quarters be called "absolutely unacceptable." Strauss has dealt fully with both of Laslett's objections.

The other answer is: He meets it by legerdemain, i.e., by a piece of sleight-of-hand that attempts to prove that Kendall 1941's "latent premise" is not latent in Locke at all, but actually "there," and to refute Kendall's major thesis (p. 109, *n.*). Political power comes into being, according to Locke, when a "band of rational creatures"[42] form a community, with the "power to punish transgressions against the law of nature and offences against their property" (p. 106).[43] ". . . This will be done by consent, the consent of every individual concerned," and the effect will be to set up a "judge on earth," i.e., a legislative power, which will promulgate rules "in accordance with the law of nature," and will "have at its disposal the mingled force of all the members . . ." *(ibid.)* The individual consents constitute a compact, which will "imply" majority-rule, since the "gravitational logic" of the state that thus comes into being "requires that those who are part of it shall not resist its final direction" (p. 107); and the compact thus made is "fair to everybody, since everybody makes the same sacrifice for the same benefits" (p. 103).[44] Government "comes into being at the same time," but "every effort must be made [by whom?] to ensure that . . . [the governors] shall never develop an interest separate from that of the community . . . ;" the "power [of government] is given for attaining an end and limited to that end" (p. 107). Let the government neglect that end, and it is dissolved; power then "devolves" to the people *(ibid.).*[45] This, though "it has had to be *interpreted* somewhat for purposes of straight *exposition,"* is the "major theme of Locke on *Government"* (p. 108).[46] Is Kendall 1941 correct then in making Locke a "majority-rule authoritarian" (p. 109, *n.*)? No, this would be to ignore Locke's "intention," which is to "lay down a doctrine," namely: the doctrine of "natural political virtue" *(ibid.),* and this doctrine "goes some way to justify in ethical terms [Locke's majoritarianism]" (p. 109). ". . . [A] majority . . . will

[42]The sleight-of-hand begins: He was distinguishing a little earlier between the "rational" and the "irrational"; the irrational now suddenly disappear as if indeed by magic.

[43]The statement is very wide of Locke's own precise definition of political power, which does not so much as mention the laws of nature: It is the "Right of making Laws with . . . penalties, for the Regulating and Preserving of Property . . . and in the defense of the Commonwealth from Foreign injury, and all this only for the Publick Good." See *Second Treatise,* 2.

[44]What matters if we toss in a little stray Rousseau doctrine, *en passant?*

[45]Which, as Laslett has already conceded, must mean the majority of the people.

[46]Italics added. "Interpreted somewhat," as we shall see when we have the entire argument before us, is putting it mildly.

under this doctrine act with *some* responsibility towards those in the majority" *(ibid.).*[47] Why? Because

> We *all* possess natural political virtue, both because we are disposed favorably towards each other in our very make-up, ... and because, when we cooperate, the tendency of what we do and what we say will *inevitably* be towards the politically efficacious, that which will work out for all of us *(ibid.).*[48]

Or again:

> .... [All] individuals ... will have some *tendency* to allow for the existence, the desires, actions, and needs of other men.... (p. 108).[49]

The individual in society, we are to understand then, is thus assured that there will be no "arbitrary" or "absolute" exercise of power by the majority, while Kendall 1941 had argued that the individual in Locke's society precisely has no such assurance. Kendall 1941, accordingly, stands "refuted"—but, I repeat, by a feat of legerdemain. The "doctrine of natural political virtue," Kendall's latent premise, is produced out of thin air, and *attributed* to Locke in a fashion that can only be called wholly gratuitous. At no point in which Laslett's account of Locke on majority-rule varies from Kendall 1941's does Laslett, though he is usually quite liberal with documentation, offer any supporting passages from, or references to, the actual text of *Second Treatise.* Laslett almost admits this: "This would seem to be the most probable and sympathetic [!] reading of the text, though *not all that is said is quite consistent with it"* (p. 108).[50] Or, as he puts it elsewhere: "... [This] interpretation is suggested by the whole tenor of his doctrine, rather than demonstrated by his statements" (p. 115).[51]

We can now re-open the question, "What *has* happened to Locke over the years since 1937—that is, to the Locke literature?" It seems

[47]Italics added. Why only "some"? Laslett appears to have no answer.
[48]Italics added. Note the "all": the "irrational" are again spirited away, thus not in position to form a majority.
[49]Italics added. This, Laslett comments, brings Locke very close to Aristotle, as the preceding quotation brings him very close to Hobbes (p. 109).
[50]Italics added.
[51]Goodbye, text!

to me that several "firm" statements are warranted.

(a) A sharp issue has been drawn, an issue unknown in 1937, between first, those scholars who take it for granted that there is a "real meaning" in the *Second Treatise* (if only, as I put it earlier, one has the wit to find it), to be arrived at by "universal confrontation of the text," and, second, those scholars who find the *Second Treatise* full of "inconsistences," "contradictions," "confusion,"[52] and content themselves with a "best bet," based on picking and choosing their "passages."

(b) A sharp issue has been drawn (not merely, of course, with respect to Locke) over the theory of "secret writing"[53]—i.e., between first, scholars who use the "secret writing" approach, and, second, scholars who deem that approach nonsensical.

(c) Judging from Laslett and the "mainstream" of political theory scholarship, neither Kendall's 1941 Locke nor Strauss' Locke, the two "revolutionary" developments in the literature during the period considered here, in question, have had any perceptible impact on the mine-run political theory scholars. The latter's general practice would seem to be either first, to ignore the two developments altogether, or second, to mention them *en passant*, only to dismiss them as "extravagant," "far-fetched," "tendentious," but never, third, to enter into public debate with them.

Whether or not the following not firm but tentative statement is also in order, by way of a conclusion, I leave the reader to decide.

(d) The fate of Strauss' Locke and Kendall 1941's Locke raises this urgent question: Assuming that "political theory" is a "profession," are the *mores* of that profession such today that writing a book of which mine-run political theory scholars can say "who ever heard of such a thing?" is, to use a favorite phrase of mine, a pastime on the same level with dropping pebbles in a bottomless well? I think, as I ask the question and refer to *mores*, partly of the now-fashionable 700-1000 word book review in the professional journals, which in the very nature of the case cannot come to grips with a book before it can get off the ground. But I think mainly of the *mores* that permits the profession to form, on the basis of such brief reviews, an unfavorable judgment about a book, and perpetuate that judgment as the

---

[52]Laslett rejoins Sabine in this regard.

[53]By no means, at this writing, only Strauss. See the recently published Joseph Cropsey, ed., *Ancients and Moderns* (New York: Basic Books, 1964), for evidence that there is now a school of scholars who follow Strauss in this regard.

consensus of the profession—without anyone's feeling obligated to forward and support that judgment with reasoned argument and documentation. Two frightening recent examples of how this works are Leo Strauss' *Thoughts on Machiavelli* and Harry V. Jaffa's *Crisis of the House Divided*,[54] which should, each of them, have kicked up a debate of major proportions, but have produced scarcely a ripple on the placid surface of what I called a moment ago the mainstream of political theory scholarship. I conclude that the political theory profession is suffering from a mortal sickness.

[54]Harry V. Jaffa, *The Crisis of the House Divided* (New York: Doubleday and Co., 1959).

Thoughts on Machiavelli

THOUGHTS ON MACHIAVELLI. By Leo Strauss. Glencoe, Ill.,
The Free Press, 1958. Pp. 348. $6.00.

It would be an exaggeration to say that Machiavelli can be cited
on both sides of all the issues in political philosophy. He cannot, for
instance, be cited on the side of that rule by "gentlemen" which the
classical political philosophers regarded as the best régime short of
rule by the philosopher-king; or in favor of the view, common to both
the classical and the biblical tradition, that rulers, as they go about
the business of ruling, should practice moral virtue; or even in favor
of the time-honored doctrine according to which tyranny is to be
condemned because it subordinates the common good of a political
society to the private good of one of its members. It is not an exaggeration to say that Machiavelli can be cited on both sides of so many
of the issues in political philosophy as to have made him, over the
centuries since he flourished, the major enigma among political philosophers—so that, as of the moment when the book here under
review was published, our vast Machiavelli "literature" had become
an impenetrable jungle of conflicting, not to say contradictory, answers to the questions "What *was* Machiavelli up to?" and "Was
Machiavelli a 'good guy' or a 'bad guy'?" It is not an exaggeration to
say, either, that that literature had become a scandal, and seemed to
place a question mark beside the very possibility of scholarship—that
is, of inquiry leading to a consensus at least among experts—in the
field of political philosophy, in a way in which the continuing scholarly debate about, for example, Plato's political philosophy did not.
With respect to the latter debate, one might indulge the hope that
some things at least were being clarified, that with each generation
there took place a net advance toward *the* correct reading of the
important documents, that the conflicting "positions" were not ut-
terly irreconcilable, and that, some time off in the future, the debate
might therefore be stilled. With respect to the debate on Machiavelli,

the movement seemed to be in the other direction: the rival interpretations of the texts seemed to get further and further apart; and to
the extent that there was a prevailing view, its very expositors
seemed less than confident that they had got hold of the "essential"
Machiavelli.

One of the marvels of Professor Strauss's *Thoughts on Machiavelli*
is not so much that it dispels the confusion as to what Machiavelli was
up to, and whether he was or was not on the side of the angels
(though it does both these things), as that it makes of the previous
confusion itself a means to the understanding of Machiavelli and his
place in the history of political philosophy, which is to say: as the
reader of *Thoughts on Machiavelli* comes to understand the reasons
for the conflicting interpretations of Machiavelli (including the reasons why he, the reader, has in the past been unable to make any
sense of *The Prince* and *The Discourses*), as he comes to see that the
misunderstandings of Machiavelli are Machiavelli's own handiwork,
he finds himself moving closer and closer to the core of Machiavelli's
thought, and growing in intimacy with Machiavelli the teacher.
(Whatever else Machiavelli was or was not, Strauss leaves no doubt
that he was one of the great teachers of all time—and, *mirabile dictu,*
like most great teachers, a teacher of morals; no reader of *Thoughts
on Machiavelli* will ever again flirt with the notion that Machiavelli
"drove a wedge" between "politics" and "ethics," or was the "first"
political philosopher to eschew "value judgments.") For there have
been no misunderstandings about Machiavelli that Machiavelli did
not invite and encourage; the misunderstandings are, therefore, one
phase of what Strauss calls Machiavelli's "plan" or intention, and, as
such, they throw decisive light on the plan as a whole.

Where did the pre-Strauss commentators on Machiavelli go wrong
in their attempts to decipher Machiavelli's writings? We must, I
think, pause to notice at least the major reasons. The commentators
have, over the centuries, paid insufficient attention to Machiavelli's
"nonpolitical" writings—*The Art of War, The Florentine Histories,*
the correspondence and, most especially, the little comedy entitled
The Mandrake Root, which are indispensable to a correct reading of
The Prince and *The Discourses.* They have paid insufficient attention
also to the "Epistles Dedicatory" of *The Prince* and *The Discourses,*
or at least have not taken them seriously enough as statements of
Machiavelli's intention. They have frittered away their energies on

a problem, a question-begging problem at that, which they have themselves (with Machiavelli's encouragement, to be sure) manufactured—namely, the problem of the "relation" between the political philosophy of *The Prince* and the political philosophy of *The Discourses*—refusing to consider the possibility that they are alternative statements of one and the same political philosophy. They have sought to pin Machiavelli down on a whole series of "issues" that he certainly regarded as *questions mal posées* or, worse still, nonsense questions, overlooking the fact that in one decisive dimension—the dimension in which we decide whether there are "permanent" problems in political philosophy and, if so, what the permanent problems are—Machiavelli had little or no quarrel with the classical political philosophers. They have sought to solve the problem of the "relation" between *The Prince* and *The Discourses* without first exhausting the problem of what, taken separately, each of the two books actually says. They have failed to correct, in their reading of Machiavelli, for possible error arising from the fact that they themselves, to an extent unknown to themselves, are pupils of Machiavelli, unable to read him objectively or to recognize Machiavelli's innovations as innovations. Above all, they have failed to decipher Machiavelli's writings because they have not realized that the task of deciphering Machiavelli is just that: a venture in *deciphering,* in the unraveling of an incredibly ingenious, deliberately devised puzzle, so constructed that 999 out of the 1,000 rare readers who will stay the course will never suspect that it is a puzzle.

Since that is the point at which most readers of *Thoughts on Machiavelli* will cavil (not to say lay the book aside as preposterous) as also the point on which the book must stand or fall, let us pause for some examples of how Professor Strauss reads Machiavelli.

(1) *The Prince* appears to be, and has always been read as, a "tract for the times," hair-raising because it seems to defend the wicked notion that the "end" justified the "means." As a tract for the times, however, it adds up—see (2) below—to something just short of nonsense, obliging us to raise the question whether it is in fact not a tract for the times, but a venture in political philosophy *sensu stricto,* dealing obliquely with one of political philosophy's permanent problems. Now, if we break the book up into parts dealing with different subject matters, which proves easy to do, and look at them with the "hypothesis" that Machiavelli, imitating a well-known device of the

classical writers, situates the important in the "center," we finally see
that all the central chapters deal with the same topic, namely, the
problem of the "founder," or the foundation of society. Then *The
Prince* does fall into shape as a treatise, hidden behind what appears
to be a tract for the times, on the greatest of the great permanent
problems of political philosophy. Machiavelli has given us, in "secret
writing," a major hint as to how to read his book.

(2) The famous final chapter (26) of *The Prince,* upon which the
commentators have relied most heavily in attempting to construe the
book, proves upon examination to be "sour": Machiavelli suddenly
turns "pious," speaking of "miracles" as if he actually believed in
them; Romulus suddenly disappears from the list of great "founders"
as he has given it to us earlier; the chapter appears to be a summons
to Lorenzo to lead Italy to the Promised Land, but great emphasis is
placed on Moses (of whom, beginning to catch on, we will remember
that he precisely did not reach the Promised Land, but died on its
frontiers); the chapter says nothing of the political obstacles Lorenzo
would have to surmount in order to liberate and unify Italy, though
these have been stressed in earlier chapters. If, however, we refer the
chapter to the dominant theme of the book as identified by the
central chapters, and then re-examine it, it falls neatly into place as
necessary to Machiavelli's plan, though only because it now takes on
a meaning quite different from what it seems to say. More: if we look
at Chapter 26 of *The Discourses,* we find that it deals with the topic
of the central chapters of *The Prince* and "rounds out" the central
argument of *The Prince* very nicely indeed. Machiavelli, by giving
the two chapters the same number, tells us that we must look hard
at that final chapter of *The Prince.*

(3) If we read *The Discourses* with a view to bringing together all
the "statements" Machiavelli makes on a given topic, we are obliged
to recognize that either Machiavelli was a stupid and careless fellow
who contradicted himself all over the place, or that the contradictions are intentional and have their role in the "plan" of the book.
The typical series of such statements turns out to move from a more
or less "respectable" opinion, through "qualification" after "qualification," to a final statement, decidedly not respectable, that is, *not*
qualified by any other statement and that rests upon that fuller understanding of the complex topic in hand that is, so to speak, provided
by the qualifications. Machiavelli leads us, along a path marked out

for us by apparent contradictions, to the position that he is in fact urging on his readers.

(4) *The Discourses* have an explicit "plan": the book will deal with such and such topics in such and such order. That plan, however, turns out to be a piece of deliberate deception; there is a second, "secret" plan, which we discover by, for example, identifying series of chapters linked together by references forward in concluding sentences and backward in initial sentences, or, again for example, by identifying series of chapters dealing with a single topic (for example, gratitude) not mentioned in the explicit plan. The hidden plan is the "real" plan of the book; in the act of hiding it, Machiavelli again points the way to the core of his teaching.

(5) The meticulous reader of *The Discourses* will come finally to recognize that Machiavelli is playing some kind of game as regards (a) that to which he appeals as authoritative (the example of the "ancients," the example of Rome, and so forth) and (b), more specifically, his "use" of Livy (sometimes he quotes Livy in Latin, sometimes he quotes him in Italian, sometimes he merely refers to him, sometimes he does not refer to him but uses an example so clearly taken from Livy as to be tantamount to a reference to Livy, sometimes he quotes Livy inaccurately, sometimes he changes or embroiders upon matter taken from Livy, and so forth). On one level, the problem of reading *The Discourses* becomes that of deciding whether Machiavelli is being "careless" or, once again, pointing us along toward hidden doctrines. ("It is fortunate for the historians of ideas," writes Strauss, ". . . that there are not many books of this kind.") And, here again, we find we are dealing with a pedagogical device that, off at the end, we can see to be indispensable to the realization of Machiavelli's "plan."

Thoughts on Machiavelli stands or falls, I repeat, on the issue: are *The Prince* and *The Discourses* elaborate ventures in "hidden writing," or is Strauss "seeing things"? Many readers, as this reviewer knows already from personal experience, will be able to resolve that issue—unfavorably to the book, of course—if not a priori then at the end, say, of Chapter Two ("Machiavelli's Intention: *The Prince*"), on the grounds that grown men do not "play games" of this kind in philosophical writings. Who, they will ask, ever heard of such a thing? For that reason, and the further reason that the reader who open-mindedly sets down to check it all may give six months of his life a goodbye kiss, *Thoughts* will not, for many a long day, still the debate about Machiavelli's political thought. I can only say, having checked out most of it, that in my opinion Strauss will win any future argument on the basic issue as I have stated it, that anyone who henceforth attempts to write on Machiavelli without taking *Thoughts* as his point of departure will be wasting his time, and that the "new" Machiavelli which Strauss conjures up for us out of the cryptograms, along with the "new" Hobbes, the "new" Spinoza, the "new" Locke, and the "new" Rousseau that we get in consequence of the "new" Machiavelli, will ultimately sweep the field of all competitors. The Strauss revolution in the interpretation of modern political philosophy is the decisive development in modern political philosophy since Machiavelli himself.

Does Strauss ask us to believe that he alone, among the tens of thousands of readers who have read Machiavelli's works over the centuries, has really understood him? He would, I am confident, answer that he could only wish that that were true, that on the contrary Machiavelli has been understood over the centuries, and understood precisely as Strauss understands him, by the kind of men for whom Machiavelli in fact wrote, that these men have grasped Machiavelli's plan and contributed to its execution, and that the result is nothing less than modern political philosophy. The world, I think he might add, would be a vastly more pleasant place in which to live—with philosophy itself as the major beneficiary—had the Machiavelli puzzle indeed never been solved before the mid-twentieth century.

Why did not Machiavelli (and Hobbes, and the others) just come out and say it? Why "hidden writing"? Great political thinkers, answers Strauss, are "stepsons" of their time: were they to express themselves candidly and unambiguously they would speedily run afoul of the authorities or, if not that, then be torn limb from limb by their neighbors. Indeed, one might trace the history of modern political philosophy by tracing the disappearance of the need so to hide thoughts like Machiavelli's where none but the select few can dig them up, or, to put it the other way 'round, by tracing the emergence of the need to hide thoughts unlike Machiavelli's where the unselect many, risen to the high places in the world of the intellect, are unlikely to notice them.

What was the "new" Machiavelli up to? Quite simply, if I understand Strauss, Machiavelli was out to do what Machiavelli and his "great successors" (Strauss's own phrase) have in fact done: to destroy the influence of the Great Tradition (that is, the classical-biblical tradition) in the world of the intellect. Machiavelli "imitates" the Socrates of the *Republic:* he addresses himself to the best of his young contemporaries, and through them to the young of future generations, engages them, fascinates them, and leads them by the hand, never arguing with them, into a new way of thinking about politics and morals. Socrates leads the young into classical political philosophy; Machiavelli leads the young into modern political philosophy as we know it. Neither Socrates nor the "new" Machiavelli, I repeat, sets out to "refute" the tradition he would destroy: Socrates' great skill, imitated by Machiavelli, is that of conducting his pupils through, so to speak, the "paces" of the new way of thinking, and so *habituating* them to it. The Machiavelli "problem" therefore becomes that of identifying the strategic points at which, on the very deepest level, which is that of the great permanent problems, Machiavelli takes issue with the tradition he challenges, since Machiavelli's "statements" on these issues become the axioms of the new political geometry, as they are also the only propositions in Machiavelli that Machiavelli leaves to stand without qualifications. On one side, one might say, Machiavelli's great achievement is to isolate the propositions, not necessarily explicit propositions, that are so central to the tradition that, once they are removed, the tradition crashes to the ground; the essence of Machiavellism has nothing to do with nonsense questions like that of the end justifying the means (for the "new" Machiavelli no end could justify wholly "good" means), but consists of the denial of those propositions. Machiavelli's thought, in other words, rests on an astonishing prior analysis of the classical tradition, as one may see from the following examples of the propositions Machiavelli identifies, through his denials, as strategic: Good things, the classics held, came from good beginnings; not so, replies Machiavelli, good things come precisely from bad beginnings: morality depends, alike for its birth and its sustenance, on immorality. Good things, the classical writers believed, are good simply; not so, according to Machiavelli: all good things have their characteristic defect, inseparable from their goodness. Man and political society, the classics fondly supposed, are simultaneous; not so, counters Machiavelli, thus opening the door into which Hobbes and Locke will disappear: man precedes, society, which is the handiwork of those men of great brain whom we call "founders." Man is a political animal, to whom society is natural; not so, insists Machiavelli: man is merely malleable, merely capable of a wide range of self-regarding responses to the carrot and the stick. Virtue, the classics taught, should be practiced for its own sake, and consists in habituation to good behavior; nonsense, says Machiavelli: true virtue consists in being good and bad by turns, as the "situation" may require. The desire for wealth, for glory, for freedom to do what one pleases, should according to the classics be subordinated to the requirements of the good life; not so for the new way of thinking about politics and morals: precisely what is needed, in order that there should exist that paltry minimum of good that is in fact possible, is to emancipate the desire to acquire. In order to think about politics, the classics taught, you must think of man not in terms of what he is but what he might become; not so, teaches Machiavelli, anticipating Rousseau and the entire apparatus of reductionism: in order to make sense about politics we must take men as they are, not as they might be. That Machiavelli's denials fit together into a "position" which, once you concede the axioms, is airtight (that is, impenetrable from outside), Strauss leaves no doubt. That they are the foundations of the political philosophy that today dominates the intellectual world, Strauss will convince all who do not close their ears.

Would it be too much to expect so skillful a decipherer of ciphers as Professor Strauss to write a book without including a little secret writing of his own? I think so—do not, indeed, exclude the possibility that some future Strauss will be needed, after modern political philosophy has run its course, to ferret out the "essential" Strauss, who no more than Machiavelli is a man to blurt things out. Certainly he nowhere tells us, in *Thoughts,* how the mischief the Machiavellians have done can be undone. But Strauss's silence on this point is perhaps as explicit a statement as the "situation" and the "quality of the times" call for, and what it says is: the mischief can be undone only by a great teacher who feels within himself a strength and a vocation not less than Machiavelli's own, who possesses a store of learning not inferior to Machiavelli's own, who will take the best of the young, of this generation and future generations, and, leading them by the hand without arguing with them, habituate them to the denial of Machiavelli's denials.

What Killed the Civil Rights Movement?

Where—so reads the typical last sentence of the typical letter I get these days from young students—where is that "Constitutional crisis" you predicted some months ago?

Well, I did indeed publish, two years ago (in ISI's *Intercollegiate Review*), an article entitled "The Civil Rights Movement and the Coming Constitutional Crisis"—did, indeed, therefore, by choosing that title, invite the needling. The words "coming constitutional crisis" did seem to say that the American constitutional system was heading for a major, and possibly fatal, storm,—which, let me agree at once, has not presented itself, so that I am indeed left accountable for an answer to the question, "Where's your constitutional crisis?" And I have thought I might do worse, *Phalanx* having asked me for an article on "civil rights," than to bring my thinking on the matter abreast of recent developments. That is, offer an answer to my correspondent's question. Namely this: the "forecast" I put forward two years ago was a "contingent forecast." I did not really say "there will be a constitutional crisis," but rather: "Unless one or more of the following things happen, which now seem improbable, there's a big storm ahead"—and, to my own great relief, the judgment that all those things were improbable has turned out to be incorrect. And since it is precisely such contingent forecasts that enable us to understand history as it "happens" to us—and, sometimes, to control the events that make up history—they can prove very "wrong" (the dreaded event does not occur) and, yet, eminently "correct" (because of them we "see," in retrospect, why the dreaded event did not occur).

What were those apparently improbable developments that have proved more probable than I anticipated? Well, what my article in fact said—I imitate the insurance companies and appeal to the fine print—is this: One or more of five things would have to happen in order for us to avoid a storm: (a) The Civil Rights leaders must step down the level of their demands to a point where they cease to be "openly revolutionary." (b) The Civil Rights leaders must desist from proclaiming "we will not take 'No' for an answer." (c) The American people—in the North as well as in the South—must undergo a change of mind and heart that will dispose them to say "yes" to the Civil Rights leaders. (d) The Civil Rights leaders not only get a majority of the American People on their side, but also persuade the minority to become believers in majority-rule democracy. (e) The Civil Rights leaders get their way through a series of fiats by the United States Supreme Court, and these fiats, unlike other recent Supreme Court fiats, fail to evoke widespread resistance and defiance from persons and groups, out over the country who do not like them.

Now: let's take those "developments" in reverse order, and ask where I went wrong in declaring all of them improbable.

As for (e)—the Supreme Court gives the Civil Rights leaders their "yes" by judicial fiat, and widespread defiance of judicial fiats suddenly ceases to be fashionable—I doubt if there has been any significant change in this regard since I wrote. The Supreme Court has, if anything, been less active of late than formerly on behalf of the avowed objectives of the Civil Rights leaders. Nor do I see any evidence that recalcitrants out over the country are today willing— as yesterday they were not—to concede to the Supreme Court the last word as to what the law is. *On the Contrary* (I shall make the point clearer as I proceed): the effect of recent developments has been to shift authority over the Civil Rights issues out of the hands of the Supreme Court and into other hands—a change whose significance, let me confess, I had only just begun to appreciate at the time I wrote.

As for (d)—the Civil Rights leaders get a safe majority on their side, and Americans-in-general suddenly decide to accept majority-rule democracy—here again I should say that I was right in judging such a development improbable: Far less than a year ago do the Civil Rights leaders have the ear of a majority of their fellow-countrymen and—again a point about which I shall have more to say below— *majority-rule democracy rides less high under the Johnson administration than under its predecessors.* Avoidance of the crisis cannot, then, be explained on these grounds.

As for (c)—the American people suddenly undergo a sea-change of mind and heart, and the generality of Americans suddenly decide to say "yes" to the Civil Rights leaders—well, I see no evidence of such change of heart, and certainly not in the Civil Rights Acts of 1964 or the Voting Rights Act of 1965. For I believe the meaning of those acts, as I shall try to show, about the opposite of what it seemed to be when they were enacted.

That leaves us, then, only (a)—the Civil Rights leaders step down the level of their demands, and (b)—the Civil Rights leaders begin to omit from their pronouncements the emphasis "we will not take 'No' for an answer" and the emphasis—for that also, remember, used to be present in their pronouncements—"The 'Yes' we demand must be forthcoming if not today then at the very latest tomorrow." This, I think, is the area in which the improbable has, almost imperceptibly, gone ahead and happened, the area in which recent history has brought our big surprises, the area, therefore, that we must seek to understand if we are to comprehend the lessening of tensions that now makes a constitutional crisis less and less likely.

The improbable, I say, has happened, but not because of any change *within* the Civil Rights movement: For I think the truly significant changes, the changes that will fix the future of the Civil Rights movement and postpone, probably indefinitely Kendall's constitutional crisis, have taken place *outside* the movement and almost without our taking cognizance of them. And I believe that it is those changes—not the change in tone and character of the Civil Rights movement itself but the events that have induced that change—that want talking about. Let's tick some of them off:

First, I believe the Civil Rights movement, as we knew it two years ago, has lost its steam because, in its crucial dimensions, it has been deserted by the *White* Liberals. I do not mean by that, of course, that the White Liberals, especially the White Liberal Intellectuals, have repudiated the movement, or disavowed its avowed objectives. They haven't and, given their commitments, can't repudiate it, or publicly disavow its objectives. In a very real sense, it is and always has been *their* movement, not that of its titular owners, the unavoidable result of *their* teachings about equality, about the meaning of the Fourteenth Amendment, about the incompatibility of the American Dream and the *status quo* South of the Mason-Dixon line. Given those teachings, one can safely say, indeed, that had the Civil Rights movement not come into existence the White Liberals would have had to invent it, because—well, because (to paraphrase James Burnham) he who says A must say B, and he who says B must say C, etc.,

but only, let me hasten to add, down to a certain point, and a point
likely to fall more or less short of Z. Let me put it this way: When the
Civil Rights movement did come into existence, when it first began
to describe itself as a Revolution and first began to proclaim that it
would not take "No" for an answer, there was nothing for the White
Liberals to do except go along with it, and go along with it on a "the
sky's the limit" basis. A Civil Rights demonstration violates a local
ordinace in, say, Birmingham? Well, you can't make an omelet without breaking some eggs, now can you? In general, we in America
don't approve of minorities that won't take "No" for an answer—that
is, minorities that seek to dictate policy. Well, the grievances of the
Negroes are intolerable, aren't they? One gets the impression, as one
rethinks the early history of the Civil Rights movement, that no
White Liberal spokesman or leader took the trouble to ask himself—
certainly none asked himself out loud—"Might this business go too
far? Might there come a point where I'd have to get off the train? If
I say C I must say D—but how if I say J, Must I also say K?" Most
particularly, I think—for somewhere along the line *I* should be entitled to do a little needling—no White Liberal spokesman seems to
have asked himself, "How strongly can the Civil Rights leaders count
on me once, if I may put it so, the movement gets out of the South
—once, if I may put it so, support of the Civil Rights movement isn't
one and the same thing with striking at those White Southerners,
whose Senators and Representatives block the whole Liberal program in Congress?" I do not, let me emphasize, *blame* the White
Liberals for not asking those questions early-on: their strengths are
many, and I admire them, but foresight is not one of them. And, in
any case, what is more natural than their letting their emotions get
the better of their good senses in such exciting times? What more
natural, if you like, than their overestimating, during such times, their
own revolutionary vocation? (Let that man cast at them the first stone
who has himself never overestimated his future dependability as a
hero!) And my own picture, for what it is worth, is that in the past
two years the message has gotten across, loud and clear, to the Civil
Rights leaders: Don't, from now on, expect from us the *all*-out support we've given you heretofore. We will support you, henceforth,
only when, only insofar as, the steps you take strike us as responsible,
reasonable; and we call upon you—tacitly of course—to act accordingly. And the unavoidable effect was to take much of the wind out

of the sails of the Civil Rights leaders, who were well aware—if not in their heads, at least in their hips—of their ultimate dependence on the support of the White Liberals.

Second, the Civil Rights movement has lost steam *because* of its very victories under the Johnson administration, especially the Civil Rights Act of 1964 and the Voting Rights Act of 1965. Political movements, to be sure, usually thrive on successes, whether electoral or legislative—as, at first blush, we should expect them to: such a movement, having shown its muscle by gaining first this objective (the opening of public accommodations to Negroes) and that objective (a voting rights act whose intended purpose is to get hitherto-disfranchised Negroes on the voting rolls)—what more natural than it should proceed, propelled now by forward inertia, to use that same muscle for gaining still further objectives and do so successfully? At some point, however, a movement's forward inertia becomes a matter of diminishing returns: as the number of its objectives it has already gained increases, the number of objectives still to be gained decreases, and it has, in consequence, less and less to offer to its followers; it thus loses, little by little, its capacity to mobilize them, to appeal to their hopes and expectations, to spur them into action, and thus, ultimately, its capacity to wring from its opponents the further concessions it demands. The correct statement, in other words, is that political movements thrive on success up to a point, and then, for obvious reasons, choke on it; but not, I am saying, the Civil Rights movement: success appears to be killing it long before its proper point of diminishing returns, long before it has gained so many of its objectives that we might fairly expect its muscle to go soft. And not, mind you, because the two acts of legislation were, from the standpoint of the Movement's immediate objectives, and as far as they went, "objectively" other than real victories (real victories, moreover, directly attributable to the Civil Rights leaders). They were real victories—as testified to by the opening of public accommodations throughout the South, and the addition of a million Negro voters—a smacking million—to the Southern voting registers. Nor would they ever have happened but for Dr. King, Mr. Farmer, Mr. Young, and Mr. Wilkins. But they were victories that carried with them a price, and one that has proved, I imagine, a good deal higher than any but the shrewdest observers appear to have anticipated. Let me put it this way: The Civil Rights Act and the Voting Rights Act outlawed the major *legal* disabilities of the Southern Negroes. They went a long way toward putting the Southern Negro in the same legal position as the Negro north of the Mason-Dixon line—not all the way, of course, but at least far enough to drain most of the drama off the Civil Rights leaders' onslaught against Southern legislatures and city councils, Southern courts, and Southern law-enforcement. And that, I think, was destined to be an important turning-point for at least two reasons: a) Henceforth the Civil Rights movement would no longer find itself in the politically powerful positions of demanding, from the Nation, the removal of a long series of legal anachronisms, of demanding, that is, a uniform legal treatment for Negroes throughout the United States, and of requiring, from the White Southerners, concessions which, as they themselves knew in their own hearts, they could not hold out on indefinitely. Henceforth, the Civil Rights leaders' major objectives could no longer be expressed in terms of demands for purely legal "reforms," or an insistence that their constituents were entitled to equality before the law (much, no doubt, remains to be done in that direction, but most of it, clearly, is on the undramatic side: local struggles for equal and full enforcement of laws already on statute books; lawyer's battles—that is battles in courts of law—which though potentially important collectively and in the long run, will, taken singly, prove too small and immediate to capture the attention of the general public). To put it a little differently: Henceforth the Civil Rights leaders must shift their emphasis from the *legal equality* for Negroes to *other types of equality* for Negroes (about which I shall have more to say in a moment). And b) —a similar but not the same point as that which I have just made, and perhaps a far more important point—the Civil Rights leaders must henceforth, must I repeat because of their victories, shift not only the content but the geographical focus of their demands. Yesterday, before the victories, they were taking on merely the South (for all that the pressure they brought to bear on the South blew down from the North); today and tomorrow, after the victories, they must—in their struggle for those other, non-legal forms of equality for Negroes— take on not merely the South, but the entire Nation. The victories were real victories, in short, but they were gained (as we shall see in more detail in a moment) at the expense of vastly increasing the size of the opposing forces, and of moving the major future engagements onto more difficult terrain. If, then, the victories have slowed the movement down, we—as its leaders and their constituents—should be something less than astonished. In politics, as in war, that is how the ball sometimes bounces.

Thirdly (again a similar but by no means the same point), the movement, in the act of forcing itself onto new terrain—out of the South and into the North or, if you like, into the nation as a whole —and of shifting its demands over from legal equality for the Negroes to what let's call *substantial* equality for the Negroes, has saddled itself, willy-nilly, with two problems that would give pause, forward inertia or no forward inertia, to any movement. The Civil Rights movement can't do anything much for the Northern Negro, leaving the Southern Negro aside for the moment, save as it can crack, first, deeply-rooted patterns of segregated housing all the way from California to Maine, and, second, the general problem of poverty. Put otherwise: winning *substantial* equality for the American Negro, once you have won for him his equality before the law, means first getting him out of the ghettoes in Chicago, Los Angeles, Detroit, Philadelphia, and New York (to say nothing of helping him penetrate the white ghettoes characteristic of Northern conurbations—for the ghetto, as the reader must learn to realize, is not a typical Southern institution), and, second, putting money in his pockets; and both of these are "objectives" that are going to require drastic action that must, on pain of killing the movement off, show "results" in the short term. (No sneer intended here with respect to the training and re-training programs, the Head Start programs, etc.; but, for purposes of keeping up steam, of maintaining the forward inertia characteristic of the Civil Rights movement at its moment victory in the Voting Rights Act, such programs are too slow.) Put otherwise again: The Civil Rights movement must henceforth, if it is to deliver the goods to its supposed constituents, go into the business simultaneously of reforming—nay, re-making—the American economic system, and of eliminating the existing American bias (by no means a monopoly of the American whites) against desegregated housing. And this must force the movement to pit itself against resistances of a kind it never had to face when its target was the South, and its rhetoric the rhetoric of equality before the law. To ask the nation to help force the Southerners to stop using the American legal system for purposes of discriminating against Negroes is one thing; to ask it to surrender its own strongly-held prejudices, and to launch itself on unprecedented ex-

periments with a deeply-cherished economic system, is quite another
—if only because the movement doing the asking acquires, overnight, tens of millions of opponents, many of them occupying positions of power, who yesterday may well have seemed to be its friends.
Again I say: small wonder that the Civil Rights movement has lost
steam, and that the mass communications begin to hold it at arm's
length. Small wonder, too, that my constitutional crisis has failed to
put in its appearance.

Fourthly—we must drive our analysis to still deeper levels if we are
to understand what has happened to the Civil Rights movement—we
can, I think, say this: The movement—again in part because of its
victories—has become, with certain unavoidable consequences, a
prisoner of the traditional American political system and thus of
consensus politics. Let me be very clear what I mean by that (LBJ,
I take it, does not have a monopoly on that word consensus): The
traditional American political system (as I argued in that article I
referred to above) lays down some very simple but also very severe
rules to political movements seeking drastic changes, if you like, in
the American way of life. The system has, to begin with, a profound
built-in bias against drastic changes through legislative and governmental action, thus in favor of leaving drastic changes (they do happen in America, often more swiftly than they could happen
anywhere else) to free, spontaneous action by individuals out in
American society. Industrialization, for example, a "drastic" change
if ever there was one, was brought about in America, for the most
part, by individual decisions to do things this way rather than that
way; so too with what learned people call urbanization, which happened because individual Americans decided, quite independently
of governmental action, to move themselves and their families to the
cities. The system has, secondly, a built-in bias, where change is to
be brought about by governmental action, against both legislation
dictated by minority pressure and against legislation, important legislation, that goes through by bare majority vote in Congress (as also
against legislation by one or both of the non-legislative branches of
our government). To put it a little differently—I paraphrase my out-
dated article—the American political system says to the movement
seeking drastic change through the rewriting of the nation's laws: you
must cool your heels in, so to speak, the legislative ante-chamber until
(a) the legislation you demand can pass Congress, both houses of

Congress, with overwhelming majorities, and until (b) the legislation can go into effect with the acquiescence not merely of Congress but of the President and the Supreme Court. Put the other way 'round: The system says, to the movement seeking drastic change through governmental action, you must settle, from moment to moment, year to year, decade to decade, whatever the three branches of our government (one of them, I repeat, acting by overwhelming majorities) are willing to give you; for whatever, in the first instance, the generality of our Congressmen and Senators can get together on. And that means, in practice: you must settle, from year to year and decade to decade, for just as much, just as much and no more of your "objectives," as you can "sell" to the generality of politically-active men and women out in American society.

The system, in short, has a built-in conservative bias, and has no machinery for "handling" the movement that answers: We are unwilling to wait that long; sure as we are that we are right, we want our way at once—regardless of whether we have actually won the generality of our fellow-countrymen over to our side; and, what is more, we propose, since we will not take "no" for an answer, to make an intolerable nuisance of ourselves until our demands are met. The system, I repeat, has no machinery for handling the movement that gives it that kind of answer, because the movement that makes that kind of answer in effect reads itself out of the system, enters into open rebellion against the system and, most particularly (where for whatever reason it appears to have the support of the White House and Supreme Court) against Congress, which, whatever is said in the textbooks you studied in college, remains the very heart of the system. Now: I am not saying there's any ultimate ban against rebelling against the system; that has been done now and then in the past, and will, no doubt, continue to be done through an indefinite future. I am saying that the system—it has been doing business successfully at the same stand for a long time, and knows a thing or two about maintaining itself—is likely to take steps (not necessarily punitive, or at least not openly punitive) to cut the movement down to size, to bring it back into the system's fold and so to speak, re-subordinate it to the system's rules. The system moves—moves out of its own forward inertia—to restore its own equilibrium when that equilibrium is disturbed, and it is by no means necessary to my position to say either that it takes the required steps consciously, craftily, in a "Machiavellian" manner, or, I repeat, that those steps need necessarily be openly hostile (the system might, for example, restore equilibrium by drowning its rebellious movement in cream, might kill it with kindness). Also, however, it is not necessary to my position—which is that you get the same result either way—to say that Congress does not act in a Machiavellian manner when it needs to restore equilibrium, or that the cream in which it drowns a rebellious movement is necessarily the real article—that is, cream.

Perhaps the best way to make the point here in question is this: Let's suppose—let's play like—Congress used the Civil Rights Act and the Voting Rights Act as "Machiavellian" means for killing off the Civil Rights movement insofar as it was a threat to the equilibrium of the American political system, and let's ask: What would have been going on in the minds of those crafty Congressmen? What exactly was their strategy? They would, I think, have been saying to themselves something like this: We are not about to settle in this country for government by demonstration, that is, government by minority dictation. Our job is to stop the demonstrations, or at least stop them insofar as they take a form, get by with things, that—to put it baldly —we in America would not put up with for a moment from any other minority amongst us. What we, we Congressmen, have to do, in other words, is to maneuver the movement into a position where it will have to play the game of American politics according to the rules applicable to everyone else; and—to put it baldly again—perhaps the easiest way to do that is to give in to the movement up to a certain point, and thus take away its trump cards. Maybe, just maybe, we could write and pass a couple of bills which, without changing things much as regards our way of life, without putting us in the business of enforcing a drastic change in the day-to-day behavior and habits of the generality of Americans, would nevertheless look like great victories for the movement we have in mind. What are the movement's trump cards? As we see it, they are two in number: the fact that it can appeal to the slogan "equality before the law," and the fact that it can concentrate its fire on a single, highly vulnerable geographical area, namely the South. To restate the problem: Might we pass a couple of bills that would concede, *in principle,* the whole business of "equality before the law," that, nevertheless, would not be unpalatable to the White Southerners, and that would, at the same time, get the movement, so to speak, out of the South? The poser, of course, is that phrase "not too unpalatable to the White Southerners". The bills must meet that test, because the alternative to meeting it is—to put it still baldly—the military occupation of the South; but we believe we can take care of that by, as we said a moment ago, giving in on equality before the law *in principle,* but, at the same time (a) being stingy with funds for enforcing the bills in question, and (b) so writing the new laws that they leave the White Southerners plenty of room for playing their favorite game, which is finding more or less legal means for dragging their feet as regards genuine compliance. Perhaps—just perhaps—we might even drive a wedge between the movement and its White Liberal supporters—who are, clearly, its greatest strength—by doing all that without giving the White Liberals the thing they want most, namely, to crack the power of those Southern Democratic committee chairmen. Perhaps—just perhaps— we might so write these bills that the Civil Rights leaders would even hail them as great victories, and appear, the day the President signs the bills, to collect their ball-points. Will they realize—they are smart fellows, but we think we're smarter and that they won't—will they realize that in the act of boasting of the victories they have just won they will automatically subordinate themselves to the rules of the American political system, to, among others, the rule that the system calls for government by consensus, *not* government by demonstrations? Will they realize—we, at least, don't think they will—that in praising Congress they subordinate themselves, resubordinate themselves, to Congress, and must henceforth settle, as regards muscle, for such strength as they can pile up by persuading not coercing their fellow-citizens, by relying not upon demonstrations but rational argument, upon the discussion process as we know and revere it here in America? We think we can bring that off by throwing open to Negroes the best hotels and motels and restaurants in the South—not, of course, Mrs. Murphy's boarding house; by giving Negroes in the South equal access to public facilities, and by getting enough— enough, but not too many—Negroes on the voting rolls in the South to keep that from becoming, ever again, a major or at least a very dramatic issue. Let's finagle the White Southerners into behaving not so much like Northerners—that can't be done—but at least like Texans (who ever heard of a Civil Rights demonstration in Texas?). And perhaps—just perhaps—by giving in on the Civil Rights' short term demands (for this or that that comes under the heading of "legal equality") we can divide the Civil Rights leaders, get them to fighting one another, over where to go from there.* (The present writer was alone, I think, among Conservative spokesmen in America, in hailing both the Civil Rights Act and the Voting Rights Act as great Conservative victories, thus as defeats for the Civil Rights movement and the political philosophy it represents; but I continue to think I was right, and other Conservative spokesmen wrong, on that point.)

To summarize: I have offered you four explanations of why Kendall's constitutional crisis (Which Kendall, of course, never wanted) hasn't happened. My favorite among the four, of course, is the fourth, namely: that the muscle of the Civil Rights movement had to be softened in order to restore equilibrium in the American political system, quarterbacked as it is, always, by a basically anti-egalitarian Congress. Note that I have not taken sides as to the merits of the demands of the Civil Rights leaders; what I do take sides on is the thesis of the *Federalist Papers,* namely: That America's mission in the world is to prove to the world that self-government—that is, government by the people through a representative assembly which, by definition, calls the plays—is possible. What I do take sides on is our solemn obligation, as Americans, to value the good health of the American political system—the system we have devised in order to prove to the world that self-government is possible—above the immediate demands, however just and right, of any minority. What I do take sides on is government by consensus, which, I repeat, requires of minorities demanding drastic change that they bide their time until they have pleaded their case successfully before the bar of public—not merely majority—opinion. What I do take sides on is the Preamble of the Constitution which gives equal status to justice and domestic tranquility, and so pledges us to pursue them simultaneously and not even in the "case" that seems "dearest" to a protesting minority, subordinate domestic tranquility to justice.

*This, of course, is what has happened. What is left of the Civil Rights movement is, to use the old phrase, rushing off furiously in all directions at once; and even the Meredith march, for all that it was clearly intended to, fails to restore so much as the semblance of unity.

The "Intensity" Problem and Democratic Theory*

(with George W. Carey)

Dinner is over. Mr. and Mrs. Jones and Mr. and Mrs. Smith are having coffee. The question arises: What shall we do this evening? Play bridge? Go to the movies? Listen to some chamber music from the local FM station? Sit and chat? Each, in due course, expresses a "preference" among these four alternatives but with this difference: Mr. and Mrs. Jones and Mrs. Smith, though each has a preference, "don't much care." Their preferences are "mild" or "marginal." Not so Mr. Smith. His preference is "strong." He is tired, couldn't possibly get his mind on bridge, or muster the energies for going out to a movie. He has listened to chamber music all afternoon while working on an architectural problem, and couldn't bear any more. If the group does anything other than sit and chat, he at least will do it grudgingly. He "cares enormously" which alternative is chosen.

Now: which is the "correct" choice among the four alternatives? Which, "distributive justice" to one side, is the choice most likely to preserve good relations among the members of the group? Some theorists, it would seem, find these two questions easy to answer. Mr. Smith *ought* to have his way, and good relations are likely to be endangered if he does not; and these answers are equally valid whether the other three all prefer the same thing or prefer different things. Since, for the latter, the choice is a matter of indifference, it is both "more fair" and "more expedient" (less likely to lead to a quarrel) for the group to do what Mr. Smith prefers to do.

To another but highly related point. At the Philadelphia Convention, some of the delegates drew a distinction between "temporary" or "snap" or "frivolous" majorities on the one hand, and what we may

*EDITOR'S NOTE: After this article had been accepted for publication, Willmoore Kendall died in June, 1967. I am grateful to his co-author, Professor Carey, for having assumed the entire burden of preparing this final draft. As Professor Kendall's friend and sometime collaborator, I am proud that his last published scholarly article should appear in this *Review—The American Political Science Review*.

call "serious" or "deliberate" majorities on the other. The Convention in consequence, wrote into the new Constitution severe limitations upon temporary majorities, and left the path to the statute-book open only to serious, deliberate majorities—that is, majorities able to keep themselves in being long enough to gain control of both houses of Congress, of the Presidency, and of the Supreme Court. Why penalize the frivolous majorities? One possible answer seems to be this: Frivolous majorities will, in due course, prove to have been more or less indifferent on the policy-issue being decided because they will *not* remain in being long enough to gain mastery of the constitutional machinery. In other words, they will show, by their subsequent behavior, that they "didn't much care," in contrast to serious majorities which will, because their preferences are "strong," "stick to their guns."

The two situations sketched above, the one posing a problem in "moral" theory the other a problem in "political" theory, have not always been regarded as *in pari materia*. There is no evidence that the 55 at Philadelphia, though they certainly distinguished between frivolous and deliberate majorities, rested the distinction on the supposed relative strength of the preferences, or the opinions, of the individuals involved. They did not, on the record at least, go behind the distinction to ask, why does the frivolous majority turn out to be frivolous, while the serious or determined majority does not? But "we," in mid-Twentieth Century America, see at once the comparability, nay the identity, between the two situations. Because our "democratic theory" is more sophisticated than theirs, we readily bring the two situations together as illustrations of the "problem of intensity": Mr. Smith's "preference," being more "intense" than that of the others, should "weigh" more than theirs. Frivolous majorities, because they reflect "preferences" that are not "intense," must bide their time in favor of majorities that reflect "preferences" that are "intense."

What we fashionably call the "problem of intensity" *is* a problem for democratic theory. We today are indeed more sophisticated about it, as a matter of explicit theory, than the Framers seem to have been. But that does not necessarily mean we have a more sophisticated solution of the problem than theirs. It may be we have greater sophistication. The Framers, however, may have had the better answers. One purpose of this article is to investigate that possibility.

It would be difficult to say when the phrase "the problem of intensity" first began to be heard in the land.[1] But we can say when, and in what book, it appears first to have been hauled out into the open and made the topic of a self-conscious venture in theoretization.[2] And we may safely add that it is a problem that had to arise, in due course, once people had begun to speak pejoratively of "apathetic" majorities, and to question the validity, or legitimacy, of the latter's claim to act for the entire electorate. For from the concept of the "apathetic" majority it is a brief step to the concept of the "non-apathetic," that is, "intense" majority, and the idea that "intensity" is the dimension in which to measure the difference between the apathetic majority and the majority that is not apathetic. Concretely, the "intensity" problem, as we know it, arises out of analysis of a "special case" under the theory of majority-rule, or "populistic" democracy. This theory assumes, as Professor Dahl put it, that decisions should be made according to "The Rule,"[3] or, as one of the present writers put it many years ago, the "majority principle," the principle that the majority should "have its way."[4]

Now: the Rule does not, in its pure form, make qualitative distinctions among members of the group. For purposes of constituting the majority that is to have its way, all are equal to every other one. Each in voting gives his consent to the proposed decision, which only he can give or withhold and which, for that reason and because consent is the only possible basis for right, for legitimacy, must be counted equally with everybody else's consent. Translated into the more sophisticated language of the recent literature, the Rule becomes: The decision-making group adopts the decision that is "preferred by most members," each member deciding for himself what he prefers, and each expression of preference being counted as of equal "weight" with every other. What is being weighed are preferences, and vote-taking is the scale on which they are weighed. So matters stood in

---

[1] The senior author of this article first became aware of it in the course of a conversation with Charles Hyneman, in 1937 or 1938.

[2] Robert A. Dahl, *A Preface to Democratic Theory* (Chicago: University of Chicago Press, 1956), whose reasoning we have attempted to reproduce in our two "situations." See, in particular, Ch. 4.

[3] Dahl, *op. cit.* See, also, Ch. 2.

[4] Willmoore Kendall, *John Locke and the Doctrine of Majority Rule* (Urbana: University of Illinois Press, 1941). See also: Austin Ranney and Willmoore Kendall, *Democracy and the American Party System* (New York: Harcourt, Brace and Company, 1956), Chs. 1-4.

majority-rule theory for a long while—until, we repeat, doubts began
to arise in some minds about decisions backed up not by a majority
tout court but by an "apathetic" majority. Again translating into the
more sophisticated language of the recent literature, an apathetic
majority is a majority made up to a greater or lesser extent of persons
who indeed "prefer" the proposed decision, but do not prefer it
"strongly." And the question arises: If what we are weighing is preferences, does it make sense to let a "weak" preference count equally
with a strong one. Perhaps the Rule should speak not of the decision
"preferred by most members," but of the decision "most preferred
by members," which, clearly, is not necessarily the same thing. And,
once that possibility is conceded, a number of further questions unavoidably arise: Is there a way of "telling," at the moment the vote is
taken, which members have "strong" or "intense" preferences, and
which "weak" or "apathetic" preferences? If there is, can we go
further and somehow distinguish between "stronger" preferences
and "less strong" preferences? Can we, that is to say, "weigh" preferences at all? And if the answer to both questions is "Yes," does it
become incumbent upon us to devise the electoral machinery of the
future populistic democracy, assuming we can do so, in such fashion
as to make sure that the policy alternative shall prevail which is "most
preferred?" What then happens to the "political equality" that is the
point of departure of the theory of populistic democracy? Are citizens to be made "less than equal" just because the issue being voted
on is one on which they do not happen to feel strongly? More, though
here we venture perhaps into less familiar territory: If political equality is to be compromised to take into account differences in intensity,
are there—might there be—other differences of which the electoral
machinery should take account? Should differences in knowledge (a
strong preference, after all, might be based on ignorance, while an
equally strong preference may be based on sound knowledge) also be
considered? What about differences in probity? An individual's
strong preference for a given measure might—just might—be born of
deeply-rooted anti-social tendencies on his part. Should it nevertheless be counted equally with the equally strong preference of the man
motivated by thoughts of the general welfare? Is it true that a system
that does not take intensity into account is probably headed for
trouble? And, *per contra,* would a system that does take intensity into
account generate problems peculiar to itself? All of these, clearly, are

questions that are inescapable, and they are, demonstrably, questions that lead us to the very heart of political theory as it is generally understood in our democratic age. More: they point, in our opinion, to new and potentially fruitful areas of inquiry, the exploitation of which would broaden and deepen our understanding of democratic institutions and precedures.

In the hope, first of all, of clarifying the problem on which these questions touch, we shall: (1) try to show that the "intensity" problem is all too easily and frequently confused with certain other problems to which it bears a superficial cousinly resemblance, but which are, in fact, unrelated to it and, simultaneously, endeavor to show what the problem, once correctly formulated, does and does not involve; (2) put forward and defend the thesis that differences in "intensity" do indeed pose certain problems, problems as to the relation between majority and minority in the self-governing political community, of which the political theory of such a community must take account and in so doing, attempt to evaluate the effort, on the part of previous theorists, to deal with those problems; (3) raise and attempt to answer, again with an eye to the democratic theory of the past, the question: Can we conceive of a political system that, while remaining faithful to the axioms of populistic democracy, would "measure" and take into account differences of intensity? Or to put it otherwise: What minimum requirements would such a system have to meet; and (4) with the foregoing in mind, venture to suggest certain standards or criteria, by which we can assess the "performance" of this or that political system over against the problem of intensity.

I. The Nature of the "Intensity" Problem

The problem of intensity as we know it has, as noted above, arisen as a special problem in the theory of populistic democracy. It is not, however, peculiar to that theory. Any theoretical answer to the question "How is the self-governing community to govern itself?" must, soon or late, make a decision as to the extent to which policies are to reflect the individual preferences of members of the community, and as to whether, in order to be reflected accurately, those preferences are (as we have now learned to state it) to be merely counted, or *both* counted and weighed. Moreover, any answer to the question, "How is a *non*-democratic political system to be viable?" can ignore differences in the intensity of individual preferences at its peril. (A Stalin, and even more certainly a de Gaulle, well knows that the stability of his regime requires him, first, to see that not too many individuals out among the governed become too disaffected, and, second, to see that enough individuals out among the governed view his policies with a degree of approval well above the "average.") The intensity problem, then, emerges as a universal problem of politics.[5] To put the same point a little differently: Although we are accustomed to hear of the intensity problem from writers who speak out of a concern for "individual rights," "the rights of the minority," the "prerequisites" of democracy, etc., we must not conclude that the problem arises exclusively out of those concerns, or that it is exhausted once those concerns are taken care of. Put otherwise again: The question "Should there be limitations on the powers of the minority in a democratic political system?" is by no means congruent with the question, "Should a democratic political system take into account differences in the intensity of individual preferences?" The first of these questions does, to be sure, readily translate itself into the second in certain circumstances. For example, where existing limitations on the power of the majority themselves become, at a given moment, an "important" political issue; or where, again for example, the legitimacy or meaning of this or that claim to "individual rights" or "minority rights" is in dispute, and the attachment or non-attachment of individuals out in the community to those rights is put to the test. Clearly, however, there is a wide range of political issues, about which the self-governing community must make decisions, that have nothing to do either with rights or with limitations on the power of the majority and that, nevertheless, pose the dilemma: "Are we merely to count preferences, or weigh them?"

Another point is this: it must be clearly understood that the intensity problem is not and cannot be exhausted by focusing attention, as theorists have shown a marked tendency to do, on the "extreme case," namely, the "apathetic majority" *versus* the "intense minority," and then proceeding to show that in such a case the

---

[5]For the most part we will discuss the problem in the context of the populistic model of democracy. However, most of what we have to say is also applicable to other "models" of democracy.

minority must, whether for "ethical" or prudential reasons, be given its way. Far from exhausting the real problem, the "extreme case" merely exposes the Achilles heel of the theorists who have yielded to its fascination, which we may put as follows: Up to a certain point in the argument, everything is simple: One man, one equal vote; in the absence of unanimity, the majority decision is accepted as the decision of the community. Suddenly, however, the "extreme case" presents itself, at least as a theoretical possibility that the theorist must not ignore, and he finds himself unwilling to administer to the patient the medicine his prescription calls for. Suddenly, that is to say, merely counting preferences is not good enough, and they must be weighed as well as counted, and weighed in such a manner that the heavier ones tip the scale more than the lighter ones. "The Rule" then gives way to another rule—which, we are told, is called for by considerations alike of fairness and of expediency. Now: no theorist of the extreme case—such at least is our thesis—has ever faced up to the difficulties that, so to speak, cry up at one out of this sudden transition: How is it to be justified?[6] If it can be justified in the extreme case, why not in the case somewhat short of the extreme, and if in the latter why not in the case that is not extreme at all—that is, in *all* cases? The extreme case, to the extent that it is taken into account at all, can only drive home the following theoretical unavoidable truth: The choice between merely counting on the one hand, and weighing on the other hand, is an *exhaustive* choice, about which you simply can *not* have it both ways. Having once made his choice between "preferred by most" and "most preferred," the theorist is, so to speak, stuck with it, and must apply his rule to all cases that present themselves. Nor is it any answer here to say, "Ah! we

[6]See Henry Mayo, *Introduction to Democratic Theory* (New York: Oxford University Press, 1960). Mayo writes: "It is often objected . . . that to count each person . . . equally is absurd: some people feel more strongly about certain issues than others. Would it not fly in the face of common sense and elemental fair play to argue that 50% plus one of the lukewarm should overrule 50 percent minus one consisting of passionate dissenters? In such artificial terms the answer is yes" (p. 178). Mayo offers no justification for this stance except that such a condition would not arise save possibly in the case of "alienated or permanent" minorities.

Dahl writes: "Even an individual who finds the Rule reasonable in cases where he believes the intensity of desire is about the same among the individuals in the minority and majority might find it intolerable in the type of cases cited above, where x is only slightly preferred by a bare majority and y is very strongly preferred by a bare minority. Indeed, probably no one would advocate the Rule for every situation": *op. cit.*, p. 49. Dahl offers no justification for the switch on ethical grounds but does introduce the value of stability. See our comments below.

shall devise a system that both counts and weighs preferences" and not merely, or primarily, because no theorist of populistic democracy has yet brought forward any suggestion as to how this might be done (though that is a not uninteresting fact), but rather because the two rules are mutually incompatible, so that to move from the first to second is to repudiate, not merely compromise, the first. In other words, if it *were* possible to devise a procedure that would simultaneously count preferences and weigh them, that procedure would be outlawed by each of the two rules—or, if you like, by each of the two principles that, respectively, underlie the two rules.

Nor is that all: The argument for the sudden switch from counting to weighing, or from counting to some combination of counting and weighing, owes much of its plausibility, we believe, to a tacit assumption on the part of some that intensity is a "discrete" not a "continuous" variable; that is, more precisely, an intensity curve may be neatly chopped up into sections, which may be labelled "low," "medium," or "high." Perhaps this explains the emphasis in our literature on minorities whose preferences are of "high" intensity, together with the implication that you move from the first rule to the second at the point on the curve that divides "medium" intensity from "high" intensity.[7] But this assumption is clearly unwarranted, since there is no such point; for intensity, in the very nature of the case, is a continuous variable which affords no point in particular at which "things become different" in the manner assumed. The moment at which the political system is to shift gears from the first to the second rule cannot, if we start with the assumption that intensity is a continuous variable, be formulated in operationally significant language. (See text below.) Nor can this difficulty be circumvented by shifting attention from the absolute level of intensity of minority or majority preferences over to the ratio or proportion between the intensity of the one and the intensity of the other. In our view, that would make it more difficult to define, in operational terms at least, the point at which to make the transition, since the ratio in question is again a continuous variable, and, on the face of it, more complex

[7]Such a conception of intensity has been fostered by polls which measure *direction* of opinion (agree-disagree) and also attempt to measure *depth* by asking the respondent "how much" (i.e., to what extent) he agrees or disagrees—e.g., strongly, mildly, etc. For reasons we will note below it is highly doubtful that such polls measure intensity in terms that are meaningful for a political system designed to handle the intensity problem.

in character than the curve that measures absolute intensity.

In speaking of the incompatibility of the two rules, and of the principles underlying them, we have of course been emphasizing the so-called "ethical" aspect of the problem. The conclusion we have reached is that any arguments used to justify weighing instead of counting in the "extreme case" would be equally applicable to any case short of the extreme. But we reach the same result if we forget about "fairness" and attempt to state the case for weighing, or counting and weighing, instead of merely counting, in terms of the "stability" of the political system, and content ourselves with the plea: Let us, in the extreme case, weigh instead of count, because otherwise the system will, like London Bridge, come tumbling down. Here we encounter, to begin with, two baffling "technical" difficulties: First, the "stability" that now becomes the "goal" of the political system must, if it is to do useful service as a goal, be given an operationally precise definition, which (a) probably cannot be done, and (b) would, if it were done, merely give rise to further problems. Is "stability" to be equated with the perpetuation of existing formal institutions, structures, and processes, governmental and social? Is it, rather, to be equated with compliance on the part of the governed with the laws and regulations the system produces—that is, with the absence of violent resistance on the part of individuals to policies to which they are opposed? If the former, are we to understand that the political system we seek is, *a priori*, to exclude "change" except by unanimous agreement? If not that, then we must ask "How much change can the system accommodate and yet be called 'stable'?" If the latter—if, that is, we equate "stability" with the absence of violent resistance—we run hard up against the difficulty that no system can reduce violent resistance to the zero point. So we must again, soon or late, define in operationally significant terms the point on the continuum at which the amount of anticipable violent resistance warrants the shift from counting to weighing.[8] And, since different persons in any community are certain to place different valuations upon "stability" (as opposed to change) no matter how defined, as also upon the elimination of violent resistance (as opposed to bringing to bear the coercive force necessary to prevent it) no matter how defined; since, more-

---

[8]This job remains for our present day "behaviorists." Though apparently determined to remain ethically neutral, they are still forced back upon stability or "system persistence" for justification of their enterprises.

over, the differing valuations will be projected on differing levels of intensity; we find once again that the answer we have before us raises more problems than, even ideally, it can be said to solve. To all of which we must add this: The "case" for weighing preferences in order to assure "stability," whatever its merits or demerits, is clearly incompatible with the case for weighing preferences in the name of "fairness," save as we are prepared to assume that fairness and stability always come down, in politics, to one and the same thing.

There are, let us notice, several readily discernible difficulties involved in any proposal, brought forward in the name of "stability," for identifying a point on the curve at which a populistic democracy must cease to merely count votes and begin to weigh them because they are intense:

a) Suppose, *arguendo,* that we have identified the "strategic" point on the curve, and have been able to formulate the necessary rule in operationally meaningful terms, so that we can now recognize, with confidence, the set of conditions in which the system must shift gears. Suppose, again *arguendo,* a series of decisions in which this set of conditions is approached but not quite reached. There would then seem to be no need for the system to shift from counting to weighing. But we are compelled to ask: Would such a system really work? Would stability, no matter how defined, be insured? We can easily imagine the following state of affairs: Individuals with intense preferences just slightly below the point or level at which we are supposed to make the transition from counting to weighing being frequently thwarted or denied by the system. This could well create a very special type of intensity, not related to any specific policy issue before the population, but rather with respect to the very system itself. At this point, of course, the intensity might be of such a degree as to warrant a shifting of gears. But we can also readily imagine at this stage of the process a second group consisting of the highly intense "victors" in the series of decisions that has produced this state of affairs, exhibiting a degree of intensity for the system that would also warrant a shift from counting to weighing. What now? It seems clear to us that by recognizing intensity as a factor to be taken into account, the system, through the cumulative effects of its own operation, might very well paint itself into such a corner. In the last analysis, it has no means to solve this kind of problem.

b) Because, first, the system as envisaged here is an open invitation to minorities to "fake" the symptoms that identify it as a threat to stability; because, second, a significant number of individuals caught up in the system may, in any case, get to feeling intensely on any side of any question; because, third, the system can, since it is by definition indifferent to all ethical considerations except the maintenance of stability, exclude no decision desired by a minority that meets the conditions for shifting gears; and because, fourth, we cannot imagine a population whose rank and file members are themselves so emancipated from ethical considerations as to be willing to elevate stability to the position of a *summum bonum* (which is what the system calls on them to do)—for all these reasons, we submit, the shift-gears-for-the-sake-of-stability system has a built-in potential for generating an instability all its own. It will, predictably, produce legislation that a (to be sure) greater or lesser number of voters will deem ethically outrageous, thus intolerable, and thus reason enough for upsetting the applecart. The stability-at-any-price system, on the face of it, emerges as an ingenious machine for the *manufacture* of the kind of intensity that produces instability. That perhaps helps explain the fact that no democratic theorist has ever actually assigned to stability as such the high "rank," amongst democracy's goods, here in question. (And, we may note in passing, the point we have just made would be equally applicable if the system's founders built in its arrangements for weighing votes not in the name of stability but in the name of fairness. It would still leave intense minorities free to force on it legislation that would produce a countervailing intense minority and, at the margin, a countervailing intense majority.)

Let us now confront the central difficulty in all this: Populistic democracy (or, if you like, the theorists of populistic democracy) cannot take intensity into account. Populistic democracy's bets, unlike those of the traditional political philosophy against which it is in open revolt, are on the notion that a political system can be adjudged good or bad according as authoritative decisions within it emanate from a certain "source" (to use Bertrand de Jouvenel's terminology) —from, concretely, the majority of a voting population made up of political equals, and not some minority. Its bets are on the notion, that is to say, that the majority must get its way. Its (and its theorists') only possible answer to the question, Suppose the majority doesn't much care, while the minority cares "intensely"? is: "So much the worse for the minority. If it feels so strongly about the matter, let it get out and win a majority over to its side." For a theorist of populistic democracy even to flirt with the idea of giving the minority its way is to appeal to "values" (e.g., justice or stability), and this he cannot do because the theory has cut itself off, once and forever, *ab initio,* from such considerations. The theorist can appeal to these or similar values only at the cost of admitting to himself that he has been wrong all along. In sum: If it is justice we are interested in, or stability, or justice and stability, and not merely equality, then we had best, as constructive founders of a democracy, build from the first moment with those goods in mind. The "intensity" problem, we repeat, merely exposes the Achilles-heel of the whole populistic democracy approach to the problem of how a people is to govern itself, that Achilles-heel being an exclusive concentration, for purposes of evaluating political systems, upon the "source" of decisions rather than the quality of their "content." It cannot, for the reasons we have been expounding in this section, meet the problem by switching to a new "source" (even if that new source could be justified on its principles, which the intense minority cannot be). It must go back to the beginning, and make a fresh start.

This is not to say that the "intensity problem" is not a real problem of democratic theory, or that any democracy could be viable that failed, in some manner, to take it into account. It *is* a real problem, but one that populistic democracy cannot solve. Put otherwise: it remains true, as a matter of history, that the intensity problem has arisen as a special problem in the theory of populistic democracy; but it has not, on our showing here, arisen there properly, because populistic democracy has no hooks for grappling with it.

II. Theoretical Consequences of Differences in "Intensity"

We are not, let us reiterate, denying that there is an "intensity problem" in politics, of which democratic theory, the theory of the self-governing society, certainly must take account. All we are saying, up to this point, is a) that the theory of populistic democracy cannot, on its own basic premise, properly recognize it as a problem; and b) that, even if it could, it cannot, on its own basic premise, conceivably "do" anything about it (i.e., the only "principled" answer it can give to an outvoted "intense" minority in political society is, as indicated above, "So much the worse for you"). To those two points we may now add this one: contemporary democratic theory, because of the parochialism that lies at its very heart, has uncritically committed itself to the assumption that democratic theory and the theory of populistic democracy are one and the same thing—that, if you like, any theory that refuses to accept the populistic-democracy model, at least as a paradigm that all self-governing societies must seek to approximate at the earliest possible moment, is *ipso facto* anti-democratic, or if not that, non-democratic.[9] One purpose of the present article, let us confess, is to combat that manifestation of parochialism.

With that in mind, let us approach our topic from another angle: The majority of the enfranchised in the self-governing society, we are told in a now vast corpus of political literature, might use its power to determine the result of an election as a means for writing rules into the statute-book (or even into the Constitution, if there be one), or for implementing policies, which violate the "rights" of "minorities" or of individuals; it might violate this or that allegedly indisputable principle of morality (or, what is equally reprehensible, perpetuate injustices); it might act foolishly, or out of ignorance, or out of momentary passion; and it might, all that entirely apart, ignore potential minority resistance to its legislation or policies and so produce defiance of the law, resistance to governmental action, and, at the margin, civil war. So the question gets itself asked: Is it possible, through the electoral process, to have it both ways, that is, somehow restrain the majority when, for any of the foregoing reasons, it "ought" to be restrained, and yet not challenge its "right" to "control" the government and, through the government, both legislation and policy-making? Much of the theory of the self-governing society handed down to us from the past (i.e., from the days before the advent of the theory of populistic democracy) insists, as is well known, that the correct answer to that question is "Yes, you can have it both ways." Calhoun's "concurrent majority" system, for example, says in effect, "Yes—by giving the minority the power to veto acts of the majority; that is, by letting the minority, any minority it would

[9]We need hardly document the fact that one of the major preoccupations of many political scientists, since at least the turn of the century, has been advocacy of reforms calculated to bring our institutional fabric more in line with the seeming requirements of populistic principles. Proposals for the reform of Congress, of the party system, and of the electoral college, as also the current reapportionment movement, reflect this.

seem, decide when the majority 'ought' to be restrained."[10] Similarly, John Adams' theory of the balanced constitution says in effect: "Yes, by giving the 'natural aristocracy' the power to veto acts of the majority and thus to decide when the majority 'ought' to be restrained."[11] Clearly, however, neither succeeds in having it both ways, since neither is in the slightest concerned with the majority's "right" to control the government (though it is always amusing to remember that Calhoun appears to have had no quarrel with that right on the level of state government). Equally clearly, neither seems about to lose any sleep over the distinction between "intense" minorities and minorities that are something less than intense, or that between majorities that are "apathetic" and minorities that are something less than apathetic. Alike, Calhoun's veto and Adams' veto could be wielded by a minority only marginally concerned with the issue at stake. J. S. Mill, though he perhaps moves a trifle closer to the theory of populistic democracy, seeks a solution to the problem in an "artificial balance" between "classes," maintained through a system of "plural voting" which, again, reflects an indifference to the "right" of the merely numerical majority to control legislation and policy, and demands of the plural voters only that amount of "intensity" that will call them away from their normal pursuits, whether of foxes or of learning, long enough to cast their "extra" votes.[12] Aristotle's polity, looking as it does to a "natural" rather than "artificial" balance, that is, to a situation in which the middle-class is as large as, or larger than, the poor class and the rich class, does depend upon the majority, that is, the middle class, conceived as possessing qualities that will dispose it to restrain itself, and therefore "saves" majority control of the government—though at the expense of any minority veto, and without regard (save as the majority itself may take it into account) to the "intensity" of the minority. (In the absence of such a natural balance, Aristotle is fully prepared to subordinate majority-rule to "justice" and "stability." Here, also, "intensity" figures in his formulations at most by implication, and of course even then only as bearing upon "stability," not "justice".)[13]

---

[10] *A Disquisition on Government.* R. K. Cralle (ed.), *The Works of John C. Calhoun,* Volume 1.

[11] *Defence of the Constitutions of Government of the United States.* Charles Francis Adams (ed.), *The Works of John Adams,* Volume IV.

[12] *Considerations on Representative Government* (London, 1861), *passim.*

[13] *The Politics of Aristotle,* Ernest Baker (trans.) (New York: Oxford University Press, 1962).

Now: Let us hold all that aside, and do a little thinking of our own. If the majority is to be restrained when it ought to be restrained, the power to restrain it must vest either (a) in the majority itself; (b) in some minority; or, if that means anything (as we believe it does) (c) in the people as a whole, thought of as acting through what some of us like to call "consensus." Any proposal for lodging the power to restrain in some minority, on the face of it, ends you up with minority *dictation*. Instead of solving the problem of the self-governing society, it merely sweeps it aside. To paraphrase *The Federalist,* the self-governing society cannot vest the "last say" in a minority and must never forget that the basic principle of the self-governing society is *some* form of the majority-principle—which, as Publius well knew and as our contemporary parochials forget, can take many forms. It cannot vest the "last say" in any minority, moreover, as the adverse critics of Calhoun and Adams are quick to point out, because no minority can be counted on not to abuse its veto power, and use it to its own advantage at the expense of the common good. It cannot, again, vest the power to restrain the majority in the majority itself, because there is no more reason to expect the numerical majority to restrain itself when and only when it ought to be restrained, than to expect this or that minority to restrain it when and only when it ought to be restrained. What, then, about the third possibility we mention —that of the majority being restrained by the whole people? Is it nonsensical on the face of it, since it calls upon the whole people to perform an action that the majority of the whole people is opposed to? We shall return to this below. For the moment, we can only say that *if* the idea is nonsensical, then so is the whole idea of restraining the majority when it ought to be restrained without ending yourself up with minority dictation. The restrained majority becomes a will-o'-the-wisp.

Let us now hold all that also aside, and do a little further thinking of our own. Let us imagine a society, determined to be a self-governing society, with a total population of only two individuals, X and Y, with differing notions about legislation and public policy, and let us fix our attention for the moment on X. *To the extent* that X is to have his way (we are about to see why he will not have his way completely), he will get it only if, and to the extent that, he enlists Y's cooperation, alike in the short and long term. Now: Is it not clear, Y having by definition ideas (or "preferences") of his own, that one of the "prices" X is going to have to "pay" for Y's cooperation is that of not proposing, and certainly that of not doing, things that he knows Y will find absolutely unacceptable? And if that is clear, is it not also clear that Y's potential sense of outrage is merely the "extreme case," at one end of a continuum, the other end of which is X's proposing and doing things to which Y will respond with enthusiastic approval? Which is to say: another method by which X can enlist Y's cooperation is to propose and do things that will please Y. And in between the two extreme cases lie an infinite number of courses X can adopt, that will, in descending order, please Y less and less and, beyond a certain point, an infinite number of courses that, in ascending order, will displease Y more and more. Y the more pleased is the more likely to cooperate; Y the more displeased the less likely to.

Now, if these propositions be correct, the following corollaries and inferences seem to us to follow:

a) If X needs Y's cooperation in order to effectuate purposes of his upon which he places value, yet ends up so displeasing Y, or failing to please him, as not to get him to cooperate, X must recognize, retrospectively, that he has acted irrationally. The more irrationally, we hasten to add, to the extent that he had means of knowing, beforehand, that his behavior would lose him Y's cooperation. Similarly X will have acted rationally if, needing Y's cooperation, he behaves in such manner as to please Y, or not to displease him, to the extent needed in order to carry Y with him. It is by no means a matter of the stability of the system and, at the margin, of X avoiding a set-to with Y; it is a matter of X being able to use the system, through time, for the realization of the purposes he cherishes. And, of course, all that we have said of X with respect to Y goes for Y with respect to X. Each, to the extent that he has purposes he expects to realize through the political system, and recognizes a need for the other's cooperation, must give thought to pleasing and/or not displeasing the other enough to keep him from withholding his cooperation.

b) Both X and Y will, clearly, always be deciding for themselves whether to give or withhold their cooperation—and whether, insofar as that is the determining factor (it is not, of course, the only one; see below), and to what extent each is pleased or displeased by the other's legislative-and-policy-proposals. Each, moreover, knows this about the other. Either, therefore, might—just might—attempt to deceive the other, or even himself, as to the "price" the other must pay for his cooperation; that is, either might—just might—try to get out of the other a little more of what pleases him, or to shoo the other off a little further from that which will displease him, by exaggerating the likelihood of his withholding his cooperation unless *his* wishes are met, his "preferences" recognized and ministered to. One major component of the art of politics in the self-governing society is skill in raising and answering the question: "This *démarche* I am about to propose—whom is it going to please, whom displease, and how much?" And that question, clearly, leads to the further question: "How can I tell?"

c) The "intensity problem" in democratic theory is, then, by no means merely a matter of a people feeling strongly *against* legislation or policy; it includes, as an equally important dimension, people feeling strongly *for* legislation or policy. (This fact is implicitly, but only implicitly, recognized in those formulations of the problem that set the "apathetic" majority against the "intense" minority, which is always thought of as being against what the majority is about to do. We do not hear explicitly—such at least is our impression—of intensely pleased minorities, or of intensely displeased majorities.) And, what is more important, the "intensity problem" is by no means peculiarly a problem of majorities over against minorities. One is tempted to say, indeed, that the normal situation in democratic policies *is* the "apathetic" majority, the majority not sufficiently concerned with or informed about the issues at stake, over against *two* "intense" minorities. Put otherwise: the X and Y of our two-man self-governing society have as their normal counterpart, not a majority and a minority, but two minorities, neither of which can hope to effectuate its purposes without eliciting some degree of cooperation from the other, with the majority playing pretty much a spectator's role until the intense minorities (in the U.S. Senate, for example, the ADA'ers and the major Southern senators plus a Hruska or two) work out a frontier treaty. One is tempted to say, in other words, that the "apathetic" majority is the normal majority, not only out among the enfranchised but even in the legislative assembly of the self-governing society; but that it stands over against not *an* "intense" minority, but two or more intense minorities.[14]

[14]Virtually all of the survey studies to date testify to the fact that the American people are "apathetic," at least in the sense that they do not know or care about the major issues of public policy. Our conception of the political process runs along these lines: The proponents of change and the resisters of change have to plead their cases

d) One interesting and unavoidable complication that suggests itself, in the light of the foregoing, is that an "intense" X may transform an "apathetic" Y into an intense Y by seeking to exact too high a "price" for his cooperation—i.e., by overestimating Y's need for him. Another component of the art of politics, therefore, is skill in not making that kind of mistake. Both X and Y must continually put to themselves, and try to answer correctly, such questions as: "How badly does he, the other, need my cooperation? Am I demanding more, in the way of being pleased or not being displeased, than I can get?" Each X and Y—dropping now our supposition that there are only two individuals involved in the system—has his own hierarchy of purposes, and, we repeat, must arrive at his own judgment as to the price he is prepared to pay, perhaps in the form of giving up on some of his purposes, for the cooperation of other X's and Y's. Thus a "passionate minority" of X's might, for example, by seeking to exact too high a price for its cooperation, or failing to offer a sufficiently high price for the acquiescence of an "apathetic majority" of Y's, transform the latter into a "passionate majority" (a fact that certain leaders of the contemporary Civil Rights movement may now be pondering). In short, any group, minority or majority, in the self-governing society, must, to the extent that it is rational in the pursuit of its objectives, constantly ask itself: "Are we going too far—are we, so to speak, over-bidding our hand?" And since groups are made up of individuals, the same thing is true of each individual member of any group. To spell the point out completely in terms of our original model, with the addition of Z: X knows that there are issues about which he feels more (or less) strongly than Y and Z appear to feel about them, and knows that his own decision as to whether to give to or withhold from Y and Z or Y or Z the cooperation they wish from him, must be made in terms of a calculation that he must make for himself—erroneously, perhaps—with an eye to the intensity of his own feelings; and he will probably assume that Y and Z, who appear to belong to the same species of animal as himself and are, presumably, much like him, are making similar calculations. The problem, we may fairly say, is common to all political systems, whether the theorists of the system are aware of it or not. Nor is it by any means confined to the "politically active" (e.g., in a democracy, the "elector-

before what may aptly be termed a "jury" of persons non-involved in or non-affected by the "issue" at stake.

ate"). The "non-voter," or even the slave, can, if only by resisting, rock the boat, and this brings him also within the confines of the "intensity problem." Only to the extent that the system "handles" the problem well is the cooperation it requires likely to be forthcoming.

e) Returning now to the "special case" of "the majority" over against "the minority" or "minorities," there emerge, in the context of the foregoing, a number of apparent paradoxes that are highly relevant to that general problem in any self-governing political society, and suggest certain minimum conditions that the latter must meet if it is to avoid tripping itself up over the "intensity problem" (a matter to which we shall return in Section III). Specifically, these apparent paradoxes are significant because they help us to understand not only why majority-rule systems (we do *not*, we repeat, equate "majority-rule system" and "populistic democracy") have not only shown a capacity to survive, but also to survive in a general atmosphere of willing cooperation and "good feeling."

First: the majority-principle and the unanimity-principle are not, though they appear to be and are generally thought to be, *ipso facto*, mutually exclusive. On the contrary. What makes a democracy workable, and hence viable, is precisely the apparently impossible combination of these two principles in a "system" whose characteristic feature is this: it gets its decisions made by the majority, but in such fashion that those decisions elicit what amounts to unanimous, or virtually unanimous, support or acquiescence. Just as the individuals X and Y, though disagreeing about this or that policy issue, may both, the one who does not get his way equally with the one who does, string along with the decision arrived at by the "system," so the minority may string along with the majority's decision—whether because of devotion to the majority-principle as such, or because it finds itself, overall, not too discontented with the results the system produces.

Second, "restraints" on the power of the majority need not be thought of exclusively (as some, at least, are in the habit of thinking of them) as either (1) of necessity imposed from some "outside" quarter (e.g., a Constitution, or a Supreme Court), or (2) as self-imposed out of devotion to the idea of "minority rights," or (3) as necessarily "anti-majoritarian," "anti-majority rule," in their bearing. The majority may very well impose such restraints upon itself, and subsequent majorities may respect and perpetuate them, because, quite simply, they deem them necessary for reasons falling within the "intensity problem" as we have defined it. It may, that is to say, restrain itself without in the slightest writing a question mark beside the majority-principle, or in any sense abandoning its claim to a capacity to make whatever decisions it sees fit to make, but rather out of a determination to keep the majority-rule "show" on the road. In doing so, what it may be doing is to re-assert, rather than abandon, its claim to be the ultimate caller of the shots.[15] We too often forget that in all political systems—monarchies, aristocracies, democracies, dictatorships even—the power to govern is frequently exercised (if only for convenience's sake)—through the elaboration of "procedures," established ways of doing things or handling problems, that have, operationally, the effect of limiting necessarily only for the short term. Concretely, the decision-making authority(the king, the nobles, the majority in a democracy) may deem it prudent, may even find itself obliged, in order to achieve the maximum possible in the light of its "goals," to yield on this or that policy issue to one or more groupings out in society with a view to obtaining its, or their, willing cooperation in other areas of policy—that is, to "restrain" itself. And if its calculations in this regard are correct, which is to say based on a realistic appraisal of what it is up against, it does not, in restraining itself, undermine the "system" or compromise the principle upon which the system is based. On the contrary, what it does is to enhance the efficiency of the "system" and, at the same time, the chances of its perpetuating itself as that kind of "system."

Third, the decision-making authority, including again the majority in a majority-rule "system," may restrain itself (not always "prcfcr"

---

[15]The point we are making both here and above is, we believe, similar to that made by Almond and Verba in accounting for the success of "civic culture." "In general," they write, "[the] management of cleavage is accomplished by subordinating conflicts on the political level to some higher, overarching attitudes of solidarity, whether these attitudes to be the norms associated with the 'rules of the democratic game' or the belief that there exists within the society a supraparty solidarity based on non-partisan criteria."

"This balance, furthermore, must be maintained on the elite as well as the citizen level. Though our data are not relevant here, it is quite likely that similar mechanisms operate on the elite level as well. The elaborate formal and informal rules of etiquette in the legislatures of Britain and the United States, for example, foster and indeed require friendly relations.... And this tempers the intensity of partisanship": Gabriel Almond and Sidney Verba, *The Civic Culture* (Boston: Little, Brown and Company, 1965), pp. 359-360.

its own "preferences") out of regard to a constitutional morality, or a morality *tout court*, or even a tradition or custom that it "values." This point will, to be sure, be lost on those who insist on reducing everything to preferences; especially those who are unable to distinguish between what "I" would give my right arm to feel free to do and that which I know, or believe, I ought to do.[16] But it is, we contend, a valid point, and an indispensable one for understanding the actual functioning of viable majority-rule systems. More: the decision-making authority, monarchy, aristocracy, or popular majority, may seek to bind its successors, may seek to stack the cards in such fashion as to limit their freedom of choice, without prejudice to the principle it appeals to in exercising its authority.

Fourth, philosopher kings are indeed (as we have lately been reminded by Professor Dahl) "hard to come by." But to concede that that is true is by no means to concede that every minority empowered to restrain "the majority," or every *parlement* empowered to restrain a king or an aristocracy, will as a matter of course end up acting in its own "selfish interest," or abusing its power, or "upsetting the apple-cart," or undermining the decision-making authority it restrains. The king, the aristocracy, the majority may, for reasons of prudence or morality, among others, itself establish arrangements calculated to cut itself off from the possibility of hasty or ill-considered decisions, and these may involve putting some minority in position to exert pressure upon it, and to keep it reminded of its obligations and responsibilities—so long, of course, as it retains the power to abolish the restraint when, in its considered judgment, it no longer serves the purpose for which it was intended. Just as it can, by creating machinery that will subject it to pressures on behalf of a constitutional morality, a morality *tout court*, a tradition or custom, or the need, arising out of the "problem of intensity," to carry others along with it, so also it can place a restraining minority in such a position that it too will be subject to such pressures and can be

---

[16]See F. H. Bradley, "My Station and its Duties," in *Ethical Studies* (Oxford: At the Clarendon Press, 1937). *A*, a paycheck in hand at the end of the month, may wish above everything to chuck it all, disappear, and start all over again, yet still go home to his tawdry and sullen wife and the five sons and daughters who drive him to despair —out of a sense of duty. Those whose idiom excludes such a distinction, and will have it that in going home to the wife and kids he "prefers" to do so, have, in our view, become so "scientific" as to cut themselves off from all possible communication with persons who "prefer" to preserve the traditional relationship between language and common sense.

counted on to respond to them. Philosopher kings, we repeat, are indeed hard to come by; but we are by no means ignorant as to the steps we can take, in establishing a "restraining" minority, in order to force out of it "behavior" sufficiently like that of philosopher kings to be worth our while.

With all this in mind, we can lay down certain conditions that, in particular, a majority-rule "system" must fulfill if it is to handle the "problem of intensity." We turn now to this matter.

III. Means for Taking Account of Differences in Intensity

At least the following conditions, it seems to us, leap to the eye, on the above showing, as among those that a political system must meet if it is to handle the "intensity problem."

1) The system must have built-in facilities for *correct reciprocal anticipations,* on the part of groups and, ultimately, of individuals, of the intensity of each other's reactions, favorable or unfavorable, to the alternative courses of political behavior open to each. In our view, to the extent that the system fails to facilitate correct reciprocal anticipations, it is likely to encourage courses of action, on the part of groups and individuals, that will prove to be self-defeating, and that may easily lead to the breakdown of the system itself. And this applies equally to the "governors" and the "governed."

2) The condition just laid down does not mean, of course, that the system must never permit groups or individuals to take action that, because of the intensity of the reaction to it in this or that quarter or quarters, will deny them cooperation, or that it must never permit groups or individuals from attempting to exact, for their cooperation or compliance, a higher price than they can get. The important point is that groups and individuals shall not base their choice among various courses of action on *false* anticipations as to how others will respond; that, if you like, insofar as that is possible, they should not act in ignorance of foreseeable unfavorable reactions. The "governors" may well decide that they are *not* prepared to pay the price that this or that group will end up demanding for its cooperation or compliance. The "governed," on the other hand, may well decide to take, over against this or that legislative or policy *démarche,* retalia-

tory action that will bring down upon their heads disagreeable consequences. Our condition merely stipulates that such decisions must be taken, if the system is to work "rationally" from the standpoint of the participants, with the maximum possible knowledge of the consequences they will entail.[17]

3) The condition does *not* require that a democratic system weigh "preferences" instead of counting them. As far as elections are concerned it can, in the end, do nothing *but* count, though democratic systems of course differ enormously as to who is counted, and how, and with respect to what. What it requires is merely that the "counted" shall, as they cast their votes in elections, be so situated as to be able to reckon, beforehand, with the intensity of the reaction in various quarters to the use they make of their votes. In other words, a democratic system does not fail to meet our major "condition" merely by not itself weighing preferences, but does fail to meet it when it affords groups and individuals insufficient opportunities, before their votes are cast, to do their own "weighing." Above all, our condition does not require that people be given their way on this or that issue because they happen to feel intensely about it. The decision as to when, and about what, to give them their way, is one that the "governors" must make according to their lights; it does require that those lights, when issues are "up" about which some of the governed happen to feel strongly, be dimmed as little as possible by the system's machinery.

4) Correct reciprocal anticipation requires, clearly, a high degree of mutual knowledge and understanding among the participants. The science and technology of politics, despite its great leaps forward in recent decades, has yet to invent a thermometer-like device that can

[17]While many have contended that the Civil War was the great failure of the American political system, there is, within the framework we suggest here, reason to dispute this. Calhoun's last speech to the Senate in 1850 certainly reflected an awareness of things to come.

"I have . . . believed from the first that the agitation of the subject of slavery would, if not prevented by some timely and effective measure, end in disunion. Entertaining this opinion, I have, on all proper occasions, endeavored to call the attention of both the two great parties which divide the country, to adopt some measure to prevent so great a disaster, but without success. The agitation has been permitted to proceed, with almost no attempt to resist it, until it has reached a period when it can no longer be disguised or denied that the Union is in danger. You have thus forced upon you the greatest and the gravest question that ever can come under your consideration: How can the Union be preserved?" We repeat: All that a well constructed political system can possibly do is to provide the means for correct reciprocal anticipations, and with respect to the Civil War the American system probably rates an A+ on this score.

be inserted in people's heads, much less into their hearts, to "measure" the intensity of their preferences. The only preferences we actually "experience," and can calibrate with great accuracy, are our own; and there is indeed "no conceivable way" to "directly observe and compare the sensate intensities of preference of different individuals [or groups]," or even to correlate them with observable "changes in facial expression, words, posture or even the chemistry of the body."[18] Yet people do, and on our showing must if their political activity is to be other than counter-productive, attempt to make such correlations. The correlations they arrive at are often "proved out" by subsequent events, as, also, they are sometimes belied by them. All we are saying, for the moment, is that the critical variable here, the variable that results now in correct anticipations and now in incorrect ones, *must* be the knowledge-understanding the "anticipator" possesses as to what makes the other "tick." (The supreme example of the process at work, and the one most of us are likeliest to have experienced, or at least observed at first hand, is the smoothly-running family, in which each participant, husband or wife, brother or sister, parent or child, precisely because of the intimacy of their life together, can predict with a high degree of accuracy how the "others" will react to various alternative courses of action on his or her part.) The successful politician, one might say, is, other things being equal, successful just to the extent that his anticipations in this regard approach the degree of accuracy achieved, day in day out, by the members of a smoothly-running family. And, from the standpoint of our overriding condition, a political system is to be judged "good" or "bad" according as it facilitates, or renders difficult, accurate anticipations of this kind.

5) A further corollary of the foregoing line of argument would be the following: The more "diverse" or "heterogeneous" the political society, the greater its need for elaborate and complex "machinery" to facilitate mutual knowledge and understanding of the kind here in question. Put otherwise: to the extent that a society is relatively homogeneous, so that people can safely assume that the "others" are pretty much like themselves, any given individual may fairly be expected to come up with fairly accurate forecasts as to the reactions of those others to any given political gambit he is contemplating. This

[18]Dahl, *op. cit.*, pp. 99-100.

for at least three basic reasons: First, the chances are greater, just to the extent that the society is homogeneous, that the legislative act or line of policy in question will affect the "others" pretty much as it will affect oneself—that, if you like, the individual will possess first-hand personal knowledge as to the extent to which the contemplated step will or will not elicit cooperation. Second, and allowing now for the fact that a society can be highly homogeneous (non-diverse, in the sense of *Federalist* 10) and still have in its bosom groupings that will be differently affected by a given policy decision, it remains true that the participants in a society have, to the extent that the latter is homogeneous, the greater opportunities to comprehend the composition and structure of the society, the "lay" of the potentially conflicting interests, goods, and "values." Third, just to the extent that the homogeneity of the homogeneous society is a matter of *shared* interests, goals, and values, we may fairly expect from the participants a higher degree of sympathetic "identification" with each other, thus a greater desire or willingness to understand beforehand the probable effects of the action contemplated, and thus, finally, a greater effort to feel the others out and seek some kind of accommodation with those who, predictably, will, if not accommodated, "cause trouble." The "extreme" case here, of course, is the "tightly-knit," "primitive" society which seeks, and obtains at whatever cost, unanimity, that is, does not submit issues to majority determination.[19]

[19]See on this point Bertrand de Jouvenel, *Sovereignty* (Chicago: University of Chicago Press, 1957), Ch. 8. He makes a similar point when he writes: "The wider and more developed a society is, the less can the climate of trustfulness (such as should always prevail among its members if they are to confer on each other all the benefits possible) be the fruit of a spirit of community; the widening of the circle and the growing diversity of personalities tend to destroy that spirit. For that reason the climate of trustfulness comes more and more to rest on the guarantees provided by Law. I know nothing of Primus and am emotionally neutral in regard to him. No element of personal sympathy, no feeling of our belonging to each other will induce in him a certain course of conduct as regards me—only the abstract feeling of obligation as such" (p. 132).

That Madison was fully aware of this principle is beyond dispute. "Those who contend for a simple Democracy, or a pure republic, actuated by the sense of the majority, and operating within narrow limits, assume or suppose a case which is altogether fictitious. They found their reasoning on the idea, that they have all precisely the same interests and the same feelings in every respect. Were this in reality the case, their reasoning would be conclusive. The interest of the majority would be that of the minority also; the decision could only turn on mere opinion concerning the good of the whole, of which the major voice would be the safest criterion; and within a small sphere, this voice could be most easily collected, and the public affairs most accurately managed. We know however, that no society ever did or can consist of so homogeneous a mass of Citizens. In the savage state indeed, an approach is made

6) Having mentioned *Federalist* 10, with its emphasis on "diversity" as one of the two pre-conditions for a democratic republic that will not lead to tyranny, we must (a) say a word about the second of Publius' two pre-conditions, and (b) face the question whether, and to what extent, our own emphasis on mutual self-knowledge places us (as at first blush it seems to) in opposition to Publius. As for (a), all that we have said about heterogeneity as an obstacle to successful handling of the "intensity problem" evidently applies, *mutatis mutandis*, to "extensiveness." An individual or group in, say, Florida, has scant opportunity, other things being equal, to make an accurate forecast concerning the reactions of an individual or group in, say, Washington (as we have largely been reminded by Watts, which seems to have surprised its neighbors in "extensive" Los Angeles hardly less rudely than it did its constructive neighbors in Portland, Maine). Distance, like diversity, is then a genuine obstacle to the kind of mutual knowledge and understanding that emerges as desirable in the light of our analysis of the "intensity problem." And this analysis certainly appears to point to the thesis—a truism in much of what we call "traditional" political theory—that self-government can thrive only in the "small" state. Such, certainly, was the teaching of Aristotle, who, as every careful reader knows, is echoed on this point by Rousseau, with his insistence that in a true democracy each of the citizens must be so situated that he can come to know and understand the "others" whom he will encounter in the assembly. (Rousseau, we feel sure, would have construed "know" and "understand" to be a matter not merely of the "head," but also of the "heart.") We do not suggest, of course, that the traditional argument for the non-extensive republic necessarily rested, even in part, on considerations akin to our overiding condition. Far from it; we suggest merely that the traditional argument would have been strengthened *had* it explicitly taken "intensity" into account, and that contemporary democratic theory would find itself less helpless, in the presence of the "intensity problem," had it given more weight to the considerations on which the traditional theorists did rest their argument. One might add (anticipating a little what we shall say in Section IV) that democratic *societies* have, in practice, departed notably less from the traditional teaching in this area than has democratic *theory*. As for (b), whether,

toward it; but in that state little or no Government is necessary": Madison's letter to Jefferson, Gaillard Hunt, *The Writings of James Madison*, Volume IV, pp. 222-224.

on our showing here, we must end up taking issue with Publius in regard to his most celebrated doctrine, the answer is "No, indeed!" For our money, the case Publius makes out in *Federalist* 51 is, quite simply, unanswerable, and the conclusion at which he arrives beyond challenge:

> In [an] . . . extended republic, and among the great variety of interests, parties, and sects which it embraces, a coalition of the majority of the whole society could seldom take place on any other principles than those of justice and the general good.[20]

At worst, our analysis merely exposes a weakness of the *Federalist* 10 model, which Publius and his adepts must do something about lest their system come a cropper over the "intensity problem." (Again to anticipate a little: Publius, regardless of whether he had anything like the "intensity problem" in mind, *did* do something about it.) In brief: just to the extent that a system does not meet Publius' two conditions, it will require special machinery to meet our condition, since mutual knowledge and understanding on the part of the participants, comprehension of the general workings of the system, sympathetic reciprocal identification, etc., will to that extent be, as a matter of course, the more difficult to achieve. For Publius' system, as Professor Burns has brilliantly demonstrated in a recent book, does tend to generate intense competition among the "diverse" groups that it deploys over the "extensive" territory, thus increasing the danger that a group or combination of groups will, in the "heat of the battle" and with the righteous zeal that intense competition is likely to engender, try to ride rough-shod over intense preferences on the part of other groups.[21]

7) It is impossible to mention the participants' attempts to calibrate the intensity of the preferences of the "others" by observing

---

[20] *The Federalist,* Jacob E. Cooke (ed.) (Cleveland: World Publishing Company, 1961), *Federalist* 51, pp. 352-353. Incidentally, this view is not so much at odds with Rousseau's as one might imagine. Rousseau does indeed teach that there should be *no* subsidiary groups in the true democracy. But he hastens to add that where that condition does not obtain, i.e., everywhere, "they should be made numerous and prevented from being unequal in size. . . .[Only in this way can you make sure] that the general will shall always be enlightened and the people never misinformed": Jean-Jacques Rousseau, *The Social Contract,* translated with an introduction by Willmoore Kendall (Chicago: The Henry Regnery Company, 1954), p. 29.

[21] *The Deadlock of Democracy* (Englewood Cliffs, N.J.: Prentice-Hall, 1963).

their behavior (the expression on their faces, the noises they make, etc.) without running hard up against this difficulty: The participants have nothing *except* observable behavior to go on in arriving at their anticipations. Yet the observable behavior may tell us more about the histrionic talents of the agonizer than about the intensity of his feelings on the issue that is up. (One thinks, as a matter of course, of Senator Dirksen, whose tear-glands would seem to be equipped with spigots.) The "others," in a word, may be bluffing about their intention to rock the boat if they can't get their way; may, for example, be using an issue about which they do not in fact feel strongly in order to gain this or that strategic advantage. And such bluffing is the more likely to be successful just to the extent that the participants have had insufficient opportunity to come to know and understand each other well. In order to meet our overriding condition, therefore, the system will require rules and procedures, analogous to those of a poker game, that impose potentially heavy penalties on the player who would like to win the pot with the weaker hand. To the extent that the system permits the bluffer to win the pot, it is unnecessarily exposed to varying degrees of instability; partly because it will run the danger of overlooking tomorrow's real boat-rockers, and let itself in for trouble it might have avoided, and partly because it will run the danger of not mobilizing, behind the goals of the decision-makers, the maximum possible cooperation available to it given the "lay" of the "intensity problem" it faces. For the majority that can be bluffed will never be in position to make accurate forecasts as to the future reactions of the "others."

Can we conceive of rules and procedures that will minimize successful bluffing? Not easily, of course; but (a) the structure of the system can take into account the fact that X is likely to get by with his bluff just to the extent that Y and Z do not know and understand what kind of poker he plays, and (b) it can, through rules formal or informal, exact sacrifices from those who, in the course of playing out a political hand, demand that the intensity of their preferences be made a *ratio decidendi*—can, that is to say, put the costs of injecting such a demand so high that no one who does not have a genuinely intense preference will be willing to pay it. One possibility: give each member of the assembly n number of votes at the beginning of the session, and let him "spend" them as he sees fit—all of them if he likes, on a single issue, with the understanding that once they are gone he can cast no further votes. Another: encourage the "horse-trading" and "log-rolling" for which the Congress of the United States is so frequently denounced, thus maximizing the opportunity on the part of the participants to "trade" their votes on issues about which they do not feel intensely for votes of the others on issues about which they do. Viewed from the standpoint of our overriding condition, "log-rolling" may well play a beneficent role in the political system by helping to handle the "intensity problem."

We turn, in Section IV, to the implications of our analysis for scholarly inquiry, whether "normative" or "empirical," into the institutions and procedures of those contemporary democratic systems that appear to have demonstrated their viability.

IV. Criteria for Evaluating Political Systems

The questions that want asking in the light of the foregoing would appear to. be these: First, to what extent do the "going" democratic systems meet the overriding condition we have laid down in Section III? And second, insofar as these systems fail to reflect accurately the "models" elaborated in democratic theory (i.e., insofar as they represent departures from those models), to what extent can we say that the models themselves meet that overriding condition? We can, we trust, pose those questions without seeming to suggest that democratic models and systems should be viewed, and judged, exclusively on the basis of their handling of the intensity problem. Our point, from first to last, has been merely that a democratic system which fails to provide facilities for accurate reciprocal anticipation among the participants does so at its peril.[22]

Let us take up these questions in reverse order, speaking first of the models, and, following Professor Dahl, assuming that after you clear

[22]By doing so, it both renders itself inherently unstable (an "empirical" judgment) and lays itself open to the charge (a "normative" or "ethical" judgment) that, by failing to elicit the maximum of cooperation available to it for the achievement of its objectives (which, *arguendo,* we assume to be "good"), it is self-defeating and therefore "bad." We hope to have dissociated ourselves sufficiently from the view that intense preferences should get the green light just because they are intense.

away the smoke, there remain only two: "populistic democracy" and "Madisonian democracy,"[23] the first of which underlines the bulk of contemporary empirical research by American political scientists, and may fairly be called the current orthodoxy, while the second is that embodied in *The Federalist.*[24]

First, then, the model of "populistic democracy." Its essential characteristics are: (a) it treats *elections* (in which *all* the citizens cast equal votes) as the be-all of democracy; (b) it conceives of elections as a means through which the voters express their "preferences" on matters of policy; and therefore (c) it understands elections as having no other function, properly speaking, than to eventuate in policy "mandates" that are, *sensu stricto,* governing, and, governing precisely because they express the *will* of a majority of the voters.

Now: reminding the reader that we are not concerned here with the model's "merits," either from the standpoint of ethics or from that of "workability,"[25] we ask only: What about it from the standpoint of the intensity problem? And our answer must be: The populistic model, just to the extent that it *is* workable and therefore capable of achieving its primary objective (a one-one correspondence between governmental action and the "preferences" of the majority), is, on the face of it, incapable of handling the intensity problem, and for the following crystal-clear reasons: (a) the constitutional morality implicit in the model encourages voters—nay, imposes upon them the obligation—to consult their *own* preferences about policy as they cast their votes, so that, just to the extent that they live up to that morality, they precisely do *not* take into account the preferences of the "others." Why should they, since the avowed purpose of the model is to translate, into legislation and policy, the preferences of the victorious majority? The role of the minority in the model—again on the face of it—is to say to itself, after the election, "so much the worse for us," and then obey the "mandate." (b) If we abstract from (a), and do impute to the majority a disposition (with a view to gaining its objectives) to take into account the preferences of the minority, and "weigh" them with an eye to their "intensity," the eristical clash

[23]Subject to correction by Professor Dahl, "polyarchy," on our reading of the *Preface,* is a variant of the model of "populistic democracy."
[24]Whose author was not, of course, Madison, but a creature with three heads who answered to the name "Publius."
[25]Professor Dahl is well aware of the difficulties involved in midwifing a "mandate" out of the electorate, as he indicates in the last chapter of his *Preface.*

between two idealogico-programmatic "alternatives" at election-time, which the model's admirers deem necessary for a clear "mandate" that must at all costs be executed, is—still again on the face of it—the worst possible arena for working out the kind of accommodation needed for handling the intensity problem.[26] What such a clash is likely to produce is more or less angry determination on both sides to have one's way and, at the margin, a fanaticism that is only too willing for the chips to fall where they may. Nor is it possible to answer either that the "leaders" will make the needed accommodations in the act of drawing up the alternative programs (*their* job, as the model's explicators understand it, is to elaborate a program that will win a majority by appealing to the preferences of the larger number), or that the needed accommodations will be made, after the elections, in the assembly or by the executive (exactly the point about the model is that the real decisions about law and policy get themselves made at the polls, so that decision-making "history" is, so to speak, over when the polls close). (c) The "preferences" of the majority are, of course, in the last analysis the preferences of the individuals of which it is composed, which the model treats, if we may put it so, as "givens." But to say that is to expose the great

[26]In this connection a comparison of the writings of Clinton Rossiter and James Burnham is instructive, as concretely illustrating how the differences in the two models manifest themselves with respect to American institutions.

Rossiter writes of the Presidency in the following terms: ". . . he is . . . the Voice of the People, the leading formulator and expounder of public opinion in the United States. While he acts as political leader of some, he serves as moral spokesman for all." Or: "Throughout our history there have been moments of triumph or dedication or frustration or even shame when the will of the people—the General Will, I suppose we could call it—demanded to be heard clearly and unmistakably. . . . No effective President has doubted his prerogative to speak the people's mind on the great issues of his time, to act, again in Wilson's words, as the spokesman for the sentiment and purpose of the century": *The American Presidency*, rev. ed. (New York: Harcourt, Brace & World, Inc., 1960), pp. 32-33.

Contrast this with Burnham's description of Congressional operations. "Many who complain about congressional slowness and inefficiency have not stopped to reflect that many of the ways in which Congressmen 'waste their time' are apt methods for accomplishing the tasks of a representative legislature in a democratic republic: by the chats and correspondence with constituents, the encounters with the press, the lunches with experts from the bureaucracy and even the cocktails with the lobbyists, the informal hours with each other and the staff professionals, the lecture trips to cities and universities, the travel junkets at home and abroad, the members are not merely helping to get themselves reelected . . . but getting to know—or, better, to feel—the myriad problems and interests, the competing needs and desires, complaints and demands, that the legislature, if it performs its function, must try to weave into some sort of working resolution": *Congress and the American Tradition* (Chicago: Henry Regnery Company, 1959), pp. 264-65.

weakness of the model from the standpoint of the intensity problem, the handling of which calls for, on the one hand, the wish for states-manlike accommodations insofar as they are needed in order to prevent rocking of the boat, and the kind of knowledge and under-standing, partly "intellectual," partly having to do with the (not-very-intellectual) capacity for empathy, needed for working out such ac-commodations. Now: the wish, or if you like the disposition to entertain such a wish regarding this intellectual know-how and em-pathy do require qualities with respect to which we should expect a log-normal distribution out among the population. Which is to say: the larger the number of people a party attracts into its projected majority, the further it must dip into strata of the population where these qualities are present in more and more modest quantities. To state this another way: the very fact that the majority is by definition made up of lots and lots of people, incapacitates it for "feeling out" the intensity of the minority's preferences.[27] (d) Decision-making history, we repeat, is over when the model's polls close, and this has the following further consequence: "Inter-election" policy decisions on issues included in the mandate (i.e., on the very issues that are most likely to produce unanticipated intense reactions that want placating) are out of the question. Concretely, the model hauls out into the open and emphasizes the kind of situation that cannot be handled consistently with its own basic principles of majority-rule: a majority preferring X, whether apathetically or intensely, standing over against a minority that intensely prefers Y, each committed, by the election, to a course of action irreconcilable with that preferred by the other; and in a context where nothing can be done about it short of the next election—a situation that is, of course, the more threatening the longer the interval between elections. The model first divides the voters into warring camps, then prevents their ranks from closing.

Does the *Federalist* model come off any better, from the stand-point of the intensity problem? Its characteristics, as we understand them, are: (a) It treats *deliberation,* that is, dialogue back and forth among members of the assembly and among the "branches" of the government, as the be-all-end-all of the democratic process, and

[27]Our voting and public opinion studies have shown, over and over again, that the rank-and-file voters are incapable of expressing, through an election, even their own "real" preferences. To impose upon them the further obligation to anticipate the impact of their mandates upon the cooperativeness of persons with different prefer-ences is, clearly, to overburden them.

claims for it that it will produce the "sense" (*not* the will) of the people as a whole. (b) It regards elections as means through which the voters express not their "preferences" on issues of policy or their "will" as to what the government is to do tomorrow, but their considered judgment, amongst the candidates who present themselves, as to which is the "best" man they can send forward to participate in the deliberative process contemplated in characteristic (a). (c) It postpones actual decisions concerning policy issues until a relatively tardy moment in the process of deliberations. (d) It places no premium upon an all-inclusive electorate, or upon an equal impact upon policy for each member of that electorate; it contemplates, rather, a citizenry divided into the two categories "voters" (i.e., persons able to meet whatever "qualifications" subordinate legislatures may have set for admission to the electorate) and "non-voters," and is not *ipso facto* unfriendly to "qualifications" that tend to make entry into the first of these categories more or less difficult. And (e) while it does not prohibit capture of its governmental machinery by a bare majority of the electorate, or legislative and policy decisions imposed by a bare majority of its bicameral assembly, it discourages both and, by clear implication, seeks decisions by "consensus."

Now: to return to our question. Just as the model of populistic democracy looks as if it had been devised to prevent handling of our intensity problem, because it renders grossly improbable correct reciprocal anticipations as to how the "others" will react to decisions by the "governors," so the *Federalist* model affords maximum facilities for such anticipations. And this for the following reasons: (a) Its implicit constitutional morality, which cannot be stated in the language of "preferences" or "will," is so to speak a summons to "statesmanship" understood as the eliciting of maximum cooperation—that is, as a matter of *not* ignoring the feelings of the losers in elections. (b) Since it does not encourage voters in elections to suppose, in casting their votes, that they are making actual policy decisions (i.e., since it tells them, in effect, that it is theirs only to choose the men who are to make those decisions at a later date), it is far less likely than the populistic model to divide the voters or, for that matter, their representatives, into warring camps committed, as we put it above, to irreconcilable positions. (c) By spreading actual policy-decisions out over a period of many months or even years (for so the inventors of the model conceived of it), it affords the participants in the decision-making process maximum opportunities to know and understand one another, to "feel each other out," and thus to arrive at correct reciprocal anticipations about future reactions to current policy alternatives. (d) Because it clearly takes a dim view of decisions by a bare majority, it puts the participants (whom it *expects* to arrive at a "consensus") under severe pressure to come to know and understand one another, to "feel each other out." (e) Decision-making history, far from being over in the *Federalist* model once the polls are closed (the word "mandate" does not appear in the model's dictionary), happens precisely in the intervals between elections, so that the model is at all times highly flexible as regards accommodations with potential boat-rockers. (f) To the extent that the qualifications for admission to the electorate make any sense whatever (= to the extent that the distinction between voters and non-voters is made meaningful, which, to be sure, cannot be guaranteed beforehand), the model may indulge the hope, impossible under the populistic model, of "creaming off " from the people, to become politically active, those whose scores would put them in the upper reaches of our log-normal curves (see above)—in the hope, in short, of not making demands on the participants that they are incapable of meeting.

But, the reader may object, have you not, insofar as you have proved anything, proved too much? Is there not every reason to believe that the British system of government (and its imitators in Australia and Canada) handles the intensity problem about as well as the American system? And is not the British system the very embodiment of the populistic model, as the American system is, traditionally at least, the embodiment of the *Federalist* model? Have you not, somewhere along the line, misled us, and proved to be impossible in theory that which every reader of the *New York Times* sees, under his very nose, in daily dispatches from London and Ottawa?

These are, evidently, questions that demand treatment on a scale far exceeding the limitations of a single article. But we can at least indicate the shape of the answers called for as follows: Let us concede, *arguendo* but reluctantly, that the British system handles the intensity problem about as well as the American system—that the former, like the latter, does bump along from decade to decade without creating pockets of irridentism that produce crises. But that is by no means to acquiesce in the main thrust of the objection, for two reasons: First, the governments in question do *not*, in our opinion, "embody" the model of "populistic democracy" to anything like the extent that some writers like to suppose. The British parties, at least as we see them in the dispatches from London, neither offer the voters at election-time the clear choice between alternative policies that the model calls for, nor make the unabashed appeal to "preferences," i.e., self-interest (as opposed to supposedly irrelevant considerations such as the "wisdom" and "virtue" of the competing candidates), which some textbook descriptions of the system would lead one to expect. The party that wins the election does, to be sure, win it on a "program," and does come to power with a "mandate" of sorts to carry out the program. The majority principle does, no doubt, command in Britain a kind of allegiance it has never enjoyed in America. Votes in Parliament do, *when they are finally taken,* no doubt reflect a very high degree of party "regularity." But the two major parties, each of which notoriously has its "left" and "right" wings, are by no means the national monoliths of the populistic model, which is to say: Electoral contests remain to a very considerable extent "local," with great differences of emphasis between candidates of one and the same party from constituency to constituency, and, in any case, are (from, e.g., the point of view of an American Conservative) more similar "ideologically" than dissimilar. Parliament, moreover, has by no means yet been reduced to the "rubber-stamp" role that the model would attribute to it. It remains essentially a *deliberative* body in the strict *Federalist* sense of the term, and its deliberations certainly turn, in very large part, on the majority's recognition that concessions must be made to the views of the minority. It gives M.P.'s on the two sides of the House all manner of opportunities to get to know and understand one another. The M.P.'s, if only because their constituencies are closer to hand, do, if anything, more constituency "nursing," more "feeling out" of the drift of voter opinion between elections than their American counterparts, and one who follows the dispatches gets the impression that the M.P. at home for the week-end by no means confines his attention to members of his own party, and is by no means without sources of information as to what measures will result in irridentism; and not a few writers on the British system have suggested that the "week-end" house-parties bring the leaders of the parties together in a kind of intimacy that, say some, has no equivalent in the American system. In sum, the British system involves a great deal of machinery that brings it, in point of fact, closer to the *Federalist* model than to that of populistic democracy. Viewed in the light of our analysis of the problem of intensity, this clearly facilitates accurate anticipations, back and forth among the M.P.'s, of one another's future reactions. Secondly, Britain remains, by contrast with America, a relatively homogeneous (i.e., non-"diverse") society that lives and has its being on a relatively tiny (i.e., non-"extensive") piece of real estate and therefore has, on our own showing, less need than the American system for *ad hoc* procedures to take care of the intensity problem. The fact it nevertheless takes the trouble to provide procedures that come off very well when referred to our overriding condition, rather fortifies than weakens the main argument of the present article.

One might argue, similarly, that if the American system is beginning, of late, to show signs of tripping up over the intensity problem, these are to be explained, in large part, in terms of a certain "slippage" in the direction of the populistic model. While we cannot fully explore this matter here, this much seems worth saying: Small wonder that—let's call it the Law of the Pinching Shoe—in any democratic system those institutions that enable it to handle the intensity problem are the ones most likely to become the target of "reform" proposals whose adherents press them with impassioned zeal, and the more certainly when those institutions are part of the very fabric of government and thus highly visible to participants in the political process (as they are in America, and are not in Britain). We have already expressed skepticism as to whether anybody ever gets to believing in the majority-principle in the sense of being ready, as a matter of course, to accept any and every majority determination, no matter how outrageous or disagreeable it may seem.[28] It nevertheless remains true that the idea "unanimity being impossible, the majority must decide" is likely, in an age when egalitarian notions pervade the intellectual climate, to commend itself to many people as axiomatic, self-evident, etc., and as, therefore, ultimately the essence of the democratic process; and from there, there is indeed nowhere to go, logically, except to automatic condemnation of institutions that "frustrate" the "will" of the majority as, *ipso facto*, "undemocratic." In other words, solutions calculated to prevent intense minorities from

[28]An exception would perhaps have to be made here for situations, such as that in the bosom of the Supreme Court, where the participants really regard each other as pretty much equals. But we have yet to see a national democratic system in which that condition is fulfilled.

kicking up a future fuss are likely to displease the large number of persons who, because of them, end up politically with something less than the jackpot; and it is only natural that they should direct their fire not merely at the substance of the decisions in question, but also at the rules and procedures that produced them, and that they should make noises about "minority dictation." And, in absence of a certain understanding of, and commitment to, *Federalist* political philosophy,[29] efforts will be made to bring the system in line with the populistic model. We hope to have shown, however, that proper evaluation of such reform proposals is an extremely difficult and delicate undertaking, and that it must, at some point, face up to the question: What, if you clear a wide-open path for the majority, will happen to the cooperation the majority needs from the minority or minorities that will take exception to its policies? And let that man think twice who is tempted to say either that cooperation is not needed, or that it will be forthcoming as a matter of course. Those answers tempt him precisely because he has not done his homework. And the literature of political reform in America seems to us to rest, to a frightening degree, upon some such tacit premises.

In our view, at least the following questions are highly relevant when dealing with the problem of reform. To what extent do existing deviations from the populistic model facilitate correct reciprocal anticipations? Given the social, economic, cultural, and political structure of the society, what means are available for the majority to impose its will after gaining full knowledge as to the possible reactions to its decisions? Is there reason to believe that certain identifiable minority groups are permanently advantaged or disadvantaged by the existing rules for making decisions, and in a way that does not facilitate handling of the intensity problem?

Finally, we submit: (a) The foregoing analysis of the intensity problem lays bare a whole series of heretofore neglected questions with respect to populistic democracy. (b) Contemporary studies of existing political systems, whether "empirical" or "normative," all too fre-

---

[29]Again, not necessarily in the heads of the participants. Such understanding and commitment can, in Lincoln Steffen's phrase, lodge itself in the "hips"—and not merely the hips of isolated individuals, but those of the generality of men in a democratic society. The American people, who up to now have turned a cold shoulder to most reform proposals of the kind here in question, despite the pleadings of the most knowledgeable writers on such topics, certainly do not do so out of an intellectual understanding of Publius; but they do so, all the same.

quently overlook the complexities introduced by the intensity problem. And (c) we can hope to understand existing democracies only to the degree that we are prepared to take into account the dimensions of the intensity problem and the complexities it introduces.

The "Roster Device": J. S. Mill and Contemporary Elitism

(With George W. Carey)

Political theorists, when faced with certain types of problems, often move in their thinking from the tacit assumption that one is entitled, having fixed attention on any human quality or characteristic, to take for granted the following premises: (a) That the individual members of any political society possess that quality or characteristic in different degrees. (b) That every political society may, therefore, for certain purposes be treated as a huge roster, on which the names of the society's individual members have been duly entered in "correct" order—that is, with that man who possesses most of the quality in question at the top and that man who possesses least of it at the bottom and everybody else just where he belongs in between the top and the bottom. (c) That, finally, one may draw horizontal lines through this roster and so divide the membership of society into significant groupings, especially for the purpose of allocating the individual members of society to the various functions that must be performed within it. The quality in question may be, as in the early pages of *The Laws,* the capacity to carry one's liquor well, and the roster may then be used, as Plato uses it, as a basis for the proposal that masters of ceremonies at banquets be drawn from the top of the relevant "roster." Or the quality may be wealth, as in Aristotle's *Politics,* and the roster may then be used for a variety of purposes such as classifying types of government, or assuring stability, or preventing revolution. We could name any number of examples.

Now there are, we shall contend, many unnoticed difficulties involved in the use of this "roster" technique. It can, let us notice first, be brought into play in two quite different contexts. Plato, in the illustration cited above, is "model building": he is speaking of a hypothetical situation, that is, no situation in particular, and his roster is merely a theoretically satisfactory solution to a purely speculative problem. He is, on the showing of the present article, operating within the "rules of the game." But if, say, a capacity-to-govern-well roster is put forth, as it usually is, with the assumptions that those at the top of the roster can actually be identified in a particular place and time, great difficulties arise. It now becomes incumbent upon the theorist to offer proof either that the roster he appeals to actually exists (like that which lists West Point graduates according to their "standing"), or that it can be more or less readily produced, if and when needed, without expenditure of time, effort and money out of all proportion to the benefits it is likely to confer. To the extent that the theorist attempts to incorporate existential reality in his assumptions, that is to say, he must assume responsibility for proving that his roster is not impractical, and must recognize, to go no further, that the various rosters one may posit on the level of abstract theory differ enormously as regards the resources of time, energy, money, etc., it would take to construct them in an actual political situation. This for several reasons: The "quality" in question, for one thing, may or may not be "measurable," as, for example, tallness is measurable. If measurable, it may be more easy to measure, or less easy. If not measurable, it may still have quantitative dimensions, like the capacity to compose great music, of which Beethoven presumably had more than, say, Rossini.[1] Again: the quality in question might be, e.g., "kindness," but the relevant roster could be constructed, for practical purposes, only after agreement has been reached as to how to decide who has more of it and who has less of it. And there are further difficulties, which arise even in connection with qualities we are accustomed to think of as readily measurable. A "richness" roster, for instance, reaching from the richest to the poorest member of a society, would, at first blush, seem easy to construct because we think of wealth as measurable. But in some societies, including the United States, people do not necessarily know how wealthy they are, and so might, if "polled," misinform the roster-builders. Or even if they do know how wealthy they are, they might attempt to deceive the roster-builders, and describe themselves as richer or poorer than they in fact are, thus getting themselves on the wrong line. Finally, even

---

[1] Cf. R. G. Collingwood, *An Essay on Philosophical Method* (Oxford: Clarendon Press, 1933), pp. 69-72. Collingwood distinguishes between that which is "measurable in principle" and "measurable in practice." He believes that philosophical concepts are, typically, unmeasurable in practice.

if we assume an accurately constructed roster, baffling problems arise when it comes to drawing significant lines across it (i.e., dividing it into significant sections). For rosters differ enormously as regards the extent to which they yield up groupings that are other than purely arbitrary.[2]

Another and less obvious problem is this: Political theorists sometimes talk as if one and the same roster could simultaneously list the individual members of a society in their right order not merely with respect to a single quality, but two or even three qualities. John Adams comes quickly to mind here as an example, since much of the controversy surrounding his "natural aristocracy" may be seen to turn on just this point. At one juncture Adams asserts that his natural aristocrats (that is, those at or near the top of his aristocracy roster) are those who "rate high," as we would put it today, in "birth, fortune, and fame." Push him further, and the relevant "qualities" turn out to be, among others, "merit," "talents," "wisdom," "learning," "eloquence in council," "confidence and affection of the citizens," "sense of duty," "virtue," "advantages of education," "respect of the public," "skill," "industry," "great knowledge of public affairs," and "honour."[3] Now: Adams' roster is intelligible, we see at once, only if (a) the qualities in question are inseparable and, in addition, come in constant proportions, or (b) he can show us how to "trade" x units of one quality for y units of the second, z units of the third, and so on.[4] (One of Adams' natural aristocrats might, on the basis of such trading,

[2]Many of the difficulties noted here also plague our social scientists, particularly our sociologists, when they try to deal with the problem of "social stratification." In our terms, they are engaged in constant controversy as to how many horizontal lines must be drawn on such and such rosters in order to delineate significant "classes."

[3]See his *A Defense of the Constitutions of Government of the United States of America,* particularly Volume III.

[4]Leadership and power studies frequently illustrate this difficulty. Alvin W. Gouldner notes, "Those proposing trait units [of leadership] usually do not suggest which of the traits are more important and which least. Not uncommonly, lists of more than ten traits are presented. In most such lists it seems very unlikely that each of the traits is equally important and deserves the same weighting." See *Studies in Leadership,* ed. Alvin W. Gouldner (New York: Harper, 1950), p. 23.

Cf., in this connection, C. Wright Mills' trenchant criticism of Lloyd Warner's definition of "class," which, he says, "absorbs at least three analytically distinct items," namely: economic, status, and distribution of power. Comments Mills: "From the insistence upon merely *one* vertical dimension and the consequent absorbing of these three analytically separable dimensions into the one sponge word 'class' flow the chief confusions [of Warner's study]." See his review of W. Lloyd Warner and Paul S. Lunt, *The Social Life of a Modern Community,* in the *American Sociological Review,* 7 (1942), 264-65.

turn out to be an uneducated and illiterate but supremely virtuous man.) Adams may well have supposed that the selfsame men could be counted on to rank very high with respect to each and every one of the qualities in question; but once such an assumption is hauled out into the open we see at once that it is unwarranted.[5] Given the number and disparate nature of the qualities he compressed into his aristocracy roster, we should expect them, in the absence of evidence to the contrary, to turn up in all manner of combinations. A "multi-quality" roster, then, places upon the theorist using it very special demands; and any failure on his part to meet these demands, as we have just noted them, renders his roster virtually meaningless.

Yet another difficulty associated with the roster technique leaps to the eye when we find a theorist drawing a single line across a putative roster, and claiming for it that, so to speak, it divides the sheep from the goats. Consider, for instance, the following age-old argument against majority rule: Assuming a roster that ranks individuals on the basis of virtue, we see at once (so we are told) that those at the top of the roster are as a matter of course a minority of the members of society; and, that being the case, that majority rule will result in the rule of the less virtuous.[6] But if we look a second time we see that the argument cuts both ways (i.e., can easily be turned against the man using it), as follows: those who possess little virtue, that is, the wicked, are a minority in society; and, that being the case, majority rule will evidently give us rule by the more virtuous. The truth is, of course, that neither argument proves anything at all, because each involves what we may now identify as an improper use of the roster device

[5] Adams may well have had occasion to reflect on some of the difficulties on this score. When he was a student at Harvard, class rank was determined "not according to scholastic ability but according to the social standing of a boy's family." According to Catherine Drinker Bowen, "No sooner was the [class rank] list posted than a flood of protests poured in. President Holyoke wished mightily that the grading depended on brains, color of hair, size of a boy's feet—anything but this vague and unholy thing called 'social position'." *John Adams and the American Revolution* (New York: Grosset & Dunlap, 1949), p. 78.

[6] Aristotle's *Politics* is one of the earliest works to advance this line of argument. "It is possible for one man, or a few, to be of outstanding excellence; but when it comes to a large number, we can hardly expect a fine edge of all the varieties of excellence." *The Politics of Aristotle,* ed. and trans. Ernest Barker, Book III, chapter VII, p. 114. Aristotle does concede this: "It is not clear, however, that this combination of qualities [to deliberate wisely and judge soundly], which we have made the ground of distinction between the many and few best, is true of all popular bodies and all large masses of men. . . ." Aristotle is, however, convinced that there is nothing to prevent this combination from occurring in *"some* popular bodies" (italics added). *Ibid.,* Book III, chapter XI, p. 124.

—improper because there is no justification for treating individuals above and below a certain point on the roster as constituting a homogeneous group, and no justification for assuming, as the arguments do, that society, if and when it divides over a political issue, will automatically (a) keep the individuals at the top of the roster together, and (b) set them "against" the other homogeneous mass that makes up the remainder of the roster. There are, in this connection, three points that seem worth making: First, we must look askance at any alleged "Great Divide" on any roster, because with respect to any quality what we are usually up against is a "log-normal" distribution, with each individual ranking just a little below the individual above him and a little above the individual below him, and so capable of being assimilated to either. Secondly, "continuous" minorities (i.e., minorities made up of persons whose names "belong together" on a roster) can be carved out anywhere along the line from top to bottom, as can continuous majorities. Whatever the case may have been in ancient Greece, for example, the societies we know do not automatically, or even usually, pit those at the top of an assumed "richness" roster against the remainder (as many of Aristotle's arguments assume they will). Averell Harriman and Nelson Rockefeller pull themselves out of the grouping in which they fall on the roster, and carve out of the roster a majority that is an unpredictable mixture of rich *and* poor; and, similarly, the British Conservatives, the party of the rich in Britain, have, notoriously, always had a vast following among those toward the bottom of the richness roster. The majorities and minorities divisions that we find in existential reality, that is to say, do not bring together persons whose names belong together on any particular roster, hypothetical or actual. All the lines theorists draw across their rosters thus begin to appear, for purposes of political analysis, highly suspect.[7]

[7]Madison showed his awareness of this when he argued in the Constitutional Convention that division and subsequent conflict between large and small states would be highly unlikely and that, therefore, there was no need to provide for the protection of the small states in the structure of government. Besides noting that there were no differences in basic interests between these two groups of states that would serve to divide them, he commented: "Experience suggested no such danger. The journals of Congress did not present any peculiar association of these States in the votes recorded. . . ." Madison did foresee, however, that there would be cleavages between the northern and southern states. See Madison's *Notes in Documents Illustrative of the Formation of the Union of the American States,* ed. Charles Tansill (Washington, D.C.: G.P.O., 1927), pp. 290-94 and 828.

The debates in the early state conventions over extension of the suffrage to those

The point at issue in the foregoing paragraph is by no means one
of merely antiquarian interest. Comparable, on our showing, to the
classical distinction between the virtuous few and non-virtuous
many, or the rich and the poor, as politically significant groupings is
the distinction, currently dear to the hearts of many social scientists,
between the "urban" population and "rural" population. The standard operating procedure here is to construct a putative "urban-rural"
roster, which ranks communities according to population (the largest
community being most "urban," and the smallest, most "rural").[8]
Allegedly significant lines are then drawn through the resulting roster, usually for the purpose of showing that the "rural" communities
are "overrepresented" in the state legislature as well as in both
houses of Congress.[9] The tacit assumption is that the "underrepre-
sented" urban areas have different interests from, and are ranged
over against, the "overrepresented" rural areas—whence it is a brief
step to the concept of "urban-rural conflict" that permeates most of
our political science texts. Yet the empirical evidence at our disposal
would indicate that the lines on the urban-rural roster do not possess,
in existential reality, the significance commonly attributed to them

without property also illustrate clearly how it is possible to shudder over imaginary
cleavages that never subsequently materialize. According to one of the most frequently
used arguments against expansion of the suffrage, the propertyless, being a majority
of society, would unite to equalize property holdings. Those who contended that
society would not divide in such fashion (thus questioning the relevance of the assumed roster) have, of course, proved to be correct.

[8]Probably the best known of these endeavors is Gordon E. Baker's, *Rural versus
Urban Political Power* (New York: Doubleday, 1955). A critically important question
regarding the procedure which is under discussion here is whether the population
index actually measures degree of urbanness or those dimensions (way of life, political
and social outlook, interests, etc.) that presumably are significant for social and political
theory. We strongly doubt it. Anyone familiar, for example, with Oklahoma City and
Tulsa, or Dallas and Fort Worth, is aware of great environmental and cultural differences that are in no way reflected in the population index.

[9]As Alfred De Grazia makes abundantly clear, rural "overrepresentation" can be
exaggerated or played down, depending upon how many lines are drawn, and where,
through the urban-rural roster. See his *Essay on Apportionment and Representative
Government* (Washington, D.C.: American Enterprise Institute, 1963).
    John G. Grumm, after analyzing the voting patterns in the 1959 session of the Kansas
legislature writes: "From the substantive standpoint, the analysis produced no evidence that an urban or rural 'bloc' of legislators existed in either house. Certainly there
was not a continuous antipathy between the two groups that reflected itself over a
broad range of issues. . . ." "The Means of Measuring Conflict and Cohesion in the
Legislature," *Southwestern Social Science Quarterly*, March 1964, p. 387. Cf., for much
the same view, David R. Derge, "Metropolitan and Outstate Alignments in Illinois and
Missouri Legislative Delegations," *American Political Science Review*, 52 (December
1958), 1065. And cf. also Robert S. Freedman, "The Urban-Rural Conflict Revisited,"
Western Political Quarterly, 14 (June 1961), p. 481.

(as, we predict, certain persons will learn once our state legislatures have been made over in the image of the urban-rural roster). The "continuous" minorities and majorities on the rosters of amateur political theorists have, we suggest, little if any relevance to the actual political divisions out in society.[10]

II

Let us, by way of illustration, turn to liberal democratic theory of recent decades. One of its standard operating procedures, prefigured in Mill's *Representative Government,* is as follows: The theorist (1) states the case for democracy, and the claims for the exercise of power in it by the people themselves, in terms not of a roster (as defined above) but of, so to speak, a census—which lists the entire adult population of the society in some fashion (e.g., alphabetically, or by street address) involving no invidious distinctions between the individuals concerned; then (2) presents a picture of the problems government must cope with that warrants the conclusion that they cannot be solved by just anybody whose name appears on the census list; then (3) appeals, at long last, to a roster (as defined above), with reference to which the theorist is prepared to argue that the problems in question can be solved only by placing the persons whose names are at the top in certain strategic positions in government and society; then (4) contends that these persons, once in these strategic positions, will in fact be able to prevent the disasters that would unavoidably ensue if all decisions were made by persons taken at random from the census list.

Great controversies and baffling problems are associated with this procedure. One perennial issue in the theory of democratic government has to do with the extent to which step 3 above, the sudden imposition upon the "census" of a "roster," is compatible with the fundamental "value" embodied in step 1, namely, the intrinsic equality of citizens within a democratic political system.[11] The position

---

[10]We do not forget that the "urban-rural" conflict might *become* a reality if the supposed issue continues to be agitated in certain quarters. But if that happened, it would be a clear case of what W. I. Thomas called the "self-fulfilling prophecy."

[11]On this point see Giovanni Sartori, *Democratic Theory* (Detroit: Wayne State University Press, 1962), chapter XVI. Sartori contends: "... [The] democratic postulate that politics does not involve special qualification is valid insofar as democratic politics remains, we might say, a middle-range politics. If a political system is grounded on the assumption that everybody is able, by birthright, to handle political affairs, then it must

any theorist adopts on this issue, we may now say, must turn on his understanding of the relationship between the "people" (conceived in census terms) and the elite (that is, the individuals at the top of this or that roster). Take, for example, the critics of modern "mass society," who according to William Kornhauser fall into two camps: that of the "democratic critics," who defend "democratic values against the rise of elites bent on total domination," and the "aristocratic" or elite critics, whose theories center on an "intellectual defense of elite values against the rise of mass participation."[12] The "democratic" critics, are, clearly, concerned about the introduction of any roster at all, and deny that the individuals at the top of this or that proposed roster should ever be the controlling elements in society by preference over the majority of the "equal" citizens. The aristocratic or elitist theorists, on the other hand, contend that the democratic values now hold such sway in our democracies, particularly in the United States, as to tie the hands of the individuals at the top of the "competence" roster, and prevent them from staving off disaster. As Lippmann writes, the egalitarian values associated with democracy have made it virtually impossible to bring competence and expertise to bear upon our problems, and have led to a "morbid derangement of the true functions of power. The derangement brings about enfeeblement, verging on paralysis, of the capacity to govern."[13] (Note, in

comply with its own assumption, and thereby recognize that certain boundaries are not to be crossed; namely, that the range of the political decision-making allowed by the system must exclude the sectors and types of intervention which would require a qualified and specialized leadership" (p. 403).

[12] *The Politics of Mass Society* (Glencoe: Free Press, 1959), p. 21.

[13] *The Public Philosophy* (New York: New American Library, 1955), p. 19. Also see José Ortega y Gasset, *The Revolt of the Masses* (New York: Norton, 1957). "Today we are witnessing the triumphs of a hyperdemocracy in which the mass acts directly, outside the law, imposing its aspirations and its desires by means of material pressure. It is a false interpretation of the new situation to say that the mass has grown tired of politics and handed over the exercise of it to specialized persons. Quite the contrary. That was what happened previously; that was democracy. The mass took it for granted that after all, in spite of their defects and weaknesses, the minorities understood a little more of public problems than it did itself. Now, on the other hand, the mass believes that it has the right to impose and give force of law to notions born in the café. I doubt whether there have been other periods of history in which the multitude has come to govern more directly than in our own. That is why I speak of hyperdemocracy." Ortega's analysis is, we may note in passing, a straight roster-type analysis (as the latter is defined in the present essay), pointing up a Great Divide between the select minorities, who make "demands" on themselves, and the "masses," who do not. It is this book that has given Ortega, who was certainly a Leftist in Spanish politics, his generally undeserved bad reputation for being a "Conservative." ("Mass," or "masses," has according to Ortega's definition no numerical connotation, though he

terms of our statement in Section I, the appeal to a "two-qualities" roster.)

As Kornhauser further notes, the elitist critics state their case against democratic systems more or less as follows: Democratic systems, because they allow the (merely equal) citizens "high access to elites," not only prevent the elites from "performing their creative and value-sustaining functions" but also generate and encourage the belief that "anyone is qualified" to participate in making policy decisions, even those that require special competence. The people, moreover, are not ordinarily content to intervene "only at certain points in the decision-making process." Rather they feel free to intervene at any and every point in the process, thus depriving the elites of the protection and isolation necessary for carrying out "their critical functions." In sum, the aristocratic critics bemoan the "loss of exclusiveness of elites," which results in the sovereignty of "public opinion."[14] These observations may be taken as reflective of the present status of the roster-*versus*-census issue in the literature of contemporary social science.

Now one of the very first treatises ever to deal with the question as to the proper respective roles of the people and elites in a democratic political system was John Stuart Mill's *Considerations on Representative Government.* Written at the height of the English industrial revolution, when there was an increasing demand for democratic "reforms" such as expansion of the suffrage to the urban "masses," this work to an astonishing degree anticipates the concerns which seem to be uppermost in the minds of the modern elitists. This is not to say, of course, that Mill is the "father" of modern elitists. Rather, as a later section will make abundantly clear, Mill differs sharply from modern elite theory on the most fundamental questions. We do contend, however, that close textual examination of this work clearly reveals techniques, especially those relating to roster construction, which, though in fact used by many modern elitists, are not so readily discernible in their writings. Mill's book, moreover, displays what may fairly be called the "mind-set," or "frame of mind," of the modern elitists that disposes them to adopt their present posture concerning the proper role of elites. This mind-set is a matter of

appears, in the passage quoted, to equate "mass" and "multitude." His point is that "mass-man" has now *become* the majority.)

[14]Lippmann, *op. cit.,* pp. 28-29.

certain fundamental "values" and assumptions that, as we shall see,
virtually dictate the positions of present-day elitists, but are all too
seldom brought out into the open and are, therefore, left to lurk
between the lines as unarticulated premises. Mill's arguments, we
suggest, lay bare these "values" and assumptions.

III

Let us take a close look, then at Mill's *Representative Government*,
and pursue further the point we were making about it: Toward the
end of Chapter 5 ("Of the Proper Functions of Representative Bodies"), Mill identifies two "benefits" to be conferred (in the jargon of
our day, "maximized") by his proposed system. First, there are the
benefits of "popular control" over government, and, second, those of
"skilled legislation and administration" which are "no less important" and grow "ever more important" as "human affairs increase in
scale and complexity."[15] He proceeds:

> There are no means of combining these benefits except by
> separating the functions which guarantee the one from those
> which essentially require the other; [that is] by disjoining the
> *office of control* and criticism from the *actual conduct* of affairs,
> and devolving *the former on the representatives of the Many,*
> while securing for the latter, under strict responsibility to the
> nation, *the acquired knowledge and practiced intelligence of a
> specially trained and experienced Few.* [Italics added.][16]

Several phrases in this passage merit all the attention we can give
them. The appeal to the "acquired knowledge and practiced intelligence of a specially trained and experienced Few" is, quite clearly,
an appeal to our "roster" device. Mill is going to devote the rest of
the book, as he has just devoted the last few pages, to claiming one
strategic position after another for the "Few" at the top of the roster
he has begun to construct. Moreover, he *sounds* as if he had already

---

[15]Mark the words "scale" and "complexity," which are to become the common coin
of subsequent elitist theory.
[16]*Utilitarianism, Liberty and Representative Government* (New York: Dutton,
1950), p. 323. All subsequent citations are to this edition. The division of function
suggested here is reflected in the cliché, "Keep the bureaucracy on tap, not on top."

made up his mind as to who "they" are, and why it is they, not some other Few, who must be placed in those positions. That Few, in any case, are to be charged merely with the "actual conduct of affairs"; and they must, he insists, act "under strict responsibility to the nation"—that is, under constant "criticism" and "control" by the elected representatives of the "people." Mill thus commits himself to the view, probably unprecedented in political philosophy, that it would be a good thing to have a knowledgeable and intelligent Few *conducting* affairs, and (as we will see shortly) a far less knowledgeable and intelligent Many *"controlling"* affairs. Furthermore, there is no skepticism on Mill's part as to whether this can be brought off— that is, as to whether he can work out an allocation of functions between the Many, regarded as not merely numerous but as, *ipso facto*, possessing a certain quality or certain qualities in low degree, and the Few, regarded as not merely unnumerous but as, *ipso facto*, possessing that quality or those qualities in high degree. But which is it? A "certain quality," so that Mill would not, on the strength of this passage, be open to the charge that he appeals to a roster that cannot be constructed (as we have defined such a roster above)? Or is it "certain qualities," so that he would be open to that charge? "Specially trained" and "experienced" sound, to be sure, like two specifications, but *might* be only one, and so might be construed as conforming to the rules of roster construction as we have explained them. "Experience," that is to say, *might* be relevant experience, experience relevant to the "training," and thus so much further training. He might be thinking, as our Civil Service Commission does, of units of the one as indefinitely "tradeable" for units of the other. (We leave the question open, that is, declare it impossible to answer on the basis of the passage we have before us.)

Mill is, let us notice, apparently quite serious about "popular control," that is, about seeing to it that his Few shall not be a law unto themselves. Representative government is in his eyes the "ideal polity," and representative government is precisely government in which

the whole people, or some numerous portion of them, exercise through deputies elected by themselves the ultimate controlling power. . . . [They] must possess [it] in all its completeness.

They must be masters whenever they please, of all the operations of government.[17]

By "whole people, or some numerous portion of them," moreover, he means just that:

> In proportion as any, no matter who, are excluded from . . .
> [participation in the benefits of freedom] the interests of the
> excluded are left without the guarantee accorded to the rest,
> and they themselves have less scope and encouragement than
> they might otherwise have to . . . exertion of their energies for
> the good of themselves and of the community.[18]

What he wants, and misses no opportunity to emphasize, is

> [ultimate]sovereignty . . . vested in the entire aggregate of the
> community; every citizen not only having a voice in the exercise
> of that . . . sovereignty, but being, at least occasionally, called
> upon to take an actual part in the government, by the personal
> discharge of some public function, local or general.[19]

And we will not raise here the fashionable post-Freudian question whether he means it. He says it, and it would be presumptuous for us to suggest that he does not mean it.

There is (as we shall see) good reason, however, to raise some slightly different but related questions, namely: Just *how* does he mean it? Or, What *in toto* does he mean on this point? We may not ask Mill "Are you for democracy?" since he has told us he is; but we can ask him "Why are you for democracy?" Here are some relevant passages:

> We may consider . . . as one criterion of the goodness of govern-
> ment the degree in which it tends to increase the sum of good
> qualities in the governed, collectively and individually; since,
> besides that their well-being is the sole object of government,
> their good qualities supply the moving force which works the
> machinery.[20]

[17] *Ibid.*, p. 305.
[18] *Ibid.*, p. 282.
[19] *Ibid.*, p. 278.
[20] *Ibid.*, p. 259.

And a second criterion:

> This leaves, as the other constituent element of the merit of a government, the quality of the machinery itself; that is, the degree in which it is adapted to take advantage of the amount of good qualities which may at any time exist, and make them instrumental to the right purposes.[21]

And:

> We have now . . . obtained a foundation for a two-fold division of the merit which any set of political institutions may possess. It consists partly of the degree to which they promote the general advancement of the community, including under that phrase advancement in intellect, in virtue, and in practical activity and efficiency; and partly of the degree of perfection with which they organize the moral intellectual, and active worth already existing, so as to operate with the greatest effect on public affairs. . . . A government is to be judged . . . by what it makes of its citizens, and what it does for them; its tendency to improve or deteriorate the people themselves, and the goodness or badness of the work it performs for them.[22]

Now: There are great difficulties here, and we must hold Mill to account for them. He clearly has, in the first place, two different definitions of "the community." There is, on the one hand, the community regarded as a whole (which has, in our terminology, the characteristics of the "census" or "directory"). And there is, on the other hand, the community regarded as made up of the Many on the one hand, and the Few, on the other—the community, that is to say, with its members' names entered upon a roster, with a horizontal line through it, above which Mill is prepared to call all the individuals listed "specially trained and experienced," and below which everybody is merely somebody who must not be "excluded." And the difficulty—a very revealing one as regards his state of mind—is that Mill's general position takes on different meanings according as one or the other of these definitions of the community is foremost in his mind.

[21] *Ibid.*
[22] *Ibid.*, p. 262.

Democratic institutions, Mill is saying, are to be judged according as they organize the "worth" of the community that already exists, so that that worth can have the greatest effect on public affairs. And the question will not down: In "organizing" the existing "worth" of the community, can the "worthy" be drawn from below as well as from above the line that separates the Many from the Few? Or are we to assume that the worthy are to be found only above the line? To put the point otherwise: When Mill speaks of *promoting* "the general mental advancement of the community" ("potential" worth, presumably), he seems to be thinking of *the community as a whole,* regarded without invidious distinctions among its members (so that everybody, ashman equally with Oxford don, is to get his mental advancement promoted). Not so, however, when he speaks of organizing the community's existing worth, since we soon learn that it is only "worth" above the line that is going to get organized. One of the things we must find out from Mill, then, is this: Are those below the line devoid, then, of "existing worth"? Is the worth of the Many, as contrasted with the Few, merely potential worth?

A second and third difficulty, both of which cry up at us out of Mill's language, can be briefly noted. Wherever the existing "worth" is, whether above the line exclusively or both above and below it, it is sometimes described by Mill as worth of one kind, *intellectual* worth, sometimes as worth of two kinds (*intellectual* and *moral*), sometimes as worth of three kinds (*intellectual, moral,* and *active*), and sometimes, once again, as worth of a single kind, "mental worth" —which, as the above passage makes clear, includes, on occasion, all three of the other kinds. Worse still "active," "practical," and "efficient" worth all bob up now and then. And, as we shall see shortly, the inclusion of "moral" worth poses, in due course, very considerable problems. That is the second difficulty.

A third difficulty, at least from the standpoint of other theorists of the democratic state such as Rousseau, is that Mill speaks of directing the worth of society to "right" purposes, of the "well-being" of the community as the sole object of government, and of the "goodness" or "badness" of the work government performs, and speaks of them as if these were matters about which there are *correct* answers, which remain correct even when trampled on by the judgments of the "community as a whole." That is, to be sure, an intelligible position, in support of which we might cite many a great political philosoher, but not, perhaps, one that can be reconciled with a proposal for "criticism" and "control" by the Many—for, to go no further, the following reason: Unless the Many possess as of now—not off in the future, not potentially, but as of *now*—"qualities" that would enable them to exercise control intelligently and to "good" purpose, there is *no* reason to expect them to come up with correct judgments on these matters. Now: Mill never intimates, never once, that the Many do, as of now, possess these "qualities." Even as to the future, indeed, Mill offers us no grounds for optimism on this point, rather the contrary: human affairs will increase in "scale" and "complexity," will accordingly, make greater and greater demands upon the "qualities" of those in control. The implication would appear to be that the Many must, with the passing of time, become less and less competent to control human affairs, and Mill never gets around to disclaiming that implication. He has, in short, come out for popular control, but he has rested his demand for it on grounds that, we repeat, leave him wide open to the questions: What "qualities" do the Many actually possess, since by definition they are not "specially trained" or "experienced"? And, would Mill really be prepared to turn society over to their "effective" control?

At least the outlines of answers to these questions are, happily, to be found elsewhere in the book, and because of the light they throw on the remainder of Mill's argument they are worth setting forth in some detail. Let us turn especially to the chapters on "The Proper Functions of Representative Bodies" and "The Infirmities and Dangers to which Representative Government is Liable"—where, if only by indirection, he points to the decisive considerations.

As for the "infirmities" and "dangers," Mill sees two great positive evils to which representative government is heir. The first of these is "insufficient mental qualifications"[23] in the "controlling body"— where, significantly, "controlling body" does not mean the electorate, as we might expect it to from the definition cited above, but the representative assembly, and where, furthermore, the "mental" in "insufficient mental qualifications" does not appear to be used in the broad "catchall" sense we noted a moment ago. He is, rather, equating "insufficient mental qualifications" with, quite simply, "general ignorance and incapacity."[24] Yet, in his subsequent discussion of this problem, Mill hardly touches upon the topic he has posed, that is, the "insufficient mental qualifications" of the "controlling body." What

[23] *Ibid.*, p. 326.
[24] *Ibid.*

we are given, instead, is a little essay on the strengths and weaknesses of governments that are entirely in the hands of aristocracies of public functionaries—of, in other words, "bureaucracies." And this essay in turn, leads not into a demonstration (which is what we are expecting) that representative assemblies have insufficient mental qualifications, and not into an explanation of what the phrase means exactly, but rather into a homily on the need of combining popular control with control by—and here note a new twist—"skilled persons, bred to it as an intellectual profession."[25] And this, in turn, leads Mill to stress the importance of getting *into the representative assembly itself* "an amount of mental competency sufficient for its own proper work."[26] We must not, he warns us, settle for anything less than "an adequate amount of intelligence and knowledge in the representative assembly."[27] And the implication, confirmed in his statement on "the representation of minorities" and "pledges," is that unless we take drastic steps calculated to sluice the requisite amount of intelligence and knowledge into the assembly, it won't get there. And so we come at last to an answer, and a very surprising one, to *our* question if not Mill's own: *with respect to intelligence and knowledge drastic steps must be taken to secure a representative assembly as little like the Many as possible.* Put otherwise: the dangers to which Mill alludes become real dangers only when the representative assembly resembles the Many, which perhaps tells us all we need to know about Mill's estimate of the worth of the Many. The assembly controlled by the Many, he says at long last, "will countenance, or impose, a capricious and impulsive, a short-sighted, ignorant, and prejudiced general policy, foreign and domestic; it will abrogate good laws, or enact bad ones, let in new evils, or cling with perverse obstinacy to old. . . ."[28] The conclusion seems inescapable: Mill believed (a) that the intelligence that needs to be "organized" for governmental purposes is to be found exclusively in the Few (i.e., "above the line"), and (b) that the consequences of turning government over to effective control by the Many (i.e., those "below the line") can only be disastrous.

Mill, as any reader of *Representative Government* knows well, did

[25] *Ibid.*, p. 332.
[26] *Ibid.*
[27] *Ibid.*
[28] *Ibid.*, pp. 332-33.

want to provide representation in the assembly for a broad range of interests; and it could be argued that, in this sense at least, Mill sought to provide for a national forum as much like the Many as possible. But even in the act of advocating that broad representation of interests, he was careful to insure that these interests would "balance out"— so that the Few, those acting on "reason, justice, and the good of the whole" would always have the decisive say. His exact words here are as follows: "The representative system ought to be so constituted as to maintain this state of things: it ought not to allow any of the various sectional interests to be so powerful as to be capable of prevailing against truth and justice and the other sectional interests combined."[29]

And, if there be any doubt about Mill's reluctance to allow for control by the Many, even after trying to see to it that the Few would hold a decisive balance of power in the assembly, Mill's views as to the "proper functions" of representative bodies would seem to settle the question once and for all. We can only guess at his motivation here (one guess: he feared that, despite the precautions which he advocated, the Few would lose control of the assembly); what is certain is that he wished to minimize the assembly's role vis à vis the bureaucracy—which, because of its composition and nature, was more apt to act as unlike the Many as possible. What is certain is that Mill thought the assembly ill "fitted" to administer, or even to "dictate in detail to those who have charge of administration."[30] Why? "Every branch of public administration is a *skilled* business, which has its own peculiar principles and traditional rules . . . , none of them likely to be appreciated by persons not practically acquainted with the department. . . .[31] There are many rules of the greatest importance in every branch . . . of which a person fresh to the subject neither knows the reason nor suspects the existence. . . .[32] All these difficulties are sure to be ignored by a representative assembly. . . .[33] Besides, an assembly never personally experiences the inconveniences of its bad measures until they have reached the dimensions of national evils. Ministers and administrators [by contrast] see them approach. . . ."[34]

[29] *Ibid.*, p. 343.
[30] *Ibid.*, p. 310.
[31] *Ibid.*
[32] *Ibid.*
[33] *Ibid.*, p. 311.
[34] *Ibid.*, p. 312 (all italics added in quoted passages beginning with no. 30).

The representatives, in other words, do not *know* enough about any branch of administration, and are not sufficiently skillful forecasters of the consequences of administrative measures, to be turned loose in this area. Their proper duty is merely to see to it that the persons who make administrative decisions "shall be the proper persons." But even this they cannot hope to do well, since there is "scarcely any case in which less attention is paid to qualifications, partly because [average?] men do not know, and partly because they do not care for, the difference in qualifications between one person and another. . . .[35] A man is appointed either because he has a reputation, often quite undeserved, for *general* ability, or frequently for no better reason than that he is personally popular."[36] Let the assembly, then, recognize its limitations in this regard also, and confine itself to deciding "who shall be prime minister, or who shall be the two or three individuals from whom the prime minister will be chosen."[37]

More: The assembly is "as little fitted for the direct business of legislation as for that of administration. There is hardly any kind of *intellectual* work which so much needs to be done by experience and exercised minds . . . as the business of making laws . . . [besides which] every provision of a law requires it to be framed with the most accurate and long-sighted perception of its effect on all the other provisions. . . . It is impossible that these conditions would be fulfilled when laws are voted clause by clause in a miscellaneous assembly."[38] In short, intellectual "worth" of the kind actually needed, needed not merely for the conduct of affairs but even for legislation (which, at first blush, would appear to come under the heading of "control"), recedes back up the roster to where it was before. Only the above-the-line Few, the "specially trained and experienced," have it. And

[35] *Ibid.*
[36] *Ibid.*, p. 314 (italics added).
[37] *Ibid.*
[38] *Ibid.*, p. 315 (italics added). Some American commentators, including the present writers, would contend that our much-criticized congressional committee system overcomes many of the difficulties cited by Mill. Not only (so they would insist) are the committees able to consider bills "clause by clause" with an eye to their effects "on all other provisions"; these committees, because of the rules that dictate their composition and leadership, develop an expertise that the "permanent" bureaucracy, for all its "training" and "experience," can seldom match, if only because of the rapid turnover in its upper echelons. At the retirement ceremonies of Carl Vinson, for example, Secretary of Defense McNamara noted that he had not yet been born when Vinson first entered the House of Representatives.

because they have it, they stand in sharp contrast to even the "well-constituted" assembly.

The second positive evil over which Mill agonizes has to do with the "evils arising from the prevalence of modes of action in the representative body, dictated by sinister interests . . . , that is, interests conflicting more or less with the general good of the community."[39] Why must such evils arise? Well, replies Mill—he is more than usually difficult to follow in the discussion we are about to analyze—for this reason: We can count on the citizens of any community ripe for representative government for "a *certain amount* of conscience, and of disinterested public spirit"[40] (moral worth, surely?). Not, that is to say, much. And, that being the case, "it would be ridiculous to expect such a degree of it, combined with such intellectual discernment,"[41] as would provide against the evils in question.[42]

Three comments are in order. (1) This time around, Mill is going to speak at last of the electorate itself, not of the representative assembly—so that we shall not, this time, have to infer his answer to the question before us from his answer to a different question. What he is out to prove, to be sure, is that sinister interests will prevail in the assembly unless steps are taken to prevent their doing so. But the discussion itself centers on the citizens who elect the assembly. (2) Since Mill's thesis does concern the assembly, we might fairly have expected him, in this context, to speak in terms parallel to those he has used earlier—that is, of "insufficient *moral* qualifications" as formerly he has spoken of "insufficient *mental* qualifications" (italics added). But he does not do so, for all that the point he ends up making is much the same kind of point he has made in the earlier section. And while the word "moral" does finally creep into the discussion, it does so for the first time in the following chapter, "On the Representation of Minorities." (This, as we shall indicate below, is no small matter.) (3) Mill is, let us notice, clearly reluctant to speak of "conscience and disinterested public spirit" as something separate and distinct from

[39] *Op. cit.,* p. 333.
[40] *Op. cit.,* p. 340 (italics added).
[41] *Ibid.*
[42] Here we should note once more a difficulty with Mill's theory to which we must return below. For all that his system is putatively designed to encourage participation in governmental affairs, and so "foster in the members of the community the various desirable qualities, moral and intellectual," our reading of Chapter VI ("Infirmities and Dangers") commits him to the view that the Many could *never* exercise unrestrained control in an intelligent *and* just manner.

"intellectual discernment." The potential evils he is calling attention to, he emphasizes, arise from insufficient conscience and disinterested public spirit *in combination with* insufficient intellectual discernment. No matter what degree of conscience and disinterested public spirit may be present in the citizens, he seems to be saying, the dangers would still exist because of the citizens' "insufficient mental qualifications." But let us turn back to the text and follow the argument step by step.

There are, says Mill, two "dispositions" that have a bearing on this problem: First, there is the "disposition to prefer a man's selfish interests to those he shares with other people." Second, there is the disposition "to prefer . . . immediate and direct interests to those which are indirect and remote."[43] Both dispositions, moreover, "are called forth and fostered by the possession of power," and both tend, so to speak, to repeat themselves on the "class" level—so that classes, like individuals, suffer from both dispositions, and suffer from them the more certainly to the extent that they possess power. Nor will Mill have any nonsense about the second disposition (i.e., preferring immediate to remote interests) being a matter of *intellectual* discernment, not conscience and public spirit: "It is only," he insists, "disinterested regard for others . . . for the idea of posterity, of their country, or of mankind . . . which ever direct the minds and purposes of classes or bodies of men toward distant or unobvious interests"; and this disinterested regard we must not expect from "average men," or even, he adds, from "much more cultivated minds than those of the numerical majority."[44] The latter, we learn in the end, simply will not have "so delicate a conscience, or so just an appreciation of what is against their own apparent interest, as not to follow their own selfish inclinations and short-sighted notions of their own good."[45]

Here, then, is at least a preliminary answer to our question: Average men, whom Mill proceeds to equate with the numerical majority, the Many, do not have the disinterested regard, or the delicate conscience, or the just appreciation for what is against their own interests, that alone restrains men from using power for selfish purposes —at the expense of the community as a whole. The same thing is true even higher up the roster, where consciences are "more delicate"

[43] *Ibid.*, p. 339.
[44] *Ibid.*, p. 340.
[45] *Ibid.*, p. 341.

and—though he does not explain what this has to do with the matter
—"minds" are "more cultivated." Once again, therefore, we find Mill
saying, in effect, that the worth of the community—this time, clearly,
the "sufficient" *moral* worth—is in a Few at the top of a roster, and
predicting, in effect, that genuine control by the Many will lead to
disastrous results.[46]

Note, now, the speed with which Mill moves—now he has a second
Many and a second Few on his hands: a Many with indelicate consciences over and above the Many with insufficient mental qualifications, a Few governed by higher considerations over and above the
Few with special training and experience. What he is out to do, as
we should expect from what we have said about multi-quality rosters,
is to regularize the situation, as soon as possible, by getting rid of one
of the two pairs; and, equally important for our purposes, to decide
which pair to get rid of. The reference to the morally superior Few
—and superior intellectual discernment is not so much as hinted at
in his descriptions of them—occurs at page 255. But by page 256 the
concept has already begun to crumble: the Few are a Few—not two
Fews but just one—who "act on higher motives and more comprehensive and distant views"—which, any way you look at it, readmits
"intellectual discernment" through the back door, whence we are
about to watch it move to the front of the house. By page 259 we find
a reference to the "constituencies to which most of the *highly educated and public spirited* persons belong"—not the highly educated
on the one hand and the public spirited on the other, but the highly
educated *and* public spirited (italics added). Through pages 260-63
he is outlining his plan for "abating" the two great dangers he has
been telling us about—a low grade of intelligence in the representative body, and class legislation by the numerical majority; so that by
page 264 he is ready to lean back in his chair and explain the predictable advantages that will accrue from his plan's operation. But the
first thing that the attentive reader will notice is that conscience and
disinterested public spirit seem to have disappeared from his purview—in favor, of course, of intellectual superiority. His plan (page
264) will "afford the best security for the intellectual qualifications
desirable in the [individual?] representative." Under the plan, "hundreds of *able men of independent thought*" will offer themselves for

---

[46]Meaning by "genuine control" by the Many simply this: The Many pursuing a
policy without securing the support of a "large proportion of those who [unlike the
Many] act on higher motive and more comprehensive and distant views."

the first time as candidates, and the consequences will be that Parliament, more certainly than under any other plan, will contain "the very elite of the country" (italics added). The plan will "raise the *intellectual* standard of the House of Commons" (italics added). Then, first on page 266 and second on page 269, the following telltale passages: "But though the superior intellects and characters will necessarily be outnumbered, it makes a great difference whether they are heard. In the false democracy ... the voice of the *instructed* minority may have no organs at all in the representative body" (italics added). Superior intellects and characters, clearly, are now equated with the *instructed* minority. Finally, "The instructed minority would, in the actual voting, count only for their numbers, but as a *moral* power they would count for much more. . . . A democratic people would in this way be provided with leaders of a higher grade of *intellect and character* than itself" (italics added). The transition from "instructed minority" to "higher grade of intellect and character" is, we notice, accomplished without so much as a "by-your-leave." And henceforth, the second roster, or if you like the confusing second quality for a two-quality single roster, can be dispensed with. What counts is *instruction;* other things, morality for example, will take care of themselves provided that is taken care of.

Secondly, as the reader will already have noticed, Mill is confused as to what name to give to the quality on which to base the single-quality roster to which he is moving. Here it is a matter of being "specially trained and experienced." There it is a matter of possessing "superior intellect." Yonder it is a matter of having "knowledge." Further on, it is a matter of being an "able" man of "independent thought." Here it is a matter of being "skillful," or having been "bred" to the conduct of affairs as an "intellectual profession." There it is a matter of "intelligence" or superior "mental qualifications." Now: it *might* be, of course, that Mill regards these qualities as interchangeable for all practical purposes—or, to put the matter in terms of the roster device, as yielding up not several Fews but only one, that is, *the* Few; and, the fact that he does not pause to clear up the confusion, which he would certainly have been compelled to do if he were thinking in terms of separate rosters, does seem to bear out that possibility. More: as he moves further and further into the realm of concrete proposals, the somewhat vague terms we have just mentioned get pushed out of the way in favor of two new terms, namely:

"highly educated" and, as an ultimate refinement, "instructed"—
which at last so situates him that he can give an affirmative answer
to the question, Can your roster actually be constructed, so that we
can in fact identify your Few and put them to work? To search out
the "instructed" is to search out the men with "credentials." A candidate for a high place on the roster either has them or he doesn't. And
the credentials he has are either better credentials or worse ones
(Oxbridge or Redbrick, Yale or Oklahoma, as we might say today).

IV

To what conclusions have we been leading up in the foregoing
analysis? Not, we hasten to assure the reader, to the superficially
tempting conclusion that Mill, despite the opening pages of *Representative Government,* is the direct ancestor of our present-day elitists and, despite certain idiosyncrasies of emphasis, ought himself to
be classified as an elitist. That conclusion we willingly forego as an
oversimplification. Mill did, to be sure, use arguments hostile in their
bearing to majority rule, especially the argument that the generality
of men are, and will continue to be, a poor lot. (He is, for example,
innocent of the notion, dear to many of his admirers, that the generality of men are as they are merely because they are brought up in an
unfavorable environment.) But we must take into account here his
practical proposals concerning the machinery of government, which
are *not* what we would expect from a man out to forestall majority
rule—or even, for that matter, universal suffrage. Mill did, of course,
"come out" in favor of plural voting, proportional representation, and
unpledged representatives (that is, representatives upon whom the
electorate has not imposed its own policy directives). But over against
all that we must place the role that Mill was ready to accord to the
representative assembly: His parliament would "throw the light of
publicity on the government's acts"; it would compel the government
to explain and justify any act that it deemed questionable; it would
censure the government for any act that it found condemnable. It
would, to be sure, channel most of its energies (as Mill puts it) into
"talk." ("Talking and discussion," he says, "are their proper business,
while *doing,* as the result of discussion, is the task not of a miscellaneous body, but of individuals specially trained to it. . . . [The] fit office
of an assembly is . . . [not] to interfere with [those individuals] . . .

except by unlimited latitude of suggestion and criticism, and by applying or withholding the final seal of national assent." [Italics added.]) Or again: "A place where every interest and shade of opinion can have its cause pleaded, in the face of government and ... can compel them to listen, and either comply, or state clearly why they do not, is in itself, if it answered no other purpose, one of the most important political institutions that can exist...."[47] But the assembly's powers, on that showing, greatly exceed those of a mere "talk-shop."

The question therefore arises: How can Mill's commitment to "control" by a representative assembly be reconciled with the elitist "tendency" we have noted above? The answer, it would seem, must be this: Mill is urging upon us, along with certain practical proposals, a "constitutional morality."[48] He did indeed wish to keep the assembly as such out of the actual business of day-to-day policy formation, and did wish to play down the "plebiscitary potential" of the form of government he outlines. But "wish" is the operative word in both contexts, and what Mill really wishes is that the electorate (which is not to exact pledges) and the assembly (which is to remember there are functions it cannot perform well) should *discipline* themselves— this in accordance with a teaching that stands quite apart from Mill's machinery-of-government proposals.[49] This distinction (between ma-

[47] *Ibid.*, pp. 321-22.

[48] Our point here should not be confused with that upon which other recent critics have rung the changes—e.g., Currin V. Shields, who writes: "Contrary to Mills' thesis, elite rule may or may not be desirable in theory, but in practice it is not desirable— for a person who believes in the consent of the governed." See his "Introduction" to *Considerations on Representative Government* (New York: Liberal Arts Press, 1958), p. xxxiv.

On our showing, the supposed inherent contradiction in Mill's theory does not exist. He is, quite simply, trying to persuade his readers, potentially a majority, to subscribe to the system he proposes and, once the system is adopted, to limit their participation in the normal operations of government—in the interest, he would have them believe, of their own well-being. Such a position allows him to advocate simultaneously and without contradicting himself; *both* popular sovereignty and, to use Shield's phrase, "elite rule." In the "showdown" situation—that is, where an issue arises that calls for a choice between popular sovereignty (majority rule) and "elite rule"—there can be no doubt that Mill would opt for popular sovereignty. See our further argument in the text.

[49] For confirmation of this point, one has only to look at his other writings, principally, *Dissertations and Discussions:* "... [It] is not possible that the constitution of the democracy itself should provide adequate security for its being understood and administered in this spirit [i.e., 'That political questions be not decided by an appeal, either direct or indirect, to the judgment or will of an uninstructed mass, whether of gentlemen or of clowns; but by the deliberately formed opinions of a comparatively few, specially educated for the task.']. This rests with the good sense of the people themselves. If the people can remove their rulers for one thing, they can for another.

chinery of government and constitutional morality) is, we believe, of decisive importance for understanding Mill. His electorate, and the parliament it elects, are to be left free, as free *constitutionally* as any majoritarian could wish them to be, to exact pledges, vote laws clause by clause, and intervene in the administrative process at every turn. Mill, on the showing of *Representative Government,* would place no barriers in their way. They can take over the decision-making process any day they are prepared to take the trouble to organize for that purpose and "move in"—and anyone who comes away from *Representative Government* with a different impression from this had better go back to the text. Furthermore, the whole system has an Achilles heel of pure majoritarianism that, however reluctant Mill may have been to call attention to it (which he certainly was), is inescapable. Mill sums up: ". . . if the men who compose the government abuse their trust, or fulfill it in a manner which conflicts with the *deliberate sense of the nation,*[50] the assembly's proper function is to expel them from office, and either expressly or virtually appoint their successors."[51] This is all that the majoritarian has any sensible reason to ask for, since it opens the door to the full plebiscitary potential in representative government.

Nor is that all: Mill refuses, again and again, to "follow through" on the Few-Many dichotomy that we have been analyzing. This is readily apparent to anyone who considers the ambiguous position in which he leaves his "government"—which is precisely not the bureaucracy, not the skilled and experienced John Stuart Millses from the great government departments, but rather a committee of the parliament that Mill's electorate is in a position to bring to heel any time it wishes to take the trouble. There is, moreover, no suggestion in the book that Mill would have it otherwise, nor that he has any quarrel with the notion of completely subordinating the permanent personnel of each department to his committee. In a word: the Few-

---

That ultimate control, without which they cannot have security for good government, may, if they please, be made the means of themselves interfering in the government, and making their legislators mere delegates for carrying into execution the preconceived judgment of the majority. If the people do this, they mistake their interest; and such a government, though better than most aristocracies, is not the kind of democracy which wise men desire." See *The Works of John Stuart Mill* (London: Routledge and Sons, 1905), IV, 387.

[50]Had Mill perhaps been reading *The Federalist,* and borrowed from it the idea of government "by the deliberate sense of the communty"?

[51]*Op. cit.,* p. 321 (italics added).

Many problem as we know it today (in, e.g., the writings of our sages in the field of Public Administration), the problem of the layman and the expert and the relationship between them with respect to policy, simply does not arise in *Representative Government.*

To put Mill down as an elitist *tout court,* then, is, we repeat, an oversimplification. But we can say that *Representative Government* is an early expression of the state of mind, the mind-set, which permeates contemporary elitist thinking (especially as regards the layman-expert relationship). And that mind-set, as we find it in Mill, boils down to the following propositions:

1. The "intellectual" and "moral" resources (that is, "worth") of the citizenry of the democratic state, which must be "organized" for purposes of government, is, like it or not, to be found in the Few, not the Many, above the roster's Great Divide, not above and below it.

2. The particular roster the democratic state should reach for, when it organizes for governmental purposes, is a "knowledge" roster, that is, one on which citizens' names are entered according to how much they are presumed to *know.*

3. For all practical purposes, training and relevant experience are the proper yardstick for measuring the individual citizen's knowledge.

4. If the community's intellectual worth is effectively organized for governmental purposes, we can safely and sensibly forget about organizing its moral worth.

Now: the crucial step in this series of propositions is, let us be clear, that which gets you over from (1) to (2)—from (in Mill's language) intellectual and moral worth to intellectual worth simply, that is to "knowledge," as the decisive quality that must be mobilized. Now again: one may take this step on either the tacit premise "intellectual and moral being inseparable, those who possess the former will as a matter of course possess the latter," or on the tacit premise "something must go; let us dump moral worth and settle for intellectual worth." That, making the transition from classical political philosophy, whose roster is always a two-qualities roster that recognizes *both* knowledge and virtue, to the elitism of the modern intellectuals, is what we have seen Mill in the process of doing. One might say, in the language of the present article, that the transition is a *flight*, understandable as we know, from the clumsiness and uncertainty of the two-qualities roster (which the man who wants to get things pinned down cannot bear to live with) to the neatness and uncertainty of the one-quality roster. Mill, as we have seen, makes the transition only after great and probably agonizing hesitations, which are duly reflected in his refusal (as we have just put it) to "follow through" when he comes to his practical proposals (which by no means give the knowledgeable a completely free hand). One might say that he knows better than to make the transition at all, and that this is the major difference in emphasis between him and his successors. The latter do not have to dump "moral worth," because they do not profess (as Mill does) to know what it is to begin with. Are not one man's "values" as good as another's?

Our conclusion, then, is this: That series of passages in which Mill spirits away moral excellence, by absorbing it into intellectual excellence, and then equates the latter with being highly educated,[52]

[52]The following passage, from another of Mill's writings, takes on great interest in this context: "If it is asserted that all persons ought to be equal in every description of right recognized by society, I answer, not until all are equal in worth as human beings. It is the fact, that one person is *not* as good as another; and it is reversing all the rules of rational conduct, to attempt to raise a political fabric on a supposition which is at variance with fact. Putting aside for the present the consideration of moral worth, of which, *though more important even than intellectual,* it is not so easy to find an available test; a person who cannot read, is not as good, for the purpose of human life, as one who can. A person who can read, write and calculate, but who knows nothing of the properties of natural objects, or of other places and countries, or of the human beings who have lived before him, or of the ideas, opinions, and practices of his fellow-creatures generally, is not so good as a person who knows these things. A person who has not, either by reading or conversation, made himself acquainted with the wisest thought of the wisest men, and with the great examples of a beneficent and virtuous life, is not so good as one who is familiar with these. A person who has filled himself with this various knowledge, but has not digested it—who could give no clear and coherent account of it, and has never exercised his own mind, or derived an original thought from his own observation, experience, or reasoning, is not so good, for any human purpose, as one who has. There is no one who, in any particular matter which concerns himself, would not rather have his affairs managed by a person of greater knowledge and intelligence, than by one of less. There is no one who, if he was obliged to confide his interest jointly to both, would not desire to give a more potential voice to the more educated and more cultivated of the two" (italics added). "Thoughts on Parliamentary Reform," *Dissertations and Discussions* (London: Longmans, Green, Reader, and Dyer, 1867), III, 19-20.

The notion that in organizing intellectual superiority you organize moral superiority at the same time is not, of course, inherently absurd. For example, where the educational system makes it part of its business to inculcate moral along with intellectual excellence, and weeds out the morally inferior as it is able to spot them, such a combination of qualities would presumably result. Mill may have believed that some such circumstances obtained in Victorian England.

prefigures an entire epoch in modern political theory[53]—and becomes, therefore, the *locus classicus* for the mind-set that dominates most contemporary political speculation. The latter, in its most "evolved" form, boils down to these assertions: the issues that arise in politics are intellectual issues, that is, issues that can be declared "settled" once we have come to grips with them intellectually, that is, in abstraction from "value judgments." The proper persons to deal with these issues are, therefore, the persons who possess intellectual superiority, and have done time in the places where such superiority is, notoriously, acquired—which is to say, translating into the idiom of current American political debate, the permanent officials and the Supreme Court justices, *not* the members of Congress.

[53]As it re-enacts part of the argument in Book I of *The Republic,* Mill, not surprisingly perhaps, is capable of the following gross caricature of Plato's argument: "In the political theory thus conceived by Plato—confining ourselves to his scheme of the ideally best, and neglecting his compromise with existing obstacles in the comparatively tame production of his decline—there are two things specially deserving of remark. First, the vigorous assertion of a truth, of transcendent importance and universal application—that the work of government is a Skilled Employment; that governing is not a thing which can be done at odd times, or by the way, in conjunction with a hundred other pursuits, nor to which a person can be competent without a large and liberal general education, followed by special and professional study, laborious and of long duration, directed to acquiring, not mere practical dexterity, but a *scientific* mastery of the subject" (italics added). See *ibid.,* pp. 371-72. Cf. Leo Strauss, *The City and Man* (Chicago: Rand McNally, 1964), chapter II, *passim.*

Part III

PREVIOUSLY
UNPUBLISHED SPEECHES
AND ARTICLES

The Function of a University

Speech before the John Dewey Society of Yale University, October 21,
1957

Let me begin by sketching in a few assumptions—all of them, I like
to think, about matters on which there should be no disagreement
between Professor Weiss and myself:

(1) I assume we are talking primarily about the university as both
of *us* know it best—that is, of the American university in its typical
present form (Columbia and California and Harvard and Illinois, not
Notre Dame, or Southern Baptist University, or the University of
Utah with its special relationship to the Latter Day Saints).

And I assume, second, without in any way prejudging the relevance or importance of the statement for our purposes here (but
merely by way of definition), that the crucial change that has come
over that typical American university in the past century—crucial in
the sense that we can no longer regard as typical those universities
in which no such change has occurred—has to do with the relation
of the university to the Christian religion. I think it probable that the
typical American university of a century ago *did*—to quote a recent
letter to the *News*—take it for granted that universities and churches
"both witness to the one final authority of truth," that is, one and the
same final authority of truth, and that the typical American university
today does not—so that, in a sense in which its predecessor was not,
it is an "open forum in which any honestly-held opinion is enter-
tained." (I stress the words "in a sense in which its predecessor was
not," because I by no means agree that it is that kind of forum really.)
To put it otherwise, and in the language of another's recent letter in
the same correspondence, I assume that the typical American university today does not "slant" its teaching or research in the direction
of Christian belief—and that, again in the language of that letter, any
move to restore the typical university of 100 years ago would be

widely regarded, and on by no means unreasonable grounds, as "a step backward into bigotry."

(3) I assume that we could engage in no less profitable activity here this evening than to discuss the *merits* of that change—as contrasted with, say, the *precise* character of it, or the question whether, if it be so far-reaching as some people suppose, the change poses some problems that are receiving insufficient attention. My own view is that the battle that might have prevented the change, assuming, *arguendo*, it should have been prevented, would have had to be fought not in the university but out in American society itself, where, like it or not, the teaching function of the Churches has gone through some bad innings. Those who deplore the change, and feel a vocation to undo it, and think they can *undo* it by rearguard actions fought within the typical university itself, are for my money wasting their time; I for one hold no brief for them. In an age when Theodore Green can write, as he does in his recently-published book, "America has become a country half-Christian, half-secular," the Christians *can*not expect to call the turns at the universities in the way their great-great-grandparents did.

(4) I assume, in that background, that our prime task this evening is to identify those issues concerning the future of the typical American university that are worth talking about; *and* that an issue is *not* worth talking about unless (a) there is enough genuine disagreement about it to provide fuel for discussion, and (b)—here I repeat myself a little—unless it is the kind of issue that involves water still this side of the dam. I do *not* profess to know with any certainty what these issues are; and I shall be pleased with our discussion this evening if we do no more than identify them.

(5) I assume, finally, that there are two promising places to look for such issues, namely: (a) the general range of questions relating to the function of the university that men have actually fallen out over in recent years; and (b) what I am going to call the official literature of our topic—the books, the articles, the lectures, and commencement addresses in which accredited spokesmen for the typical American university undertake to communicate to others that university's picture of itself. Under (a) we can, as it seems to me, fix upon at least the following: the continuing controversy in recent years over the loyalty oaths imposed by certain state legislatures; the question whether there are *any* circumstances in which a congressional investigating

committee might properly look into what is going on at our universities; the whole question of the propriety of eliminating Communists and Communist-sympathizers from the faculties of our universities, and the kindred question as to the grounds on which, once the decision to eliminate them had been made, the executioner's axe was to be wielded; and, finally, the question—let me state it as carefully as possible—as to the status of the restrictions imposed by the Government of the United States upon normal channels of communication among scholars in different countries. These *are* questions on which I can imagine Professor Weiss and myself as having held rather different views in recent years; but most if not all of them I would favor excluding from tonight's discussion because they are water on the wrong side of the dam: we are not, in our time, going to see Communists back on the faculties of our universities; we are not going to see Communists excluded from our faculties any the more hesitantly because some say they are being eliminated as conspirators not heretics; and we are not going to see any successful challenge to the Government's power to interfere with scholarly communications in the interests of national security; at most we might expect an occasional new flare-up of the loyalty-oath controversy, and of the issue concerning congressional committees; but even those are not lively issues at the present time, and I earnestly hope—as I am sure Professor Weiss does—that we have heard the last of them. But I feel quite otherwise about the grounds upon which the more vocal academic spokesmen in these controversies adopted their positions—about, if you like, the state of mind they revealed concerning the relation between the university and the broader society of which it is a part. So, too, though there is considerable overlap, with what I have called the official pronouncements about the kind of "freedom" (I can sidestep the word no longer), freedom of inquiry and freedom of teaching, that the typical university can or does or ought to extend to the members of its faculty. The relevant and potentially controversial issues, in a word, have to do with the claims being put forward in the name of academic freedom—the freedom of the university, vis-a-vis the broader society within which it functions, to pursue its way without regard to the present and future state of public confidence in what it is doing, and the freedom of the faculty-member of the typical university to initiate and execute just any old type of inquiry he may take it into his head to initiate and execute, to arrive at just any old type of conclusions that just any old method of inquiry may lead him to, and, having arrived at those conclusions, disseminate them "freely" in the academic journals and in the classroom. I believe that the typical American university, however it may square off to specifically theological questions, is from the standpoint of tradition-alists a far more sense-making enterprise than it describes itself as being and, what is worse, thinks of itself as being; that a great deal of foolishness is being talked—and in high places—about both types of academic freedom; that the most casual glance at the realities of its operations will reveal that the things being said about it *are* fool-ishness; and that the time has come for the foolishness to stop being talked, and for three reasons:

First, a university—Thomas Hobbes to the contrary notwithstand-ing—is above all a place where the talking of foolishness should be discouraged as a matter of course; *second,* in misrepresenting its function the university cuts itself off increasingly from the possibility of understanding it, and so becomes less capable of performing it; and *third,* in misrepresenting its function it endangers the position of privilege—not freedom but yes, independence—it enjoys in the broader society that wills and maintains that independence—and, by endangering it, does the university a great and undeserved disser-vice.

Let me be as clear as possible as to the *kind* of point I seek to raise with Professor Weiss, not in the hope or expectation that he will disagree with it and do battle against it—no one who has ever stood in the presence of his wit and dialectical skills would lightly bring upon himself such a misfortune—but in the hope *and* expectation that he will agree with it. We are not going to fall out, as far as I am concerned, over the desirability of free inquiry at the typical univer-sity; *I'm* for it too—provided we do not understand ourselves to mean by free inquiry, inquiry so free that it ceases to be inquiry. We are not going to fall out either over the desirability of autonomous status for the university vis-a-vis its broader society—provided we do not understand ourselves to mean by autonomy a right on the university's part to defy the broader society *ad libitum,* and without calling down on its head retaliatory measures by that broader society. Freedom of inquiry and university autonomy let us have by all means—provided they do not contemplate the reduction of the university to improvisa-tion and farcicality, and provided they do not contemplate a suicidal irresponsibility vis-a-vis the tacit understandings, between the university and the general community, on which the former's continued existence, with *any* kind of autonomy, clearly depends. Freedom of scholarship and freedom in the classroom let us have by all means— provided we mean by it merely the kind of freedom of scholarship and teaching that the university not preaches but actually practices; not any other kind of freedom, or more freedom, because more freedom, or any other kind of freedom, would speedily deprive us of the benefits we have learned to expect from free inquiry. *Both* kinds of academic freedom let us have—provided we keep ourselves reminded that with freedom go commitment and responsibility that keep freedom from being nearly so free as it is sometimes made to sound.

Let me, in that background, endeavor to point up the issues that seem to me worth discussing with a series of questions to Professor Weiss—so worded, I hope, as to leave no doubt as to my own position about them.

First, is it or is it not true that the general impression that our universities are the guardians of no orthodoxy—that within them all questions are open questions and no mind really a mind unless it is an open mind—is it or is it not true that this impression results from what is in fact an optical illusion? Whatever may appear to be the case about the university as a whole, what of the several departments of which the university is made up, each of them the carrier of a discipline, each belonging to a national, or even world-wide, academic community dedicated to the dissemination and development of the findings of that discipline? If the university appears to have no orthodoxy that it jealously guards against all challenge, what, I ask, of the sum-total of the orthodoxies of the departments? In a word: whatever the university and its spokesmen may think or say about the *university's* having no orthodoxy that it seeks to impose, does it not remain true that it is the carrier of a congeries of orthodoxies, so organized as to perpetuate themselves in substantially their present form, and to that end placing—each of them—formidable obstacles in the way of any save the most marginal challenge to *its* orthodoxy. Do they really, over in the biology department, grease the wheels for the young man who has decided that no matter what others may think Lysenko was right, and everybody else wrong? Do they really provide him the fellowship support he requires in order to exercise his freedom of inquiry, encourage him not to bow to authority handed down from the dead past, and urge upon him his duty to follow the bent of his instincts wherever they may lead him? Do they really, over in the English department, lay down a red carpet, as at a Polish wedding, for the graduate student who has got himself convinced that Arthur Miller is a finer playwright than Shakespeare, or that the late Edgar A. Guest was a more accomplished poet than Donne, and make it their business to provide him the facilities he needs in order to do the research necessary for establishing his novel hypothesis? Or do we find, in point of fact, the reverse situation— where the graduate student is likely to thrive, grades- and fellowship-wise, to the extent that he identifies and feels at home with his department's orthodoxy. Is it not the same when, having satisfied a committee of his elders of his mastery of the content and methods of inquiry of his discipline, he turns to seek a teaching or research appointment—when, a little later, he aspires to promotion, and when, all along the line, he turns to his professional journals to ask for publication of his findings? Is it not true that freedom of inquiry is really a privilege reserved for the most part to the Elders of the various disciplines, and that the punishment meted out to the youngster who challenges prevailing opinion among those Elders is sure and swift? Does the whole not add up to something more like an apparatus of censorship than to one of freedom of inquiry? And, most important of all, since the presumption in favor of the discipline and against the youthful innovator is necessarily overwhelming, is it not desirable that this should be the case? And if that be true, mightn't we find some more accurate word than freedom with which to describe what actually happens in the bosom of our universities?

Second, have we, in the course of outgrowing God and Holy Scriptures, outgrown *all* absolutes? Are we, in the typical secular-age university, "free" to question not merely the existence of God and the validity of Truth that rests merely upon Revelation, but also everything else? Including, if so, the scholar's obligation to serve and seek and, having sought successfully, to tell—the Truth? Are we free to suppress knowledge, or to advocate the suppression of knowledge because it is uncongenial to, say, our political purposes? Are we free, as individual scholars selecting our topics of inquiry, to ignore the best long-term interests of the respective disciplines to which we are nominally dedicated? Is there, or is there not, such a thing as the scholarly conscience—and if there be such a thing, are its demands absolute or merely relative? If so again, do we invent it anew with every sunrise, and are those who insist upon the prescriptive character of its demands—like those who still speak of God and Revelation —asking for a return to some outmoded bigotry? In a word: is it desirable that our universities should vouchsafe to their faculty-members a freedom to deny the value of scholarly inquiry itself? And if not, is it not desirable—to go back to my earlier form of words—to stop talking as if it were?

Who Should Control Our Public Schools?

———✌———

Transcript of address before the Montgomery County (Md.) Conservative Club

They say that in France (so centralized is public education there) —at every minute every day throughout the academic year—every first year public school student is looking at the same word on the same page of the same book; and so with every second year student and every third year student, etc., right up to the top.

That, I agree, is a dismal thought with which to begin our discussion of the topic "Who Should Control Our Public Schools?" We in America shudder—or like to *think* that we shudder—at the prospect of that kind of regimentation. We have in America—or like to *think* that we have—*no* public school system in the French sense. We have, so we tell ourselves, *thousands* of public school systems, each founded and financed by the local community it serves; each free to have its first year students doing at a given hour of the day whatever it has decided locally *for* them to do; and so with the second and third and fourth year students right up to the top. We have—or used to like to think that we have—a Constitution forbidding the creation, in our midst, of a public school system on the French model; and we have—or at least *I* like to think that we have—a firm intention to preserve that Constitution, and so keep *on* forbidding, the creation of a public school system on the French model. We take our stand on our Tenth Amendment, which reserves to the states and the people all powers not delegated to the Federal Government; we read the Tenth Amendment as meaning that the power to found and maintain public schools is one—perhaps the most important one—of the powers thus reserved to the states and the people; and, with minor variations in the Departments of Education from state to state in our union, we think of that power as one largely reserved to the people —the people, that is, as organized in their several counties and cities and towns and villages.

All that being the case, the question "Who Should Control Our Public Schools?"—which we in America equate with the question, "Who Should Control Each of Our *Thousands* of Public School Systems?"—that question, I say, would *appear* to be a silly question, one of those questions that are silly because they admit of only one possible answer, and that an obvious one. We do not ask ourselves, "Who Should Control Our Local Fire Department"; we do not ask "Who Should Control Our Local Traffic System"—that is, who should write our local traffic ordinances? We *know* the answer about the fire department and the traffic system, namely, We the people of our community through our regularly elected officials, and don't, therefore, bother to ask the question. With the schools, however, it is quite otherwise; for people in local communities all over the United States are finding it necessary, these days, to ask themselves, again and again, who actually should control the public schools they pay taxes to support, depend upon for the instruction of their youngsters, and point to with pride as *their* testimonial to America's faith in, and devotion to, the idea of free public education. And perhaps the best way into tonight's topic is for us to understand each other as to why that does not seem to them, any more, a silly question—why they do not find the answer to it obvious, and why it bids fair to become one of the major issues in our public life—as, according to your President, it has become already in the public life of *this* community.

The reasons for this strange difference between the way people think about fire departments and the way they think about public schools—the reasons for it, I say, seem to me fairly easy to pin down; they are, I believe, three in number.

First, the public schools are now staffed (let us not ask quite yet how this came about) by men and women—teachers, principals, curriculum-supervisors, superintendents, etc., who are able, with at least *some* show of reason, to say to the people *and* their elected representatives, in effect, something like this: "The public school system, of course, does, like the fire department, *belong* to *you;* ultimate control of it is in *your* hands, in the sense that if you interfere with it there is no one, ultimately, who can say you Nay. For a number of reasons, however, you would be very foolish to exercise that control. For one thing, you are too busy to give to it more than your sporadic and—if we may say so—amateurish interest. We, by contrast, give to it our lives, and every moment of our attention; besides which we have been trained to make, and to make wisely, the decisions in-volved in operating a school system. And, for another thing; we have not only taken the trouble to educate ourselves better than most of you, and as well as the best of you; we have also pursued—at our universities and colleges and normal schools—certain *courses* that bear very directly on the school system's problems. We have, for instance, taken courses in Educational Psychology, and know, as you do not, what is involved in learning. We have taken courses in Educa-tional Theory, and consequently know, in detail, what a school is for, what kinds of things it ought to teach, and what kinds it ought not to teach. And we have courses in which attention is fixed upon a very special problem; namely, the relation between public schools and democratic government—the very special problem, if you will, of educating the community's youngsters for successful participation in democratic government and democratic living. Thus we confront the school system's problems as *professionals*—as, if you will permit the term, experts in a field in which even the best of you are laymen and the worst of you are (dare we say it?) illiterates. Thus while you *can* control your public school system, we are here to tell you that you *must* not control it; that if you try to control it you will merely defeat your own purposes, and get done badly what could otherwise be done well. *You* run the community's grocery stores, its cleaning es-tablishments, its garages, and its pharmacies—which you are presum-ably competent to do else you'd have been put out of business—and let *us* run the schools, which only we are competent to do. Moreover your argument about the fire department is not a very good one: running a fire department is a lot easier and a lot less important than running a school system; besides which the argument points in a somewhat different direction than you suppose; the fact is that you don't run your fire department either; rather you entrust it to some person or persons whose competence and dependability you have confidence in; and all you ask of it, and quite rightly, is that it put out our fires efficiently. Well, something similar to that is what you had better ask of us; namely, that we run, and run well, the kind of schools you would *wish* us to run if *you* had *our* training."

These claims are, perhaps, seldom put quite that sharply and can-didly; but if you pause to think it over a minute you will, I believe, agree with me about this: these claims are always *there,* implicitly if not explicitly; they are put forward by honorable and loyal men and women who would not *dream* of putting anything over on us; and what the claims mean is just this: we have ended up in this country, whether we intended to or not, with an alternative answer to the question, "Who Should Control Our Public Schools?" It is no longer a question with only one answer, and an obvious one at that. For there are those among us—not all of them teachers and administrators, either—who would now answer: "The professionally trained educators should control them; they alone know how to!"

I come now to the second reason why the problem before us has come to be a real problem, which is: that the claims of the professional educators (whether valid or invalid, for let's not raise that kind of question quite yet)—those claims, I say, whether valid or invalid, are now backed up by a very considerable apparatus of nationwide power. The superintendent of public schools who assures the members of the school board that he knows all the answers about how to run a school system might, at first blush, appear to be at the school board's mercy; he, it might appear, is one against their many, besides which they normally have the power to remove him and send him packing. That, however, is not quite how it works; he in fact speaks for a nationwide army of men and women who happen to share his notions of what a school is for and how it ought to be run; they are the creators and carriers of a body of literature on education which —since *they* regard it as authoritative, that is, as embodying the last word on educational problems—*is* authoritative, *does* to all intents and purposes embody the last word. The local school board that dares to challenge their local representative, the superintendent, finds itself up against a vast array of forces presumptively capable of policing it back into line. Unless it goes back in the literature to the Age of Lincoln or thereabouts, it will fail to discover arguments with which to back up its position; looking out over the country it sees ten thousand docile school boards being jumped through the hoop it is refusing to be jumped through, and it begins to feel a little foolish and peculiar. If the board has rebelled on points that the nationwide army regards as crucial, it may well run afoul of our nationwide system of mutual accreditation, and have to back down before the threat that its pupils will suffer, when they go elsewhere to school, for its rambunctiousness. Between it and the nationwide army, in any case, stands the Department of Education at the State Capitol, whose views on the issue at stake are pretty certain to correspond with those of the nationwide army because it is part of the nationwide army. If it fires the superintendent for *his* defiance, moreover, it must replace him; his replacement must possess the same credentials, else he is not eligible for the job, and that means he will have undergone the same training, under the same kind of teachers holding the same kind of authoritative books in their hands as he has undergone; predictably, therefore, the replacement will entertain the self-same ideas as the man he is replacing. Most important of all, perhaps, the army—its name, of course, is the National Education Association, or NEA—is, among other things, a large and extremely effective pressure group, with large numbers of skilled spokesmen at its disposal, who operate directly upon that intellectual climate I mentioned a moment ago, and have had a great deal to do with making it what it is. "NEA has today"—I quote from a recent book written and published under its own auspices, "nearly 700,000 members"—yes, 700 *thousand*—"who function through 66 state organizations and 6,000 local associations, elect 4 to 5 thousand delegates to a Representative Assembly, and act through an executive secretary with a 440-man staff." Back in 1870 it was still small enough to rest content with four departments through which to conduct its operations; today it has no less than 30. And, as any one can tell you who has looked into it a little, it knows what it is after, and has quite a history of getting what it is after. Our public schools today reflect like a mirror the objectives the NEA had formulated for itself as of, say, fifty years ago; so that, to go back to my point about France, we *do* have today what amounts to a nationwide school system—the differences between ours and the French being simply these: first, the center of our system is not a government agency but an extra-legal one, operating not by legal command but by influence and persuasion; and second, our system controls from the center not the details of classroom activity, but the goals, the philosophy, the level of difficulty, and the content of the education offered in our many thousands of local school systems. These systems —though theoretically free to experiment and invent—have for the reasons we now have before us long ago ceased to do that. As you and I well know, today's variations from school system to school system are almost entirely a matter of differences in wealth and resources from community to community, and of differences in just plain luck. Youngsters in conservative communities get the same kind of education as youngsters in politically radical communities; youngsters in religious communities, the same kind of education as youngsters in communities where the majority of the population are unbelievers; youngsters in Louisiana (which still retains its French legal system, and in other areas of its life, its French traditions), the same kind of education as youngsters in Scandinavian-dominated Minnesota. Either our local school boards are not so free over against the NEA as we used to think of them as being, or they are not making use of their freedom. We have become regimented by regimenting ourselves.

Thirdly—we are, you remember, noting the reasons why the question before us is not necessarily an easy one to answer. And now for the third reason, namely, that the old answer to the question which was that the people of the community should control the schools, is, whether correct or not, less and less likely to spring to the minds of the ordinary people of whom communities are mostly made up. To give the old answer is to challenge those claims of the professional educators that I summarized a while ago—that is, to challenge the claims of experts; people are now too accustomed, in area after area of their lives, to having experts do their thinking for them to be disposed to kick up a fuss against any particular set of experts. Experts tell them how to care for their bodies, and they obey. Experts tell them what books to read, and they obey again. Experts make the decisions about foreign policy that get them into the wars they fight, and the decisions about tax policy that determine how much of their incomes they can selfishly spend on themselves; and they no longer even know the words they would have to use in order to argue back. They are out of the habit of bringing to bear their own cherished convictions, their own preferences and prejudices. The experts tell them, indeed, that they shouldn't have prejudices—their own value-judgments, as they are now fashionably called. People are, I say, out of the habit of bringing these things to bear on any matters more grand than choosing their personal friends or deciding whether to paint the garage door. The experts—*any* expert—have them, with each passing day, more and more at a disadvantage; how expect them, then, to do battle with a set of experts so entrenched, so respected, so sure of themselves, so articulate, as the professional educators? To which let me add one other, intimately connected, point, which again has to do with the intellectual climate most of us live in, namely: the slogans and catch-phrases on the lips of the educators—about democracy and equality and successful living and adjustment and so on—are the very slogans and catch-phrases they have dinned at them, day and night, by the newspapers, the television and radio programs, the political leaders, the sermonizers, who provide most of their intellectual fare. They think they believe those slogans (I do believe it necessary to distinguish between what a man believes and what he thinks he believes); and they feel, therefore, scant temptation to take issue with the educator who assures them that those are the slogans on which he is running their schools.

So much for why and how the tide has set against the traditional answer to our question; which brings me, at last, to the heart of what I have to say to you this evening: the professional educators *do* control our public schools; but I hold that the people—yes, the ordinary people—in our numberless local communities should recapture from the professional educators the control over the schools that they have usurped. I hold that the claims of the professional educators to special knowledge, based on special training, that entitles them to name the goals, determine the content, establish the standards, and call the turns on the political philosophy that is to prevail in our public schools—I hold that those claims are false claims, false claims, moreover, that ordinary people are plenty capable of detecting and exposing once they have set their minds to it. I hold that the major effect of the professional education movement has been to complicate what is essentially a simple matter. Let us remember that there were teachers, good teachers, moreover, long before there were professional educators, and not only good teachers but well-educated men and women who had been taught by them. And I hold, finally, that once ordinary people, acting through school boards they have elected for this purpose, do stage their rebellion against the professional educators, they can get lots of help from a strangely-forgotten quarter, namely: the nation's great teachers at the nation's great universities, who as I have known them over the years are sick beyond belief of the farce to which the so-called experts have reduced our public school education. And I hold that the future of America, no less, depends on whether the American people get around, soon enough, to staging such a rebellion.

Let me defend that general view of our problem by pressing briefly the following three points:

First, I believe that ordinary people know *better* than the educators—as what the educators have done to our schools amply demonstrates—the difference between an educated and an uneducated man. They know, perhaps because of having failed at them themselves, that good education is education, the more of course the better, in what youngsters are likely to call the "hard" subjects: languages—especially the dead languages, mathematics, physics and chemistry, history, the *disciplined* use of English. They know, though they may have forgotten momentarily, that these are the things that are taken seriously at the great universities the nation supports—the things a knowledge of which wins a man reputation as a great teacher in what, by common consent, we call the highest level of education. For these are the things, the subjects, that develop the specifically intellectual skills upon which depends the continued expansion of man's knowledge and understanding; yet they are also the subjects that our public schools, after 50 years under NEA auspices, are failing to get across, partly because of the addition, under NEA pressure, of new so-called practical subjects, partly because of the introduction of the elective principle, also under NEA pressure, enabling youngsters who choose to, to avoid or underemphasize the hard subjects, partly because of the relaxation, still again under NEA pressure, of the standards that make the hard subjects hard, and partly because of the attempt, yet again under NEA pressure, to give more education to more people than we have, or can have, good teachers to provide. Our public schools, in NEA hands, have become a major assault upon the nation's intellectual skills; and I do not believe for a moment that ordinary people ever wished them to become that, or would have consented, if consulted, to their becoming that. All of it happened, moreover, over continued and vociferous protest from our university faculties, whose members are today appalled at the ignorance and intellectual incompetence of the normal product of our public schools. Only ordinary people, and they only by rebelling against the educators, can put the schools back in the business they ought to be in; namely, educating, which means weeding out those who are incapable of receiving education, and, above all, holding the teaching force to the available supply of persons who have mastered the hard subjects. And I repeat that they can get lots of help, as regards carrying the rebellion through, from the nation's university teachers.

Secondly, I believe that ordinary people know, even if they have

temporarily forgotten, that the other big job of a public school system, besides teaching the hard subjects, is that of perpetuating the
community's way of life: its basic beliefs, its moral standards, its
religious convictions, its political philosophy, and, yes, its prejudices.
I said, mark you, perpetuating its way of life, which anyone but a
professional educator knows is the opposite of imposing upon the
community, through its youngsters, a *new* way of life—which is what
I believe our public schools to be doing, or anyhow trying to do,
today. I accuse the professional educators of having permitted their
NEA to be captured, lock, stock and barrel, by what is still—but short
of the rebellion I demand may not long be—a minority political
movement, dedicated to the remaking of America in the image of
Left-Wing Liberalism. That, incidentally, is the significance of the
nationwide uniformity in education that I have referred to: it *proves*
that our schools are *not* perpetuating from community to community,
our way of life; for our communities differ enormously in basic beliefs,
attitudes, and preferences; but the content and outlook of their education is everywhere the same. I accuse the educators of having for
many years now used the schools for purposes of sheer indoctrination
—indoctrination, moreover, in ideas about equality, freedom of
thought, collective security, socialism, that continue to be repugnant
to the best judgment of ordinary people in most of our local communities. And I call upon ordinary people in all communities to serve
notice on the educators that they will tolerate it no longer, that they
wish, nay, are determined, to bring up their children with beliefs and
ideas and attitudes and loyalties as nearly as possible like their own,
which they cling to because they believe them to be best, and that
the essence of a community is that it has a way of life it intends to
perpetuate because it loves it.

The educators of course will at this point begin to make noises not
about their expertise but about something called "academic freedom", but let our rebel's hands not be stayed by that; no community
can afford a freedom for teachers to undermine its way of life, can
afford it or will afford it once the community realizes what there is
that is involved. Here again, no one except ordinary people can put
a stop to the harm being done by the professional educators and they
will do it by transforming the significance of our elections of members for boards of education. Those elections should be genuine debates about the goals, the performance and the impact of our schools.

If there are different points of view about these things in the community, there should be candidates representing each point of view. The final vote should be a plebiscite on the issues involved. But the ordinary people must demand a board of education that will represent their views and call the educators to time. Neither they when they confront the board nor the board as it confronts the educators can or should take "no" for an answer.

(delivered February, 1958)

American Conservatism and
Right-Wing Dictatorships

Speech given at a Hollywood Symposium on Freedom, Fall, 1961

It is a great honor to follow my colleagues and friends William Buckley, James Burnham, and Frank Meyer, at this podium.

I come to you, as our chairman has indicated, direct from the Dominican Republic—not, to my good fortune, by way of Cuba, though my plane flight used to stop in that country back in those pleasant days before we knew the names of Fidel Castro and Che Güevara. I come to you, a little more remotely, five weeks to be exact, from two happy years in Spain, so that I stand before an English-speaking audience for the first time in a long while—not only out of practice but also out of touch, so that when we come to question-time I should be asking you questions, and listening to your answers, rather than the other way around; and I for one wish it might be that way. For I come with my mind full of two sets of related questions—one set about the so-called upsurge of conservatism in the United States: Is it an upsurge? Is it conservative? And another set suggested to me by my more or less recent experience: Both Spain and the Dominican Republic are, and have been for over 25 years, so-called Right-wing dictatorships, where basic policy-decisions have been made by one man, and not necessarily with much opportunity for other men to discuss and criticize, and little or no opportunity for other men to compete freely for political power—so that the second set of questions has to do with conservatism and Right-wing dictatorships: What about Right-wing dictatorships in general? What attitude should conservatives—the conservative upsurge if it is an upsurge, and perhaps therefore able to have its way about American policy, and if it is conservative, that is based on a clear grasp of conservative purpose and conservative principle—what attitude should conservatives adopt toward Right-wing dictatorships in general and the Dominican Republic in particular? And you will readily see, putting it that way, why I say the two sets of questions are related: in order to deal with the last of them, What attitude should conservatives adopt toward Right-wing dictatorships, we must tell ourselves sooner or later what conservatives believe in and are trying to accomplish, which is going to be the main business in tonight's address. Then, weaving back and forth between that and a clear picture of what Right-wing dictatorships are, we can hope to decide whether conservatives should support them, or oppose them, or—a third possibility of course—adopt toward them a position of neutrality, or indifference.

First, then, let us get before us some general statements about contemporary Right-wing dictatorships in general. We have, I think, four major instances to get in mind: the Franco dictatorship in Spain; the Chiang Kai-shek dictatorship in Formosa; the Syngman Rhee dictatorship in South Korea; and the Trujillo dictatorship in the Dominican Republic. And, with their names in front of us, several arresting points leap to our minds. 1) They have all, throughout the period of history in which they have figured, been staunch allies of the West, and so of the United States—nay, more, they have 'been allies of the West, even been on the West's side, even at those moments when some of us have wondered whether or not the West was on the West's side; they have been on the West's side, and ready and eager to fight and spill blood against the West's great enemy the World Communist movement, any and everywhere there has been fighting to be done, or blood to be spilt, against the Communists. We may fairly take as our symbol of this point Chiang and his half-million man army, pawing the ground year after year in Formosa, impatient to resume the war against Red China (whether on the mainland or in Korea), and being forever restrained by a West so frightened by its own shadow that it will not even permit others to fight for it. Second, the four Right-wing dictatorships are *uniquely and exclusively* associated, in the events of our day, with the handful of victories—how strange the word falls on our ears, we who are in the habit of always losing to Communism!—that have been achieved over Communism, modest victories perhaps, but victories all the same and, however remote the second-hand, *our* victories. Tick off the major thorns in the side of the Communists: The Communists' complete inability to reverse or begin to reverse the defeat they suffered at Franco's hands in Madrid, represented by the American Strategic Air Command bases in Spain; the Communists' impotent battering away at Quemoy and Matsu, which to their consternation don't seem to mind much, with Chiang safe and supreme there on Taiwan, untouchable, and Red China's coveted membership in the UN as a symbol of political frustration; the consolidation of the frontier between North and South Korea (not the thorn perhaps that some of us would have liked to thrust into the side of the Communists, because the point of that thorn would have penetrated to the Yalu River, but still a horn and one that the Communists do not know how to get rid of) and, lastly, the Dominican Republic, still there after twenty years of Communist scheming and conspiring and invading and character-assassinating—these, I repeat, are apart from Berlin *the* thorns that draw blood out of the side of World Communism; and in each case we have the Right-wing dictators to thank for them. Third—a similar but not identical point—the countries we have named as Right-wing dictatorships are, again uniquely and exclusively case by case, *the* countries in which the Communists have suffered what is for them the least acceptable of all defeats, namely: the defeat that makes it impossible for them to operate, except underground and upon well-understood pain of the severest punishment, on the home territory of an enemy they intend to destroy. "Right-wing dictatorships" is, then, merely another name for the countries in which there *is* no Communist movement, the countries that have made so firm a decision against Communism that they refuse to hear the so-called merits of Communism so much as discussed, and refuse to leave at large persons so mad, or so evil, or so misguided, as to wish to gain adherents for the cause of Communism, or to organize on Communism's behalf. Fourth, they are or have been—let us not trip up over the grammatical difficulty that the Rhee dictatorship is gone, and that the status of the Dominican Republic is at present in doubt—they have all been countries, regimes if you like, that have brought down on their heads the hatred and distrust of American and European Liberals, *all* Liberals, one is almost tempted to say all Liberals dead, living and unborn, and hatred and distrust in its most venomous and vindictive and voracious form—hatred and distrust that never never sleep, that demand the total destruction of the thing hated and distrusted, hatred and distrust that know no scruples about the means—misrepresentation, trickery, what have you—with which to accomplish the desired destruction. Fifth—let us think now not about whether American Conservatives *should* support the Right-wing dictatorships but whether they have supported them and do support them, thus coming a little closer to the heart of the matter—the history of American Right-wing support (to say nothing of Right-wing support in Europe) for the Right-wing dictatorships, as also the picture as regards present support, is strangely, almost incomprehensibly, checkered. Syngman Rhee was driven out of Korea, almost certainly at the instance of left-wing ideologues in the DOS and CIA, without a single Right-wing voice being raised in his defense—as, in the subsequent chaos in Korea, no Right-wing voice has shown the good sense to wish for him back. Trujillo also never succeeded in striking any responsive chord in the heart of Right-wing America: no Right-wing tear was shed over his assassination, nor has any Right-wing organization or publication—with one honorable exception—shown any concern about what might happen, in the post-assassination period, to the interests (if any) Trujillo defended. With Franco and Chiang, however, the situation is quite different: each can today count on a hard-core of Senators, Representatives, publicists, and academics in Right-wing America who are constantly mobilizéd on their behalf, who keep a constant eye on the machinations—anti-Franco, anti-Chiang as the case may be—of their enemies, who if not always able to get all they want for Franco and Chiang are always there to ward off any new blow directed at them by the Liberals. To put it otherwise: if Rhee went down, if Trujillo's collaborators in the Dominican Republic prove unable to pursue Trujillo's policies, the reason is or will be that they failed to win for themselves the vigorous and vigilant kind of support that some American conservatives regularly give to Franco and Chiang, and the question arises, Why does the American Right, not all of it of course but enough, support Franco and Chiang but refuse to go to the assistance of Rhee and Trujillo or, if you like, Trujillo's heirs? I do not, as I have already intimated, know the answer to that question, which is why I used the word "incomprehensible" a moment ago. At most I am sure (very sure, however) that the answers that come most readily to mind will not wash, for example: That Rhee and Trujillo were conspicuously more wicked than Franco and Chiang, so that we, nice fellows that we are, can touch Franco's and Chiang's pitch without being defiled, but must not touch Rhee's and Trujillo's because it is so much blacker: all four have been charged with, and have probably been guilty of, the same alleged crimes, with only minor differences of detail. Not, either, because American interests, or even American Right-wing interests,

are more directly involved in Spain and Formosa than in Korea and
the Dominican Republic (if that seems so today, it is *because* of
Right-wing support for Franco and Chiang, *not* the other way round).
And not because we are more ignorant about Korea and the Dominican Republic. More ignorant we are, but not more ignorant than we
were once about Spain and Formosa (here again we must not mistake
the result for the cause). The reason, I imagine, is something like this:
that Franco and Chiang have been more intelligent and more assiduous in seeking and finding that original core of Right-wing American
support that, by effort and education, can be snow-balled into the
"enough" I have spoken of. Or if not more intelligent and assiduous
then luckier, in the sense that *some* American Right-wingers just
happened, in their cases but not in the others, to get busy and do the
job. But it has been, in all four cases, the *same* job, and I think we
may soon be paying very dearly for the fact that the job has *not* been
done for the Dominican Republic. If it makes sense, makes sense that
is on Conservative principles, for the American Right to frustrate
Liberal and Communist designs on Franco and Chiang, then on those
same principles it would have made sense to frustrate Liberal designs
in Korea, and would today make sense to frustrate Liberal designs on
the Dominican Republic. The issues at stake there are the same, and
the American interests at stake are if not identical at least of the same
character. And those issues are: First, whether a political regime that
is more on the West's side than the West is, a regime that is a thorn
in the side of World Communism that really hurts, is to survive, or go
down the drain. And whether a situation that the Communists are
determined to dominate is or is not to be thrown open to Communist
and Communist-front infiltration, subversion, and mischief-making.

To put it otherwise, the Liberal and Communist designs on the
Dominican Republic, especially the Liberal designs right now because they must succeed before the Communist designs become
relevant, are certainly present, and seem to be carrying the day
—seem to, that is, in the absence of Right-wing efforts to frustrate
them.

Let me sketch the main facts we need to flesh out that statement.

Item. Trujillo was assassinated at the end of May—assassinated,
incidentally, late at night, on a lonely road, without a guard, though
he must have known himself to have more enemies, who desired his
death, than any man in the world. The assassins, so far as we know,

were local soreheads, since no evidence has come to light of foreign intervention in the plot.

Item. Shortly before Trujillo's death the Office of American States —whether at the Department of State's instigation we need not say —had found Trujillo guilty of participating in an assassination plot against President Betancourt of Venezuela. The Office of American States had called upon its members to break off diplomatic relations with the Dominican Republic, and had imposed economic sanctions upon it. The United States, for example, has today no diplomatic representation in Cuidad Trujillo, and the Dominican Republic did not benefit from the transfer of coveted sugar quotas from Cuba to other sugar producers. And let us pause over that item a minute: the Office of American States, with U.S. approval and participation, has gone into what we may call the ostracism business, claiming the power, so to speak, to read nations out of the American community, and to do so, so to speak, on grounds of moral turpitude. But the first victim of its ostracism is the Right wing, anti-Communist dictatorship in Hispaniola, not the quasi-Communist, pro-Communist dictatorship in Cuba.

Item. The economic sanctions against the Dominican Republic have begun to draw blood: foreign exchange is scarce, and the formerly solid and proud Dominican peso is under pressure; business is slowing down, unemployment is growing, much-needed imports are in short supply; the pace of the deceleration is, moreover, rapid, and may within the near future run the Dominican Republic into insuperable economic difficulties, with political repercussions unpleasant to think about. What Castro is doing to the Cuban economy in the name of nationalism, which is to say ruining it, the Dominican Republic's neighbors are doing to it in the name of some newfangled international morality; and our government, yours and mine, is helping every day to pull the noose tighter.

Item. No-one, least of all the Dominicans, knows what the Dominican Republic must do to purge itself of its guilt and rid itself of the hated sanctions; all one can say is: attention has shifted from Trujillo and the assassination plot against Betancourt to—by what magical process of transubstantiation no one can say—the quality of the "freedom" enjoyed by the individual citizen of the Dominican Republic as such. As matters originally stood, with the Dominican Republic being punished for a personal act by Trujillo, one might have expected the punishment to cease with Trujillo's death—as, clearly, the victim of the punishment is the Dominican people, who certainly had not participated in the famous assassination plot. But no, the point now is that potential opponents of the existing regime are not as free to "oppose," to speak their minds and organize, as certain persons outside the Dominican Republic think they should be, and that the Dominican Republic is to purge itself by improving matters in that regard—or, more accurately, by convincing persons outside that matters have been improved in that regard. Improved how much? The Dominicans do not know. Over how long a period? Again the Dominicans do not know. How establish the fact of the improvement? That they know least of all; for there is no established tribunal to which the relevant proofs might be brought.

Item: The Office of American States did, after Trujillo's death, send a commission of observers to the Dominican Republic—to look into that little business of freedom to oppose. The commission's report has yet to be published, some cynical observers say because it gave the Dominican Republic a cleaner bill of health than the commission's masters expected and desired, while other observers offer no explanation at all.

Item. The press—what we at *National Review* call the "Establishment Press"—has clamped down on the Dominican Republic a news blackout unlike anything this speaker has ever seen. The only way the Dominican Republic can get its name in the newspapers these days is by some "incident", of one kind or another, which suggests or might seem to suggest that the Dominican regime's opponents, known or potential, are being terrorized. Outside opinion, in other words, learns about the Dominican Republic only those facts, or alleged facts, that would appear to justify, under the present rules of the game, continuance of the sanctions.

Item. The castigation of the Dominican Republic has given joy in Liberal and Communist circles comparable only to that which, we are told, the soul of the sinner saved gives to the heavenly hosts on high. The Dominican government—it is, indeed, made up of friends of Trujillo, so the fact that the Generalissimo is six feet under need not be overstressed—is over exactly the barrel they have always wanted it over: it must set the people free! or else starve—or, as we have noted, perhaps *both*. And it is worth pausing over the apparent logic of the joy, which is: The victors in a really-free Dominican election, it is confidently believed, will be the opponents of Trujillo and all his works—that is, a government with policies as unlike his as it is possible to imagine; that is, a government—for this surely is the point—with ideas as like as possible to those of, say, Trujillo's great enemy the Venezuelan government; that is, a Leftist government, not likely to offend anyone by its excessive and hysterical anti-Communism; that is, a government acceptable within the sacred precincts of the Office of American States. In a word: the Dominican Republic is to purge itself by getting itself a Leftist government.

Item: The Liberals and Communists should be joyous about the barrel the Dominican government is over, but for a different reason, out of a different logic, than that just named—should, that is, if all they want is to get rid of the Trujillo regime and the devil take the consequences. For the barrel, when carefully examined, turns out to be this: The elections are many, many months off. During those months, unless it is to abandon the hope of getting rid of the sanctions, the Dominican government must admit to its territory pretty much any exiled Dominican who alleges a political reason for wishing to return, or who might, if not admitted, claim that he was refused on political grounds. And it must not only admit him: it must leave him free to speak and to organize, to agitate and incite, to do any of the things that by the widest stretch of the imagination can be brought under the term "electoral freedom." Let the government turn someone down; let it try to silence someone on the grounds that what he is saying is *not* electoral activity within any civilized definition of the term, but incitement to hatred and violence; let it—oh most unthinkable of thoughts—crack down on some demonstration that has got out of hand, on some meeting that threatens to turn into a riot; let it do any of those things, and they will say, out over the Hemisphere: just as we thought. The terror continues. Let it do any of those things and then win the election, and they will say out over the Hemisphere that the elections were not democratic, and that the officers newly elected have no proper mandate. The Dominican government has been dealt a hand with which it must lose even if it wins.

Item. Either the present rulers of the Dominican Republic are the most accomplished liars this speaker has ever listened to lies from, or they have no fear of a fair election. They are confident they will win such an election, and win it hands down, against any opposition movement that might offer a serious alternative to existing policies, that will participate in fair debate as to what the Dominican Republic ought to do. What they are afraid of is Communism—not of course electoral victory by a Communist Party with a Communist program that is offered as frankly that to the Dominican people, but long-run *military* victory by a Communist movement that will act largely by conspiracy and in secrecy, that will do its business as, at first, it did in Czechoslovakia, by infiltration of strategic positions in Dominican society, and that will express itself not in votes but in a military *putsch*—probably like Castro's, off in a corner of the country, from which—with arms supplied in all likelihood, by Castro himself or his Soviet allies—it will proceed to conquer the country. What the Dominicans fear is, in a word, Civil War; what they see clearly is that the recipe of electoral freedom being imposed from outside is a recipe for disorder, and disorder from which only the Communists can emerge victorious because only they know how to profit from disorder, how to turn it to strategic advantage in the naked struggle for power, how, progressively, to disarm a government in its attempt to prevent disorder. And—for we have come full circle—American Conservatives seem content to leave the Dominicans to their fate, to withhold from them the support they would surely give to Franco and Chiang if they were put over such a barrel; and I ask, Can the withholding be squared with Conservative principle? And if not, should not the struggle against the Dominican sanctions be raised, in the months ahead, to the highest level of priority for the Conservative upsurge—if indeed it is an upsurge and if indeed it is Conservative. And I propose to try to say, briefly, what Conservative principles are—a question that we can best work our way into by asking, quite simply, Who are the American Conservatives?

Now:

1. The usual procedure for dealing with that question—even among people who ought to know better—is this: "the Conservatives" are people who are trying to "conserve" something handed down out of the past; and the problem is to identify that moment in the past when men we know to have been conservatives were making their voices heard. Let us study attentively what those men said, and get clear in our heads what their principles were; and let us, thereafter, apply the word Conservative to those men and movements in the present who have remained faithful to those principles.

You are, I am sure, familiar with this way of slicing the problem;

and the first point I want to make tonight is that it won't do. There *is* no moment in history you can point to and say, "This is when the Conservatives showed their true colors"; we can, perhaps, identify voices out of the past that were articulating Conservative principles; but the only way to recognize them is by knowing, *before*hand, what principles we are listening for.

Another mistaken procedure rests on the simplistic notion that Conservatism is sheer opposition to change. Among the writers of our day, Professor Clinton Rossiter—that Trojan Horse that the Liberals have spirited into the Conservative camp—has done most to popularize it, and to conceal the fact that it is root and branch wrong. Wrong, first of all, because it identifies something called Tradition, about which Conservatism is passionately concerned, with something with which Conservatism has no concern whatever, namely, a merely static state of affairs. Wrong, secondly, because it makes no distinction between opposition to change and opposition to change in undesirable directions. And wrong, thirdly, because it conceals the fact that the essence of Conservatism often expresses itself in an insistent demand *for* change—sometimes, indeed, in a demand for *drastic* change. Professor Rossiter and his allies merely obscure our problem before us. Their purpose is not to explain or define Conservatism, but to make it look foolish.

Nor, thirdly, can we define Conservatism, as some people are always trying to do, by spotting the "real" American Conservatives of the present. I take no pleasure in recording the fact, but the *dramatis personae* of contemporary American politics includes no adequate spokesman of the Conservative approach. Senator Bricker, for example, did yeoman's service for Conservatism when he pressed the struggle for the famous Bricker Amendment, and any Conservative worth his salt had to wish him well in that struggle; but we must not forget that Bricker's voting record on many other matters was hardly less Liberal than, say, that of Senator Douglas. The late Senator Pat McCarran earned the undying gratitude of all Conservatives when his Internal Security Committee forced the facts of the Communist conspiracy upon American public opinion and, later, when he initiated the rapprochement between the U.S. and Spain, but McCarran was also the spokesman of the silver states, and by playing that role made the sort of compromise with principle that Conservatism most deplores. Senator McCarthy's battle against the bureaucrats for a tough loyalty-security program in the government service was a Conservative battle; but his voting record on, say, agricultural subsidies was one over which the Conservative can only shudder. Representative Francis Walter, whose task it is to fight off the Liberals' semiannual attacks on our traditional immigration policy, can be sure that the nation's Conservative elements will always rally behind him; he is, for that one purpose—the purpose of preventing further inroads upon our nation's cultural homogeneity—a Conservative: but I seldom encounter his name in connection with other Conservative causes. Senator Byrd, similarly, speaks for Conservatism on the budget; Senator Knowland used to speak sound conservative sense on foreign policy and, most particularly, on the falsity of the ideal of world government as Barry Goldwater does today, and as Barry Goldwater has been doing of late on the very different topic of Newburgh; both Knowland and Goldwater, however, have cast many a strange Senate vote on many another issue.

In short: one of the peculiarities of American public life is that whereas there *are* Liberals (Senator Humphrey, Senator Douglas, Representative Celler, the learned justices of the United States Supreme Court come to mind) who go down the line with Liberalism, so that the stand they will take on any given issue is readily predictable, there is no comparable phenomenon on the Conservative side.

Nor, fourthly, can we get far into the problem with the idea, a prominent Liberal propaganda theme, that the American Conservative tradition is a "Conservative tradition" with a "Liberal content." Like the other heresies to which I have alluded, this one has, to be sure, its element of truth, namely: The great political decisions of recent decades *have* to some extent reflected Liberal ideas, and Conservatives have gone along with them to some extent. But to leap from this statement about the immediate past to the conclusion that the content of our Conservative tradition is Liberal—that, as Myrdal would have us believe, what Americans are bent on conserving out of the past is a frenzied zeal for Liberal reforms—is in my opinion to miss the point about our politics, which is: The Conservative tradition in America is not only Conservative but profoundly Conservative, with a profoundly Conservative content; which, if I may put it so, explains why our politics in this country tend to be about Liberalism. To put it otherwise: The basic inertia of our politics is a forward Conservative inertia. When American society "changes" it changes for the most part—as Conservatives wish it to—in the proper direction; that is, in the direction in which it must change in order to become more and more like itself at its best. Changes in that direction —the various steps in the evolution of our present party system are conspicuous examples—tend, however, to take place quietly, unobtrusively, and without becoming sharp political issues. Of late, to be sure, our politics have tended to be very noisy indeed; but the reason is that the Liberals, here as everywhere rebels against our Tradition, do not wish American society to become more and more like itself —wish it, rather, to become something very different from itself. They are, therefore, constantly putting forward proposals for making it over in their image of what a society should be like—proposals born of their instinctive dislike for the American way of life and for the basic political and social principles presupposed in it, and certain, therefore, to run up against vigorous and uninterrupted Conservative resistance. And "presupposed," come to think of it, is just the right word. For the fundamental beliefs involved in a way of life tend, I believe, to remain inarticulate—to be lived rather than spoken or argued about—until a political force arises that is capable of destroying it. Liberalism is not (or at least not yet) such a force. But its proposals are, increasingly, the subject-matter of American political discussion.

'Ism Without 'Ives

And this explains, it seems to me, why we have in our political life no consistent and articulate spokesmen for Conservatism. Since the American political tradition itself *is* a Conservative tradition with a Conservative content, and *is* clearly understood as such by those who live the American way of life and love it, it has—up to now at least —required no political party to represent it, no political theorist to set it down in black and white, no statesman to embody and symbolize it. The "Conservative" political leaders who arise to fight off Liberal attacks upon the tradition's content do not vote together, do not support each other, indeed, do not particularly like each other; they do not go down the line with a corpus of Conservative doctrine, because there *is* no line to go down, no corpus of Conservative doctrine to be faithful to. Senator Byrd rallies the resistance on this

Liberal proposal, Senator McCarran on that one, Representative Walter on yonder one; and because Liberalism, though not strong enough to dominate our politics, is strong enough to keep them confused and on the defensive, each tends to play out his Conservative role merely with respect to the one or two issues *he* happens to have got mobilized about and understands. The Conservative position, in consequence, is the sum-total of their respective positions on the series of issues the Liberals are pressing; and up to now, I repeat, no greater unity among them has been needed. They make up, so to speak, the machinery through which our Conservative people defend their way of life. And the absence of unity among them is a sign not of weakness but of strength; as the mood, the animus, and the political philosophy that underlie their stands on their respective issues add up to Conservatism.

Let me illustrate what I mean by trying to put into words what seems to be the Conservative position on three of the current Liberal attacks on the American tradition, namely:

First, the Liberal attempt to construe the First Amendment as a firm mandate for an *"open"* society, which involves the entire Liberal stand on such matters as the current persecution of the Communists, academic freedom, and the fundamentally religious basis—that is, the Judaeo-Christian basis—of American society. Second, the Liberal attempt to transform the American political system into a *plebiscitary* system. And, third, the Liberal attempt to construe the American tradition as an egalitarian tradition, friendly to the kind of levelling whose predictable result would be world-wide uniformity—of economic status, of subordination to something called the Conscience of Mankind as expressed by something called the United Nations, of religious or rather irreligious belief, and of political philosophy or organization.

On the first of these matters, the question whether the First Amendment to the Constitution is to be treated as a mandate for an open society, the Conservative takes his stand in line with the Great Tradition in political philosophy. He assumes, with Plato and Aristotle and Hobbes and Rousseau, that any viable society has an *orthodoxy*—a set of fundamental beliefs, implicit in its way of life, that it cannot and should not and, in any case, *will* not submit to the vicissitudes of the market place. He assumes, again with the tradition, that no society can survive—or should survive—without foundations driven deep in religious belief. And he assumes, with the authors of the Declaration of Independence, that no *good* society can be conceived that does not regard itself as moving through History—I take the phrase from Eric Voegelin—under God, ultimately therefore under a law whose source is the divine will, for a purpose that lies outside History. He finds in the First Amendment no mention of a right to think and say whatever one pleases, or of a duty on the part of American citizens to tolerate and live with and interminably discuss any and every opinion that their neighbors may take into their heads. And he holds that if the First Amendment *does* recognize such a right and such a duty, then the moment is coming when the First Amendment will itself have to be brought into line with Conservative principles regarding the character of the good society.

The Conservative, then, views with pride the fact that the American people have always construed the First Amendment, despite what it says about an established religion, as *not* forbidding them to acknowledge God on their coins, or in their oath of allegiance, to exempt religious institutions from taxation, to open sessions of their national legislature with prayer, or to retain chaplains in their armed forces. The Conservative views with horror the thesis of Mill's *Essay on Liberty,* according to which a man can hold and publicly defend any opinion, however repugnant to morality, and still be regarded as a good—or even acceptable—citizen. And—to come to the main point—he regards the present clear determination of the American people not to permit the emergence of a Communist minority in their midst—their determination, as I like to put it, to place the price of being a Communist so high that no American is likely to pay it—as a manifestation of good sense that he can only applaud.

In a word: If by an open society is meant a society built on an unlimited right to think and say what you please, with impunity and without let or hindrance, then Conservatism holds that American society is *not* such a society, and must not become such a society. And, to tie that back to the Dominican Republic, we should expect the Conservative to take a dim view of, to oppose, Liberal attempts to force other societies to become open societies.

Secondly, Conservatism views with profound disapproval American Liberalism's increasingly clear intention to realize what let's call the plebiscitary potential in the American Constitution. Conservatism does not deny that that potential is present in the Constitution:

Article V, which deals with amendments, is obviously an authorization for—if not an invitation to—the submission of even our most fundamental institutions to popular debate and, ultimately, majority-rule. The plebiscitary potential—the majority-rule potential—is, I say, there as far as the Constitution is concerned, but the American political tradition, happily, has always taken a dim view of it; and the American people—who, I repeat, have proved themselves to be better carriers of their political tradition than any individual among them—usually choose to operate their Constitution as if its plebiscitary potential were absent—and have, to that end, developed four political *habits* that have been clung to in a way that enables us to regard them as established American institutions. First, the habit of not abolishing the filibuster in the U.S. Senate. Second, the habit of not upsetting the apple-cart as regards the seniority system in congressional committees. Third, the habit of not organizing themselves —we are speaking, remember, of the American people—in political parties of an ideological or programmatic character, which might separate them off into huge, sharply-opposed groupings, capable of turning American elections into plebiscites. And, fourth, the habit of being difficult to mobilize for political purposes, especially the political purposes of amending the Constitution.

Here, entirely outside and independent of the Constitution, are the real guarantees in America against plebiscitary elections and unlimited majority-rule; and they reflect, as I see it, a sober and sustained judgment on the part of the American people that nationwide plebiscites are not good instrumentalities for making public policy, and that even if they were, we must not use them because of their tendency to divide us, to make us bad friends with one another.

These four habits, however, are precisely the points in the American political system upon which the Liberal intellectuals keep up their most insistent pressure. The filibuster, they repeat over and over again, must go, for how else can we get integration in the South? The seniority system, they shout from the roof-tops, must go; for how else can we get rid of Representative Walter? What the nations needs, they tell us, alike in their speeches and in the textbooks they write for our political science courses, is two parties that *really* disagree, so that every election will provide a real *mandate* for a clearly understood program. The instinctive refusal of the American people to mobilize for political purposes, they assure us, is just what is *wrong* with American politics; let us, therefore, tie more and more people into the political process, into a mass-communications network that keeps people's minds on politics to the virtual exclusion of all else.

Well, on all four points, Conservatism can only say: You are breaking with the American political tradition, which is Conservative and therefore not that sort of thing at all; and we will resist you to the last. And, again tying back to the Dominican Republic, we should expect Conservatism to take a dim view of, to oppose, Liberal attempts to force majority-rule on other countries.

Which brings me to my third and last issue, namely, the increasing tendency of Liberals to appeal, if I do not misunderstand them, to the principle of equality in its crudest form. I for one seem to sense such an appeal in much of the current argument in favor of foreign aid, where the idea seems to be that *because* we are rich and they are poor, it is our duty to share our riches with them. I seem to sense such an appeal, again, in much of the current argument against segregation, where the idea seems to be that if anybody enjoys privileges everybody else doesn't have then something ought to be done about it. I seem to sense such an appeal in the current propaganda in favor of a United Nations Bill of Rights, each draft of which seems to come closer to saying: nothing will do except a world-wide cooperative commonwealth of equal men.

Well, either the appeal is there, or it is not; either the Liberals are saying, in effect, one drunken wife-beater equals one gentleman, one ignoramus equals one scholar, one lazy pauper equals one hard-working merchant; either they are saying that, or they are not. But if they *are* saying it, Conservatism can give only one answer, which is the answer it believes the American people have consistently given to Liberal leveling proposals. *Rights and privileges are correlative to duties: a man has a right to those rights and privileges that he earns by the performance of his duties.* People differ enormously, moreover, in their capacity and disposition to discharge duties, and in the energy they can put into the attempt; and the good society is good just to the extent that it confers rights and privileges on those of its members who perform their duties, and withholds right and privileges from those who do not perform them.

And this, of course, is the point that should make it easiest for American Conservatives to identify and accept their obligation to go to the assistance of their beleaguered allies in the Dominican Republic. All that can possibly come out of the present American policy toward the Dominican Republic, that American policy which I believe American Conservatives could yet call a halt to were they to act *soon,* must be to level the Dominican Republic as Castroism has leveled Cuba, as the USSR has leveled Russia and the Iron Curtain countries, as Mao Tse-tung has leveled China—to destroy those meaningful distinctions of rank, of privilege, of wealth, of prestige and position that any decent society develops and builds into itself as it grows toward achievement of the purposes that called it into being as a society—to snuff out of existence one further component of that West, that Christendom, that Communism and Liberalism set out to obliterate more than a century ago. We of the American Right —stupidly, irresponsibly—permitted it to happen in Cuba; we must not permit it to happen again in the Dominican Republic. All of our principles—the three basic principles I have tried to lay on the line tonight—require us to rescue the Dominican Republic from our own Department of State.

(Fall, 1961.)

Basic Issues Between
Conservatives and Liberals

The topic of this article: those two groups of politically-conscious people out in American society, the "Liberals" and the "Conservatives," and the whole question of what the disagreement between them is about. Should I tarry to argue with the man, ex-President Eisenhower for instance, who insists that no such groups actually exist—as witness the impossibility of drawing a meaningful line between them? I think not: the groups seem to have little difficulty identifying themselves, and can, paraphrasing Descartes' enthymeme, say "Nous nous identifions, donc nous sommes"; and as for the contention that no-one can say what they disagree about, let us dismiss it as question-begging.

My thesis is, then, that we know what we mean when we make to one another such statements as the following: The Liberals support Medicare; the Conservatives oppose it. The Liberals would like to broaden and deepen our social security system until it is finally applicable from womb to tomb; the Conservatives think we'd have been better off if we had never gone in for that sort of thing to begin with. The Liberals take seriously the so-called disarmament negotiations with the Soviets, and take them seriously because they favor disarmament—would, if the Russians too would only be serious about disarmament, actually *disarm* the U.S.; the Conservatives regard the disarmament negotiations as essentially fraudulent, and would not think of disarming even if the Russians were willing. The Liberals dream dreams of out-lawing war, of establishing an international authority empowered to prevent war, of an indefinite future in which the nations will live side by side in peace and unity; the Conservatives dream no such dreams; they regard even the existing United Nations organization with suspicion, would not hesitate to challenge its authority if ever it tried to call the United States on the carpet, and take it for granted that wars have quite a future on this planet just as they have had quite a past—in short, Conservatives dislike the orientation of American foreign policy toward pacifism and world govern-

ment. The Liberals have nightmares about the future nuclear holocaust and, meantime, about nuclear fallout, and, naturally enough,
favor such measures as the nuclear test-ban treaty; the Conservatives
are given to no such nightmares: they face the nuclear age with, so
to speak, strong stomachs, dislike the test-ban treaty, and demand
that the United States maintain overwhelming nuclear superiority
over the Soviet Union. The Liberals look with favor on any and all
proposals for equalizing the *soi-disant* "civil rights" of Americans,
insist that the federal government not the state governments assume
responsibility for equalizing civil rights, and demand that the federal
government bring to the enforcement of civil rights measures the full
weight of the federal government's power and authority (right up to
and including the military occupation of the South); the Conservatives drag their feet on equalizing civil rights to start with, certainly
do not want the federal government forever in the business of equalizing civil rights, and view with horror such spectacles as those federal troops in Little Rock and Oxford. The Liberals support
ever-expanding federal aid to and control of the public schools; the
Conservatives would, like the Constitution, leave responsibility for
education to the states and the local communities. The Liberals are
pleased when, for example, the learned Dr. Oppenheimer gets a new
lease on respectability by receiving—from the hands of the President
himself—the Fermi Award, and rub their hands when they hear, as
we do now and then, that a still unrepentant Alger Hiss is prospering,
and applaud when, as happens oftener than now and then, the
United States Supreme Court wipes out still another part of the internal security system bequeathed to us by the late Senator McCarthy,
or appears to be drawing a bead on the House Un-American Activities Committee; the Conservatives, by contrast, are appalled at the
rehabilitation of Dr. Oppenheimer and the well-wishing for Mr. Hiss:
they would like to strengthen not weaken our internal security arrangements, and if one must go, HUAC or the Jefferson Memorial, the
Conservatives will opt for saving the Committee. (Only an extreme
Conservative, like myself, would say that there never should have
been a monument to Jefferson to begin with.) We do, I say, know
what we mean when we make such statements about the "Liberals"
and the "Conservatives.

Now: for purposes of this article, let us call issues like those we have
just been noticing "policy" issues between Liberals and Conserva-

tives. "Policy" issues, let us say, are the issues that are *out in the open* in American politics, issues that actually and visibly *divide* Liberals and Conservatives in the day-to-day struggles over legislation, over what foreign-policy measures to adopt in the Cold War, over current Supreme Court decisions as, Monday after Monday, the justices let us all in on what the Constitution means *this* week. "Policy" issues, let us go further and say, are the issues over which, normally, people seem to be choosing sides in our politics, the issues with an eye to which most people appear to *become* Liberals or Conservatives, that is, make up their minds as to which of our two groups, *the* Liberals and *the* Conservatives, they are going to join, and, what is perhaps most important, choose their *heroes* in politics (which will you have, Bobby Kennedy or Ronald Reagan?). But, having said all that, we must now add: these policy issues are not our real problem in this article; they are precisely *not* the "basic" issues between Liberals and Conservatives; nor shall we, I think, ever understand why we have on our hands those two groups of people, the Liberals and the Conservatives, unless we drive our analysis down to a level deeper than that of the policy issues, that is, to the level of those fundamental (or, to anticipate a little, *irreducible*) political beliefs and attitudes that cause men *to* differ, *to* take different sides, on the policy issues. John F. Kennedy and Adlai Stevenson, for example, favored the test-ban treaty, yes, and Barry Goldwater, for example, opposed it, but not, I contend, because John F. Kennedy liked treaties and Barry Goldwater didn't, or because Barry Goldwater wanted the skies full of nuclear fall-out and John F. Kennedy didn't. Down deep within John F. Kennedy and Barry Goldwater, I contend, there were—*must* have been—some basic beliefs and attitudes that made their respective stands on this policy issue not only intelligible but also *predicta-ble*. Beneath the policy issues, I contend, there are, *must* be, some deeper issues on which Conservatives and Liberals take different stands and, having taken them, *have* to disagree about the policy issues. The stands men take on the policy issues, I contend, are *derivative* from the stands they take on the *basic* issues. And the task I have set myself in this article is that of identifying at least some of the major basic issues that, as I see it, underlie our differences about what concrete *policies* we are to adopt in our day-to-day conduct of government.

That task cannot, for several reasons, be an easy one. Conservative-

Liberal differences over the policy issues are (as I have indicated) visible, audible, "out-in-the-open"; not so, by ordinary, Conservative-Liberal differences about the basic issues. The latter, in our present intellectual climate, do not, for the most part, come to the surface at all—so that I owe it to my readers, to admit, *ab initio,* that the burden of proof, not only as to the role the basic issues play but as to their very existence as issues, is on me. Put otherwise, I owe an answer to any objector who may say: if the issues you speak of are all so basic as all that, we might fairly expect them to be constant topics of discussion and debate in our public forum—which, you yourself tell us they are not; and we want to know, first off, how that can be? How, he may continue, can your issues be basic in the sense intended and yet, as you have intimated, somehow hidden.

Now: that is a matter, quite simply, of what I called a moment ago the "intellectual climate" in which we live, and have lived so long already that it is difficult for most of us to imagine any other intellectual climate. It is, however, a very peculiar intellectual climate—at least when viewed from the standpoint of those, like myself for example, who do not feel altogether at home in it, and peculiar above all in its way of handling, and appearing to dispose of, my basic issues. It is, to begin with, an intellectual climate now wholly dominated by Liberals—that is, by authoritative voices whose owners are committed to the Liberal side on both my policy issues and my basic issues. It is, secondly, an intellectual climate that tends to discourage discussion and debate about my basic issues—not, I hasten to add, by suppressing them, by never bringing them up, which would be one way to discourage such discussion and debate, but rather by treating them as issues that have already been decided, as issues that are no longer "up", that is, as issues that may have been "up" at some moment in the past but have ceased to be "up" because they are issues about which, nowadays, reasonable men could not possibly disagree. The situation is not, then, that my basic issues are never mentioned or referred to, rather the contrary: public discussion is full of references to them, but precisely not as issues that require further discussion, precisely not as proper topics for continuing debate. It is an intellectual climate whose chief characteristic, then, is an elaborate pretense that we are—all of us—in fundamental agreement on the basic issues; and that the Liberal position on the basic issues is not only right, but so patently and indisputably right that there is nothing further to be said about it. The Conservative position on the issues in question, in other words, may fairly be called the *silent* position. *Qua* silent, it has to be ferreted out, Nay, more: Its very existence has to be inferred, that is *deduced,* from the following fact: Despite that elaborate pretense that we all agree on the basic issues, Liberal proposals deriving from the Liberal position on the basic issues run up, politically speaking, against constant and on the whole successful resistance, and that resistance, I contend, entitles us to affirm the existence of a Conservative position that, however silent, is nevertheless *there.* And that position is silent, I contend, because in our intellectual climate it is outflanked—because, I repeat, most of the articulate people on the horizon are Liberals, and Liberals who take it for granted that a Conservative position on the basic issues is impossible to defend, either intellectually or morally. And No, I must not be understood to be suggesting (as we Conservatives are so often accused of suggesting) that there is anything conspiratorial or inherently sinister about the intellectual climate as I have just described it. I only wish, indeed, that the matter were that simple, since were that the case all that would be needed to reopen discussion of the basic issues would be to expose the conspiracy. Those authoritative voices, I should say rather, are those of men deeply and sincerely convinced that the basic issues have indeed been disposed of once and for all: the Conservative position has to be ignored, has to be treated as non-existent, because to treat it otherwise would, for them, itself be intellectually dishonest, itself be a conspiracy against the public good. What I am pointing to is not a conspiracy but a fact, which it is mine not to complain about but to try to understand and square off to, namely: the virtually complete domination of our intellectual climate by the Liberal position on my basic issues. Which, I repeat, is why the Conservative position on those issues has to be first fished up and then hauled out into the light of day. My task, as I began by saying, cannot bè an easy one.

II

Perhaps it would help if, at this point, I paused to do two things: First, to point to some issues that I am *not* going to put forward as "basic" between Conservatives and Liberals, though I know that some of my readers may well be expecting me to put them forward.

For instance: we hear, sometimes, that the essence of Conservatism is to be found in its *religious* basis—with the implication that Conservatives and Liberals are somehow divided over such questions as the existence of God, or the status amongst us of Judaeo-Christian religious beliefs in general, or our subordination to divine will, or what have you in and around the whole business of politics and religion. That I take to be nonsense, since many practicing Christians are Liberals, and many convinced Conservatives unbelievers. For instance again: We are often told that the essence of Conservatism is to be found in its dedication to free enterprise, or capitalism, or private property—with the implication that all the Liberals are Socialists, and mean business about Socialism; where my answer is that there is nothing as dead amongst us today as Socialism, and that the one thing we owe to Communist effort is that private property has been made safe for our time. Still again for instance: There are those who would like us to believe that the essence of Conservatism is its distrust of political power, its dedication to limited government, its opposition to centralized authority, and that the Liberals are totally indifferent to the dangers of centralized authority and big government—to which I answer that alike Liberals and Conservatives want centralized authority for some purposes but not for others, that therefore the issue, as just stated, is for the most part spurious (how much centralized authority would it take, for instance, to bring the Soviet Union to heel, as Conservatives would like to do?). I shall not be speaking, then, of religion or capitalism or decentralized authority as basic issues in the sense I intend: I doubt whether they in fact divide Conservatives and Liberals in the neat way that some people claim.

What then are the issues I have in mind? Let us, instead of listing them, keep things simple by taking them up one at a time—speaking, to begin with, of the basic difference I believe to exist between Conservatives and Liberals over the nature and extent of our dedication, here in America, to the political goal of *Equality*. For I believe that the aforementioned policy differences between Liberals and Conservatives derive to a very large extent from their difference about—as I like to put it—the meaning we are going to impose upon those words in the Declaration of Independence: All men are created equal.

My point here is *not*, I hasten to add, that there is an issue between Conservatives and Liberals as to the *status* of the all-men-are-created

clause: Conservatives no less than Liberals, I think, accept the Declaration of Independence as an initial but authoritative statement of
our political creed, think of it as laying down doctrines to which We
the People stand wholly committed, and recognize an obligation on
our part to *act* in our political life consistently with those commitments—of which the all-men-are-created-equal clause is certainly
one. But there, I think, the agreement stops, because Conservatives
do not accept, do not regard as a commitment of theirs, the principle
of politics into which the Liberals have sought to translate the all-
men-are-created-equal clause, namely: It is our duty to assure to all
of our citizens genuine *equality of opportunity*, to remove from our
national life, and that at the earliest possible moment, all identifiable
barriers to equality of opportunity, to leave nothing undone that
could contribute to equality of opportunity; and not merely our duty
to do these things, but also to place that duty at the very top, so to
speak, of our roster of duties; not merely our duty to do these things,
but our duty in a very special sense—our duty in the sense that when
we leave these things undone we should be deeply troubled in our
consciences, should plead ourselves guilty of having failed to do that
which we should have done before anything else, and should move
speedily, or at least not stand in the way of others as they move
speedily, to undo the wrong that has been done to those who have
been denied equal opportunity (or, if it is too late for that, at least see
to it that the wrong shall not in the future be inflicted upon others).
My readers will, I think, recognize that series of propositions as
familiar counters in our current political discussion—nay, as *potent*
counters, in the sense that any measure called for by one or another
of the propositions ceases, once that is made clear, to be deemed a
proper topic for futher argument, which is to say: Show that a given
measure *is* called for by one of the propositions I have named, and
—in our intellectual climate—no further justification of the measure
is deemed necessary; those who oppose the measure must do so not
on the grounds that it is unjustified in principle, but on some other
grounds—for example, that we can't afford it for the moment, or that
it is unconstitutional, or that there is a simpler or cheaper or more
promising way to accomplish the purpose in hand. The equality-of-
opportunity doctrine, I am saying then, rides high in contemporary
America. It has been promoted to the status of an axiom; if it is
anywhere being challenged on its merits, we do not hear about it; and

if it were openly challenged on its merits, I think it a safe bet that
the man who challenged it would soon find himself publicly discredited—as reactionary, or heartless, or selfish, or unavailable to the clear
call of duty, depending on which of these sticks were handiest for
beating him over the head.

So much, I think, is indisputable: the Liberals, judging from what
we hear out in the public forum, have won any argument that they
may once have had with the Conservatives over equalization of opportunity as a basic, settled commitment of We the People of the
United States. How, then, can I claim, as I am about to do, that
equalization of opportunity is, nevertheless, a basic issue between
Conservatives and Liberals? Well, let me say first that the apparently
universal acceptance of the equalization doctrine leaves a good deal
to be explained: Any way you look at it, progress on the equalization-
of-opportunity front, if there be progress at all (which I doubt), is
glacially slow. New-born babes in the United States are *not* born to
the equality of opportunity that Liberals claim for them as, literally,
their birthright, but what is more, nobody thinks they are. More
important still: even measures that might move things just a little
towards making good the supposed right to equal opportunity are
stoutly—and on the whole successfully—resisted all along the front.
Most important of all: really drastic measures on behalf of equality of
opportunity are not even proposed—not, I imagine, because the Liberals can't think up such measures, and not, I imagine, because they
wouldn't be in favor of such measures, but because sound strategic
instinct tells them that such measures are not politically possible.
Why? Because vast numbers of Americans simply do not accept the
supposed moral obligation to equalize opportunity as binding upon
them, as a duty of theirs; and they do not accept it, I suggest, because
they do not believe, down deep in their hearts, that any such duty
exists. No other explanation of the slow progress toward equalization
of opportunity will, I believe, hold water. Despite their elaborate
pretense to the contrary, the proponents of equal opportunity have
not—not yet anyhow—pled their case successfully at the bar of public opinion. You can, to be sure, silence argument with the equalization doctrine as I have stated it: but you cannot get people to support
the measures the doctrine calls for. There is, then, for all that we
never hear of it, a Conservative position on equality of opportunity,
and it stands in flat and unyielding opposition to the Liberal position.

Equality of opportunity, far from being a matter of settled doctrine amongst us, is a basic issue between the Liberals among us and the Conservatives among us, and in order to begin to understand contemporary American politics we had best begin to recognize it as just that. For I am sure, I repeat, that a very high percentage of Conservative-Liberal differences over policy issues are derivative from this basic difference over equality of opportunity.

"But all you are proving," some reader may object, "is that Conservatives are political *sinners,* not that they deny the moral obligation to support equalization measures." "The sinner," that reader may proceed, "is seldom a man who tells himself in his heart that he is acting virtuously. He sins because he is weak, or because he is lazy, or because he is selfish, and cannot or doesn't want to make the sacrifice that his duty demands of him; the sinner is usually a man who knows better than anyone else the sinfulness of his behavior." "And," my objector may conclude, "I believe that to be the case with your Conservative who opposes equalization measures. He cannot make out an intellectual or moral case for what you call his position, and he knows that he can't. Properly speaking, therefore, he hasn't *got* a position; he is silent because he doesn't have a leg to stand on." Now: that is a persuasive objection, and before passing on to my second basic issue I owe it to the reader to indicate, briefly, at least, the grounds upon which, in a less hostile intellectual climate, Conservatives *would* defend their opposition to equality of opportunity as a goal for American society. (I shall attempt to do that with each of my basic issues—drawing for this purpose on what Conservatives say to one another when they talk together; for Conservatives do talk when they are beyond the reach of Mr. Walter Cronkite and those microphones.) The equality of opportunity goal, they would say, is unrealistic, impossible to achieve, *utopian*—and because utopian, *dangerous.* In order to equalize opportunity in any meaningful way you would have, first of all—as clear-headed political philosophers have always seen—to neutralize that great carrier and perpetuator of unequal opportunity, the *family,* and you can do that, really do it, only by abolishing the family, which we will not let you do because that would be wrong. You would have, in the second place, to abolish poverty, and we do not believe anybody knows how to do that—the pie, if I may put it so, just isn't big enough to go 'round; and the schemes one hears of now and then for making it big enough to go around do not commend themselves to us, either intellectually or morally; usually they involve one kind or another of *socialism,* about which we believe *both* that it is morally wrong and that it won't work —that it will in fact impoverish people rather than improve their lot. In a word, you can't equalize opportunity, and it is wrong to talk as if you could—wrong, to go further, because you encourage many people to think themselves entitled to things they cannot have, to think they are being treated unjustly when in fact all is being done for them that can be done—more, indeed, in many cases, than ought to be done because more than is good for them. All that creates unnecessary and unwarranted resentment, and causes dissension among us, kicks up trouble. Finally, we repudiate your equality of opportunity goal because it rests on a false reading of the all-men-are-created-equal clause, and makes us forget, keeps us from acting on, the true meaning of those words, which commits us *not* to equalizing opportunity as the Liberals understand it but rather, to use a favorite phrase of ours, to providing for every American the kind of equality to which Abe Lincoln was born—to the kind of equality that, we think rightly and wisely, he sought to extend to the whole of our population rather than only some of it. That kind of equality means leaving people free to equalize their own opportunities, as Lincoln certainly equalized his—to equalize their own opportunities to the extent that they have the ability, the energy, and the determination to do it. Such equality is a matter not of doing things *for* people, but of leaving them alone—of seeing to it that even the highest places in our society are there for anyone, everyone, to win if he has the wit and strength to win them, and of seeing to it, beyond that, that everyone is given maximum encouragement to develop, out of himself, that necessary amount of wit and strength. We believe that by equalizing opportunity *for* people, by releasing them from the responsibility to equalize their own opportunities, you will penalize the best of them, the Abraham Lincolns, in a futile attempt to do something for those who will be only too willing to settle for what you do *for* them, and let it go at that. You want to turn the American dream of a career really open to the able into an American nightmare of mediocrity, and we will not let you do it. But enough—it is no part of my task in this article to prove that the Conservatives are right on the "basic issues"; I seek only to persuade the reader that there is a Conservative position on each of them, and that it deserves a hearing.

I seek only to persuade him that the basic issues I speak of are by no means already decided—that, rather, there is with respect to each of them room for a great and continuing public debate; and, for the moment, that that is certainly the case with Equality.

My second basic issue calls upon us for a quick shift of gears; it is of a quite different character from my first, and may seem to some of my readers not to be a political issue at all. Let me, for that reason —without putting a name to it quite yet—work my way into it by posing, "socratically", the following series of questions: Surely I am right—am I not—in saying that those Liberal spokesmen who dominate our intellectual climate are constantly telling us, in one way or another, that the moral imperatives of our age are in the very nature of the case "different" from those of past ages? Surely I am right— am I not—in saying that one of the axioms of contemporary Liberal political discourse is, quite simply, that morally speaking we have outgrown our grandparents, transcended our grandparents, risen above our grandparents? Surely I am right—am I not—in saying that our Liberal spokesmen are forever telling us "We must do this, and that, and that yonder, because *the time is past* when—how naturally the words fall on our ears—without turning back the hands of the clock, without repudiating the moral demands of the Twentieth Century, without refusing to live up to the responsiblities—the special and unprecedented responsibilities—of our time, we can say 'No' "? Surely I am right—am I not—in saying that we are constantly told that we must, for example, "abolish war", with the clear implication that our grandfathers failed to abolish war because morally speaking they just weren't up on our exalted level, because though free to choose between the higher level of morality and the lower, they chose, and settled for, the lower? Surely I am right—am I not—in saying that we are forever being told that we must, for example, liquidate the last vestiges of Colonialism, or must recognize our obligation to minister to the "expectations" of the underdeveloped peoples, or what have you, because there is a new morality abroad in the world, better by far than the morality of our grandfathers, a new morality to which we must subordinate ourselves, lest someone accuse us of not knowing what century we live in; must subordinate ourselves to it, *cost what it may, wherever the chips fall, Come Hell and High Water?* Surely I am right—am I not—in saying that discussion of these matters normally proceeds on the premise, none the less

oppressive because often tacit, that there is only one decent attitude
to adopt toward those grandfathers of ours, namely, to bow our heads
and be ashamed of them, to repudiate them as teachers of morality,
especially political morality, and—well, get on with the job of building that better world that they were too obtuse, morally, to envisage?
Surely I am right—am I not—in saying that the tacit premise, not the
less placed beyond challenge because tacit, is that we, we sons of the
Twentieth Century, are historically speaking a very superior breed,
projected upon a place of moral excellence the like of which mankind
has never seen before? Surely I am right—am I not—in saying that
one of the rules of the New Morality is: "Thou shalt not speak up in
defense of our grandfathers—they were a poor and benighted lot,
and there's an end to it"?

Let us, without pausing to argue whether the correct answer to all
those questions is "Yes", call all that line of chatter the "Appeal-to-
the-Century stopper"—"Appeal-to-the-Century" because the "century", *this* century, is the supreme tribunal to which appeal is being
made, and "stopper" because wherever the appeal is made it is
understood, by the appellant, as putting an end to the argument. Our
age is, to be sure, more lenient than most ages as to whom you can
talk back to—it has no objection if you talk back to Authority, or to
Revelation, or even, I suppose, to Walter Lippmann. But its strategically-situated spokesmen will not let you talk back to the Century.
Here again my point is, quite simply: There is a silent Conservative
position that flatly denies the whole line-of-chatter and so gives us
what is indeed a second basic issue. Here again my point is: The
apparently universal acceptance of the Liberal position, the new
morality, leaves altogether too much to be explained, since the generality of men amongst us seem to regard the new morality as an
attempt to impose upon them obligations that they find unacceptable. The new morality—the imperatives of the age—leaves them
unmoved. The Century commands us to do something about the
underdeveloped countries? Our Congressmen probably won't put up
much argument about it on the level of so-called principle; they will
merely vote down the relevant provisions of the foreign aid bill. We
must abolish war? The Congressmen, and their constituents as well,
will again refuse the gambit on the level of principle, but will see to
it that the Pentagon keeps on getting ready for that next war that the
Century forbids us to fight. I could multiply examples of this kind

indefinitely, but I will spare the reader that and pass on to the question, "What goes on in the minds of those Conservatives that makes them refuse, when called upon to do so, to climb aboard the Twentieth Century Limited?" Something like this, I think: The Conservatives believe, with Burke, that the important discoveries in morals and politics were made long before our generations put in their appearance. They believe, again with Burke, that anything that purports to be a new discovery in morals or politics is, for that very reason, suspect. They deny, with Burke again, that there are fashions in morality as in women's wearing apparel; and, like Burke, look upon their grandfathers, even their remote ancestors, with respect and reverence. They insist, following Burke, that the man who has no respect for his ancestors is unlikely to have much respect for himself, and they believe that we shall be well-advised, we sons of the Twentieth Century, to try to live up to our grandfathers before we try to surpass or transcend them—that, indeed, our grandfathers ran a better world than we seem to be running, and that the big reason we run a worse world is that we have failed, failed in the crucial dimensions, to measure up to the moral standards we have inherited from the past. As Robert Penn Warren has put it: "The past is always a *rebuke* to the present; it's bound to be, one way or the other; it's your rebuke. It's a better rebuke than any dream of the future . . . *The drama of the past that corrects us* is the drama of our struggles to be human, or our struggles to define the values of our forbears in the face of their difficulties" (italics added). The Conservatives believe that the new morality usually turns out, upon examination, to be *immorality;* and they feel confident, as they make that judgment, because in making it they speak out of a morality that *boasts* of its rootedness in tradition. They dislike especially the way the rules of the new morality end in phrases like "Cost what it may" or "Come Hell and High Water," because for them such phrases have only one meaning and that a shocking meaning, namely: Let us adjourn considerations of prudence—we are so right, we up-to-date moderns, so absolutely and marvellously right, that we do not have to raise questions about the consequences of applying our rules; if the rule is right, as it must be since it is ours, then the consequences of obeying it must be right. All of that, for the Conservative, is impudent moral nonsense, since he knows that one of our major obligations in politics is to act prudently, as one of our major obligations in morality is to walk in the ways of humility. But again enough: I believe I have already shown that there is an issue here, and one which, if debated publicly, would not find the Conservatives without intellectual and moral arguments. It remains only to put a name to it; and I suggest that we call it the issue of *piety toward the past*—and that, here again, we should all be better off if it were fished up to the surface of our public debate and talked about, instead of being constantly brushed aside as if it did not exist.

For my third basic issue, we must again shift gears. I am going to call it the issue of the "Open Society", and I think of it as the issue that underlies (and renders unavoidable) Liberal-Conservative differences on, for example, McCarthyism, the House Un-American Activities Committee, the censorship of allegedly indecent or pornographic books and films, loyalty oaths, and many another problem involving, in one way or another, individual freedom of thought and speech. Just as my first issue, Equality, boiled down to an issue as to the meaning we are going to give in America to the words "All men are created equal", that is, to a form of words handed down from the past, so this one boils down to an issue as to the meaning we are going to give in America to the First Amendment of the Constitution. The Liberals see that amendment as a guarantee of certain *individual* rights—the right of each to think and say what one pleases, the right of each to the free exercise of one's religion even if that religion be irreligion, the right of each to live under a governmental system that in no way favors one religion over other religions or even religion-in-general over irreligion. Some Liberals, indeed—Mr. Justice Black for instance—go so far as to say that these rights are *absolute,* so that no governmental agency in America can infringe or limit them in any way by indirection. Other Liberals, avoiding that rather frightening word "absolute", would permit the government to interfere with, *e.g.,* freedom of speech if and when it can be shown that free speech is posing a clear and present danger to public order and the civil peace. (Even these more moderate Liberals, however, are likely to shift in the direction of an absolute right when it is a question of the free exercise of religion, or of government action that appears to favor religion at the expense of irreligion.) At first blush, therefore, the Liberal position here would seem to be less "neat" than the Liberal position on my other two issues, and the Liberal-Conservative clash, accordingly, might fairly be expected to be less sharp than on the other two. But these difficulties disappear, I think, if we insist on forcing the question down to a deeper level, where the Liberals cease to fall out over questions of detail and unite in opposition to my silent Conservatives (who are, just possibly, a little less silent on this issue than on the other two). And we arrive at that deepest level, I believe, when we state the issue not in terms of individual rights, with their long history in the decisions of the United States Supreme Court, but, I repeat, in terms of the "case for" and the "case against" the Open Society (as it is called in one of the most influential Liberal books of our time). The question then becomes whether (I take my language from Mr. Justice Douglas) we in America have or do not have an "orthodoxy", a "creed" of some kind, that we seek to "prescribe" (again I use Justice Douglas' term) to our "individual" citizens. Nearly all Liberals would agree, I think, that we have no such orthodoxy, and that our governments never have any business acting as if we did. America is to be an *open society,* in which differing opinions compete freely with one another in an "ideas"-market as merchants freely compete with one another in a vegetable-market. Government, public authority, must not seek to give the inside-run to any opinion, any point of view—whether by suppressing one opinion at the expense of another, or by seeking to inculcate one opinion at the expense of another. And here, as with my other two issues, the Liberals seem to me to be saying: The discussion—the intellectual and moral discussion—is over; we *should* be, have our minds made up to be, an open society. If there are people in America who hold some different position, let us recognize that that position cannot be supported by sense-making intellectual or moral arguments, since any different position is, on the face of it, rooted ultimately in prejudice and bigotry.

Is there, in point of fact, no issue about the Open Society? The answer, once more, is that the universal agreement to which our Liberal spokesmen appeal leaves too much to be explained: the continuance on our statute-books of rules requiring loyalty oaths; the religious observances in public ceremonies and in the public schools (now, to be sure, in open defiance of the Supreme Court); the chapels at our service schools; the chaplains in the Armed Forces and in Congress; the exemptions of church property from taxation; the "In God We Trust" on the nation's coinage; the exclusion of Communists and Communist sympathizers from government employment—indeed a thousand disabilities under which we place the Communist movement in all its forms and manifestations. There is, in other words, a whole list of things that, as the Liberals always find when they try to get rid of them, enjoy widespread support that can only be described as Conservative. And it remains only to ask, once more, and to answer briefly, the question: Are not the Liberals right when they say the discussion is over, that the Conservative support I speak of is rooted exclusively in prejudice and bigotry, and that there is no Conservative position here that can be defended with intellectual and moral argument?

Once more my answer must be "No"; the discussion, properly speaking, is not over; the Conservatives are for the most part silent because up on the level of public discussion they are momentarily outflanked, not because they have nothing to say that is worth listening to. Were the discussion reopened—as I am pleading in this article that all three discussions ought to be reopened—the Conservatives could, for example, claim the support of most of the great-name political philosophers who, through the centuries, have addressed themselves to questions relating to the public orthodoxy. They could argue that the doctrine of the Open Society is, in point of fact, an upstart among political doctrines, since it is as old as, and no older than, John Stuart Mill's *Essay on Liberty*. They could insist that there are great intellectual difficulties in Mill's position, that Mill's critics have repeatedly exposed those difficulties, and that none of Mill's epigones has stepped forward to do honest battle with those critics. The Conservatives could argue, again with considerable show of reason, that the Open Society is on the face of it unworkable, because its very idea presupposes a demonstrably false view of human nature since human beings as we know them, and particularly as we see them in America, cannot be prevailed upon to behave as the Open Society expects them to behave (*i.e.,* to tolerate the dissemination of opinions that they deem outrageous). They could demonstrate and back up the demonstration with overwhelming evidence that the open-society conception of America is, on the record to date, unacceptable to vast numbers of Americans, and that this is a fact that the Liberals, however right they may be in theory, ignore at their peril. (Vast numbers of Americans, as I like to put it, have yet to make up their minds whether America is a political society like other political societies, or something rather more like a church.) The Conservatives could argue, as Boston argued in effect with Roger Williams, that they have yet to hear why the right of a people to adopt an orthodoxy, to seek to hand it down to their descendants, to take steps against those who would undermine it, isn't as good a right as the right of the "individual" to freedom of thought and speech. But again enough: my point is not that the Conservatives would necessarily win the debate if the issue were ever reopened, but merely that it would be quite a debate.

Will the debates for which I am pleading ever actually come off? Not, you may be sure, for so long as the Liberals retain their virtual monopoly of the mike—in the mass communications and, above all, in the college and university classrooms.

(University of Dallas)

Is Violence a Human Necessity?

Speech in Berkeley, California, as a member of a panel, in 1965

Let me speak first about how we are to construe that word "Utopian": We *might* read it, of course, as synonymous with "absurd", or "impossible to realize"—the word is, of course, sometimes used in that sense. But were I to read it that way for present purposes I should be assuming too great a burden—to say nothing of delivering myself into my opponents' hands. Let me concede at once, then, that we simply do not know enough about human beings, and the workings of human affairs, to warrant the statement that all proposals for eliminating war are impossible to realize, and thus absurd. I, for one at least, should not know how to go about defending such a statement. One of the things my opponent and I would most easily agree on, I think, is that while we can often extrapolate from the past and say that such and such is *possible*, because it *has* been done, we can never—never if we are talking about a question worth discussing—extrapolate from the past and say that such and such is *impossible*, because it hasn't been done. What we can do and often do do, is look at the past—at man's history and what it seems to teach us about man's nature, about man's behavior, about socio-political reality—and make such statements as: Given what we know, such and such a proposal is *improbable* of realization—or even so *grossly* improbable of realization that we'd be ill-advised, especially where the stakes are big and valuable, to go putting out bets on it. Or, variously, that to date we know nothing about people that disposes us to believe that they can ever be brought to behave in the manner called for by such and such a proposal. Let me, then, mean just that by "utopian": A proposal is utopian—more or less utopian, if you like—to the extent that we find ourselves obliged, in terms of what we know of the record, to say that the *chances* of its being adopted, and, once adopted, carried into effect, seem more or less slender—too slender, for example, to dispose us who listen to the proposal, and weigh it, to risk much of anything on it. In making such a judgment, let me add, we do not necessarily involve ourselves in any quarrel with those who, enamored of the proposal, wish to keep on urging it. Often, indeed, we can admire them for the courage and public spirit that enable them to keep up a struggle against such overwhelming odds, provided they show a certain amount of good sense as to how overwhelming the odds are, and do not use the argument: "I see all that, but it *mustn't* be true; the consequences would be too horrible to contemplate; your 'grossly improbable', where this question is concerned, is shockingly immoral, and betrays a callous indifference to the sacrifice of human life, to the destruction of civilization." That, of course, is an accurate *précis*—not a caricature but a *précis*—of much of what we hear these days about the topic before us. The argument starts out from what is moral, or at least sentimentally appealing, and argues from the moral to the probable; its underlying logic reduces to the axiom: If that which is probable is immoral, then it ceases to be necessary. Not so, either, with the man who argues: The consequences being too horrible to contemplate, people will *see* that they are too horrible to contemplate and take the steps necessary for avoiding them, so that the improbable will become the probable. Not so, finally, with the man who wants to say to us: In thus dwelling upon what we know from study of the past, do you not end up insisting that might is right, that that which must happen, that which is unavoidable, is in fact *good*—that since that which must be will be there's no point in talking about morality at all? Do you not, in a word, end up justifying all existing evils? That man is simply avoiding the question before us, and all we can say to him is this: No, we must not be understood as saying that the probable is good, but merely that it is probable; the question as to what is good, what is morally justifiable, though an urgent question, is a separate question and, for most purposes at least, a *posterior* question; take the moral question up first, and what you end up with is not sound moral speculation but utopianism, which is the intellectual equivalent of the sin of Onan. Put otherwise: let us not hesitate to brand as evil that part of the probable that our consciences condemn—to brand it as evil, to denounce it, even do what we can to bring about a state of affairs in which what now seems improbable will seem so no longer. But you will get nowhere with that by denying, in the teeth of convincing argument, that, for the moment, the probable *is* probable. Not so,

finally, with the man who says: You are taking refuge in sheer determinism; you are denying freedom of the will; you are insisting that
there's no point in trying to do anything about anything, that man is
the helpless prisoner of so-called forces that he cannot hope to control. I am, I believe, more than ready for such a man, for no one is
more deeply convinced than I that man, exercising his free will
under the God that gave it to him, makes his own history and can,
within certain limits, guide that history where he pleases; I shall say
nothing of forces, or historical trends, or the like, that reduce man to
impotence. On the contrary: my position is, quite simply, that so far
as we know proposals for eliminating war are utopian because man's
will *is* free—that so far as we know war is unavoidable because man
wills it to be unavoidable, and commits *freely* the acts that lead to
war.

Now down to business—that is, the grounds on which I assert that
we had best, since so far as we know all proposals for eliminating war
are utopian, all denials of the human necessity of force specious, we
had best, I say, keep our powder dry.

First, then, the chances of eliminating the use of force in domestic
affairs and the use of war in international affairs are just as good as,
and no better than, the chances of teaching the generality of men
that *discussion, debate, talking things over,* followed, presumably, by
some kind of vote whose verdict all have agreed to accept, is a better
way of settling differences than fighting them out; and the historical
record would seem to suggest that those chances are not very good.
(No-one, let me say in passing, seems to have come up with a third
alternative, that is, one over and beyond talking it out and fighting
it out.) What historical record? Well, to take the simplest case (and,
one would have thought, the easiest one), namely, that of the spread,
over the face of the earth in modern times, of government by discussion *within* national frontiers. Thirty-odd years ago, in the aftermath
of World War I, when all civilized nations seemed, for the moment,
to be "going democratic", a reasonable man might, just conceivably,
have indulged a moderate degree of optimism about this; since then,
however, things have pretty well settled down to the pre-World War
I normal state of affairs, that is: on the one hand a tiny handful of
"civilized" nations (nearly all of which, curiously, speak either the
English language, or a Scandinavian language, or, at the extreme
margin, Dutch or Flemish), and all other nations governed by more

or less open dictatorships resting unabashedly upon force, upon the physical might necessary for crushing any potential dissenter. Nor are the reasons for this reversal hard to seek out: Government by discussion, as we know it in the English-speaking and Scandinavian countries, depends for its smooth functioning upon deeply-ingrained political habits, upon a stern discipline, upon elaborate arrangements for confining discussion, for the most part, to that minimal percentage of the population that is capable of discussing to begin with, upon, above all, the kind of trust and confidence, and I am tempted to say affection, back and forth among the citizens that dispose them to accept, beforehand, the verdict of the future vote. These are, in the main, phenomena that are present and accounted for only in the tiny handful of countries that I have mentioned; and where they are not present they can, so far as we know, be called into being only as they are taught and inculcated, which calls for (a) a dedicated elite to do the teaching and inculcating, (b) a population willing to listen to them and be persuaded by them, and (c) that scarcest of all the world's goods, namely, time, and more time by far than we are likely to have before the present crisis in world affairs comes to a head. And let me remind you: I have been speaking thus far of the simplest case, namely, the elimination of the use of force, in favor of government by discussion, within national frontiers (all those dictatorships I speak of, remember, will just as they rest on force be overthrown one day by force, that is, by civil war); even here, I say, the chances of getting the case for government by discussion over to the generality of men in the generality of the world's nations, and within the foreseeable future, are pretty slender. Yet there are those amongst us who dream —and dream, alas, aloud—of extending government by discussion into the realm of international affairs—where, as we shall be noticing in a moment, the issues at stake are, demonstrably, issues that are far more difficult for the discussion process to handle.

Secondly, the chances of eliminating the use of force in domestic affairs and the use of war in international affairs are—again so far as we know—as good as, and no better than, the chances of transforming human nature as we know it, in precisely that one of its dimensions in which, as I believe, it displays its greatest resistance to change; and no, I am not about to say what, as I suspect, you think I am about to say. I am, as you perhaps know, a Roman Catholic, and hold what I take to be normal Catholic views about original sin, and

thus about the role in human affairs of envy, of cupidity, of predatoriness, of, at the margin, just plain thirst for blood, just plain lust for
lording it over others, just plain orneriness; I do, therefore, believe
that a powerful case could be made out, as regards the human necessity of war, on the grounds that the best-laid schemes for perpetual
peace will, soon or late, smash themselves against the stone-wall of
innate and ineradicable human viciousness. I shall not, however,
bring that case, and shall not avail myself of any strength that might
accrue to my position tonight from an appeal to any such line of
reasoning. Put otherwise: I am more than willing to assume, for purposes of tonight's panel, that the psychiatrists and social workers and
city-planners can—can even within the foreseeable future—prevail
upon the generality of men to cease to be predatory in domestic
affairs and, at one further remove, upon the generality of governments not to engage in predatory wars—more than willing not because I believe any such thing, which of course I do not, but because
I am convinced that, in our immediate situation, the situation that is
in fact at the back of all our minds, predatory war is not the problem.
Put otherwise again: the chances of eliminating the use of force from
the conduct of human affairs, above all the chances of avoiding an
ultimate arbitrament by force between the United States and the
Soviet Union, are as good as and no better than that of eliminating
from the hearts of man *not* the worst that is in them but, paradoxical
as that may seem, the best that is in them. For that future war between the United States and the Soviet Union, when it comes, will
not be a predatory war, a war of conquest for conquest's sake, but a
war rendered unavoidable by dramatically-opposed views as to the
nature of man, diametrically-opposed views as to man's relatedness
to God, diametrically-opposed views as to what is good, and what is
true, and what is beautiful, and what is valuable, diametrically-
opposed views as to what man should revere and humble himself
before, diametrically-opposed views as to what kind of world our
descendants shall be living in a thousand years hence. Now: those
diametrically-opposed views arise not out of man's viciousness or
predatoriness, but precisely out of his noblest aspirations—the aspiration to understand, the aspiration to penetrate the meaning of the
universe in which he lives, the aspiration to distinguish between the
good and the bad, the true and the false, the beautiful and the ugly,
the aspiration to *identify* himself with the good, the true, and the

beautiful, the aspiration, finally, to sacrifice himself, to give the last full measure of devotion, in order that the good should prevail. Ask me to believe that the would-be reformer of human nature can produce for us a breed of men who will turn their backs on predation, and I shall not accuse you of insulting my intelligence; ask me to believe that they can produce for us a breed of men who will not rally to the standards of a Jesus, a Mahomet, a Marx, who seems to minister to their highest aspirations, and you ask me to believe the unbelievable. Ask me to believe that you can elaborate an international organization that will get across to the predatory the idea that the world will not tolerate wars of conquest, and you merely tax my credulity; but ask me to believe that men will ever bow before an international authority when what is at stake is not a piece of real estate but the very survival of the true religion, and you ask me to unlearn all that I have learned about how history works and how human beings behave. Make no mistake about it: the great arbitraments of history —the decision for example as to whether the Roman Empire is to be Christian or pagan, the decision as to whether Europe is to be Christian or Mohammedan, the decision for example, for we do stand on the threshold of another such arbitrament, as to whether Christendom or Communism shall inherit the earth—are *always* arbitraments by force, that is, by war. They *have* to be, because arbitrament by discussion between conflicting world-views is out of the question: the contestants possess no common vocabulary in which to speak to one another, and no common set of axioms in the contest of which to conduct a debate, above all, perhaps, no common willingness, where the big issues are at stake, to be swayed by mere reasoned discourse.

(Berkeley, Calif.—1965)

The Future of Individual Initiative in America

Lecture delivered November 29, 1966, the fourth in a series of
Wingspread lectures on "Individual Initiative in America's Future"

I find myself wondering, as I begin this lecture, what is my announced topic likely to mean to the average member of my audience? The topic implies a question, namely, what *is* the future of private initiative in America? But that question, clearly, might mean different things to different people (depending, I suppose, on what literature they have read, what they themselves are interested in, etc.) and —a point of considerable importance for my purpose—different things at different times to one and the same person (depending, if he is a friend of individual initiative, or what, at the moment, he identifies as the threat to individual initiative). The future of private initiative is, so to speak, one face of a coin, the other face of which is the future of the things that threaten private initiative.

It might mean, for instance, what is the future of capitalism in America? Or, looking at the other side of the coin: what is the future of socialism in America? That, certainly, is what the question meant to most of us thirty-odd years ago, when the late Lawrence Dennis was writing his book *Is Capitalism Doomed?* It might mean, to a man less interested in economics and more interested in, say, politics: what is the future of political freedom? Or, again turning the coin over: what is the future of big government, centralized authority, and bureaucratic controls in America? It might mean—to the man interested in both economics and politics—what is the future of hierarchy, of unequal distribution of goods and privileges, or, again flipping the coin, what is the future of egalitarianism, of levelling, of taking from the rich and the privileged and giving to the poor and the underprivileged? It might mean, to the man interested above all in what we call culture: what is the future amongst us of freedom to innovate in the realm of ideas and art? This is the obverse of conformism, of thought-control, and manipulated opinion and sentiment. (Though let us not fail to notice, as we canvass the various possible meanings, how often that word "freedom" keeps cropping up.) It might mean —though perhaps we shan't understand each other very well about that until a tardy moment in this lecture—how about access to existing information?, access to the kind of information private initiative needs if it is to initiate other than blindly and with the cards stacked against it, where, as I shall be arguing, the threat would seem to be governmental monopoly of information about the future itself. Furthermore, all these ways of construing my question are legitimate and defensible in the sense that each points up an issue, a problem in which each and every one of us ought to be deeply interested. More still: each of these questions is likely, on a given pair of lips, to conceal a value judgment (let us be fashionable and call it that) as to how much freedom there ought to be in the area in question. More again: one man will ask his question on the tacit premise that freedom is a good thing—the more of it we have the better—while another may ask it on the premise that too much freedom leads to anarchy and, beyond that, to tyranny.

But perhaps I have now said enough along that line to prepare the way for the following general statement about my purpose in this lecture: I am concerned not only about my overall question, but about each and every one of the subsidiary questions into which I have just broken it down.

I think the time long past when we dare to mean by the overall question anything so simple as: what is the future of capitalism, that is, of socialism, in America? While I shall not neglect that question (I am myself a product of the age when it seemed to be *the* question), I shall not tarry over it very long. I shall, indeed, be content if I can make clear my reasons for feeling that that form of the question is now outmoded and that the man looking for the threat or the threats to private initiative at this juncture of our history will waste his time looking at the socialist movement. The threat or the threats lie elsewhere, in quarters where we are not in the habit of seeking them. The threats lurk in dimensions of the individual initiative problem of which all too many of us are largely unaware. I shall try to put names to them, as we proceed, and try to indicate where efforts must be directed if we are to forestall them, as I hope we will.

But let me, before getting into that, dwell for a moment on that word "forestall," because that will give me an opportunity to situate myself with respect to some of my Conservative confrères, whose ideas on these matters differ greatly from my own. I do not believe, as they seem to, in historical inevitabilities, that is, historical laws that somehow settle questions like that of the future of individual initiative in America beforehand. I do not think of history, as they seem to, as something already printed up on a roll of ticker-tape, and of ourselves as being called upon merely to guess how the tape reads down on its unexposed layers. I do believe, as they seem not to, that men make their own history, that great historical events such as, for example, the coming of socialism, are determined by men's ideas and opinions rather than the other way around, and that just as historical events are not pre-determined, neither are men's ideas and opinions pre-determined, but rather formed in the process of debate and discussion. I do not, as they seem to do, look upon the future or immediate past of individual initiative in a mood of black pessimism. I am, as they seem not to be, distrustful of all the so-called laws of history to which the prophets of doom appeal in the attempt to justify their prophecies—the idea, for example, that it is inherent in the very nature of government to try to expand its powers, and to expand them indefinitely; or that a democratic government, in order to expand its powers indefinitely, has merely to up and up the ante with regard to handouts for the poor and underprivileged; or that, since ordinary men and women value pork-chops above freedom, the enemies of freedom are, unavoidably, the wave of the future. I believe, as they seem not to, that we Conservatives, if we but use our wits and mobilize our energies, have it in our power to *forestall*—I deliberately repeat the word—all the threats to individual initiative today readily discernible on the horizon. Our cause being just, and our debating skills considerable, we have nothing to fear except our own pessimism—as bequeathed to us by Alexis de Tocqueville and nurtured, from year to year, by Liberal psychological warfare.

My first point on what we will call the optimistic side of our topic is this: if we equate the future of private initiative with the future of capitalism or free enterprise; if the great threat to private initiative is government ownership of the means of production; if the issue is a future made up of Sears and Roebuck plus GE plus IBM, versus a future made up of TVA's, all that is two or three decades out of date, and we should quit losing any sleep over it. There was a time, as I have suggested repeatedly, when it certainly wasn't so, or at least was not as obviously so as it is now. During the great depression a very plausible case could be made of the notion that capitalism had failed us, that by its very nature it was incapable of delivering the goods— so that the intelligent thing to do was, as rapidly as possible, to turn responsibility for production and employment over to the government. We began to hear about something called the private sector, destined because of its inefficiency for euthanasia, and something called the public sector, destined to replace production for profit with so-called production for use. At the time TVA was established, that is how we Conservative and Liberal intellectuals all thought it was going to be. Nevertheless, we have yet to see our second TVA, and it might be profitable for us to pause to remind ourselves why things have fallen out as they have.

There was, first of all, the great post-war depression that never happened (although all the economists, including, amusingly enough, Lord Keynes, were telling us that it was inevitable), because the capitalism that everybody had been busy burying displayed a vitality and forward thrust that promptly began to pour out goods and services in quantities of which no one had ever dared to dream. There was, secondly, the progressive failure of the socialized economies, especially that of the Soviet Union, which has yet to get back to the level it had reached under the czars, so that my friend Bertrand de Jouvenel can say, in his best epigram, that we owe a deep debt of gratitude to the Soviets because it is they, beyond anyone else, who have made private property safe for our time. There were, thirdly, the German and Japanese economic miracles, which were certainly *capitalist* miracles. There was, fourthly (to come back to a theme to which I shall return again and again), the fact that these great events —the new triumphs of capitalism, the ubiquitous demonstrations of the inability of socialism to minister even half-adequately to people's needs—were brought home to people generally so that they were left in no doubt that the unexampled prosperity they were enjoying, and that they saw other nations enjoying, was due precisely to the fact that free enterprise had *not* failed us.

The consequence was the death of the socialist movement, apart from its last refuge in some of the classrooms of our universities where the indictment against capitalism now runs not in terms of its alleged inefficiency but rather in terms of its alleged immorality. That is, as the intellectuals like to put it, capitalism places a premium upon greed and property rights as contrasted to public service and human rights. The socialist movement is as dead as Queen Anne, and dead *because* public opinion is no longer open to its appeals; and public opinion is no longer open to its appeals *because* Conservative spokesmen have, in economics, taught people in general how many beans it takes to make five and made the lesson stick. So I repeat: if the threat to private initiative were socialism, we might safely adjourn our worries about its future.

I move on now to my second point on the optimistic side, which is: if we equate safety for private initiative with safety for the rewards of private initiative—if we believe, as I certainly do, that private initiative is fed at its roots by the promise of wealth and income and privilege for the potential innovator, and that, being so fed, it can be starved by legal onslaughts on economic and social inequality—if, accordingly, we believe that the threat to the future of private initiative is redistributive taxation, confiscatory inheritance taxes, and such measures—then I say again: let us adjourn our worries. I know, I know: the government, on paper at least, already takes quite a large discriminatory bite out of high incomes and hefty inheritances. The bite might keep on getting bigger and bigger, and might conceivably get big enough to cause the man who can build a better mousetrap to say to himself "Why bother?" Worse still: many of my Conservative confrères, who don't want that to happen, join the Liberals, who do want it to happen, in proclaiming its inevitability. My answer to both, however, is this: the years go by, one by one, and it doesn't happen. The years go by, one by one, and yet year by year the rich among us grow relatively richer and not only relatively richer but more numerous and by the same token, the poor amongst us grow relatively poorer and also more numerous. Nor have I ever seen any evidence that the average American's eagerness—for me, admirable eagerness —to make a buck has yet been restrained by the income tax he is going to have to pay on it, or that his equally admirable eagerness to pile up an estate has been notably curbed by the thought of those inheritance taxes. Indeed, the continued forward thrust of American free enterprise is inexplicable, but we believe that what the Liberals call greed and the Conservatives call entrepreneurial incentive remains, in our part of the world, vigorous and robust.

This is not particularly difficult to understand. The people who elect the congressmen who write our laws believe, quite simply, that it is wrong to steal, even if the thief be poor and the victim of the theft rich. They have never, like their cousins across the Atlantic, gotten it through their heads that stealing ceases to be stealing if the poor have the government do their stealing for them. We have our discriminatory taxation which appears to strike hard at the rich, but, first of all, the tax laws that authorize such taxation are never, if I read our legislative history correctly, enacted out of devotion to *egalitarian principle.* Congress taxes the rich hard simply because, within limits, they are the handiest source for that extra tax dollar.

Secondly, the tax laws in question are notoriously as full of loopholes as the Pentagon is of whiz kids. Like the Almighty, Congress taketh away but also it giveth, so that an expert writing in *The Reporter* three or four years ago was able to conclude that any rich American who pays more than a 40% tax on any of his income had better get himself a new tax consultant. However the laws may appear to read, it does remain possible for a rich American with a good lawyer to bequeath sizable forturnes not only to his children but to his grandchildren—who, we like to think, will take it from there.

Thirdly, we have in America a great many taxes of the type the economists call regressive, that is, taxes that, like the sales tax, fall heavier not on the relatively rich, but on the relatively poor.

Fourthly, let it be said to our eternal credit as a nation that no American political party with any chance of coming to power has ever staked its fortunes on schemes for plundering the rich in order to line the pockets of the poor. That, politically speaking, just isn't pay-dirt in America.

Fifth, and finally, it seems not unlikely that England, which had indeed made a career out of plundering the rich, will end up playing, in this matter, a role similar to that of the Soviets with respect to private property. No American who has watched the British economy stumble, through crisis after crisis, all the way from prosperity to penury, from elegance to frayed collars, is going to be eager to imitate its tax policies. As with income and wealth, so too with privilege and unequal opportunity, which is one of the things the innovator wants to buy for his children and bequeath to his grandchildren. As more Americans grow affluent, more and more of them are turning their noses up at the education offered in our public schools, sending their youngsters to private schools, where they have not only the privilege of that better education that will give them the inside-run in the competitive race out there in American society, but also the privilege of identifying one another and establishing the *connections,* the *access,* which permit privilege to breed privileges, at least in the professions, in an unending imitation of the so-called population explosion.

And so we arrive at a second conclusion, parallel to our first: if the future of individual initiative depends on keeping alive the motivations of the entrepreneur, and if that is a matter of containing the advance of levelling for the sake of levelling, of principled egalitarianism, then the future of private initiative in America looks pretty good. And here too, returning to that minor theme of this lecture that I don't want to let disappear, we can safely say that private initiative is safe for the foreseeable future because, as far as this threat is concerned, there exists in America a healthy public opinion which, when the chips are down, is against levelling. Healthy public opinion exists because the Conservatives among us have taken the steps, in the public forum, necessary for keeping it alive. American opinion perhaps nibbles at the cheese of levelling, but as far as I can see, its *heart* is never really in it.

But enough, for the moment, about capitalism, that is, about private initiative as equated with the entrepreneurial function and the security of the innovator's rewards. Let us turn now to that phase of our topic in which we equate individual initiative with freedom to innovate and compete in the *political order*—that phase of the problem that the pessimists about the future of private initiative in America seem to be least aware of and least concerned about. Let us mean by individual initiative in politics, at its lowest level, the freedom to become a precinct captain in one of our two great political parties. At its highest level let us mean, on one side, the freedom of every American who dislikes our present parties, and feels a vocation for it, to go start a new political party and enroll in it each and every other American whom he can persuade, hypnotize, or cajole; and, on the other side, the freedom to rise, according to his wits and energy, to enlist the necessary supporters to any legislative or executive office in the land and, once he is there, offer and plead for any proposal— intelligent or unintelligent, prudent or foolish, therapeutic or suicidal —that he gets into his head. The precinct captain is no less an entrepreneur, an enterpriser, no less a symbol of individual initiative than the man who makes a better mousetrap.

One wonders why we hear so little about him in this connection, though perhaps the reason is not too hard to formulate: as I have already intimated, the American university classroom is the last refuge of Marxist-type economic determinism, and too many articulate people have convinced themselves that private initiative in politics *depends* on private initiative in economics. They feel that once free economic enterprise goes, political freedom will go too—that political freedom is never any safer than economic freedom. Dare I confess, in the teeth of my Conservative confrères, that I imagine it to be the other way around? Dare I record my belief that there isn't a shred of proof for the supposed law of history to which they appeal? (I have already said that I am suspicious of historical laws, to which I can now add that I am infinitely distrustful of laws about how politics work when, like this one, they originate in the writings of economists who have forgotten the location of the fence that divides their back yard from that of their neighbors.)

In America, certainly, the causation seems to have operated in the opposite direction: draconian restrictions on private initiative in the economic order lasted until a much more recent moment than most people realize. When they were removed, they were removed by the repeal of the relevant laws and ordinances, which repeal would never have occurred but for individual freedom to propose and agitate in the political order. Nor does the more conspicuous evidence from abroad point to a different conclusion: in pre-war Germany it was democracy that went first, then capitalism; in Russia, the Communists moved first to abolish political freedom, after which the rest was easy, leaving to one side the legal slaughter of a few million people. In Germany it was post-war German democracy that reconstructed German capitalism and produced the miracle. And if we shift our attention to England—well, she is far gone in pregnancy with a controlled economy that may well finish off the entrepreneurial function; but according to my *Sunday Times*, British political freedoms remain intact. Given an appropriate public opinion I see no reason why a free political system and a socialized economic system couldn't coexist on one and the same piece of real estate.

Are there threats to private initiative in the political order comparable to socialism and egalitarianism in the economic order? Of course there are, although here, too, I count myself among the optimists. The typical nemeses of free political systems in our time are,

I suppose, two in number, namely: government by television, as we see it operate in France and Egypt, and perhaps in Cuba; and government by the Praetorian guard, as we see it operate in Africa and Latin America. It is also quite possible for them to overlap, as they appear to do in Egypt.

The characteristic feature of government by television is, on the one hand, a more or less, but mostly less, benevolent monopoly of mass communications; and on the other hand a more or less, but mostly more, durable, illicit love-affair between a great and persuasive leader like de Gaulle or Nasser and a safe majority of the masses. Similarly, the characteristic feature of government by the Praetorian guard is an openly non-benevolent monopoly of firepower by a cohesive military caste which, in a manner of speaking, elects and on occasion replaces the top guy. The two nemeses possess, however, one common pre-condition, namely a population psychologically and emotionally capable (because it has no long experience and thus no tradition of genuine political freedom) of being jumped through the hoop, which is why I think neither constitutes any real threat here in America. The American people I grew up with can't be jumped through the hoop in the Egyptian or Latin American manner. They can, indeed, be counted on to cause a great deal of trouble to anyone who might have a try at jumping them through the hoop. I would therefore conclude that in this area, too, private initiative is safe in America for the foreseeable future. Going back once more to my *leitmotif:* there is a bed-rock Conservative public opinion, carefully nurtured by Conservative opinion leaders who value freedom and know how to defend it, which will settle for nothing less than freedom.

As I have been implying all along, there are some "pessimistic" points that I must lay beside my three "optimistic" ones. I must now say a few words about them, although too briefly, since they are a little more difficult than the points I have been making.

First, I believe, with Richard Cornuelle, that the future of private initiative looks a good deal less bright if we include in the problem (as we are *not* in the habit of doing) private initiative in that wide range of activities men engage in for reasons that have nothing to do with the so-called profit motive. We are wrong, thinks Cornuelle, when we make it a matter of the "private sector" and the "public sector" (as we *are* in the habit of doing). There are, in fact, two private sectors, not only one: one private sector that, quite properly, mobilizes, for the public purposes of increasing the production of saleable goods and services, man's laudable desire for wealth and income and unequal privilege; and another that mobilizes, for the public purpose of increasing the flow of things that are *not* saleable, man's equally laudable *neighborliness,* his desire to extend not the hand that grasps but the hand that helps. The great traditional symbol of that second private sector, on Cornuelle's showing, was the old-fashioned American barn-raising, which involved John Jones' neighbors saying to themselves, "John needs a barn? Well, let's all go over on Saturday and, for free, help him build it." Its great contemporary symbol is, perhaps unfortunately, the non-profit foundation, performing this, that, or the other type of good works.

Over the long pull, Cornuelle thinks, Americans have channelled into this sector vast and *beneficent* energies, which we can classify only under the heading, "private initiative." What we really ought to be worried about, he thinks, furthermore, is the fact that if present trends continue, those energies are soon going to have no place to go. Why? Because the second private sector is today struggling for survival, and struggling for survival precisely against government encroachment, much as, thirty years ago, we thought the first private sector was struggling for survival against government. Again why? Because more and more, with government taking over on the whole matter of good works, Americans come to think of good works as wholly and exclusively the responsibility of the government and obviously, therefore, not their responsibility. Help for the poor, the sick, the imprisoned, the stricken, becomes increasingly a matter not of face-to-face neighborliness in the local community, but of the paid services of the government-employed social worker. People feel increasingly that any intervention on their part, even where such intervention is clearly called for, would be a matter of their butting in.

Even the foundations, with their self-perpetuating governing boards of private citizens, come increasingly to be run by experts, that is, by bureaucrats who allegedly know the field in which the foundation's founder intended it to operate. The board member's job becomes increasingly a matter of approving the recommendations of the paid expert, not that of pouring his own energies and imagination into seeing to it that the foundation's money is wisely used. Worst of all, the typical foundation project, especially the typical project of the typical large foundation—and such foundations now account for a huge percentage of the available funds—tends to be conceived in terms merely of showing that "it," the good work it has in hand, can indeed be accomplished and ought, therefore, in due course, to become a further government responsibility.

The key point is that the typical private citizen who feels within himself the unselfish urge to do something for others, to take new steps to enrich and soften and beautify our society, finds his role reduced to that of contributing his money to organizations slated for government take-over. Let him look around for that something extra he can do, over and above contributing his money, and he will find himself hemmed in from every side. Cornuelle's objection, if I understand him, is not so much that this makes for big government (though it does), and that big government is in the nature of the case bad (that is true only of government that is pointlessly big), but rather that a) government good works are inefficient in the sense that they don't get the job done; b) government good works are expensive in the sense that a dollar's worth of government good works tends to be much smaller than a dollar's worth of good works accomplished by private initiative; and c) the system into which we are drifting snuffs out private initiative, with its infinite capacity to innovate, to use imagination, to stay with it until the task is accomplished, thereby inhibiting our citizens' growth and development in the direction of freedom and creativity.

Cornuelle believes, as I do, that one way to destroy freedom is to cut people off from free competition in good works. He asks: when the word goes out over the radio after a big fire for 50 blood donors, why do 1,000 people turn up at the hospital, 950 of whom end up having wasted their time, and go home no less frustrated than if they had missed an opportunity to make a buck? Because, he answers, there are vast stores of human energies, rooted in sheer human magnanimity, that are going to waste because the system has no use for them. And this is what I like best about Cornuelle's argument: they are going to waste because here the Conservatives, the friends of freedom, have neither done their homework nor performed the educational task that makes homework worth doing. They, even the most intelligent of them, do not in general understand what is at stake, what good things they are trying to conserve, and why present trends add up to a threat that we should indeed be losing sleep over.

Secondly, I see considerable grounds for pessimism about the future of private initiative in two current developments that are already far advanced and that seem likely to loom larger and larger on our horizons as time passes, namely: the bureaucratization of business enterprise and—a related but still separate phenomenon—what Michael Young calls the rise of the meritocracy.

As for the bureaucratization of business, the late Joseph Schumpeter already saw the way things were moving, and the danger involved, as long as three decades ago. As capitalism pushes production to ever higher levels, so runs Schumpeter's argument, the number and urgency of unsatisfied human wants tend, progressively, to shrink, so that there are fewer and fewer areas in which profitable innovation by entrepreneurs is even so much as possible. We seem to come ever nearer to the day when existing enterprises need only keep on churning out, with this or that slight improvement from year to year, already familiar goods and services. Even those year-to-year improvements tend increasingly to be thought up, developed, and ushered into the market by men who are job-holders (one is tempted to say time-servers) in firms that have been long established. "The management of industry and trade," Schumpeter wrote, "... becomes a matter of current administration, not innovation ... and the personnel ... unavoidably acquires the characteristics of a bureaucracy." Progress itself, he continues, even technological progress, becomes mechanized, that is, reduced to the mere continuance of lines of research and experiment that are themselves reduced to repetition and routine.

There is no longer any place for the man who, in an earlier age, would have become a real entrepreneur—would, that is, by "exploiting an invention or ... an untried technological possibility for producing a new commodity or producing an old one in a new way," or "opening up a new supply of materials or a new outlet for products," or "reorganizing an industry," make his way in the world. Increasingly, too, the bureaucratized industries finance themselves from their own coffers and, failing that, have an inside-run, as regards access to financing, with which the "outsider" is less and less able to compete. Economic progress, in short, becomes increasingly the "business of teams of trained specialists who turn out what is required and make it work in predictable ways;" it becomes "depersonalized and automatized;" "personality and will power" count for less

and less and (here I go beyond Schumpeter) have less and less opportunity and less and less reason or incentive to break out of their
chrysalis and take wings. "Private initiative," in virtue of its "very
achievements," makes itself "superfluous and breaks to pieces under
the pressure of its own success."

We are, to be sure, still some little distance from the day on which
everything, or even most things, will work in quite the way I have just
described. But the interesting question is not how soon industry and
trade will be *totally* bureaucratized in the Schumpeter manner, but
whether the trends leading in that direction begin to appear irresistible, and whether anything is visible on the horizon that might conceivably arrest those trends, and whether, as I believe, the only
possible answer to those questions is "no."

Let us now superimpose on the second of the two developments,
namely the rise of the meritocracy, which ought to be the topic of a
separate lecture, and which I have time to speak of only in the most
nakedly suggestive terms. Let us take as the meritocracy's defining
symbol the descent on our college campuses, each spring, of representatives of those same organizational giants Schumpeter was thinking of. We conduct a frantic competitive search for the seniors who
have shown *merit,* the kids with the best marks and the best credentials from the best institutions, where they happen to be because they
had won, by merit, the marks and credentials that the best institutions require for admission. Those kids, each spring, are promptly
whisked off to the nearest company installation and put through a
highly elaborated ordeal of *psychological* testing. Here again it is a
question, for the most part, of who makes the highest marks. The kids
with the highest marks will get the offers from the best companies
because of their demonstrated *merit*—they get the offers, accept
them, and are promptly absorbed—with everything they could ask in
the way of security and high incomes in the future—into one of those
bureaucracies. These, in turn, are asked, save possibly on the highest
levels, that above all they should fit themselves into the routinized
procedures, and display, with regard to making those procedures
work, the same kind of ability that won them those high marks from
their professors and their psychological testers.

Nobody cares who their parents are, or what wealth or position
they have inherited. The smart kid from Yale now avoids the corporation where his uncle, or his father-in-law, is a member of the board

of directors. Nobody even cares what their moral standards are. What the system puts a premium on and what, because of the rich rewards bestowed on it, increasingly sets the very tone and atmosphere of society is *merit*, and merit defined as sheer *measurable* brain power (how few people realize how young such a definition is!). The system's pervasive influence reaches horizontally out to the universities (whose job becomes that of producing the men the giant organizations are looking for) and, vertically, not only down to the university freshman, who quickly learns that innovation and originality are seldom the shortest paths to those high marks he needs in order to get ahead in the world, but also to the youngsters in high school and grade school, who from an early moment are shooting for high marks on the college boards.

I have not suggested, let me emphasize, that bureaucratization and the premium on brain power are necessarily bad in their *economic* effects. On the contrary: if productivity is the watchword, as I am told it now is, both are perhaps called for. My topic for this lecture, however, is the future of individual initiative, and my point, as some of you will have guessed, is that both bureaucratization and the premium on merit, defined as brain power, bode ill for originality, for inventiveness, for creativity and, ultimately, for freedom in any meaningful sense of that term. For I contend, and only wish I had time to develop the point, that the glorification of merit, as we know it today, does not take on its full meaning until we understand that it is an oblique attack on the criteria by which former ages decided who was to get ahead in the world. Those criteria were, quite simply, inherited status, inherited wealth, moral desert (or "virtue," as our Founding Fathers were in the habit of calling it) and, though that was the last of the criteria to emerge, individual initiative or, if you like, originality.

And here, it seems to me, the Conservatives, who have resisted neither bureaucratization nor the rise of the meritocracy, have missed the boat, by putting economics, that is, productivity, first; by consequently trying to have it both ways about the claims of inheritance, virtue and originality on the one hand, and the claims of brain power on the other; by failing to mobilize behind the old-fashioned watchwords and so against the meritocracy which, I deeply believe, is incompatible with the old-fashioned watchwords. The Conservatives should themselves have reminded the world that there are other good things in the world besides productivity, that we must not, by over-emphasizing productivity, endanger those other good things, especially freedom, and that, when and if it comes to choosing between more productivity and less freedom, and less productivity and more freedom, the Conservative can give only one answer: let productivity suffer, and let freedom ring!

Freedom of Speech in Our Time

Let me begin by saying what I understand my role in this *disputatio* to be—lest you expect some things of me that I am unable, or unwilling, to attempt to do for you, or for my distinguished fellow-disputants (whose task, I take it, could be made easier, or more difficult, according as I do this or that). If, for example, my "billing" in your minds is that of—if I may put it so—a horrible example of someone who is just plain "against" freedom of speech, I can only disappoint you: temperamentally, I happen to be a man who in any given situation would always favor letting everybody have his "say" —temperamentally, I repeat, which is to say, not on principle but out of an essentially selfish wish to satisfy my curiosity about what there is *to* say on whatever question happens to be up, and also out of şome terrible anarchic thing 'way down inside me that always puts me on the side of the pillow-throwers and against the umpire, on the side of the freedom-riders (even though I disagree with them) against the Mississippi sheriff, on the side of George Washington against George III—and so: on the side of the let-'em-speak contingent against the censors and silencers.

Secondly, I am not a very good horrible example for you where what is in question is freedom of speech in a certain kind of community, where people have in some sense *contracted* with one another to conduct their affairs on a freedom-of-speech basis, or to treat each other as equals: The United States or England, for instance, where *other things being equal—other things being equal,* I repeat—I should say (and no longer just temperamentally, but, to some extent, on principle) that the *presumption* is for me always in favor of the let-'em-speak contingent and against the shut-'em-up contingent. (Though I would hasten to add, so as not to disappoint you too much too soon: as regards communities-in-general, situations-in-general, there is and can be no such presumption; and to add too: there are other kinds of communities, the Dominican Republic, for instance, or contemporary Spain, for instance, where the presumption for me would be very distinctly against any attempt to conduct affairs on what I just called a freedom-of-speech basis.)

I strongly feel, in other words, that the classic attempt to defend
freedom of speech as a compelling principle, applicable to all communities, that is, Mill's famous *Essay on Liberty,* is a piece of bad
political philosophy, and one that has done great harm, so that the
less heard of any general principle of freedom of speech the better.
And the fact that most American intellectuals are under the contrary
impression, so that even if they do not know Mill at first hand they
yet feel sure that the day they need conclusive arguments for freedom of speech they will have only to go to Mill and look them up—
the fact, I say, that most American intellectuals are under the impression that Mill settled *that* argument once and for all, is merely a sad
commentary on most American intellectuals. And, having said that,
I can go ahead and answer the first question on our little list, as
follows: There is *no* reason, in theory, for saying that freedom of
speech is a principle that should be defended; or, more cautiously,
if it *is* a principle that should be defended someone whose heart goes
pit-a-pat over it should get busy and find a better defense for it than
Mill took the trouble to do.

Now: I have already suggested that in a certain kind of community
where people have in some sense contracted with one another to
conduct their affairs by freedom-of-speech procedures, I should to
some extent on principle say there is a presumption, other things
being equal, in favor of freedom of speech; and I have said that for
me the United States is such a community. But you will notice that
I have stashed into my aircraft a great many verbal parachutes that
would enable me, if and when that seemed advisable, to bail out: I
say, a certain kind of community: I speak of people in that kind of
community having *in some sense* contracted to practice free speech;
I speak even there merely of a presumption in favor of free speech,
that is, a presumption other things being equal; and I speak finally of
defending the presumption *to some extent* on principle. Let me
clarify all that:

The sense in which the American people have contracted together
to conduct their affairs by freedom of speech procedures is this, and
only this: The First Amendment to our Constitution says that Congress shall make no law impairing freedom of speech and I do think
that it can be argued that that Amendment in some sense constitutes
a contract among Americans to conduct their affairs according to

freedom of speech procedures. But let us be quite clear here about several things:

a) The First Amendment, along with the rest of the so-called Bill of Rights, was not written by the Philadelphia Convention, but rather, as sort of an afterthought—like painting the front stoop after the house is built—by the First Session of the Congress, then ratified by the amendment process specified in the Philadelphia Constitution. Now: that does not make it any the less part of the law of our Constitution, or any the less, for me at least, a contract among Americans. But it does perhaps create as many difficulties about freedom of speech as it solves, and for this reason: the Philadelphia Constitution was not intended to have a Bill of Rights; the most brilliant statement we have against a Bill of Rights is Alexander Hamilton's statement about freedom of the press in the *Federalist Papers,* where he argues: What good will it do to write it into the Constitution? If Congress sees fit to violate freedom of the press it will certainly go ahead and do so; the Bill of Rights in fact changes the whole character of our constitutional system; and this is the point—the authors of the Bill of Rights were, for my money, extremely careless about tidying up after painting the front stoop. Concretely: while the First Amendment forbids Congress to impair freedom of speech, the body of the Constitution *empowers* Congress to do certain things that it may feel it cannot do without impairing freedom of speech; and most particularly it does that if, like me and unlike the Supreme Court, you regard the Preamble to the Constitution as the essence of the Contract among the American people. For the Preamble seems to announce an intention on the part of that people to do quite a number of quite sweeping things, *e.g.,* to secure the ends of justice, to promote the general welfare, and the First Amendment invites the question: Oh! What if Congress be strongly convinced that enactment X is needed in the interest of justice, or for the general welfare, and yet that same enactment X impairs freedom of speech? There is no simple answer, except to say: Under our Constitution it is always a fair argument to insist: This may seem to some people an impairment of freedom of speech, but it is *necessary* in order to accomplish the very purposes of the Constitution, and *therefore* we are going right ahead and do it. Most particularly it is not a simple answer to say: Let the Supreme Court decide. By the time *it* gets around to deciding, free speech will already have *been* impaired and Congress, as Hamilton foresaw, will have had its way.

b) In any case, the First Amendment does not properly speaking establish what I have called freedom of speech procedures in the United States: still less, for all that we speak of a Bill of Rights, does it confer on anybody a "right" to freedom of speech. At most, it confers a right not to have your freedom of speech impaired by the Congress, that is, by the Federal Government. In its original form, it did not even confer on anybody a right not to have his freedom of speech impaired by his state and county and municipal government. And it certainly did not confer upon anybody a right not to have his freedom of speech impaired by a whole series of non-governmental authorities—by, most especially, the persons most likely to impair it, who are one's neighbors.

c) The situation I have just described, where the First Amendment leaves our state and local governments at liberty to impair freedom of speech, has been greatly complicated up, if I may put it so, by a line of Supreme Court decisions which, in technical language, read the so-called Bill of Rights into the Fourteenth Amendment. These decisions, that is to say, seek to apply the limitations on the federal government involved in the first eight amendments to the states and localities, and they are so applied by the Supreme Court today. Now: by way of shoring up my image as a horrible example of an opponent of free speech, I'll confess I have never been much impressed by the constitutional logic by which that particular bit of juggling was accomplished, but that is not the main point I want to make about it. My main point is simply this: By the time we have moved away from the solid structure of the Constitution through some jerry-built lean-to of the Bill of Rights to the remote tool shed of a mere Supreme Court decision, we may have left far behind us the kind of freedom of speech that the American people may be said to have contracted with one another not to impair. I personally would still be willing to say that for me the presumption under the Constitution is against impairment, even when the latter is by a state legislature or a city council. But the presumption begins to wear a little thin; and I no longer feel sure of myself, when I defend it, as regards doing so on principle. That is why I speak, in my preliminary remarks, of defending the presumption *to some extent* on principle.

Academic Freedom

Let me leap right into the middle of things, as follows: Academic freedom—like its first cousin freedom of speech—has *become* in America, for good or ill, one of the battlegrounds in the ongoing struggle between Left and Right, between Liberals and Conservatives. It is not that, so far as I know, in other countries—not even in those countries, Germany for instance, or Spain, that still have a Right, still have some Conservatives in our sense of the word Conservative; and it has not always been that, a battleground between Left and Right, here in America. That is a quite important fact for us to bear in mind as we tease our way into the academic freedom controversy—or, more accurately, the academic freedom *controversies,* for, as we shall soon be noticing, set-to's between Left and Right over academic freedom are not always, *by no means* always, set-to's over one and the selfsame issue.

Now: it is an important fact for us to bear in mind for the following reason, very central to what I want to say tonight: Here in America, nowadays, the academic freedom issues have a way of getting themselves stated so as to make it *sound* like—*sound* like, I say, for I do not think it is or can be really true, or that the resulting discussion situation is one in which Conservatives can afford to acquiesce—the issues I say have a way of getting themselves stated so as to make it *sound* like the Liberals were in *favor* of freedom in the universities, and the Conservatives out to destroy it, out to replace academic freedom with something academic *other* than freedom. That, I repeat, cannot be true! Insofar as it sounds as if it were true it is merely because we have, as certainly we do have in America at the present time, a very confused, very messed-up discussion situation, where words like "freedom" have got torn loose from their proper meaning, or if you like where some people—the Liberals, of course—have *torn* words loose from their proper meaning and, like Humpty Dumpty, are making words mean whatever they choose to make them mean. For—let me get this said before the evening gets a moment older, lest I be struck dumb before I get it said—where words *are* being used with their proper meanings, academic freedom, I think, takes its place as a Conservative property not a Liberal one, as a Conservative ideal not a Liberal one. It was discovered—and mark that word discovered, for when I say discovered I don't mean something other than discovered, such as "invented"—it was discovered and first expounded by men who are the intellectual and spiritual ancestors of our Conservatives *not* our Liberals. It was such men—the Conservatives' spiritual and intellectual ancestors—who kept it alive in Europe through the centuries; and it was such men who brought it to America—along with the rest of Europe's intellectual and spiritual baggage, along with the concept of freedom itself, in the 17th century. It was, to be sure, discovered under another name, to wit, the *studium,* which is the phrase under which our ancestors discussed the rights and duties of universities and—derivatively, mind you— the duties and rights of individual scholars; and the chief function of the phrase was to distinguish the *studium,* the world or sphere of the university, the world or sphere of scholarship, from the *imperium,* the world of the state as distinguished from the university, the world of statesmanship as distinguished from scholarship, *and* from the *sacerdotium,* the world of the Church as distinguished from the world of scholarship and the world of statesmanship. And the point being made by those who discovered and defended the *studium,* distinguishing it from the *imperium* and the *sacerdotium,* was, quite simply, this: The world of the university and scholarship is *different,* something *apart,* from the world of the state and statesmanship; and different and apart again from the world of the Church and churchmanship. It is a different world, a world apart, and *therefore* mustn't be confused with the other two worlds. It is a different world, and *therefore* has its duties and rights, both within it and towards things outside it, different from those of the other two. But note the *therefores.* The whole business starts out from a distinction, a clearly understood distinction, between three different worlds, and therefore starts out from a state of affairs in which such a distinction makes sense. It starts out, above all, in a state of affairs in which *distinctions,* the whole business of *discriminating* between things that are different *in nature,* makes sense.

Don't, I hasten to add, be alarmed: I am *not* going to go on and on about matters that have to be talked about in Latin. And I am *not* about to say that anything much can be decided about the very-much-alive, present-day, *American* controversy over academic free-

dom by thus appealing to the remote past. My point is merely that
Conservatives have been in the academic freedom business for a long
time; that they have not sold that business, which with them is a
family business, to any Johnnie-come-latelies, any Snopeses; and that
if the Snopeses say they own it—that academic freedom belongs to
them—that is merely another case of the Snopeses, the Johnnie-
come-latelies, confusing matters, or, worse still, just plain fibbing, just
plain saying *that which is not.* The task of the Conservatives, as
people who've been around a long time and intend to be around for
quite a spell yet, is to *unconfuse* matters, to affirm *that which is* as
against *that which is not,* but to do it, however, with humility—
remembering, though we cannot do so without a shudder, that it was
they who let the Snopeses move in, they who let things *get* confused.
The Conservatives must about this be *charitable* to the Liberals, and
the nonsense they talk about academic freedom—not merely for the
usual reason that they know not what they do but for the further
reason that it was the Conservatives who let them get into a position
to do what they do.

Now: Academic freedom, I was saying, is today one of the battlegrounds in the ongoing struggle between the American Right and the
American Left; and I suggest we work our way into our topic a little
further by pausing to remind ourselves, but always in the background
of what I have just been saying, of what, in recent years, the issues
have actually been—and note, once again, that I say "issues" not
issue. And let us do that by reminding ourselves of what exactly the
Liberals, in their guise as defenders of academic freedom, have been
asserting in recent years, and of what we have been getting in the
way of Conservative *answers.*

The Liberals assert: The task of the university is to press forward
with the search for truth, and to teach students how to engage in the
search for truth themselves. But in the phrase "search for truth" the
word the Liberals stress is not "truth" but "search." No-one, they say,
knows at any given moment what the truth actually is about anything;
and the university's performance of its tasks must be subject always
to that overriding principle. And the Conservatives answer: that is to
say that the uniquely correct theory of knowledge is skepticism,
revolving-door skepticism, and we believe in no such theory. We
believe that the search for truth goes forward in the context of a
deposit of truth received from the past; that, therefore, at any given

moment there are some things we do know to be true; that, therefore
again, the university's first task is to preserve that deposit of true
knowledge intact against the possibility of loss or neglect—to press
forward with the search for truth, yes, but before pressing *forward*
with the search to make sure that no ground is lost, or, to vary the
metaphor, no capital lived up or lost sight of.

The Liberals assert that because the university's pursuit of truth is
like the greyhound's chase of the electric rabbit at the greyhound
race-track, where the greyhound (if he's smart) knows that he'll never
actually catch the rabbit; that because the pursuit of truth *is* like that,
the university's personnel policies must be tailored accordingly: it
can concern itself only with the competence of its researchers and
teachers in the *pursuit* of truth, not with their knowledge or ignorance of truth or truths that some allege already to have been acquired—not, above all, with the content or substance of that which
its teachers shall teach. The Conservatives assert first that any such
personnel policy is absurd on the face of it, that is, in the same boat
with the radical skepticism in which it is rooted; and second that the
university does not in fact apply such a policy, is not in fact so
indifferent as all that to what its scholars know, or profess to know,
or even to what its scholars profess to believe; that, to go no further,
no contemporary American university would hire, or keep in its employ, a scholar committed to Lysenko's views on biology, or to Hitler's views on racial superiority and anti-Semitism; that when the
chips are down, down at least on *some* matters, the radically skeptical
university, that radically skeptical university that figures so prominently in the harangues of university presidents to foregathered
alumni, turns out to be not so radically skeptical after all; on *some*
matters it *does* seem to know how many beans it takes to make five.
Conservatives hold therefore that a very good place at which to
begin discussing the problem of academic freedom is right *there,*
where you do catch the university knowing, and admitting that it
knows, how many beans it takes to make five.

But to go on: The Liberals assert that however all that may be,
however the university's actions or policies may, to the outsider,
seem to conflict with its avowed theory of knowledge, it must be free,
has a *right* to be "free"—free from outside supervision, free, perhaps,
even from criticism from the outside, exempt certainly from any
obligation to render to any authority or constituency beyond its por-

tals any accounting concerning its stewardship, free to set its own standards and free to be its own unique judge as regards its living up to the standards it so sets. The Conservatives answer that that, any way you look at it, is absurd; that that, any way you look at it, would begin to make sense only if the university were self-sufficient and self-supporting, only if the university could survive, there behind its portals, without regular delivery of the groceries it consumes; that it wouldn't make *much* sense, however, even if the university *were* self-sufficient; that in organized society nothing and nobody enjoys *that* kind of freedom; that nothing and nobody in organized society is entitled to declare itself thus exempt from all accountings; that organized society cannot allow any such freedom, and least of all to the institution to which it sends its future elites for training and formation; that in any case the university is *not* self-sufficient, *does* depend for survival from day to day on the groceries being delivered; that the university not only *should* not be allowed the unlimited freedom it claims, but cannot and therefore will not make good any such claim—cannot and will not because out there beyond the portals there are always people in position to withhold delivery of the groceries.

Or again: The Liberals assert that *since* no-one knows what is true, all points of view should be represented on the university's faculty; otherwise students will be "indoctrinated"; and students have a *right* not to be "indoctrinated." The Conservatives—well, some Conservatives anyway, for we enter now on more controversial ground—some Conservatives answer, I say, that that also is foolishness, that all points of view *can't* be represented; and that even if they could the resulting university would be a bedlam, a madhouse; moreover, those same Conservatives continue, the universities as we know them clearly *don't* try to represent all points of view, even all points of view distinctly visible on the horizon.

Still again: The Liberals assert—a little inconsistently with their point about representing all positions, but of course there are worse misdemeanors than inconsistency—that university administrators cannot, in hiring their teachers, take cognizance of their opinions, religious, political, or what have you; the administrators, they repeat, are interested in professional *competence,* exclusively; to take an applicant's opinions into account would indeed be to violate academic freedom; and that goes even for a situation where the applicant holds views that the surrounding community deems outrageous, intolerable. The Conservatives say they don't believe it: that the high degree of conformity one quickly observes nowadays in any faculty couldn't have come about by accident; that administrators *must* be looking, and looking hard, for men of a certain outlook, and, moreover, that everybody with his wits about him knows what that outlook is; that what you have all over the country is Liberal-dominated departments recruiting Liberals and even more Liberals; and, finally, that the conspicuous absence of Conservatives must be due to the fact that Conservatives are being passed up.

Those, I believe, are the academic freedom controversies, most of them at least, that have been up during the last couple of decades; nor, let us note, is there anything surprising about their dividing Liberals from Conservatives: The Liberal assertions, as even these brief statements of them make clear, are shot through and through with the philosophy of freedom associated with the name of John Stuart Mill—which philosophy is, notoriously, an article of faith with Liberals and, by the same token, anathema to Conservatives. But let us pass on to notice a few facts of history that will round out our picture of the controversies:

First: If we fix attention on a somewhat longer period than 20 years, we shall discover that the controversies have got themselves, to some extent, turned upside down of late. Only a while ago—how long let us not try to say quite yet—it was the *Conservatives* who were being accused of stacking the university and college faculties, and of persecuting men of non-Conservative opinions, that is, Left-wingers. What is today the prevailing theory of academic freedom was, back then, only beginning to be heard on most campuses; university administrators did not speak of representing all points of view, or of having the faculty conduct an ongoing debate with the students sitting as judges; rather it was taken for granted that the university would and should inculcate upon their charges a healthy respect for, for instance, the American economic system and the American political system; it was even taken for granted that religion —yes, the prevailing or "majority" religion, which was Christianity —was a proper concern of the university; that the university would and should provide an atmosphere in which its students would grow and develop religiously; most administrators—presidents, deans, department heads—were churchmembers, and pretty much expected

to be, and so to set a good example (so it was called, back then) to
their pupils. Now: Was that old-fashioned university "intolerant", as
it was often accused of being, or rather "tolerant"? Let me answer
that firmly: if it was *not* intolerant, that was *not* because its image of
itself was rooted in radical skepticism; put otherwise: if it was tolerant
of the non-conformist, that was not because it thought or suspected
or feared he might be right; if it was tolerant, and it must've been,
since it let the Liberals take over, from inside, in due course, that was
because it had some built-in reasons for being tolerant that, if I may
put it so, no-one seems to remember any more, that few people would
understand any more. And again: if it was tolerant—and I repeat it
must have been—it was, or intended to be I think, tolerant subject
to a severe limitation that again I think few people would understand
any more, namely: dissidents, and there were dissidents, were free
to disagree with the prevailing orthodoxy, but only if they recognized that there *was* an orthodoxy, a set of dominant views, that so
to speak had a right to be and remain dominant—short, anyhow, of
a sea-change in the beliefs of the American people. Dissidents were
free to criticize the orthodoxy, but not to proceed as if it did not have
a proper claim to special treatment, favorable treatment, in the university. Did such a university practice academic freedom? Here let
me give, before I pass on, a very brief answer: It believed it did. But
not, of course, academic freedom as defined in the way that is fashionable today.

A second fact of History: The academic freedom controversy entered a new phase with the publication, in 1950, of a book by a young
man named William F. Buckley, Jr. Buckley you might say had gone
to Yale thinking it was the old-fashioned kind of university I have just
described. He soon found out it wasn't—that what it was trying to do
to him was *undermine*—yes, undermine—his, and other students'
belief in the orthodoxy that had once ridden high at Yale. He found
that this was being done under the slogan "Academic Freedom!"—
with an exclamation point, of course. He also found that nobody
much besides himself seemed aware of what this showed to be happening to the American idea of the university, and along with it, to
the whole American idea of higher education. And he found this
paradox, or rather pair of paradoxes. The administrators of Yale, the
President, the important deans, were all men who themselves still
appeared to believe in the orthodoxy their university was undermin-

ing—paradox one. And the money for running Yale not only had come in the past but was *still* coming from men who believed in the orthodoxy. They were still in position to say "No more of this, or *we* give no more money, and where'll your university be then?" They were still in position to, yet didn't. Paradox two. So Buckley wrote *God and Man at Yale*—to demand that Yale's alumni bring her to heel. And Yale, the Yale faculty, met Buckley head on: Running the university, deciding what kind of university it should be, was, it said, the faculty's business, not the alumni's. What Yale was doing—what, concretely, it was doing about the old orthodoxies, was—well, exactly what it *should* be doing, and certainly what it was going to keep on doing. And, overnight, Buckley got what I imagine to have been *the* surprise of his very surpriseful life: For the alumni, instead of rallying behind him, tacitly rallied behind the faculty. Instead of themselves becoming angry, at being told that Yale was none of their business, they tacitly accepted that view of the matter, and still kept on giving their money—soon, indeed, were giving their money more generously than ever. Buckley, at least on the battleground he had chosen, took a licking. Soon, indeed, Yale had a President who, unlike his predecessor, was the very embodiment of the new ideas on academic freedom; and Yale became, even more unabashedly, the kind of university Buckley had accused it of being. Moreover, people became aware, under the impact of Buckley's book, that the nation's other colleges and universities, with a greater or lesser timelag from campus to campus, were also becoming the kind of university Yale was. And nobody in position to arrest the process—indeed, nobody, except Buckley, seemed to be about to raise a finger to do so. Only in one sense—how important a sense remains to be seen—did Buckley not take a licking. His book, his challenge to the new definition of academic freedom, became one of the roots from which contemporary American Conservatism, as we know it, has sprung; just as, soon after, Senator Joseph McCarthy's challenge to a new definition of freedom of speech and thought in America became another such root. Too late? So many people would certainly say; and certainly nothing has happened in the colleges and universities that would suggest the contrary. All we can say is, I think, this: Thanks to Buckley —thanks to him and later writers like Russell Kirk and Stanton Evans —conscious Conservatives in America know that one of the things they must fight for, must wrest from the Liberals, is the restoration of that older kind of university I speak of. Or maybe we can also say this. If Buckleyism hasn't accomplished anything yet on its battle-ground, the other root of the contemporary American Conservative movement, McCarthyism, has accomplished much, remains strong in America, and must some day interest itself in the issues Buckley raised. And when and as it does that, things *will* begin to happen at the university. Let me say that still more sharply: Buckley, in this speaker's view, carried his battle to the wrong people, that is, the intellectuals, where his few converts were always easily outflanked by the Liberals. But Conservatives now know, from McCarthy's ex-ample, who are the right people to carry battles to. And that they must in due course learn to do with the problem of the university.

A third fact of History, at which I have been hinting for some while, but must now bring out into the open: The Liberal take-over of the American university is much more recent than we are in the habit of thinking. Buckley, for instance, seems to think of it as having been far advanced already by the 1930's. But it is to the 1930's that the "Walsh Sweezey case" belongs; and the Walsh Sweezey case, the biggest academic freedom squabble of recent decades, concerned the right of Harvard University to fire two men who merely held mildly Left-wing opinions on economics! Harvard, in other words, was still pretty Conservative as late as 1936; and 1936 is less than 30 years ago.

Let me turn now to the theses I want to present tonight, concern-ing matters, all of them, on which I believe the Conservative intellec-tuals to be wrong, and to be proceeding on an incorrect analysis of our university problem.

First. The reason why Conservative intellectuals like to think of the take-over as *less* recent than it was is this: There were plenty of Liberals around, by the 1940's, to do the taking-over, and what more natural than to assume that those Liberals were Liberals because they'd been *taught* to be by Liberal professors they studied under; and the same logic leads to yet another idea current in the circles I speak of. Pretty much all professors are, admittedly, Liberals. Now: won't their students all become Liberals under their influence, so that the take-over process will be self-perpetuating forever and ever? I feel sure myself that the question enormously exaggerates the influ-ence professors exercise on their charges. *And* that the faculty "im-balance to the Left" we hear of these days is, by that token, a far less

serious problem than Conservative intellectuals like to think. Serious
enough, in all conscience, but not hopeless, as such a picture of
Liberals breeding more Liberals, on and on to the end of history,
would suggest.

Second, if the Liberals who did the taking over were *not* brought
to Liberalism by Liberal professors, what *did* fetch them? And my
answer is: By the late 40's we of the West—not just we Americans,
perhaps we Americans less than other peoples—had moved far into
a period we may describe as follows: It was a period during which,
increasingly, the *heroes* the intellectuals were likely to admire happened to be—I know no other way to put it than that—Left-wingers;
and to the extent that was true the intellectuals tended, for that
reason, to move sharply to the Left. Think of them, those heroes!
Albert Einstein. Albert Schweitzer. André Gide. Pablo Picasso. Ernest Hemingway. Thomas Mann. Liberals, or if not Liberals then
socialists or even Communists, *all* of them. And they were, I repeat,
the men you *had* to admire—so good were they at their businesses
—if you were going to feel at home in that climate. By the 40's their
reputation was so solid that—what more natural?—intellectuals in
America were not only admiring but imitating them. But those 40's
heroes are, most of them dead now, less likely to engage admiration,
and I doubt if it could be demonstrated that their successors, as
heroes, are predominantly Left-wing. Perhaps, indeed, for good or ill,
the climate that is replacing that one is less given to having heroes
at all. On either showing, the Einstein-Picasso kind of hero-worship
is by no means certain to be self-perpetuating. Here again, the Conservative who removes his blinders can see hope: It is Faulkner they
go into ecstasy over in Paris these days—Faulkner not Hemingway.
And while one swallow doesn't make a summer, it isn't a fact to be
ignored. And I predict the American intellectuals will follow the fad
next time around too!

Third—I can name one further reason for optimism about the future: The academic freedom Buckley exposed is a *bluff*—a fundamentally indefensible DEMAND that American universities be given
all the rights of the medieval *studium* in conditions where those
particular rights no longer make any sense. The medieval university,
the medieval Church, and the medieval state stood over against one
another in a context of deeply shared beliefs and common purposes.
It could be trusted with freedom, with the right to govern itself

without outside interference, because it was willing and eager to discharge the duties correlative to that right, and to discharge those duties as not only itself but other people understood them. It knew that it was there to inculcate beliefs, to *indoctrinate,* and precisely did *not* feel itself free to improvise the beliefs it inculcated. Not so the contemporary American university: it does *not* any more share the beliefs and purposes—so I confidently think anyhow—of the society in whose bosom it functions. The right it claims is a right to *remake* the Nation's belief system, according to its *own* ideas as to what it ought to be. It is, I repeat, *bluffing,* and the bluff it is attempting is the kind of bluff nobody ever gets by with in America, and for reasons we Americans have well understood ever since Publius wrote Federalist 10. Nobody ever gets by with it because we Americans are wise in the ways of taking people, individuals or institutions, down a notch or two when they get to throwing their weight around. One wonders, indeed, what ever made the American university—dependent as much of it is precisely on appropriations from state legislatures, which are made up of men not so easy to jump through the hoop as the late Whitney Griswold found the Yale alumni—what ever made the American university even *think* it could get by with such a thing? I predict that it can't: it can either go back willingly to its proper business of communicating American beliefs, American traditions, to the nation's youth, or someone will have to *make* it go back to it. And remember: the ultimate weapon—refusing to deliver the groceries—is always in the hands of the people the American university is trying to bluff.

One more point, which I have already made by implication. In my opinion it is just not true—though most Conservatives now believe it to be true—that the American university's present imbalance to the Left is a matter of Liberal cardstacking, of Liberal conspiracy, of the deliberate excluding of Right-wing scholars by Liberal-dominated departments. And it is just not true, though most Conservatives believe it to be true, that the American Right has anything to gain by talking any such line of chatter. The reason the universities are staffed mainly with Left-wing scholars is, quite simply, that today most American scholars are Left-wingers, so that no matter what recruitment policies administrators might adopt, they would end up with a conspicuous imbalance to the Left. Put otherwise: The Right-wing scholars that would be needed to correct the imbalance, to give fair representation to the Conservative position, simply don't, for the most part, exist. They need—if I may put it so—to be *created,* as Ann Arbor's Relm Foundation is today, almost alone, trying to create them. There is no other solution to the problem, and the Right must —just *must*—get that through its head. Which means: get busy providing the funds it'll take *to* create them.

World Government

Proposals for voluntary world government—for I suppose it is the voluntary kind we are here to discuss, and *not* the kind we are pretty sure to get, which is world government by the Russians or ourselves —proposals for voluntary world government, I say, are to political philosophy what schemes for *perpetual motion* are to *physics,* what attempts to *square the circle* are to *mathematics,* what plans for creating wealth and prosperity by *manipulating the currency* are to *economics.* All four of them, however, world government, perpetual motion, circle-squaring, wealth by way of the printing press, exercise an unending fascination for a certain type of mentality, which we may characterize as follows: it assumes that if we *want* something hard enough, *will* it with sufficient *determination,* then, reality— whether it be political reality, physical reality, mathematical reality, economic reality—*must* not and therefore *cannot* stand in our way. The ideas in question, accordingly, will not down; neither logic nor events ever quite dispose of them; refuting them, therefore, is a never-ending task for practitioners of the relevant sciences—a *veritable* task of Sisyphus, which is no sooner completed than it must be begun again, and begun again with the knowledge that the rock will roll once more down the hill. The task calls not so much for strength or skill as for patience, which it becomes the duty of those practitioners to develop at whatever cost—the *kind* of patience, moreover, that bears up under the necessity of repeating again and again, each time in more simple language, principles of such simplicity that they seem, almost, to explain *themselves*—the kind of patience that does not flag even in the presence of apparent incorrigibility. It is, properly speaking, a task for a teacher not a debater, a task for the gentle guiding hand of the pedagogue not the cruel dexterous hand of the disputant. Let us, then, as we reason together this afternoon about world government, about one-worldism, keep it simple—partly in the hope of recalling my opponent to the *real* problems of contemporary politics (which are already difficult enough, in all conscience, without his complicating them further), partly to clarify our own minds in preparation for tomorrow's inevitable encounter with the next one-worlder. Let us keep it simple and, I repeat, cultivate the virtue of patience. (We are likely to need it before the end of the afternoon.)

Now: one of the issues about which we must keep it simple, despite the one-worlder's tireless efforts to complicate it, we may put as follows: The one-worlder believes—nay, hammers you over the head with the idea—that the growth and development of nuclear weapons have somehow clinched the case for world federation and world government. The case, he argues, was always strong, so strong that it is hard to see how reasonable men ever rejected it even back in the days of the conventional bombing-raids over Hamburg and Tokyo, even conceding—the one-worlder is never more dangerous than when he adopts that pose of sweet reasonableness—that back in those days the case was *not* open-go-shut, that back in those days there were objections we could not answer to everybody's satisfaction, that, in a word, back in those days it was *not* easy to show that world government would yield benefits so great as to justify the sacrifices it would call for. Let us, he says, concede that, but also let us face the fact that the state of the question shifted, and shifted once and for all, when the United States lost its monopoly of the nuclear weapons—when, that is to say, the military future assumed the shape of an all-out nuclear war between the United States and the Soviet Union. Formerly the case for world government had to be put in terms of the ravages, the pointlessness, the inhumanity of war; but that was a difficult argument to grasp, especially for people who had not actually experienced the ravages of war. The fanatical nationalist, or anti-Communist, or whatever, could still argue: the war I propose will accomplish goals that will justify the ravages. But now it is no longer a question of ravages; the question now is whether we are to have, on the one hand, peace through world federation, or, on the other hand, *total destruction;* and between those two alternatives no man in his senses can possibly hesitate. Nuclear weapons have ushered in a new world in which federation is no longer just desirable, which it *always* was, but *necessary, indispensable* for our survival, forced upon us by circumstances about whose implication no disagreement is possible. In saying this, moreover, the one-worlder is *not* ignorant of the fact—so often urged upon him in the past by opponents who, as he would put it, fancy themselves as political theorists—that the successful federations of the past have been built on a basis of shared principles, common convictions, etc., that federation is probably impossible without such shared principles, and that the absence of such shared principles has been, up to now, a major barrier to federation. His point is that the nuclear weapons have taken care of that also. They have, simultaneously, made federation an absolute necessity and provided the grand principle around which the federating nations can rally, namely, the principle: There must be no nuclear war, and only federation can prevent nuclear war. That is a principle on which all can agree, and no further principle is needed. Or, to state the principle otherwise, from now on it is one world or *no* world; only through federation can mankind hope to survive.

It is, let us note at once, a shrewd argument. It gets the one-worlder, for debating purposes, completely around what used to be the major difficulties in his position. He no longer has to answer the question, Is world government desirable? Or the question, Would the world government be despotic? Or the question, How are we going to *get* world government? It no longer matters whether world government is desirable; it no longer matters whether it would be despotic. And as for how we are going to get world government, well, once we recognize world government as necessary, once everybody recognizes it as necessary, the barriers to world government will simply disappear because nobody will have any interest in maintaining them. The means, once we go at the end as a necessity not a mere choice, will be found. And the problem becomes: is there an answer to the case for world government when it is put in those terms? Does the political philosopher *still* pretend that world government is the political analogue of perpetual motion? And if so, on the basis of what so-called principles does he take such a stand?

Well, let us read the one-worlder the political science lesson he needs:

a) Even if we Americans were to agree to world federation under the proposed new principle—let us postpone for a moment the reasons why we would *never* agree—the Politburo of the USSR will *not* agree to it save as it is assured it will itself control the new federation —that is, save as it is assured that the new world government will be a Communist world government. To suppose otherwise is to ignore, to forget, all that experience has taught us and all that scholarship has taught us about the nature and meaning of the World Communist Movement, about the grit and intelligence and determination of the

men it moulds—I use Frank Meyer's phrase—to lead it, about the
nature of the historical dilemma we face, which is not Federate or
Perish, but rather Surrender to World Communism, or, *cost what it
may*—cost what it may, I repeat—Defeat World Communism. The
Communists, though the one-worlder cannot get it through his head,
mean it when they say they will bury us; they will stop at nothing;
they are not available to rational appeals calculated to divert them
from their appointed course, which is that of world conquest. In
short: the principle around which we are asked to rally has in it a
hidden premise about World Communism, and that premise is false.
Let the one-worlder first learn what everyone else knows about Communism, let him enter the discussion prepared to talk in realistic not
fanciful terms about the Communist enemy, and then, but only then,
shall we be prepared to listen to his proposals about world federation.

   b) Even if we were to agree to world federation, and even if the
Russians were to agree to world federation, and even if the agreed-
upon world federation were to be a *non-Communist world federation,* the resulting world government would be a despotism. This
flows as a necessary consequence from the principle around which,
in the nuclear age form of the one-worlder's proposal, we are asked
to rally, namely, the principle: there *must* be no atomic war. This
principle would not be, could not be, in the proposed federation, a
mere policy, even a mere alternative end, that the world government
would pursue along with, for example, the purposes laid down in the
Preamble of the Constitution of the United States (such purposes
would, for the rest, be as unacceptable to the Russians as Communism
as a purpose would be to us). That principle is, rather, elevated to the
status of an Ultimate Moral Imperative, beside which all else pales
into insignificance or irrelevance; that principle, by definition,
becomes the Be-All and End-All of the new federation, to which all
other considerations, all other values, must as a matter of course be
subordinated. Organizations, as we know, all organizations and
therefore the world federalist organization, too, derive their mood,
their quality, their character from the *purpose* for which they have
been created—indeed, the more rationally devised an organization
is the more faithfully it reflects, even in the minutest details of its
activities, its central purpose. Now: in the world federation, as we
know, the central purpose is the prevention of destruction by nuclear
weapons, which will mean first of all, of course, a world government

monopoly of such weapons. Ah! but that is only the beginning. The world government must *protect* its monopoly of nuclear weapons against all possible infringement, which means it must see to it that no nuclear weapons get manufactured. That is, moreover, a matter about which it must sho-nuff mean business: the price of preventing manufacture of nuclear weapons by potential rebels is not merely vigilance, not merely eternal vigilance, but eternal and universal vigilance, vigilance which must, in order to accomplish its purpose, reach into every nook and cranny of the new society's life. That means, at the very least, a secret police—not an FBI, since FBI's are mild stuff by comparison with what this calls for—that would make the MVD associated with the name of Stalin look like a Boy Scout troop, and this alike from the standpoint of the number of operatives required, the powers of arbitrary search and seizure and arrest that the organization simply must have in order to perform its function, and of the clearly necessary circumventions of due process, judicial tribunals, and suchlike outmoded niceties of the *ancien régime*. The police must, in the very nature of the case—does not the Supreme Moral Imperative demand it—act and act vigorously not upon proofs of guilt but upon the mildest breath of suspicion. So great and good is the purpose, that the MVD must not hesitate to use every known technique of intimidation, of recruiting informers, of manufacturing and twisting evidence so that no person who even *might* be guilty shall go free. Nor is that all: bombs are most likely to be manufactured precisely by the dissidents, the discontented minorities, by the opponents of the existing world government. They must be struck at even before they have time to become suspicious, because of the suspicion that they *might* become suspicious. And even that isn't all: Before there can be dissidents, discontented minorities, opponents of the existing government, there must first be criticism of the existing government; and the existing government, if it takes its mission seriously, must see to it that criticism shall never begin, that nothing shall be spoken or printed except that which expresses approval of existing policies—nay, if it is really serious, that nothing shall be *thought* save "loyal" thoughts. The proposal for a world federation is, on the face of it, a proposal for a world police state, in which the very memory of what used to be called freedom will not, because it cannot, be tolerated.

Finally (c), *because* the world government proclaims itself—proclaims itself, I repeat, on the face of it—as a despotism, *we* Americans, we the second of the great powers whose acquiescence would be needed for world government to be born, would not agree to it, *should* not agree to it, *will* not agree to it; and let not the one-worlder think that by dwelling upon the horrors of nuclear warfare, by harping on the destructiveness of nuclear weapons, he will ever blackmail us into doing so. He is, as we know, a great *connoisseur* of those horrors, a great propagandist for that destructiveness, a great accumulator of the relevant statistics; he will, at or even before the drop of a hat, tell you all, absolutely all, about them. Sometimes, indeed, he seems to be licking his chops over them, as the rest of us, even the best-bred among us, do at the thought of dinner at our favorite restaurant. He finds it difficult to remember that other people read the newspapers and journals too, and take in and comprehend anyhow part of what they read; another of the things he cannot get through his head is that the people who drag their feet on world federation do not drag their feet because they are less seized than he of the annihilation-potential of the new weapons, less impressed than he by that potential—that, indeed, they would still drag their feet if tomorrow, by some miracle, the new weapons were to become 10 or 20 or 1,000 times *more* destructive than they are today; that, indeed again, the foot-draggers are as ready as *he* to suppose that a nuclear war would snuff the human race out of existence or even, as we are sometimes assured, blow up the world. One of the things he cannot get through his head is that the foot-draggers do not drag their feet because they repudiate his premise about nuclear warfare, but because, for them, the conclusion he wants to draw from those premises does not follow from those premises, cannot by any feat of logic be extracted from those premises, would not flow from those premises even had they been communicated to us by Revelation and even were they more horrible to contemplate than they actually are; and I say, Let us, even if we do not get anything else done this afternoon, be clear, both with ourselves and with the one-worlder, as to *why* the conclusion does not follow from the premises. Let us do that although, admittedly, it involves the most difficult lesson we have to try to teach to the one-worlder.

It is, fortunately for pedagogical purposes, a lesson that we may divide into two parts—both, as we know from experience of debates like this one, equally difficult for him to grasp. Part One consists of the simple principle: Survival, in itself, is *not* the highest value; on the *contrary:* under the ethos of Western civilization as revealed to us by that civilization's central teaching, survival is a relatively *low* value; above it, for example, ranks truth; above it also, for example, ranks beauty; above it, far above it, ranks justice, and along with justice true religion; above it finally, and perhaps most appositely for our purposes here, ranks *freedom,* and along with freedom those processes of rational deliberation and discussion—we have just seen why world government would be fatal to *both*—that we know to be the characteristic features of truly civil society. All these, I say, rank above survival—your survival, my survival, anybody's survival—in the eyes of *both* the religion and the philosophy of Western civilization; and when we say that they rank above survival we understand that to mean—I said we must lay it on the line, did I not—that one does not mention survival in the same breath with them, that one thinks and schemes and plans for survival only after, in one's thinking, these higher values have been provided for, that these being the things that make life worth living, survival without them is not life but death, that, in short, the law of reason bids us regard ourselves as—I choose my words—*expendable* for these higher values. The one-worlder's conclusion does not follow from his premises because his logical progress to that conclusion involves an illicit step, involves, that is, the hidden premise that survival is the highest value, which is a *false* premise. The foot-draggers drag their feet, and rightly drag their feet, because they detect that premise in the one-worlder's position, and because they repudiate that premise. As for Part Two of the Lesson, it rounds out the teaching of Part One as follows: Not only is survival a low value, which rightfully yields precedence to truth, to beauty, to freedom, to self-government, but also we—the "we" that I started out by saying will never accept the proposals of the world federalists—*know* that survival is a low value, can be counted on to *treat* it as a low value, can be counted on, above all, to reflect in our *actions* the low esteem in which we hold survival as a value, can be counted on, therefore, to reject the proposals of the one-worlders. Those proposals, insofar as they involve the premise that we, Western man, can be blackmailed into a one-world despotism by the slogan "Federate or Perish," are, for one thing, a *libel,* since they do not do us justice, and for another thing a *lie,* because they deny the facts of the history of Western man, who has never refused, when the highest values are at stake, to die for them. We suspect the man who so libels us, and so lies to us, of judging us by himself. We suspect him of being a man who, having nothing to die for, can only babble about survival. We suspect him, in a word, of being a Liberal.

Index